The Winn L. Rosch Multimedia Bible

Winn L. Rosch

PUBLISHING

201 West 103rd Street
Indianapolis, IN 46290

To Deborah.

Copyright © 1995 by Sams Publishing

FIRST EDITION

International Standard Book Number: 0-672-30670-0

Library of Congress Catalog Card Number: 94-74886

98 97 96 95   4   3   2   1

Interpretation of the printing code: the rightmost double-digit number is the year of the book's printing; the rightmost single-digit, the number of the book's printing. For example, a printing code of 95-1 shows that the first printing of the book occurred in 1995.

Composed in AGaramond and MCPdigital by Macmillan Computer Publishing

Printed in the United States of America

Trademarks

Publisher	*Richard K. Swadley*
Acquisitions Manager	*Greg Weigand*
Development Manager	*Dean Miller*
Managing Editor	*Cindy Morrow*
Marketing Manager	*Gregg Bushyeager*
Assistant Marketing Manager	*Michelle Milner*

Development Editor
Sunthar Visuvalingam

Software Development Specialist
Wayne Blankenbeckler

Production Editor
James Grass

Editorial Coordinator
Bill Whitmer

Editorial Assistants
*Carol Ackerman, Sharon Cox
Lynette Quinn*

Technical Reviewers
*Lewis C. Eggebrecht, John Goodman,
David Reichert, Nick Stam*

Cover Designer
Tim Amrhein

Book Designer
Alyssa Yesh

Vice President of Manufacturing and Production
Jeff Valler

Imprint Manager
Kelly Dobbs

Manufacturing Coordinator
Paul Gilchrist

Production
*Angela D. Bannan,
Georgiana Briggs, Michael Brumitt,
Charlotte Clapp, Terrie Deemer,
Cheryl Dietsch, Teresa Forrester,
Michael Henry, Louisa Klucznik,
Clint Lahnen, Kevin Laseau,
Steph Mineart, Tim Montgomery,
Casey Price, Brian-Kent Proffitt,
Bobbi Satterfield, Dennis Sheehan,
Greg Simsic, SA Springer,
Susan VandeWalle, Susan Van Ness,
Mark Walchle, Angelina Ward,
Jeff Yesh*

Overview

Quick Reference		IV
Introduction		XX
Section I:	**Hands-On Multimedia**	**1**
1	Defining Multimedia	3
2	Applying Multimedia	21
3	The Multimedia PC	39
4	Getting Started	59
5	Authoring Multimedia	83
Section II:	**Software Guide**	**115**
6	Software Concepts	117
7	Operating Systems	137
8	Device Drivers	201
9	Data Storage	227
Section III:	**Hardware Guide**	**299**
10	The Basic PC—Hardware Essentials	301
11	Input and Output	353
12	The Compact Disc	387
13	Images	415
14	Cameras and Monitors	477
15	Sound	511
16	MIDI	555
Section IV:	**Appendixes**	**579**
A	Multimedia Law	581
B	Production Issues	595
C	Distribution	599
	Index	605

Quick Reference to Your Multimedia Bible

Audio

Topic	Page
Acoustics: nature of sound, frequencies and wavelengths, air pressure, hearing	513
Basics: basic PC sound, sound boards, audio quality, compression	526
DSPs: MWave, Signal Computing Architecture, VCOS, Windows DSP Architecture	544
File format (types of): descriptor, control, and waveform files	282
File formats (specific formats): AIFF, .IBK, .MID, .MOD, .RMI, .SBI, .SND, .VOC, .WAV	283
Loudspeakers: baffles, multi-speaker systems, location and coupling, passive and active systems	515
Microphones: technology (dynamic, condenser, piezoelectric), directionality, physical and electrical characteristics, quality, connectors	521
MIDI: background, hardware, channels, voices, messages, operation, synchronizing, playback	255
Recording: system sounds, OLE (background, operation, using), voice annotation	72
Soundboards: installation, setup, speaker wiring	530
Standards: compatibility, Ad Lib, Sound Blaster	537
Synthesis: subtractive, additive, FM, Wave table, Advanced techniques	532
Technology: Digitization, sampling rate, resolution, compression	256
Video recording: annotation, microphones	81, 491

Authoring

Topic	Page
Authoring: software, hypertext, presentations, CBT, programming, preproduction	87
Computer-based training: TourGuide, TIE Authoring System	99
Hypertext (Microsoft): Multimedia Viewer 2.0, MediaView Libraries, WinHelp 4.0	90

Hypertext (other vendors): Guide, Multimedia Toolbook 92

Pre-production: still images, video, morphing, sound (SoundForge) 107

Presentations: Aldus Persuasion, Astound!, Authorware Professional for Windows,
ForShow, IconAuthor, ImageQ, Macromedia Director, Q/Media 93

Programming: languages, Rapid Application Development, toolkits 101

Programming aids: MCIWnd, Media Control Interface (MCI), OpenGL,
WinG, WinToon 104

CD-ROMs

Topic	Page
Connections: control, data, audio, power	408
Drives: transfer rate, access time, buffers, mechanism, controls, interface	402
Drivers	410
Interface: SCSI, IDE, parallel port, proprietary	406
Players	67
Standards: CD-DA, Photo CD (color, resolution, compression), CD-ROM (format)	394
Technology: media, recordable CD, physical format	388
Troubleshooting: startup, audio, video	413

Communications

Topic	Page
Modems: background, standards, configuration, advanced technologies, fax	378
Parallel ports: standard, bi-directional, enhanced, extended capabilities	372
Serial ports: UARTs, interrupts, initializing, maximizing speed	366

Data Input

Topic	Page
Keyboards: layout, ergonomics, technology, interface	383
Mouse: technology, buttons, interfaces, protocols, trackballs	358
See other entries: lightpens, digitizing tablets, scanners, game ports	362

Data Storage

Topic	Page
Audio: Digitization, Sampling rate, Resolution, compression	256
Audio file formats: AIFF, .IBK, .MID, .MOD, .RMI, .SBI, .SND, .VOC, .WAV	283
Audio file format types: descriptor, control, and waveform files	282
Format conversion	296
Images: Vectors versus bit images, resolution, color depth, 2-D versus 3-D	246
Image compression: color mapping, Run Length Encoding, dictionary-based, JPEG	250
Image file formats: .BMP, .EPS, .GIF, .JPG, .PCD, .PCX, .TGA, .WMF	259
Text: BCD, EBCDIC, ASCII, word processor formats, Rich Text Format, numbers	228
Video compression: Cinepak, Indeo, Microsoft Run-Length Encoding (RLE), Microsoft Video 1, Motion JPEG, MPEG	253
Video file formats: Audio Visual Interleaved (AVI), Quick Time Movie (MOV)	277

Graphics

Topic	Page
Accelerators: register width, bus type & width, memory handling, memory type, resolution support, color depth support, speed rating, VGA support, bus connections RAMDACs display control interface (DCI)	451
Color: planes, coding, mapping, Windows, compression and codecs	435
Compression: color mapping, Run Length Encoding, dictionary-based, JPEG	250
File formats: .BMP, .EPS, .GIF, .JPG, .PCD, .PCX, .TGA, .WMF	259
Hardware: video controllers, graphics accelerators	447
Images: background, video, memory mapped systems, color, standards	415
Images: Vectors versus bit images, resolution, color depth, 2-D versus 3-D	246
Linking scanned and memory-mapped systems: rasterization, time code	443
Optics: human vision, moving images, image geometry	416
Rasterization: overlay boards, step capture	443
Scanning signals: retrace, blanking, vertical interval, synchronizing signals color, RGB, composite video, S-Video, international standards, recording	421
Video boards: VGA, VESA, signals, connectors	457

Hardware

Topic	Page
486 clones: Cyrix 486 SLC/DLC, IBM 486SLC2 and Blue Lightning	315
486 family (Intel): 486DX, 486SX, 486SL, clock-doubled and clock-tripled models	313
AT attachment: Fast ATA, Enhanced IDE, speed, capacity, packet interface	339
Expansion bus: function, history, standards (ISA, MCA, EISA, VL, PCI, PCMCIA)	323
Floppy disk: double-density, high-density, extra high-density, Distribution Media Format, drive compatibility	349
Graphics accelerators: register width, bus type and width, memory handling, memory type, resolution support, color depth support, speed rating, VGA support, bus connections RAMDACs display control interface (DCI)	451
Hard disks: speed, AV drives, capacity, interfaces, AT Attachment, SCSI	335
Memory: technology, addressing, parity, chip count, sides, speed, logical types	332
Microprocessor: definition, Intel architecture, operating principles, chips	302
Microprocessor: registers, bus connections, clock speeds, caching, coprocessor operating voltages, power management	303
Pentium: Intel (OverDrives), AMD K5, Cyrix M1, NexGen 586	316
SCSI: making connections, troubleshooting	345
Video: boards (VGA, VESA, signals, connectors), controllers, accelerators	457

Multimedia

Topic	Page
Basic applications: Windows Help, Multimedia Viewer, players, OLE, annotations	62
Basic PC requirements: MPC 1.0, MPC 2.0	40
Defining: philosophic foundation, digital convergence, hardware standard, software interface, the media, the future	4
Making multimedia: music, home movies, audio and video production	36
Mass-market categories: education, reference, training, entertainment, games	24
Recommendations: processor, memory, storage, Plug-and-Play, expansion bus, video, sound, ports, physical concerns	44
Upgrade strategy: system approach, all new?, false savings, status seeking	54

Operating Systems

Topic	Page
BIOS: boot sequence, input/output, hardware, resource allocation, Plug-and-Play	128
Device Drivers: DOS, Windows 3.1x, Windows 95, OS/2	201
MS-DOS: history, structure, file system, memory, installation	139
MS-DOS: essential files, booting, applications multitasking, command processor	143
OS/2: history, kernel, file system (Super-FAT, HPFS), device drivers, Plug-and-Play	189
Operating systems: function, structure, configuration	133, 138
Windows 3.1x: history, structure, updating, upgrading to 32-bit, disk features	155
Windows 3.1x device drivers: DOS drivers, DLLs, standard, VDX, MCI, installation	208
Windows 3.1x memory: system resources, DOS session memory, VMM, requirements	162
Windows 95: compatibility, structure, memory, file system	168
Win95 configuration: registry, hardware, old devices, Plug-and-Play, BIOS, SCSI	178
Windows 95 display setup:	509

Software

Topic	Page
Multimedia players and viewers: Multimedia Viewer, CD Player, Video Players	64
Programming: languages, Rapid Application Development, toolkits	101
Programming aids: MCIWnd, Media Control Interface (MCI), OpenGL, WinG, WinToon	104
Programming concepts: languages, tools, APIs, tasks and threads	118
Software: definition, programming, user interface, BIOS, OS, applications	118

Video

Topic	Page
Camera Electronics: scanning, encoding, white balance, effects, viewfinders	489
Camera optics: sensors, color resolution, lenses, focal length, field of view, iris shutters, zooming, focusing, stability	478

Cathode Ray Tubes (CRT): phosphors, color temperature, persistence, electron guns, convergence, shadow masks, aperture grilles, matrix color, projection systems 494

Compression: Cinepak, Indeo, Microsoft Run-Length Encoding (RLE), Microsoft Video 1, Motion JPEG, MPEG 253

Flat-panel displays: nematic twists, active versus passive, color, resolution 499

Monitor electronics: synchronizing, frequencies, bandwidth, overscan and underscan, aspect ratio, image sizing, image controls audio inputs 503

Players: Video for Windows, QuickTime for Windows (installation, compatibility) 69

Scanning signals: retrace, blanking, vertical interval, synchronizing signals color, RGB, composite video, S-Video, international standards, recording 421

Contents

Quick Reference IV

Introduction XX

Section I   Hands-On Multimedia   1

1 Defining Multimedia 3
  Philosophic Foundation 4
  Digital Convergence 6
  Hardware Standard 8
  Software Interface 10
  The Media 12
  The Future 14

2 Applying Multimedia 21
  Scope 22
  Production and Consumption 23
  Mass Market Multimedia 24
    Education 25
    References 28
    Training 31
    Entertainment 32
    Games 34
  Making Multimedia 36
    Music 36
    Home Movies 37
    Audio and Video Production 37

3 The Multimedia PC 39
  What You Need 40
    MPC 1.0 40
    MPC 2.0 42
  What You Really Want 44
    Microprocessors 45
    Memory 45
    Mass Storage 47
    Plug-and-Play 49
    Expansion Bus 50
    Video 50
    Sound 51
    Ports 52
    Physical Concerns 53

New or Renew—Finding the Best Strategy 54

    System Approach 55

    All New Beats Partly New 55

    False Savings 55

    Status Seeking 56

    Adding in Multimedia 56

4 Getting Started **59**

  System Kick-Start 60

  Basic Applications 61

    Windows Help 62

    Multimedia Viewer 64

    CD Players 67

    Video Players 68

    System Sounds 72

  OLE 74

    Background 74

    Operation 76

    Using OLE 77

  Voice Annotation 78

    Recording 78

    Embedding 81

  Video Annotation 81

5 Authoring Multimedia **83**

  Overview 84

  Authoring Software 87

  Hypertext 88

    Microsoft Offerings 90

    Independent Offerings 92

  Presentations 93

    Aldus Persuasion 96

    Astound! 96

    Authorware Professional for Windows 97

    ForShow 97

    IconAuthor 97

    ImageQ 97

    Macromedia Director 98

    Q/Media 99

Computer-Based Training 99
    TourGuide 100
    TIE Authoring System 100
Programming 101
    Languages 101
    Rapid Application Development 103
    Toolkits and Programming Aids 104
Pre-Production 107
    Still Images 107
    Video 109
    Morphing 110
    Sound 111

Section II   Software Guide   115

6 Software Concepts **117**
    Definition 118
    Programming 118
        Languages 119
        Tasks and Threads 123
    User Interface 125
        History 126
        Design 127
    BIOS 128
        Boot Sequence 128
        Input and Output Control 129
    Operating Systems 133
    Applications 135

7 Operating Systems **137**
    Function 138
    MS-DOS 139
        History 139
        Structure 143
        File System 148
        Memory 151
        Installation 153
    Windows 155
        History 155
        Structure 158
        Memory 162
        Configuration 167

Windows 95 168
   Compatibility 169
   Structure 171
   Memory 172
   File System 174
   Configuration 178
OS/2 189
   History 190
   Structure 192

8 Device Drivers **201**
Background 202
DOS 203
   Loading 204
   Mandatory Drivers 206
Windows 3.1 Family 208
   Background 208
   DOS Drivers 208
   Dynamic Link Libraries 209
   Standard Drivers 211
   Virtual Device Drivers 211
   Media Control Interface 212
   Installation 215
Windows 95 218
   Installation 221
OS/2 222
   Memory Use 223
   Installation 223

9 Data Storage **227**
Text 227
   EBCDIC 228
   ASCII 237
Word Processor Formats 241
   Rich Text Format 242
   Numerical Storage 244
Images 246
   Vectors Versus Bit Images 247
   Resolution 248
   Color Depth 249
   2-D Versus 3-D 249
   Still Image Compression 250
   Video Compression 253

Audio 256
   Digitization 256
   Sampling Rate 257
   Resolution 257
   Audio Compression 257
File Formats 259
   Still Image Formats 259
   Video Formats 277
   Audio File Types 282
   Audio File Formats 283
Format Conversion 296

Section III   Hardware Guide   **299**

10   The Basic PC—Hardware Essentials **301**
Microprocessors 302
   Definition 302
   Intel Architecture 303
   Operating Principles 303
   Commercial Chips 309
Expansion Buses 323
   Function 324
   History 324
   Standards 325
Memory 331
   Technologies 331
   Memory Characteristics 332
Hard Disks 335
   Speed 336
   AV Drives 336
   Capacity 337
   Interfaces 338
Floppy Disks 349
   Double-Density Disks 351
   High-Density Disks 351
   Distribution Media Format 351
   Extra-High Density 352
   Drive Compatibility 352

11   Input and Output **353**
Keyboards 353
   Layout 354
   Ergonomics 355

Technology 356
Interface 356
Mice 358
Technology 358
Buttons 359
Interfaces 360
Protocols 361
Trackballs 361
Lightpens 362
Digitizing Tablets 362
Scanners 363
Ports 365
Serial Ports 366
Parallel Ports 372
Game Ports 377
Data Modems 378
Background 379
Standards 379
Configuration 382
Advanced Technologies 384
Fax Modems 385

12 The Compact Disc **387**
Background 387
Technology 388
Media 389
Recordable CD 391
Physical Format 392
Standards 394
CD-DA 395
PhotoCD 396
CD-ROM 401
CD Drives 402
Transfer Rate 403
Access Time 404
Buffers 404
Mechanism 405
Controls 405
Interface 406
Drivers 409

Troubleshooting 413
    Startup Problems 413
    Audio Problems 414
    Video Problems 414

13 Images **415**
    Background 416
        Human Vision 416
        Moving Images 417
        Image Geometry 418
    Video 418
        Scanned Video Systems 419
        Scanning Signals 421
        Cabling 432
    Memory-Mapped Systems 434
    Color 435
        Color Planes 436
        Color Coding 438
        Color Mapping 439
        Windows and Color 439
        Compression and Codecs 440
        Standards 442
    Vector Graphics Systems 443
    Linking Scanned and Memory-Mapped Systems 443
        Rasterization 443
        Time Code 445
    Image Hardware 447
        Video Controllers 448
        Graphics Accelerators 451
    Video Boards 457
        VGA 458
        VESA 463
        Signals 468
        Connectors 471

14 Cameras and Monitors **477**
    Video Cameras 477
        Optics 478
        Electronics 489
        Recording 492
    Monitors 493
        Cathode Ray Tubes 494
        Flat-Panel Displays 500

Electronics 503

Setup 508

15 Sound **511**

Acoustics and Transducers 512

Acoustics 513

Loudspeakers 515

Microphones 521

Audio 526

Basic PC Sound 527

Sound Boards 530

Audio Quality 531

Synthesis 532

Subtractive Synthesis 533

Additive Synthesis 534

FM Synthesis 535

Wave Table Synthesis 535

Advanced Techniques 536

Compatibility and Standards 537

Compression 543

Digital Signal Processors 544

Installing a Soundboard 551

Soundboard Setup 551

Speaker Wiring 553

16 MIDI **555**

Background 556

Hardware 556

Channels and Voices 558

Messages 566

Operation 570

Synchronizing 575

Playback 576

Section IV Appendixes   **579**

A Multimedia Law **581**

Copyright 582

Subject Matter 582

Issuance 584

Notice 585

Term 586

Protection 586

Infringement 586

Fair Use 587

Work for Hire 587

Rights 587

Public Domain 588

Licensing 590

Subject Matter 590

Permissions 591

Protecting Your Rights 592

Contracts 593

B Production Issues **595**

Doing It Yourself 595

Studios 596

Contractors 597

C Distribution **599**

Commercial Distribution 599

Self-Distribution 600

Creating a Product 601

Shareware Help 602

Index **605**

About the Author

Winn L. Rosch started writing about personal computers back in 1981 when IBM introduced its first PC. Since then, he has contributed nearly 1,000 articles to a number of magazines. At one time or another, he has been (or is) a contributing editor to various computer publications, including *MacUser, PC/Computing, PC Week,* and *Computer Shopper.* He also contributes to *PC Magazine* and *PC Direct* in the United Kingdom as well as *PC Direkt* in Germany. In its annual awards, the Computer Press Association voted one of Rosch's stories in *PC Magazine* as the best feature of 1987.

Rosch also has written a number of books about PCs, including the best-selling *Winn L. Rosch Hardware Bible,* now in its third edition (Sams, 1994). He also has moderated symposia at NetWorld and PC Expo personal computer conventions.

In his spare time, Rosch designs perpetual motion machines and is working on a related project, a perpetual stillness machine. He also is a founding member of the Trilobite Breeders Association.

Introduction

Something is different about your new multimedia PC. But you know that. That's probably why you bought it.

If it's your first computer, you probably feel a bit of reverence or awe for it. Perhaps not quite to the extent of making a ritual sacrifice before it (besides, you already sacrificed a good deal of your savings in honor of the hardware), but you can sense its overwhelming presence. The feeling is something more than an appreciation for the machine itself and its technology, something that lifts your spirits and makes you feel a sense of accomplishment or of coming accomplishment. It isn't a mere hunk of hardware but something that can change your life. You have finally brought yourself into the information age and stand poised to take advantage of a new technology that promises to revolutionize your life. At least that's the gist of the spiel the sales staff at the computer store spoon-fed to you, right?

Even if your multimedia PC is only the most recent of a long line of personal computers, you can still see the difference. This new multimedia PC is probably the most powerful computer you've ever bought for yourself. It likely has capabilities far beyond any other machine you've bought, the capabilities that give effect to the "multimedia" in its name. It has a big, new voice thanks to a set of stereo speakers. Its monitor is probably sharper and clearer than that of any other machine you've had. And there's a new slot for sliding in CDs. Inside is a microprocessor that's more powerful than the mainframe computers that terrorized the world in the horror films of the 1950s.

Should your multimedia machine be your first machine, you probably approach it with a bit of reverence and awe because it *is* a computer—and that means it's something that you're going to have to learn to use, a new skill to develop, a challenge, and possibly a frustration. Take heart. That's what sets a multimedia PC apart. From the very start, multimedia was designed with you in mind. It thinks the way you think and responds the way you expect. You don't have to know 10,000 esoteric commands, each a bit more confusing than the last. You don't even have to learn to type. Multimedia software is so accessible that you can enjoy and learn from it no matter your skill level. Even people who are too young to read or those not fluent in English can work their way through the graphic control systems of many multimedia programs. At that, multimedia is sort of like television but with you in control instead of an ungodly alliance of writers, producers, and programming executives. A multimedia system is simply more fun to use, and it makes learning to use it fun.

Unlike the lunch that is never really free, multimedia doesn't force you to give up anything to gain its almost-instant accessibility. Multimedia systems are not the crippled kin of real PCs, second-rate systems reserved for home use. In fact, they are typically more powerful than the computers that businesses plop on employees' desktops. A modern multimedia PC can to do things that ordinary computers cannot—and can do them faster.

The general trend among PCs of any sort is, of course, toward ever faster and more powerful hardware, but that doesn't mean ordinary PCs—those without multimedia pretenses—will overtake multimedia systems. There is no competition. It's a changeover, a metamorphosis. As it becomes more powerful, the average PC is turning into the multimedia PC. Multimedia is, in fact, the new standard for personal computers. Buying a new computer without multimedia capabilities today chains you to a box of regrets. You'll put yourself behind before you start. You severely limit what you can do with your PC, the programs you can run, and even your future options.

Fortunately, a wrong decision or yesterday's lack of clairvoyance about the computer you'll need tomorrow need not be fatal. You can always upgrade an ordinary PC to gain multimedia capabilities. After all, every PC is upgradable by some means (although some crotchety old systems require more expense and effort to upgrade than can be justified in face of the low prices of today's multimedia systems). Upgrading enhances rather than restricts your options. You have your choice of an entire range of upgrades, from all-in-one-box kits to individual components you can mix and match like fashion accessories. None takes installation skills beyond the abilities of anyone who knows how to grasp and turn a screwdriver. The latest systems that understand the new *Plug-and-Play* standards make expansion and upgrades easier than ever before.

Hardware alone does not multimedia make. Far from being an end in itself, computer hardware is only the means by which you gain access to multimedia. The real experience of multimedia is in the media itself, the software you run on your system. Just as you buy a VCR to show movies and not decorate your shelf, you buy a multimedia PC as a playback system for multimedia programs. Unlike the VCR, however, your multimedia PC is a universal playback system. It can handle just about any software written for PCs—video, sound, text, charts, even synthesizer sequences. Your choice of software determines exactly what your multimedia PC does and how it does it.

With the right software, your multimedia PC can do anything. Slide in the appropriate disk, and it can become a movie projector, action or adventure game, music synthesizer, or encyclopedia. Moreover, because of the built-in power required for the rigors of running multimedia, any multimedia PC is more than adept at handling an ordinary word processor, spreadsheet, or database. It can do anything that any other system can do—and more. It can even do them all at the same time.

Software defines not only what your multimedia PC can do but also how it works. Software provides the command system. And that's good news. The control system that's used by most modern multimedia software finally makes the computer understandable, even intuitive. In fact, you'll probably find your multimedia PC to be easier to program than the typical VCR (although the Space Shuttle probably is, too).

The change in controls is sufficient alone to revolutionize PCs. Systems before multimedia were obstinate beasts demanding that you tell them every detail of what you wanted them to do. They differed little from ancient, room-size computers that each required a platoon of programmers to keep running. They made you change to suit them—you had to learn their language, and you had to learn how to type in their commands exactly the way they expected. You, your way of working, and your needs were subservient to those of the computer. With a modern operating system like Windows 95 or OS/2 Warp, however, your multimedia PC becomes an obedient slave. You get pushbutton operation and few hassles. Running a program or choosing an option requires nothing more than pointing and clicking. To install and run most multimedia applications, about all you have to know is how to slide a CD into the drive slot in your PC. It's hardly more complicated than operating a toaster.

Of course, if simplicity were all there is to multimedia, you'd probably expect to quickly leave it behind like your first tricycle and kindergarten class. But ease of use is only one aspect of multimedia. It's important because it makes multimedia usable by anyone and opens the technology to the mass market. But it's only a thin surface layer, a pretty face that makes it attractive but belies a deeper complexity.

Beneath the surface, multimedia computing is fundamentally a communications medium, one the likes of which the world has never seen before. It has the potential to change the way you express yourself and your ideas, even to change the way you think. As with any communications medium, multimedia has another side—creation.

Perhaps the best thing about multimedia is that the only difference between using it and creating it is you. You decide on your involvement. If you're content to learn and entertain yourself with multimedia software, you can sit back and run commercial applications. Should you be a bit more adventurous, you can add multimedia touches to your everyday work—a voice annotation to a spreadsheet, a greeting video enclosed in an electronic letter. If you're *really* ambitious, you can create your own multimedia software, perhaps the first million-selling title. Best of all, you can do any of these things on just about any multimedia PC. Every multimedia system is equally adept at creating and displaying. You don't need an elaborate studio and piles of equipment to get started in making multimedia. The primary requirements are only patience and your own personal drive.

This Book

This book is meant to be your companion as you explore and take command of the world of multimedia. No one book can tell you everything about such a complex topic. What we can do is gain an overview, get a firm foundation in the essentials, and look at the details that are most relevant to your getting the most from your investment. This book will attempt to answer most of your questions even before you ask them and provide a reference for minutiae that may be needed in the future.

We'll examine exactly that, how to make multimedia including the hardware and software tools you'll need, how to go about putting together the various pieces of media needed to make a full production, and what to do with it when you're finished (marketing). Along the way, we'll check the many options available to you—acquiring sound and images, where to do the work, hiring others to help out, and protecting your rights when you work with other people or hire others to work with you.

Section I: Hands-On Multimedia

If your multimedia system is your first PC, the initial chapters will help you get started. Rather than a step-by-step guide, however, the emphasis will be on exploring and experimenting so that you can discover the basics of multimedia, what it is and what you can do with it. Rather than intimate knowledge, which best develops naturally as you explore on your own, the goal is to gain an overview and show you multimedia's potential so you can find your own direction. We'll leave it open-ended because there's no end in sight for multimedia technology.

Chapter 1, "Defining Multimedia." We'll start by examining what multimedia is and what you can do with it. Although this is supposed to be a practical book, this first look will be essentially philosophic. We'll examine the roots of the technology and see just exactly what multimedia is—the reality and the promise. We'll see that the constituent parts of multimedia are only now coming together from diverse sources, that multimedia is here but still embryonic, defining itself, and that no one really knows what mature multimedia will be. That's the whole point of looking at multimedia today. The technology is still so young and malleable that you can play a role in forming its future.

Chapter 2, "Applying Multimedia." If you're going to invest in multimedia—still not an inexpensive proposition these days, despite plummeting PC prices—you need to know what you're going to do with it. We'll take a look at multimedia applications, the software you can buy to run on a multimedia PC. We'll examine the different types of programs you can get— educational, entertainment, reference, game playing—and take brief looks at some of the commercial programs currently available. Applications are, after all, the best introduction to multimedia. They will show you what the technology can do—or at least what today's authors have thought of doing with it. Seeing what's available will whet your appetite and probably fire your imagination. You'll see what you can do and maybe what you can do better making your own productions. Even if you plan to write multimedia yourself, you need to check around to see what's available to avoid the problem that makes so many people think that they are geniuses: they don't know what they don't know. Only when you see what others have and have not done can you appreciate the potential for your work in the medium.

Chapter 3, "The Multimedia PC." Next we'll look at what you need to bring these multimedia applications to life: a multimedia PC. The personal computer industry has developed a strict definition for what a multimedia PC must be, and that's where we'll start. But as computer hardware gets ever more capable, the standard is little more than guidance to the least computer you'll want to buy. We'll examine what you really need to be multimedia-ready, what you really want to be happy with modern multimedia technology, and how to get there—whether you need a new PC or should upgrade your existing system to multimedia abilities.

Chapter 4, "Getting Started." Once you have a multimedia PC sitting in your office, den, or kitchen, you're going to want to see what it can do as quickly as you can. After all, patience is no virtue when technology is rushing past you too fast to let you catch up. We'll see what you can do with multimedia in the first few minutes after you switch on your PC. You can explore commercial applications or put multimedia into your more conventional PC work. All you need to know are a few basic secrets, what to look and which buttons to press, and you'll be on your way. There's no need to learn about computer programming even if you want to meld sound and images with your worksheets and letters or turn your PC into a stereophonic multimedia playback system. In a few minutes you can master some of the most powerful concepts in multimedia software, like Object Linking and Embedding. You can even use your multimedia PC to make digital audio recordings.

Chapter 5, "Authoring Multimedia." The best part about multimedia is its accessibility. Not only can you easily use it, you can just as easily make multimedia productions of your own. The field is wide open, and your multimedia PC gives you all you need to get in on the ground floor. Using authoring software, you can create multimedia books, references, presentations, games, and even adventures that exist nowhere but in your imagination. We'll look at the various styles of multimedia and what you need to write them, focusing on the tools that are available to let you put your ideas in action with a minimum of busy work. We won't bog ourselves down in the minutiae of line-by-line programming—that's well beyond the scope of this book, a black art that takes years to master and entire libraries of guides and references. Again, our goal will be the overview that will help you find your way through the morass of multimedia tools.

Section II: Software Guide

Once we've got the basics out of the way, we'll examine the technology behind multimedia with a combination of guide and reference to software. We'll start at the beginning, what software is and how programs are constructed, then examine the various software elements involved in multimedia, from BIOS to operating system to application software. Along the way we'll look at the details of your multimedia PC's software so you can set up your PC and configure it and your system for optimum performance.

Chapter 6, "Software Concepts." Understanding how multimedia works requires a knowledge of computer software, what it is and how it works. In this chapter, we'll lay a foundation for that understanding and examine how software controls a computer and what a computer program really is. We'll examine important underlying concepts like program threads and the user interface. From there, we'll look the types of software that make a multimedia PC work—the Basic Input/Output System or BIOS, the operating system and its components, and application software.

Chapter 7, "Operating Systems." The actual software on a PC that enables multimedia to work is the operating system. Some say the operating system gives a computer its personality. More than that, however, the operating system defines exactly what you can and cannot do—and how easily and well you can do it. New operating systems have made multimedia possible, and the latest crop of operating systems make multimedia an integral part of the everyday operation of your PC. We'll try to stay agnostic about which operating system is best, treating the three main venues for multimedia on essentially equivalent terms. Windows 3.1 and its progeny (Windows for Work groups) remains the multimedia platform with the widest installed base, and will likely stay the leader for the next couple of years—if just from inertia and the cost of memory. Windows 95, the designated successor, will put multimedia into the hands of the masses, with 32-bit performance and ease of installation and use (notwithstanding its appetite for memory). OS/2 Warp bridges the gap with sturdy multimedia work. In truth, more than a common thread unites them, and most multimedia applications will run on any of the three. Our discussion will start with a look into the background of each then dig into practical details. We'll cover the origins and history of each of the three most popular PC operating systems, discuss its underlying structure, then look at its memory usage and file systems, and finally how to get each one going.

Chapter 8, "Device Drivers." Multimedia links more different devices, both hardware and software, to your PC than ever before. Each one requires a device driver of some kind to link it to your operating system and the rest of your PC. Today's operating systems load your PC down with more device drivers than ever before. This chapter will discuss what device drivers are, how they work with each operating system (and how you manage them), and which ones you absolutely need to get your multimedia PC going.

Chapter 9, "Data Storage." To make multimedia work, you need to deal with the media. PCs store everything—ordinary bytes of data, sound, or video—in files. This chapter will help you understand and work with all the different files used in multimedia systems. After dispensing with a few basics, we'll look at the structure of all the major kinds of files used by multimedia software for data, audio, and video storage.

Section III: Hardware Guide

From there, we'll look at multimedia hardware with two goals in mind: a basic primer so that you know enough not to be outflanked by an eager sales force and enough technical background so that you can wisely use the tools of multimedia in your work—or in making multimedia your work.

Chapter 10, "The Basic PC—Hardware Essentials." The basic personal computer is the system unit, which is made from a microprocessor, memory, expansion bus, and mass storage system. This chapter will look in turn at each of these components so that you can determine which of each is best for you. We'll compare all of the available microprocessors so you can see which performance level is right for you. We'll check the different kinds of memory and see how you can expand the native endowment of your system with exactly what it needs. We'll compare the major expansion buses (including the PCMCIA system used by portable computers) to see how they work and what you need to get the most from your multimedia system. And we'll check out disk storage so you know the important differences in performance and interface. We won't slight on the practical issues. For example, we'll look at how you can add a second or third hard disk to your PC and how to keep it working at peak efficiency.

Chapter 11, "Input and Output." Your multimedia PC needs to link with the outside world—you need a way to communicate with it, and it needs a way to communicate with multimedia sources beyond its internal confines. This chapter will look at the input devices that you use to control your PC including the keyboard, pointing devices such as mice, trackballs, and digitizing tablets, and joysticks. In addition, we'll consider the external links, both that connect to devices in the immediate vicinity of your PC (the serial and parallel ports) and services at remote locations (modems). We'll follow the connections from microprocessor through your PC's BIOS all the way through the wires. You'll learn the differences within each connection type such as the performance limits on serial ports, the four kinds of parallel ports, and all the varieties of modems. In addition, you'll see how to wire things together and solve common port problems.

Chapter 12, "The Compact Disc." With the megabytes of storage afforded by the compact disc, what we know as multimedia would not be possible. The CD has become today's leading multimedia distribution medium. This chapter explains the technology behind the CD as well as the variety of formats that are grouped under the CD banner. These include not only the familiar CD-ROM but also digital audio discs, interactive CDs, and the Kodak PhotoCD system of image storage.

Chapter 13, "Images." Multimedia combines PC and video technologies. This chapter looks at the video half of multimedia. We'll start with a discussion of imaging technologies and show how the digital revolution has completely transformed video. In the digital video systems used by PCs, for example, dots and lines have no relevance to resolution. Compression is king, and codecs are key to making it work. We'll examine the major types of modern video systems, from conventional raster-based television to bitmapped digital video and how your PC converts images from one format to another. We'll trace PC video signals from memory to the screen, looking both at the technology and hardware.

Chapter 14, "Cameras and Monitors." Putting any kind of video to work in a multimedia system requires some means to acquire pictures and some way to display them. This chapter examines both ends of video system. We'll take a look at all the requirements of video cameras from optics to output. And we'll look critically at monitors so that you will know the differences that lie behind the screens.

Chapter 15, "Sound." The sound board is one of the defining elements of the multimedia PC, but sound is more than a mere card you slide into a slot. We'll examine what sound really is so that you'll know why PCs sound so bad even though they are capable of quality on a par with any stereo system. We'll examine the recording and synthesis of sounds and the various technologies involved. From there we'll see how microphones detect sound waves, how audio is digitized, and how speakers try to reconstruct the sounds you record. We'll run through all the considerations in finding the best microphone and using it to make multimedia recordings, how to connect speakers to your PC and get the best possible sound, and how to get that reluctant sound board working in your old PC.

Chapter 16, "MIDI." A mandatory part of any real multimedia PC, MIDI is a connection system, a communications system, and a storage system. It's a standard that links music and computer technologies. This chapter will look at the various sides for MIDI, from the details of the hardware interface to role in synthesizing music from commands in your multimedia applications.

Section IV: Appendixes

Once you get serious about multimedia, you can get yourself in serious trouble if your not careful. Going professional—whether you pen an multimedia program you share with friends or write a system that some media giant publishes in 15 languages—is fraught with pitfalls for the unwary. This set of appendixes will help you step carefully through these trouble areas.

Appendix A, "Multimedia Law." This appendix will examine what your rights are in your multimedia creation and how to protect those rights with copyright, patent, and trade secret laws. It will also look at the other side of the issue, what can you do with multimedia without infringing the rights of others. We'll look at the different kinds of programs, whether you can use the sounds and images you acquire, and obtaining (and giving) permission to use the property of others.

Appendix B, "Production Issues." If you want to put sound and images into a multimedia work, you need to get those sounds and images in digital form. For casual use you can capture what you need with your sound board and video capture card. But if you want to make a truly professional multimedia products, you may need to set your quality standards far higher. You need professional production that you can get only at a dedicated facility—a photography studio, recording studio, or television studio. This appendix takes a look at what you need to know to get the best.

Appendix C, "Distribution." If you decide you want to make your own multimedia and sell it, you must somehow deliver it to your audience. This appendix looks at the most workable and affordable outlet for individuals who want to self-publish their multimedia creations.

Icons

To help you find your way through this tome, the publishers have developed a number of icons to highlight subjects of particular interest, emphasize points, and just generally decorate gray pages. You can use them to zero in on subjects of particular interest and skip over topics that might not be relevant to your PC or current state of mind.

To highlight issues relevant only to particular operating systems, we've used the following:

Windows 3.1x

Indicates a section dealing with issues regarding the Windows 3.*x* system, which includes Windows 3.1 and Windows for Workgroups 3.11.

Windows 95

Indicates subjects relating to Windows 95.

Macintosh

Highlights discussions pertaining to the Apple Macintosh.

OS/2 Warp

Indicates sections devoted to OS/2.

Other icons will help you zero in on your own concerns and avoid things that veer away from your interests. These icons include the following:

Performance Issue

Draws your attention to issues influencing the performance of your multimedia PC.

Buying Tip

Flags buying tips that will help you get the most for your multimedia dollar.

Upgrading Advice

Points our upgrading advice that will aid you in revamping your PC to make it better match the demands of multimedia.

Trouble-shooting

Highlights troubleshooting advice so you can quickly find solutions to problems within a given topic.

Standards

Indicates a discussion of technical standards, including both definitions and applications.

Technical Note

Warns where things get really deep into technical discussions. Most of the time, you can avoid these sections and still know what's going on. But these discussions will give all these details to those readers who want them—and live by them.

The final three icons are more general in nature.

Indicates a general tip, good advice, or some information that can make your life a little easier.

Warns you about critical issues, such as common mistakes and frequently occurring problems. You should pay special heed to the text following this icon.

Indicates a special note that may be off the track of the text, but needs saying anyway.

And yes, I restrained the editors from putting the last icon in front of every paragraph.

The programming information in this book is based on information for developing applications for Windows 95 made public by Microsoft as of 9/9/94. Since this information was made public before the final release of the product, there may have been changes to some of the programming interfaces by the time the product is finally released. We encourage you to check the updated development information that should be part of your development system for resolving issues that might arise.

The end-user information in this book is based on information on Windows 95 made public by Microsoft as of 9/9/94. Since this information was made public before the release of the product, we encourage you to visit your local bookstore at that time for updated books on Windows 95.

If you have a modem or access to the Internet, you can always get up-to-the-minute information on Windows 95 direct from Microsoft on WinNews:

On CompuServe: `GO WINNEWS`

On the Internet:
`ftp://ftp.microsoft.com/PerOpSys/Win_News/Chicago`
`http://www.microsoft.com`

On AOL: keyword `WINNEWS`

On Prodigy: jumpword `WINNEWS`

On Genie: `WINNEWS` file area on Windows RTC

You can also subscribe to Microsoft's WinNews electronic newsletter by sending Internet e-mail to `news@microsoft.nwnet.com` and putting the words `SUBSCRIBE WINNEWS` in the text of the e-mail.

Section I
Hands-On Multimedia

Chapter 1   Defining Multimedia *3*

Chapter 2   Applying Multimedia..................................... *21*

Chapter 3   The Multimedia PC *39*

Chapter 4   Getting Started... *59*

Chapter 5   Authoring Multimedia.................................. *83*

Chapter 1
Defining Multimedia

What is multimedia? As with all questions about modern technology, the answer is neither simple nor easy. Multimedia is many things—that new personal computer you just bought with the gaping toothless mouth begging for a diet of CDs, the software you buy to run on it to avoid drowning in your own wealth, a new technology so wonderful writers have to cart in superlatives by the truckload, an insidious plot to steal your few remaining productive wakeful hours, the long-awaited merger of mindless video and incomprehensible computer technology, a buzzword to get you to go out and buy what you steadfastly resisted as the "home computer," a godsend that will keep the floundering hard disk industry afloat as you push against the capacity limits of almost obscenely large drives, the first truly new publishing system since Gutenberg retired the town crier, a technological *tour de force* that puts more power at your fingertips than Captain Nemo in league with the giant squid, a topic so confused that its admittedly plural name is universally regarded as singular, a subject so immense that no single book can hope even to define it. Multimedia is all of these, except maybe the last, because we're going to start our exploration into the subject by attempting our own definition of sorts, actually an overview aimed at giving you an idea not only at what multimedia is but also where it came from and, more importantly, where it is going. Just by buying this book you've made multimedia part of your life. You should get yourself prepared for the huge role it stands to play.

With one look, you know multimedia is different. Compare what you see on the screen to the pages of a book. While the traditional media just lie there, black-and-white and inanimate paper, multimedia literally glows.

Even at this superficial level, the difference is more than between turning pages and pressing the scroll button. In multimedia, as in any art, form dictates content. Printed images have no choice but to be silent and static, reality flattened and all too often grayed to fit on paper. The multimedia screen adds one dimension and at least one more sensory experience. Although screen images have two physical dimensions exactly like those on paper, the mutability of the screen adds a third, temporal dimension. Images change in time—they appear, move, shake, morph, and disappear. The time dimension is the difference between life and death—and living and dead presentations. Action makes things move, be they living creatures or the hours spent communicating.

One common definition in the electronics industry is that multimedia is the combination of computer and video technologies. Much of today's multimedia software does exactly that, giving you a computer control system for viewing substandard video images. But if that were all there were to multimedia, you could buy a new VCR and be done with it. Multimedia would be no more than video with a keyboard.

For some people, multimedia means little more than its concrete representation, the Multimedia PC. For them, multimedia is a hardware standard, the collection of features and power that you should expect from your next computer system. If that were the case, multimedia would already be a memory. PC performance doubles about once every 18 months. The term "multimedia" was first applied to PCs several years ago, and those systems have already been left far behind.

The truth is that multimedia is hard to define because there is no such thing as multimedia. Oh, great. Now you've bought a book that tells you its subject matter doesn't exist. You've wasted your money both on the book and on that multimedia system that has suddenly vanished like the photo image in a science fiction movie in which the past inadvertently gets changed. But despite those ominous words, your system lingers on in reality and the title of this book says it right there in big print—"Multimedia." So there must be such a thing. Nope. Might as well stop reading right here. Nope again.

There is no such thing as multimedia because multimedia is not *one* thing. It's a combination of ideas and technologies. Far from being a weakness, the absence of a singular entity that is multimedia is its great strength. The combination brings multimedia its versatility. It lets you and the entire software industry gradually move into the future. The ultimate multimedia program has yet to burst on the scene. Instead, software is gradually incorporating multimedia features, more in every new release. The multimedia combination accommodates them all.

Philosophic Foundation

Multimedia isn't anything new, either. It's not the child of the PC. Even the term "multimedia" predates the PC. The word was born in the old-fashioned, low-tech world when a "business presentation" meant a dark room filled with grey smoke, snoring executives, and a dozen carousel slide projectors, at least one of which was sure to malfunction.

The *multimedia experience* was usually a special event reserved for presentations to the Board of Directors of some faceless corporation because only large corporations could justify such a waste of effort. If nothing else, it was an experience. It typically went something like this: Along with the slide projectors, somebody lugged along a tape recorder—not one of your neat little cassette machines with the tapes that fit into your pocket, but big open reel tapes, the kind that dangled a trail of plastic behind to help you find your way home and ensnared your fingers when you tried to thread it around the heads and capstan. (You're probably too young to remember that. In fact, no one wants to remember that.) One of those tapes held a sound track that played back through speakers only a bit smaller than Iowa, and always turned up too loud in an attempt to deafen the audience into ignoring the lack of content in the slides, the lack of synchronization between the slides and the sound, and that someone had accidentally slipped in a roll of his vacation pictures from Acapulco in place of the projected sales of tail-fin ornaments for '59 DeSotos. If only the photographer had picked the right beach, he might have generated some real interest in the audience. As it was, no one even noticed the Acapulco slides. At least no one said anything. They didn't even cough as they did at the inevitable upside-down slides. (You can always tell an upside-down slide, but you can never be sure if a right-side-up slide is not supposed to be there, even if it pops a game of beach blanket bingo among the monthly sales charts.) Then again, if someone actually did speak up, no one would have heard because the entire audience was deaf from listening to the soundtrack.

Even in such early efforts that tiptoed carefully between boredom and disaster, you can see the germ of today's multimedia systems. If just from faith, the hardworking (if overly optimistic) authors of such slide shows knew that a presentation made more impact when it assaulted more than one sense at a time. Even before MTV arose to capitalize on on-screen chaos, these pioneers knew instinctively that if you had enough things going on, each person in the audience might find something interesting enough to keep him awake.

Another, more mundane, truth arose from these primeval multi-projector presentations. Despite the name and the promise, multimedia really meant just two media—sound and pictures, or in today's terms, audio and video. Smell-o-Vision notwithstanding, none of the other five senses needed apply.

This realistic view is not that dismal. These two senses are the ones that count, and the ones that take the expressway to your intelligence. Taste (with the tongue) and smell are aimed at more the animal level—helping find pleasure in meals and frolic, alerting you to panic with the aroma of smoke. Touch is in between, a kind of technician of the senses, what you need for building walls and draining crankcases more than negating Nietzsche and finding the meaning of life. After all, sight and sound are the senses of language and communication. And that's what multimedia is all about.

But multimedia is more than just sounds and pictures. Motion pictures had long combined sound and images. Your television set can handle that, and even the most primitive PC can deal in those terms—at least in terms of beeps, squeaks, and coarse graphics.

The real difference and innovation of the multi-projector multimedia presentation goes deeper than just the combination of media. In fact, the power of primitive multimedia presentations was not the combination of media itself but the way the two media were presented. They created a new, different form of narration, almost as if you dropped a reel of a movie and the individual frames and sound track jumbled together. Instead of a single flowing stream of images, you get flashes of scenes and bursts of sound no longer linked by a single narrative thread. The multimedia pioneers showed that not only can you make sense out of such a seeming mess, the puzzle of putting it all together made you more a part of the presentation. It kept you involved and interested. It made your mind active instead of lulling you to sleep.

Consider for a moment that the most important trend in PCs before the multimedia juggernaut rumbled out the advertising offices of computer makers was *multitasking*, the ability to run more than one program at a time, and you'll immediately recognize why PCs and multimedia are made for one another.

Multimedia itself has its binary aspects. As with all modern technologies, it is made from a mixture of hardware and software, machines and ideas. More importantly, you can conceptually divide technology and function of multimedia into control systems and information. In today's terminology, the representations of the two sides of multimedia are the user interface—the means through which you control the presentation of information—and the storage system—where the ideas are kept until ushered out by the control system.

Digital Convergence

The enabling force behind multimedia is digital technology. Multimedia represents the convergence of digital control and digital media—the PC as the digital control system and the digital media being today's most advanced form of audio and video storage and transmission. In fact, some people see multimedia simply as the marriage of PCs and video. The courtship has been a long one, but chaste. The two technologies have flirted for years but only recently have they become intimate.

Digital control came first in the guise of the computer, behemoth engines conceived in the 1950s as a faster way to calculate the trajectories of artillery shells. Their exquisite number work led to them taking over any arduous mathematical chore. They worked digitally, turning numbers into patterns of pulses, based on the absolute certainty of the binary dichotomy—by making everything one or zero, on or off, white or black, the machine could suffer no confusion of shades of gray. Numbers could be encoded by assigning a specific pattern to each.

Of course, they had to save their work—or else making calculations would hardly be useful. The natural form for that storage would match that of the calculations, digital patterns of pulses. Soon any business worth its ranking on the Fortune 500 had a library of computer tapes that, stretched end to end, would extend to somewhere outside our solar system.

Digital media are based on the underlying principal that anything that you can perceive with your senses—size, weight, length, color, or sound—can be measured and given a numerical representation. In other words, we can describe our world numerically. Engineers have been doing that for centuries, drawing blueprints for buildings, machines, and sometimes societies (with varying degrees of success). After all, people have been measuring physical quantities since before the Pyramids.

During most of civilization, people have only measured the static—miles between cities, acres of farm, feet of siding. About the time scientists started calculating the trajectories of artillery shells, they discovered they could measure the dynamic phenomena if they measured often enough. How fast depends on the accuracy of the representation, and the need for accuracy depends on our limited human ability to perceive differences. After all, if you can't tell a difference, what does it matter?

In the early 1980s, sound came into the digital realm, quantified and recorded on tape. In 1985, digital music made its American premiere on the compact disc. In 1991, when America started thrashing through proposals for High Definition Television (HDTV) systems, truly digital television became a possibility that quickly grew into reality.

Media and control remained separate at the consumer level because affordable equipment could not process and move digital data fast enough to overwhelm your senses. Thanks to increases in PC power and visionaries willing to diminish your expectations by delivering only partly—or slowly—on their promises, multimedia was born. PC power has reached a level close to that needed for processing television and sound data streams in real time—but not quite. Instead, a number of technical tricks reduce the need for handling really high data rates—small images that change less often, sound by-passing the calculating engines—have brought data rates within the abilities of today's advanced processors.

The main marvel of digital technology is its resistance to noise in transmission and duplication. Digital data holds the potential of truly lasting forever. The information content of a digital signal gets coded into a pattern of only two states, usually represented by electrical or magnetic signal strengths such as a voltage level. Noise, on the other hand, is by definition a random occurrence, so it can take on any voltage level. Engineers have designed digital equipment to ignore signal levels of any but the two states used in their digital systems. In analog systems, the noise gets mixed in with the signal. This noise masks or obscures part of the signal, usually the fainter or more detailed parts.

The advantage of digital technology comes into its own when signals are retransmitted, amplified, or copied. When an analog signal passes through equipment that actively processes it, the noise is amplified or copied right along with the signal. Worse, each stage of processing adds its own signature to the signal in the form of noise and distortion, and these effects are cumulative. Each pass through processing equipment marks a generation in the evolution of the analog signal, and after several generations, the analog signal is apt to become so noisy and distorted that it is unusable.

Digital processing, on the other hand, eliminates noise instead of adding it. Digital processing equipment simply ignores everything but the two desired signal levels, regenerating them. The noise is left behind. Distortion, too, is never allowed to creep into the digital signal.

If enough noise sneaks into a digital signal, there is a chance that it might get confused with one of the logical signal levels. But most digital systems minimize this possibility, too. Many depend on not only signal levels, but also its timing. Noise occurs randomly, so the chance that noise of the right level will blast into a signal at exactly the right instant to be confused with the signal is almost incredibly small.

Almost. There's always a tiny possibility that exactly the right conditions will conspire to push in a pulse of noise that will be misinterpreted as part of the information of the signal. As with analog signals, the possibility increases with every step in transmission or processing. However, digital engineers can reduce this possibility of errors by adding redundancy, extra information that can be used to detect or correct errors. With modern error-handling techniques, the potential for errors in digital systems is often reduced to a chance on the order of one in a billion, as close to a sure thing as you can get outside the world of fiction.

Digital technology does, however, make some major sacrifices to achieve its noise immunity. For one, it loses all subtlety. In theory, an analog system can transmit or reproduce any level and the finest of changes. Its resolution, at least in the abstract, is unlimited. The resolution of digital signals is limited and fixed in the design of the system. In any case, it is less than infinity.

The more resolution or fidelity required in a digital system, the more digital information it must carry, which means more bits, which means more bandwidth. In fact, digital signals typically require many times the bandwidth of their analog equivalents.

That's wonderful if you have a lot of bandwidth with which to work. But engineers rarely have the bandwidth they want. And that lack of bandwidth stymied the development of digital equivalents of analog phonograph records and tapes, as well as analog television signals.

Brute force engineering finally ushered in the digital audio systems we know today. After years of development, engineers found how to fit megabytes of data on small plastic discs. Video requires more finesse. Instead of just increasing the number of bits available for storage, engineers learned how to minimize the bits they needed to store using data compression techniques. Without these innovations, modern multimedia systems would not be possible.

Hardware Standard

All those bits demand processing power to move and control them, dozens of times more processing power than available from the first generation of PCs. That need for power has raised the bar for what's acceptable in a new computer. Instead of an ordinary PC to run today's multimedia software, you need something better, a higher standard. That something is called the *Multimedia PC* or *MPC*, a term that will become numbingly familiar long before you finish this book. For many people, that's what multimedia means: the hardware, a new standard for the next generation—the true second generation—of PCs.

Multimedia PCs are special and different. They stand out from the various odd machines sold over the years chiefly through their power and features. A Multimedia PC requires some abilities that, before the concept of multimedia was accepted, were not available in general purpose computers. In fact, for most of the history of the PC, these capabilities were unavailable, if not technically impossible. Among the features now required by a modern multimedia machine are the ability to store hundreds of megabytes of files, to further exchange hundreds of megabytes on a single disc, to display movies with near-realistic action, to generate sounds with more range than death throes of a penny whistle. Moreover, wielding those new abilities requires more raw data processing power. From nearly every perspective, a Multimedia PC need be more powerful than the mainstream computer—at least until the Multimedia PC defines the mainstream. And that's already happening.

Certainly, standards are rising for all PCs, leading to the convergence. Among contemporary PCs, about the only things that separate an ordinary computer from multimedia are a sound board and CD-ROM drive. Plug 'em in and, gee, Windows will chime instead of beep. Isn't the miracle of multimedia wonderful?

Certainly hearing that chime for the first time will be somewhat less than the transcendent experience the multimedia vendors promise. But don't give up. The strength of multimedia lies deeper and only comes into play when called for. By itself, the Multimedia PC is a machine of promises and potentials.

Two of those potentials arise from a common source: the compact disc. The CD drive that multimedia grafts onto a PC gives you digital audio and a storage medium with large, transportable capacity. Before the advent of the CD, audio was being digitized but not as a mass market item. Only recording pros used it to produce special, extra-price, limited-edition vinyl record albums. (Remember vinyl? Remember the Sixties? Remember anything? No? Then you *do* remember the Sixties.) When it was introduced, the CD system finally did set a standard for consumer digital audio—and a high one at that. Today the CD is not only a distribution standard but it is a quality standard to which all other audio systems are compared.

Today, the CD also serves as multimedia's chief storage and exchange medium. Without the convenient CD, the PC industry would lack a means of distributing the hundreds of megabytes of audio, visual, and textual data that make up today's multimedia titles. Without the CD, you couldn't buy multimedia because publishers would have no way of getting it to you.

The quality and acceptability of multimedia systems has gone hand-in-hand with the CD drives they contain. A slow, first-generation CD player in your PC makes a system that's tedious and frustrating to use. A second-generation double-speed drive moves performance into acceptable territory. But the real excitement of multimedia begins with today's triple-speed and quadruple-speed CD drives. It's not so much simple access to information that makes multimedia so desirable—after all, an ordinary book gives you true random access—but the speed of accessing what you want. Computer technology helps you scan books and libraries as fast as paging to the index of a conventional book. Better performance from your multimedia hardware better fulfills the goal of multimedia systems.

Performance Issue

Disc-based sound isn't the only aural dimension to multimedia hardware. Digitizing sounds to store them is particularly inefficient when precise reproduction isn't necessary. For games, one explosion (of a given magnitude) is good as another. When you're sequencing square dance repertory, it doesn't matter whether the fiddle you play is a Guarneri or Stradivarius. In such situations, synthesized sounds using a sound board has its advantages—it's fast, and storage is compact and more versatile.

With only a CD drive and sound board as its defining endowments, the Multimedia PC is nothing more than a banner that's waved above an array of personal computer hardware and software. It serves more as a marker, or milepost, than a thing in itself. The Multimedia PC is not multimedia. It's only what you need to get multimedia, much as you need paper and ink to have a book.

Even so, the Multimedia PC label does serve a purpose. It sets a *minimum standard* that you'll need for multimedia—or for any modern PC application. The official MPC imprimatur was designed as an assurance of compatibility, that a given computer system had the features and power required to run multimedia software. At that, it set a standard that was a quantum leap ahead of the first generation of personal computers. It sets the minimum for the second generation of PC in terms of microprocessor power, storage, interfaces, and features. It finally puts the steam-powered pioneering attempts at PC-making of a decade ago in their proper place: as memories of things long past.

In all likelihood, the Multimedia PC will prove to be even less than that. Rather than a real computer generation, in retrospect, it will more resemble a bridge that linked the PCs with the next revolution, whatever it may be.

Probably the most important influence of multimedia in the long run will be drawing the line between past and future. The era of the modern PC started with multimedia. Everything before doesn't matter. Operating systems before Windows 3.1 don't matter. Microprocessors before the 386, needed to run Windows 3.1, don't matter. And all the baggage of days before can be safely ignored for the PC's new major market.

Take a look at a graph showing the increase in PC performance over the years. What you get from a contemporary PC is logarithmically ahead of that available only three or four years ago. The numbers aren't important. The direction and the trend speak for themselves. Changes are coming faster and faster.

We put hardware first because the hardware determines the capabilities of the system—what you can do with it. But software determined what you actually get, the image on the screen, the sounds gurgling in the speakers. Software, perhaps, is what makes multimedia.

Software Interface

Defining multimedia in terms of philosophy and hardware skirts the real issue, however. The *media* must have something to do with multimedia, and media in computer terms means software—the words, the sounds, the music, and the images that make up a story, discussion, explanation, or presentation. Defining multimedia as software seems a bit closer to reality.

Software is what makes your multimedia PC come alive. It paints the images on the screen, blasts the sound from the speakers, confuses your keystrokes and generally keeps your life interesting.

But every piece of that software has its own mundane existence. All those words in a multimedia encyclopedia have their counterparts on paper. The images flicker to life as computer graphics, as scanned-in slides, or maybe as little shreds of colorful construction paper glued into a collage, photographed, and sent to the PhotoCD developer. Video images begin with a camera exactly like movies and television. Even the program code of a multimedia application gets written the same way with the same languages as any other computer software—late at night by bleary-eyed hackers jazzed up on Jolt cola. There's nothing unique about any of the constituents of multimedia software. The essence of multimedia really isn't the software.

Nor does multimedia arise from the combination of hardware and software or where the two come together—the interface. What terrible shape we would be in if multimedia were the interface—because what we'd have then is chaos. Multimedia involves not one interface, not two, but dozens. Every place where two somethings come together—computer and disk drive, program and operating system, keyboard and typist—lurks an interface of some kind. Worse, many of them come in more variety than canned vegetables and are about as standardized.

For example, when a designer builds a piece of multimedia hardware, he uses the interface that he thinks is best and leaves it to someone else to figure out how to deal with it. Sound boards, graphics adapters, and modems all have their own particular twists to their interfaces that vary among brands and even within product lines.

The software interface is somewhat saner. Just as you can pop the cap off any beer bottle, no matter its shape with one opener, Microsoft Windows is increasingly the interface of choice for multimedia. Even many OS/2 multimedia programs use the Windows interface.

Notwithstanding that Microsoft autocrat Bill Gates would like to make multimedia mean only Windows, it doesn't. Like your multimedia PC, Windows is only a tool that helps you get multimedia. It's an organizer and standard bearer—at least it helps sort out all the different standards. Windows is pretty much what it says it is when it comes to multimedia: a window, something that you can look through to see what you want to see—that something being multimedia.

So what is multimedia? By now you should agree that multimedia isn't any one thing but a complex (and hard to define) entity that involves many things: hardware, software, and the interface where they meet. But we've forgotten the most important thing that multimedia involves—you.

Yeah, sure. The recipient is part of any communications system. That must be the first thing they teach in Communications 101, right after the professor writes his name on the blackboard. (Remember blackboards?) But multimedia does more than blast information at you. Just like those old, disjointed, multi-projector slide shows, a modern multimedia display involves you. You become part of it, at least until you pass out from boredom. With multimedia, however, you don't have to be a passive recipient. You can take control. You can interact. You can make it do what you want it to. It involves you, you become involved in it, you become part of multimedia.

The college professor types who want to add an academic aura to their observations will tell you that "interactivity" is a feature of multimedia. You might want to call it "fun." At least it will keep you awake, like an unexpected beach picture in a boring business presentation or a welcome sound bite or video clip as you dig through days of research.

That interactivity means more, however. It means you can tailor a multimedia presentation to your own needs. You can cut through the chaff and dig directly into the important data in a report, pull together reports and video clips from around the world that interest you, or just skip over the kissy parts of a video and languorously revel in the terror evoked by the man in a rubber suit stomping on Tokyo. Interactivity is a form of control, the control that multimedia gives you.

The Media

Any stand-up comic knows (or should) it's not the joke but the delivery. And that's the strength of multimedia and what distinguishes it from traditional media like books and television. Multimedia tells the same stories and teaches the same facts, but does it differently. It can make the mundane truly exciting or the boring tedious. Making something in multimedia doesn't necessarily make it better. Success depends, as with the stand up comic, with the storyteller.

Rather than taking multimedia apart and trying to analyze the pieces, a better way to understand it is by what it does as the storyteller. In other words, forget any idea you have about the separate elements of hardware and software. That kind of deconstruction won't get you any closer to understanding the whole. It's like disassembling a clock. Pry off its face and dig in. When you're done, you'll be left with a box full of gears, levers, and springs and still be no closer to understanding time.

The place to start is with one telling question: What does multimedia do? It presents information, shares ideas, elicits emotions, makes you laugh, makes you cry, makes you bored. It enables you to see, hear, and understand the thoughts of others. In other words, it is a form of communications.

The range of communications methods available today starts with the simple spoken word and gesture. Everything else is built on those primitive concepts—language and image. Multimedia combines the most technically advanced forms of those basic communication concepts.

Anything you view on a computer screen is obviously different from the most traditional of media, printed paper. Your first look at the computer screen tipped you off. It glows. It's colorful. And it changes itself instead of demanding you change it as you would page through a book. In fact, a multimedia screen can change second to second, or in a fraction of a second to produce animated images. At that, multimedia sounds like video. But multimedia is different from ordinary video, too. Even on the surface you can tell the difference. To be honest, most of today's multimedia titles look poor when compared to the look of the average video. Most animated computer displays are tiny compared to full-screen video pictures, and the computer images often jerk along, abruptly changing from frame to frame while video is smooth (unless some auteur decides that a rough look will give his video the look he is after). Despite the minuscule screen, multimedia gives you something more. For one thing, you can put multiple images on your screen. Even the default case for multimedia is exotic in the realm of television and video—you can put a picture inside a picture. That's exactly what you do when you have a video window glowing in your desktop or document.

More than multiple images, however, multimedia lets you combine multiple *sources*. Only a few years ago, combining video images required expensive professional equipment that was safely housed in television studios to keep it from falling into the hands of people who might have fun with it. Although that began to change with the advent of the camcorder, the Multimedia PC puts the same power at your fingertips. In fact, you can mix and manipulate video images on your PC in ways that only the most progressive television stations can duplicate—that is, the ones progressive enough to have Multimedia PCs of their own (and staff members creative enough to use them!).

As with the television producer, your multimedia system lets you add sound to your videos, but multimedia does more. Instead of just giving you a soundtrack, with multimedia you can combine sound sources—add in your voice, sounds you've sampled or synthesized, or music from a CD. With the right software, you can alter any of the sounds you work with. You can filter them, change the pitch, add echo, or stretch out a sound without altering the pitch.

The most important difference between ordinary video and multimedia is not the sounds and pictures but the links between them. A movie and a soundtrack are unchangeably linked for their whole length, in sync for their length. That's the whole point of the soundtrack. It's a great arrangement, at least if you want to listen to a story that you've never heard before and have enough time on your hands and attention in your head to listen to it all. Time, however, is something we all have too little of. Little wonder, then, that the fast forward button on your VCR brought a new perspective to movie-watching. When things got too boring or gross, you could press fast forward and leave them far behind. (Wait. Maybe the gross scenes were the inspiration for the pause button and still-framing. At least for male teenagers.) Multimedia takes you the next step, to true random access. You can venture to any picture, any sound, at the moment you want. Sounds can be linked to videos or keep their own separate existence. Not that all the rules of movies and video get broken—they just get redefined with you in mind.

Instead of being linked by time, multimedia lets you connect text, sound, and images by meaning. Instead of standing by as a presentation passes slowly before your eyes, you pick the parts that are important to you.

Nearly all of the ingredients of multimedia have been around for a long time. Movies, records, even CDs have been around for at least a decade. Even the PC is more than a dozen years old. If all the elements have been around for so long, how come multimedia is becoming viable only now?

The performance needs of a Multimedia PC are so great, in fact, that they have turned the traditional view of processing power upside down. Once upon a time, PC makers believed that the home computer was the weaker cousin of the business machine, less costly and less powerful. These same people must have believed in dragons and unicorns, too, because the weakling home computer proved a mythical beast.

In truth, the demands on the home computer are more onerous than on most business machines (the big exception being graphic workstations). Intel's late 1994 Pentium fiasco proved the point. The damage of defective double-precision division was minimal because most Pentiums were serenely ensconced in homes where math errors didn't matter. While the fate of the world might be balanced on a subtle calculation carried out in one of those machines, the world in question was most likely imaginary and generated by Myst. The lesson to be learned from the Pentium problems is not a guide to everything you should avoid in public relations but the understanding of the fundamental shift in the computer industry. PCs are consumer machines, and multimedia has been the driving force.

After all, the average worker doesn't need a powerful machine in business. Except for the top-rung of sharks, the measure of quality has nothing to do with speed. Dedication equates to hours spent in the office, not the number of spreadsheets crunched through a computer. Good judgment doesn't require speed, only accuracy. The longer getting the answer takes, the more difficult the problem must be, the more diligent the worker.

Only with today's cheap, powerful PCs can you get the performance you need to make multimedia palatable. (Even so, the shortcomings are obvious, attested by the tiny, jerky windows of video you see on most monitor screens.) The view will only get better—the performance of the typical PC doubles about every 18 months or so. By the end of the decade, century, or millennium you may not be able to tell the difference between your PC and real video—maybe even between it and reality.

The Future

Multimedia holds promise, so much promise a lot of smart, aggressive, or just plain greedy business people have bet their companies on it. Wise as they may be, they may lack a bit of perspective and see multimedia as an end rather than as a mile marker. Truly understanding the future of multimedia requires a visionary. As envisioned today, multimedia remains a tantalizing first glimpse at what could come.

The first thing the visionary will tell you is that no matter how powerful the PC on your desk or compelling the video on its screen, multimedia remains embryonic. The technology is evolving faster than its application. Or, to put it in more familiar computer terms, the hardware is being developed faster than the software. Most of what's offered today as multimedia is repackaged from old-fashioned print and video, tarted up with buttons to press, coarse animation, and out-of-context sound.

To work over an already overworked comparison, multimedia is now at the same point the printing press was in the time of Gutenberg. It is being used to extend traditional ideas and concepts. The printing press initially served to mass-produce the same works scribes individually scribbled out. The printing press became a more efficient means of handling traditional soft-ware—liturgies and chronicles.

Over the years, however, printing and publishing changed dramatically. Printed works developed into an art form unimagined at the time the press was conceived—the novel. Other book genres evolved out of the technology including the textbook, dictionary, and encyclopedia. Moreover, the form of printed material changed. Book technology enabled the development of the magazine and newspaper (replacing the town crier).

The printing press, in itself an outgrowth of the technologies of etching and engraving, expanded beyond the written word into images and combinations of words and images. By extending the ancient concept of labeling, the print press helped introduce the packaging revolution, which has brought us consumerism and the shopping mall. It also brought us the mall's arch-nemesis, the mail-order catalog. The power of the press is pervasive and appears where you least expect it.

Multimedia currently has developed about as far as Gutenberg pressed printing technology. We've figured out the equivalents of carving individual letters and duplicating their impressions with ink, but we have not yet even conceived modern typefaces or the rotary press. Despite the huge sales volume of computer and multimedia equipment, today's efforts remain tentative. The PC holds its place as the centerpiece of the multimedia system the same way as did the first typeface that attempted to emulate the pen strokes of scribes. It's more familiar and traditional than necessary, and once someone unleashes a better idea, we will never look back (except, perhaps, for the sake of novelty or nostalgia).

Today's multimedia presentation emulates the old technology, the book. Much of the available software is, in fact, centered around the book concept. That's hardly unexpected. For eight centuries we've thought in book terms. More venturesome software jumps ahead about five centuries and attempts other metaphors—the slide show or movie—progressive, perhaps, but neither new nor matched to the technology.

More important than the metaphors themselves is the lesson that they teach. The first efforts at printing with the mechanical press carried the old information and methods of presentation into a new technology that was truly a radically different communications channel. You can see the same concepts in today's first steps at multimedia.

The printing press dramatically changed the role of paper in society. Before the advent of the press, paper was a one-on-one communications medium. You wrote a letter (if you could write), and a courier carried it to a recipient, often the intended one. The printing press made paper a broadcast medium that spread the same message to the multitude. It ushered in the age of mass communication, the paper industry, and many other modern sins. Similarly, multimedia redefines the computer (or its successor) as a new broadcast channel.

Before the advent of multimedia, the PC was seen chiefly as an input mechanism for personal information. Certainly yesterday's PCs churned out reams of paper, but the most significant part of the information coursing through them traced its origins back to the person running the machine. You bought a spreadsheet, database, or word processor to run on your PC so you could fill it with your own numbers and words.

With multimedia, however, the direction of the flow of information is changing so that the computer is becoming a conduit that brings information to you. If only by definition, this reversal in the direction of information flow makes the computer into a consumer device. Thanks to the compact disc, we have a means of acquiring the vast amounts of data that multimedia requires. But the CD is only a short-term solution. It's a force that has helped launch multimedia off the ground and will give multimedia its first big boost. In all likelihood, CDs will continue to be a major force in multimedia for the next few years.

Helping the CD fade from fame will be its successor, already on its way to the market—new CD formats using technologies that may push up capacity more than ten times. Two industry consortia are promoting their visions of the successor to the CD storing up to 10 gigabytes (10GB). Currently the new formats are a long way off.

Just as Beta and VHS butted heads in the early days of home video, each of the two proposals are vying to be the high capacity standard, and such matters will have to be sorted out before you can expect to buy your multimedia on a multi-gigabyte CD. While you're waiting, you can spin ordinary CDs. Or you can try what may be the real direction of multimedia.

For example, you can sniff the first flowering of the alternate technology by logging onto the World Wide Web of the Internet. You'll find a huge library of multimedia awaiting your download. You can find nearly anything, no matter where in the world it lurks, with electronic speed. You can even interact with on-line multimedia, if you don't mind the dropped frames and squeezed sound forced on you by a modem connection. You can exchange video messages, in real time if you're lucky enough to have a fast enough connection.

As you can see, most of the elements of a communication revolution are already present. But a big barrier blocks the path to making multimedia the next mass medium—economics. The price of multimedia still makes it a toy for the privileged. Figure at least $1,000 and probably $2,000 for an acceptable Multimedia PC, another $50 every time you look at a CD, even more if you find one you really want, bills for line charges that make you want to adopt CompuServe as a family member for the purposes of discount calling.

One underlying problem is that today's distribution system is cost-ineffective in the dispensing of data. The CD-ROM is simply a horribly inefficient means of distribution. You can ignore the CD-ROM's slow speed (technology will fix that, right?) and that disks are out of date the day you buy them. (Technology will fix that. Yeah, right.) But the price? If you're buying a reference work, you'll probably have to buy that $50 CD-ROM to get about a nickel's worth of information that you can actually use. Some bargain. Even if you buy a CD for entertainment, you're not cutting such a good deal. Think of the video rental industry—a tape of a movie costs about the same as a CD, but the real value of the entertainment most tapes hold is much less, about the price of a rental. (You may watch a movie more than once, but you probably share your rentals with someone else. It all evens out.) If you actually buy a tape, you're paying for the privilege of having the movie sitting around. Sometimes you may be willing to spring for the additional expense, if the movie means a lot to you or if it's a particularly effective narcotic for the kids. But most of the time, one viewing is enough. If you had to buy outright all the movie tapes you want to watch, you'd be going to the theater more often. Similarly, you pay for the honor of collecting CDs of which you use little of the content. Not that this situation is any different than with the most conventional medium of all, books. You pay for the right to keep the dust off your bookshelves with a set of encyclopedia even if you only use a handful of the facts locked inside.

Multimedia doesn't have to be that way. On-line technology holds the potential for dramatically altering its economics. Multimedia will really blast off when a new, more efficient cost structure works itself out as it has with other media. The printing press freed the information in books from the monastic library. The corner video store made movies-on-demand affordable (if not yet the ultimate in convenience). For the multimedia revolution, some new technology must take hold to change the cost of information from the high cost of CD-ROM.

The wired-in world holds the hope. It could radically alter the cost of information.

By itself, the promise of the oft-touted information superhighway is minuscule. It's a shortcut to the library for the elite who actually need or want to look things up. Like multimedia, however, the Internet and its kin are just another part of the coming revolution and not the revolution itself. As with multimedia's slide-projector heritage, personal digital communications are older in concept than you might think and undergoing exactly the same troubling adolescence. The Internet has been around in one form or another for decades, and anyone with a PC has long had the ability to somehow link up. With a little effort, you can send a message to just about any PC in the world that logs into any bulletin board, university computer system, or information service. Dial up any bulletin board with your PC's modem. You'll find an anarchistic distribution system, promise, and potential not yet ready for prime time.

Media moguls know that once the wired-in world sorts itself out, it will likely be your primary connection with the information universe, with information defined as anything man and machine can translate into bytes—facts, news, videos, movies, games, even the ruminations of visionaries. Instead of depending on a local CD drive as your source of multimedia data, you'll be linking with distribution systems either through your telephone line, a cable TV connection, or other high-speed data channel be it a local area network or (some day) fiber-optic wire linked to your telephone or cable company. In hopes of cashing in on this future, telephone and cable companies are diligently wiring up every loose end of the world. (But they'd missed an important point: the connection is not what's important. The important piece is what the connection brings. The revolution is in the information, not the hardware.)

Traditional information distributors like publishers and production houses see this as the most important part of the future of their industry and are locking up rights to the software. More enlightened telephone companies are pairing with them. They are getting ready. But these link-ups aren't the breakthrough that will unleash the next computer revolution.

Having the information available doesn't mean anyone will use it. Right now, today, you can probably ferret out any fact you need, if you have the time and know who to hire to help you. You could build a stadium in a cornfield, but no one will come to it—unless, of course, you hire Kevin Costner to attract them. Right now the media moguls are trying to find the equivalent of Costner to lure you to their webs so they can, spider-like, suck your wallet dry.

If you fall into the web, you can be rudely surprised at how fast anemia can set it. For example, you can grab nearly any magazine article off-line right now. But in the end you'll pay more than the cover price of the entire magazine for that one article, even if you don't count the charges for connect time. That's not such a good deal, either, particularly when you're looking for one fact in the article. Finding one fact you need typically costs about $10 to $20 worth of searching and downloading—while that's better than buying an entire CD-ROM, it's a roadblock to casual curiosity or simple consumerism. Add in the bulky data requirements of digitized video, and commercial on-line multimedia just doesn't make sense today.

The cost of connecting is changing, however. Ten years ago, data service companies regularly billed you a premium for a high-speed connection—that is, one faster than the 300 baud rate that lets you read the message as it scrolls lazily down the screen, drum your finger, and get a manicure between pages. Today, data services are shifting to one-price-fits-all, even to the extent of billing high-speed ISDN lines (64KB bits per second) the same as ordinary modem connections. Connect time has never been cheaper. And as competition between services becomes more focused and intense, it will likely continue its downward spiral. Meanwhile publishers will discover the magic of demand elasticity, that lowering prices increases demand, purchases, and profits. Suddenly, the lid will explode off.

How big will the multimedia revolution be? The best we can do is put it in perspective for today. It will be bigger than video games. Certainly there is a viable games industry, but it is dwarfed by conventional publishing. It's not just that people are lazy, however. Games are reusable; every time you play you have a new challenge. Pure information is closer to a one-shot affair. My point is not to make any judgment about this difference but to look at the economics. Electronic games are a multi-billion dollar industry.

The annual sales of conventional PC software is measured in tens of billions of dollars. But today's software is aimed in the wrong direction: input. It's simply part of the PC. The electronic distribution of multimedia promises to be much larger.

In fact, the device that brings this information to you will likely be a true computer only in the short term. The computer is useful today in this context; it gives you an available means for accessing information, and it enables you to manipulate and use that information for your own purposes after you receive it. But the needs of computing and information delivery are not the same (instead of the classic garbage in/garbage out, the garbage is already there and you just pick through it for what you need).

But we've forgotten one thing in painting this rosy future. You can't make a store succeed, no matter how low its prices, without something to sell. Translating from one medium to another and pushing the old chestnuts to market only works for a while. The chestnuts get stale and tastes change. The cable television industry never could have succeeded—or probably survived— if all it had to offer were Hollywood's cast-offs.

The on-line distribution systems need a breakthrough equivalent to round-the-clock news (CNN), music videos with an attitude (MTV), or neurasthenia on demand (C-SPAN). The web will be the distribution channel and multimedia the technology. What will put that pairing to work hasn't been sorted out. A lot of important people have ideas and hopes (most of which are based on repackaging what's already around—a cheap, expedient solution you can exploit without much vision (or taste, for that matter). The real breakthrough will be something revolutionary, something no one has yet thought up. Unless you have an idea.

That's perhaps the number one reason for getting involved in multimedia right now. The technology is young, and everyone is still crawling around, feeling his own way. You and your ideas could dramatically change the direction of technology. You could mold the future. You could write the definition of multimedia yourself.

Chapter 2
Applying Multimedia

The box lies empty in the corner, eyed warily by your 2-year-old as a prospective fort. Cables stream from it down the sides of your desk wrestling with the electrical outlet like a pugnacious octopus. Finally everything is in place and plugged in, so you flip the switch. And your multimedia PC comes to life with a rattle from the disk drive and a bright new face on its screen. It glows before your eyes, waiting, just waiting for your command. So what are you going to do with your multimedia PC? What can you do with it? Change your life? Change the world?

You probably did have grand goals when you decided to move up to multimedia. Perhaps not that grand, but you may have bought into multimedia based on expectations of wonder and delight. After all, multimedia is today's hot toy for the technology set—but it's more than that. Or maybe you bought your multimedia PC because that's about all that's being sold for personal use anymore. Maybe you haven't bought a machine yet but are looking to get a running start on the next revolution. In any case, your first question should always be what you're going to use your new machine for.

The answer is obvious: you want your machine to show you multimedia. But what multimedia? Do you have a specific application in mind or is your multimedia machine an answer looking for a question, a PC in search of software, a lost soul looking for meaning in life?

Nothing about a multimedia PC precludes it from running non-multimedia software. In fact, your multimedia PC is probably an excellent platform for any program you choose to run. Meeting multimedia standards assures that your PC has the power to run nearly all current software—and run it fast. A multimedia PC has all the memory and microprocessor power needed to race through nearly all PC applications.

Scope

Above all else, multimedia is a means of communication, a tool for conveying information. It stands out from all other communications systems in that its strength is in the presentation—multimedia has more impact; multimedia is more exciting; multimedia can be just plain fun. The real value of multimedia, however, lies in the substance behind the flash. After all, if you found no value to what you get from multimedia, it would have quickly shriveled and died, just another fad like disco, pet rocks, and the international communist conspiracy.

In fact, there's a lot more than flash to multimedia. Behind the pretty video face lies a wealth of information, the content of the communication. Of course, exactly what constitutes information is in the eye and mind of the beholder. The range runs the gamut of modern mindspace, everything from complete encyclopedia of every fact a normal human being can digest (or tolerate) to an interactive description of an imaginary world in which you can frolic. Multimedia can convey anything that any other communications channel can—only multimedia can do it better.

Even though compared to other communications means, the infant we call multimedia is still teething, it's already chewing up older technologies. After all, it has hybrid vigor thanks to being a breeding of the best features of older technologies. For example, its electronic roots add instant accessibility to information. You can find what you need fast. You can dig out the details what you need to know or simply what interests you quickly and simply using modern search algorithms. Instead of running your finger down an index and flipping through pages, you can almost instantly zip to references—without holding your place with your thumb. You can logically link search criteria to narrow things down and catapult yourself from one reference to another. Better still, you can search through the entire library as easily as through a single book.

Multimedia gains, too from the depth of content permitted by today's highest-density storage systems. With today's CD-ROM-based multimedia systems, you have immediate, on-line access to about 650MB of readily exchangeable data. Most optimistic observers equate that to 325,000 pages of text (based on the rather spurious assumption that a page holds 2,000 characters)—that's the equivalent of several shelves of ordinary books. Of course, the only optimists left in the modern world write advertising copy for computer systems. Realists know that single CD capacity hardly equates to 1,000 books because a true multimedia disc includes information that ordinary books cannot. CDs give over their megabytes to movies and sounds as well as ordinary text. Still, one CD easily holds a complete encyclopedia linked to a library of film clips.

The flash of multimedia is not without its value, either. Sounds, illustrations, and animations help you learn. One picture is worth a lot of understanding—it can clarify concepts, help visualize relationships, and just keep you from falling asleep. A drawing makes the parts of a flower plain; a chart can outline the relationships between the House of Lancaster and House of York; a map can illustrate the military importance of Gibraltar.

Multimedia on CD-ROM is just the start, however. Couple the search and illustrative abilities of today's multimedia technologies with the reach and scope of the growing international data network, and all the knowledge of the world will soon be at your fingertips. You'll be able to search not just across a shelf of books but all books. And play games with anyone, anywhere, any time—providing your partner is willing, of course.

Today much of multimedia's potential remains untapped. Video means different things in the context of television and multimedia. The marriage between computers and video is still a courtship—neither is certain it wants to make a commitment. Neither gives its all.

What you can capture with your camcorder puts the professional moving images in most multimedia discs to shame. Too much of the time you get small images with jerky motion that lasts only briefly. Broadcast television—even cable—is to multimedia as the Louvre is to Sunday comics. But even today's rudimentary software commands interest, just as the comics may be the first part of the Sunday newspaper you delve into. The sound of multimedia is similarly second-rate, but not because of technical limitations (as is the case with video). Most multimedia systems simply shirk on sound with barely adequate speakers at fad-level prices. All that said, multimedia may today fall far short of its potential but still is useful and entertaining. Better still, it can only get better.

Production and Consumption

As with any communications medium, multimedia has two sides, sending and receiving, just as every conversation involves someone talking and someone else listening. Although the process often is symmetrical with each participant taking turns speaking and waiting for others to speak their minds, in practice communications as well as conversations tend to be one-sided. In multimedia, matters are no different. Sending and receiving often involve different people, technologies, software, and concerns at each end. Some people look at multimedia as a means of getting their message across. Others want only to listen in.

In its current form, commercial multimedia works most like an electronic lecture, a *broadcast* medium. It distributes information from a single source to many people just as a television stations transmits from one studio to (the station manager hopes) millions of households. In this scheme of things, most people will be recipients of multimedia. They will view, interact with and (the publisher hopes) enjoy material prepared by others. That's as it should be. Unless you are omniscient (and few of us who have passed our teen years are), you always stand to learn from others.

Participating as the multimedia audience is the practical approach. After all, preparing a single multimedia presentation takes hundreds or thousands of hours of work. Elaborate productions now have budgets approaching $1 million.

But multimedia is more than just commercial software. You don't have to make a mass-market multimedia show to put the technology to work. You can use the power and features of multi-media to embellish the work and fun you already do. Just as including charts and graphics in letters was unheard of 10 years ago and now is common (if not expected) practice, voice and video annotation will likely become part of your personal correspondence and business reports in the coming decade. Already you can attach sound bites and film clips to your correspondence as easily at charts and graphs. Eventually the animations may replace the rest of your message.

Of course, even if you don't aspire to commercial distribution you can always prepare your own multimedia presentation for your own entertainment, for a business purpose (such as training), or simply as a learning experience to get ready to make it into the commercial multimedia market. Current technology makes production easy.

If you do decide to go professional, opportunity abounds because the market and medium are new. With practice and an adequate supply of free time you could create the first multimedia million seller on your own PC, today, with software costing only a few hundred dollars.

Mass Market Multimedia

On the receiving end, the software you need for multimedia is simple—if you have a PC capable of running multimedia and a multimedia-capable operating system, you need nothing more. The multimedia CDs you buy bring with them everything they require, not only the information but the programs required for reading, displaying, and searching same. Slide the disk into your CD-ROM drive, run through a quick, automatic installation process, and you're ready to explore, interact, and learn. Commercially-distributed software aimed at you on the receiving side of the multimedia broadcast includes reference works like encyclopedia, games, and even training and instructional lessons.

On the sending side, multimedia's widest application is annotation—adding sounds and images (still and moving) to other work you do on your PC. For the most part, you don't need anything other than the software that came with your multimedia PC to add sounds or images to your ordinary work. Today's operating systems have those functions built right in.

Writing your own applications is another matter. It's more complex than penning a novel or even scripting a movie because you have to add in a new element: programming. You can't get the full power of multimedia features without tangling with programming issues. Although for most multimedia presentations you probably won't have to actually write in programming code, you will need authoring software. We'll consider this side of multimedia separately in Chapter 5, "Authoring Multimedia."

Commercial multimedia software falls into several application areas. The most common are education, training reference, entertainment, and games. Inevitably these areas overlap. After all, most multimedia software can be so much fun to use that it's entertaining—even if its primary goal is education or reference. But we need some kind of organization to put the multimedia puzzle together, and these classifications are as good as any. Let's take a look at some of the most important of today's commercial multimedia applications and some examples of what publishers offer in each area. With so much software available—and more crushing into the market—our view is necessarily scattergun. We'll look at the more visible titles, those that you are more likely to have heard about because of publicity or reviews.

Education

Apple started it all. The message hidden in the company's early advertising was hardly subtle: without a computer your kid will grow up dumber than a box of sedimentary rocks. Without a computer to serve up the latest digital data, the knowledge your kid absorbs will be hopelessly out of date, pre-industrial rubbish that can only pollute the mind and hold the child back from an Ivy-league education. Without computer stimulation, the modern brain atrophies to the point it can only receive signals from MTV and comic books. Such pleas to your parental guilt work well, particularly when your offspring joins in as a co-conspirator, jockeying for a venue to play DOOM by portraying it in the guise of a diploma machine.

Fact: by high school, education turns so gray that the only things that a PC does usefully work perfectly well in ancient text mode. The PC works as a word processor for reports and, rarely (though this should change) as a research engine that can connect to on-line databases. Any kid that thinks he can base a report on what he finds in the shallow confines of Microsoft's *Encarta* is destined to earn the same "C" as was awarded to his parents when they cribbed from their dog-eared desktop encyclopedia. Today's multimedia reference works are mostly educational enticement rather than in-depth information sources.

Although an admission, that's not a condemnation. Anything that encourages learning should be applauded. If buying Microsoft's *Dinosaurs* inspires your child to want to be a paleontologist, it's done as much as the best teachers ever aspire to. Education is more than learning—finding and memorizing facts. Moreover, becoming familiar with computers—and particularly those that use the latest technologies—is now a mandatory part of education because computers are intrinsic to the workplace. Even playing DOOM will help your child gain the right attitude toward the PC—not to hold it in awe but to put it to work.

If there is one rule to follow in using a PC in your child's education it is that the computer should become part of your child's life early on. Multimedia works wonders with pre-literate children. They don't have to read to use it because they can recognize images on the screen (with a sophistication many parents fail to understand or appreciate) and through spoken accompaniment. Animation and color can hold even the most itinerant attention. Pre-literate kids can identify icons and push a mouse around to control their own software. They can play games to entertain themselves. Better still, the games they play can aid in their learning more advanced skills. Although many of today's early childhood learning applications are a bit heavy-handed—spelling things out with all the pomposity of a college lecture—as programmers and educators become more skilled in getting young children involved and learning (even in spite of themselves) multimedia holds the promise of entertaining, educating, and occupying the wandering minds of youngsters better than the other great electronic babysitter, television. Mastering a simple multimedia system gives children a sense of accomplishment that television cannot. It involves them physically and intellectually—at which television utterly fails on the former and you be the judge of the latter.

At higher education levels, multimedia is an inspiration to exploration and rumination. It can make you want to discover and learn. It can make you think. Even if you don't believe that multimedia is anything more than flash, you must remember that the flash can be motivation, and motivation is the most important aspect of learning. As with the old joke about psychiatrists and light bulbs (How many shrinks does it take to change a light bulb? One, but it has to want to change.) you have to want to learn, and the electronic excitement of multimedia provides the motivation.

Commercial educational multimedia runs a wide gamut in itself. The least desirable of the software follows the old rote learning model of teaching with drills, hoping to open a hole in the densest head through which knowledge may pour in. Most of these program seek to minimize the tedium of their chores by turning the drill into a game. Answering a question properly earns you points until finally you graduate to the next level. Done with wit, it can dull the edge of the drill. Better educational applications turn learning into exploration and let your child discover while journeying through some kind of intellectual adventure.

The range of topics covered by today's educational multimedia software is large, though a few topics have inspired multiple publishers to take their own approaches. Among these popular topics are human anatomy, geography, and history.

The approaches taken by individual products may be dramatically different, and nowhere are individual differences more apparent than in the human body. A few of these products are:

> **A.D.A.M. The Inside Story** (A.D.A.M. Software, about $50) translates the infamous visible man into the multimedia world. It gives you a layer by layer look at the human body including skeleton, nerves, circulatory system, organs, and glands. Its static-graphics approach, reminiscent of better illustrated books, is augmented by simulations and narrations to help explain how the body works. The naughty parts are present, but parents can restrict how much of the really interesting stuff that kids can view.

> **The Magic School Bus Explores the Human Body** (Microsoft Home, about $50), on the other hand, mixes in more television-based entertainment as it takes you for a ride through the various conduits inside each of us. With full-screen animation almost on par with the PBS Magic School Bus series, you can go with the flow or poke around with your mouse. Click objects, and they may take a surprising turn. In case the learning gets too serious, the Bus brings a number of games to play.

Publishers have taken a number of different tacks in teaching history, too. Some rely on the power of images themselves to make impact, others mix in games to sugar-coat the learning experience. Some available products are:

Exploring Ancient Architecture (Medio Multimedia Inc., $59.95) takes the straightforward approach and acts as your tour guide through seven architectural wonders from Stonehenge to the Parthenon. Not static pictures, you walk through a three-dimensional photo-realistic rendering of each, complete with a floorplan that lets you choose the route.

Museum Madness (MECC, $49.95) aims for more involvement by challenging you or your kid's deductive abilities to help bring order to a museum with a computer run amuck and exhibits that come to life. The program is presented as an adventure game that requires you to solve puzzles as you work your way into a locked museum that hold exhibits that have mysteriously come to life. While you work your way through the program, you learn about ecology, energy, history, and space as each challenge confronts you.

The Yukon Trail (MECC, $69.95) attempts to make learning an adventure, too, but a more true-to-life experience. It follows a historic model, putting its pre-teen audience into the role of gold-rushers trekking from Seattle to Alaska in search of Yukon gold. They start with an outfitting, book passage, and make their ways through the wilderness to find fortune while keeping a journal along the way. The fun comes when the PC challenges them with a surprise turn of events such as a natural calamity. To reach the goal, they have to work their way around the problem, learning along the way.

Of course, the best way to scare kids away from something is to let them know that the something is good for them or—worse—educational. Several developers have chosen to make their kid's software obstensibly games belying the educational content.

Where in the World is Carmen Sandiego? (Brøderbund Software, $59.95) is a classic in this regard, a game that teaches geography. This latest incarnation lets your kids stalk arch-criminal Carmen across the territory of CD-ROM. The object is to chase Carmen's gang around the world, gathering clues to solve a crime before the clock runs out. Of course, no one cannot travel dozens of times around the world without learning landmarks and locations, particularly considering making progress requires answering geographic questions. Unlike early floppy-disk versions, this CD-based version is a true multimedia experience complete with enough exquisite photographs, foreign languages, and folk music to make education almost inadvertent.

Morgan's Trivia Machine (Morgan Interactive, $34.95) shows a more conservative approach, turning a question-and-answer quiz into a humorous learning game. Its 1,000+ questions are drawn from science, geography, and a miscellaneous grab bag and can be tailored as to difficulty between players so parents can compete fairly with pre-teen kids (the parents, of course, get the easy questions).

Hands-on education means learning by doing, and multimedia helps here, too. A program can simulate a modern-day real-life experience and let kids participate. Or multimedia can be the subject itself.

The Musical World of Professor Piccolo (Opcode Interactive, $69.95), for example, teaches about different kinds of music by taking you or, better still, your children to visit various venues, including the concert hall, a church, and jazz club. Thanks to the multimedia simulations, you get an in-context foundation in musical basics such as jazz improvisation and rock riffs.

Multimedia Workshop (Davidson & Associates Inc., $79.95) gives young folk the real thing to work with—it's a true multimedia authoring tool, adapted for kids. They can build their own presentations from text they write, illustrations, photographs, and video clips using an automated storyboard called the Sequencer. By actually building multimedia works, they will learn about PCs, authoring, and whatever subject they choose to explore.

References

The search power of the PC makes it the perfect venue for encyclopedic research, so it's little wonder that among the first reference systems brought into the multimedia fold were encyclopedias. At least four publishers quickly introduced multimedia versions of encyclopedias: Brittanica, Compton's, Grolier's, Microsoft. The rapid entry of these players is natural. The first three had their encyclopedias already prepared, complete with illustrations. The last had the best grasp on the technology, its implementation, and its potential. All knew that the PC was the perfect reference mechanism. The capacity of the CD-ROM to store dozens of books makes encyclopedic storage a natural. The graphics, animation, and search abilities make multimedia versions superior to the paper predecessors.

There is a downside to adding multimedia to reference databases, however. Although a CD-ROM holds a lot, graphics and animation require a lot of storage. As a result, most multimedia augmentations can cramp out information as each tries to find space in the confines of a CD. Something has got to go and typically it's not the show—after all, multimedia images are the prime selling point of these systems. Consequently the multimedia encyclopedia that include extensive collections moving images usually lack the depth of information of their paper-based counterparts. Of course, this same shortcoming is an advantage if you're surfing rather than searching out in-depth research—the electronic versions are more accessible and don't hold you back with dead weight—heavy facts that weigh down your progress.

As with old-fashioned paper books, CDs, too, quickly grow out of date. Many CDs are updated yearly just as books come in new editions. But the world continues to change even after books and CDs find their final form in printing or stamping. Such obsolescence is inevitable, but with multimedia it's not unavoidable. By combining on-line communications with CD-distribution media, you can keep electronic references continually up-to-date. These combined systems give you the advantages of each constituent part. CD storage gives you a huge database that enables you to dig through years of historical data. The on-line connection brings updates that can reasonably be kept on your hard disk. When you disk fills, you can update to the next edition of the CD and clear out all of the update files.

The five principal encyclopedias now available on CD run a broad range.

Britannica CD (Encyclopedia Britannica, $995) is the most conservative, the most in-depth, and the least multimedia influenced. It puts the full contents of what many regard as the most authoritative encyclopedia on disc, a full 16 million references in 82,000 articles. Heavy on the information, it includes relatively few illustrations. It's best as an quick-search enhancement to the paper version and marred by hardware copy-protection.

Compton's Interactive Encyclopedia (Compton's NewMedia, $395) emphasizes depth more than flashiness, making it a better choice for serious research (though not in league with Brittanica). True multimedia, it includes video and a few animations in addition to its generous hyperlinked text base that enables you to instantly seek out individual topics. In addition, its "idea search" feature will let you find related topics in which the item of your interest plays a secondary role. It's at its best helping your kids prepare single-page homework assignments.

Grolier Multimedia Encyclopedia (Grolier Electronic Publishing, about $100) attempts to be an in-depth research aid with multimedia capabilities. In fact, it is essentially a from-paper translation enhanced with some video (such as interviews with contemporary figures like Buzz Aldrin and Kurt Vonnegut, Jr.) and multimedia overviews of broad topics like architecture, the human body, and world history. Although it uses many of the usual search methods, it's sometimes quirky.

Microsoft Encarta, *issued annually,* (Microsoft Home, about $100) is Microsoft's demonstration of what multimedia reference should be—lots of flash and excitement and even some reference material. If you're looking for information, you might find it obscured rather than enhanced by 100 videos, 83 animations, 6,500 photographs. Consider it as an exploration tool rather than reference work.

Webster's Interactive Encyclopedia (Cambrix Publishing, about $40) is a low-cost way of peeking at the technology, although it's weak in the exact places you would want strength. Rather than seeking depth, it's built around short, light articles and accented with many multimedia features. Unfortunately what it lacks in depth it also lacks in polish, and accessing the multimedia is sometimes inelegant.

The same trade-off between depth and flash carries over in other reference areas.

Microsoft Bookshelf, *issued annually,* (Microsoft, $79.95), sounds promising from what it includes—seven major reference works: The Columbia Dictionary of Quotations, The American Heritage Dictionary of the English Language, The People's Chronology, The Concise Columbia Encyclopedia, The Hammond World Atlas, The Original Roget's Thesaurus, and The World Almanac and Book of Facts. Better still, the work as a whole has been augmented with video animation and sound clips. Unfortunately, although the breadth is wide, none of the references delve very deeply. It's sort of the *USA Today* of reference works. The encyclopedia introduces new topics, the almanac adds a bit of perspective to recent events, the dictionary gives quick definitions, the atlas includes rough maps that will help locate major cities and nations but little more. It holds promise of being exactly what you need when you are immersed in research and something unfamiliar appears that you're assumed to know. The interface of the latest version of Bookshelf has honed this function by adding a new program called QuickShelf which drops a Windows toolbar on top of your other Windows applications so you can visit this reference with a single click. Too often, however, you have quick access to nowhere when you discover what you're looking for isn't covered.

McGraw-Hill Multimedia Encyclopedia of Science & Technology (McGraw-Hill Inc., $1,300) shows the other extreme. It's an expensive collection of in-depth information that delves into more than 100,000 entries, 7,300 of them as full-length articles, on hard-core scientific topics suitable for penning college-level papers or helping shore up professional research. Although generalist in coverage, articles zero-in on specifics such as individual chemical compounds. Emphasis is on depth and ease of access using searching and hypertext links. But what you gain in depth you lose in flash. Multimedia power is minimal, limited to coarse full-screen bit-mapped illustrations, tiny, short animation, and low-quality sound.

Beyond general references, publishers have attempted to find topics that interest you as multimedia titles. One of the leading choices is health care. Even in such a well-defined area, however, the available titles run a wide range.

Complete Guide to Symptoms, Illness & Surgery (Great Bear Technology, about $30) is not a diagnostic aid but a medical reference. Arranged by name rather than symptom, it's complete enough to support a term paper but won't help you discover what ails you.

Dr. Schueler's Home Medical Advisor Pro (Pixel Perfect, $69.95) is best regarded more as entertainment than a substitute for a real MD when it attempts to identify ailments from symptoms, which is always risky to rely on. Even though the program concentrates only on more common ills, you'll find it's not always right. Better is its drug reference, which can pinpoint some interactions that may be dangerous. For your multimedia entertainment, Dr. Schueler will regale you with a collection of still and video images of a multitude of medical conditions, all in vivid enough detail to make you genuinely ill.

PharmAssist (SoftKey International, about $40) is like having your local druggist on call. Start with the brand or generic name of a drug, and you can discover significant (and potentially dangerous) interactions and side effects. In addition, you'll find suggested medications for some common conditions, first aid help, even advice on drug abuse.

Other multimedia reference titles run the full range of human interest, from the practical (home improvement) to trivial (movie lore). Here are some examples:

Home Survival Toolkit (Books That Work Inc., $49.95) gives you much more than a hypertext repair manual. Not only do many of the topics include animated illustrations with icons to lead you to related topics or tell you the tools you need for repair, but also several survival guides to help you through common difficulties and estimators to help you calculate material you'll need for common repairs and home improvements.

Microsoft Cinemania, *issued annually,* (Microsoft Corporation, $59.95) will overwhelm you with movie trivia as well as guide you to the perfect rental. You can search out your favorite stars or select film by genre. Covering more than 20,000 films, this compendium laces together reviews and biographies with stills, video clips, dialog and soundtrack excerpts, you may find the disc more fun than the films.

PhoneDisc PowerFinder (PhoneDisc USA, $249) is not really multimedia, but it will put your Multimedia PC to work finding just about any telephone subscriber in the country. Essentially a nation-wide white pages, its five CDs list about 91 million home and business phone numbers as well as the corresponding addresses. The Windows-based program maintains everything in database format, which enables you to search by name, number, address, or business type.

Select Phone (Pro CD, $150) similarly collects the business and residential telephone numbers of the complete United States on a five CD set. Although it lacks some of the business-oriented data of other packages, it's workable and low-priced.

Small Blue Planet: The Real Picture Atlas (Cambrix Publishing, $79.95) is a photographic atlas of the world that doesn't so much show you where things are as how they look when viewed from on high. Visual only, Small Blue Planet exploits your multimedia PC's power to give you a spy satellite view that lets you progressively zoom in on a particular city, geographic feature, or even meteorological event. This is a collection for gawkers rather than researchers, however, because the images essentially stand on their own.

Taxi (News Electronic Data, $79.95) is a compendium of maps of five major American cities—Chicago, Los Angeles, New York, San Francisco, and Washington, D.C. More than putting you in your place, Taxi will help you enjoy it by giving you appraisals of hotels and restaurants drawn from Zagat-Axxis CityGuides. You can search out your favorite cuisine, ambiance, quality of service, and price range with electronic speed, get the address, and print out a map showing you how to get there. It's the perfect justification for a Multimedia notebook PC.

Warplanes: Modern Fighting Aircraft (Maris Multimedia, $69) brings together technical data on 500 modern airplanes and 200 of their weapons systems presented in the form of move than 1,000 full-screen photos, video clips, and technical details like dimensions, performance, armaments, and costs. The text is fully searchable and includes hypertext links. You can even walk around any of 25 three-dimensional models created from engineering drawings or put your hands on the sticks of three of the planes in flight simulations.

Training

Because multimedia is fun as well as educational, it serves well as a training medium. Instead of submitting the unlearned to an ordeal as dull as home movies but without the potential for catching embarrassing incidents, multimedia can bring trainees into the material. Interactivity demands their attention. The buzz word you'll most likely see is *CBT*, which stands for *Computer Based Training.*

Just as a picture is worth a thousand words, an animation is worth a thousand pictures—particularly if it goes on for 20 seconds or so. (At motion picture rates, a 20-second cartoon clip comprises about 1,000 frames.) Animation allows the trainee to see the process instead of just the preparation and result. Multimedia lets you watch cartoon-like animation or actual film clips as part of your training presentations, in context and in detail. You see how all those statuesque poses in the golf book work together as a proper swing, how you can actually reach that impossible to grab spark plug squeezed between the manifold and firewall, how you can whisk a roué into a perfect sauce without setting off the smoke alarm. Moreover, because multimedia training is interactive, you can stop the show and examine each step (at least with some multimedia presentation software).

In addition, hypertext links in training let you instantly dig as deeply as you want when you need more information or explanation. Click a word, and you get the background you need to clarify confusion issues or fill in gaps in your understanding.

Because multimedia training presentations are interactive, you can course through them at your own speed. The material responds to your needs instead of pushing your pace to the spin of a movie projector's reels. You can scroll ahead past familiar explanations and linger on the turgid details. You need not fret about frying your neurons into a headache or boring your gray matter into blubber. The one personal who knows your brain's learning capacity and rate is in control—you.

Training is, of course, a two-way street that involves both learning and teaching. Today's multimedia systems are adept at both. The same hardware that lets you learn can also let you teach. You can create your own training presentations with little more effort (or, perhaps, even less) than you would with classical media such as film or booklets. The multimedia PC gives you an integrated environment for developing your work. You can work with text, sound, and images in the same software and interface.

Entertainment

Drawing the line between education and entertainment in multimedia can be almost impossible. After all, multimedia can make learning so much fun it becomes entertainment. That's enough reason for investing in it. For example, you can listen to Microsoft's Beethoven just for the aural pleasure, but information about Beethhoven's symphonies are always just a keystroke away.

But multimedia has a pure entertainment side, as well. At its best, you can consider it MTV on demand or a video jukebox. Anything that's possible in sound and images is possible on a multimedia CD.

Sound is the easy part. All multimedia CD drives can play the same discs that you slide into your stereo system. You can make your PC do double duty as both workplace and entertainment system. In fact, you can replace your entire stereo with your multimedia CD. Add an FM receiver board and your PC can do anything your stereo can—play CDs, tune in your favorite FM stations, or record (although on your hard disk).

In fact, electronic integration has already sneaked in the back door. You can add PC components cheaper than buying stereo add-ons. CD-ROM drives are now competitive with the stereo system CD players. FM receiver boards are available with a street price under $50. If you want, you can even add-in a TV tuner for about the same price as a small television set. Your PC can take the place of your entire entertainment system. (In fact, it can mastermind all the electronics you need—add in a communications board and your PC can put both your answering machine and fax machine out of work, too.) A brief overview of a few multimedia programs that represent cross-overs from other, more traditional media, follow:

Beethoven's Fifth (Interactive Publishing, $59.95) performs the aforementioned symphony complete with an accompanying explanatory text keyed to the music so you can stay abreast as Beethoven developed his themes. In addition you'll find the requisite biography of the composer to help you understand the position of the symphony in the panoply of orchestral compositions, an orchestra seating chart to help you listen for particular instruments, and a glossary of musical terminology.

Detroit (Impressions Software, $69.95) lets you try a turn as the next (for first) Henry Ford and build your personal auto industry. Starting in 1908 and bankrolled to the tune of $60,000, you have 100 years to set up the assembly line, develop the technology, build the cars, and sell them. Monitor your progress with profit-and-loss statements, market comparisons, and sales reports.

European Racers (Revell-Monogram, $69.95) puts your PC in the place it will occupy in the future, a presentation medium that helps out with more mundane and traditional pursuits—in this case, model-building (as you might expect from the publisher). The multimedia CD itself presents you with exploded views of the pieces of four Revell-Monogram car kits including the Bugatti EB 110, the Lamborghini LP500S, the Nazca M12, and Porsche 911 Slant Nose (the last accompanies the disc) and the instructions for assembling same. Putting some of the power of your multimedia PC to work, you can preview paint schemes on-screen. Once you're done with the car (or tired of the tedium of assembly), you'll find a multi-level race game that puts your choice of the four cars on the track with you behind the wheel.

Gettysburg Multimedia Battle Simulation (SWFTE International Ltd., $69.95) lets you experience or even control the three-day battle that changed the American Civil War. Start with a narrated historical simulation complete with movie clips, statistics, and other details. Short documentaries present background on weaponry, terrain, strategy, and leadership. Switch to interactive mode, and the troops—blue or gray—carry out your orders, even to rewrite history.

J.F.K. Assassination: A Visual Investigation (Medio Multimedia, $59.95) lets you concoct your own conspiracy theory or put your mind to rest about the circumstances surrounding the 1963 death of President John F. Kennedy. In true multimedia form, this CD collects newsreels, home movies, videotapes, and sound recordings to tell the story of the assignation. You can do your own research from the included Warren Commission report or actual footage of the shooting, including the Zapruder film and two others (which you can analyze one frame at a time).

Supersonic (Interactive Publishing, $79.95) is a collection of both still and video photographs of fighter jets and helicopters in action complemented with listings of their firepower and specifications. If you get bored gawking, you'll find an interactive section complete with some primitive games.

Twain's World (Bureau Development, $39.95) compiles all known writing of Mark Twain including everything from his great novels to minor speeches and essays. In addition, the collection includes an array of images and an almost unbelievable film of Twain himself, the only known footage of the author that may have been shot by Thomas Edison. The included readings of Twain's works are, however, by a modern narrator.

Games

Multimedia means interaction, and to many interactive entertainment means games. Don't look down your nose at the computer game. The best games show new computer technologies at their finest.

In fact, computer games were a multimedia experience even before multimedia was hatched. The first PCs lashed primitive graphics and sounds together to create a challenging (in many ways) experience.

Game designers didn't just embrace multimedia early, they have continually pushed the limits of every technology they've bumped into. For example, games were quick to take advantage of the capacity of CD-ROM storage; now games are pushing into multi-CD packages. Game makers should be credited with priming demand for sound boards and realistic graphics.

Multimedia games differ from video games the same way a PC differs from a typewriter. While good at what they do, the video game promises nothing more. The multimedia PC promises the world.

Video games mean action. The primary control you get is a joystick (or gun or something with a similar point-and-punch function). The game is rigidly structured and presents a series of fixed tasks, although in variety. Typically you scale levels based on accomplishments that require a high degree of control and, sometimes, a bit of strategy. But the entire game world is pre-ordained. The goal is set and you are channeled into the one true means of solving it.

Video games incorporate the latest in technology. In fact, the leading video game processors have some characteristics more advanced than those in many PCs. For example, video games now exploit 64-bit technology while nearly all PCs have 32-bit logic cores.

Let's be honest. If you just want to play action games, the dedicated video game systems are superior. Thanks to things like that 64-bit technology, they present superior—that is, more realistic and faster moving—graphic images. Of course, the graphic used in video games get their edge from slighting somewhere else. They only need generate resolution at the lowest end of the PC range. The multimedia games on your PC have to deal with the overhead of an operating system, several times more pixels, and probably a lot more creativity on the part of the program-mers. On the other hand, a video game is solely an investment in neuro-anesthesia. A multimedia PC is a full-power system that can also play games when the left side of your brain needs to recharge. For example:

Iron Helix (Spectrum Holobyte Inc., $99.95) gives you the chance to save a planet from a doomsday weapon streaking toward it out of control. You can't shoot it down, but you can outsmart it—if it doesn't get you first. This multimedia tour-de-force includes top-quality video and music that will challenge all but the most powerful PCs.

The Journeyman Project (Quadra Interactive, $79.95) takes you into a 21st Century that's happy in having finally found world peace and unsettled because the creating of a time machine could potentially rewrite history and end the new Nirvana. Your role in the game is as a member of the Temporal Protectorate, going back in time to undo the dastardly deeds that may unravel time's fabric. The game itself mixes adventure with arcade-style action (slow and sometimes jerky because it runs directly from CD) mixed with enough sardonic humor to keep your soul alive.

Rebel Assault (LucasArts Entertainment, $79.95) takes action gaming into outer-space and into a galaxy far beyond our own. You sit in the hot seat—the cockpit of a *Star Wars* X-wing fighter. You start as a neophyte and earn your wings on training flights. Eventually you work your way up through several levels of difficulty in half a dozen scenarios until the final challenge, an attack on the Death Star that by rights (and script) only Luke Skywalker should succeed at. The simulations are as good as the *Star Wars* special effects, with three-dimensional graphics combined with video images that will make you believe that you're actually there, wherever there might be.

Video Cube: Space (Aris Multimedia Entertainment Inc., $49.95) combines Rubik's cube with images and video. Instead of colors, you rearrange the cube to form pictures on each of its six sides, earning the display of a space-age video when you win. Each of the 18 levels of this single-player game are timed and increase in difficulty, although you don't need extraordinary skill to win.

Making Multimedia

The other side of multimedia is production, using the technology and your talents to create works of your own. You don't have to be so ambitious (and optimistic) as to strive to develop your own encyclopedia or even a commercial product that would require real multimedia authoring. You can work on a more personal level, for example adding vocal comments or snapshots to your electronic journal.

Music

Long ago musicians learned that electronics are a creative tool, one that amplifies and synthesizes instruments. The PC (and more usually, the Macintosh) gave them even greater control. The same programming power that solves the toughest problems can take command of an orchestra of synthesizers. Your multimedia PC plays the same role.

All PCs that claim the epithet multimedia must have all the pre-requisites you need to make music. A multi-voice music synthesizer is mandatory. Moreover, all multimedia systems have connections that let you plug in virtually any other electronic musical device—musical (as opposed to typing) keyboards, sequencers, synthesizers, what have you. A few top-notch programs include:

> **Midisoft Multimedia Songbook** (Midisoft Corp., $39.95) plays any of near 200 songs through your multimedia PC's MIDI sound board. The selections range from holiday and kids' songs to classics, jazz, and inspirational music, more old than new. Arrangements vary from plain piano to synthesized (that is, unconvincing) General MIDI orchestrations. When you want to go interactive you can switch to Midisoft Noodler to improvise along with the music on your MIDI keyboard. You can also learn about different instruments and their history from the Songbook's Instrument Gallery.

> **Midisoft Music Mentor** (Midisoft Inc., $49.95) gives you a grounding in basic music theory and musicianship. Included are tutorials covering basic musical concepts like notation and harmony, basic music appreciation, a music history timeline, even short biographies of famous people involved in music from composers to contemporary performers. The package plays short, representative pieces by important artists and its dictionary even guides proper pronunciation. The package also includes a basic MIDI editor and instrument gallery.

> **MusicTime** (Passport Designs Inc., $99) combined a musical education with a notation package that is essentially a stripped-down version of highly regarded Encore used by many professional songwriters, limited to four voices on eight staves. Designed more for recreation and entertainment, you can enter music from mouse, MIDI or character keyboards, listen to it through your sound board, and transcribe it in standard musical notation. In addition, you can edit arrange your opus using built-in tools that include a basic sequencer and MIDI editor.

Sing-Along with Elvis (The King) (Sirius Publishing, $19.95) gives you 10 Elvis hits from the rollicking "Hound Dog" and "Jailhouse Rock" to ballads like "Love Me Tender" with fully orchestrated backup. All that's missing is your voice, which you can croon into your multimedia PC's microphone while reading lyrics off the screen. It's computer karaoke, and you're in the spotlight.

Soloist (Ibis Software, $59.95) teaches you to sight read music. Designed as a game, it shows you the notes on the screen, and you are supposed to respond by playing or singing them at the proper pitch. It listens to the microphone you plug into your multimedia PC and determines whether you've hit the right notes.

Home Movies

Although multimedia holds the potential for being the home movies of the new generation, it currently faces a problem in distribution at the individual level. Certainly you can gather together friends, family, and random people off the street to torture with your personal computerized cinematic efforts and huddle them all around your 12-inch monitor. Not only will questions of halitosis and personal hygiene immediately come to mind and nose, but you'll see the impact and potential disappear faster than your audience. Remember, multimedia is supposed to be a personal, interactive experience. The VCR by itself captures better quality than your PC can, stores it more compactly on inexpensive tapes, and has a potentially wider audience. Anyone with a VCR can play a tape but only the chosen few will be able to view your home movie multimedia.

Audio and Video Production

But your multimedia PC can play a role in home movie-making, not as the capture or presentation system but in producing them. A multimedia PC can give you the power of a Hollywood production house to edit and augment your home movies and even audio recordings. In fact, the ultimate application of the multimedia PC is almost a contradiction—using its computer power to work with conventional media, dare we say "unimedia." Movies, television, radio, and music products are today routinely handled on PCs hardly a step above the ordinary home multimedia machine. The professional production engines have the same microprocessors, the same displays, the same storage systems as ordinary multimedia PCs. The software they run looks amazingly like the stuff that you use to play Myst. Yup—good old Windows.

Television special effects are more and more often originating in ordinary PCs. Editing systems based on ordinary PCs help produce some of today's highest tech television shows like *Babylon 5* and *SeaQuest DSV*. Radio production, once the realm of crazed men with razor blades and splicing tape, now takes place behind the Windows interface on PCs specially enhanced to pass professional-level sound quality.

To give them professional aspirations, these unimedia machines have one or another special hardware endowments that you won't find on consumer level multimedia PCs. Video editing stations typically get hundreds of megabytes of RAM, gigabytes of hard disk, and special TV-compatible video boards. Audio production machines demand sound boards with top digital quality. What once was done with rack upon rack of audio production equipment—compressors, limiters, filters, equalizers, and noise gates—now requires only the right software package. Moreover, effects engineers could once only dream about are routine—changing the tempo of music without affecting pitch, shaving seconds from commercials imperceptibly, transposing tenors to bassos profundos.

Not only is the functional difference between professional audio and video production gear and your multimedia PC slim, it's disappearing as technical standards for consumer components improve. The big difference between the editing suites used to produce hi-tech television shows and your multimedia PC is mostly a matter of memory—full-length video productions require hundreds of megabytes of RAM and thousands of megabytes of disk storage.

The bottom line is that you can make multimedia into whatever you want it to be. If you want merely to enjoy the technology, you can take advantage of the wide array of commercial software. But if you want to push the limits, you'll find that multimedia makes you stretch out even to catch a glimpse of a constraint. Multimedia is what you want to make of it.

Chapter 3
The Multimedia PC

Putting on a multimedia show in your home or office should simply be a matter of sliding the appropriate software into the PC you already have. After all, PCs all follow the same standard and run the same software. There shouldn't be anything standing in your way. In the same vein, however, there's nothing standing in the way of your competing in the Olympics—well, nothing but years of training, special skills, and maybe a good dose of native endowment.

Compared to ordinary computer programs, multimedia applications are the Olympics. The software stretches the capabilities of your PC to its limits much as athletic contests explore the limits of human abilities. In theory the Olympics are open to anyone who meets the most basic of criteria—membership in the human species. But getting to the level at which you can compete (indeed, to a level at which you are allowed to compete) takes more. The emphasis is on youth—you might be too old to start training once you've graduated from elementary school. PCs have quickly become too old for multimedia, too. A machine two years old may strain at the latest applications, if it's fit to run them at all.

The problem you face is that without additional guidance you cannot be sure whether the hardware you have will run the software you really want. The mere PC label is not enough. And trial-and-error requires either an understanding dealer or a charge card with a limit only slightly less than the Pentagon's. Worse, many people might not realize the shortcomings of their systems even after loading their dreamed-of applications comes to naught. They may blame the software publisher and waste needless hours with technical support people only to determine that their PC just doesn't make the grade.

What You Need

To avoid such costly problems and eliminate the frustration in matching program to PC an industry group called the Multimedia PC Marketing Council created its own standard of assurance. The group designed a minimal set of specifications that would guarantee compatibility with most multimedia applications. Systems conforming with these specifications were given a special name, the *Multimedia PC* or MPC. Then the group designed a readily recognizable trademark that would let innocent consumers immediately know that a given PC was multimedia capable, the MPC logo. In fact, the group set the standard even stricter. To put the MPC logo on a product, a manufacturer must be a member of the Multimedia PC Marketing Council, which helps guarantee that the organization generates enough dues to keep its programs going.

The first of the MPC specifications, version 1.0, was released in November 1991, the dim, early days of multimedia. Back then, few people cared about the new novelty. By the time multimedia applications had gained prominence in the market, this original standard was aging. Like an athlete gearing up for his third or fourth Olympiad, PCs meeting the original minimum standard were faced by the increased challenges of age. Although they might run through the expected course, they might not do it in record time (or without risk of myocardial infarction). In fact, the challenge was even greater. As new applications pushed the envelope defining what multimedia meant, they strained the performance limits of any PC on which they ran.

To assure that the multimedia software you chose will not just run but also run fast enough that you won't give up on multimedia technology as unworkably slow, the product council published a revised set of specifications, MPC 2, in November 1993. The new standard (which remains the current standard) sets higher performance and storage requirements that not only broadens the range of software that will run but also improves the performance of all multimedia applications.

MPC 1.0

Today the bottom line MPC 1.0 specification reads like a recommendation for a minimal PC for any applications (which hints that multimedia is now the mainstream).

Although the first incarnation of the MPC specification allowed for the use of 286-style microprocessors (but only those running at speeds of 12 MHz and higher), the original MPC 1.0 formula was updated without altering its numeric designation to demand a 386SX microprocessor as the acceptable minimum. This chip choice automatically guarantees a minimum speed rating of 16 MHz, the lowest rating Intel gives the 386SX chip. For memory, a system complying with MPC 1.0 must have at least 2MB of RAM, enough to get Windows 3.1 off the ground. The specification also required a full range of mass storage devices, including a 3.5-inch floppy disk drive capable of reading and writing 1.44MB media, a 30MB hard disk (small even at the time), and a CD-ROM drive.

Because at the time MPC 1.0 was created, CD-ROMs were relatively new and unstandardized, the specification defined several drive parameters. The minimum data transfer rate was set at a sustained 150KB/second transfer rate, the rate required by stereophonic audio CD playback. The standard also required the CD-ROM drive to have an average seek time of one second or less, which fairly represented the available technology of the time (although not, perhaps, user expectations). For software compatibility, the standard demanded the availability of a Microsoft-compatible (MSCDEX 2.2) driver that understood advanced audio program interfaces as well as the ability to read the fundamental CD standard (mode 1, with mode 2 and forms 1 and 2 being optional). (See Chapter 12, "The Compact Disc," for more information.) The drive needed to be able to read an embedded data channel (called, in CD parlance, *subchannel Q*) with optional support for subchannels P and R-W optional (with matching software support in the driver). The spec also required a mean time between failures (MTBF) of 10,000 hours for MPC-compliant CD-ROM drives. Translated to English, this part of the standard essentially means that the CD-ROM drive in a multimedia PC must be able to play ordinary music CDs.

Because audio is an implicit part of multimedia, the MPC 1.0 specification required an extensive list of capabilities in addition to playing standard digital audio disks (those conforming with the Red Book specification). The standard also required a front panel volume control for the audio coming off music CDs. Evidently the MPC organization wanted you to listen to your CDs while you worked on other multimedia. They also required that the CD drive be capable of maintaining a sustained transfer rate of 150KB/second—the speed needed for music CD playback—without stealing more than 40 percent of your PC's microprocessor power so that reading data from CD wouldn't bring the rather anemic chips required by MPC 1.0 to their knees.

Another part of MPC 1.0 is the requirement for a sound board that must be able to play back, record, synthesize, and mix audio signals with well-defined minimum quality levels.

So that your multimedia PC can capture and play its own digital sounds, the MPC 1.0 standard required a digital-to-analog (DAC) converter (for playback) and an analog-to-digital (ADC) converter (to sample and record audio). Under MPC 1.0, the requirements for each differ slightly. The DAC (playback) circuitry requires a minimum of 8-bit linear Pulse Code Modulation (PCM) sampling with a 16-bit converter recommended. Eight-bit sampling means noisy, distorted sound, better than telephone quality but not up to the level of a good radio.

Playback sampling rates of 11 KHz and 22 KHz are mandatory and hi-fi quality 44.1 KHz "desirable." The lower of the two standard sampling rates is a bit better than telephone quality; the higher falls short of FM radio quality. The analog-to-digital conversion (recording) sampling rate requirements include only linear PCM (that is, no compression) with low-quality 11 KHz sampling; both 22 KHz and 44.1 KHz being optional.

In effect, the MPC 1.0 specification froze in place the state of the art in sound boards and CD-ROM players at the time of its creation (1991) while allowing the broadest possible range of PCs to bear the MPC moniker. The only machines it outlawed outright were those with technology so old no reputable computer company was willing to market them at any price. The specification was not forward-thinking but an endorsement of the hardware on the market, fulfilling the goal of any specification: protection of the interest of those proposing it. But what did you expect?

Despite its underlying self-serving nature, the MPC 1.0 specification really did benefit you as a consumer. It gave you an incentive to ignore your most frugal tendencies and avoid buying a low-priced PC that would be obsolete as soon as you pulled it from the box. Far from perfect, far from pure, MPC 1.0 did draw an important line, one that showed backward compatibility has its limits. In effect, it said, "Progress has come, so let's raise our expectations." In hindsight, the initial standard didn't raise expectations or the MPC requirements high enough.

MPC 2.0

To help you locate a more responsive multimedia system, MPC 2.0 ratcheted the standards up a notch. It doesn't overrule MPC 1.0 but instead gives a second level of compliance. Some products will bear the MPC 1.0 moniker, but more advanced products can wear the MPC 2.0 banner.

As with the previous specification, MPC 2.0 is held back by practical considerations—keeping hardware affordable for you and profitable for the manufacturer. Although it sets a viable minimum standard, something for programmers to design down to, it does not represent a desirable level of performance for multimedia systems.

On the positive side, MPC 2.0 raises the performance level required by a PC in nearly every hardware category. It requires more than double the microprocessor power, with a 486SX chip running at 25 MHz being the minimal choice. More important, MPC 2.0 requires 4MB of RAM, which will give you acceptable performance with Windows 3.1. However, the standard recommends an additional 4MB, and the recommendation is a wise one. The additional memory will do more than a faster microprocessor in speeding up Windows.

While MPC 2.0 still required a 1.44MB floppy so that multimedia software vendors need only worry about one distribution disk format, it pushed its hard disk capacity recommendation up to 160MB. This huge, factor-of-five expansion reflects both the free-for-all plummet in disk prices as well as the blimp-like expansion of multimedia software.

CD-ROM requirements are toughened two ways by MPC 2.0. The standard demands a much faster access time, 400 milliseconds versus a full one second for MPC 1.0, and it also requires double-speed operation (a data transfer rate of 300KB/second). Although triple- and quadruple-speed CD-ROM drives were already becoming available when MPC 2.0 was adopted, most multimedia software of the time gained little from them, so the double-speed requirement was the most cost-effective for existing applications.

Under MPC 2.0, the CD-ROM drive must be able to play back commercially recorded music CDs and their track identifications (using data embedded in subchannel Q). In addition, the specification requires that the drive handle *extended architecture* CD-ROMs (and recommends the extended architecture capabilities include audio) and be capable of handling PhotoCDs and other disks written in *multiple sessions.*

The primary change in the requirement for analog-to-digital and digital-to-analog converters was that MPC 2.0 made CD-quality required all the way. Sound boards under MPC 2.0 must allow both recording and playback at full 44.1 KHz sampling in stereo with a 16-bit depth. Lower rate sampling (11.025 KHz and 22.05 KHz) must also be available. MPC 2.0 also required an integral synthesizer that can produce multiple voices and play up to six melody notes and two percussion notes at the same time.

In addition, the sound system in an MPC 2.0 machine must be able to mix at least three sound sources (four are recommended) and deliver them to a standard stereophonic output on the rear panel which you can plug into your stereo system or active loudspeakers. The three sources for the mixer include Compact Disc audio from the CD-ROM drive, the music synthesizer, and a wavetable synthesizer or other digital-to-analog converter. An auxiliary input is also recommended. Each input must have an eight-step volume control.

An MPC 2.0 system must have at least a VGA display system (video board and monitor) with 640×480 pixel resolution in graphics mode and the capability to display 65,535 colors (16-bit color). The standard recommends that the video system be capable of playing back quarter-screen (that is, 320×200 pixel) video images at 15 frames per second.

Port requirements under MPC 2.0 are the same as the earlier standard: parallel, serial, game (joystick), and MIDI. As you should expect with any new PC, both a 101-key keyboard (or its equivalent) and a two-button mouse are also mandatory. Table 3.1 summarizes the requirements of both MPC 1.0 and MPC 2.0.

TABLE 3.1. Multimedia PC requirements.

Feature	MPC 1.0	MPC 2.0
Microprocessor type	386SX	486SX
Microprocessor speed	16 MHz	25 MHz
Required memory	2MB	4MB
Recommended memory	No recommendation	8MB
Floppy disk capacity	1.44MB	1.44MB
Hard disk capacity	30MB	160MB
CD-ROM transfer rate	150KB/second	300KB/second
CD-ROM access time	1000 milliseconds	400 milliseconds
Audio DAC sampling	22.05 KHz, 8-bit, mono	44.1 KHz, 16-bit, stereo

continues

TABLE 3.1. continued

Feature	MPC 1.0	MPC 2.0
Audio ADC sampling	11.025 KHz, 8-bit, mono	44.1 KHz, 16-bit, stereo
Keyboard	101-key	101-key
Mouse	Two-button	Two-button
Ports	Serial, parallel, MIDI, game	Serial, parallel, MIDI, game

Source: Multimedia PC Marketing Council

What You Really Want

Despite the best intentions of the Multimedia PC Marketing Council, its MPC specifications don't reflect what you'll really want in a multimedia system. It's not just that the standards reflect compromises meant to satisfy the conflicting needs of the organization's members. The price of power is plummeting quicker than the best predictions of just a few years ago, faster than even an informed marketing council might have judged. In 1995, Intel imagines only two levels of microprocessor in the PC mainstream: the price leaders, logging in around $1,200, which will come equipped with DX4 microprocessors; and everything else, which will be Pentium-based. In comparison, the 25 MHz 486SX is anemic at best.

The MPC Marketing Council hasn't come up with a third-generation standard yet, but we can speculate at what it might include. Table 3.2 lists some of the features to aim for.

TABLE 3.2. Multimedia PC target requirements.

Feature	Recommendation
Microprocessor type	486DX2 minimum
Microprocessor speed	66 MHz minimum
Required memory	8MB
Recommended memory	16MB
Floppy disk capacity	1.44MB
Hard disk capacity	420MB
CD-ROM transfer rate	450KB/second
CD-ROM access time	100 milliseconds
Audio DAC sampling	44.1 KHz, 16-bit, stereo

Feature	Recommendation
Audio ADC sampling	44.1 KHz, 16-bit, stereo
Keyboard	101-key
Mouse	Two-button
Ports	Serial, parallel, MIDI, game

Although such a table is a useful reference, a better way to approach buying a Multimedia PC is with a better understanding of each of the elements you should be looking for. So let's take a quick view of some of the necessities and niceties in PCs for multimedia. You'll find in-depth treatment of all of these hardware issues in the Hardware Guide section of this book, starting with Chapter 10, "The Basic PC—Hardware Essentials."

Microprocessors

The fast pace of microprocessor development means that there is only one hard-and-fast rule in selecting the chip to power your next multimedia PC: buy the quickest chip you can afford. You'll never regret having a faster PC, and you'll probably add months—maybe even a year—to its life by opting up the scale of chips. Certainly any PC will last a decade, but if you get the best you can, you'll grow tired of laggardly performance later rather than sooner. No matter what you do, your new PC will probably be functionally obsolete (though still operable) in three to five years. But buying the quickest chip means fewer regrets later on.

Intel's predicted price leader, the 486DX4, is a good beginning. A Pentium-level chip is the state-of-the-art choice—at least for the next year or so. (By the end of this year you should be able to buy PCs equipped with Intel's unnamed Pentium successor, code-named the P6.) You can save $100 or $200 by selecting a chip from an Intel competitor. Although the 586-class chips lack full Pentium architecture compatibility, they will run all multimedia software written for Intel 486 chips (only faster). Few programs optimized for the Pentium's parallel design currently are available, so the quicker core processors of the competitors can actually hold an advantage on typical multimedia applications.

Buying Tip

Memory

Even more important than microprocessor choice is memory. Adding memory is the least expensive way to accelerate multimedia. Even if your favorite multimedia applications claim that they will run in 2MB or 4MB of RAM, you will be far happier with 8MB. The performance of Windows 3.1 and OS/2 Warp is noticeably faster with a basic 8MB instead of 4MB. Adding an additional 8MB (to 16MB) will further improve speed, although not as dramatically as the 4MB to 8MB move. The faster your microprocessor, the bigger the boost you can expect from adding RAM. A Pentium PC may gain 60 percent to 70 percent by increasing RAM from 8MB to 16MB, which a 486 might gain only 15 percent to 20 percent with the same memory increase.

Performance Issue

Most multimedia applications strain at the edges of a 4MB system. In fact, a typical Windows multimedia session requires much more than 4MB, but Windows takes advantage of virtual memory to simulate greater amounts of RAM using disk storage. It swaps bytes not immediately in use by its programs to disk to free up space for its immediate needs. Disk access is more than a thousand times slower than RAM access. Every time Windows avoids swapping bytes, it saves dozens of milliseconds, and those milliseconds really add up. Given more bytes of RAM, you can cut memory swapping to a minimum and get the most performance out of your PC and its processor.

The same situation as applies to Windows holds for OS/2 Warp. Windows 3.1 benefits from up to 16MB of RAM. It won't take advantage of more for typical user environments, so there's little point in investing in more. Windows 95 and OS/2 can take advantage of more, but 32MB is the most that most applications (and combinations of applications) require, at least for now.

Performance Issue

Besides amount, you have two other memory concerns: matching with caching and expandability. The mismatch between microprocessor and memory speeds is the biggest drag on overall system performance. A cache helps overcome this limitation. The internal (primary) cache in most modern microprocessors is not sufficient for adequate performance in today's top-end systems. You need a secondary cache—a block of high-speed memory. Most systems start with 64KB secondary caches. You'll want at least 256KB for a standalone PC, 1MB or more for a server. Better still are newer systems that use EDO burst-mode memory. They can access their entire RAM at high speed and eliminate the need for a secondary cache. Although EDO alone is not as good as a big cache, pairing it with a secondary cache will give you the best memory performance generally available today.

Caches differ in quality, too. *Set-associative caches* are superior to *direct-mapped caches*, and the more ways the better. (Many PCs now have four-way set-associative caches. Write-back buffers are superior to write-through because the latter don't accelerate memory writing operations. For more information, see Chapter 10.)

Memory for modern PCs comes in the form of *Single In-line Memory Modules* or SIMMs. The root of your memory expandability concerns are SIMM sockets. More sockets means more memory expansion potential. For adequate expansion every PC motherboard needs at least eight. Besides the number of sockets, however, you'll want to know what kind of SIMMs—8-bit, 9-bit (both 30-pin) or 36-bit (72-pin)—they accommodate.

Eight-bit SIMMs lack *parity-checking*. Parity-checking protects you from a single bit-error in memory creeping into your data or programs by stopping your system when an error gets detected. Some people argue memory is now so reliable, insuring its accuracy is unnecessary. Others argue that the consequences of one bad bit—calculation errors or system crashes—are so scary that a bit of protection is common sense. Remember, when you walk barefoot you don't expect to find broken glass—you only regret it later.

The chief distinction between 9-bit and 36-bit SIMMs is that you need four of the former to make a 32-bit bank of memory and only one of the latter. You can expand a PC that uses 36-bit

SIMMs in more affordable increments. You can expand systems with 9-bit SIMMs in increments of 1MB (4×256KB SIMMs), 4MB (4×1MB), 16MB (4×4MB) and 64MB (4×16MB) while you can add RAM to 36-bit systems in 1MB, 2MB, 4MB, 8MB, and 16MB increments. With eight sockets, a 9-bit system can have a total capacity of 1MB, 2MB, 4MB, 5MB, 8MB, 16MB, 32MB, 64MB, 128MB. Using 36-bit SIMMs, any 1MB increment capacity up to 79MB is possible, then larger increments to 128MB.

The added flexibility of 36-bit SIMMs has given them increasing acceptance. Moreover, 36-bit SIMMs also have speed detection pins so that PCs can automatically configure themselves for the ratings of the SIMMs you install. On the other hand, 9-bit SIMMs are generally less expensive. The 64-bit memory systems of Pentiums (and newer microprocessors) make the wider SIMMs the only practical approach.

Consider reality in addition to potential when you look at the memory in the PC you want to buy. One particular configuration to avoid: 8MB of 9-bit SIMMs because you'll have to toss something out to add RAM because all the sockets will be filled from the start.

Mass Storage

Disk storage, too, has pulled far ahead of the MPC specifications. Of course, every PC today needs a 1.44MB floppy disk drive, and almost universally every PC is equipped with one. Because 3.5-inch floppies have become the universal distribution medium and the choice for program exchange, you have little need for a 5.25-inch floppy disk drive. If you can avoid cluttering your office with yet another media type, why not? Once you get into multimedia you'll probably have too many CDs around as it is.

The alternatives to the now-traditional 1.44MB floppy disk all have their own problems. Extra- or ultra-density 2.88MB 3.5-inch floppy disks don't merit the extra money—the media cost much more, but software doesn't come on ED disks and 2.88MB still isn't enough when graphic files are megabytes more. Floptical drives lack both capacity (only 21MB) and acceptance to be a candidate for a multimedia system; MO drives cost too much; and Bernoulli Boxes and SyQuest drives are proprietary beasts—excellent in particular applications but second-string for primary storage. New 100MB floppy disks rate as a good backup and exchange medium but are too slow for playing multimedia.

Hard disks are another matter. Even the 160MB recommendation of the MPC 2.0 specification doesn't make much sense in a world where hard disks are near 50 cents per megabyte and multimedia data files grow by 50 percent every time you get a new idea. The place to begin today is about 320MB. The better choice is about 500MB. As long as you're not planning on developing a complete multimedia application yourself, that capacity is probably enough for a few years. It also avoids the thorny issue of addressing limits and interfaces. Venture beyond, and you'll have your hands full juggling specifications and standards.

The addressing limits are several. DOS allows no more than 512MB per disk partition, although you can slice a drive into up to four partitions or use disk management software to use more. Both OS/2 and Windows 95 strong-arm their way past that limit.

The original AT Attachment (IDE) specification combined with your system's Basic Input Output System (BIOS) restrictions effectively limits drive addressability to 528MB. (See Table 3.3.) The problem is a conflict between how most BIOSs and AT interface (IDE) drives address storage. New ATA or Enhanced IDE hard disk drives are designed with a new addressing scheme that effectively bumps the limit to 8.4GB, but they will only work with BIOSs with similar accommodations or special software drivers. (Because larger manufacturers almost universally match system BIOSs and hard disks, this issue arises only with off brands or when making upgrades.)

TABLE 3.3. Restrictions in head/track/cylinder addressing of IDE drives.

	BIOS	*IDE*	*Effective limit*
Max sectors/track	63	225	63
Number of Heads	255	16	16
Number of Cylinders	1024	65536	1024
Maximum Capacity	8.4GB	136.9GB	528MB

After capacity, the biggest hard disk decision you face is interface. As noted above, the original AT Attachment standard tops out at 528MB, so you'll want to look beyond it if you want more bytes now or tomorrow. Western Digital's Enhanced IDE proposal adds speed as well as addressing—it provides the means to boost the maximum transfer rate of the interface and drive to about 13MB/second (16.6MB/second using mode 4 E-IDE transfers (either PIO or Multi-word DMA)), which gives it an edge even on standard SCSI systems. The same technology is used in Seagate's Fast ATA specification. In fact, most new AT interface drives support this faster transfer mode. To take advantage of it, you'll need a PC with a matching BIOS or have to add a driver software to empower older machines.

Performance Issue

To avoid these worries, you can opt for a SCSI interface and gain a whole new set of worries. Current versions of SCSI allow for up to 8GB of storage, although some host adapters may top out at lesser amounts with some operating systems. Rather than ordinary SCSI, you'll want SCSI-2 in your hard disk drive and host adapter. For best performance, you'll want to be sure to get a Fast SCSI-2 (10MB/second transfer rate) interface. The actual throughput with Fast ATA (or E-IDE) and Fast SCSI-2 will be about the same because of the leveling effect of software overhead.

To take full advantage of these higher transfer rates, a host adapter must use a local bus connection. Local bus helps match E-IDE speeds to your PC. If you want to squeeze the most speed possible from your old IDE (not E-IDE) hard disk, you'll want a host adapter that incorporates 2MB or more of hardware disk caching. You'll also want to opt for software caching, which is included in all newer operating systems, (as from DOS/Windows SMARTDRV) or an after-market product like Super PC-Kwik.

Any multimedia system requires a CD-ROM drive, at least a double-speed (300KB/second data transfer rate) drive to comply with MPC 2.0. With current software, double-speed CD-ROM drives often outperform early triple-speed (450KB/second) units. Newer software should, however, tax the abilities of double-speed drives and use every bit of performance delivered by triple- and quadruple-speed (600KB/second transfer rate) drives.

Some new PCs will include CD-ROMs using the ATA Packet Interface (ATAPI), a variation on the AT Attachment interface. Although the new interface by itself won't in itself improve performance (but compliant drives can take advantage of the speed of E-IDE or Fast ATA host adapters), it will trim overall system cost by eliminating the need for a SCSI host adapter. The new drives will plug into a standard ATA (IDE) cable—which means you can add one less ATA hard disk to your system.

Plug-and-Play

In years past, you had few motherboard worries when looking for a new PC. After all, the available chipsets and BIOSs delivered everything you need to run all modern software. An emerging new standard changes that. Plug-and-Play, the specifications for which first appeared last year, is now appearing in PCs. Plug-and-Play is built into Windows 95, so you may regret buying a PC that lacks it.

Plug-and-Play is not a singular thing but a collection of technologies, standards, and potentials with a common goal: making the setup and configuration of your PC as easy as plugging in cards and cables—no concerns about jumpers, DIP switches, interrupts, and base addresses.

The simple goal belies an arduous journey. Plug-and-Play requires changes in the your PC's BIOS, PC bus, expansion boards, and the operating system. The transition will take time as compliant products course into the market and older equipment retires. The design of Plug-and-Play products eases the transition: all will work with non-Plug-and-Play equipment by sacrificing some Plug-and-Play abilities. In other words, a new Plug-and-Play PC will accommodate old expansion boards and give you true Plug-and-Play operation with compliant peripherals. A PC without Plug-and-Play can't ever take full advantage of the technology.

Your next system will need two levels of Plug-and-Play support. You'll want a Plug-and-Play BIOS so that your PC knows how to make itself self-configuring. (You may be able to upgrade a PC with a Flash memory BIOS to Plug-and-Play, but getting Plug-and-Play to begin with is a better strategy.) In addition, the expansion bus of a PC must be Plug-and-Play compliant.

Buying Tip

The standard ISA bus is not enough by itself; the bus requires a new slot-specific signal—which means you must look for a PC that declares it has bus-level Plug-and-Play support. EISA has slot-specific signals already. So do VL Bus and PCI. Because all the slots in a PC generally do not use local bus technology, you'll need to be sure all slots support Plug-and-Play.

Expansion Bus

Follow one simple rule when deciding on an expansion bus: Don't settle for anything but local bus. This choice assures the best possible performance as well as helping you get Plug-and-Play.

Whether PCI or VL Bus is a tougher call. Performance and number of slots is not an issue: both offer effectively the same alternatives when you compare the most recent standards (PCI 2.0 and VL Bus 2.0). The difference is that PCI came to the market later, so you'll find more VL Bus (at least version 1.0) accessories. Although PCI is rapidly catching up, you're unlikely to be stranded with local bus within the useful lifetime of your next PC. Even if one standard eventually dominates, you won't face that prospect until you buy your next PC. If you can get the expansion boards you want, PCI is the better long-term choice.

If you want to hedge your bets and get both local buses in your next PC, think twice. The initial machines that promised double-barreled local buses stumbled on bus accesses and did not deliver the throughput on par with ordinary local bus systems.

You might also want to consider PCMCIA slots for compatibility with notebook computer expansion. A growing number of desktop machines sport slots that accept credit card-size expansion boards. For memory, network interface, modems, and sound boards, you'll want PCMCIA Type 2 slots. Type 3 slots accept card-size hard disk drives.

Under DOS and Windows 3.1, PCMCIA has a severe handicap: the required driver software takes about 100KB of DOS memory. Neither OS/2 Warp nor Windows 95 suffer this handicap. Moreover, both have built-in PCMCIA support that allows automatic configuration and recognition of hot-swapped cards. The new operating systems make PCMCIA expansion very desirable.

Video

Multimedia demands the fastest possible video system, and you'll want the highest possible resolution to get the most from your system. The performance standard today requires both local bus technology and a graphic accelerator. In fact, if you don't get a graphic accelerator, you might as well buy black glasses, a tin cup, and a handful of pencils. A graphic accelerator can speed up today's graphic operating systems more than moving up a notch or two in the micro-processor spectrum. In general, picking the quickest accelerated display adapter is a chip choice: faster chips make faster boards. You'll want a graphic accelerator chip that uses a 64-bit design.

The amount of video memory you need on a graphics board depends on resolution level and the number of colors you want to see. Sixteen color images require one-half byte per pixel; 256 colors, one byte per pixel; 64KB colors, two bytes per pixel; True Color (16.7 million hues), three bytes per pixel. Multiply the horizontal and vertical resolution value by the color require-ment, and you'll have your minimum video memory requirements. For example, 1280×1024 resolution in True Color would require 3,932,160 bytes (that's 1280×1024×3) bytes. Rounding upward, you'd need a video board with at least 4MB. Just to confuse matters, some system designs use more (or less) memory for the same video data.

Once upon a time your graphics adapter alone determined the resolution you'd see. Now viewable resolution is a matter between you and your monitor, and the critical issue is the screen size. You can put 1600×1200 pixel resolution on a 12-inch monitor, but you won't see all the detail that you've paid for.

Assuming normal working distances, you'll want a 14- or 15-inch screen for 800×600 pixel resolution; a 16- or 17-inch screen for 1024×768 pixels; or a 20- or 21-inch screen for anything higher. If you want to make as well as view multimedia, the smallest screen you should consider is 17 inches operating at 1024×768-pixel resolution. Remember, you'll probably outgrow your multimedia PC in two years as systems get ever more powerful and speedy. Your monitor, however, is a longer term investment, so you can afford to spend more on it. Moreover, changes in monitor technology are subtle and slow-paced. The monitor you buy today is not apt to become obsolete until flat-panel LCDs or elongated screens (like those of High-Definition Television systems) take over.

When you choose a new monitor, watch the frequencies it can handle so you can assure yourself that the monitor you choose can display high scanning and refresh rates at the resolution you choose to use. At the new VESA ergonomic 75 Hz refresh rate (vertical frequency) standards, you'll need a monitor capable of a 47 KHz horizontal scanning rate at 800×600 pixel resolution; 60 KHz at 1024×768 pixels; or 80 KHz at 1280×1024 pixels.

If you're planning to make multimedia, you need to consider capturing as well as displaying video. To grab images from conventional video sources like tape and camcoder, you'll want a *video capture board.* If you want to monitor and edit your video output on your computer screen, look for an *overlay board* that can put full-screen, full-motion video on your display.

Sound

By definition alone, any multimedia PC requires a sound board. The MPC 1.0 specification requires a board that will be most useful for adding voice notations to presentations and spread-sheets. Its minimal, monaural requirements won't cut it when you want music.

The MPC 2.0 level of sophistication for digital-to-analog and analog-to-digital converters will let you approach CD-quality audio in your multimedia work. You won't get all the way there because consumer-quality sound boards suffer high levels of background noise and distortion. For critical audio applications (for example, editing music professionally), you'll need a specialized sound board that guarantees a high signal-to-noise ratio (aim for 96 dB).

If you intend on playing games, you'll want the basic Ad Lib and Sound Blaster compatibility implied (but not specifically required) by the MPC standard. But today's Windows-based multimedia applications will benefit more from a sound board with full *wavetable synthesis*. Look for large on-board ROM to give you a full range of voices.

Many multimedia systems are packaged with their own speakers. These all-in-one systems won't rock the room with the latest rap, but they'll give you a painless way to unlock the audio power of today's multimedia software. With them you won't have to tangle with the hassle of installing a sound board or search for the right cables to plug into your stereo system. Although you'll want to listen for speakers that don't sound too awful, fidelity is not now a concern in mainstream multimedia systems.

Ports

Every PC should have a basic endowment of ports, and multimedia requires a little extra beyond the basic two serial ports and one parallel. A PC with less cheats you on the peripherals you'll want to plug in (parallel for a printer; serial for a mouse, a modem, a scanner, or whatever). More is always better. Parallel ports should be both bi-directional and enhanced in conformance with at least the Intel/Xircom/Zenith EPP or IEEE 1284 standards, or Microsoft ECP (Extended Capabilities Port) standards—the difference is more than a factor of 10 increase in transfer speed (200KB/second versus 2MB/second). Multimedia machines also require game (also known as IBM joystick) and MIDI ports. All multimedia machines require a mouse or other pointing device (such as a trackball), but you'll be better served if it's a bus mouse that leaves your serial ports free.

If you want to extend your multimedia reach to Internet and other information super-duper-highways or just glom images and sounds from the local bulletin board service (BBS), your multimedia PC needs a high-speed modem, either as standard equipment or one that you add immediately after you uncrate your system. A modem is no big deal in that you can find an internal board that will add 57,600 bits-per-second throughput to any PC for under $100. The vital standards to look for are V.34 (a top speed of 28,000 bits per second) if you want the most speed and are willing to pay a premium, or V.32 bis (which allows a raw data rate of up to 14,400 bits per second) to appease your budget. Other important numbers include V.42 (which provides error correction), and V.42 bis (which gives the data compression that pushed the maximum communications rate to 57,600 bps with V.32bis and 115,200 with V.34). You need both.

Be wary of interim modems that wedged in between V.32bis and V.34. You'll find modems following two interim almost-standards (V.32 terbo and V.32 FC) at budget prices. V.32 terbo was AT&T's brainchild that pushed V.32 technology to its limits; V.32 FC (for Fast Class) is a Rockwell development that fell inches short of full V.34 compatibility. V.32 FC modems use the same technology as V.34 but don't quite make the standard (different handshaking). Both work but only amongst themselves at their top speeds. The best strategy is to think of the interim higher-speed modes as a bonus—these modems will work with the other V.32 and V.32bis standards just fine.

Fax tags along free. Even bottom-end modems include full 14,400 bps Group 3 fax. Nearly all data/fax modems include both data communications and fax software. But if you have hopes of linking your fax to other software, take care of class concerns, too. The broader Class 2 standard will assure a given fax modem will work with the widest variety of software.

Physical Concerns

In that you will have at least three mass storage devices in your multimedia PC (a floppy disk for exchanging data and installing software; a hard disk for on-line program and data access; and a CD-ROM player), you'll need a PC physically large enough to hold them all. That means at least three drive bays—four when you add in a backup system, a good idea for any computer system. Although the hard disk will tuck away in the bowels of your system, any CD-ROM drive will require a system large enough to give you at least one 5.25 inch bay.

You'll also need expansion slots, a lot of them so you can add new multimedia innovations as creative engineers think them up. To allow yourself the greatest flexibility, you'll want at least six expansion slots in your PC: three local bus (one each for video, mass storage, and the future), three ISA or EISA base bus (sound board, modem, network adapter). You'll want only the standard I/O ports and floppy disk interface built into your new PC's motherboard, not video or disk control because technical changes in these products are coming too fast. Every year graphic accelerator performance doubles, and disk interface performance is now following suit. You need the flexibility of slot-mounted accessories to ease your upgrades.

The physical requirements of a modern PC mean you'll probably want a mini-AT desktop case or mini-tower as a minimum for multimedia. Smaller boxes just don't have the space it takes for all you need.

Despite the space requirements, you can go lightly on power. No longer does a desktop system need 200 watts to bake your daily bread. Disk drives need a dozen, motherboards little more than that. A modern PC gets along fine on about 50 watts; 30 watts makes it Energy Star; a dozen watts make it a notebook machine. Even so, the typical Pentium PC comes with a power supply rated from 200 to 250 watts—more than you'll likely ever need.

New or Renew—Finding the Best Strategy

If multimedia has lured you to buy your first computer, you have reason to be happy, if not ecstatic. You're about to get into a new technology with unlimited potential and you don't have to carry any baggage along with you. As easy as signing a MasterCard chit, you can have a complete multimedia system in your home or office with no headache other than the worry how to pay the monthly bill.

But if you've been hooked on PCs, you may think that multimedia is something you can add to your PC the same way you plugged in a modem or more memory. You'll be sorry to know that it is. Plug in a multimedia kit, and your ordinary PC becomes a true multimedia engine, so you can fret and worry about all sorts of multimedia expansion options. You'll have more choices than making a chess gambit. You'll also have the chore of matching multimedia peripherals and reconfiguring your system.

Of course, you have other alternatives, too. You can always buy a new multimedia PC to replace or augment the machine you already have. Or you can buy a new PC and instantly upgrade it into a multimedia monster. Before you move into multimedia, you have to decide which strategy makes the most sense for you.

The choice can be a tough one. You have to temper your dreams with reality. Although your PC may be like a family heirloom, with more sentimental than monetary or functional value, sometimes you have to let go of the past. While adding multimedia to your existing PC sounds like the economical move, in the long run buying a new machine may make more sense. You can simply toss out the old machine and invest in one with all the modern amenities. Or you can upgrade, take what you have and make it better. Modernize. Accelerate.

Without a doubt, buying a new multimedia PC makes your move easier. Fewer decisions. Fewer headaches. And the headaches can be great: sound boards alone can take hours—days if the stars are in a particularly evil configuration—to get working properly. Choose a new multimedia system and the only skills you need are writing a check and opening a box.

But upgrading your old system or customizing a new one has a lot going for it, too. The end result will be custom tailored to one tough customer—you. You can save by choosing exactly the components you want and shopping for them with a sharp eye for ads and the bottom line. You can get the best possible performance by selecting only the fastest peripherals. And if you already have a PC, upgrading to multimedia means less waste, and that means easier on the environment and easier on your investments. Your PC won't add to the mountains of castoffs overflowing the landfills. Do it wisely and you can squeeze enough more life out of your existing PC that you can hold out till the next generation of multimedia systems hits the streets.

System Approach

The direct approach—buying a new PC as a multimedia system—has several advantages both for people new to PCs and those who have grown up with silicon under their fingernails. It's fast, easy, effective, and foolproof.

No decisions. No brains. If you don't want to think—or think you want to avoid a migraine—then buying a prefab multimedia PC is the choice for you. You don't have to worry about what you need or how to connect it together. The manufacturer has taken care of those details for you. You can be sure that everything will work together, and if it doesn't, you have one number to call for help or complaints.

Choosing an all-in-one system doesn't mean you're dumb. You may just have better things to do with your time. Or you may have learned your lesson the hard way, sitting inside a circle of manuals and expansion boards, scratching your head and praying yet again to the gods of silicon for an answer late into the night.

All New Beats Partly New

When you upgrade your PC, you still have the same computer you had before your upgrade. Certainly part of it will be brand new—a new sound board and CD-ROM drive—but everything else will be the same old stuff. And that can mean everything from just plain ugly to a disaster waiting to happen. Mechanical components like floppy disks suffer with age and slowly wear out. Hard disks fill up until their seams bulge and access time climbs as the last clusters get filled. Buy a new computer and new disk drives will come with it. Slide a multimedia upgrade kit into your old machine, and you still have your same old disk drives. Even though your old drives may have a lot of life left in them, a new machine will bring a new warranty.

False Savings

Of course, no one and nothing forces you to keep the rest of your system intact when you add multimedia. For example, a new floppy disk adds only about $50 to the total cost of your multimedia move. You can add a new hard disk and video system equally easily. So with a few simple changes and a multimedia kit, you can have everything you need.

You may not save as much as you think with such a system work-over. The prices of new multimedia PCs are low—frighteningly low to some system makers who have watched their profit margins slip past the point of no return. Add up the cost of all the upgrades you need to bring your 2-year-old PC to the state of the art, and you're likely to find a totally new system is less expensive. You get more, pay less, and have a second PC to give to a friend so he will have the expensive joy of upgrading it to multimedia abilities later on down the line.

Status Seeking

If you own a PC simply for the status it affords, you probably won't deign to get your hands dirty installing a multimedia upgrade yourself. Besides, an older system, even if equipped with the latest multimedia features, won't impress your friends and cow your competitors as will a brand new machine with a Pentium processor and more flashing lights than a 1930s theater marquee.

Of course, how many status points you score depend on the game you are playing. If you want your coworkers to think you a sub-god who need not soil his hands, you'll want the new system. But you could also impress your coworkers—if not yourself—by making a multimedia upgrade yourself. More effective still, you can buy that shiny new machine but tell everyone that you scratch-built it yourself. After all, you've been telling the same lie about the full-rigged wooden schooner model sitting on your desk all these years, haven't you?

Adding in Multimedia

Selectivity is the key reason to piece together your own multimedia PC, either as an upgrade to your existing system or as a customized new purchase. You need install only the multimedia components that your specific application requires. You don't have to follow the multimedia PC specifications to the letter, paying for features you will never use. For example, if you don't really need MIDI but want the highest quality sampling possible for sound editing, you can get a professional sound board that perfectly fits the bill. If your eyesight is so poor a seeing-eye mole guides your way, you can tailor a system with a simple but oversize graphic display. Or you can get a system with Cinerama pretensions.

The place to begin in selectively upgrading your system to multimedia capabilities is to assay what you have—the features and facilities of your current PC—and compare them to what your new application demands. Making this first inventory is easy if you don't already have a PC. The second part of the inventory requires an excursion through the system requirements listed on the boxes of all the programs you hope to run. As with any PC, you're better off buying the software before the hardware. You may even have a week or so to read through the manual before you start. And you may be the first person in recorded history to turn a page in the documentation before a problem crops up.

If you're improving your current PC, you should also look for fundamental weaknesses. A standard multimedia upgrade kit won't do anything to extend the capacity of a too-small hard disk, slow video display, or modem left over from medieval times. Make a list, check it twice, and hit the catalogs. Figure out your upgrade costs, and compare them to the new machine offerings.

Remember that upgrades differ in difficulty. A quicker microprocessor or additional memory require only that you plug them in. A new hard disk demands more physical labors—mounting the drive in a bay and possibly deciphering your SCSI chain.

Be prepared for the worst even when buying a multimedia package. Although manufacturers assemble multimedia upgrade kits for the mass market and make them as easy as possible to install, the underlying products are often unforgiving of machines that vary slightly from the industry norm. For example, most sound boards will plug right in to any PC but require device driver mumbo-jumbo to get talking with your applications. If your PC varies the slightest bit from plain vanilla—for example, say you've installed a network adapter—the carefully wrought automatic installation procedure may leave you guessing and regretting your purchase. You can spend hours or days sorting through the I/O port, interrupt, and memory options before discovering an irresolvable conflict. One source notes that 25 percent of multimedia upgrades get returned because of installation problems.

Don't try to be a miracle worker. In PCs, the brain dead have no hope of recovery. Any PC more than about two years old is an unlikely candidate for a multimedia upgrade. It will likely have a microprocessor inadequate for routine multimedia chores. Compare what you have to the MPC minimums. If your old system doesn't have at least a 386 microprocessor—or a 486 if you don't have godly patience—you'll be wasting your time installing a multimedia upgrade kit.

If your system can handle the MPC requirements, the piecemeal approach to multimedia will let you ease your way into greater power. Instead of gouging your purse for a multimedia upgrade, a new microprocessor, new memory, a new hard disk, and a new display system all at once in a single tin box called a new PC, you can add what you need as you require it or as you can afford it. For example, buy the multimedia kit today, then add in more megabytes when the cost of memory again falls to the affordable range.

The only problem with a selective approach to multimedia is that your plans will quickly change once you whet your appetite. As soon as you plug in the multimedia upgrade kit, you'll want more speed—no matter how fast your system is already. Instead of waiting a couple months for more memory, you'll want it now. Of course, you'll also want a whole shelf of multimedia applications now, too. But you can always make room in your budget by giving up little luxuries (like lunch, breakfast, and dinner) and putting off that mortgage payment for a few more days. The bank can't yell any louder, anyhow, and if you turn up your multimedia system just a little bit more you won't be able to hear them anyway.

Chapter 4
Getting Started

Now that you have a Multimedia PC sitting on your desk, table, counter, or lap, what are you going to do with it? Run multimedia, of course. Whatever that means.

In fact, it means a lot. The wonder of multimedia is that the range of applications extends at least half a parsec beyond the edge of your imagination. It's one of the basic facts of life. Someone, somewhere, will think up an idea that you never conceived and instantly become wealthy. Although barring a change in governmental policy or a sudden decline in your own moral turpitude, you can't partake in that wealth; with multimedia you can at least take advantage of the ideas and parlay them into your own fortune. Or you can simply increase your knowledge and self-worth by increasing your knowledge or extending your cultural horizons. You can simply blast away the next few decades of your life with a game extravaganza.

What you use multimedia for depends on your desires and dedication. At the lowest level, many people consider multimedia merely as a PC with more features—a throatier tone and wider program access thanks to its CD-ROM drive. At this level, multimedia is a reactive, one-way experience. You slide a CD into the drive and obey its commands, probably playing a game by its rules. Although there's nothing wrong with simply being entertained, it shortchanges on the possibilities locked in a Multimedia PC.

The next step is to put your multimedia PC to work as a command center for digging into classic media. It can play music from your CD collection, movie clips you download, or dig into electronic books and references. As easily as sliding your mouse, everything in the digital electronic universe comes under your command. But that everything is pre-existing, gathered up from diverse sources but nevertheless nothing new under our sun.

Vertical applications take this aspect of multimedia a level higher. The Multimedia PC substitutes for an audio mixer or television switcher. The production work that might have meant twisting a hundred knobs becomes a matter of hitting the right keys. In the same vein, your multimedia PC plays the role of sequencer in your electronic music studio.

The top level is making multimedia yourself, bringing together words, sounds, and images to make a cohesive experience. You don't have to craft an Imax presentation that leaves your audience melted into a puddle of sweat after each show to be working in multimedia, however. The first time you add a voice note to a spreadsheet or clip a moving image into a report, you become a multimedia producer. With a bit of practice (okay, a lot of practice) and motivation, you could produce your own multimedia software.

That's the final stage of multimedia—authoring. You conceive a grand project, script it, bring together all the pieces—the multi- of multimedia—and create a cohesive presentation.

System Kick-Start

Before you can partake in the multimedia experience, you've got to get everything running on your PC. If you're an old pro at PCs, that's easy. You've already endured the headaches at the front-end of the learning curve. Boot into Windows (or wherever), load your application, and go!

For the uninitiated, the multimedia experience begins with toggling on the power switch and waiting for the PC to come to life. Nearly any system sold today as a Multimedia PC will come with DOS and Windows pre-installed, so you won't have to deal with the intricacies of the first time load of the operating system or the patience test of installing Windows. With Windows 3.1, you'll face a couple layers of software. First, DOS will turn your PC from mineral to vegetable, then Windows will give it some intelligence. With Windows 95, you'll just start up and be ready to go. Slide a CD into your drive, and Windows 95 can immediately start running software from the disc. You don't even have to worry about setting up your PC. With a Plug-and-Play PC, your Windows 95 system will even configure its own hardware.

If you're starting out with Windows 3.1 or 3.11, your entry point to multimedia will be at a Program Manager screen rife with icons and pull-down menus. What to do next? Experiment, of course. Slide that new CD into the drive if you haven't already. With Windows 3.*x*, however, your screen won't change after you load the disc. You have to tell your system what to do. PCs are not self-motivated, at least those not running Windows 95. Before you can run a new multimedia CD, you'll have to install or configure it. The process is easy once you know what to do—and impenetrable if no one reveals the secret.

Here's the easy way of getting started:

1. Grab your mouse and point it at the File selection in the upper left of the screen, which should make a menu drop down.

2. Slide the mouse to the Run entry and click. Magic is already happening—you get a box that's asking you for the name of a program to run.

3. Move your mouse to the Browse button and click. Now things get tricky—you have to find the right drive to browse. You'll see a list of available drives on the right of the screen. The last drive in the list is likely your CD-ROM.

4. Click twice on the name of the last drive. The left-hand list of filenames should abruptly change. And among them—probably the top of the list or the only name—you'll see SETUP.EXE or INSTALL.EXE.

5. Move your mouse over and double-click whichever of those two appears. You'll snap back to the Run box.

6. Click Okay, and you're done. The hard work is left for your PC.

What you've done is tell your PC to look at your CD-ROM drive, find the installation program, and load it. Your PC then switches its attention to the installation procedure, and starts to set up your multimedia application. If all goes well (as it normally will) you'll be ready to run your multimedia application in a few minutes.

The one big problem you face is that your PC may not be properly setup for multimedia. In particular, you may find that all the required software drivers have not been loaded. (For more information about setting up your PC's device drivers for multimedia, see Chapter 8, "Device Drivers.")

Basic Applications

You don't have to buy a multimedia software package to get started. Any new PC probably has everything you need to start exploring and using multimedia technology. Just about any commercial multimedia CD you buy will incorporate all the software you need (besides your operating system) to use it effectively. Even if you could teach Scrooge a severe lesson on frugality and abstain from buying anything additional for your PC, you can still enjoy multimedia. All the latest operating systems come fully equipped with multimedia presentation software for showing movies and listening to sounds and music you can grab for free from your favorite bulletin board system. Moreover, most modern software readily accommodates multimedia. You can add video or audio clips to documents or databases as simply as pasting in a static image or table.

All you need do is spend a few minutes getting comfortable, and multimedia will be second nature to you. If you don't quite feel like a pro, you'll at least know that multimedia is the way that PCs ought to be.

Windows Help

One way to ease yourself into multimedia is to look at one of the most basic constituents of the technology, hypertext. If you're running Windows, you have a hypertext system already available on your PC—the Windows help function.

Although Help at first seems mundane, it is a very powerful information access system, and Microsoft has spent great effort into making it useful and usable. More than just a crutch to lean upon when you can't figure out the "intuitive" Windows interface or the operation of a Windows application, Windows Help is a true publishing system. The software core of Windows Help, called the *WinHelp engine*, is Microsoft's preferred multimedia hyptertext publishing tool. This engine has gone through several generations of development. The current and most powerful form is WinHelp 4.0, the help system that accompanies Windows 95.

Windows Help is easy to access. Simply click the Help entry in any Windows menu, and the engine starts running, loading context-sensitive help for the application or function that you are currently using. Help can do much more than give you guidance in what you're doing, however. Using its File function, you can select any compatible help file for reading any time Help is running. Help files normally have the filename extension HLP, and their icons typically wear a bold question mark. Newer WinHelp engines are backwardly compatible with help files created for older versions of Help. Because the latest help system adds new features older help engines don't understand, newer help files may be inaccessible by older help systems.

As an introduction to Help, Figure 4.1 shows you something you ordinarily should never see—the Windows 95 Help program reading the help file for Windows 3.1 Program Manager:

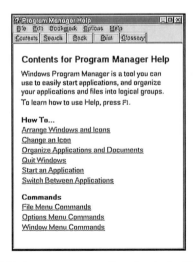

FIGURE 4.1. Windows 95 Help program reading the help file for Windows 3.1 Program Manager.

This initial screen shows you one way of accessing information through Help, the Table of Contents view. You simply click the topic of interest, and Help tells you all about it.

Alternately, you can find information using the WinHelp search engine. Clicking Search from the main menu of Windows 95 Help will give you an index, a categorized listing of topics available through the help system, something like that as shown in Figure 4.2.

FIGURE 4.2. Clicking Search displays a categorized listing of topics available through the Help system.

Click a topic to highlight it, then click the Display button to take you to information about that topic. Or simply double-click the topic.

The Table of Contents and Index provide fast access to information, but the real power of hypertext appears inside the text itself. Key words and phrases called *hyperlinks* are highlighted in green and underlined. Move your mouse pointer over one of these hyperlinks, and the normal arrow transforms into a hand pointing its index finger. Clicking the left button of your mouse with the finger pointing at a hyperlink and Help will take you to a cross-reference that is linked to the word or phrase. The cross-reference itself may also contain hyperlinks that will take you to more cross-references, which may have more hyperlinks until you're so far astray you've forgotten what you're looking for. Clicking back will step you back through the hyperlinks to your point of departure.

Hyperlinks with dotted underlines are a special case. These link to definitions, which pop on your screen as small windows to explain to you the meaning of the linked word or phrase.

The Windows 95 incarnation of Help can include more than mere text. Graphics, sounds, and videos can all be included in a help file for presentation by Help. Currently, help files that mix in sound and video are uncommon. However, the same engine that runs Help also powers one of the most popular multimedia display systems, Multimedia Viewer, that is used in a wide range of commercial multimedia software that includes both text, sounds, and moving images.

Multimedia Viewer

Install any of the multitude of book-based multimedia titles, and odds are you'll find Microsoft's Multimedia Viewer in control. Viewer gives you an easy way both to skim through long texts and to zero in on a subject of interest. It brings together text, still and moving images, and sounds through a single cohesive interface. Figure 4.3 shows the opening screen of Multimedia Viewer.

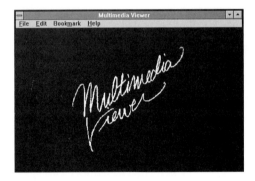

FIGURE 4.3. The opening screen of Multimedia Viewer.

As with Help, Viewer is a hypertext-based system that allows embedded bitmaps, sounds, and animations. It displays the visual elements on your screen (text, graphics, and animation), supplies you with a search engine so you can quickly find words and phrases of interest, and gives you hypertext links so you can instantly dig deeper into topics of interest.

Most Viewer-based applications will install from the multimedia CDs you buy. Under Windows 3.1, simply select File and Run from your Program Manager screen and run the program SETUP.EXE from your CD drive. Windows will install the appropriate icons (and often a program group) under program manager. It will also add a copy of Viewer and a Viewer subdirectory to your hard disk. Selecting the application icon automatically launches Viewer and opens your multimedia program.

Microsoft has steadily improved Multimedia Viewer through a number of versions, the last of which is the current version, 2.0. With commercially distributed compiled applications, you don't get to choose the version you use. When a publisher develops a multimedia CD, it compiles its product with a specific version of Multimedia Viewer which accompanies the product on the CD. When you install your application, you get the version to match. Early versions of Multimedia Viewer would make a copy of themselves on your hard disk—you'll find it lurking in a directory called Viewer after you've installed an older multimedia CD. Newer Viewer versions run from your CD drive without scattering files across your hard disk.

In its current form, Multimedia Viewer also operates as a freestanding application. It reads files created especially for it with the filename extension .MVB. You can run Multimedia Viewer 2.0 either through Windows (click its icon) or from the command line by running the program MVIEW2.EXE, in which case it will automatically load Windows then the Viewer file you specify on the command line.

The only important differences between Multimedia Viewer versions are the features you get. Newer versions offer you more options, making the application more versatile. The differences are meaningful only to programmers, however. Commercial applications typically include a run-time module for the version of Viewer under which they were written and only use the features of that version.

Viewer typically lets you dig into your multimedia text in any of three ways: jumping from its table of contents, probing from its index, or searching for a match. In addition, specific applications may offer their own means of accessing information. For example, Figure 4.4 shows the control screen from *The Ultimate Business Reference,* published by Allegro New Media:

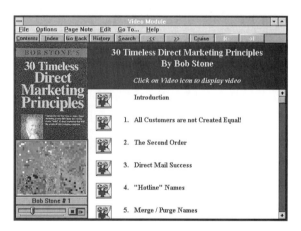

FIGURE 4.4. The control screen from *The Ultimate Business Reference.*

Buttons give you the options of selecting the Table of Contents, Index, or Search engine. Or you can click the movie projector icons to select a video clip.

The table of contents mimics that of a printed book and gives you an array of topics to choose from. Instead of flipping across pages, however, you only need to click the entry you want to access. Viewer takes you there by express. You can even pretend you have a paper book and start at the beginning and cruise through to the end using Windows scroll bars or your PgDn key to read everything in the order the author thought you should.

The search engine requires you to type in a word or phrase to find. The engine will then look through all the text for a match, and present you with a list of topics in which your choice appears. Double-click your selection, and you'll be transported to the proper place in the book.

Start your search by clicking the Search button. Viewer will respond with a dialog box that lets you choose what you want to find, like that shown in Figure 4.5.

FIGURE 4.5. The search dialog box of the Multimedia Viewer.

Viewer obediently searches through all the topics or groups that you specify, in this case all the self-help business books on the CD. Once it has found all the mentions of the word or words you've indicated, the search engine presents you with the results, listing each chapter in which your chosen word appears. Highlight a topic by clicking it with your mouse, then click Go To, and Viewer will take you to the reference. Or you can save a step and simply double-click the topic. If you don't like where you get to, you can always go back to Search Results and try another topic by choosing the Back option from the button bar. If none of the topics in Search Results look particularly promising, you can start another search by selecting To Search. (See Figure 4.6.)

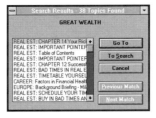

FIGURE 4.6. You can start another search by selecting To Search.

The Index is essentially a search with the word to use selected for you.

The hypertext power of Viewer is subtle. It doesn't appear in any menu. You'll just find some words in text highlighted in green. These are keys to the hypertext side of Viewer. Highlight your choice and click Go To or simply double-click any green word or phrase, and Viewer will take you to an explanation, elaboration, discussion, or reference about the topic. (See Figure 4.7.)

The multimedia side of Viewer is more mundane. Normal static illustrations spice up the text. Some of these are animated. You start the animation by clicking the appropriate illustration. Buttons or icons enable you to hear the sounds embedded in the Viewer document.

Viewer is popular because it gives developers a complete system for making their multimedia titles work, as we'll see in Chapter 5, "Authoring Multimedia."

FIGURE 4.7. Attaching a page note under Multimedia Viewer.

CD Players

If any one application is de rigueur on every Multimedia PC, it is the audio CD player. After all, by definition every such system must have a CD player, so putting it to work is only natural. Moreover, the CD interface is so simple and plainly documented that creating CD players appears to be a favorite hobby for multimedia hackers. Cruise through the multimedia section of any electronic bulletin board system, and you'll find a profusion of shareware and freeware players. You'll probably get one free with your sound board as well. If you upgrade to Windows 95 (or get it installed on a new PC), you'll find a CD player built-in and ready to run.

The universal point of departure appears to be the classic CD player in your stereo system. Most of these programs emulate those easy-to-use controls, tapping the Windows interface for the images and point-and-shoot control. The difference between the programs is little more than that between Pioneer and Panasonic stereo gear—more cosmetic than a matter of quality. (They're all good, right?)

In fact, the difference is even less. The CD player software never touches the sound you hear at all. All you get in CD player software is a control system for starting, stopping, and cruising across your CDs. Your CD-ROM drive does the rest, translating the bits on disc to the audio that plugs into your headphones or stereo system. In other words, the drive controls the quality of what you hear; the software only unlocks the possibilities built into your drive. (See Figure 4.8.)

FIGURE 4.8. Example of CD Player software.

The start, stop, and track access pushbuttons are little more than a remote control—but one with a difference. Because they are linked to your PC, you can use the computer's memory and scheduling abilities to program the tracks of the CD you listen to. You can skip the dogs or repeat play the hits until your ears bleed. You can even target a favorite riff and loop through it again and again until your mate packs up for saner surroundings.

If you're an audiophile, consider CD player software only for its novelty value. The sound quality delivered by PC-based CD-ROM drives falls far short of the level you would expect from stereo components. The chief culprit is noise. CD-ROM drives are built as data readers and operate at digital levels with digital signals that are impervious to the influence of noise. Unfortunately, the inside of your PC is awash with high-level signals—10,000 and more times higher than the faintest pianissimo your on-disc music calls for—that seep in to signals everywhere. Digital circuits ignore them; analog circuits amplify them so when you listen closely to the output of your CD drive you hear something akin to the brainwave patterns of Venusians percolating behind your favorite symphony.

Because CD player programs do little more than send commands to your drive, they steal almost zero microprocessor power while your music is playing. Run one in the background of your Windows session and you'll never notice. Couple a CD player with an inexpensive AM/FM tuner board and powered multimedia speakers, and your PC can double as a stereo system.

Video Players

Next in line as a leading multimedia application is the video player that lets you view small clips through Windows.

Playing a movie on your PC is easy. Just pull up Window's media viewer, select the movie, and press the buttons for the function you want. Of course, from the box, Windows 3.1 won't do anything, and you'll be stuck twiddling your thumbs trying to figure out what you need. (See Figure 4.9.)

FIGURE 4.9. The Windows 3.1 Media Viewer.

To get the media viewer to work, you need video driver software. As with any budding PC technology, you have your choice. Fortunately the choices are few—two—and both produce good results. Unfortunately, the two are not compatible, and movies made for one will not play on the other.

Choice one was the first media viewer for any desktop computer system, Apple's QuickTime, which was first introduced for the Macintosh in 1991. Although less impressive than Cinemascope with full THX sound—the first views it gave were limited by the performance of that vintage Mac hardware to tiny, quarter-screen images at frame rates that gave images the look of an old-time disco strobe show—QuickTime for the first time integrated video into a PC operating system. It was designed to be built into newer versions of the Mac operating system, much like the QuickDraw graphic routines were, and is now a standard feature.

Macintosh

With the success of QuickTime on the Mac, Apple began to work on a version for the PC. This aggressive move by Apple inspired Microsoft to develop as expediently as possible (which means buying someone else's software, tinkering, and gluing on the Microsoft label) their own movie viewer, now known as Video for Windows, built into Windows 95 as Media Player (which, by default, gets installed in the Multimedia folder inside the Windows Accessories folder). Video for Windows is the standard; Media Player the application.

The Apple and Microsoft products are essentially similar, but most people believe that QuickTime is superior in that it runs faster at a given hardware level and has more low-level features to help developers. Video for Windows has the advantage of Windows compatibility (in fact, it runs only under Windows), which means it is a major market force. You can also use OLE to embed Video for Windows movies in other Windows applications.

Performance Issue

If you want to create movies on your PC, you don't have a choice. Video for Windows includes video capture and editing modules. QuickTime does not enable you to create movies on a PC— all image-making must occur on a Macintosh. On the other hand, QuickTime enables you to easily transfer movies made for (or on) the Mac to your PC. Using QuickTime, developers can easily cover both platforms.

The two standards are completely independent and require movies to follow their own standards. You can usually distinguish files meant for one or the other by their extensions. Movies meant for playback under Video for Windows usually have the extension .AVI; movies meant for QuickTime playback under Windows generally use the extension .MOV.

Video for Windows

To play back a Video for Windows movie, you need a run-time module to install under Windows 3.*x*. The required module is available nearly as many places as bootleg copies of DOS. Media Player under Windows 95 is essentially the same run-time module. Neither is the complete Video for Windows package. Each lacks the capture and edit modules that let you make your own video clips. But the Video for Windows run time has a couple of advantages. It's free, widely available, and distributed legally.

Under Windows 3.1*x*, Video for Windows comprises two separate on-screen elements, its control panel and its display screen. The control panel that follows is simply a glorified electronic VCR, with buttons to control common functions (play, fast forward, rewind, pause, and stop),

Windows 3.1x

menus for controlling the display and selecting files, and a thermometer-style display showing how far through a video you've progressed (and enabling you to quickly access any given point in a video presentation). The control screen looks like that shown in Figure 4.10.

FIGURE 4.10. The video for Windows control pane in Windows 3.1*x*.

The image itself appears in a separate window which you can move and expand independently from the Media Player controls. The window itself is spartan, with only the image and minimal controls for sizing, as shown in Figure 4.11.

FIGURE 4.11. The video for Windows display screen in Windows 3.1*x*.

QuickTime for Windows

The run time for QuickTime is also generally available free. You can find it on AppleLink and directly from Apple through Internet (at `ftp.apple.com`). It is also available from the Macintosh Developer's Forum on CompuServe (`GO MACDEV`) in Section 8 (Apple System Files). Generally, you'll want to download two large files, QTDSK1.ZIP and QTDSK2.ZIP, which are compressed images of the QuickTime disks distributed by Apple. To create QuickTime movies, you'll want Apple's QuickTime for Windows developer's kit, available from APDA at (800) 282-2732.

The basic QuickTime package includes a movie player and a still picture viewer. As you would expect, the movie player enables you to view movies made under the QuickTime standard. It permits you to scale the image, sacrificing speed as you increase size, and play it. Its editing function is aimed not at altering the image but the presentation, enabling you to carry out only simple alterations such as removing the frame and looping the movie so that it plays continuously. The still picture viewer displays images stored as Macintosh PICT files or JPG format. Its image manipulating abilities are limited to little more than scaling from 25 percent to 400 percent in discrete increments. (See Figure 4.12.)

FIGURE 4.12. The Quicktime Movie Player.

Installation

To install QuickTime for Windows, you'll first have to unzip the disk images from the distributed compressed files. Use PKUNZIP.EXE (which is probably available from the same source that you get the QuickTime software) using its -d option so that it recreates the original directory structure of the disk image. You'll want to unzip each file in a separate subdirectory. When you're done unzipping each subdirectory, move the original compressed files out of the directory and copy all the files in each directory to a separate floppy disk (use XCOPY with the /s option to preserve the directory structure). The two resulting floppies will be your installation disks. Run the install routine from Windows by selecting the Run option from the Program Manager Files option. The installation program is called SETUP.EXE, and it is on the first floppy, the one unzipped from the file QTDSK1.ZIP.

Cross-Platform Compatibility

Although part of the lure of QuickTime for Windows is the ability to play the same movie on both PC and Macintosh platforms, you can't view all QuickTime movies on your PC nor will you see the same results on a PC as you would on a Mac. In native mode, QuickTime movies are meant for the Macintosh. To play on a PC, a QuickTime movie file must have its system-specific features generalized. This process is called flattening and PC-compatible Mac movies are generally termed "flattened." You can only carry out the flattening process on a Mac, so you can't deal with unflattened movies on your PC at all. When you download movies, check the comments for each to be sure it is a flattened file before you waste connect time. Otherwise you'll have to invest in a Mac or find a friend with one to flatten the file for use on your PC.

Note that Mac QuickTime files are often compressed with StuffIt and have the filename extension .SIT. Chapter 9, "Data Storage," covers this and other compression schemes. Other QuickTime movies wear the filename extension .BIN as ordinary binary files. These are usually not compressed but may or may not be flattened. In some cases, you can play them back under QuickTime for Windows simply by renaming them with the extension .MOV. These files may have a Macintosh header (called a "MacBinary header") which prevents QuickTime from properly recognizing it. You can remove this header with a utility like UNMACA.COM, available through the GRAPHSUPPORT forum on CompuServe in Library 14.

Performance Issue

If a QuickTime movie was not specifically made for viewing on PCs, they may look too dark or have too much contrast on your PC monitor. The problem is that the Macintosh handles the gamma of image files differently than does the PC. The only solution is to adjust the monitor to make the image as pleasing as possible. You'll probably want to twist up the brightness, twist down the contrast, or both.

System Sounds

One difference you'll immediately notice between a Multimedia PC and machines of old is that the multimedia system has a voice of its own. Rather than uttering only alien beeps, it bursts forth with chimes and crescendos at opportune moments. Start Windows, for example, and your PC announces its readiness with a burst of electronic orchestra suitable for a Cinerama production. Make a mistake, and it obstinately burps a hollow ding at you.

The various noises that modern operating systems make at these decisive instants are called *system sounds*. Although the same events consistently key them to play, the assignment between sounds and events is not forever fixed. Moreover, the repertoire of sounds you can link to events is essentially unlimited. Anything you can get into the proper digital format—a standard sound file called a .WAV file—will work. If you wanted to (and had a big enough hard disk to hold all the data) you could key Beethoven's Ninth Symphony to play every time you started Windows. Unfortunately, some sound systems are single-minded and won't let you do anything else while they play their themes (the SPEAKER driver that coverts the beeper/speaker in your PC to a playback system) is such a one-track-at-a-time playback system) so you'll want to keep most common system sounds short. Even when you use a multimedia sound board that plays along as you work, you'll find long exclamations at every error to quickly lose its charm.

You can change the assignments between events and the sounds supplied with your operating system or add new sound in much the same way whether you run Windows 3.1, Windows 95, or OS/2 Warp. Each gives you a control screen that lists events and sounds, and you make the assignment.

Windows 3.1x

In Windows 3.1*x*, you make your choices by choosing Sounds from Control Panel, and you get a screen like that shown in Figure 4.13.

The events are on the left, sounds on the right. Click an event, and the corresponding sound gets highlighted. Highlight another sound for that event, click OK, and you've changed the link. Windows lists all the available .WAV files in the current directory. You can search through other directories for additional sounds to assign. You can preview each sound by clicking the Test button.

FIGURE 4.13. Setting system sounds from the Windows 3.1*x* control panel.

Under Windows 95, you make these sound assignments by selecting Settings from Control Panel (which you can access from the Start button). From settings, double-click the Sound Events icon. You'll see the Properties screen for Sound Events which will look similar to that shown in Figure 4.14.

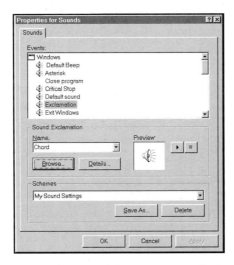

FIGURE 4.14. Properties screen for sounds events in Windows 95.

As with Windows 3.1*x*, start by selecting the event that you want to key to a specific sound. To make a new assignment, click your sound choice. If you want to save several different collections of sounds, you can organize them into a *sound scheme* that you can select and deselect as a group. To make a group of assignments into a sound scheme, select a scheme name from those Windows lists for you under Schemes, then click the Save As button.

You can get additional sounds to assign to events from commercial collections, by downloading them from bulletin boards, or by recording them yourself. Windows supplies a tool called *Sound Recorder* which will let you use your sound board to capture sounds from a microphone or other source. Sound Recorder is discussed later.

Adding events is another matter. In order for an event to start a sound playing, the software controlling the event must send a message to the operating system, essentially an alert that a specific event has occurred. Without the message, the operating system would never know it needs to take action. Unfortunately, an application must be specially written to send the appropriate messages. You can't just add an event.

OLE

Object Linking and Embedding (OLE) is one of the greatest strengths of the Windows system and a promise for the future of personal computing and multimedia. OLE brings unity to the applications on your PC and the work that they generate. It enables you to incorporate data from one application into another and have the two applications control their respective data interactively. Although OLE works with mundane matters like pulling spreadsheet cells into weekly reports, its finest flowering is in multimedia. Using the power of OLE, you can add voice annotation to your documents or drop a movie into your spreadsheet. If you later change your mind or improve your aesthetic sensibilities, any change you make to your original voice tracks or movies gets instantly reflected everywhere it appears, even in multiple documents and presentations.

Functionally OLE extends your basic ability to move information between applications beyond simple pasting. The most rudimentary form of data interchange between applications is reading the data from one into another using the file system. Through the Clipboard, Windows improves this basic interchange by providing an easy-to-use mechanism for moving information.

Background

Simple cut-and-paste lets you take text, numbers, or illustrations between applications. But like any good glue, a paste operation fixes the material with which it works in place. Computerized cut-and-paste is more convenient than the old glue pot because you can always move what you've laid down at any time without messing up your fingers. But in another way, the data subject to this rudimentary paste is fixed—not in place but in time. Once you've moved data from one application to another, the data is locked into final form, as permanent as anything resident in your PC. The only way break through this time barrier is to go back and cut-and-paste a new version all over again.

One step above the simple paste is embedding. The data you embed—called an object in the Windows schemata—runs deeper than what you see. In addition to the visible display, the object includes its pedigree. The object tells your application what application created it and where that application can be found. Using that pedigree, you can access the program that created an embedded object by simply clicking the object. The OLE system takes note of the origins of the data and calls up the creating application so that you can immediately work on the object's data using its original creating application. The mundane example of embedding is a range of spreadsheet cells in a text document—click them, and the spreadsheet loads so that you can edit the numbers. A multimedia example would be to embed a movie in your monthly report. The movie appears as a stationary image, but clicking on it can bring up the media player that will let you start the image in motion and run it forward and backward.

In effect, embedded objects respond like the data files you click using Windows File Manager. Pick a file, and File Manager automatically loads the application associated with its data and drops you in. The difference is that information that File Manager uses to make its link gets stored independent of the data files you choose. File Manager simply uses the filename extension to target an application and can easily get fooled. An embedded object contains the source information itself, so it knows exactly how to get home.

The data associated with an embedded object becomes part of the application it gets embedded into. Every time you embed an object you make a new copy which gets added into the file in which it is embedded. As with a simple paste operation, the object data is essentially fixed in time. When you change the original, its embedded offspring retain the data stored in them when they were originally created.

The next step is linking objects. When you link an object, it looks outwardly identical to one that is embedded (in fact, it looks like data that you've simply pasted). Even when you click the object, it responds as you would expect from an embedded object. The difference is the mechanism through which the object gets connected to your application. While an embedded object becomes part of your data file, a linked object has a life of its own. Instead of lumping the object's data with the rest of your data file, the linked object only leaves behind its pedigree. Through the magic of OLE, the data for the linked object gets combined with the rest of your data file as you work with or display it. From the pedigree, OLE hunts down the object's data as it is needed. Click it, and it digs up the application that originally created it.

This seemingly tentative link offers a pair of advantages. Every object needs to be stored only once. The same data gets shared by every file or document that uses an object. As a result, you save on storage space. In addition, because all occurrences of the object's data represent exactly the same data, any change made to the data will be reflected in its every appearance. Blot out a face on a video to protect the outwardly innocent, and the face will disappear wherever the video appears.

Of course, along with these advantages you get disadvantages. Eliminating the duplication of data means the end of the protection afforded by redundancy. Make a mistake and damage the original object, and it dies everywhere. You can't recover from errors by lassoing another copy that you pasted into another file. OLE also demands more from your PC. Simply displaying a document becomes an elaborate scavenger hunt for Windows as it races across your hard disk to find all the objects, then to regenerate them on the screen. Moreover, a system built around OLE can be a house of cards. Every object depends on its own files and applications, and a complex document can involve dozens or hundreds of separate links. Every link requires an exact knowledge of your PC and the directory structure of its storage system to find the files it requires. Change that structure—move a file, rename a directory, or reorganize your disk hierarchy—and the system collapses.

OLE doesn't grow automatically. Programmers must specifically build OLE abilities into their applications. In order to link an object into an application, both the program creating the object and the application to which you want to link the object must support OLE. Because of the relative newness of OLE and its complexity, relatively few applications support OLE fully. Fortunately, multimedia applications are leaders in OLE support.

The OLE standard now has two levels: OLE 1.0, the original version introduced with Windows 3.*x*, and OLE 2.0, which is part of Windows 95. As you would expect, the newer version is more versatile and refined. It is backwardly compatible with applications that use OLE 1.0, but getting the full power of OLE 2.0 requires using only applications that support the newer standard. Both versions can use the same objects, but the function of the link is limited to that of the OLE 1.0 standard when either side of the link supports only that level.

Operation

OLE isn't a program or application itself but a model or standard that describes how objects interact. It gives your PC's software a channel through which to move objects as they are needed. In addition, it defines the way object data gets saved to disk and retrieved again and how to mix types of data into a single file (which Microsoft calls compound files). The program STORAGE.DLL manages these compound files and the links between the files originating and using objects under Windows 95.

To allow the interactive editing of an embedded object, both the application into which the object is imported and the application in which it originates must comply with Microsoft's OLE specifications. If both applications conform with OLE 2.0, you can use the OLE visual editing interface to edit the object. If, however, one of the applications only meets the older OLE 1.0 standard, then the application that created the object will automatically get loaded when you choose to edit the object, and you'll use that application for your editing.

A given application may not implement all the features of the visual editing interface, so the editing tools available to you can vary with the software you use for working with an embedded object. The exact range of features you can use depend on the application in which you embed the object, not the object itself or where it originates. For example, when you embed an object in a word processor you might not be able to zoom in on the object or scale it (depending on the word processor, of course), but should you embed the same object in a desktop publishing document zoom and scaling may be available. Because OLE uses filename extensions to key applications to objects, if it does not recognize an extension, it may not enable the editing of an object because it won't know where the object came from.

When objects are linked, the OLE system must update the links if the files in which an object originates or gets used is moved. Windows 95 automatically maintains object links when you move files; older Windows versions do not. If you have Windows 95, you can link an object to a file, then move that file elsewhere in your system, and the link will be maintained.

In Windows 95, the Registry, (described in Chapter 6, "Software Concepts"), tracks OLE objects. Windows 95 gives each object a unique identification tag and stores it along with the identification of the program that created the object in the Registry. Simply moving a file can't break the link. (The object identifier becomes the class name of the object should the object be linked with an OLE 1.0 file.)

If you choose to move a file containing a linked object, you can check that the link does, in fact, stay with the file. You can verify the link by taking a look at the file and the linked object and check its field codes. This is usually a choice on the Options, Tools, or View menus. Select Links (typically from the Edit menu) and press F9 to check the path of the link.

Using OLE

The easiest way to use OLE is through the Windows clipboard. The clipboard is a temporary holding place for edits that you make. Whenever you mark a block of text or an image and select cut or copy from the edit menu, the data in the block gets copied to the clipboard. The information is held there until you replace it with another cut or copy (or until you switch off your PC). You can later move the data in the clipboard to another location in the file from which it came or into a different file using the paste function.

With applications that support OLE, you can use the clipboard to embed as well as paste objects. Programs that follow the OLE specification package the data you cut or copy with information describing the type of data and its origin. In pasting the data, you can choose Paste Special instead of plain paste from the edit menu. A dialog box then offers you the choice of data type to use for the object you want to paste. When you choose Paste Special from the Edit menu, you can choose which data type you want to use for the object. For example, in pasting an image you might choose between a bitmap (essentially a plain paste) and embedded picture format that will allow later editing. The dialog box offers rough guidance about the advantages and disadvantages of the data types available to you. In some cases, you can embed an object as an icon that masks the underlying object. The document displays with an icon that operates as a hot spot. Click it and choose convert. The complete object then appears on the screen.

Once you've embedded or linked an object into a file, you can drag and drop it like any other block of data, even from one file to another. When you use applications that follow the OLE specification, dragging a block of text from one file to another automatically makes the block of text an embedded object unless both the source (the application used for making the object) and that of the destination share an understanding of the data type. (If both applications understand the data type, the object can be freely edited in either application without a link between them.)

Voice Annotation

Multimedia enables you to add another dimension to your documents—sound. With voice annotation you can add vocal comments to spreadsheet entries or monthly reports. You can use your voice to add emphasis, explanation, or entertainment. Better still, it can be so easy you might use voice annotation to take quick notes for yourself, to capture your thoughts as you read or edit.

At heart, voice annotation is a direct extension of OLE. Your voice becomes the object that you embed in your work. The degree of OLE support offered by your application determines the means by which you can add annotation. If a program does not support OLE, it won't accept voice annotation through Windows.

Programs that are not written using the Windows or OS/2 interfaces ordinarily cannot accept voice annotation unless this feature has been explicitly built into the application by its publisher or have voice add-on available from third parties. Because of the popularity and convenience of Windows, this sort of application is rare.

Similarly, some Windows applications have built-in voice annotation links. In these you'll find a Voice Annotation menu entry. Adding an aural note to a document is easy. First, put the cursor at the place in the document at which you want to add your note. Then click Voice Annotation menu selection. Windows will then pop the Sound Recorder application on the screen. Just click the > button to start recording; the square to stop. When you're done, your note will appear as an icon embedded in the text. When you're done, you only need click the note to hear it.

Recording

The hardest part of voice annotation is the preparation. Before you can add a voice to a document, you have to have a recording in a form your system can use: a digital file. A decade ago, digital recording was something even professional recording engineers held in awe (and even envy). Today, the only extra equipment you need to make a digital recording with your multimedia PC is a microphone. The specifications for any true Multimedia PC require a microphone input on the sound board. Plug your microphone in, and you're ready to go.

The only program you need to capture your voice and turn it into a file is called *Sound Recorder*, and it is a standard part of every Windows version since 3.1. You'll find an icon installed as the default in your Accessories group. In Windows 95, you'll find *Sound Recorder* in your Multimedia folder, inside the Accessories folder. The only effective difference between the two versions of *Sound Recorder* is the graphic look, reflecting the aesthetic update between Windows 3.*x* and 95.

Once you open sound recorder, you'll see a control system that looks like that shown in Figure 4.15.

FIGURE 4.15. The Sound Recorder control panel in Windows 95.

This relatively little screen combines elements of the overall Windows control system, a cassette recorder, and an oscilloscope.

The buttons at the bottom are the control system. In order, they represent the digital equivalents of rewind, fast forward, play, stop, and record (the eye-dropper, indicating taking a sample). Click Record, start speaking, and you're making a recording. Click the Stop button to stop. To save your dulcet tones, just select Save As from the File menu just as you would save words or images in any other Windows program.

The standard sound format is a .WAV file. Sound files can be very large, and disk capacity often determines how long you can record. (The timer in the recorder in Windows 3.*x* may stop after three minutes, but your recording continues until you click the stop button.) The quality of the recording you want to make influences the file size—the better the quality, the bigger the file. Quality gets gauged by such technicalities as sampling rate, bit depth, and coding (discussed in Chapter 15, "Sound"). Your choices are essentially three, matching what you'd hear through a telephone, FM radio, or CD player. Each quality level doubles the data requirements and file size. Stereo recordings double file size once again.

For voice quality recordings, Windows 95 also gives you two compressed recording formats which approximately halve your storage requirements. Windows 95 defaults to making mono-phonic voice recordings with FM radio quality. You can change this selection by selecting the New option from the File menu before you begin your recording. (See Figure 4.16.)

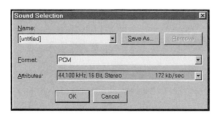

FIGURE 4.16. Selecting compressed recording formats in Windows 95.

Selecting Name enables you to choose quality level by name. If you want to be more frugal or take command, the Format and Attribute options enable you to adjust the details of the digital encoding process. Format determines the code method and gives you a choice of uncompressed (ordinary Pulse Code Modulation or PCM) or two forms of compressed (Adaptive Digital Pulse Code Modulation or ADPCM) encoding. Attributes lets you choose sampling rate and bit-depth. It lists the data rate, which directly translates into file size for each selection. Choose a lower data rate to conserve disk space, higher data rate for better quality, or just accept the default as a good compromise that lets you get your work done without unnecessary decision-making.

In the center of the *Sound Recorder* control panel you'll see either a horizontal line or a madly squiggling curve. The line is a representation of the analog waveform, the same as an oscilloscope display or an old-fashioned optical movie soundtrack. It shows you how loud your voice (or other sound) is—the fatter the line becomes, the louder the sound. For your first recording, you'll be safe as long as the line bulges like a snake rapidly swallowing random-sized cookies. The lumps simply serve as a confirmation your microphone is working. Ideally, however, you'll want the line to swell as viciously as possible without spreading the full height of the display.

If what you see is a flat or barely quivering line—your snake is starving—for best recording quality you need to increase the sound level, either by speaking louder, closer to the microphone, or increasing the recording level. If, on the other hand, what you see is a batch of square blobs with flat tops, you need to speaker more softly, back-off from the microphone, or decrease the recording level.

To adjust the recording level, *Sound Recorder* enables you to make coarse adjustments from its Effects menu. If you want finer control or to mix other sounds with your voice, you need to deal with another application. Most sound boards include their own software for this function, typically called a *mixer,* for use with Windows 3.*x.* The look and implementation of mixers vary with each maker. Windows 95 has its own mixers that take care of setting levels. You'll find them under the Volume Control in your Multimedia folder. From Options menu in the initial Volume Control screen (which does not give you a microphone entry), you can choose two other mixers which will enable you to adjust the microphone level and/or mix with other sounds, Recording Control, and Voice Commands. All work the same, give you control over similar functions, and interact. (See Figure 4.17.)

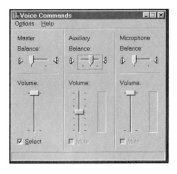

FIGURE 4.17. The Voice Commands mixer in Windows 95.

You adjust volume settings by dragging the slider, up for louder. The horizontal sliders at the top are pan controls, which adjust the balance of levels between your two stereo speakers when you make (or play) stereo recordings.

Embedding

Once you have a digital sound recording, you may still need to prepare it so that you can embed or link it to another file. Under Windows 3.*x,* you ordinarily cannot embed raw recording in files using OLE because OLE works only with objects. By packaging your voice file as an object, however, you can embed the file in any OLE-compliant application. The trick you need is the *Object Packager* that's included as a standard part of Windows 3.1. It installs in your Accessories window as a default.

To use the Object Packager, click its icon. It will open into a split window, like that shown in Figure 4.18.

FIGURE 4.18. The Object Packager screen in Windows 3.1*x.*

The left side is the object, the right its identification. Select the voice file you want to package— you can just type it in or browse through your directories to locate and add it. The packager creates an object, a file containing your voice note and directions telling Windows what to do with it—specifically, to load the Sound Recorder when you click the object icon so you can play back the sound from within the other application.

Once you've embedded a voice note, you can edit it as well as listen to it with the Sound Recorder. If you want, you can even re-record the note. For example, you could use a single icon within a file to pass notes back and forth between yourself and someone else editing your file. The Object Packager permanently links the object icon with the file name you choose to use. You cannot alter this association from within your application using the sound recorder, although you can with the Object Packager.

Video Annotation

You can add video clips to applications that support OLE as easily as you can audio files. The procedure is the same, only the object packager will give you a different icon to start with—a movie projector—and you'll specify an .AVI file instead of a .WAV file. No big deal. Make the appropriate substitutions, and you're on your way.

The problem you'll face is coming up with the video to add. You need a source of video files to capture a moving image yourself. The latter can be a challenge because you will need additional hardware and software to get you going, a video capture board, and a control program to match. You can get video files on disk, like clip art, or download them from on-line services.

After you make your first few steps into multimedia, you should take a look around and see where you want to go. If you're having enough fun with commercial software and system sounds, great! But if you're willing to make a bigger commitment—if you want to wring out the real power of multimedia—you'll have to consider true multimedia authoring, the subject of Chapter 5.

Chapter 5
Authoring Multimedia

Your friends all know that you can animate better than Disney did with *Pocahontas*, create special effects more convincing than *Jurassic Park*, and write plots more gripping than the best work of Stephen King. After all, you've told them often enough. But why waste your talents on those conventional media when multimedia beckons? With your native skill, your multimedia PC, and a few hours of otherwise spare time you could craft the first multimedia title to sell millions. You'll become instantly wealthy, so you can quickly retire to build the most elaborate house this side of Xanadu or found a chain of pizza restaurants populated by wise-cracking animitronic characters.

Of course, the only thing holding you back is your moral upbringing. Your soul knows you don't want to sell out at your young age. That, and the fact that your best efforts at capturing your voice with Sound Recorder resemble nothing so much as the squawks of oddly ill African parrots.

Take heart. Few multimedia titles are go-it-alone efforts. Most involve work by many people, each of whom specializes in a painstaking craft. Many of the most prominent publishers of multimedia have had head starts in getting to market. While you might be a bit hard-pressed to come up with the filling for a 650MB encyclopedia by tomorrow's deadline, the folks at Encyclopedia Brittanica have only to carry their typesetter's tapes across the room.

Creation is a personal process, one that we each carry out in our own way. Just ask God. Some people start with the germ of an idea, maybe a situation (man and woman shipwrecked on a desert island offshore from Toledo) or title (say *Saddlesore in Manhattan*), and elaborate their way to a feature film. Some just pile words and images in a bin, reach in and pull out a stack of clips, then organize whatever they get into a revue. Others diligently craft outlines with sharp quill pens, then slowly flesh out the scene with careful descriptions and apt characterizations, and finally sketch out illustrations in drypoint and their own blood.

Authoring in multimedia is no different. The best way to work is the way you work best. The one difference is that you have a wide choice of tools to help you with multimedia authoring. You may find that one tools suits your creative style while another impedes your progress.

Your choice of tool depends, too, on what sort of multimedia you hope to craft. Some tools can take command of external devices like video disc players and combine them with PC-based sound and text. Others restrict your media choices.

Overview

The creative process has no hard and fast rules. If it did, it would hardly be creative. Most of the guidelines for authoring multimedia are the same as for any creative process. Basically, the guidelines ask you to get yourself and your ideas organized before you begin. The authoring process involves several steps; some obvious, some subtle. Consider them all before you start.

Set a goal. After all, if you don't know where you're going, you won't know when you get there. Your work is apt to be pointless. You have to set a focus when you begin. Consider what your work is meant to accomplish, even if in vague terms like educate or entertain. Most of the time you can be very concrete in your goal: to teach about the flight speed of the African swallow, to keep viewers white-knuckled with non-stop action, or to make an easy-to-search visual reference of the complete works of Vaughn Bode.

Define your audience. Keep in mind who you're creating for. Your audience will determine the vocabulary and diction to use, the references and assumptions you can make, even the sensibility (and sensitivity) to humor. Consider whether your audience will put up with your ravings or will even stay away if you don't plaster the screen with exotic images and arcane sounds.

The place to start is with scripting, which may take the form of a conventional text-based script or something more suitable like a mix of media. Perhaps the best way to build an overview of a multimedia presentation is with a *story board*, the workday world's version of the comic book or cartoon drawings, a visual outline. The story board lays out decisive images in order of presentation, sort of like static scenes taken from a movie script.

Capture your words. The text of your multimedia presentation has to come from somewhere. In general, the old reliable tools are sufficient for capturing words from your mind and fingertips. Any word processor or editor, even Notepad, will do to collect your keystrokes and convert them into file form that can be imported into nearly any multimedia authoring package.

When you're goal is transferring an on-paper work to the multimedia screen, you should consider a scanner equipped with Optical Character Recognition software to convert ink to bytes. The OCR system takes care of the keystrokes and gives you relatively clean and pre-formatted text suitable for editing and updating.

Format text. As with preparing any document, multimedia requires formatting of your text to suit your presentation, if just for aesthetic considerations. Layout, fonts, and headings are as important to organizing multimedia as paper publications. Multimedia authoring in one way is like desktop publishing for the screen. But because the way you browse through traditional paper documents and course across your monitor screen are so different, desktop publishing software doesn't really work for multimedia. Instead of multiple columns, you use multiple Windows. Instead of footnotes, you use hypertext links.

Multimedia authoring software typically includes all the formatting power you need. In some cases, however, you can prepare the final format for a hypertext title using a conventional word processor. For example, if you're planning to use one of Microsoft's hypertext authoring tools (Multimedia Viewer, MediaView libraries, or WinHelp, see the following sections), you need to start with your document in Microsoft Word for Windows format. (You can't blame them for wanting to keep it in their family, can you? The "it" being your money, of course.)

Create or capture the graphics. You create still images for multimedia exactly as you would for any other sort of electronic presentation. The best way is to build simple graphics with the same software you've used all along for charting and graphing. If your multimedia authoring software can't read the native format of your graphics programs (many directly import the more common presentation graphic file formats), you can always save your charts and drawings as bitmapped files, if just using Alt+PrtSc under Windows to capture an image. Anything that will make a presentation slide will make a multimedia-compatible image.

You can also bring conventional art into your multimedia presentations, although you'll need extra equipment or services to make the conversion from physical to digital. A color scanner will turn your sheet-size flat artwork into disk files. If your original art is more elaborate or three-dimensional, simply take a snapshot. A digital still camera will directly produce a file that you can use, although the quality may not be as high as you'd like. You can also take moderate quality snapshots with your camcorder and a video capture board if it supports single frame. Even conventional silver-based photography works, typically producing the best-quality images for multimedia. You'll need a slide scanner to convert negatives or slides into digital files, or you can let your photo dealer transfer your image into digital form on a PhotoCD, Kodak's standard for storing images on compact disc.

Define hot spots. If you want your audience to interact with your graphics so that clicking on an object will elicit a function—for example, play a song, run a movie, or drive the host PC into meltdown—you must define the *hot spots,* the areas in which the mouse cursor is active. Using s hot spot editor, you outline the area on the screen corresponding to the location you want to be active. You also must associate the appropriate action with the hot spot.

Capture the video. Getting video into your multimedia production requires more work than adding mere static graphics. Not only do you need software for converting video into a digital file, you'll also need special hardware. Although video playback is an inherent capability of all Multimedia PCs, video capture is not. You need a video capture board. Any source with a video output that matches the standard followed by your video capture board should work, be it a video camera, camcorder, VCR, or video disc player.

A camcorder gives you versatility. You can carry it anywhere and capture images without lugging your PC behind. And tape is a lot less expensive for storing videos than hard disk space. Although the quality of video tape is always lower than that pouring directly out of a video camera (videotape is an analog medium that adds noise as part of the recording process), the difference is inconsequential for multimedia purposes. In general, your videos will fill a small windows and use a low frame rate because of your PC's limitations in data handling speed. You might consider a digital still-frame camera.

One important consideration when capturing video is its format. Overlay-style video capture boards grab images with high quality (for instance, in JPEG video format) that can only be played back with compatible hardware, that is, another overlay board. To reach the widest audience, you need to be able to translate your video images into Video for Windows or QuickTime for Windows formats. The following paragraphs briefly describe the steps used in making a video.

Produce the video. Here's where you play television director, making transitions between shots, accelerating or slowing the action, shading the colors, even distorting shapes. All those special effects you've become oblivious to on MTV and commercial television commercials can be duplicated on a PC—with varying degrees of success, depending on your budget and talent.

Sample sounds. Making .WAV files that can be incorporated into multimedia presentations is one of the easiest sides of production. Both sound boards and sampling software (such as *Sound Recorder*) are a standard part of any multimedia system. All you need is a source, which can be a microphone plugged directly into your sound board or an auxiliary audio source such as a tape recorder or CD player—even the CD-ROM drive built into your multimedia PC.

Produce the audio. Raw sounds and images work for some kinds of presentations but for others, you'll want to enhance the source material. Image and sound processing software allows you to quicken the pace of videos, brighten or dull sounds, morph between images, or combine individual effects into something the world has never seen before.

Compile the complete product. You can create a multimedia presentation with ordinary Windows software. If your word processor is OLE-compliant, you can integrate images, videos, and sound with your text. Most presentation graphics programs let you create slide shows and even integrate sounds and video with them. You can even use Visual Basic to make a custom presentation. But if you're planning to distribute your multimedia work, you'll want to seriously consider compiling it as a finished application using true multimedia authoring software. You'll gain power, flexibility, convenience, and protection.

Authoring tools give you power to do things with multimedia that your word processor or presentation package cannot. You can add hypertext links and search abilities to your text. Pull multiple Windows with hot-buttons into your presentations. Or combine the best of both into a single cohesive whole. An authoring package gives you a solid foundation to build on with screen management, searching, and titling power built in. The features that your audience most wants come almost automatically, requiring little effort on your part.

Your multimedia title will be more manageable once you've compiled it. All the required files will be brought together so you won't have to worry about copying every single one that you need if you choose to duplicate what you write. Moreover, authoring packages typically supply you with run-time modules to distribute with your product so your audience won't need the software you used to create your work. You can usually license a run-time package for distribution more easily (and at a lesser expense) than a full-blown application.

Compiling your multimedia title also gives you a measure of protection. Your audience won't be able to edit your work with ordinary software, dropping in surprise expletives before passing it on under your byline. Nor will most folks be able to lift text or images directly from it for their own plagiaristic purposes.

Authoring Software

Before you go too far, think about how multimedia fits into your creation. For example, you might want to build your work mostly from text, perhaps basing it on an existing book, and only add hypertext links and video illustrations. Or you might work in the mold of a training film, expanding it with the random access abilities of multimedia. You might even want to create an animated game that's all multimedia sound and fury. Understanding the relationship between the multimedia presentation technology and your work is more than a matter of preparation, however. It will help guide you to the proper tools to use to bring your work to life. Although you can use the same software tools to build a hypertext book and an action game, the effort will be less and the finished work more polished if you choose the right authoring tools.

With multimedia, you also have to weigh the amount of flash you want to put in your work against the effort and expense involved in creating it. Adding more hot spots and video clips makes sense when they enhance your overall effort and make it work better, but are a waste if they serve as nothing more than frills (or worse, are there just to show that you could put them there).

Most multimedia productions fit one of four common styles: hypertext, presentations, computer-based training, and no-holds-barred multimedia programming. Hypertext involves mostly text or is text-oriented. The presentation is mostly image-oriented. Computer-based training adds interactivity to the presentation. No-holds-barred multimedia programming can be anything, but mostly it is an exploration of the capability and power of multimedia technology. Each of these applications has its own authoring needs.

Hypertext. If you plan to build from a traditional base of the printed word, you will probably be working with *hypertext*, basically the book of the information age. Primarily text-based, hypertext endows normal or nearly normal books to logically link concepts and ideas together. Instead of presenting everything in a simple linear arrangement, hypertext allows easy sequencing in whatever order best suits the reader's appreciation of the content. Hypertext works are primarily text, using multimedia graphics, moving images, and sound as adjuncts that clarify points.

Presentations. The multimedia presentation relies mostly on images to make its point. As an outgrowth of the classic slide show and training film, it augments them by combining multiple images and sound with random access abilities. Again, although the author puts an initial ordering to the images and their presentation, the audience organizes or sorts the images of the presentation to better its own appreciation and understanding, for example, dashing from image to image for clarification.

Computer-Based Training. Education and training can use all the resources of multimedia but add their own demands. To work at the student's pace, computer-based training systems must be interactive. They must have hypertext abilities to elaborate on points that might not be understood in the first telling and incorporate presentation-like graphics to clarify murky issues. In addition, a complete system requires integrated test abilities so you can determine what's been learned and whether a student is ready to advance.

Programming. Today's conceptions of multimedia fall far short of its potential. The technology is too young to have been tapped out of its creative possibilities. After all, when Gutenberg slid the letters in place for the first impression of his Bible, he could never have foreseen the advent of the modern novel, encyclopedia, or comic book. Similarly, only the most prescient of us have any idea what creative writers and programmers will do with multimedia technology.

One thing is for sure, however. Wherever multimedia is going, today's accepted tools won't take us there. A tool designed to cut circles does you little good when you need squares. Hypertext and presentation authoring software are fine for crafting hypertext or presentations but can never go further than the imaginations of their creators.

When you want to push the envelope rather than simply address and mail it, you need all the power and flexibility you can muster. That means taking direct and intimate control of your PC with a programming language. Obviously, this is not a strategy for sissies. You have to make a large investment in time to master the intricacies of computer programming. But the rewards for your efforts are great.

Hypertext

The chief difference between ordinary text and hypertext is *linking*. Most conventional text is meant to be read in sequence from beginning to end. At most, it may be a collection of essays divided into freestanding sections that you can read in any order you choose. Hypertext allows greater freedom. Although you can access it in straight sequence as ordinary text, it also allows you to leap from section to section related by context and reference rather than the written order. Instead of confining yourself to individual articles, hypertext lets you lead yourself through several in your quest for information or answers. Instead of following a sequential order fixed for all time by the author, hypertext enables you to dig through words in a logical order made by jumping along the links.

Authoring hypertext differs from ordinary writing primarily in that you, as the author, must define the links as well as the rest of the text. You have to connect related concepts that may or may not appear continuously in your text.

Because of the text basis, the primary authoring tools for hypertext-style multimedia are text-based. You start with the familiar word processor. For the most part, you'll be writing as usual, typing into the word processor and editing, as you always have to get the information you want into your PC.

Even at this early stage, you can mix in multimedia. With a modern word processor that lets you use OLE, you can mix in sound and video hot buttons as easily as importing paragraphs of boilerplate. You'll also want to format your text for the right "look," be it formal paragraphs for a scholarly presentation or a looser format with random bold-faced words for emphasis targeting a more general audience. You may want to add in headlines, subheads, and other such typographic conventions. For personal consumption or sharing with a few friends, you don't have to go further than building a file with your word processor.

The big difference in authoring hypertext arises when you start to make the links. The hyperlinks don't spring into existence by themselves. You have to key them to your work, indicating which word will be highlighted and where a click will take you. You have to build a roadmap for journeying through your work. Some links will be little more than redefined footnotes, which are explanations that pop on the screen instead of lurking below a page full of text. Others will weave together and nest into a web so complex that every reader's path will likely be unique. You will have no way to test or even predict every possible route.

Although you could share ordinary text with your friends and expect them to read it with their own word processors, you can't make that assumption with hypertext. An ordinary word processor has no idea what to do with a link. It probably doesn't even know what a link is. Reading through hypertext requires special software. To produce a hypertext work, you have to convert your ordinary text that has been embellished with multimedia elements and link indications into a form that can be properly read. The process is called *compiling* and works just like compiling a program. You can use any of several commercial applications to compile your hypertext work. The end result will be a hypertext work in a standard format that other people can read with the appropriate software—the Windows Help program is one widely available hypertext reader—or a file meant to be distributed with its own reader program. This reader typically takes the form of a *run-time* version of the software you used to compile the hypertext. The run-time version includes only the parts of the compiler needed for reading through the file.

If you want to produce a hypertext work, the place to start is with the words themselves. Any editor or word processor will get you going. Since the most popular PC hypertext development tools are sold by Microsoft, that company's word processor, *Word*, would appear to be the best choice. In fact, Microsoft's multimedia tools are designed to work best with text files created by that program. You can, however, do preliminary work in simple ASCII files using any editor or word processor and later reformat them with Word.

After you have your text in order, the next step is to establish the links and compile it. Several programs are available for handling these chores.

Microsoft Offerings

Microsoft supplies three development packages oriented toward the needs of the text-based multimedia author: Multimedia Viewer 2.0, MediaView Libraries, and WinHelp 4.0. The three are inter-related and reflect the continuing development in multimedia thinking at Microsoft. All three can trace their heritage back to Microsoft's WinHelp 3.1, the help system designed for Windows 3.1. The core of WinHelp serves as the engine for these hypertext programs, giving them the power to let you jump between links and search for key words.

Multimedia Viewer 2.0

You'll find a number of commercial hypertext applications based on Multimedia Viewer. One reason is that Multimedia Viewer makes a solid stand-alone package with powerful linking and search abilities as well as the ability to handle individual multimedia elements. It gives the hypertext you write an easy-to-understand user interface and features advanced text-rendering and layout to let you make appealing presentations from ordinary paragraphs and graphics that automatically adapt to the display system in use. You don't have to worry whether the people reading your files have VGA, SuperVGA, or some weird display system. Multimedia Viewer optimizes display quality.

At its heart, Multimedia Viewer 2.0 is an elaboration of the WinHelp 3.1 design. It automatically endows the applications you create with it with the full power of the WinHelp engine. Unlike WinHelp, however, you can customize the user interface to suit the needs of your application. Of course, this customization has its price. It requires you to do actual computer programming.

Otherwise, creating applications with Multimedia Viewer requires little knowledge of programming. You only need to add special codes—lots of them—to your text. You write your text using Word for Windows formatting and embed graphics, sounds, and video in it just as you would prepare an ordinary document. When you've finished your draft, you save the result as Rich Text Format (.RTF) files, which converts formatting and embedding commands into ASCII text. To produce a distribution version, you compile it using the Multimedia Viewer software.

The downside to authoring with Multimedia Viewer 2.0 is that it's the end of the line. Microsoft has announced that the package will be supported only for Windows 3.1 and some special Sony multimedia hardware. Although the applications you create using it will run under Windows 95, you won't see further development of the Multimedia Viewer 2.0 to enhance its operation with newer Windows incarnations.

MediaView Libraries

If you're not content with the look and operation of presentations you author with Multimedia Viewer 2.0, MediaView Libraries give you tools for making your hypertext work look and act exactly the way you want. You can customize the user interface to suit your purpose and presentation. That way, you can give your work its own individual identity so that it stands apart from everything else on the market rather than just being another Viewer application.

To take advantage of this flexibility, however, you need programming skill. The MediaView Libraries is a compiler and run-time library, that is, a collection of routines that you use in writing C, C++, or Visual Basic programs that mimic the functions of Multimedia Viewer 2.0 while letting you toy with the outward look and feel. The MediaView Libraries give your multimedia applications index and searching, a file system, navigation features, multimedia rendering, and capability to control the screen presentations so you don't have develop those common multimedia features anew. Moreover, because you do the essential programming behind your application, you can build upon the MediaView Libraries to take your application anywhere you want without limitations imposed by Multimedia Viewer.

You start construction of a multimedia presentation exactly as with Multimedia Viewer 2.0. You embellish your text in Word for Windows format and save the result as an .RTF file, although MediaView understands some enhancements that Viewer does not. On the other hand, MediaView does not understand some Viewer features (specifically, panes and macros). Once you have the RTF version of your file, you add commands to the MediaView Libraries as text strings to link it to the user interface that you have developed yourself. When you're done, you compile the RTF so that it is displayed with your interface instead of the standard Viewer menus.

Unlike Multimedia Viewer, MediaView will be fully supported in upcoming Windows versions. Microsoft reports that it is working to supplement its Windows 3.1 product with versions written for Windows NT, Windows 95, and the Apple Macintosh.

WinHelp 4.0

The next generation of Microsoft's text-based multimedia development tools is represented by WinHelp 4.0, the help engine that Microsoft has built into Windows 95. Authoring hypertext to work with WinHelp offers the advantages of simplicity and convenience. Because Windows comes with its Help engine built in, there's no need for you to package it with your hypertext.

You can distribute a compiled file without a runtime and have reasonable expectations that it can be read and enjoyed (at least by people with Windows). Your WinHelp hypertext gets the full benefit of the powerful WinHelp search and linking engines. Compared to earlier versions, WinHelp 4.0 makes your hypertext more accessible by giving your audience a single entry point for navigating by using the table of contents and index.

WinHelp 4.0 starts with and builds upon the basic functions of Multimedia Viewer 2.0, although a few features (such as Viewer's panes, and the ability to open multiple windows on a screen) didn't make the cut into the first release of Windows 95 because of constraints on development time. WinHelp 4.0 includes all of Multimedia Viewer's text searching and multimedia abilities and adds several new features of its own, including support for keyword indices, full-text search indices, and a contents window that works across multiple files. It can even make hypertext links across multiple files. WinHelp 4.0 also enables users to print an entire book or several nested books.

In the Microsoft scheme of things, the new version of help replaces both Multimedia Viewer and older Windows help. The new Help reader included with Windows 95 is fully backwardly compatible with files created for earlier Help versions. When older Help files are read by WinHelp 4.0, however, you can only take advantage of the features that were originally compiled into them. For example, old Help files do not allow full text searches. However, you can recompile the original source files for older Help hypertext under WinHelp 4.0 to gain all the features of the new version.

Although Multimedia Viewer is based on the WinHelp engine, files compiled for Multimedia Viewer 1.0 or Multimedia Viewer 2.0 will not run under WinHelp 4.0. If you have written Multimedia Viewer hypertext, however, you should be able to recompile your source files to yield WinHelp 4.0 files. Microsoft has promised to provide tools to convert Viewer files.

Independent Offerings

The glitz of hot graphics have made them the darlings of the multimedia software industry, so mere hypertext authoring has been almost abandoned by most software publishers. After all, it's hard to compete with a product like WinHelp that comes free with the operating system. Nevertheless, a few publishers have developed programs aimed chiefly at creating hypertext applications. These include the following:

Guide

Guide (OWL International Inc., $495) starts with simple hypertext and enables you to add sound, video clips, and animation to create a multimedia production. Guide lets you type in text or import it from your word processor, then embellish it with buttons to trigger hypertext links. The Note button enables popup footnotes; the Expansion button expands on a topic listed in a heading; and the Reference button jumps to explanatory text elsewhere in the document.

You can build your basic hypertext system and add graphics to it using Guide's menu system. To mix in multimedia or take greater control, however, you'll need to do programming in LOGiiX, the authoring system's command language. Among its other powers, LOGiiX lets you take advantage of dynamic data exchange with other Windows applications. After you've compiled your hypertext system with Guide, you'll need a separately licensed run-time program, Guide Reader, to display it.

Multimedia ToolBook

Multimedia ToolBook (Asymetrix Corp., $895) is based on a book metaphor but extends far beyond hypertext with the ability to incorporate databases, financial functions, and custom interfaces. It permits running external applications and sending and receiving data from other applications.

The program works in two modes: author and reader. In author mode, you start building a book with a blank page to which you add text, links, controls, and multimedia elements. To extend your work, you add more pages. You can define background properties to maintain consistency across all pages of your book. Reader mode lets you view and test your book before you compile it for distribution.

As with Microsoft's authoring tools, ToolBook can import text in Rich Text File format. It also understands most standard graphic formats, including PhotoCD and Video for Windows, QuickTime, and motion JPEG, in addition to bitmaps.

The latest versions of ToolBook incorporate its own multimedia engine to handle animation and full-motion video. It includes a bitmap, icon/cursor, palette, .WAV file, and video editors. The last of these, Digital Video Producer, enables you to mix Video for Windows files, synchronize sound from .WAV files, and add titles.

You can build a book using nothing more than menus and dialog boxes. For more advanced control, with Toolbook's programming language, OpenScript, you can build menu bars, control buttons, and hypertext links. The package includes a library of common functions and minimizes your need for actual programming.

When you're finished building your multimedia book, ToolBook collects and compresses the files it requires for CD-ROM mastering and makes an installation program. ToolBook will compile your book into an .EXE file that can be distributed without royalty.

Presentations

Where hypertext deals primarily with words, presentation products are chiefly visual. As a consequence, you need a completely different array of tools for writing presentation-style multimedia, and authoring programs that are image oriented.

The starting point with most presentation programs is making the images. Most presentation packages grew from basic graphic software designed to make drawings, charts, and word-based slides for converting to film and projecting. As PC-based on-screen presentations became accepted in business (and helping them become accepted) these programs added on-screen slide show abilities. Modern multimedia presentation software goes beyond these mere slide shows by integrating in-depth hypertext as well as sounds and moving images.

In building a presentation, commercial authoring tools most commonly use a slide show metaphor for their primary interfaces. A slide show is simply a presentation of images arranged in a pre-determined sequence, the end of one slide triggering the start of the next.

Early presentation software did little more than that. As presentation packages have become more sophisticated, they've enhanced their ability to bring images together. They offer a variety of *transitions* between slides. The basic transition cuts between two slides; a second image totally replaces the first in the blink of an eye. A *dissolve* extends the transition, fading out one image while the other fades in so that both images mix together across the entire screen. A *wipe* replaces one image with another by sweeping the new image across the screen so that it take the place of the first instead of mixing with it. Wipes are the most dynamic transition with the edge between the two images moving across the screen. Any direction is possible, from left to right, top to bottom, diagonally, and even in odd patterns like exploding stars. More exotic effects include *tile transition* that replace an old image with new as a sequence of individual blocks and *louver transition* that updates the image in a series of synchronized broadening bands.

Originally, slide show software painted a single image across the full display screen. Modern packages enable you to fill your screen with multiple images and change each one independently. You can even superimpose a small image over a larger one—today's most popular use for video in that most systems still are not fast enough for full-screen video. In fact, most presentation-style authoring packages enable you to incorporate video images along with graphic stills. During playback of the show, the run-time will sequence through the slides, automatically running the video clips as just another image.

Although creating real animation requires another kind of authoring software, presentation preparation software typically gives you several methods of adding action to slide shows. *Sprite animation* enables you to move a small bitmapped image called a Sprite across the screen to draw attention to an image or issue. Basic Sprite animation moves the image only in straight lines (because linear motion is the easiest to program). *Spline-based animation* enables you to shoot Sprites across the screen in curved trajectories.

You can also make images animated by rapidly cutting between two similar stills, thus alternating two similar images on the screen. The success of this effect depends, of course, on the ability of your PC to rapidly repaint the screen. With many presentation packages, the only way to achieve high performance is by limiting the size of images. By *double-buffering* video frames, some software can speed repaints sufficiently to make convincing two-frame animation across the full screen. Double-buffering manages two frame buffers: one for the on-screen image and one off-screen for storing a second image that can be rapidly streamed to the on-screen buffer.

A few presentation preparation applications are based on a movie (or more accurately, animation) metaphor rather than the slide show. Although they enable you to put together a presentation in much the same way—generally by dragging and dropping icons representing the individual elements of your presentation—they use different terminology and synchronize events using actual timings rather than one slide triggering another. Using time codes, the movie metaphor gives you precise control. You can key events to individual frames, which are typically called *cells*, as with individual frames of an animation. Similarly in this movie parlance, a slide becomes a *scene*, and multimedia objects like video clips are *actors*.

Movies uses essentially the same transitions as slide shows. In addition, you'll find several programs also allow *morphing* of images—making one face or shape transform into another. Morphing is more than a simple dissolve. It actually distorts forms from one face or shape into another, using critical areas like the eyes as foci for the distortions. For the morph to be effective, these key areas must remain fixed while the rest of the image changes. Professional morphing software lets the control artist tag as many foci as are required for a compelling illusion. PC software does a good job of automatically choosing the right points to fix in the transition. The effect works best, of course, when you carefully match images beforehand.

Some presentation authoring applications are built around a *flowchart metaphor*, though it may bear some other name (one calls it a river). To take control with this sort of package is a true programming effort. After all, most complex programs begin life as flowcharts outlining their function. Most multimedia authoring offerings don't require you to write actual program code, but instead let you work graphically. You build a flowchart using icons representing the logical flow, then move text, sound, and images to the positions you want in the flow of things. Instead of slides or time keying the various multimedia events, your audience takes control by pressing an appropriate key or moving the mouse. Developing a presentation using this metaphor can be less intuitive but rewards you with greater interactivity with your audience.

Commercial presentation authoring software tends to fall into one of three classes based on power and price. The least expensive programs, which are typically priced under $500, offer first-time authors easy entry to multimedia programming. Most are based on a slide-show metaphor but can incorporate any standard multimedia object. Moderately price packages, generally in the range of $500 to $1,000, may give you a choice of control systems and often give you a programming language that you can optionally use for greater flexibility and control. Most of these packages will gather together the files you need for your presentation to help you package and master a CD-ROM and enable you to compile a distributable program. The high-end authoring packages, which cost from $1,000 to $10,000, give the serious multimedia professional a complete array of tools, a programming language, and extensive links to all sorts of multimedia devices. Most of these packages are designed to help develop training systems. Nearly all provide runtime versions that you distribute with your compiled presentation and many, despite the high initial price of the development system, also require a royalty for each run-time copy you distribute.

The following sections detail a selection of the presentation-oriented multimedia development programs currently available.

Aldus Persuasion

Aldus Persuasion (Adobe Systems Inc., $495) expands on the basic presentation program design to include such multimedia abilities as hyperlinks, animated displays, and embedded videos.

At heart, Persuasion is a slide preparation program with charting and drawing capabilities. You start with basic text slides or with one of 84 chart types that you can visually edit to suit your needs. Drawing abilities include freehand and the usual vector tools for arcs, circles, lines, and rectangles in color with fills.

Persuasion works through a three-view interface. The outline view helps you prepare your presentation, letting you enter text, edit by dragging and dropping to arrange your thoughts. The sorter view lets you see the various elements of the presentation in a glance to gain an overview. The slide view lets you prepare individual slides using templates for quick, preformatted designs or from scratch. You can add text and format it and bring in charts, tables, hyperlinks, and other multimedia objects.

Multimedia abilities include typical slide transitions, adding movement to slides (for example, having text interweave from opposite sides of the screen), and adding hot spots and video clips. Basic media players are built-in so you rely on OLE links to external functions to play sounds or videos, though you lose some flexibility (like the ability to adjust sound levels) in the process.

Although the program on the whole is easy enough to use that a few hours will give you enough mastery to make a presentation, you'll find that controls aren't completely consistent, particularly when adding multimedia elements.

Astound!

Astound! (Gold Disk Inc., $399) is an entry-level authoring package with a bonus of 1,200 sound and image clips. A set of more than 50 templates and a simple drag-and-drop control system helps you get started fast. You build your presentation either with a slide sorter or outline metaphor, arranging your presentation as a slide show. Display all your frames at once on a virtual light table and drag-and-drop to rearrange them. You similarly edit a graphic timeline to control transitions, synchronize events, and add pauses.

A far-ranging understanding of graphic file formats (including the ability to directly import Microsoft PowerPoint and Lotus Freelance files) lets you build upon what you already have. Or you can make your own slides with Astounds' built-in drawing and charting powers. Astound imports nearly any still image format and movies in Intel Digital Video Interactive DVI), QuickTime for Windows, or Video for Windows formats. Sounds can be added from .WAV files, CD audio, or MIDI.

The built-in text editor is aimed primarily at producing slides, with rulers, bulleting, and a spell-checker to help avoid embarrassment. Interactive features are limited to creating control buttons which can initiate jumps between slides, start sounds and videos, and pause the presentation.

Authorware Professional for Windows

Authorware Professional for Windows (Macromedia, $4,995) takes some time to learn but rewards you for your effort. Priced for multimedia professionals, it excels at handling video, both in Video for Windows format and through MCI control of external devices like laser disc players. It lets you quickly build interactive applications complete with hyperlinks, drag-and-drop controls, and integrated animation. Files made with the PC version of Authorware can be shared with those made with the Mac version (and vice versa, natch), and compiled files can be distributed with a run-time module without royalty.

ForShow

ForShow (Bourbaki Inc., $79) ranks as an oddity if just because it's one of the few multimedia authoring tools that doesn't require Windows. Rather, it simulates Windows with many of the same features such as a menu bar and drag-and-drop control. It lets you package together multiple bit-image files into a slide show, add sound in the form of .WAV or .VOC files, even add animation using Animator FLC or FLI. (Note ForShow uses these file formats but cannot make sounds or animations itself.) When you're done, you can compile your presentation with a DOS runtime or encapsulate it in Bourbaki's own Windows screen-saver format. Although you won't want to use ForShow to make a commercial application, it's an interesting tool to explore the technology.

IconAuthor

IconAuthor (AimTech Corporation, $4,995) gives you a graphical interface with popup dialog boxes that will get you authoring in a hurry. Using its Smart Object Editor, you will be able to build objects like buttons, timers, and scroll boxes quickly and easily so you can make multimedia programs that perfectly fit the Windows mold. Obviously, IconAuthor is also priced for professionals.

IconAuthor is best at building training programs for which it can link standard dBase files (which it directly reads) with other objects through Window's OLE. If you choose to use IconAuthor to compile multimedia for internal distribution, you'll pay $50 for run-time license for the first 249 copies and $10 each for more. Commercial distribution rates are negotiable.

ImageQ

ImageQ (Image North Technologies Inc., $749) controls rather than creates images for presentations. It gives you drag-and-drop control of its slide sorter, called Slide Strip. It lets you simultaneously work with up to six series of slides, letting you sequence them and control transitions between them. A text-based control mode is also available. Other windows scattered on your screen store notes, image thumbnails, and scripts for each slide.

Although ImageQ has only rudimentary sound and image editing abilities (it can adjust the color and size of your graphics), it can control all Media Control Interface (MCI) multimedia devices. (MCI is Microsoft's standard for controlling multimedia devices from Windows.) Building a presentation requires no programming expertise—using ImageQ's Standard Function dialog box, you can build a presentation by selecting icons. You can edit any of its 250 or so standard functions. If you want more intimate control, ImageQ incorporates its own object-oriented programming language so you can reach into other Windows applications and even build your own interface or database access system.

ImageQ enables you to put up to 25 images anywhere on the screen simultaneously, even overlaying them. You can overlay animations on bitmapped screens or add sprites with spline-based movement.

When you are finished with a presentation, you can compile it into a single EXE that incorporates its images and control information. ImageQ can automatically convert image color and resolution for the best match between stored and displayable formats. It will build its own Windows installation file and can package your presentation for CD-ROM mastering.

Macromedia Director

Macromedia Director (Macromedia Inc., $1,195) uses a movie metaphor instead of the slide show as its basis for building multimedia presentations. The Hollywood side of the program runs deep, infecting the product with a language of its own that will become familiar as you build your multimedia projects.

In fact, the presentations you shoot with Director are called movies, and the multimedia objects in starring roles, such as bitmapped Sprites, scripts, music, sounds, and palettes are called the cast. You write a script by placing these objects on a stage and setting the timing of their movements and transitions.

Director includes tools for manipulating bitmapped images, adding text, and writing the script. It aids in animation by *tweening* (interpolating in-between frames of a changing image). It can import just about any bitmapped file format. You can also hyperlink elements for interactive control.

You can take intimate control using Director's own object-oriented language called Lingo that includes its own debugger and enables you to control not only devices in your PC but external hardware such as VCRs and video disc players. Power always has its price. Although it uses English-like commands, Lingo is complex enough to require a two volume manual—definitely not an afternoon's reading.

Director compiles runtime files called projectors. Alternately, you can share movies in their native DIR format. Movies made on PCs will also play on the Mac Director version, allowing for subtle differences in platform (such as palette variations).

Many people regard Director (or its Mac-based sibling version) as the best program for developing presentation-style multimedia.

Q/Media

Q/Media (Q/Media Software Corp., $199) extends the slide show abilities of ordinary presentation products into the realm of multimedia by enabling you to add animated objects and sound. You start by building a presentation from scratch or importing one from another presentation program. You can then drag in multimedia objects from a dialog box or any application that supports OLE 2.0 and precisely set the instant the object appears in a scene and disappears. Q/Media allows interactive branching so you can let your audience jump from scene to scene, run programs or play video clips. Basically a beginner's program, Q/Media is easy to use but lacks many of the fine control mechanisms of more expensive presentation packages.

Computer-Based Training

In the wonderful early days of the PC, some of the first folks to embrace the PC were teachers. They discovered early on how readily the technology could be adapted to their own particular field. They saw the computer as an iron-willed task master with limitless patience. The machine could accommodate the most dim-witted student without melting in frustration. Better still, the computer made education back into an individualized project. The machine could adapt its pace to match the least or most gifted of students, letting the individual student determine the pace of his own education.

Computer-based training plays on this virtue and adds even greater refinement. Properly written programs not only test what the student has learned but also discover where further training is needed. Based on test results, the computer can repeat or reinforce a lesson as necessary. Consequently, testing is an integral part of any computer-based training application. Authoring programs must be able to construct the tests but make applications that automatically check the answers and adjust themselves to the responses.

Multimedia isn't necessarily part of this process at all. But adding multimedia to computer-based training brings the same benefits as it does any other application. Graphics and animation can clarify confusing issues, add impact, and lighten the heavy load of education. A video clip can show process and progress.

Most computer-based training gets written for a specific purpose in a specific business, teaching how to run a punch press or smile politely at the most obnoxious counter customers. Moreover, most of it is prepared by education professionals who have their own preferred ways of working. Consequently, the authoring software is specialized and exists in a rarefied realm of its own. Most of it has developed through several generations and often across several platforms, gradually stepping down from minicomputers and workstation-class machines to PCs. As with any product undergoing long development in a specialized area, it has developed its own idiosyncrasies, which may have become institutionalized. In other words, most computer-based training authoring software is powerful, quirky, and expensive. Most people don't need it, but those who do can't live without it.

The following sections include a brief look at a few PC-oriented computer-based training authoring tools.

TourGuide

TourGuide (American Training International, $3,370) lets you build training suites based on the metaphor of a road trip. You build a tour by stringing together scenes made of multimedia elements. The control logic that dictates the direction the tour will take is stored as a graphical flowchart, termed a map. The map determines when and how long scenes play, change variables, and play multimedia elements. Events controlled by the map can be triggered by keystrokes, mouse clicks, or MCI messages. You draw your map by linking together icons that obtusely represent your chosen function—a traffic-circle for a loop, for example.

To help you create and grade tests, TourGuide features a powerful string pattern-matching function that can analyze what users type in. The package also provides excellent scoring and performance analysis tools. It can readily construct training suits that tailor themselves to the abilities of the student.

Although TourGuide includes tools for manipulating bit-image, video, and sound files, its text-handling is handicapped. It doesn't readily import text files and limits formatting options. You can create royalty-free Windows run-times, although the process is cumbersome and requires numerous files.

TIE Authoring System

TIE Authoring System (Global Information Systems Technology Inc., $2,450) lets you build complex training systems easily using icons, as suits its name (TIE stands for Training Icon Environment). Each icon represents an element or action involved in your final project. You construct your project by putting together icons to make basic building blocks called units—the icons provide the structure, and you provide the content. The TIE programmer can use units as subroutines, debug them separately, and recycle them in multiple projects. Students see the units as training modules, displayed linearly, and click them to expand and view them.

The icons are actually a convenient way of dealing with Tutor, a proprietary programming language used by TIE. Once you've constructed your training application, you compile the code behind the icons. Global licenses a run-time modules that can play your projects in a variety of computer environments (such as UNIX) in addition to Windows.

In that TIE is aimed at training, its multimedia capabilities are less than dazzling. Besides its modest range of native effects, it lets you mix in audio, animation, and video from external sources using its Output Presentation icons. The system also includes a rudimentary paint program that can add titles to graphics imported through Windows' Clipboard.

On the other hand, TIE offers an extensive array of testing tools and options. It makes building multiple choice, true or false, and other styles of test easy. You can key branching to test answers to reward/punish appropriate/inappropriate responses.

Programming

Computer programming takes you to the land of no restraints. All things are possible when you take complete control of your PC. You're not bound by the pre-defined rules of the creator of an authoring package. Instead, you become the magician, conjuring up any effect you can imagine—if you have the patience to learn and develop a facility in programming.

Programming can take place at several levels. For example, IBM built multimedia control into its batch programming language for OS/2, REXX. You can operate multimedia devices from the command prompt using REXX even without extensive knowledge of programming.

OS/2
Warp

The bottom level of programming language control is running your multimedia devices through the standard MCI functions. Any language that is compliant with MCI commands will serve at this level.

Controlling the image requires more power, both from the language and your abilities to use it. Not only must your language of choice be able to route video data to specific screen locations, but you must also know how to write instructions to do it. Learning a computer language is no less trivial than learning to speak a second or third language.

Languages

Out of the profusion of languages available for programming a PC, only one plays a significant role in writing multimedia software: C. Its dominance is easy to understand. C is the language in which Windows and OS/2, the leading multimedia operating systems, are mostly written. Its commands and syntax define the way that modern multimedia applications (and most programs in general) are written. And it's something most multimedia authors will want to avoid. Learning to write C is like learning a new language: closer to Klingon than French because it's entirely contrived. C earns is name as the successor to the B language, which in turn got its one-letter name from the first initial of the place where it was developed, Bell Labs.

If you're serious about multimedia programming, you'll end up learning C sooner or later. Although the various authoring aids and toolkits do much of the work for you, at some time or another, you'll need to take direct control.

The current incarnation of the language is C++, which is built on the same foundation as the rest of the C family but is designed for *object-oriented programming* or OOP. One of the popular buzzwords of programming, object-orientation means that the language enables programmers to define *objects* that they can use in their programs as individual units simply by calling them by name. Functionally, an object is a black box into which the program pushes data and out of which comes results. The object is typically built of a block of C language code.

OOP makes code writing easier, particularly when you need to create many similar applications. Instead of typing out lines of code, you build code and data into independent objects, which you can then generalize into object types called *classes*. You can use classes to create new objects or subclasses. A subclass *inherits* the characteristics of the class used to create it, that is, the essential code and data is retained, so you need only write new code for the parts of the subclass you change. For example, if you already have a class that plays movie clips in Windows AVI format in your application, you can build a new class to display MOV format clips by changing only the code that deciphers the file format. The rest of the image handling and display programming automatically gets carried into the new class through its class inheritance. By recycling objects and taking advantage of *class inheritance*, you can quickly expand existing applications and develop new ones with a minimum of programming work.

If you're writing multimedia, you probably won't want to use unadorned C++. Unless you have a particular reason for building your applications from scratch, it just doesn't make sense when you can eliminate much of the "busy" work of building an application by using application development software. For example, when writing a Windows applications you need to create all the accouterments that are expected from every application, Windows resources like dialog boxes, icons, cursors, and the like. Application development tools make these everyday programming chores easy.

The tools available to you depend on the version of C you use. You have to modern choices, Borland C++ and Microsoft Visual C++. Borland includes its Object Windows C++ Class Library, usually abbreviated as OWL, to speed development of your applications. A related set of objects is called a class, and OWL is a collection or library of Windows classes that gives you a full array of object with which to begin programming. In the Microsoft scheme of things, you use the Microsoft Foundation Classes that accompany Visual C++.

Building a program with class libraries is a matter of writing code—typing in characters. Later you compile the code to see what errors you've made, and after you do it often enough you get a running program. You can't see the effect of your work until after your code is compiled and debugged, which means you have to take the aural and visual effects of multimedia on faith until you're done.

Rapid Application Development

When you want to build a graphic application, it's only natural to want to work graphically. And several programming aids help you do exactly that, enabling you to build a Windows interface as easily as working with a Windows program. Called *rapid application development* or RAD tools, they let you choose your resources from menus and drag and drop them into place. Most of the commercial development kits are aimed at programmers in business who need to work with database files that follow the Structured Query Language (SQL) standard. Their prices, typically at the $3,000 level, reflect this orientation. Although primarily designed to build programs for accessing corporate databases, they also enable you to build user interfaces and integrate multimedia elements. The most prominent of these development systems include the following:

Delphi (Borland International) is the only development tool that lets you compile your application into stand-alone machine language .EXE or .DLL files, which give a potential performance advantage. Some developers say the compiled code runs faster by a factor of two (Borland says more, others say less). Delphi is unique in other ways, too. Unlike other development systems, its code generation works two ways—when you modify an object, Delphi alters the resulting code. Edit the code, and Delphi changes the object. Unlike most development tools, Delphi is based on Pascal rather than BASIC. As you would expect, Delphi best complements Borland's own C++ compiler as it uses the same editor and debugger. (Its compiler is based on Borland's Pascal.)

ObjectView (KnowledgeWare, $2,899) runs midway between code-based design and a visual development system. For the most part, it makes construction of Windows objects parameter driven—to change the size of windows, for example, you call up a dialog box and type in the new coordinates. Although much quicker than doing all of the dirty work yourself, getting the right size and look takes longer than simply dragging the window outline, the method the other development systems allow. ObjectView works better as a tool for database development (for which it can automatically generate source code) than a multimedia design tool.

PowerBuilder (PowerSoft Corporation, $3,595) combines its own powerful BASIC-like scripting language, called PowerScript, with a suite of visually oriented graphics tools called Painters. The combination lets you build an application with quick programming and add a graphic user interface by pointing and clicking from on-screen choices. Although not fully object-oriented, the package gives the Windows objects with which it works a limited form of inheritance so that new windows, menus, or custom objects assume the code and variables of that from which it was developed.

SQLWindows (Gupta, $3,795) makes developing a graphical interface somewhat more work but fully supports C++ class libraries and multiple inheritance even in its scripting language, SQLWindows Application Language (SAL). Its Outliner is particularly helpful when you build an application from multiple interlinked modules in that it gives you a expandable tree-structure overview. Although basically a database system, it lets you add multimedia capabilities. It's best viewed as a professional's tool.

Visual Basic (Microsoft Corporation, $199 standard version; $499 professional version) is the official programming system for Windows. With Visual Basic, you can quickly design Windows screens using all common features (buttons, toolbars, icons, and so on) using an interactive drag-and-drop system. You write the tougher parts of your program—for example, the algorithms that do the actual work—with a language derived from familiar old BASIC. The applications you write support all Windows features including OLE 2.0. The design of the Visual Basic system makes it easy to build and reuse modules in multiple applications. Microsoft enables you to freely distribute the applications you write using Visual Basic to anyone who has Windows to run it. (The Visual Basic package even includes a wizard utility to help you build a setup program for your application that installs all the files you need.) What Visual Basic lacks is a compiler, but then again, that's what Microsoft will tell you C++ is for.

Toolkits and Programming Aids

Most development aids are aimed at helping you create ordinary Windows applications. They don't go out of their way to accommodate the needs of multimedia. However, several tools are available from Microsoft to assist in the development and control of multimedia systems. These are discussed in the following sections.

MCIWnd

MCIWnd is Microsoft's highest level multimedia interface, a window class that includes a library of functions, macros, and messages for operating multimedia devices in a 32-bit Windows environment. The commands associated with the MCIWnd function let you set up a simple control system that your multimedia audience can use to play videos, CD or MIDI files. You can also alter the appearance of the control window, limiting your audience's control to a single button, should you wish.

Your multimedia audience sees MCIWnd as a window that allows the playback of video and animation. At your command, MCIWnd will put a toolbar with media control buttons (Play, Stop, and Record), a trackbar to control the file position of playback, and a button that will pop up a menu with more choices. MCIWnd lets you give your audience the ability to open and close Video for Windows files, adjust playback speed and volume, change the size of the image, reconfigure the playback device, copy the playback to the Windows clipboard, and issue MCI commands. (See the following section.)

Media Control Interface (MCI)

Media Control Interface or MCI is Microsoft's standard way of communicating with multimedia devices; not a wire or connector but a set of commands. Although strictly speaking, MCI is not a programming tool, use of MCI commands makes writing multimedia programs easier and the programs themselves are more transportable. MCI is designed to be device-independent so that you can use a single command no matter the model and manufacturer of the hardware you want to use. The list of devices that MCI can control is lengthy and includes any CD players, MIDI sequencers, digital video playback systems, and .WAV file playing audio devices. Your program sends out the standardized MCI commands to your PC's MCI driver, which passes them along to the hardware driver associated with the device meant to carry out the command. The hardware driver translates the standardized MCI command into the equivalent device-specific instruction that the hardware can perform.

MCI commands take the form of strings and messages. MCI *command-message interface* is a set of C language constants and structures. To send a message to a multimedia device, you use the `mciSendCommand` function. MCI *command-string interface* puts the command messages into text form. To send a text command to a multimedia device, you issue a `mciSendString` function. The difference is purely in the look of the command and your comfort in using it. Windows automatically converts command strings into MCI messages before it sends them to the MCI driver to be carried out. Another difference is that command messages retrieve information in the form of data structures that can contain a wide variety of information that's readily processed by the C language. Each command string can retrieve only a single string of information which must then be properly parsed before it can be processed by a C language program.

The MCI mechanism requires several steps to command a device. First, you must open the device, then send the commands, and finally close the device. A single set of core commands is shared by all MCI devices for the most common functions, for example, play and stop. Devices are also grouped as to MCI *device type,* which share a common command set for features shared by that class of devices.

OpenGL

OpenGL is a set of three-dimensional drawing commands that was developed by Sun Microsystems for its workstations and later released as a device-independent graphics standard. Microsoft first adopted OpenGL for Windows NT 3.5, and the technology is likely to radiate through the company's product line.

In the Microsoft implementation, OpenGL comprises about 120 commands for drawing basic graphics primitives such as points, lines, and polygons. In the programs you write, you call the OpenGL commands to build 3-D still and animated images. The operating system then translates the commands into images either through the Window's Graphic Device Interface or by directly controlling (through an appropriate driver, of course) an OpenGL video board that can carry out the commands in its hardware.

OpenGL enables you to create realistic renderings that give the illusion of actually existing in three dimensions. For example, OpenGL tracks the "depth" of pixels, so it knows when one part of an image would appear behind another and consequently be covered up. Because it has become an open, industry-wide standard, the code is portable. You can use the same commands on any system that supports OpenGL to draw identical images.

WinG

WinG speeds up the performance of Windows applications by adding a library of high performance graphics techniques to recent and future Windows versions. According to Microsoft, it was designed to be the absolute fastest way of moving device-independent bitmaps to the screen, and often pushes image data through your system at memory access speed.

It accomplishes this goal by providing a means to handle double-buffering through Windows whereby programs can paint images off the screen, which are then quickly transferred to the display. In addition, WinG adds halftoning abilities to the Windows repertoire so that the applications you write can imitate 24-bit true color on display systems with a limited palette 8-bit display system.

You use WinG as a set of program calls when you write an application. Microsoft enables you to distribute the WinG run-time library (WING.DLL for 16-bit Windows, WING32.DLL for 32-bit implementations, as well as drivers and other support) without royalty. The WinG development kit is available free from Microsoft through several channels, including CompuServe and Internet.

WinToon

WinToon is a set of extensions to Video for Windows that enables you to create smooth animations by layering a moving foreground image over a static background. It allows you to create full-screen animations by minimizing the update needed to each screen. It achieves its efficiency by updating only areas in a given frame that have changed since the last frame. These changed areas are called "dirty rectangles" and they are mapped out when the cartoon is compiled. During playback, Video for Windows sends the video data stream, audio stream, and dirty rectangle data stream to the WinToon run-time program. WinToon then puts the data together to paint the frame in an off-screen buffer created by WinG. WinToon then allows the application that uses it to make changes to the image in the buffer. Finally, WinToon takes charge of moving the bit-image data from the buffer to the screen.

WinToon lets you work with scanned-in images as well as frames generated by animation tools. The animated part of the cartoon is a standard .AVI file, and the background is a device-independent bitmap static image. Both the foreground cartoon and the background share the same palette, one color of which is reserved to key the cartoon over the background.

WinToon is not a cartoon authoring tool but a means of managing animation frame data. The advantage of WinToon is that it enables you to produce a cartoon as an .AVI file with standard image manipulation tools instead of delving into heavy-duty programming. Microsoft imagines that you will outline key frames, scan them in, and fill in the color electronically to assure your on-screen palette stays consistent. You can tween frames for smooth animation and produce an .AVI file to store the animation and play in the foreground. This method requires less programming skill than working with most computer animation tools, although bringing a complete cartoon to life will still require familiarity with C and Windows programming.

WinToon relies on WinG to provide off-screen buffering and fast composing of images and uses Video for Windows to supply compression, synchronization, and streaming of data to the display screen.

The WinToon routines move the bits of the changing foreground image into the frame buffer for display without otherwise affecting the image. Its dirty rectangle stream handler tracks screen changes, and only when necessary repaints the screen.

WinToon comprises a run-time support library (WINTOON.DLL), a scanning tool, header files for the programs you write, an import library, and samples of applications, code, and cartoons. The WinToon development kit is available free from Microsoft through various channels (including CompuServe and Internet). Microsoft grants those who use WinToon to develop applications the royalty-free right to distribute the application with the run-time support library.

Pre-Production

In the motion picture and television industries, the process of making a film or video is called *production* and includes everything from arranging props and scenery to the final splice of the last cut of the finished film. Production in multimedia brings together diverse sources, one of which may be video or film segments that have undergone their own production process—though in multimedia, more appropriately part of pre-production.

All of the external media that get collected into a final multimedia production needs to be created and prepared for their final roles. This pre-production can involve any sort of effort that lets you capture ideas into sensory and sensible reality. For example, a video clip may originate as a traditional film, shot with a movie camera and edited on a moviola. Increasingly, however, the creation and pre-process takes place inside the PC. Each of the major media inclusions has spawned its own array of software that may be used during multimedia pre-production to create still images, video clips, and sound recordings.

Still Images

The slides that you put into your multimedia extravaganza will likely originate with your favorite presentation program, and you can probably squeeze out all the effects you need as you make the slide. But if you plan to incorporate scanned photographs or still images grabbed from the screen, you may want to exert more control over the image.

Photo prep software gives you the ability not only to heighten reality but to change it as well. Using a technique called *cloning*, you can duplicate shapes and textures from one part of a photo to another (or from one photo to another). You can use cloning to retouch simple flaws in the image or move pyramids halfway across the Sahara. Using *filters,* you can change the tonal and color balance of an image, heighten its sharpness, blur it into obscurity, or mix in a special effect (such as the spherical warp shown in the Corel sample screen in Figure 5.1). Most photo editors also let you change the size and shape of images and to perform complex functions using *masks* or *roll-ups*. You can edit down to the bit level of the image. Photo editors also enable you to prepare images for making color separations for printing, although a paper printout is pretty much irrelevant to a multimedia production. On the other hand, most photo editors enable you to change the file format in which an image is stored to match the needs of your multimedia software.

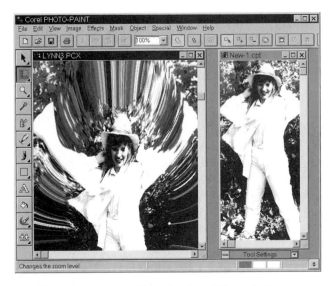

FIGURE 5.1. Using filters for special effects in Corel PhotoPaint.

Corel PhotoPaint 5 Plus (Corel Systems, $199) is a new photo painting tool introduced by Corel to augment its highly regarded CorelDraw program. It links into the Corel family of image software and follows many of the same conventions of its kin, such as the use of roll-ups (essentially floating menus). It includes a wealth of filters for color, tone, sharpness, and artistic effects and a full range of tools including blur and cloning using your choice of hard- or soft-edged brushes. It shows its newness, however, in the pointillistic quality of some of its transformations of file format in some color depths.

Image-In Professional (CPI Inc., $399) ranks as a mid-level product: not as powerful as professional image editors but more than adequate for occasional use. In addition to its photo editor you find a lot of utilities for scanning, optical character recognition, raster-to-vector conversion, and digital copying (turn your scanning into a Xerox machine) particularly welcome. You'll need to experiment for a while to get used to its tricky user interface. Keeping the photo editor from professional status is its weakness to make precise masks. Better are its abilities to retouch photos, with a full range of cloning and painting abilities, though you'll regret it's inability to save the custom tools you design for reuse in later sessions. The program also gives you a full range of filters, although some lack the degree of control professionals needed.

Picture Publisher (Micrografx Inc., $595) ranks as one of the top photo editors and has won many hearts with its ease of use. In fact, Picture Publisher may be the most intuitive photo editor: one that lets you calibrate scanners and screen hues without preaching color theory, and one that lets you browse through image thumbnails when searching graphic files. It includes a full range of professional-level tools that are readily customized and includes some welcome touches such as the ability to paint in extra sharpness in selected details. On the other hand, it tends to blur rather than smooth diagonal lines. In its most recent incarnation, Picture Publisher includes a unique Command List that records every change you make while editing. You can replay the list to recreate the image, editing the list in the process so that you can rethink any step you make in editing an image. A new multithreaded version is scheduled for release at the same time as Windows 95.

Photoshop (Adobe Systems, $895) is almost universally regarded as today's premiere photo editing program. It ranks as the most powerful, with a fast graphics engine and built-in abilities to take advantage of multi-threading (available in Windows NT and Windows 95 operating systems) and its own plug-in API that has become an industry standard for adding on utilities. Photoshop uses its power to good advantage, giving you the ability to make nearly any manipulation you might need to a photo with the most painstaking detail. It can undetectably edit reality or make truly surreal images from ordinary photos. In its latest incarnation, it has more alpha channel control (to let you store effects with image data) than ever before and new anti-aliasing algorithms for banishing jagged edges. If Photoshop has a fault, it is that power requires knowledge to wield wisely, and you face a steep learning curve with Photoshop.

Video

ImagePals (Ulead Systems, $129) serves as an all-in-one toolbox for still image capture. You start with its Capture module to grab screens (or definable parts of screens) and convert bit-image graphics file formats. Its Image Editor includes 20 special effect filters, dodging and burning tools, and a clone mode that works within and between images. Its Album catalogs your images as thumbnail images that you can assign a title and description, helps you group related images together, and searches for exactly the one you need.

After you've gathered your images, you can check them out through ImagePals' slide show viewer that includes 18 transition effects. To help you manage other multimedia files, the package works with Media Player to store and play .AVI, .MID, and .WAV files.

MediaRecorder (Lenel Systems International Inc., $149) captures video signals and takes intimate control of external video devices (including computer-controllable VCRs, camcorders, and video disc players), allowing you to grab single frames, and multiple frames for real time or time-lapse display. It generates .AVI files that can be played back through Video for Windows Media Player or incorporated into presentations.

You take control of your video system with your PC's mouse, using it to search a tape or disk, mark segments to capture, and command fast forward or rewind motion. When you mark a segment you want to capture, MediaRecorder displays its first frame, compiling single-frame thumbnails of the segments in a capture session as a video story board, which helps you to keep an overview of your work. When you've finished selecting segments from a tape or disk, MediaRecorder puts your video system on autopilot, going back and capturing only the clips you've designated so you don't waste hard disk space with out-takes.

Morphing

A morph is a transformation, a change in form, short for *metamorphosis.* Just as a tadpole changes into a frog or a caterpillar into a moth, images change form through the morph—but they make their transformation before your eyes instead of in a swamp or cocoon. One face transforms into another, a man becomes an animal or chair; any image can become another.

As simple as it sounds in concept, making a compelling morph in practice is a challenge. Fading from one image to another doesn't make a morph. It only looks like a dissolve. The morph looks like one object *grows* into another. The trick is to lock certain key points in place and let all the shapes around them change. When faces morph, for instance, the eyes are likely to be locked in place and the rest of the face distorts from the old shape into the new. To make a successful morph, you've got to pick the right key points to lock in place.

Morphing software either lets you pick the key points or makes its own guess at what's best. It then generates the steps in between the starting and ending images, tweeking the intermediate frames. Morphing programs differ in the flexibility and control they offer you, both in selecting key points and in the formats they handle.

Elastic Reality (Elastic Reality Inc., $495) makes you a morphing magician. With this professional-level product, you can transform anything in a few short steps. You use conventional drawing tools (for example rectangle, ellipse, Bezier, or freehand) to select an image area to morph, putting barriers around what you want to keep from changing. Elastic Reality then tweens the intermediate frames to make the transformation. You can make multiple simultaneous transformations, and even run each at a different speed for truly complex changes. Included in the package are 32-bit extensions to bring Windows 3.1*x* up to full speed and a package of editable 60 transitions called Transjammer. This is probably the most powerful morphing program currently available for the Windows platform.

HSC Digital Morph (HSC Software, $149) is better at warping effects than actually morphing. You can drag vertices of an overlay grid to expand, contract, or reshape images. In making morphs, it's slow and cumbersome. For example, editing key points is difficult. Source and destination images must be the same size. Then again, HSC Digital Morph supports some advanced morphing features like line weighting and adjustable line strength. Each morph stands alone—you cannot link several together—although you can save individual frames.

Morph (Gryphon Software Corp., $169) is designed solely for morphing. Using reverse cross-hairs, you define key points, select functions from a single toolbar, and Morph makes the transitions. You get excellent control over the speed of the change of shapes and colors using Morph's tension slider control. You can link a series of morphs to run in a single sequence at a wide variety of frame rates, and save the entire clip or single frames in a variety of standard file formats.

PhotoMorph (North Coast Software, $149.95) only starts with morphing. In addition, the package includes animated transitions, distortion effects (such as swirls, ripples, spheres, and waves), screen capture, and titling. PhotoMorph is powerful enough to transform images of different formats, bit depths, or even sizes. Control is easy: point and shoot with your mouse to set key points, choose a transition effect, and start the morph. PhotoMorph displays starting and ending images side-by-side so you can easily find the optimal key points. You can link morphs into mini-movies (in AVI or Animator formats) or save single frames. Best of all, it's one of the fastest morphing programs.

Sound

The raw sounds that you record with the microphone plugged into your PC's sound board are okay for adding notes to a spreadsheet or adding snide comments to memos, but in making professional presentations, raw sounds are the equivalent of a dot-matrix printout. There's an indescribable something about them that hints they weren't captured by a prime-time player.

Professional recording engineers refine and doctor raw sounds with a variety of tools. They use equalizers to balance the bass and treble, add reverb to give life to flat sounds, shift pitches for dramatic effect, flange sounds for alien effects, add in choruses and echoes, and maybe even stretch sounds to perfectly match a visual effect. A classic recording studio may have rack upon rack of specialized equipment to get these effects.

Digital technology is changing that. Most of those audio effects can be synthesized digitally with a few pieces of gear. In fact, once the audio is digitized, all you need is a computer to create the special effects that you want. With the right software, you can do the audio preparatory work yourself in your PC.

The most advanced of the digital audio production programs available are detailed in the following section.

Sound Forge

Sound Forge (Sonic Foundry, $495) gives you full command of any sound you can get into your PC. Multimedia producers will find the equivalent of a rack of digital audio processing gear at their fingertips—the program can flange, filter, compress, limit, double, chorus, gate, stretch, and squeeze or add echo, reverb, and a wealth of other effects—while musicians can sample, sync, and synthesize.

Any sound in digital form is fine fodder for Sound Forge. It reads and writes nearly any audio file format (including files from Ataris, Macs, and Sun workstations), converts one to another, can change sampling rates and bit depths, and even synthesize MIDI files into Windows waveform (.WAV) files. You can also capture sounds through your sound board or grab samples from external synthesizers using the program.

Sonic Foundry hopes to make Sound Forge a standard platform and expects to release additional plug-in features. Third-party plug-ins are also expected.

A complete rewrite from the previous Sound Forge 2.0 (released August, 1993), this new version now completely integrates with Windows 3.1, which it requires, for full GUI control and support of Microsoft's Audio Compression Manager (ACM). The main screen of Sound Forge gives you an oscilloscope-like analog waveform display of the sound files you load and enables you to monitor what you do with standard media controls (play, rewind, fast forward, loop, and so forth). Digital effects controls take the form of sliders that will be almost too familiar to audio engineers. For example, in the screen shown in Figure 5.2, the graphic equalizer takes the form of an array of sliders, each corresponding to an octave-wide frequency band. MIDI manipulation uses an on-screen keyboard.

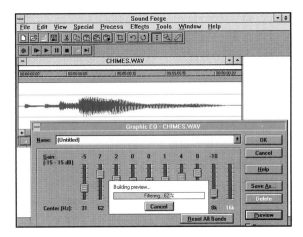

FIGURE 5.2. The graphic equalizer in Sound Forge.

Sound Forge embraces MIDI and allows patching together of other MIDI applications strictly through software using a clever virtual MIDI router. With the router, you can, for example, synchronize digital audio and MIDI files. Similarly, you can sync sounds with multimedia presentations because the program understands all forms of SMPTE time code.

Sound Forge processes from disk, so your hard disk's capacity and speed are the chief limits on its capabilities. For safety's sake, the program backs up every sound file before editing, so opening a large file can be time-consuming (a couple of minutes for 50MB). Short sequences load in seconds.

Sound Forge handles audio effects one-at-a-time and processing varies with algorithmic complexity. Simple filtering can be quicker than real-time (processing time equals playback time) even on a 33 MHz 486, though complex conversions—for example, a pitch change while maintaining tempo—may take minutes for 10 seconds of sound. Disaster recovery is exemplary—you won't lose a whisper even if your system crashes during heavyweight processing.

Although Sound Forge will work with sound systems as primitive as Microsoft's SPEAKER driver, you really need a professional quality sound board to take advantage of its power. It handles sampling rates from 2 KHz to 60 KHz (that's better than CD and even pro audio quality), and depths to 16 bits, stereo or mono.

Section II

Software Guide

Chapter 6 *Software Concepts*....................................... *117*

Chapter 7 *Operating Systems*....................................... *137*

Chapter 8 *Device Drivers* *201*

Chapter 9 *Data Storage* *227*

Chapter 6

Software Concepts

Software is the reason you buy a PC—or it should be. Software does the actual work or play for which you want a PC. It makes the graphics that appear on the screen and the sound that rolls out of your speakers. It fosters cardiac arrest when you play action games and migraines when you wend your way through adventures. It keeps track of numbers in your checkbook, watches every word you process, and bends reality when you edit images. Software does the actual brain work of running your PC. The hardware is merely its slave, doing what the software says and no more. This chapter will introduce basic software concepts.

Software is the essence of multimedia. Without multimedia software, today's fast PCs would do little more than their forebears—only quicker. The power, excitement, and enjoyment of multimedia all arise from the creative efforts of the people who create software, the people we call programmers—at least when their efforts are new and wonderful and haven't yet shown their bugs, structural deficiencies, and hidden tendency to scramble the data on your hard disk.

No hard and fast line separates multimedia software from the rest of PC programs. In fact, multimedia programs are built on the same foundation as are ordinary applications. The text on the screen starts off in a word processor; images originate in scanners and drawing programs; starting a multimedia application relies on an ordinary operating system that gets your PC running. At the level at which your PC sees the software code, multimedia applications look exactly like any other computer software. If anything, they are often more elaborate because they have to do more work all at one time to keep all your senses reeling. At heart, however, multimedia software and non-multimedia software have the same foundation and ingredients. Understanding those origins will help you appreciate the power and ability of multimedia; it will help you sort through most of the hype that infests multimedia; it may even inspire you to create your own multimedia when you find out how simple software really is. Although a nitty-gritty look at how programs work may at first seem tedious, even a bit of overkill, you'll see that most of the problems people run into in getting multimedia systems to work properly begins at a very low level. Once you know how the problems arise, they're a lot easier to understand and set right.

Let's take a quick overview of software, venturing from its origins to the capabilities of commercial multimedia products. Along the way we'll see where some of the most bothersome problems in getting multimedia to work arise.

Definition

A good place to begin is to define what "software" really means. Software is that stuff that comes in boxes with squishy sides. The boxes are kind of soft, so they call it software. At least that's a possible derivation of the term, paralleling the merchandiser's cant in which appliances are hardware and clothing is software. In truth, however, the origins of the term "software" are even dumber than that. Software is called "soft" because it's not hardware. It's not really soft. It's immaterial, even imaginary. Software has no physical existence, only a physical representation. It's an idea or series of ideas, a product of someone's mind or intellect.

Computer software is like a book, ideas represented in a more tangible form. Instead of printed paper, the software comes on a disk, either floppy or CD-ROM. The ideas in software are more like a special kind of book, a cookbook. Computer software doesn't tell a story itself but is a list of instructions that guide the making of a story.

Programming

A computer program is nothing more than a list of instructions for a microprocessor to carry out. A microprocessor instruction, in turn, is a specific pattern of bits, a digital code. Your computer sends the list of instructions making up a program to your microprocessor one at a time. Upon receiving each instruction, the microprocessor looks up what function the code says to do, then it carries out the appropriate action.

Every microprocessor understands its own repertoire of instructions just as a dog might understand a few spoken commands. Where your pooch might sit down and roll over when you ask it to, your processor can add, subtract, move bit patterns around, and change them. Every family of microprocessors has a set of instructions that it can recognize and carry out, the necessary understanding designed into the internal circuitry of each chip. The entire group of commands that a given microprocessor model understands and can react to is called that microprocessor's *instruction set* or its *command set*. Different microprocessor families recognize different instruction sets, so the commands meant for one chip family would be gibberish to another. The Intel family of microprocessors understand one command set; the IBM/Motorola PowerPC family of chips recognize and entirely different command set.

As a mere pattern of bits, a microprocessor instruction in itself is a simple entity, but the number of potential code patterns allows for incredibly rich command sets. For example, the Intel family of microprocessors understands more than eight subtraction instructions, each subtly different from the others.

Some microprocessor instructions require a series of steps to be carried out. These multistep commands are sometimes called *complex instructions* because of their composite nature. Although the complex instruction looks like a simple command, it may involve much work. A simple instruction would be something like "pound a nail;" a complex instruction may be as far ranging as "frame a house." Simple subtraction or addition of two numbers may actually involve dozens of steps, including the conversion of the numbers from decimal to binary (1's and 0's) notation that the microprocessor understands.

Broken down to its constituent parts, a computer program is nothing but a list of symbols that correspond to patterns of bits that signal a microprocessor exactly as letters of the alphabet represent sounds that you might speak. Of course, with the same back-to-the-real-basics reasoning, an orange is a collection of quarks squatting together with reasonable stability in the center of your fruit bowl. The metaphor is apt. The primary constituents of an orange—whether you consider them quarks, atoms, or molecules—are essentially interchangeable, even indistinguishable. By itself, every one is meaningless. Only when they are taken together do they make something worthwhile—the orange. The overall pattern, not the individual pieces, is what's important.

Letters and words work the same way. A box full of vowels wouldn't mean anything to anyone not engaged in a heated game of Wheel of Fortune. Match the vowels with consonants and arrange them properly, and you might make words of irreplaceable value to humanity: the works of Shakespeare, Einstein's expression of general relativity, or the formula for Coca-Cola. The meaning is not in the pieces but their patterns.

Everything that the microprocessor does consists of nothing more than a series of these step-by-step instructions. A computer program is simply a list of microprocessor instructions. The instructions are simple, but long and complex computer programs are built from them just as epics and novels are built from the words of the English language. Although writing in English seems natural, programming feels foreign because it requires that you think in a different way, in a different language. You even have to think of jobs, such as adding numbers, typing a letter, or moving a block of graphics, as a long series of tiny steps. In other words, programming is just a different way of looking at problems and expressing the process of solving them.

Languages

These bit-patterns used by microprocessors can be represented as binary codes which can be translated into numbers in any format—hexadecimal and decimal being most common. In this form, the entire range of these commands for a microprocessor is called *machine language*. Most human beings find words or pseudo-words to be more comprehensible symbols. The list of word-like symbols that control a microprocessor is termed *assembly language.*

You make a computer program by writing a list of commands for a microprocessor to carry out. Think of a program as a recipe—a list of steps that must be carried out in a particular order. First, you mix the ingredients, then bake, then lay on the frosting.

This step-by-step command system is perfect for control freaks but otherwise is more than most people want to tangle with. Even simple computer operations require dozens of microprocessor operations, so writing complete lists of commands in this form can be more than many programmers want to deal with. Moreover, machine and assembly language commands are microprocessor-specific: they work only with the specific chips that understand them. Worse, because the microprocessor controls all computer functions, assembly language programs usually work only on a specific hardware platform.

Higher-Level Languages

Just as an assembler can convert the mnemonics and subroutines of assembly language into machine language, a computer program can go one step further, translating more human-like instructions into multiple machine language instructions that would be needed to carry them out. In effect, each language instruction becomes a subroutine in itself.

The breaking of the one-to-one correspondence between language instruction and machine language code puts this kind of programming one level farther from the microprocessor, a greater or higher abstraction. Such languages are called higher-level languages. Instead of dealing with each movement of a byte of information, high level languages enable the programmer to deal with problems as decimal numbers, words, or graphic elements. The language program takes each if these higher-level instruction and converts it into a length series of digital-code microprocessor commands in machine language.

Higher-level languages can be classified into two types: interpreted and compiled.

An *interpreted language* is translated from human to machine form each time it is run by a program called, appropriately enough, an interpreter. People who need immediate gratification like interpreted programs because they can be run immediately, without intervening steps. If the computer encounters a programming error, it can be fixed and immediately tested again. On the other hand, the computer must make its interpretation each time the program is run, performing the same act again and again. This repetition wastes the computer's time. More importantly, because the computer is doing two things at once, both executing the program and interpreting it at the same time, it runs more slowly. BASIC, an acronym for the Beginner's All-purpose Symbolic Instruction Code, is the most familiar programming language. BASIC, as an interpreted language, has been built into every personal computer IBM has made.

Using an interpreted language typically involves two steps. First, you start the language interpreter program, which gives you a new environment complete with its own system of commands and prompts, then you execute your program. Although these two steps can be linked together at your point of view—for instance, when you start BASIC with the name of a program to run on your DOS command line—your PC still must run the language interpreter before it can deal with your program.

Compiled languages cut the waste of interpreted languages. The programs written using them are translated from high-level symbols into machine language once. The resulting machine language is then stored and called into action each time you run the program. The act of converting the program from English into machine language is called compiling the program and uses a language program called a compiler. The original, English-like version of the program—the words and symbols actually written by the programmer—is called the source code. The resulting machine language makes up the program's object code.

Compiling a complex program can be a lengthy operation, taking minutes, even hours. Once the program is compiled, however, it runs quickly because the computer need only run the resulting machine language instructions instead of having to run an program interpreter at the same time. Most of the time, the compiled program runs directly from the DOS prompt—you just type the program's name, and it loads and executes. Examples of compiled languages used in programming multimedia include C, C++, and Pascal.

Because of the speed and efficiency of compiled languages, compilers have been written that take interpreted language source code and convert it into object code that can be run like any compiled program. For example, a BASIC compiler will produce object code that will run from the DOS prompt without the need for running the BASIC interpreter.

No matter how high the level of the programming language, no matter what you see on your computer screen, no matter what you type to make your machine do its daily work, everything the microprocessor inside does is reduced to a pattern of digital pulses to which it reacts in knee-jerk fashion.

Programming Tools

When you start with any programming language, your PC is little more than a blank sheet of paper. While that's great for putting your imagination to work, it can be more work than a project justifies when you have to create basic functions that have been done dozens of times before (and probably better). To avoid starting from scratch with every new program, professional programmers build collections of their favorite language routines that they use over and over again with every application they write. For example, you might write a series of language instructions for drawing a box on your monitor screen, which you can recycle every time you need to draw a box.

Commercial software vendors sell program development tools that collect useful routines that have been professionally developed. These libraries of functions can save programmers hours or days of development. Modern object-oriented programming languages take this concept a step further by packaging common functions and structures as *objects* that can be shared and reused in the development of applications. A generalized collection of objects is called a *class*. In developing multimedia software, most programmers work with class libraries to create programming objects.

Typically, class libraries may be packaged with other useful software for creating programs such as editors and debuggers (which let you step through a program one instruction at a time to find errors) along with their language compilers to create *software development kits* or SDKs. Most commercial application programmers start work with at the SDK level.

Application-Level Programming

Multimedia is so demanding that even higher-level languages offer little respite for programmers. Moreover, most languages don't work at the level that developers want to operate. They want to open windows, run film clips, and clang out sounds rather than write millions of lines of code. Consequently most multimedia programmers develop at a level higher than the computer language or even SDK. Visual interfaces of developmental tools give direct, interactive control over screen elements, text, and sounds.

After all, multimedia functions are pretty well-defined and well-nigh universal among presentations: you need to be able to organize text, sound, and images; link the various elements together; and key them to user input. Whether you're developing a commercial multimedia program or just putting together a personal presentation, the requirements are essentially the same. Consequently most multimedia programs that are designed to let you wend your way through the world of multimedia also provide a means of developing commercial products.

Of course, when you put together a presentation using an application, you need to run the application to view your presentation. While that's no problem for you when you already have the software (you can't create the presentation without it, right?), it is a problem if you want to distribute your finished work commercially. You either have to distribute a copy of the application you used with your presentation (which means buying a copy for every one you distribute, which quickly gets expensive) or depend on your audience already having the required software. Sometimes the latter works—for example, when the required software is included as part of Windows.

The other alternative is the run-time module, a stripped-down version of the application you use to create your presentation. The run-time module has all the creative functions removed, leaving only the display functions. It can show presentations but not make them. Often the application publisher extends a free license to distribute its run-time module to encourage you to develop your presentations using its application.

Tasks and Threads

In the early days of PCs, programs followed the simple step-by-step style of execution called *linear programming.* They worked exactly like recipes. Each step had to be completed before the program could venture on to the next—you had to put the eggs in the mixing bowl before you could beat them. Moreover, the computer was designed to do only one thing at a time. It could walk or chew gum but never both.

As PCs became popular as the universal desktop tool, clever programmers saw the limitations of the one-thing-at-a-time approach. The PC helped out with many office chores. But a strict linear approach meant you had to finish with one task, end the program that carried it out, then start another program for the next task. Certainly the process was no different from changing gears (mentally or physically) except that it could take nearly a minute for a complete transition, long enough for you to miss a shift, lose your place, or simply fall asleep at the wheel.

The first bright idea to making shifting between tasks easy was called context switching. Instead of shutting down one application before starting another, context switching put the first program on hold, memorizing all the settings of the computer (technically speaking, the contents of each register and memory location) by copying them to an unused spot in memory or to disk. The PC could then load a second application and let you tinker around with it. When you wanted to switch back to the first program, your system would memorize the new application and reload itself with the old application. Because the PC worked at electronic speed, memorizing everything took no more than a few seconds.

The next step beyond context switching is multi-tasking. Instead of memorizing an application by copying everything down, a multi-tasking system gives each application its own place in memory. It then activates and deactivates the individual applications as they are needed. Different kinds of multi-tasking systems use different events to trigger the switch.

The most primitive multi-tasking systems work as simple context switchers, waiting for you to designate which program should run. A real multi-tasking system, however, makes your PC appear to run several applications at the same time by quickly and automatically shifting control from one application to the next.

A simple *time-slicing* system divides up the total time that your PC could be running programs into individual slices, each a fraction of a second long. It then gives each application its own slice to carry out its functions, then gives a slice to the next application in round-robin fashion. Although this simple time-slicing works, it is also inefficient. It gives slices to applications that might not need them and it makes no provision for emergencies when an application desperately needs to take control. For example, a communications program might not get the slice it needs to grab a character from a serial port. Another character could rush in and bump the first into oblivion.

In a *cooperative multi-tasking system*, applications take turns at controlling the computer. Although the multi-tasking system switches between applications, it depends on each program to yield up control of the PC when it no longer needs it so the multi-tasking system can pass control along to the next application. Programs take only the time they need, making more efficient use of the total time available to the PC. The Windows 3.1 family (and earlier Windows versions) use cooperative multi-tasking.

But cooperative multi-tasking depends on cooperation from individual applications. A greedy program can hoard system time and ruin the performance of the rest of the system. The alternative is to give the multi-tasking system complete control over which application runs, and when and how long it runs, switching with or without the cooperation of the individual programs. Because this kind of multi-tasking system can pre-empt one application and give control to another, it is called *pre-emptive multi-tasking*. This form of multi-tasking makes the most efficient use of a computer's time, preventing any one application from usurping control. Both OS/2 Warp and Windows 95 perform pre-emptive multi-tasking, though Windows 95 uses cooperative multi-tasking for handling DOS applications.

While multi-tasking puts more of your PC's time to work, it doesn't necessarily run your applications at the highest possible efficiency. The handicap is the linear approach to programming tasks. Although doing one thing after another works well for simple tasks, when chores get complex the linear approach can waste time. Think of the cookbook again. A particular entree may require a special sauce. Cook the entree then the sauce, and the entree gets congealed. Make the sauce first, and it could clot by the time you clean and cook the partridges. Moreover, while the partridges are in the oven, you don't do anything but wait for them to finish, drumming your fingers and making small talk with your spouse. Quite naturally, while the birds are baking you put the time to use making the sauce. The recipe gets divided into two separate and independent parts, which you can schedule as you see fit, even though the parts are related to and result in a single glorious finale.

Programmers can do the same thing with software. They can divide a given chore into separate parts so that your PC can carry out each part as it has time. Each separate and independently executable part of a program is called a *thread*. Modern operating systems make life easy for the programmer who needs only to break the program into threads. The computer itself keeps track of each thread and insures that all parts of a program stay coordinated. The PC runs each thread as time becomes available, even mixing together threads from different programs at the same time. This multi-threading is particularly advantageous when part of a program must wait for something—you to hit a key at the keyboard, a character to zap into your serial port, your printer to smudge and shred another ream of paper. Instead of idling along waiting, your PC puts every available cycle to work.

Multimedia applications lend themselves naturally to multi-threaded design in that they combine several time-dependent tasks running separately. For example, one thread can run the video display, another a sound track, while a third handles your input and interaction. Under

Windows 3.1 the multi-threading abilities were nascent because the environment itself (and the DOS under which it ran) was single-threaded. Windows 95 and OS/2 are designed to run multi-threaded applications.

The difference between single-threaded and multi-threaded operation is readily apparent in comparing older and newer operating systems. When you print a file under most Windows 3.1 applications, for example, you lose control of your PC until the file is processed and passed over to Print Manager. Under Windows 95 or OS/2, you can continue to interact with your PC while a document prints.

User Interface

The place where different people, ideas, technologies, worlds, or universes come together is called an interface, and interfaces abound in the realm of PCs. The one interface most important to you as a participant in multimedia is the user interface, where you and your machine come face-to-face. The user interface is not only what you see on the screen (that is, how your PC communicates with you) but also the buttons you press, the mouse you slide, and the trackball you roll to convey your wants to your PC.

What you see when you switch on your multimedia PC running Windows 95 or OS/2 is called a graphical user interface or GUI (pronounced "gooey"). With Windows 3.1, you get a GUI only after you start Windows. Otherwise you'll either stare at the unadorned DOS prompt—little more than an indicator that your computer is working and waiting for you to type a command —or a text-based shell, a GUI-like face to hide the ugly DOS command-line interface.

If you're new to computers, the term may not seem to make sense (and it might not even if you're familiar with computers) because there's very little graphical about it—you see words scattered on the screen and little images here and there. The term graphical distinguishes this kind of screen from those that came before, screens of nothing more than text. Appropriately these were called text-mode interfaces. Alternately, they are described as command-line interfaces because your PC reacts only to the command you type on a single line on the screen. Except in rare instances, however, you probably won't tangle with the command-line interface—it will pop up only during the period between when you boot up and run Windows 3.1 or when you stretch back in history to run some archaic program to take care of some detail of running your PC.

The graphical user interface has become the one accepted means of running personal computers. The reason for this, according to its developers, is that the GUI is more natural and understandable, which of course is nonsense. There's nothing the least natural about pushing a plastic mouse shaped like a soap bar around on top of your desk to move an arrow-like pointer on your screen to indicate crude miniaturized symbols. Learning to use a PC for the first time is a challenge no matter what's on the screen or under your hand.

The real advantage of the GUI has nothing to do with graphics or pointing. Rather, the GUI gets high marks because it puts the full range of functions in front of you. You don't have to guess at what command does what, a chore akin to guessing the PIN (Personal Identification Number) for someone else's bank card. You can explore everything that a computer and its software can do by pushing and prodding your mouse while watching the effects on your screen.

The other strength is that the odd control system, unnatural as it is, has become standardized. A generation of designers has grown up believing that it is, in fact, a natural interface, so they have uniformly adopted it. It is ubiquitous as paper money—and equally artificial. (As with money, the GUI has value only as long as everyone believes in it!) Look beyond its contrived roots, however, and the usefulness of money or GUI is undeniable.

Once you learn the rudiments of moving the mouse, coordinating your arm to the pointer on the screen, and how to select from menus and icons, you can figure out just about any program through experimentation. The learning curve starts abruptly. Watch someone for about three seconds and you know how to move a mouse. The art of clicking and double-clicking is a bit less intuitive, but given a couple of minutes and a modicum of manual dexterity, you'll be in full command of your PC's GUI. All that's left is exploring the possibilities, exactly what you've spent all your life doing—and what you're destined to do for the rest of it.

Each of the three leading multimedia control systems—Macintosh, OS/2, and Windows—arranges the pieces of its GUI differently. The differences are mostly matters of preference and philosophy—and intellectual property protections. The concepts underlying each are identical.

History

The GUI that's standard today among multimedia systems did not arise like Athena, fully armed with features from the first instant they sprang from some developer's head. Development went hand-in-hand with new theories of computers. Moreover, workable GUIs had to wait until personal computers were powerful to make them work quickly enough that you wouldn't be tempted to throw a fist through your monitor screen in frustration.

The first computers were slow, demanding beasts and about as accessible to neophytes as an medieval alchemical text—they responded only to programs that, when written down, more resembled mathematical formulae than the product of a normal human mind. The first step on the long road to the graphical user interfaces used by today's most powerful personal computer operating systems was a demonstration program created in 1963 by Ivan Sutherland and called Sketchpad. Instead of requiring a computer operator to type a series of commands (or punch them into a stack of cards, then feed them into a card reader), Sketchpad enabled anyone capable of pushing a lightpen across a monitor screen to make engineering drawings. Sketchpad introduced many of the concepts basic to today's most powerful software—including windows and the graphic cursor.

Another pioneer was Douglas C. Englebart, who worked at Stanford Research Institute, and explored the potentials of computer technology. In the course of his research, Englebart invented many of the elements underlying the design of today's multimedia systems. Two of the most important were on-screen windows, which enabled a single computer operator to monitor several applications running at the same time, and the mouse as a pointing device in an overall control system. Powerful as his ideas were, they didn't immediately catch on. The necessary processing power and technology simply didn't exist when he first published his work in October, 1962.

When master/monster mainframe computing was brought down to size with work on work-group computing at Xerox Corporation's Palo Alto Research Center (PARC), the GUI was part of the concept of the personal computer. Xerox developed the Alto, the machine some historians credit as the first PC, although it lacked the accessibility that characterizes modern machines. Grafting the GUI onto the desktop workstation resulted in the Xerox Star workstation, which put all the elements of today's multimedia systems in place.

Design

The GUI is based on the fundamental and frowned-on natural human inclination to point at what's important. The point of pointing is drawing someone's attention. With a PC, pointing with a mouse indicates to the machine what interests you, drawing its attention to an object, file or program.

The GUI relies on another concept, that of grouping related issues or thoughts together as a class to aid in organization. Related functions are combined into sub-menus. Files are grouped like a family tree. This organization enables you to move from the general to the specific in your quest for information.

The way the GUI looks and operates depends on who puts it together. Among PCs, the most familiar GUI is the window. Consistently throughout all GUIs, a window provides a way to look into your software, an aperture for peering into a program and seeing what it was doing. At that, the window was a convenient means of dividing your monitor screen into separate elements, each of which display a program, so that you could see and run several applications simultaneously. Without windows, multi-tasking would force you into running blind.

To give you a consistent, graphically oriented means of control, most GUI designers use icons, small on-screen graphic images, to represent the object with which you work. The depth of the representation varies with the sophistication of the interface. Early PC-based systems used icons mostly as labels that enabled you to launch programs. The latest generations use icons as true programming objects so that you can manipulate them graphically by dragging them along with your mouse.

Designers add their own variations to the windows theme. Windows, for example, began by using a special control program called Program Manager for starting and switching between applications. In the latest Windows incarnation, this function is integrated into the operating system itself. OS/2 Warp calls it a *desktop* (as does the Macintosh), and makes it the default command center of the operating system.

BIOS

The software that runs a modern PC is not a single program, no matter what you see on the screen, but a snarl of many programs each vying for control of the machine. Some wait their turn for control, others weasel their way into control by shooting out interrupts that break into the flow of other programs. The relationship between all these programs is as tangled as the combined family tree of the Jukes and Kalikaks, and only with great effort can your PC ease some sense from it. We mortals can hope only to impose some kind of artificial order.

The most common imposed structure is the layered approach. Each level of software is a layer spread across your PC's processing system piling up and up until the top layer, the frosting, appears as your operating system's user interface. The accepted picture stacks the layers from hardware to you, the bottom-most layer taking actual command of the hardware. In a simple software system, the bottom layer is the BIOS (the Basic Input/Output System), next are drivers, the operating system kernel, and finally the user interface. Modern operating systems impose more intermediate layers as well as splitting individual layers into multiple modules with separate functions. In any case it all begins with the BIOS.

The BIOS itself is a complex thing with many functions. The instructions coded into the read-only memory (ROM) of the BIOS stores three special functions: two help get your system started (a preliminary quality assurance test and a boot-strap loader) and one acts as a basic description of the input and output connections to the microprocessor. The startup code in the BIOS holds your PC's *initialization code*, a mini-program that tells your system how to start itself. When your PC is running, this last part of the BIOS is designed to provide the bottom-layer software functions, although today's 32-bit operating systems sidestep the BIOS and substitute their own low-level code.

Boot Sequence

When you switch on or reset a microprocessor, it automatically looks for something to do, some instructions to execute. Chips that power PCs always start in the same way. They are preprogrammed to look at a specific location in memory for a pointer that indicates where the first set of instructions begins. By convention (and by Intel's design) this first pointer appears not as the first bytes in memory but 16 bytes from the end of the first megabyte of memory in Intel's microprocessor. When the chip starts, it probes that particular memory location, then jumps to the address it indicates to find the first instruction it is to execute.

Of course, this system provides no way for the microprocessor to load anything into its memory before it goes looking for its first instruction. Consequently, the first thing the microprocessor does must be written in some permanent form that's assured to be there when the chip starts. Read-Only Memory chips or ROM has exactly this characteristic. Once these memory chips get instructions and data written to their addresses (using special machines), the memory contents are permanent.

The first of these functions is called the Power-On Self-Test or POST. It checks out the function of nearly all circuits in the PC to be sure that everything is working. For example, it races through memory, writing to and reading from each address to assure that all memory chips are working properly. The POST procedure typically includes a rudimentary means of reporting errors that it finds, usually as a series of speaker beeps.

Once POST has assured that your PC can function as a PC without any surprises, it passes control to the boot-strap loader. That is, after all of the test instructions finish, the next instructions in ROM tells the system to try to load a file from a disk drive. If it can successfully read the disk drive and the disk drive has further code (the operating system) in the proper place, the boot-strap loader tells the microprocessor to switch to running the disk-based instructions. At this point, POST and the boot-strap loader exit gracefully, to lie dormant and unused until the next time you start or reset your PC.

Older PCs had an ingrained sequence for looking for the operating system code. Initially they would try to read from your first floppy disk (drive A:). Not succeeding there, they would try to read from the first hard disk drive (drive C:). This floppy-first philosophy was aimed at giving you an out if you screwed up your hard disk drive. In the startup files on your hard disk, you can instruct your system to load files that don't work or will crash your PC. Since some startup files load automatically, you might possibly make your system unusable—it would start up and automatically crash itself. By trying the floppy drive first, your PC gives you the opportunity to slide in a clean boot disk so you can get your PC running to fix your hard disk problems.

Many modern PCs enable you to alter the boot sequence. For example, a setup option may enable you to boot directly from your hard disk without checking your first floppy drive—which can save you several seconds in booting up. If you then screw up your hard disk, you only need to change your system setup so that your PC first tries your floppy disk drive.

Input and Output Control

The part of your PC's BIOS that continues operating when your PC is running holds the instructions for operating some of the basic circuitry required in any PC. Rather than a single program, this part of your PC's BIOS is a set of short routines that other programs use to run the circuitry of your PC. The entire set of routines is the core of the actual Basic Input/Output System, although many people use the term BIOS to include the other two ROM functions— POST and boot-strap loader.

The purpose of the BIOS has evolved with the development of multimedia systems. With the first PCs, the BIOS was supposed to offer a single common system for accessing PC hardware for all normal system operations. Today the BIOS handles basic functions only until an advanced operating system (Windows or OS/2) takes over.

The original concept underlying the BIOS was to isolate your programs from your PC's exact hardware configuration by adding an extra layer of software. Instead of directly addressing hardware, your programs would call a routine in the BIOS that, in turn, would signal to the hardware what to do. This layered design would enable a PC maker to change the underlying system hardware by simply updating the BIOS without affecting the operation of your programs.

This layered approach suffers one substantial handicap—speed. The BIOS routines impose an extra step and probably many extra instructions on every hardware access. Consequently even in the early years of PCs, programmers wrote around the BIOS to access some system hardware directly. In modern multimedia PCs, BIOS code suffers another speed penalty. Most ROM in modern PCs uses a 16-bit data path while most microprocessors use a 32-bit data path. Accessing ROM consequently takes twice as long as would using the 32-bit memory in your PC. Windows and OS/2 replace the BIOS code with software drivers (see Chapter 8, "Device Drivers") which run in fast 32-bit memory.

Hardware Interface

In the basic PC, every instruction in a program gets targeted on the microprocessor. Consequently, the instructions can control only the microprocessor and don't reach beyond themselves. The circuitry of the rest of the computer and all of the peripherals connected to it all must get their commands and data relayed by the microprocessor. Somehow the microprocessor must be able to send signals to these devices.

Two methods are commonly used, input/output mapping and memory mapping. *Input/output mapping* relies on sending instructions and data through ports. *Memory mapping* requires passing data through addresses. Ports and addresses are similar in concept but different in operation.

A *port* is an address but not a physical memory location. The port is a logical construct that operates as an addressing system, which is separate from the memory addressing system of the microprocessor even though it uses the same address lines. If you imagine normal memory addresses as a set of pigeon holes for holding bytes, input/output ports act like a second set of pigeon holes on the other side of the room. To distinguish which set of holes to use, the microprocessor controls a flag signal on its bus called memory-I/O. In one condition it tells the rest of the computer the signals on the address bus indicate a memory location; in its other state, the signals indicate a input/output port.

The microprocessor's internal mechanism for sending data to a port also differs from memory access. One instruction, move, allows the microprocessor to move bytes from any of its registers to any memory location. Some microprocessor operations can even be performed in immediate mode directly on the values stored at memory locations.

Ports, however, use a pair of instructions: In to read from a port, Out to write to a port. The values read can be transferred only into one specific register of the microprocessor (the accumulator), and can only be written from that register. Immediate operations on values held at port locations is impossible.

To the microprocessor, the difference between ports and memory is one of perception: memory is a direct extension of the chip, ports are the external world. Writing to I/O ports is consequently more cumbersome and usually requires more time and microprocessor cycles. I/O ports however, provide a standard structure for peripheral communications.

I/O ports give the microprocessor and computer designer greater flexibility. And they give you a headache when you want to install multimedia accessories.

Implicit in the concept of addressing, whether memory or port addresses, is proper delivery. You expect a letter carrier to bring your mail to your address and not deliver it to someone else's mailbox. Similarly, PCs and their software assume that deliveries of data and instructions will always go where they are supposed to. To assure proper delivery, addresses must be correct and unambiguous. If someone types a wrong digit on a mailing label, it will likely get lost in the postal system.

In order to use port or memory addresses properly, your software needs to know the proper addresses used by your peripherals. Many hardware functions have fixed or standardized addresses that are the same in every PC. For example, the memory addresses used by video boards are standardized (at least in basic operating modes) and the ports used by most hard disk drives are similarly standardized. Programmers can write the addresses used by this fixed-address hardware into their programs and not worry whether their data will get where it's going.

The layered BIOS approach helps eliminate the need for writing explicit hardware addresses in programs. Drivers accomplish a similar function. They are written with the necessary hardware addresses built in.

Resource Allocation

The basic hardware devices got assigned addresses and memory ranges early in the history of the PC and for compatibility reasons have never changed. These fixed values include those of serial and parallel ports, keyboards, disk drives, and the frame buffer that stores the monitor image. Add-in devices and more recent enhancements to the traditional devices require their own assignments of system resources. Unfortunately, beyond the original hardware assignments there are no standards for the rest of the resources. Manufacturers consequently pick values of their own choices for new products. More often than you'd like, several products may use the same address values.

Manufacturers attempt to avoid conflicts by allowing a number of options for the addresses used by their equipment. You select among the choices offered by manufacturers using switches or jumpers (on old technology boards) or through software (new technology boards, including those following the Micro Channel and Plug-and-Play standards). With traditional technology accessories, nothing prevents you setting the resources used by one board to the same values used by another in your system. The result is a resource conflict that may prevent both products from working.

Driver software matches the resource needs of your hardware to your software applications. The match is easy when a product doesn't enable you to select among resource values—the proper addresses can be written right into the driver. When you can make alternate resource allocations, however, the driver software needs to know which values you've chosen. In most cases, you make your choices known to the driver by adding options to the command that loads the driver (typically in your PC's CONFIG.SYS) or through configuration files. Most new add-in devices include an installation program that indicates the proper options to the driver by adding the values to the load command or configuration file, though you can almost always alter the options with a text-based editor.

This complex setup system gives you several places to make errors that will cause the add-in device or your entire PC to operate erratically or fail altogether. You might make duplicate resource assignments, mismatch drivers and options, or forget to install the drivers at all. Because multimedia PCs use so many add-in devices, they are particularly prone to such problems. Sound boards in particular pose installation problems because they usually incorporate several separate hardware devices (the sound system proper, a MIDI interface, and often a CD-ROM interface) each of which has its own resource demands.

Solving resource conflicts is one of the most challenging aspects of making a Multimedia PC work. The inevitable problem of conflicts arose early in the history of the PC, and IBM attempted to solve it in 1987 by introducing Programmable Option Select as part of its Micro Channel Architecture, and a year later the consortium that developed the EISA system adopted a similar scheme. Both had the same aim, to eliminate the need for setting up hardware and the support required for sorting out hardware conflicts, but both ultimately proved unsatisfactory. Each added the need for a separate software configuration step when adding new hardware and each demanded configuration programs that were often as difficult to manage as the hardware adjustments.

Plug-and-Play

Hoping to eliminate setup problems, an industry consortium led by Microsoft and Intel Corporations developed a new standard for PCs that will allow them to automatically allocate their own resources. Called the Plug-and-Play initiative, the new standard allows a PC to determine which port and addresses are needed by each expansion board and work out arrangements that eliminate conflicts.

In its purest form, Plug-and-Play passes the work of setting up the system from you to your PC's operating system. All you need to do is slide expansion boards into the slots in your PC. A special board design prevents conflicts: all boards except those necessary for booting up the system are switched off electrically when you turn on your system. Only the video adapter stays on so that you can monitor the progress of the boot process, and the disk drive host adapter remains on so that your PC can load the operating system from disk. Once the operating system is running, it polls each board to find which ports and addresses it needs. If the operating system detects conflicts, it can force a given expansion board to shift to alternate resource values (as allowed by the board manufacturer).

This scenario shows the stiff requirements for a pure implementation of Plug-and-Play. The system has three parts, all of which must follow the standard: the expansion boards, the PC itself and its BIOS, and the operating system. Without all three, Plug-and-Play retains the conflict complications of old technology PCs. The standard does allow for adding non-Plug-and-Play boards to Plug-and-Play systems, but you lose totally automatic configuration in the process—you have to tell your system which ports and addresses the old boards require.

Various attempts have been made at creating Plug-and-Play systems since the first years of the PC. IBM's Micro Channel Architecture was an initial step into the realm of Plug-and-Play design. Micro Channel eliminated the need to set switches and configure jumpers to setup hardware—an expedient incorporated in the system design because IBM had discovered that most of its support calls arose from improper hardware settings. Micro Channel required that you start and monitor the hardware configuration process. The same design ideas were carried into Micro Channel's competitor, EISA (see Chapter 10, "The Basic PC—Hardware Essentials"), with the same user involvement. Only with the introduction of the first operating system to fully embrace Plug-and-Play technology, Windows 95, have all the worries about hardware configuration finally been lifted from your shoulders. Windows 95 automatically sets up Plug-and-Play boards and guides you in the installation of those not using the new technology.

Operating Systems

The basic level of software with which you will work on your PC is the operating system. All of today's operating systems provide your PC with its basic user interface. But an operating system is much more than what you see on the screen. As the name implies, the operating system tells your PC how to operate, how to carry on its most basic functions. Early operating systems were designed simply to control how you read from and wrote to files on disks and were hence termed Disk Operating Systems (which is why DOS is called DOS). Today's operating systems add a wealth of functions for controlling every possible PC peripheral from keyboard (and mouse) to monitor screen.

The operating system provides a common interface—actually several. Only one, the user interface is visible to you. For example, the Windows display you see on your screen is the user interface of the Windows operating system. Behind those windows, however, are program interfaces which enable the programmers who write applications for your PC to link to other software and the hardware in your system.

Considered at one level, your PC's operating system is little more than a BIOS that's loaded from disk. In fact, in some computers much of what PC owners consider to be the operating system is part of the BIOS of the machine. For example, much of the graphic look of the Apple Macintosh is stored in its BIOS memory. Once your PC's operating system loads into memory, much of its program code works like a BIOS and provides the same functions to your system. In fact, most 32-bit operating systems almost completely replace the BIOS built into your PC with their own code that handles exactly the same functions—only a lot faster.

Most of these BIOS-like functions are packaged into separate software modules called *drivers* because they take control of another part of your system (such as the hardware) the same way that you would take control by driving a car. Drivers are separate modules because they are meant to be matched to the specific needs of your PC. Each different kind of hardware gets its own special driver. The modular approach enables you to add in the one right driver for your needs and easily update it to accommodate improvements in your peripherals.

Modern operating systems use software drivers for more than hardware control, however. Drivers are part of their layered design. Drivers also link the operating system to program. A given link up may involve several layers of drivers. Drivers are so complex and important to the proper operation of your PC, they earn their own chapter in this book, where you'll find a complete discussion of their design, installation, and operation. (See Chapter 8.)

From another perspective, a modern operating system is like a library of program routines. The operating system supplies your application programs with most of the everyday functions they need to handle the basic operation of your PC. For example, instead of specifying each step of reading a file from a disk, programmers can call an operating system function that takes care of all the busy work and simply delivers the data from the desired file into a program. This part of the operating system is called the Application Program Interface or API because it is the place at which your programs link to the rest of your PC.

Most operating systems go further by providing you with tools for maintaining your PC using utility programs. The range of utilities depends on the imagination and generosity of the operating system vendor. Even the most basic operating system—early versions of DOS, for example—included utility programs for setting up and managing your disk drives. Modern operating systems include such a wealth of utilities that you need little other software to put your PC to work. The OS/2 Warp Bonus Pack includes applications sufficient to handle most of the office work you'd want to do on your PC.

With primitive operating systems, user involvement tends to be minimal because the operating system does little and most people chose to avoid it. For example, DOS is used mostly to load programs (although most programs use DOS functions once they are loaded) and to copy and erase files. Once they have an application running, these people forget about DOS—or at least try to.

Today's operating systems have a more pervasive influence. Their user interface spans across and unites programs. As a user, you regularly call upon the operating system to switch between applications and maintain order on your system.

Applications

The programs you run to do actual work on your PC are its applications, short for application software, programs with a purpose. They are the dominant beasts of computing, the top of the food chain. Everything else in your computer system, hardware and software alike, exists merely to make your applications run. Your applications determine what you need in your PC simply because they won't run—or run well—if you don't supply them with what they want.

Strange as it may seem, little of the program code in most applications deals with the job for which you buy it. The actual function of the program, the algorithms that it carries out, are only a small part of its code, usually a small fraction of it. The hardcore computing work performed by major applications—the kind of stuff that the first UNIVAC and other big mainframe computers were created to handle—is amazingly minimal. For example, even a tough statistical analysis may involve only a few lines of calculations (though repeated again and again). Most of what your applications do is simply organize and convert static data from one form to another.

In fact, the most important job of most modern applications is simply translation. They convert your commands, instructions, and desires into a form digestible by your computer system. At the same time, they reorganize the data that you give your PC into the proper form for its storage or take data from storage and reorganize it to suit your requirements—be it stuffing numbers into spreadsheet cells, filling database fields, or moving bits of sound and images to speakers and screen.

This translation is simple work but demands a great deal of computer power. For example, displaying a compressed bitmap that fills a quarter of your screen in a multimedia video involves just a few steps. Your PC needs only to read a byte from memory, perform a calculation on it, and send it to your monitor. The trick is in the repetition. While you may press only one key to start the operation, your PC has to repeat those simple steps more than 1 million times each second. Such a chore can easily drain the resources available in your PC dry. That's why you need a powerful PC to run today's multimedia applications—and why multimedia didn't catch on until microprocessors caught up with the demands of your software.

Chapter 7
Operating Systems

Most important of all software for any PC is its operating system. Even more than the microprocessor and other hardware, the operating system defines the personality of your computer, complete with all its sociability and defects. An operating system is like a friend—or at least it should be your friend—because you have to stand by it through thick and thin, good times and bad, every program that you run and crash. As with a friend, the pretty face of an operating system can seduce you, and soon, without realizing the implications, you may find yourself married. Don't laugh. An entire industry married itself to the original PC operating system, DOS. Now that the honeymoon is over, all the little annoying idiosyncrasies of the spouse have become glaringly apparent, and they're stuck together, not till death do they part.

Into this little melodrama enters temptation with the pretty face of a graphic user interface, one that makes poor DOS look plain, ordinary, and even ugly. Should we flirt? Should we succumb to the seduction? Should we cast our loyalty and common sense to the four winds and rush into a divorce?

Get real. We're talking about computer software here, not spouse, kids, and platoons of lawyers from the jackal training school. Of course you should trash that DOS that's so old that frost is caked on its code. Technology marches on, and so should you, particularly if you want the most from multimedia. Today's latest 32-bit operating systems are so superior at handling images and sounds that you shouldn't give a second thought to abandoning familiar old DOS (or even taking a look at it if you're new to PCs and never before bothered). After all, you never have to look back. And all of the new operating systems for PCs give you full visitation rights. You can always run your tired old software if your mind gets too frayed from a multimedia blitz.

Function

An operating system plays many roles. Most apparent is what you see, the user interface, the way in which it presents not just itself but nearly all of your applications to you, the mechanism through which you control the operation of your PC. In addition, the operating system also provides the same sort of link between your applications and your PC hardware in the form of an application program interface (or API). In effect, the operating system is the glue that holds you, your PC, and your software together.

The operating system does more, however. It also acts like a combination of secretary and housekeeper, assistant and butler. It helps you and your PC stay organized and takes care of the housekeeping. It sets up the logical structure of your disk, creates, copies, edits, and erases your files, and even monitors the quality and performance of your disk drives.

A modern operating system is also a negotiator. It arranges the orderly transfer of information from one part of your PC to another and coordinates the flow of related data. Your operating system assures that the sounds and pictures of your multimedia presentation stay together and get to the right place in the right form. For example, it may route image data from your CD drive through a decompressor and then channel it to your monitor screen at just the right rate to match the playback speed of you MIDI-based music system.

It also plays referee among the programs that you want to run, deciding which can take control of your PC's microprocessor. As with any referee, it ensures that everyone plays fair, that all programs have access to system resources. But it also knows your priorities and it gives the most important of your programs—the one you're working on—more time to do its job.

A modern operating system also handles the negotiations for control of your communications system and peripherals. It collects and organizes the text and images you send to your printer, doling them out at just the right rate to keep both the printer and your PC running at their optimal rates.

The first operating system for PCs was DOS, and it remained the default standard for over a decade. Although IBM offered several alternatives early on, the only serious competitor for the mass market has been OS/2, which for its first half-decade suffered slow acceptance except in specialized business applications. After a 14-year run, however, Microsoft has slated DOS for obsolescence, with the intention of replacing it with an entirely new way of looking at and using PCs, Windows 95. But the new Microsoft offering has a serious competitor in form and function in IBM's latest version of OS/2, Warp. Either one promises to be a multimedia powerhouse.

DOS, however, is where everything began and is the appropriate place to begin any discussion of operating systems. Although DOS by itself has no multimedia pretensions, it readily accepts additions and enhancements to accommodate many multimedia functions. DOS is also the platform on which you can build a Multimedia PC based on the Windows 3.1 family. And DOS continues to linger in the background of the latest operating systems with built-in multimedia.

MS-DOS

The defining characteristic of the PC is DOS, long the primary operating system of computers based on Intel microprocessors. Stark, obstinate, and opaque, the face of DOS stood between the timid and technology. DOS made the PC into an icy and demanding machine suited for the cold world of business but never really at home near a cozy fireside. Although DOS has undergone a long evolution since the first days of the PC and found itself in three competing dresses designed by different manufacturers, its reputation as unyielding still hangs over it like a spectral visage leering into an old Paris opera house.

We could dismiss all of DOS's shortcomings by saying that the operating system isn't truly evil but only misunderstood, but that begs the problem. For all too many people, DOS has proven un-understandable, a miasma of commands and concerns about memory and configurations. Despite a mask, called a *shell*, painted on its face to make its ugly interface less forbidding, DOS has consistently held back the PC from its full potential.

And yet the heart of DOS still beats in today's powerful 32-bit operating systems. They owe part of their heritage to DOS and still devote a good fraction of their code to keeping DOS alive. Far into the future, DOS will be with us in spirit, if not in fact.

By far the most popular and familiar of the various implementations has been MS-DOS, the MS indicating its origins at Microsoft Corporation. Closely related is PC DOS, a product of IBM but licensed by Microsoft. Originally identical with the Microsoft product, more recent versions have veered further and further from the Microsoft original, although it remains essentially compatible. The only clone with substantial market presence was DR DOS, created by Digital Research (hence the name). When Digital Research was absorbed by Novell Corporation, the product became Novell DOS. Although still available, Novell announced in 1994 it would release no new versions of it. The essential structure and functions of all three are identical, the variations reflecting only whim and the reach of the copyright laws.

History

The history of DOS begins in 1981 when IBM was developing its first PC. To make their novel machine work, the company needed an operating system. Trying to play it safe, executives for IBM sought out the proven standard for the desktop computers of the time, a simple operating system called *CP/M*, short for the Control Program for Microprocessors. Developed by industry pioneer Digital Research, CP/M allowed a computer to read and write and offered a few simple commands for copying, deleting, and renaming files. IBM wanted Digital Research to develop a new version of CP/M for the first PC. Although such a product was later created, IBM's initial talks with Digital Research president Gary Kildall proved inconclusive.

IBM sought out an alternate source of supply, and the software trail led to a pair of young men, Paul Allen and Bill Gates, who had developed the first microcomputer BASIC language interpreter for what is considered the first "personal computer," the *Altair*. To sell their language, they had started a new company they called Microsoft, and, in what must have been the greatest salesmanship effort in history, they sold IBM on using their own operating system as the primary choice for the first PC. Little did it matter that they didn't have one at the time. Backed by their contract with IBM, they bought rights to an operating system written by Tim Paterson for Seattle Computing, worked it over, and stuffed it into binders under the name *PC DOS 1.0.*

When introduced along with the original IBM PC in 1981, the principal claim to fame of PC DOS was that it booted up the PC and let the world see what personal computers could do. In appearance and operation, it nearly duplicated CP/M, featuring but a few innovations such as renaming the command to copy files *Copy* instead of *PIP* and altering the syntax of commands so that you specified the source file before the destination file. Nice as those minor touches might have been, one factor more than any other probably led to its domination of the PC marketplace: while IBM priced its chief competitor, CP/M 86 (which Digital Research prepared under a later contract), for $300, the price of PC DOS was just $60.

In any case, you didn't get much for your money compared to today's operating system offerings. All of PC DOS fit on a single side of a floppy disk. It had to. In its first incarnation, PC DOS could handle exactly one kind of floppy disk, specifically single-sided, double-density 5.25-inch disks that stored a measly 160KB each. (PCs never used single-density disk storage.) The history of DOS since then has chiefly been one of adding support for new disk formats and new features.

For example, PC DOS 1.1, introduced in early 1982, opened a new world to the floppy disk—the second side. The update allowed a PC to exploit either single- or double-sided disk drives with double-density disks. Adding the second side exactly doubled the maximum capacity of a disk, pushing it to 320KB.

Both of these early versions of PC DOS were sold as such under the IBM label. But Microsoft did not grant IBM an exclusive license to the operating system and reserved itself the right to sell it as well. Sold as MS-DOS (for Microsoft DOS), the first independent version released was numbered 1.25 and was shipped with the earliest clones of IBM computers. All were based on the code originally developed at Seattle Computing.

In 1982 when IBM introduced the XT with its 10MB hard disk, Microsoft upgraded DOS to version 2.0. More than merely adding instructions for handling a hard disk drive, Microsoft reworked DOS 2.0 from the ground up, building in the ability to load extra code called *device drivers* to link new hardware to the host computer and adding *tree-structured directories* based on large computer operating systems to help organize disk storage. In the process DOS also grew substantially, increasing not only the size of its memory-resident code, but also adding many new utilities which cut into the capacity of DOS system disks. To offset some of the increased storage needs, Microsoft boosted the capacity of floppy disks by adjusting their format. By writing to disks a bit faster, the new DOS was able to squeeze nine sectors of data on each disk track instead of the eight allowed previously, boosting capacity by one-eighth from 320KB to 360KB per floppy disk.

New hardware requirements forced another DOS upgrade—to version 2.1—in 1983. IBM's first attempt at a home computer, called the *PCjr*, incorporated a new style of floppy disk drive, one made by Qume Corporation that was half the height of the usual 5.25-inch disk drive but used exactly the same floppy disks. To help these drives read and write disks more reliably, the authors of DOS subtly altered the timing of the operation of some commands. Timing requirements were relaxed because early half-height floppy disk drives were not as precise as their larger forebears. The rest of the operating system remained essentially unchanged.

By 1984 big changes could be seen in PCs and the industry. People were demanding more power from individual machines, and they wanted to link them together into networks. IBM pushed ahead by developing its Personal Computer AT, the initials indicating Advanced Technology, based on Intel's advanced 80286 microprocessor. Part of the new design was a yet-again increase in floppy disk capacity, to 1.2MB per disk using special high-density media. Again the DOS developers changed the timing, reading and writing double speed (which required new hardware, floppy disk controllers, capable of handling higher frequencies). As a result, the new DOS could write 15 sectors in a single track instead of just nine. In addition, the AT used a new kind of floppy disk drive with a narrower head that allowed tracks to be squeezed closer together—two in the place of one. This closer spacing of tracks also caused compatibility problems. Although the new drives could read disks made by older drives with wider heads, older drives couldn't always read disks made by high-density drives (even when drive timing and capacity was kept to the old value that put 360KB on each disk).

Although a minor upgrade to DOS would have sufficed to take care of timing requirements of the new floppies, Microsoft and IBM jointly revamped the structure of DOS at the same time to make it more amenable to network operation. The resulting release that accompanied the AT, DOS 3.0, did not have built-in network support. A tight development schedule precluded that addition. They released the actual network version of DOS three months later as DOS 3.1.

The next DOS upgrade matched another hardware change by IBM. Version 3.2 was introduced in April, 1986, to support the 3.5-inch diskettes used by IBM's first notebook computer, the *PC Convertible*. The first 3.5-inch drives offered by IBM used only double-density floppies which could store only 720KB per disk. Support for today's dominant high-density 3.5-inch floppies, each having a capacity of 1.44MB, came only in August, 1987, to accompany IBM's new range of Personal Systems/2. Version 3.3 proved the longest lived of all DOS versions, persisting as the preferred choice even long after the introduction of its successor.

PC users viewed the October, 1988, release of DOS 4 with ambivalence. It marked a major change in the direction of DOS by being the first version to include its own shell for menu-driven operation, but most DOS users either circumvented the menus or relied on aftermarket products. DOS 4.0 broke through a major barrier and increased the disk capacity that could be accessed as a single unit (or *partition*) from 32MB to 128MB. But its means of improving disk addressability was incompatible with previous DOS versions. Boot from a floppy formatted using an older version of DOS, and a DOS 4.0 hard disk could be unreadable. Worse, many users regarded the initial release as buggy, even for a major revision of DOS. So buggy, in fact, that a cleaned-up version followed just two months later.

Real motivation for change came in April, 1991, with the introduction of DOS 5.0. In the five years since DOS 3.3 had been released, PC speed and capacity had increased dramatically while the operating system remained essentially unchanged. New software pushed at the limits of available memory, and new disks far exceeded the capacity that DOS could manage. A new floppy disk format had even been introduced. DOS 5.0 took care of all of these innovations. It added its own memory management system that helped squeeze 64KB or more useful memory from most PCs, a modest but welcome improvement. It modified the DOS 4.0 disk structure to increase single partition capacity to 528MB, allowing up to four such partitions on a single drive. And it added support for extra-density 3.5-inch floppy disks that could store up 2.88MB each using special drives (which did not catch on).

DOS 6.0, released two years later, brought another dramatic change. In the past, IBM and Microsoft had cooperated in the development of DOS. In 1993, however, the two companies split their efforts and developed their own DOS versions independently, although both used essentially the same foundation of code. Microsoft used its DOS 6.0 to launch integral *disk compression*, which could effectively double the capacity of any hard or floppy disk by packing data more efficiently. When IBM released its version, 6.1, disk compression was not included, although compression was folded in later.

Compression proved the undoing of DOS 6.0. Users reported many problems, forcing Microsoft to release an upgrade, DOS 6.2. More humbling was a lawsuit for patent infringement filed by Stac Electronics, which claimed that Microsoft stole its disk compression technology. After Microsoft lost the suit, it introduced another update, version 6.21 that omitted compression. Three months later, Microsoft released yet another version, 6.22, that incorporated a new, non-infringing compression system. IBM avoided the lawsuit by licensing a compression system for its PC DOS 6.3, released at the beginning of 1994.

Microsoft's slated successor to DOS 6.22 is Windows 95. In late 1994, however, IBM began beta testing PC DOS 7.0. The new incarnation promises several improvements but few innovations.

Table 7.1 lists the various versions of DOS and the date each was introduced or released.

TABLE 7.1. DOS timeline.

Version	Date	Features
1.0	12-Aug-81	Supports only 160KB floppy disks
1.10	17-May-82	Double-sided (360KB) floppies
1.25	17-May-82	Microsoft version of 1.10
2.00	9-Mar-83	Hard disk support
2.01	5-Jan-83	Microsoft version of 2.0
2.10	1-Nov-83	Revised floppy timing
2.11	1-Apr-84	Microsoft version of 2.10
3.00	1-Aug-84	1.2MB floppy support
3.10	7-Nov-84	Network support
3.20	2-Apr-86	720KB floppy support
3.21	3-Oct-89	ROM-based code
3.30	1-Aug-87	1.44MB floppy support
4.00	13-Oct-88	16-bit FAT entries
4.01	2-Dec-88	Bug fix
5.00	12-Apr-91	Large volume support
6.00	30-Mar-93	DoubleSpace disk compression
6.10	1-May-93	IBM version, no compression
6.20	1-Nov-93	Bug fix, ScanDisk
6.21	10-Mar-94	DoubleSpace removed
6.22	14-Jun-94	DriveSpace disk compression
6.30	1-Jan-94	IBM version, with compression
7.00	Beta	IBM version only

Structure

DOS, written to control the 16-bit Intel 8088 microprocessor, is a 16-bit operating system. Its code was written using the 16-bit commands of the 8088 instruction set, which Intel has assured to be understandable by all of its more recent microprocessors.

Modern-day DOS comprises several disks chock full of files to carry out its functions. Most of these are utilities that Microsoft or IBM supplies you mostly as a convenience. They are not essential to the everyday operation of your PC. Only a small subset of the complete DOS collection handles the vast majority of the work you do on your PC. In fact, you normally need only three files to make DOS work.

Essential Files

The heart of DOS is comprised of two files making up its kernel that resides on every boot disk. They are invisible to you—you only deal with them when you create a boot disk—but are essential to your DOS applications. MSDOS.SYS holds the essential disk operating system itself, the code your applications use (or are supposed to use) to access your disk drives. IO.SYS holds the code for controlling input and output devices as well as the bootstrap loader that starts off DOS in the first place. (IBM and Novell call these files IBMDOS.COM and IBMBIO.COM.

One more file is essential to a DOS system disk, COMMAND.COM or its equivalent. Called the *command processor,* this file is little more than a program that DOS recognizes as its shell, its outer covering by which you recognize and interact with it. It monitors what you type at the command prompt and carries out the most basic user-initiated operating system functions.

Although you need to have a command processor to run DOS successfully, you don't have to be satisfied with the COMMAND.COM that's supplied as standard equipment with DOS. You can upgrade or exchange COMMAND.COM with another command processor to change DOS's personality.

When these three essential files are available on disk—the two kernel programs and the command processor—DOS can carry out its essential functions. These include: booting up your PC, presenting you with an interface for controlling your PC—that is, calling applications—and letting you bring those applications to life.

Booting Up

The boot-up process involves an interaction between DOS, BIOS, and disk. After your PC completes its power-on self-test and other setup operations, the BIOS instructs it to read the first sector of the disk designated as your PC's boot-up disk. Typically your boot disk will be drive C:, the first hard disk drive in your system, but some PCs give you other boot options.

Most PCs have BIOSs that first try to boot from your A: floppy, then your C: hard disk. This arrangement is designed to save you from yourself. If you set up your hard disk with a strange entry in a configuration file that causes it to crash even before you can take command at the keyboard, you can always boot from a floppy disk to fix the error on your hard disk. It also enables you to prepare a hard disk that's not already bootable. With MS-DOS or PC DJOS after version 6.0, you can also step around your startup files by pressing F5 after you see the message Starting MS-DOS... (or PS DOS) on the screen. Pressing F8 instead will let you step through each command in CONFIG.SYS.

Of course, checking your A: floppy before booting also takes time and can be inconvenient should you want to keep a back-up floppy or other disk lodged in your A: drive. Consequently a number of new BIOSs enable you to select boot order or suppress booting from the A: drive. Typically this option is available under the Advanced Setup menu of your BIOS.

The guidance that your PC BIOS provides in the boot-up process is otherwise minimal. It simply tells your PC to read the first cluster from your boot drive and start executing the instructions it finds there. The first sector of the disk must contain code that tells your PC how to read anything beyond that first block of code. In effect, this first block of code tells your PC how to load and run the operating system code. From this function it gets the name bootstrap loader from the old cliché "pulling yourself up by your own bootstraps," a phrase left over from a time before Velcro and zippers when boots had straps to yank them onto your legs.

If the bootstrap loader doesn't find valid code in the first sector, it posts an error message on the screen. Most PCs prompt you to try another disk. Older IBM systems automatically switched into a subset of the BASIC language so you could waste your time typing in programs that you couldn't save.

The bootstrap loader gets your PC to load the essential three programs of the operating system into memory. The first two simply load and sit there. When the bootstrap loader finishes, it transfers control to COMMAND.COM, which (after a bit of self-configuration) puts a prompt on the screen and awaits your instructions.

For this boot-up process to work for DOS or any other operating system, one element is critical. The first block of DOS's code must reside on the first available sector of your disk. Otherwise, the BIOS won't be able to find it, and your system cannot get going. This is the only part of DOS that must reside at a particular physical location on your disk.

During the boot process, DOS configures itself to match your system. This process involves two or three special files through which you can enable options and load operating system extensions. DOS checks each of these three files in turn.

The first of these files that DOS since version 6.22 checks is DRVSPACE.BIN. (In MS-DOS Versions 6.0 to 6.2, the file was DBLSPACE.BIN.) This file holds information needed to set up disk compression. Using a separate file for configuring the compression enables you to work with your other configuration files without worrying about compression. In earlier schemes, the compression system was loaded through a startup file, so you had to keep some of your boot files uncompressed so that they could be used before the compression system was loaded. DRVSPACE.BIN assures that the compression system will always be configured first. The compression system also needs to find its own configuration information in DRVSPACE.INI (or DBLSPACE.INI) before it can successfully load.

The next file that DOS reads when booting up is CONFIG.SYS, which is the primary DOS configuration file. This file lists the drivers that DOS needs to load as well as details of how to set itself up, such as the amount of memory to allocate to housekeeping functions.

Finally, DOS checks for and reads AUTOEXEC.BAT. At the point DOS courses through AUTOEXEC.BAT, it has been entirely configured and reacts in its final form. It treats AUTOEXEC.BAT as an ordinary batch file—that is, it reads through it as if you typed its contents directly at the command prompt. Think of AUTOEXEC.BAT as a convenience feature, a way to load all the applications you'll normally want to launch every day when your system starts but before you get down to your real work.

Application Support

Once DOS boots up, most of it sits there idling as if it were under a cool green tree on a hot August afternoon. It doesn't want to move and won't do anything unless you or your software specifically commands it to. The part of DOS that sits in memory comprises a set of program routines that your programs call to carry out specific system functions, much like an extension to your PC's BIOS. For example, when a program needs to read data from a disk drive, it can ask DOS to help it out. Given only a file name, DOS will take control of your hard disk, move the head to the proper place, and find the data you want.

The process of getting DOS's help is termed a *function call.* In classic DOS, your application loads the registers of your PC's microprocessors with particular values, then it triggers a software interrupt. Most DOS function calls use interrupt 21(Hex). The interrupt tells your PC's microprocessor to jump to its interrupt vector table in memory at a location specified by the interrupt number. The program uses the address specified in the interrupt vector table to find a section of code that then determines the requested action and carries it out.

When initially conceived, DOS used a cumbersome procedure for transferring command information from your application. Since version 2.0, however, DOS has also used a system of file handles for streamlining commands. To work with a file, you first define it by telling DOS that you will be working with it. In DOS terms, you open the file. Whenever you open the file, DOS assigns the file a file handle. Your application makes subsequent references to the file by using its handle.

When DOS finishes carrying out a command, it returns control to your application. DOS then slips into the background and lets your application carry on unmolested. This non-interference policy is part of the very structure of DOS. It assumes that everything going on in your PC happens in strict sequence, one thing at a time. It follows the same basic execution design as the basic microprocessor without any elaboration. DOS provides no means for keeping track of multiple functions. It simply assumes everything will follow a single path or, as programmers call it, thread. DOS is classified as a single-threaded operating system.

Multitasking Support

Although a single program thread implies that DOS can do only one thing at a time—which is true because modern microprocessors only do one thing at a time—it can simulate simultaneous execution of multiple tasks by rapidly switching between them. Multitasking becomes a matter of time frame. From a human perspective, many things appear to happen at the same time, even though they occur one after another in sequence but shift between them quicker than you can recognize the changes.

DOS, however, provides no means for switching between applications or tracking multiple applications. The single thread of execution keeps going its own way without the interference of DOS. When one program is in control, no other program can get in a word edgewise. Only if a program chooses to look to see if another program wants to run can control shift.

Hardware, however, has a means of breaking into the normal flow of a program. A hardware interrupt will force a stop in the flow of control until the needs of the interrupt are attended to. A number of system functions require immediate attention so if the hardware interrupts, memory refreshing has the greatest priority, but the keyboard, disk drives, and even the printer have their own interrupts.

The designers of the PC had enough insight to add one more hardware interrupt, the timer tick. This interrupt is generated automatically 18.2 times per second and is key to DOS-based multitasking.

By intercepting the interrupt code, a control program can take command and see if applications are vying for command of your PC. The control program can then switch execution to which-ever application has the greatest need.

Even under this system, an application cannot steal control from another. It must await the control program which must await the timer interrupt. This form of control is termed non-preemptive or co-operative multitasking.

Command Processor

The final section of the DOS system files is the command processor, nominally COMMAND.COM. Its job is to monitor your keystrokes, decipher the commands you request, and get them started or carry them out itself. COMMAND.COM has a small repertory of commands that it can carry out itself called *internal commands* because all the code required is inside the COMMAND.COM file itself. These internal commands include those to type, rename, copy, and delete files; make, change, and remove directories; set time and date; and execute batch commands. Other DOS commands are *external*. They require the explicit loading of separate files containing their code.

For external commands, COMMAND.COM operates only as a loader. That is, it copies the bytes of the file into memory and starts executing the program code embodied by them. It then hands control of the system over to the program's code, passing along any options you typed on the command line. As external commands run, they may call other DOS functions in IO.SYS or MSDOS.SYS exactly as would other programs.

File System

To store a file on disk, DOS breaks it down into a group of allocation units or *clusters*, perhaps hundreds of them. Each cluster can be drawn from anywhere on the disk. Sequential pieces of a file do not necessarily have to be stored in clusters that are physically adjacent. A cluster is a logical construct that comprises one or more physical disk sectors. Cluster size is set when you format a disk. Using current versions of DOS, cluster size may be 4, 8, or 16 sectors—or sometimes even larger with really big SCSI and EIDE hard disks.

The earliest—and now obsolete—versions of DOS follow a simple rule in picking which clusters are assigned to each file. The first available cluster, the one nearest the beginning of the disk, is always the next one used. Thus, on a new disk, clusters are picked one after another, and all the clusters in a file are contiguous. When a file is erased, its clusters are freed for reuse. These newly freed clusters, being closer to the beginning of the disk, will be the first ones chosen by these early versions of DOS when the next file is written to disk. In effect, DOS first fills in the holes left by the erased file. As a result, the clusters of new files may be scattered all over the disk. The earliest versions of DOS use this strange strategy because they were written at a time when capacity was more important than speed. The goal was to pack files on the disk as stingily as possible.

Starting with version 3.0, DOS doesn't immediately try to use the first available cluster closest to the beginning of the disk. Instead, it attempts to write on never-before-used clusters before filling in any erased clusters. DOS keeps selecting clusters toward the end of the disk, only going backwards to the beginning when no more clusters are available (or you reboot). After all the clusters on the disk have been used at least once, DOS starts its single-direction cluster-picking once again. This helps assure that the clusters of a file will be closer to one another, a technique that improves the speed of reading a file from the disk. It also helps improve the chances that you can successfully undelete a file you accidentally erase.

To keep track of which cluster belongs in which file, DOS uses a *File Allocation Table* or FAT, essentially a map of the clusters on the disk. When you read to a file, DOS automatically and invisibly checks the FAT to find all the clusters of the file; when you write to the disk, it checks the FAT for available clusters. No matter how scattered over your disk the individual clusters of a file may be, you—and your software—only see a single file.

When disk capacities were small, it was important to keep cluster size small because clusters are the smallest possible storage unit on a disk. As a result, the smallest batch file you create will steal at least one cluster of disk space—a 10-byte batch file could occupy 8,192 bytes on the disk. On the average, every file larger than one cluster will also waste half a cluster worth of disk space. Moreover, every directory, even those not containing files, will also steal at least one cluster from a disk. Consequently, the smaller the cluster size, the less disk space will be wasted on unused storage. With today's larger hard disks, the convenience of keeping files together in one large partition often overrules parsimonious partitioning with small clusters.

Maximum disk capacity, cluster size, and the FAT are interrelated. DOS versions through 3.3 used FATs with 12-bit entries for their cluster numbers, a strategy that allows for a total of 4,096 uniquely named clusters. DOS versions before 4.0 fixed the size of hard disk clusters at 16 sectors or 8,192 bytes. This design allowed for a maximum possible disk (or partition size) of 33,554,432 bytes—long the infamous DOS 32MB limit. DOS 4.0 introduced 16-bit FAT entries, which allow a total of 65,536 uniquely named clusters. DOS 4.0 and 4.01 kept the cluster size fixed at a space-saving 2,048 bytes, allowing a maximum permissible disk possible disk size of 134,217,728 (or 128MB). With DOS versions 5.0 and later, larger disks or partitions—up to 512MB—are accommodated by increasing cluster size, stepwise, through 4,096 to 8,192 bytes to 16KB. Proprietary disk management software can extend the size of a single partition by further increasing cluster size. Floppy disks always use four-sector clusters storing 2,048 bytes.

Table 7.2 shows the relationship between disk capacity and cluster size for current DOS versions.

TABLE 7.2. Disk capacity and cluster size with 16-bit FATs.

Capacity (Megabytes)	FAT type	Cluster size (Sectors)	Cluster size (Bytes)
0 to 7	12-bit	4	2,048
8 to 15	12-bit	8	4,096
16 to 127	16-bit	4	2,048
128 to 255	16-bit	8	4,096
256 to 512	16-bit	16	8,192

DOS versions after 5.0 handle disks larger than 504MB by dividing them into logical drives using its partitioning system. Originally DOS enabled you to split your hard disk into multiple partitions so that you could install more than one operating system on a single drive. Current versions of DOS take advantage of partitioning to create logical drives. DOS understands two kinds of partitions: a standard DOS partition that can boot your PC and an extended DOS partition, which can be subdivided into multiple logical drives each of which is awarded its own drive letter and functions as if it were a separate hard disk. Each logical drive follows the same pattern as ordinary hard disks for its FAT structure, so the capacity of each logical drive is also limited to 504MB by a combination of DOS and your PC's BIOS.

In fact, the PC BIOS is the biggest limit on disk capacity. The interrupt 13 routines in the standard PC BIOS handle disk interactions using a method of locating data on the disk called Cylinder, Head, Sector (or CHS) addressing. The BIOS design is generous, allowing for disk capacities as large as 8.4GB. However, the maximum values chosen for allowable cylinders, heads, and sectors is at odds with that used by the ATA interface. The result of this interaction is that a PC can address only 1024 cylinders, 16 heads, and 63 sectors (of 512 bytes each) per track. (For more information about this, see Chapter 10, "The Basic PC—Hardware Essentials.")

SCSI and EIDE drives circumvent this limitation by using a different technique, called Logical Block Addressing (LBA). Normally, LBA works by taking a CHS value supplied by DOS and translating it into a 28-bit block address that's sent to the hard disk drive to find a sector. This expedient enables you to connect drives with up to 128GB of capacity to DOS. Of course, DOS still uses the same 16-bit FAT with these very large drives, with the result that its cluster size increases dramatically should you want to partition such a disk as a single volume—each cluster would require 4MB of disk space with a drive of maximum capacity.

Using LBA requires both a hard disk that understands the technology (any SCSI drive or a new EIDE drive) as well as a BIOS with LBA capabilities. You can either upgrade the BIOS of your old PC or add in a new host adapter for your hard disk that includes LBA in its on-board BIOS. Operating systems like OS/2 that replace the interrupt 13 code in your PC's BIOS with their own routines are not limited by CHS addressing.

Compression

Disk compression, as sporadically implemented in various DOS versions after 6.0, imposes additional structure on the FAT system. To store the compressed file data, DOS creates a virtual disk drive and stores its data in a single file called the compressed volume file. This file has a structure that mimics an ordinary disk drive using a file allocation table.

DOS works with individual sectors instead of clusters when storing compressed data in the compressed volume file. DOS takes uncompressed data one cluster at a time and maps it in compressed form into sectors in the compressed volume file. To locate which sector belongs to each file, it used a special FAT called the MDFAT (Microsoft DriveSpace FAT) that encodes the first sector used for storing a given cluster, the number of sectors required for coding the cluster, and the number of the cluster in the uncompressed volume that's stored in those sectors. When DOS needs the data for a file, it first searches for the clusters it needs in the main disk FAT, then looks up the corresponding starting and length values from the MDFAT. With that information, DOS locates the data, uncompresses it, and passes it along to your applications.

To speed up operations when writing compressed data to disk, DOS uses a second kind of FAT in the compressed volume file. Called the BitFAT, this structure reports which sectors reserved in the compressed volume file hold active data and which are empty. The BitFAT uses only one bit for each sector as a flag to indicate whether a sector is occupied.

Because disk compression is imposed on the underlying operating system, its storage suffers the limitations imposed on it by that operating system. In the case of DOS, individual uncompressed volumes can be no larger than about 504MB, depending on how you count megabytes (set by 16-bit FAT entries), and, to achieve the greatest compatibility, DOS constrains compressed volumes to about the same size. Third-party compression software (which means Stac Electronics' Stacker) allows larger compressed volumes, up to 2GB. Because of the dynamics of compression—some types of data permit compression ratios higher or lower then the nominal 2X factor.

Memory

One of the chief functions of DOS is to load programs from disk into memory. Besides reading the disk, DOS must also manage the memory used by your programs and their data to do this. The structure of DOS and programs written to use it puts severe constraints on memory usage.

DOS shows its age in memory handling. Initially conceived back in 1981, DOS was built around the capabilities of the 8088 microprocessor and the needs of the designers of the original IBM PC. The 8088 chip could address only 1MB of memory, so this limitation was built into DOS. Worse, IBM's engineers reserved half of that memory for system use and DOS was forbidden from handing any of the reserved range over to programs. When IBM's engineers later trimmed the reserved memory to 384KB, DOS was left with total memory capacity of 640KB (that is, 1MB or 1024KB – 384KB).

When more powerful microprocessors were introduced, this limit did not change because of the way DOS and programs looked at memory. Because of the way that DOS loads code, programs require that the memory they use to be contiguous, that is, without gaps in the addresses available. Unfortunately, IBM's engineers assigned the memory range that abuts the top of the 640KB assigned to DOS to the VGA display system for its frame buffer for graphics. Because of their need for contiguous memory, programs cannot jump over the VGA range to find more memory on the other side.

This problem became most apparent with the introduction of 386 and new microprocessors. These chips were endowed with the ability to remap memory addresses. They could assign new addresses to blocks of memory to the extent of filling in unused spaces in the reserved memory area. DOS programs, with their need for contiguous memory, could not jump into this re-mapped memory. However, small programs that could entirely fit into the empty spaces in this reserved range could run there. The memory managers added to DOS after version 5.0 enable you to load self-contained programs like device drivers and terminate-and-stay-resident programs in this range. A quirk in the design of 286 and later microprocessors enables them to add an extra 64KB of addresses beyond the first megabyte of memory for this kind of software.

A whole nomenclature has evolved to describe the various types of memory in PCs. The 1MB addressable by DOS is called *real mode memory*. The name comes from the designation given by Intel to the operating mode of the 8088 (and 8086) chips that allows addressing this memory.

Memory beyond the first megabyte is called *extended memory*. The 640KB ordinarily usable by normal DOS programs is termed *DOS memory* or *lower memory*. The extra 384KB range reserved by IBM for system functions is called *high DOS memory*. Ranges in High DOS that are remapped for use by programs are termed *upper memory blocks* or UMB. And the special 64KB block that sits on top of the base 1MB address range is called the *High Memory Area*.

Without further ado, DOS cannot use memory beyond the 640KB range nominally assigned to it. To make high DOS memory work in your PC, you must have suitable hardware (386, 486, or a 286 with a chipset that supports memory mapping) and a *memory manager*, a program that adds the necessary functions to DOS for assigning and tracking the extra memory. In addition, you need a special *loader* program to actually load programs into high DOS memory. DOS versions 5.0 and later include both memory managers (HIMEM.SYS and EMM386.SYS) and loaders (the DEVICEHIGH and LOADHIGH commands).

Like all computer programs, loaders mindlessly do what you tell them. Ask one to load a program, and it will, or die in the attempt. If you want to squeeze as many programs as possible into high DOS memory, however, mindless loading is fraught with problems. Each program or driver that's loaded into high DOS memory must fit into a single upper memory block to keep its memory contiguous. Two more programs will fit into a single block providing the block is big enough. Blocks, however, vary widely in size and packing the most code into high DOS memory requires matching program size to block size optimally. The order in which upper memory blocks get filled is critical, and the mindless loader pays it no heed. Intelligent loaders, like MEMMAKER, which accompanies MS-DOS 6.0 and later, or RAMBOOST, which comes with later versions of PC DOS, automatically find the best match between blocks and programs.

Although ordinary DOS programs and drivers can only use real mode memory, more modern software can be written to reach into further addresses using special DOS extender software. For extended memory to be useful, however, it must be managed. The extended memory manager that accompanies later versions of DOS is called HIMEM.SYS.

During the developmental years of the PC, another kind of memory was also popular. Called *expanded memory* or EMS (for Expanded Memory Specification), it was a hardware and software trick, called *bank-switching*, that allowed 8088 microprocessors to use more than 1MB of physical memory. Special hardware circuitry switched banks of memory in and out of the address range of the 8088 microprocessor so that the chip could read and write to it.

Originally EMS dealt with its expanded memory in banks of 16KB and mapped out a 64KB range in the high DOS memory range to address the banks. Up to 8MB of 16KB banks of expanded memory could be installed in a system. The system was later expanded as *EMS 4.0* to make available up to 32MB. Today's powerful microprocessors with their 4GB addressing ranges and new operating systems make EMS unnecessary. Nearly all multimedia programs use extended memory rather than expanded memory.

Installation

As with nearly all modern programs, current versions of DOS come complete with their own installation software. A menu-controlled interface steps you through the process, offering you a limited set of options to custom-configure your system. The installation procedure takes care of the mind-numbing details like assuring that files get sent to the proper subdirectories (at least the subdirectories that DOS's designers thought best) and that all DOS files are uncompressed. (As with most software, most of DOS's files are MS-compressed so that they fit on fewer disks. In addition, the latest DOS versions use a unique floppy disk format called DMF—Distribution Media Format—that packs more data on disk but makes the disks incompatible with most utilities and programs.) PC DOS uses a similar format, called Extended Density Format (XDF). Because DOS provides no manual mode for decompression or handling DMF disks, you're stuck using its installation procedure for getting it started the first time.

Once you have decompressed DOS files in standard disk format, however, you can manually install the operating system on other PCs and disk drives. The manual installation procedure has not significantly changed throughout the life of DOS.

Manual DOS installation on a hard disk requires three or four steps: low-level formatting, disk partitioning, DOS formatting, and installing DOS files. Making a boot floppy disk requires only DOS formatting and installing the essential DOS files, which can be combined into a single step.

All disks require a low-level format that marks sectors with special digital patterns that serve as guideposts for identifying each one so the information it contains can later be found and retrieved. Most modern hard disks that use the IDE (or AT) interface or a SCSI connection have this low-level format written to the disk at the factory after which it cannot be changed. Old-technology hard disks often left the low-level formatting process to you. You would have to create the low-level format by running special software, sometimes included with special versions of DOS or built into disk controllers. If you've used a disk for any version of any operating system, it already has its low-level format in place and you need not worry about this procedure.

Partitioning prepares a hard disk to accept an operating system. It sets up the logical structure of the hard disk to a form that is compatible with the operating system. Most versions of DOS call their hard disk partitioning programs FDISK. This program enables you to divide your physical hard disk into the equivalent of several logical disk drives. Each looks as if it were a separate hard disk. Not only does partitioning help you organize your disk, but also it enables you to keep up to four operating systems and file systems on one disk drive.

Different operating systems and file systems use their own partition types. DOS uses two partition types, the primary DOS partition and extended DOS partition. A primary DOS partition can boot your PC and is limited to only one drive letter. An extended DOS partition can be subdivided into one or more logical drives, each with its own drive letter. The partition containing the master boot record is called the active partition, and under DOS it must be the primary DOS partition on your first hard disk (drive C:). Because of the file allocation table size restrictions noted previously, each logical drive can be no larger than 504MB when using current versions of DOS and conventional cylinder, head, sector addressing.

DOS identifies each logical drive by its drive letter. Although FDISK may use drive letters to identify logical drives when you partition your disk into multiple drives, DOS doesn't track these letters. Instead, it assigns drive letters anew each time you boot up your PC. DOS follows strict rules when awarding drive letters. The boot drive (when you book from the hard disk, of course) is always assigned C:. DOS then assigns drive letters in order, starting with D:. First it gives letters to the primary DOS partitions on physical drives. Then it goes back and assigns letters to all of the logical drives in the extended partition in the first drive in your PC before going on to the extended partition in the next drive. Consequently, if you have a PC with two hard disk drives that is each subdivided into three logical drives (one as the primary partition, two in an extended partition), the assignment would be as follows: C, the primary partition in the first physical drive; D, the primary partition on the second physical drive; E, the first logical drive in the extended partition of the first physical drive; F, the second logical drive in the extended partition of the first physical drive; G, the first logical drive in the extended partition of the second physical drive; and H, the second logical drive in the extended partition of the second physical drive. DOS then goes on to assign further letters to drives installed using drivers in your CONFIG.SYS file.

Once you set up the partition structure of your disk, you must DOS-format the disk. DOS-formatting sets up the file allocation table DOS uses to assign disk space to files, sets up the master boot record, and configures the root directory, where it records file identification information. The DOS program FORMAT.COM installs the required structures on a disk. When run with a floppy disk as the target, FORMAT.COM also low-level formats the floppy disk medium. When you specify the /s option, format will also install a copy of the operating system boot files on the target disk.

To assure that you install the essential DOS files in the proper location (remember, IO.SYS must start at the first physical sector on your disk), DOS includes a manual installation utility called SYS.COM (or SYS.EXE in some DOS versions). This utility checks a disk to assure that the space that IO.SYS requires is available, then copies the essential DOS files to the disk. (Some early versions of SYS.COM only copied the hidden system files and required you to manually copy COMMAND.COM to any boot disk you made.) The DOS formatting program incorporates the sys function. By specifying the command line switch /s, you can format a disk and copy to it the operating system files essential to booting your PC.

Windows

Without Microsoft Windows, we would have none of today's leading PC-based multimedia applications. Windows is an essential enabling element. But until the introduction of Windows 95, Windows could not be regarded as a complete operating system. Rather, the critical role which Windows has played has been that of standard-setter and arbiter.

Strictly speaking, Windows provided an *operating environment*, a link between programs and an underlying operating system (good old DOS). As Windows developed, however, it shifted more and more to becoming an operating system in itself, relying on DOS only to be loaded, then replacing most of DOS's code (and even that of your PC's BIOS) with its own functions. By the time Windows had advanced to version 3.1, the difference between operating system and operating environment became purely semantic.

More important than how it's described is what it does. Windows is a bridge, one that stretches in two directions—between you and your applications, and between your applications and your PC. It gives you a uniform control system for your applications and programmers, a streamlined way of writing powerful and easy-to-use applications. Multimedia programmers get a platform upon which they can easily build the most Byzantine and powerful presentations. Moreover, Windows removes much of the doubt and a lot of the work from building any application. It has become the one leading graphic standard for PCs. Just as celebrities are people famous chiefly for being famous, Windows is successful chiefly because it has been so successful.

That success arose from the perseverance of Microsoft, which has doggedly promoted the system for more than a decade, and from need. Windows predates the needs of multimedia. It predates the viability of multimedia. It predates PC-based multimedia itself. But multimedia has been instrumental in creating the success of Windows. In fact, multimedia and Windows have developed hand-in-hand. The latest incarnation, Windows 95, has grown to be the best match for today's multimedia applications.

In the beginning, however, Windows was much less. It wasn't just a graphic operating environment. It was one of many such environments. As with its competitors, its goal was seemingly modest, to allow PCs to move from their text orientation to the ability to work with images. In addition, it promised multitasking, but was only able to run (and multitask) programs written explicitly for it.

History

The first version of Windows followed so closely on the heels of the introduction of the Apple Macintosh (which was built around a graphical user interface itself), you might suppose they developed in parallel from a common source. In fact, both had the same inspiration in the graphics-based Star workstation developed by Xerox Corporation's Palo Alto Research Center (PARC), but the two have a fundamental difference. The Macintosh made graphics code an essential element of the hardware by encoding image manipulation functions into its ROM and operating system. Windows was built as a software add-on, code meant to graft graphics onto properly-equipped text-based PCs that would otherwise run a text-based operating system. Which came first is an interesting question. Microsoft announced Windows in 1983 before the introduction of the Macintosh. But the first commercial version of Windows did not reach the market until June, 1985, a full year and a half after the Macintosh was introduced to the world in a commercial during the broadcast of SuperBowl XVIII in 1984.

Some sources speculate that Windows was inspired by a Microsoft visit to Apple during the development of the Macintosh. In any case, the original version of Windows was created with the benefit of a license Microsoft negotiated with Apple.

When Microsoft introduced Windows Version 1.0, the market was crowded by contenders. It faced competition both from multitasking systems and a rival graphic environment. Among the multitasking software, the leader was IBM's *TopView* but other available multitasking systems included *Concurrent DOS* from Digital Research, *Core Executive* from APX, *DESQ* (forerunner of DESQview) from Quarterdeck Software, *VisiOn* from VisiCorp (maker of VisiCalc), and *WindowMaster* from Indian Ridge Enterprises. The competing graphic system was *Graphic Environment Manager* (or GEM) developed by Digital Research and released before Windows in January, 1985.

At the time, programmers had no particular reason to favor one of these environments over the others outside of technical details important and interesting only to the sort of people who get their kicks defining variables and dimensioning arrays. Each seemed destined to an equal share of consumer ennui. Each attracted a few program developers who, for the most part, created esoteric graphics applications with limited appeal. All suffered a common problem: the PCs at the time hardly had enough speed to get out of the way, let alone move huge blocks of graphics around at the press of a key.

The first environments did serve to get a GUI foot in the door. Besides none-too-good graphics—at the time PCs were as likely to be text-only as have cartoon-like CGA or barely better EGA graphics abilities—early Windows did deliver one advantage. Because they substituted their own environment for DOS, they could break through one fundamental DOS barrier—memory. Even early Windows allowed programs to reach beyond the 640KB allotted to DOS. In addition, even early Windows could handle multitasking to a limited extent.

Extended addressing and multitasking alone weren't enough to overcome one handicap: a lack of software. The Windows environment worked only with applications specifically written for it. And there weren't many of those—with good reason. Windows added an extra layer of software with all of the associated overhead on top of its applications. At the time, graphic software was already too slow. Most programmers chose to avoid the extra handicap.

The second generation of Windows was born into a world of more powerful PCs in late 1987. Better still, Windows gained compatibility with DOS applications. Even better, a Windows variant introduced at the same time as 2.0, Windows 386, took advantage of the power of the 386 microprocessor to juggle DOS applications using the hardware multitasking power of the chip. More than anything else, Windows 386 established itself as a multitasking system, often used simply to shift between text-based DOS programs.

The $10 million breakthrough came with Windows 3.0 in May, 1990. With the biggest advertising budget of any software product up until then, Window 3.0 was launched with the excitement and huckster promises of a medicine show. It was a cure for what ailed your PC—no matter what ailed your PC.

Windows 3.0 grew upon the foundation of Windows 386. It was meant not as a launching pad for a few specialized applications but to control your entire PC. It was a true cooperative multitasking system that adroitly shifted between its own applications and used pre-emptive multitasking for those that ran under DOS. As with DOS, Windows 3.0 was written using 16-bit code. It attempted to be truly universal, running on whatever hardware you had, requiring as little as 1MB of memory and able to lower its aspirations to work with older microprocessors.

Microsoft groomed Windows 3.0 and 3.1 for the mass market more with advertising than with engineering. Although it could simplify the operation of your PC, getting it to work often was far from simple. Getting the most from any of the 3.*x* versions required the same tinkering as squeezing RAM from DOS. Indeed, instead of tweaking CONFIG.SYS, Windows 3.*x* mavens marched through their SYSTEM.INI file adding drivers, changing settings, and disrupting their dreams.

Windows 95 brings Microsoft into the modern age. From a technical point of view, it brings 32-bit technology to the masses, just as Windows NT put 32-bit power in elite machines. More importantly, at least from the standpoint of this book, it is the first version of Windows to fully incorporate multimedia power, not a grafted-on afterthought.

From Microsoft's viewpoint, Windows 95 is much more. It is an opportunity—not just to bring in full 32-bit power but also to make Windows the mass market PC interface. Microsoft gave Windows 95 a new face, new setup procedures, and new features. No longer would PC neophytes have to come to terms with a command line. Where the DOS prompt lingered in the background of Windows 3.1 like a persistent case of the flu, Windows 95 dashes into graphics like a teenager to a mall. Its new interface, although perhaps even more businesslike than the 3.*x* forbears, shows off a cleaner, less cluttered, and less confusing look. It borrows the best from the rest of the market.

Technically speaking, Windows 95 is a fully integrated protected-mode 32-bit operating system. No longer does it require you to first load DOS before entering Windows. Although the standard means of control of Windows 95 is its graphic interface, a command-line interface much like that of DOS is integrated into the system.

Table 7.3 summarizes the history of Microsoft Windows.

TABLE 7.3. Windows timeline.

Product	Release date
Windows 1.0	20-Nov-85
Windows 2.0	9-Dec-87
Windows/386	9-Dec-87
Windows 3.0	22-May-90
Windows 3.1	6-Apr-92
Windows for Workgroups 3.1	27-Oct-92
Windows for Workgroups 3.11	1-Nov-93
Windows 95	24-Aug-95 (Microsoft prediction)

Structure

Windows is not a single program but an interrelated and interacting group of programs. Most of its important functions are separated into individual programs. Three of these are most important for running Windows applications. The Kernel handles the actual loading and execution of Windows programs and takes care of managing the memory that they use. The Graphics Device Interface or GDI takes care of the images you see on the screen and print out. The User program manages input and output, including your keyboard, mouse, ports, sound systems. (Video is part of the GDI). These programs are all stored in your PC's WINDOWS\SYSTEMS directory.

The Windows 3.1 family operates in either of two modes, standard or enhanced. Standard mode is patterned around the capabilities of the 286 microprocessor. Enhanced mode takes advantage of features of 386 and later microprocessors. The chief differences you'll see is that enhanced mode allows the use of virtual memory to enable your system to load more programs than it has RAM to hold, run multiple DOS programs at once, and run more advanced, 386-specific applications. In standard mode, Windows uses the program KRNL286.EXE as its kernel; in enhanced mode, KRNL386.EXE. When you start Windows by typing WIN, you activate the program loader WIN.COM which will automatically pick the proper mode for your PC. You can, however, force Windows into one mode or the other by specifying a command-line option. To force standard mode, use the switch /S or /2; for enhanced mode, use /3 (providing, of course, your PC has a 386 or better microprocessor). Windows 3.0 also featured a real mode for backward compatibility with some applications written for even earlier Windows versions.

Updating Windows 3.1

Microsoft provides files that let you upgrade Windows 3.1 to the same functionality as Windows for Workgroups 3.11. The upgrade includes a revised protected-mode kernel (a replacement for the file KRNL386.EXE), improved communications support (in the form of the file COMMDLG.DLL), other drivers (UNIDRV.DLL), new graphic device and user interfaces (GDI.EXE, USER.EXE, and SHELL.DLL), and a new PostScript driver (PSCRIPT.DRV). All of these file updates are packaged together as the self-extracting compressed file WW091.EXE. You can download this file through a number of sources including the Microsoft Software Library on CompuServe (type GO:MSL) and the Microsoft Download Service (MSDL) at (206) 936-6735.

32-Bit Upgrade

At its heart and kernel, the members of the Windows 3.1 family are 16-bit operating systems. The modular nature of Windows with its dependence on downloadable libraries enables you to upgrade various parts of the operating system as new technologies become available. You can replace individual 16-bit parts of these versions of Windows with 32-bit upgrades to improve performance of your system on specific functions. The downside of these upgrades is that they work only with 32-bit microprocessors—they are off-limits to 16-bit 286 chips—and sometimes have other more stringent hardware requirements.

Microsoft provides an upgrade for the Windows 3.1 family that enables you to run many 32-bit Windows NT and Windows 95 applications. Called *Win32s* (for "Windows 32-bit Subsystem") by Microsoft, the upgrade is a complete package of several dynamic link libraries and a virtual device driver that provides an application program interface to give your 16-bit operating system many 32-bit features such as advanced memory management. (Drivers and DLLs are discussed in Chapter 8, "Device Drivers.") Programs written for 32-bit Windows will run faster under Win32s than their 16-bit equivalents will run under Windows 3.1. Execution of 16-bit Windows applications won't be affected.

It does not make your old Windows into a 32-bit operating system, however. The underlying Windows remains a cooperative multitasking system. Even multiple Win32 applications will be cooperatively (rather than preemptively) multitasked, and all share a single address space. True 32-bit Windows NT gives each its own address space and preemptively multitasks Win32 applications. Moreover, the Win32s extension still depends on the underlying 16-bit Windows for many functions including the graphic device and user interfaces, thunking its 32-bit functions into 16-bit form for execution. (Thunking is Microsoft's term for the conversion process.) Nevertheless, Win32s enables you to run many 32-bit applications under your existing Windows with minimal investment in cash or time. The entire installation takes less than five minutes.

The Win32s version 1.2 code is available from various Microsoft outlets including its CompuServe forum and Microsoft Download Service in the self-extracting compressed file named PW1118.EXE.

32-Bit Disk Features

Depending on the version of Windows you have and your installed hardware, various 32-bit enhancements are available to you. The two primary disk enhancements are *32-bit disk access* (available in all Windows versions since 3.1) and *32-bit file access* (introduced with Windows for Workgroups 3.11). Neither of these options provides a 32-bit data path to your disk storage system. Rather, they improve its performance by taking advantage of protected mode to control disk operations. In fact, the most important benefit of 32-bit disk access seems only tangentially related to your disk drive—it enables your DOS sessions under Windows to use virtual memory so Windows can free up more memory for running other software including additional DOS sessions.

In operation, 32-bit disks access substitutes for the hard disk code in your PC's BIOS that works through hardware interrupt 13. The Windows 32-bit disk access driver intercepts interrupt 13 calls and processes the functions itself. This substitution improves performance in several ways. The new 32-bit code runs faster than 16-bit ROM-based code. It runs in protected mode and minimizes time-consuming switching between real and protected mode in carrying out disk operations. Because the 32-bit disk access routines replace old DOS code that prevents Windows from copying parts of executing DOS programs to disk, it allows Windows to move the DOS applications it runs into virtual memory, moving them from physical RAM to temporary disk storage. As a result, Windows can open up more RAM for other applications so you're less likely to run into out-of-memory errors.

On the downside, 32-bit disk access is hardware-dependent. After all, it substitutes for BIOS code that links your software and hardware. The only 32-bit disk access driver Microsoft supplies requires that your disk drive controller (which may be embedded in the disk drive) be compatible with a Western Digital WD1003 controller. According to Microsoft, when Windows 3.1 was introduced, about 90 percent of all hard disk controllers were compatible with 32-bit disk access. Unfortunately, most ESDI controllers and SCSI host adapters are not. PCI-based EIDE systems often require their own drivers, too. To use 32-bit disk access with this hardware, you have to install the proper driver written by the hardware maker in your SYSTEM.INI file. In addition, 32-bit disk access is incompatible with many energy-frugal disk systems that power-down when not in use, such as those in notebook PCs.

The default setting for 32-bit disk access is *off.* You must specifically enable it to gain its benefits. To enable 32-bit disk access, run Control Panel and select 386 Enhanced, then click the Virtual Memory button. Once you see the screen shown in Figure 7.1, check the box "Use 32-bit disk access."

FIGURE 7.1. Activating 32-bit disk access.

To optimize disk performance, you may also want to choose a permanent swap file. If you prefer to make the appropriate changes to your SYSTEM.INI file yourself, break out your favorite editor and change the 32-bit Disk Access entry in the [386Enh] section to read on, like this:

```
32BitDiskAccess=On
```

Should you believe that 32-bit disk access is causing problems, you can temporarily switch it off without altering your SYSTEM.INI settings. The trick is to use a command-line switch when starting Windows. The following switch turns off 32-bit disk access:

```
WIN /d:f
```

Windows for Workgroups 3.11 adds a second degree of 32-bit storage system support in the guise of *32-bit File Access*. The underlying technology has two parts, an installable file system called the Virtual File Access Table, or VFAT, and an 32-bit disk caching system called VCache. When you enable 32-bit file access (as with 32-bit disk access, the default configuration is *off*), Windows substitutes the VCache system for SmartDrive in accessing the hard disk. You still need to have SMARTDRV installed (although you may want to reduce its size by adding parameters like SMARTDRV 2048 128). It continues to use SmartDrive for caching floppy disk drives or pure DOS if you do not run Windows. To use compression with VFAT, you must use DOS 6.2 or later; earlier versions of DoubleSpace are not compatible with it.

VFAT still uses the same 12-bit or 16-bit file allocation table structure as do ordinary DOS versions since 4.0. However, VFAT differs from the ordinary DOS FAT system in that it uses protected-mode 32-bit code instead of the standard DOS 16-bit functions. This code design adds several performance advantages. The 32-bit code offers an inherent performance advantage in that it takes advantage of the full data path capabilities of modern PCs. Moreover, because the VFAT driver runs in protected mode, it cuts out many of the time-consuming mode switches that are required when using the ordinary real-mode FAT system through DOS. Instead of just reading tracks, it looks ahead to the actual clusters used by your applications.

The VFAT and VCache system is equally effective for all hard disk technologies including SCSI-based systems, although not all hard disks can take advantage of its full range of capabilities (hence, its defaulting to *off*.) Each of the two parts of 32-bit file access requires its own driver, so the following entries must appear in your SYSTEM.INI file for this feature to work:

```
device=vfat.386
device=vcache.386
```

Should you believe that 32-bit file access is causing problems in your Windows for Workgroups 3.11 system, you can temporarily switch it off when starting Windows with the following command-line switch:

```
WIN /d:c
```

You can allocate the amount of RAM to devote to the VCACHE system using the 386 Enhanced dialog box under Control Panel. This dialog box limits you to a maximum of 24MB of cache. However, you can increase the size of the cache in systems with sufficient physical RAM by editing the [VCache] section of your SYSTEM.INI file and altering the MinFileCache= entry as shown here:

```
[VCache]
  MinFileCache=64000
```

The number you specify is the cache size in kilobytes; the example sets VCache to use 64MB of RAM. Windows for Workgroups 3.11 enables you to devote up to 2GB of RAM to VCache in this way. Microsoft has tested VCache sizes up to about 40MB and does not guarantee larger cache sizes to operate properly. The default settings are Microsoft's guess for what works best. If you have the memory, you might experiment to see if you gain performance with your specific multimedia application.

Memory

From the start, one of the biggest promises of Windows was new memory territory. Even the first version was able to give programs megabytes for their data under the original EMS standard. With later versions, Windows gained access to managed extended memory (that is, SMX brought to life by HIMEM.SYS), so the megabytes in more powerful PCs finally became useful.

Memory management has become one of the foremost advantages of Windows. For example, although Windows 3.1 and 3.11 do not use expanded memory for their own purposes, they can create it for use by the DOS applications you run within the environment when you use enhanced mode.

Unfortunately, versions of Windows before Windows 95 suffered from subtle memory limits which affect both performance and the ability to run applications. Because these versions of

Windows are not operating systems in themselves, they have to be launched by another operating system—specifically, DOS—and take over the memory environment set up by DOS.

The underlying problem is that Windows splits its time running in two microprocessor modes: the real mode that emulates the original 8088 microprocessor and suffers a 1MB addressing limit, and protected mode that gives access to the rest of the memory in your PC. Because it is launched by real mode DOS, Windows must start and set itself up in real mode, and it suffers the constraints on real mode memory. Many device drivers and other code must run in real mode. If insufficient real mode memory is available, some parts of Windows may not get properly set up or may not work at all, even though megabytes of extended (protected mode) memory might be present in your PC.

To get Windows operating optimally, you should give it as much real mode memory as possible to work with. Although most PCs nowadays are maxed out to the DOS 640KB limit in real mode memory, tens or hundreds of thousands of bytes of this get whisked away by system software. DOS code has to be running and taking up memory space to load Windows. You probably have to load several device drivers to bring peripherals to life. DOS-based PCMCIA drivers are particularly greedy, stealing up to 100KB from real mode memory. You may also give over more memory to networking software. Although the memory management software included with DOS 5.0 and later helps expand the memory available to your DOS programs, a typical PC configuration may pare down the real mode RAM available to 400KB from 500KB, and Windows may complain that it has insufficient memory for real-mode functions and programs with the message: `Insufficient memory to load this application. Close other applications and try again.` It also needs real-mode memory for system resources such as storing on-screen icons.

Windows System Resources

Although Windows is essentially free to romp through the entire range of your PC's extended memory, certain parts of the package are tightly restricted to limited memory ranges. For backward compatibility with older applications, Microsoft limited the GDI to one segment or 64KB of memory for its storage area, which is called the local heap. The GDI local heap stores data about the graphical objects used by your PC, things like pens, brushes, cursors, fonts, icons, buttons, and scroll bars.

The USER local heap stores data about windows, dialog boxes, and controls. The User program also creates two more heaps for menus and menu strings, each of which can store 64KB of information.

You can monitor the system resources available in your PC by choosing the About option from the Program Manager Help menu. You'll see a display like that shown in Figure 7.2.

FIGURE 7.2. About dialog box in Program Manager showing system resources.

The number in the last line lists the free percentage of whichever of the four local heaps has the least available memory (hence, the one most likely to fill first).

DOS Session Memory

When you run a DOS application with newer versions of Windows, the environment creates a virtual machine simulating a dedicated PC in which the application runs. Created anew, a virtual machine would be like a PC without software—no operating system, no drivers, no TSR programs, nothing to make an application useful. Instead of giving your application such a useless place to run, Windows duplicates the DOS environment that it was started in. The applications you run under Windows thus get access to the underlying operating system as well as peripherals controlled by DOS drivers. Your program gets as much memory in which to run as did Windows when it started.

Window 3.1 takes over managing memory when it is in operation, at least with cooperative DOS-based memory managers. To be compatible with Windows' memory management, DOS memory managers must support an undocumented interface called the Global EMM Inport Interface, which allows Windows to take over the page tables used by the DOS memory managers. This yielding of tables effectively gives Window control over all system memory. If a memory manager does not comply with the required interface, the memory it reserves will not be usable by Windows. Most third-party memory managers obey the rules of the interface.

Virtual Memory Management

Windows will run in amazingly little memory, as little as 1MB. You don't even need enough physical memory to accommodate all your Windows programs. Using a technique called *virtual memory*, Windows simulates extra RAM using space on your hard disk drive. When it needs more memory, it swaps code and data that is not immediately needed from physical RAM to disk storage. When a program calls for the disk-based data or code, Windows invisibly copies it back to real RAM while swapping other bytes back to disk. Your system behaves as if it had dozens more megabytes of memory—except things slow down into a flurry of drive light flashes when you switch from program to program.

The speed penalty of using virtual memory is unavoidable (except by installing more RAM) because accessing disk storage inevitably takes thousands of times longer than reaching into RAM. Windows enables you a bit of choice in setting the performance of virtual memory, the choice being between disk capacity and speed.

To hold the data swapped out of memory to disk, Windows builds a special file on your hard disk called the *swap file.* Windows gives you two primary choices in swap files, permanent and temporary. A *permanent swap file* gets assigned a fixed block of disk space, which is cordoned off from any other purpose, effectively cutting the capacity of your hard disk. A *temporary swap file* is dynamic, expanding and contracting to follow the virtual memory needs of Windows.

The temporary file imposes a performance penalty because managing it involves more overhead. Moreover, the temporary swap file is built like any other DOS file, with clusters plucked from here and there, wherever they are available. Reading the temporary swap file can send your hard disk's read/write head chattering away, wasting its time skating from cluster to cluster and track to track. The permanent swap file, on the other hand, is locked in place. Windows requires all of its sectors to be contiguous, and it cannot be larger than the largest block of contiguous sectors on your disk. Before you create a permanent swap file, you should defragment your disk to assure that its free sectors are contiguous. The overhead of disk compression severely slows disk access, so using a compressed drive for a temporary swap file is inadvisable. You cannot set up a permanent swap file on a compressed disk drive.

Performance Issue

Temporary swap files are called WIN386.SWP and are created when Windows starts in enhanced mode and erased when you properly close Windows. Because temporary swap files are ordinary DOS files, you can simply delete them if Windows fails to do so when you exit. The location of your PC's temporary swap file is set by your SYSTEM.INI file using the `PageFile=` setting. You can limit the size of the file using the `MaxPagingSize=` or `MinUserDiskSpace=` settings, the later constraining its size to keep the specified disk capacity unburdened. The best location is high in the directory tree structure—the root is optimum—so that the operating system needs to do the least work tracking it down.

Permanent swap files are always hidden in the root directory of the disk you specify for your swap file. It is called 386SPART.PAR.

If you decide at some point to change the type of swap file, for example, moving a temporary swap file from a compressed to an uncompressed drive, set the type of swap file to `none`, then restart Windows. Reconfigure your swap file, then restart Windows again. This will assure that all references to the swap file get properly changed from old to new.

How large a swap file you need depends on your system's memory, the size of your disk, and the needs of your programs. Making your swap file as large as possible is tempting because it lets Windows report a larger amount of free memory. Make your swap file too large, however, and performance can suffer. When Windows sees a lot of free space in the swap file, it may prematurely move data into it in an attempt to optimize its memory usage—and any unnecessary disk access will slow your system down. Consequently, the more memory you have in your PC, the smaller the swap file you should use. For example, if you have a full 16MB of RAM, a 2MB swap file will usually be sufficient. The one exception is when your applications demand massive amounts of memory, as is the case with some powerful graphics programs. If your swap file is not large enough for these applications, they will complain or may even not run at all. Increasing the size of your swap file should keep them happy.

Performance Issue

The rule that a smaller swap file is better does not hold to the extreme minimum. Windows is optimized to use a swap file, and its performance may suffer if you totally eliminate one from your system.

How Much Memory?

Virtual memory is no panacea. You still need at least as much physical RAM in your system as the largest program you want to run occupies. A program's code must be in RAM for it to execute, and some programs demand a great deal of memory to operate. Some multimedia programs require 8MB.

The right amount of memory for Windows for your PC depends on the applications you want to run. Some can be greedy. For the general run of programs, however, a few rules apply. You can load Windows with less than 1MB. For example, getting Windows started in standard mode requires as little as 512KB (128KB conventional, 384KB extended) to load. Enhanced mode requires at least 762KB (182KB conventional, 580KB extended). When you start Windows, the WIN.COM loader checks to see the amount of memory available in your system. According to Microsoft, WIN.COM requires at least 256KB of XMS memory in your system to load Windows at all, and it demands 1024KB to load Windows in enhanced mode when you have a 386SX or better microprocessor in your PC.

You'll need more to do anything useful, however. To get adequate performance, you'll want at least 4MB. You'll get good performance with 8MB. Adding more memory than the minimum means that Windows need not swap from RAM to disk as often (or at all, if you install enough memory). In fact, boosting Windows past its minimal memory needs can boost overall performance more than moving up the microprocessor ladder. Remember, one microprocessor step improves performance from 30 to 50 percent. Moving from disk to RAM storage increases access speed a thousandfold. Additional RAM is consequently the most cost-effective performance boost you can add to Windows—up to a point. At 16MB, the law of diminishing returns sets in, and adding more generally adds marginally to the acceleration of your work. The Windows user interface has a 24MB limit.

The recommendations for the amount of memory to install can be overruled by your applications, however. Some programs absolutely require 8MB. Some may require more than 16MB. If you have one of those and not enough memory, you'll know as soon as Windows balks. The only cure is adding to your investment in RAM.

Configuration

The Windows 3.1 family relies on a series of *initialization files* to set up and maintain its configuration. These files are often called .INI files because nearly all use those three letters as their filename extensions. Most applications that run under Windows have their own .INI files, and Windows uses two for its basic configuration. SYSTEM.INI stores overall setup parameters for the entire Windows system such as the drivers to be installed and other configuration data. WIN.INI primarily holds settings that personalize Windows to your preferences. Both are plain text files that you can alter with any editor or word processor that works with standard ASCII files, such as Windows Notepad.

Normally you need not tinker with these files. All the changes you make through the Windows Control Panel are stored as entries to these files, as are the options you choose during the setup of individual programs. Windows function calls allow applications to make, change, and read the various entries to these files. In some instances, however, interactively editing these files can give you control over parameters that installation programs hide from you. Interactive editing is also quicker when you need to make small changes, particularly when you've misplaced the installation disk for the application with which you want to experiment.

All initialization files are arranged in *sections*, and each section is identified by a name listed inside square brackets. Individual entries get listed below the section names, and each entry has one or more variables associated with it. A variable may be a number or a string of alphanumeric characters, the meaning of which is understood by the application using the initialization file. Applications use section names to find the entries they need in the initialization file. The same entry name may be used in different sections with different variables; an application checks only the one listed under the appropriate section name. Windows uses a simple scheme to resolve conflicting section or entry names—it stops looking when it finds a match for the name it's looking for. Subsequent listing of entry names within a section, or of section names within an initialization file, are ignored because Windows never reads down to them.

The order in which sections or entries within sections appear is unimportant, because Windows uses a string-matching algorithm to find the names it seeks rather than looking at the order of entries or other characteristics. This search method also results in Windows skipping over blank spaces and spurious entries. Windows also ignores all lines beginning with a semicolon, so you can make Windows and its applications temporarily ignore an initialization file entry to trouble-shoot a problem by appropriately inserting a semicolon.

Windows also uses a *Registration Database* in which programs store information about themselves that can be shared with the rest of the Windows system. The Registration Database is a binary file—its contents are data bytes that have little meaning to human eyes—that is not meant to be touched by mortal fingers. It is called REG.DAT and resides in your Windows subdirectory.

The Registration Database primarily stores associations between file types (as designated by their filename extensions) and programs. For example, when you double-click a file using File Manager, Windows checks the Registration Database for the program associated with the filename extension of the file you've picked. If Windows makes a match, it opens the designated file with the associated application. Similarly, the Registration Database associates filename extensions with programs for the File Manager print option. Select a file and choose Print from the File Manager menu, and Windows uses the Registration Database to find the appropriate program to print the file. The Registration Database permits a given file type to be opened by one program and printed by another.

Programs normally make and maintain their own entries in REG.DAT. The Windows 3.1 family includes a file to edit some of the entries in the Registration Database called REGEDIT.EXE that enables you to adjust these settings.

Windows 95

What's wrong with the Windows 3.1 family? Everyone has his own pet peeves, some of which may be toothy, snarling wild beasts. Distill the complaints and you'll have a mighty strong brew, but the chief irritations will be few and unanimous. Windows is too slow, too confusing (particularly when you have to mess with DOS to get and keep it going), and too unintuitive.

Windows 95 fixes all three, at least to some extent, and brings a new look to your screen. It adds versatility, convenience, even fun. Multimedia is even built in. About the only place it failed was getting to market on time.

To boost performance, Windows 95 moves into 32-bit territory. The centerpiece of Windows 95 is a 32-bit kernel that manages memory and controls individual processes. Unlike Windows 3.1, Windows 95 uses pre-emptive multitasking, which yields improved switching between applications and background processing. It is multithreaded, which gives it quicker response even within a single application.

To unsnarl the DOS/Windows/chaos software scheme, Windows 95 integrates the operating system into the graphic environment—consider it a Mac on disk. With Windows 95 you should never need deal with the DOS prompt again. But, if you want to, you can step back, open a window, and run your favorite DOS commands.

To make Windows 95 easier to work with, Microsoft gave it a new look. With it you can now launch applications from the desktop instead of a Window by simply double-clicking an icon. The Start Bar at the bottom of the screen lets you switch instantly between applications (or you can rely on familiar key combinations, the same ones as in earlier Windows versions). You can move, copy, and delete files simply by dragging and dropping their icons. Configuration settings are kept in notebooks, changed as easily as scribbling in a new entry.

The list of improvements goes on and on. Although Windows 95 is fully compatible with DOS's FAT disk structure, it allows the use of multiple installable file systems. Included in the Windows 95 package is VFAT (Virtual File Allocation Table), the installable 32-bit file system first introduced with Windows for Workgroups 3.11, a management system for CD-ROMs called CDFS (for Compact Disc File System), and network redirectors. Under Windows 95, filenames are no longer restricted to 11 characters.

Windows 95 also offers some subtle enhancements. For example, where ordinary MS-DOS limits the length of lines in batch files and environmental variables to 128 characters, Windows 95 pushes both up to a maximum of 1,024 characters.

If you still plan on using your old DOS applications, you'll find they never looked better than when running under Windows 95. Thanks to its TrueType fonts, you can select a sharp, clear typeface for your text mode applications that lets you take advantage of the high-resolution capabilities of your display system. Windows 95 can substitute any of a dozen different sizes of TrueType fonts or nine bitmapped fonts for the standard coarse 8X14 font DOS normally chooses, no matter the size or resolution of your monitor.

Multimedia is built in, ready to run your existing Video for Windows and QuickTime sequences, play symphonies from your CD drive, capture your voice, and mix in MIDI music.

Best of all, Windows 95 looks back happily. Just about every program you've copied onto your PC will run under it. You don't even have to change or format your disk to make the upgrade. In half an hour you'll have more speed, power, and beauty in your PC than has ever before been possible.

Compatibility

The most important aspect of Windows 95 is its compatibility with applications. Nearly all existing DOS and Windows programs will run under Windows 95. In addition, many programs written for Windows/NT will also run under Windows 95.

Windows 95 and Window/NT share the same application program interface, which Microsoft calls Win32. The important difference is that Windows 95 does not understand all of the functions in Win32 while Windows NT does. Consequently, all Window 95 programs will run under Windows NT but not all Windows NT programs will run under Windows 95—providing, of course, that the programs are meant to run in the same hardware environment. If a programmer writes a Windows NT application that calls on those features of Win32 that Windows 95 does not understand, the program will not run under Windows 95. In addition, Windows 95 requires more freedom in placing programs in memory. Applications must be written to load in memory addresses about 4MB and they cannot include their own memory relocating instructions; Windows NT applications suffer no such restriction.

Compatibility with older applications is more troublesome because Windows 95 is a 32-bit operating system and older programs are written in 16-bit code. Microsoft incorporates some 16-bit functions in Windows 95 to help run these applications. Better still, Windows 95 converts much of the 16-bit code into 32-bit instructions that can run Windows 95's faster 32-bit routines. Microsoft calls the conversion process thunking, combining the words "thinking" and "chunking" because the process intelligently processes the 16-bit code to 32-bit in chunks. The result is near 32-bit speed and full backward compatibility with older Windows applications.

Old DOS programs don't call the routines that are part of the old or new Windows interfaces, but they can pose their own problems. Thanks to the Virtual 8086 mode of the latest Intel microprocessors, Windows 95 gives each DOS application its own virtual machine in which to run. As long as the DOS software tolerates the virtualized environment, Windows 95 can run applications inside individual windows. As with previous Windows versions, some graphic video modes used by DOS applications may not be compatible with windowed screen handling and must be run fullscreen. Applications that run in text mode not only present few problems but benefit from the ability to substitute high-resolution TrueType fonts for the standard (and rough) VGA font.

A few DOS applications will not run in the virtualized Windows environment. Windows 95 does not enable you to exit the graphic environment and dip down to the DOS command prompt. Windows 95 is DOS to your system. To enable you to use these programs, Windows 95 offers its version of command mode, actually a dual-boot system. To enable a program to run in this environment, you must choose MS-DOS mode from the Advanced settings menu of the application's properties. Selecting the icon or shortcut for such an application closes your Windows 95 session and reboots your PC in MS-DOS mode. Your application has the entire machine's resources in which to run using standard DOS function calls (which report back to the program that they are running under DOS version 7.0). No other applications can run in this mode (although you can rig the DOS mode session to load TSR programs and other old stand-bys). When you type EXIT on the command line to end this MS-DOS session, your PC will reboot and take you back to Windows 95.

Although Windows 95 will run DOS, 16-bit Windows, and 32-bit Windows applications indiscriminately and will give each the same on-screen look and feel, it treats each class of program differently. Each DOS application is completely isolated from the rest—as well as Windows and all Windows applications—by the Virtual 8086 mode hardware of Intel's microprocessors. A crash in one DOS session affects nothing but the DOS session. In contrast, all Windows applications share the same virtual machine. But all 32-bit Windows applications are allocated their own memory and queues for input and messages. They are pre-emptively multitasked and each application may split its functions among multiple threads.

Older 16-bit Windows applications share memory with one another, share the queues, and are cooperatively multitasked. Each comprises only a single thread. Because of the shared memory and queues, 16-bit Windows applications are the least isolated in the Windows 95 system. A crash in one has a greater chance of affecting other 16-bit Windows applications. Moreover, a misbehaving 16-bit Windows applications can monopolize the 16-bit Windows queues and processing time. If you choose to kill a 16-bit Windows application by pressing Ctrl+Alt+Del, Windows 95 will show you a list of all running applications and lets you choose which to end. Even so, one particularly ill-behaved 16-bit Windows application can bring down all the rest.

Structure

At its core Windows 95 has a three-part structure—a central kernel flanked by its user interface and graphic device interface (GDI). This triumverate handles most of the daily work you do with Windows.

The kernel is charged with actually controlling your PC and all its applications. When you click an application icon, the kernel actually loads the .EXE file associated with the application into memory, along with the .DLL files the program needs to run. It schedules which application and thread gets control of your PC's microprocessor and arbitrates conflicting demands for system command between them. It allocates memory (in the form of 4KB pages) for each thread, divvying out individual pages as each thread requires more. It guards against memory problems, shepherding exchanges of data through the memory system while ensuring that no program trespasses into the RAM used by another. When the physical RAM in your system fills up, the kernel guides the operation of virtual memory, deciding what pages of code and data get swapped to disk. The kernel also controls disk access and maintains the file system. And the kernel acts as the emergency rescue squad. When a problem occurs and an application requires help from code that's not part of the general stream of its program instructions, the kernel can signal to the application how to solve the problem, even shutting down the application if there's no other solution.

The user interface of Windows 95 puts you in control of the system. It monitors the keyboard and captures your keystrokes, follows every twist and turn of your mouse, and listens to any other input devices you connect to your PC, passing on what it learns to the rest of Windows. It also controls the information flow in the other direction, managing the display of windows, menus, and icons on your monitor screen as well as the sounds your system makes. It also controls the timer inside your PC and your communications ports.

The interface shell—the part that you actually work with—is the file CAB32.EXE. In addition to the interface functions, this program also implements several desktop tools such as the Network Neighborhood.

The user interface is interrupt-driven. That is, it lies around waiting for something to happen. When you press a key or some other event (like a timer tick) sets off an interrupt, an interrupt handling routine in the user interface checks what's caught its attention and creates a message it sends to the rest of Windows describing what happened. It then sends the message to the appropriate application, where it sits waiting in a message queue until the application has a chance to read and act on it.

The Windows 95 architecture gives each Windows 95 application its own message queue, so applications only need process relevant messages without waiting for other tasks to take care of their correspondence. On the other hand, old applications written for previous Windows versions together share a single message queue, so a single application that fails to pull a message out of the queue can stall all the rest.

The Windows 95 GDI links applications to your screen. It provides a common set of routines for controlling all the graphic functions of your PC. In addition, the GDI extends its graphics support to printers and other peripherals that use graphics. This single-minded purpose belies the impact of the GDI. You PC probably spends more of its time running GDI functions than the rest of Windows because manipulating graphics requires all the processing power your system can deliver. The GDI is in charge of executing graphic primitives, altering and moving bitmaps, and controlling graphics drivers such as those for your video display and printer. For this reason, the GDI is one of the most reworked aspects of Windows 95, having been converted from the 16-bit form used in earlier Windows version to 32-bit power. The few 16-bit routines that are in the new GDI remain mostly to provide compatibility with older applications.

The centerpiece of the Windows 95 GDI is a new graphics engine called the Device Independent Bitmaps (or DIB) engine that directly controls the bit-images sent to your monitor (and sometimes to your printer). Built into this engine are a full set of drawing primitives optimized to the most common color display systems including monochrome (1-bit), 4-bit, 8-bit, 16-bit, and 24-bit color. All of these drawing functions (including routines for Bézier curves) are built into a new universal display driver. To match specific display adapters, Windows 95 uses a mini-driver, several of which are included with the operating system package. For color-critical applications (like pre-press proofing of color images), Windows 95 includes the built-in ability called Image Color Matching that enables it to tune its display colors to that of specific printed hues.

Memory

The handling of memory is one of the great triumphs of Windows 95 and one of the best reasons to shift to the new operating system. Although Windows 95 requires more RAM to get started, it's more frugal with what it uses and better at housekeeping. It knows enough to release memory no longer needed by applications back into the pool from which other tasks can draw.

And it can use every byte that you make available to it—Windows 95 manages the entire 4GB addressing range of Intel 32-bit microprocessors.

Windows 95 reserves the upper 2GB of addresses for its own functions, leaving a maximum address range of 2GB to your 32-bit applications.

When the needs of Windows 95 and the applications you run exceed the limits of physical memory available in your system, the Windows 95 kernel simulates additional RAM as virtual memory. As with any virtual memory system, it requires disk space—a swap file—to simulate RAM. Windows 95 simplifies the management of its swap file, however. Where previous versions of Windows forced you to decide between permanent and temporary swap files and swamped your mind with concerns about contiguity and size, Windows 95 gives you a simple, dynamic swap file which the operating system itself completely manages. This dynamic file combines the best features of temporary and permanent swap files. It can grow or shrink as the needs of your applications change, and it can reside on any disk (even those that are fragmented or compressed) without suffering performance penalties. Although you can still take manual control and specify the minimum and maximum size allowed for the Windows 95 swap file, most systems will require no change in the default values.

Windows 95 even gives your old DOS applications more memory to work with. The reliance on virtual device drivers instead of real-mode device drivers means more memory will be available to your DOS sessions under Windows 95. Each real-mode device driver you load steals RAM from every DOS session, and the more you load, the less RAM is available to your applications. Virtual device drivers draw from protected mode memory, leaving real mode RAM untouched.

The Windows 95 Virtual Machine Manager divides the resources of your system into one or more virtual machines using the Virtual 8086 mode of newer Intel-architecture microprocessors. One of these virtual machines is devoted to each DOS application that you run under Windows 95. In addition, Windows 95 itself and all Windows 16- and 32-bit applications share one virtual machine. While old Windows 3.*x* applications share a single address space in this virtual machine, each Windows 95 application gets its own address space, providing a greater degree of isolation between programs. While a warm boot (pressing the Ctl+Alt+Del key combination) to clear a stalled Windows 3.*x* application may knock out all other running Windows 3.*x* applications, the Windows 95 programs (and DOS applications) that are running will suffer no ill effects.

Microsoft provides a utility with Windows 95 so that you can determine how much memory of various kinds is available in your PC. The System Information program, which installs by default in your PC's WINDOWS\MSAPPS\MSINFO directory, lets you check various dynamic aspects of your Windows 95 system. When you start the program MSINFO.EXE, the initial screen lists your system's memory and its allocation, as shown in Figure 7.3.

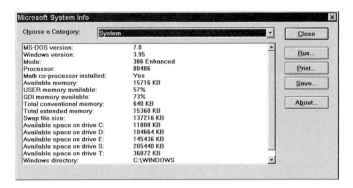

FIGURE 7.3. Microsoft System Information screen in Windows 95.

File System

In becoming a true operating system, Windows 95 required a scheme to manage disk-based files. Previous versions of Windows relied on DOS for disk management. Breaking with the DOS tradition, Windows 95 uses a layered file system architecture that allows the simultaneous use of multiple file systems. It includes two file systems of its own, Virtual File Allocation Table or VFAT, a 32-bit system that expands on the traditional DOS FAT system, and Compact Disc File System or CDFS, which handles files on CD-ROM drives. In addition to supporting installable file systems (those that can be added as modules to augment the operating system's abilities), the new architecture boasts performance and convenience improvements over DOS.

Unlike Windows for Workgroups 3.11, the 32-bit VFAT file system cannot be disabled under Windows 95. VFAT takes care of all hard disk data requests and uses 32-bit protected-mode drivers or 16-bit real-mode drivers depending on the requirements of the underlying hardware. It maintains compatibility with DOS systems by maintaining the same 12-bit or 16-bit FAT structure. The CDFS is a protected-mode, 32-bit version of Microsoft's old MSCDEX.EXE driver. It loads dynamically when Windows 95 detects a CD drive.

The Windows 95 file system is incompatible with utilities that write directly to your disk drive hardware. Because of Windows 95's protected mode cache, writing directly to disk hardware may corrupt the file system. Windows 95 makes two provisions that let you use programs that do write to physical disk hardware: a COMMAND.COM switch and its Single MS-DOS Application mode. Normally Windows 95 will run DOS applications in an individual window and, using the VFAT system, will not permit direct hardware access of the disk drives. You can convert your DOS sessions to Single MS-DOS Application mode by selecting the MS-DOS mode under the Advanced Program Settings page of the MS-DOS Properties control, as shown in Figure 7.4.

FIGURE 7.4. Advanced Program Settings page of the MS-DOS Properties control in Windows 95.

After you've made this setting, selecting the MS-DOS Prompt icon will essentially reboot your PC with the DOS command interpreter in complete control. You cannot open Windows. But you can run direct hardware access utilities without fear of corrupting your file system.

The biggest difference you'll notice is that Windows 95 enables you to use long filenames containing up to 255 characters each. (Some sources give the file length as 256 characters; the difference is that the higher count includes a null character, 00(Hex), that's used by Windows 95 to indicate the end of the file name.) Pathnames can be up to 259 characters long including the drive letter, colon, and directory backslashes (260 characters counting the terminating null character). Upper and lower case characters are preserved and spaces within filenames are accepted as any other character. In identifying files, however, Windows 95 does not distinguish between uppercase and lowercase letters and will not enable you to have two files with names differing only by capitalization in the same directory. Upper- and lowercase differences are also ignored when Windows 95 searches for a file, for example with the DIR command at the MS-DOS prompt.

Existing applications typically won't understand the new, longer names, so Windows 95 gives them a shortened version in the familiar 8+3 combination, an eight character filename and a three character extension called an *alias*. In general, the translation to make an alias works as follows: the first eight characters of the long filename are transposed into all capital letters. Spaces, periods, and other characters illegal in DOS filenames are each ignored and replaced by the next non-space character. The filename extension is reported as an all-capital translation of the first three characters following the last period in the file name.

Windows 95 requires that every long filename and the alias associated with each be unique in every directory. Sometimes under the general translation rule, two long filenames may generate the same alias. Windows 95 resolves this potential ambiguity by creating an alias using the first six characters of the long filename followed by a unique numeric tail, a tilde (~), and a numeral.

As Windows 95 encounters potential conflicts, it starts by appending a 1 to the first conflict, 2 to the next, and so on. If it finds more than 10 conflicts, it starts truncating the name to five characters and uses two final numerals to distinguish files. If it needs even more unique names, it further truncates the filename. Better still, you should find a more appropriate way of designating your files with long names.

Copying files can lead to some surprises. You can copy a file from one directory to another in which a second file has the same alias as the first. As long as the long filenames of the two files are different, Windows 95 considers the two files to be different and will not overwrite the second file with the first. Instead, it generates a new alias for the copy, one that is different from the original alias of the first file. It may appear that Windows 95 automatically changes filenames when copying. In fact, it is only changing the translation and alias to maintain compatibility with applications that don't understand long filenames, while preserving both uniquely identified files.

The following characters are preserved in alias names as all are valid FAT filename characters:

$ % ' - _ @   ~ ` ! ( ) { } ^ # &

Strictly speaking, the space character *is* valid in DOS filenames since DOS version 3.0. However, many DOS applications cannot handle a space within a filename. Consequently Windows 95 suppresses spaces in generating aliases.

The VFAT system allows several additional valid characters in its long filenames. The list of valid characters for Windows 95 long filenames includes the following:

$ % ' - _ @   ~ ` ! ( ) { } ^ # & + , ; = [ ]

In addition, Windows 95 allows characters with ASCII values between 128 and 255 in filenames, although Microsoft discourages the use of these high-bit characters. The assignment of character to ASCII code varies with the character set in use, so the same filename may have what appears to be a complete different name if you use high-bit characters and change the character set.

Note that when you run Windows 95 Single MS-DOS Application mode, it uses only the standard FAT file system. Any long filenames that you assign your files will be invisible, although the names on the disk are not changed. You cannot create long filenames in Single MS-DOS Application mode.

Old applications that are unaware of long filenames may inadvertently delete them when copying or updating a file. Windows 95 attempts to prevent such problems with a feature that Microsoft called *tunneling*. Windows 95 sends only the alias to the old program and uses the alias to manipulate the appointed file, hiding the long name from the old application. When you install Windows 95, tunneling is automatically activated, although you can switch it off.

The long filenames used by Windows 95 are compatible with those created by the Windows NT File System (NTFS), OS/2 High Performance File System, and Novell's NetWare file system.

In addition to long filenames, Windows 95 also tracks the time and date of creation and the last modification of each file. This information is used by Windows 95 to maintain the various links between programs and files. Windows 95 also stores the date that a file was last accessed using the application that created it so that you and your programs can determine which files you have not recently used.

You can assign long names to a file in three ways: from within applications that support long filenames, using Windows 95's icon-based file maintenance utilities behind the My Computer icon, or in command mode. In command mode, you can use the standard COPY or REN functions. Just substitute the long filename for a short one, putting the long name in quotes to avoid confusing the command interpreter. For example, you can rename the file ELECTRIC.EEL to A long skinny fish with a charge.txt using this command:

```
REN ELECTRIC.EEL "A long skinny fish with a charge.txt"
```

To programs that only understand 8+3 filenames, the new name of this file would be ALONGSKI.TXT. In command mode, you can use the 8+3 translation of the long filename in the commands you issue. A DIR (Directory) command will display both the long and short names, short to the left of the file statistics, long on the right.

Because the Windows 95 file handlers operate in 32-bit protected mode and use a full 32-bit path to access the disk drive, they can outrace DOS in transfer speed. The VFAT driver is reentrant and multithreaded, so it provides smoother multitasking performance. It can be entered and used by one thread before another one has been finished. In addition, Windows 95 enhances disk access time with an integrated disk cache. This cache runs entirely in protected mode, so it steals no memory from the DOS applications you might run under Windows 95. It caches both read and write operations and works with both hard disk and CD-ROM files. In addition, the memory use of the integrated cache is dynamic. The cache automatically adjusts its memory impact as the amount of free memory in your PC and file system activity changes.

The installable file system enables you to add multiple network redirectors so you can access disk drives on several networks at once. Up to version 3.1 of Windows, only one network redirector was permitted to run in a single PC. Windows for Workgroups (3.11) allowed two, one of which had to be Window's own redirector.

Although the part of the file system that actually handles writing to disk (the input/output subsystem) is fully 32-bit, it includes a mapping layer to accommodate real-mode (16-bit) DOS disk drivers. This code converts Windows 95 protected-mode file requests into real-mode requests that the DOS driver can handle. This feature is mostly for compatibility. Sixteen-bit file access by itself will slow down Windows 95. Worse, DOS drivers use serial I/O access so one request must finish before another begins. The multithreaded Windows 95 file system does not suffer this limitation.

If all the complication of the VFAT system and long filenames seems too complex to you, you can force Windows 95 to use the older DOS-based file system through its Windows 3.1 Compatibility Mode. In preliminary versions of Windows 95, you were given the option of adjusting some of the settings for the file system in the Troubleshooting page you reach by choosing File System from the Performance page of the System Folder of the Control Panel, as shown in Figure 7.5.

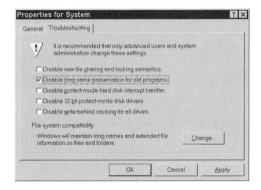

FIGURE 7.5. File System Troubleshooting page in Windows 95.

Try to alter these settings, and Windows 95 will tell you that you need to make the adjustments through the Setup program you use to install the operating system. When you choose Windows 3.1 Compatibility mode during setup, Windows 95 will eliminate all the extra file data it finds on your disk, including long filenames, file creation, modification, and last access dates. Despite such drastic disk preparation, even in this mode Windows 95 will not access direct write to disk hardware. You'll still have to switch to Single MS-DOS mode to use older utility software that takes direct hardware control.

Configuration

Windows 95 adds its own configuration system based on a single database called the Registry, designed with hopes of eliminating all of the configuration confusion of the past. Ultimately, the Registry is slated to replace the profusion of files used by DOS and previous Windows versions. Instead of a group of .INI files, the Registry uses only two that handle the system and all of its applications, a system configuration file and personal configuration file. The former, stored in a file named SYSTEM.DAT, matches the Windows operating system to your PC, its hardware, and its programs. The latter stores your preferences in using Windows and its applications in the file USER.DAT. This separation of files lets you share your PC with other people, each of whom can customize it to match the way they work without jeopardizing the smooth operation of your system. Alternately, you can setup a notebook PC to respond differently when sitting on your tray/table when in the air or in its docking station at your desk. If you work in a business with many networked PCs, you can arrange to keep your USER.DAT file centrally so that it is downloaded to whatever workstation you log into. In effect, the Registry allows every PC in your offices to be custom configured for you—as well as everyone else.

The Registry

The Registry works as a hierarchical database with a tree-like structure much like typical computer file systems with folders nestled in other folders. Configuration information is stored in the form of keys, which like folders, can contain other keys. Unlike .INI or .DOS configuration files which store only text, those of the Registry embrace both text and binary data. Where .INI files are limited to 64KB in length, the Registry can hold a nearly unlimited horde of configuration information, limited only by disk size and reasonability.

Windows 95 marks the beginning of the transition to Registry-based configuration, but it does not yet replace the older configuration systems. It can't. Older Windows applications, for example, still rely on referencing .INI files when they start up. Deprive them of their files and they won't load. Some old hardware requires real-mode device drivers complete with setup parameters passed through the CONFIG.SYS file. Consequently, the Windows 95 Registry supplements rather than replaces the older schemes. If you plan to run anything beyond Windows 95 applications, you'll still face the traditional setup systems. You'll still find a complete set of .INI files in your Windows 95 directory. SYSTEM.INI and WIN.INI are retained because many older Windows applications reference those files when they load. Each of your old Windows applications will likely have its own associated .INI file in the Windows directory as well. These files are maintained by your applications rather than Windows 95. As always, you can alter them with any text-mode editor. The only way to completely eliminate the old configuration systems is to discard all of your old applications.

In normal operation, you won't see the Registry or deal intimately with its settings. But every time you install a new program, adjust the properties of an existing application, or even change the look of your screen, you will change your Registry. Windows 95 makes the changes automatically without your express intervention.

If you like to tinker, you can edit the Register directly using a special program supplied with Windows 95. Called REGEDIT.EXE and stored in your Windows 95 directory, it enables you the ability to freeform edit the Registry. Because it enforces no syntax—it doesn't concern itself with the context of what you type; it only moves the characters that you type into the Registry without considering whether they make sense—you can make grievous errors which may prevent your system from properly working. In other words, refrain from using the Registry editor or use it with utmost caution.

Trouble-shooting

Windows 95 provides a fail-safe mechanism to help you recover from altering your Registry into oblivion. Each time Windows 95 starts up successfully, it makes itself a new copy of the registry, saving the old version in the files SYSTEM.DA0 and USER.DA0. If Windows 95 runs into problems with the Registry during boot up, it automatically tries to recover the Registry used during the last successful boot. You can restore this old version of the Registry and use it to step back one previous configuration. You may have to use your Windows Startup disk (which you made during Windows 95 installation) to get your system running. Then use the standard command-line instruction COPY to overwrite the bad data in SYSTEM.DAT and USER.DAT with the good data in SYSTEM.DA0 and USER.DA0. By default these files are stored as hidden, system files in the Windows 95 directory, although you may move your USER files to other locations.

Hardware Configuration

Windows 95 is the first operating system to fully implement the Plug-and-Play standard that was designed to eliminate the vagaries of installing PC expansion hardware. Using Plug-and-Play technology, Windows 95 can automatically configure your PC's hardware so you don't have to worry about such issues as DMA channels, base addresses, and interrupts. Better still, Windows 95 can eliminate the worry about these options when installing software drivers and applications. This technology allows Windows 95 to automatically adapt to any hardware changes you make—even those, like sliding in a PCMCIA modem, you make while your system is running.

Originally conceived by Microsoft and Intel Corporation, most of the computer industry has embraced Plug-and-Play as the breakthrough that will finally bring PCs to the masses. But Plug-and-Play is not a singular entity. It is neither hardware nor software but a combination of both. Plug-and-Play is a banner that unites several technologies, standards, levels of compliance, and residual headaches.

Because Plug-and-Play is a complete system, to completely fulfill its promises it requires all aspects of your PC conform to its various standards. This includes your PC's system board and BIOS, the various peripherals installed in your PC, and the operating system running it. To get truly automatic configuration, you'll need a new PC and new peripherals that are both Plug-and-Play compliant along with Windows 95. Fortunately, the developers of Plug-and-Play made the system as accommodating as possible to existing hardware. By design, Plug-and-Play products help ease the transition to the new technology. All Plug-and-Play PCs and peripherals work with non-Plug-and-Play equipment by sacrificing some of their inherent Plug-and-Play abilities, so a new Plug-and-Play PC will accommodate old expansion boards and give you true Plug-and-Play operation with compliant peripherals. Although a PC without built-in Plug-and-Play can't ever take full advantage of the technology, Windows 95 uses it to do a better job configuring and troubleshooting your older PC's resources than can most dedicated utility programs.

The concept behind Plug-and-Play is not new. One of the principles underlying IBM's 1987 Micro Channel Architecture design was simplified system configuration. Although the 1988 EISA consortium downplayed most of the innovations in Micro Channel, the group incorporated its own automated configuration into the EISA design. The first official effort at a Plug-and-Play specification appeared when the original Intel-Microsoft specification for it on ISA computers was released on May 28, 1993. That announcement inspired other companies to join in, and related standards are being developed to extend Plug-and-Play to other troubling configuration processes, particularly SCSI expansion. For example, Compaq Computer Corporation and Phoenix Technologies joined Intel to develop a BIOS specification for Plug-and-Play, first released November 1, 1993. The original VL Bus specification predates the Plug-and-Play announcement, but the Peripheral Component Interconnect (PCI) standard includes complete Plug-and-Play support.

The basic Plug-and-Play procedure is a three-step process: First, your system checks what resources each expansion device needs. Next it coordinates the assignments to avoid conflicts. Finally, it tells your system and software what choices it has made.

In a fully Plug-and-Play compliant PC, the process begins in the BIOS, although its role is minimal. The BIOS instructs all Plug-and-Play peripherals except those needed to boot the system (the video display and disk drive) to temporarily switch themselves off. This prevents resource conflicts because the switched-off devices make no resource demands. Old expansion boards that don't know about the Plug-and-Play standard keep working because your PC has no way of switching boards off individually (at least if it does not use a Micro Channel, EISA, or PCI expansion bus). Resource conflicts consequently can arise in these older devices. If the conflicts are not fatal, however, your PC can boot even though they are present.

Once the boot process begins, Plug-and-Play responsibility shifts to the operating system. Windows 95 uses the active boot devices to load itself. Then it begins an exhaustive search of the devices installed in your PC and the resources they use. With Plug-and-Play peripherals, this task is easy because the standard provides a mechanism for polling each expansion board individually and for the board to tell the operating system the resources it needs. Old boards lack such a mechanism, so Windows searches for evidence of what other devices are installed. It can identify some boards by their BIOS signature—the code that some expansion boards add to your BIOS routines often contains copyright information and version numbers that aid in identification. In addition, Windows can check to see what other resources are used to try to identify products. When this automatic identification of older devices fails, Windows 95 may ask you to help out.

Windows 95 then compiles a list of the products installed in your PC and the resources they use. With non Plug-and-Play devices, this information is fixed in the Registry database and is used only for reference when setting up Plug-and-Play devices. Windows 95 then sets up the Plug-and-Play devices one by one, assigning them the resources they need from what remains available. Because Plug-and-Play boards can be reconfigured at any time, Windows 95 can change the resource assignments it makes to them to adapt to PC cards you might slide in or even to match the requirements of particular programs.

Accommodating Old Devices

Implementing this procedure is complicated on older PCs because of the shortcomings of the ISA design. For example, the ISA bus provides no way of singling out an individual expansion board to determine exactly what resources it might require. Boards can be used individually only after they are configured and after your software is notified which resources they use.

ISA expansion boards, too, lack the facilities required for automatic configuration. They need some means to allow their resource needs to be set automatically. Instead of jumpers and switches, they must have software latches and must understand a common command set for making their adjustments.

In addition, an automatic configuration procedure itself needs its own control system. That is, it needs a program to step through the configuration procedure. And it requires some method for communicating the addresses and assignments that it makes to your software so your applications can reach your PC's peripherals.

These shortcomings show that building an automatic configuration system will involve changes in nearly every aspect of a PC. To individually address expansion boards, the ISA expansion bus needs revision. To permit automatic configuration, ISA expansion board design must change. The setup procedure needs to be built into your PCs test procedure, which requires changes to the system BIOS. And linking with software is best implemented by redesigning the overall operating system.

With existing PCs that lack explicit Plug-and-Play support in their BIOSs, the automatic configuration system will divide the task of sorting through resource conflicts between you and the operating system. Although the Plug-and-Play operating system will manage Plug-and-Play expansion boards, you'll still have to configure your conventional expansion boards.

Windows 95 does an exemplary job of seeking out and identifying the peripherals you've installed in your system. You can check the device that Windows 95 finds by clicking the System icon in Control Panel, then click Device Manager. You'll see a graphic display of the devices installed by type, as shown in Figure 7.6. Click the icon for the device type, and Windows 95 will show you the specific devices installed. Figure 7.6 has the CD-ROM controller listing expanded to show a Matsushita CR-52X drive present. It also shows two device conflicts, the network adapter and SCSI controller.

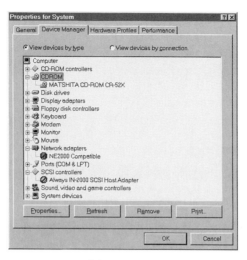

FIGURE 7.6. Device Manager page of the System Properties in Windows 95.

Click a specific device, and Windows 95 will enable you to manually adjust setup values. The changes you make only affect the parameters Windows 95 uses to access the device. They have no effect on the actual hardware itself. When you find a conflict and have to reset the resources used by an old expansion board, you'll have to pull the board out of your PC (switch your system off first!), adjust its switches or jumpers, reinstall the board, and restart Windows 95.

When Windows 95 matches the signature of a older device with its own database it then attempts to adjust the configuration of the rest of the system to avoid conflicts with the old device. Sometimes, however, it does not succeed. Even so, it tells you of the conflicts it finds so that you can reassign resources manually. For example, in setting up your system, Windows 95 might find a conflict between the port ranges used by two peripherals—your SCSI adapter and game port, for example. Double-click the device in conflict, and you'll be able to edit the settings Windows uses for the device. You'll see conflicts at a glance as shown in Figure 7.7.

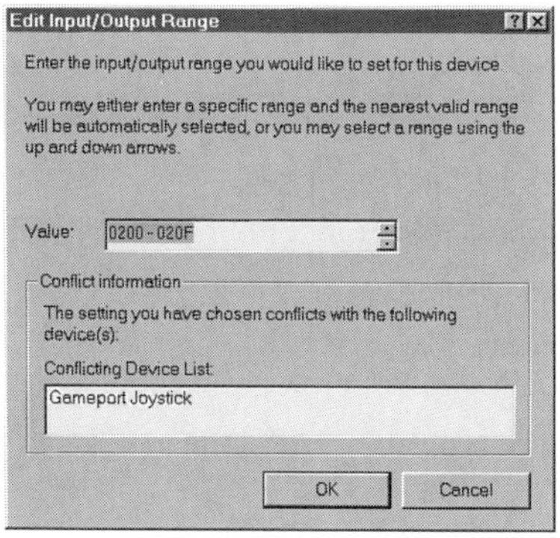

FIGURE 7.7. Editing configuration settings for a device in Windows 95.

Even if you upgrade your PC with a Plug-and-Play BIOS you won't eliminate these problems and the need for manual intervention. Windows 95 and a new BIOS can't help resolving conflicts between conventional expansion boards because the hardware-mediated resource allocation on conventional boards can't be changed by software alone. Once you've eliminated non-Plug-and-Play products from your system, however, your need to deal with these screens and your setup headaches will disappear.

Plug-and-Play Configuration

IF you wonder why Windows 95 takes so long to boot, part of the reason is the time needed for Plug-and-Play configuration. The process is neither simple nor quick, as you can see from this discussion of how it works.

The Plug-and-Play configuration process calls upon specific hardware features of Plug-and-Play expansion boards. Most importantly, each Plug-and-Play board is able to inactivate itself so that it does not respond to the normal control signals inside your PC. The board disconnects itself from all system resources so that when it is inactive, it cannot possibly cause conflicts.

In addition, each Plug-and-Play board has several new on-board registers that are reached through a standardized set of three I/O port addresses so that the BIOS or operating system can control the configuration of the board. These ports are designated Address, Write Data, and Read Data.

The Address Port functions as pointer that expands the number of control registers directly accessible to your system without stealing more system resources. Loading a register number in the Address Port makes that register available for reading or writing through the Write and Read Data ports. In other words, the address port switches direct access between several additional ports.

The Plug-and-Play specification explicitly defines eight card control registers and reserves two large ranges, one of 24 registers for future elaboration of the standard and a second 16-port range that board makers can assign to their own purposes. In addition, the Plug-and-Play specification allows cards to be configured as multiple logical devices, and it assigns ports for their control. The Address port allows the Write Data port to select which of the logical devices is active and the resources used by each.

Plug-and-Play expansion boards act in one of two ways, depending on whether they are needed for booting the system. Boards that are required for boot-up—that is, display adapters and disk controllers—start up active. That is, they come on-line exactly like conventional expansion boards using the resources assigned them as power-on defaults. They will grab the resources that they need, participate in the normal power-on self-test procedure, and let you operate your PC normally. They may also cause the same old resource allocation problems, as will any conventional expansion boards that don't support Plug-and-Play. The other Plug-and-Play devices (those not needed in booting your PC) automatically deactivate themselves when your system comes on, waiting to be told what configuration to use by your operating system.

Every Plug-and-Play board has specific circuitry for managing its configuration. This circuitry operates independently from the normal functions of the board. Unlike the functional circuits on the board that can be disconnected from the bus interface, the Plug-and-Play circuits always monitor the signals on the bus. However, the Plug-and-Play circuitry operates in one of four states—Wait for Key, Isolation, Configuration, and Sleep—regardless of whether the functional circuitry is active or inactive.

All Plug-and-Play boards, whether active or inactive, boot up in their Wait for Key state. In this condition, the boards refuse to respond to any signal on the ISA bus until they receive an explicit command called an Initiation Key. The Plug-and-Play BIO starts and governs the process. The Initiation Key is actually a precisely defined 32-step interaction between the host Plug-and-Play system and circuitry on each expansion board. A circuit on the board called a Linear Feedback Shift Register generates a new pattern at each step (by shifting its bits one at a time) and the host sends a data byte to the board. Each Plug-and-Play board compares its internal values to those received from the host. All 32 comparisons must be correct for the Initiation Key to be successful. Upon properly receiving the Initiation Key, Plug-and-Play expansion boards shift into Sleep mode.

Because an ordinary PC BIOS does not know how to carry out the Initiation Key process, it cannot remove Plug-and-Play boards from the Wait for Key state. The configuration circuitry of the Plug-and-Play boards does not activate (if at all) until the Plug-and-Play operating system loads.

In a fully Plug-and-Play PC, the BIOS automatically sends out the Initiation Key. It can then take control of individual boards, interrogates each Plug-and-Play device about the system resources it requires, and resolves conflicts between boot-up devices. The BIOS ordinarily does not, however, make resource assignments or activate the boards not involved in boot-up. Instead, it leaves that decision-making to the operating system.

In order to configure each expansion board, the Plug-and-Play BIOS or operating system must be able to individually communicate with each board to independently instruct each what to do. Ordinarily that's difficult in the ISA system because all signals are broadcast in common to all expansion boards. The Plug-and-Play creators envisioned the ISA bus being modified to include slot-specific signals to unambiguously identify each expansion board. Knowing such changes would take years to creep onto desktops, however, they also developed a board-identification system compatible with the existing ISA bus that allows individual addressing except when multiple identical boards are installed in a single PC. In this Plug-and-Play system, a Card Select Number (CSN) identifies each board. Each board is dynamically assigned its CSN by the Plug-and-Play BIOS (if your PC has one) or the Plug-and-Play operating system.

The CSN is actually a convenience that works as a handle, much like the file handles used by DOS. The ROM on each Plug-and-Play board model includes a serial identifier, an 8-byte code coupled with a 1-byte checksum. Two bytes store a three-letter manufacturer identification in compressed ASCII code (five bits per character). Two more store the model number of the board, and four more bytes code a board-specific serial number.

In contrast, the CSN is an individual byte value that is more convenient to store and manipulate. Moreover, CSN numbers enable you to install multiple copies of a given board model in one PC without conflict—providing your PC has a means of individually addressing each expansion slot.

All Plug-and-Play boards boot up with a CSN of zero (0). To assign a unique CSN to a Plug-and-Play board, the Plug-and-Play BIOS or operating system must isolate individual boards from the bus. It does this by first arousing all boards from the Sleep state into their Isolation state by broadcasting a Wake specifying the default CSN of zero to the Write Data ports of all boards.

In the Isolation state, each board interacts with your PC (and the Plug-and-Play BIOS or operating system) in a precisely defined manner called the Isolation Sequence. The Plug-and-Play BIOS or operating system uses the serial identifier to uniquely identify each board. The system merely checks the bit patterns of the serial identifiers, ignoring their information content.

The Isolation Sequences involves simultaneously scanning all serial identifiers one bit at a time in the Linear Feedback Shift Register. The host system sends out 72 consecutive 1-bit read operations (one operation for each of the 64 bits in the code plus its 8-bit checksum). At every step, each Plug-and-Play board compares one bit in its LFSR to that of the other boards by observing bus signals.

When the board has a high bit (digital 1) in its LFSR, it asserts a data signal across the bus; boards with low bits (digital 0) at that position in their serial identifiers do not. When a board with a low bit detects the signal from one or more boards with high bits in a given position in their ID codes, it drops out of the isolation sequence by slipping back into its Sleep state. This bit-comparison process continues until, at the end of 72 evaluations, only one board has not dropped off to sleep.

Once a single board is thus uniquely identified, the operating system then assigns that board its unique CSN number. The board then stores the CSN for future reference in a special CSN register and it, too, goes into its Sleep state. Then the Plug-and-Play BIOS or operating system initiates another Isolation Sequence to assign the next CSN, and so on until all boards have been assigned their CSNs. Only the boards with a CSN of zero participate in later Isolation Sequences because only they respond to the Wake command that starts the sequence.

After all Plug-and-Play boards have been isolated and assigned CSNs, the BIOS or operating system then checks the resource needs of each one. To do this, the BIOS or operating system individually switches each board into its Configuration mode to read its resource needs from the data stored on the board.

A board with a valid CSN switches into Configuration mode when it detects a Wake command specifying its CSN. Only one board is permitted in Configuration mode at a time, so other boards automatically switch to Sleep mode when they detect the Wake command meant for another board.

In PCs with a Plug-and-Play BIOS, the BIOS checks each board by reading registers through its Read Data port to compile a list of resource requirements, then finishes the boot-up process. The Plug-and-Play operating system takes over at that point. In PCs without Plug-and-Play BIOSs, the operating system merely jumps from the isolation to the configuration process.

After a given expansion board has been configured, the operating system can activate it by writing to the appropriate register on the board. A single expansion board may have several functions, each called a virtual device, which the operating system can separately activate.

After the configuration process is completed (or at any other necessary time) the operating system can switch the designated expansion board out of its Sleep state and back to its Configuration state to activate it, deactivate it, or change its configuration. It controls each board individually using the Wake command and specifying an CSN. This process allows the operating system to dynamically modify the resource usage of any board in the system as applications require.

BIOS Issues

Besides introducing several new steps to the standard BIOS-mediated POST procedure, Plug-and-Play adds a new structure to add-in BIOS code. It allows a given expansion board to include code targeted to specific operating systems so that a given expansion board can take on different personalities depending upon the operating system that's in control.

Under a convention originated by IBM back in 1981, your PC scans through the memory address range used for BIOS code to look for add-in code held on expansion boards. During its scan, the POST procedure looks for a special add-in ROM signature—the 2-byte 055(Hex), 0AA(Hex) code—which indicates a block of add-in BIOS code follows.

In the Plug-and-Play system, this signature is followed by a pointer that indicates the location of an Expansion Header in the BIOS code or a chain of several headers. Each header is identified by a special 4-byte preamble—024(Hex), 050(Hex), 06E(Hex), 050(Hex)—which corresponds to the ASCII characters $PnP. Each header can be keyed to an individual operating system using additional codes. Unlike conventional expansion boards, the operating system and not the PC's own BIOS reads through this add-in code on Plug-and-Play boards because the boards are inactive and effectively decoupled from the bus during a normal BIOS scan.

Using the CSNs given by the BIOS (or the operating system itself), the operating system can identify each Plug-and-Play board, read through its BIOS area, and find each header. Information encoded in each expansion header includes the type of devices on the board and the location of program code to boot the PC (if a device on the board can boot the computer). A Device Indicator byte in the header indicates whether the ROM on the board initializes as a device driver, may be shadowed, can be cached, operates as a boot, display, or input device. A Device Type Code helps the system BIOS figure out which devices should be used for booting the system if none is overtly specified. It identifies exactly what kind of peripheral is connected through the expansion slot. The serial identifier is also included in the header.

The Plug-and-Play specification allows each board maker a generous apportionment of the available memory and port addresses. Each board can use up to four non-contiguous ranges of memory base addresses for BIOS code and up to eight non-contiguous base addresses for input/output ports. In addition, a board can use from zero to two separate interrupt levels and up to two DMA channels. Each manufacturer determines the number of resources that a given board can use. Which it uses, however, is a matter left to the board maker. In other words, the manufacturer gives the board a list of options, but the ones that actually get used is determined by the Plug-and-Play system in your PC when you boot it up.

Resource requirements need not be configurable. A board with minimal Plug-and-Play support merely tells what resources it wants and stubbornly sticks there. Most Plug-and-Play products will, however, allow for several options in their resource requirements. Even when irresolvable conflicts arise between boards, the Plug-and-Play system can keep a PC operating by inactivating one of the conflicting boards.

SCSI

Although the initial Plug-and-Play specification promises to bring order to the chaos of resource allocation inside a PC, it did nothing to help alleviate the insanity outside the system. In particular, while Plug-and-Play could guarantee that ports and products would have access to the PC facilities they needed, it did nothing to help sort through the confusing SCSI configuration process.

Certainly plugging a single SCSI device into a PC can be simple, but more than one device sharing the same connection (and the current SCSI standard allow up to seven peripherals to share one host adapter link) insures only that your aspirin consumption will increase. Consequently five major vendors of SCSI equipment (Adaptec, DEC, Future Domain, Maxtor, and NCR Corporation) joined Microsoft to extend Plug-and-Play to embrace SCSI.

In effect, the Plug-and-Play SCSI initiative embraces part of the upcoming SCSI-3 specification termed "SCSI Configured AutoMagically" or SCAM. All Plug-and-Play SCSI devices must conform to SCAM.

The SCAM system is much like Plug-and-Play in that it allows its refined configuration system to be phased in. SCAM accommodates older, non-conforming SCSI drives but does nothing to aid in their configuration. You can use ordinary SCSI devices in a SCAM system but you'll give up some of the benefits of SCAM.

As a practical matter, you will still need to assign ID numbers conventionally to old SCSI devices even in a Plug-and-Play SCSI system. Two conventional SCSI devices (called "legacy" devices by SCAM) given the same ID will conflict exactly as they always have—and with the same repercussions. Neither will likely work. On the other hand, the SCAM devices in a Plug-and-Play SCSI system will check for conflicting ID assignments and rearrange their IDs to avoid duplication.

Under the SCAM scheme, the host adapter has sufficient built-in intelligence to assign the IDs to all conforming devices. SCAM-compliant SCSI devices come pre-set with a preferred ID number but allow the host adapter to reset the ID number to sidestep conflicts. When two devices connected to a single SCAM host adapter come pre-set with the same ID value, the host adapter normally will assign one of the device the next-lowest available ID number (one with less priority). When no lower ID numbers are free, the host adapter assigns the next higher ID number.

As with conventional SCSI systems, those conforming to the SCAM specifications require termination at each end of the SCSI cable. The SCAM system relies on external termination of all SCSI devices. That is, instead of flipping switches on the SCSI device, you plug a dummy plug filled with terminating resistors into the last open connector at each end of the SCSI chain. Although installing the termination is hardly an automatic, hands-off process, it remains the only feasible way of assuring a proper circuit termination until manufacturers incorporate mechanical arms in their PCs.

Plug-and-Play SCSI host adapters will conform with the same specifications as other expansion boards to gain access to the PC resources they need. Plug-and-Play SCSI does nothing to clear up the chaos of different device driver interfaces (CAM and ASPI, discussed in Chapter 10) encountered with DOS systems. But new Plug-and-Play operating systems will likely incorporate integral SCSI support much as OS/2 and Windows/NT already do.

OS/2

The leading alternative to Windows is—and long has been—OS/2.

Originally pioneered as a joint effort by IBM and Microsoft, the product has become IBM's own as Microsoft pursued its Windows strategy.

OS/2 was introduced to the world in 1987 as a better operating system accompanying IBM's better PCs, the Personal Systems/2. As a next generation operating system, OS/2 was designed to step beyond DOS by taking advantage of the protected mode of Intel microprocessors. This automatically gave OS/2 the ability to address memory beyond the 1MB limitation of DOS's real mode and also aided in running multiple simultaneous applications. Protected mode allows the memory used by one program to be protected so that other programs cannot interfere with it.

The initial incarnation of OS/2 pushed up the minimum hardware requirements in a PC to a 80286 microprocessor along with a hard disk drive. It introduced concepts such as a modular design, pre-emptive multitasking, and multithreaded operation.

Unfortunately OS/2 proved to be too little too soon. In the rush to get it to market at the same time as the new PS/2s, important features were omitted, including the graphic interface which would have made it a serious competitor to Windows. Its compatibility with DOS applications was limited to a "compatibility box," a DOS emulator that severely constrained the performance of programs. After a few major software vendors introduced applications that ran under OS/2 (for example, Lotus 1-2-3 and WordPerfect) to less than auspicious success, OS/2 lost third-party support.

OS/2, in fact, only became a serious contender as an operating system with the introduction of version 2.1—which integrated support of Windows applications in the 386-specific environment. OS/2 2.1 put existing DOS and Windows applications on an equal footing with the (nearly nonexistent) native OS/2 applications using a single common interface.

The current version, OS/2 Warp represents an streamlining of version 2.1. It's both faster and more compact, able to run in PCs with as little as 4MB of RAM, and is faster to load and execute.

History

OS/2 can trace its origins back to 1985 when IBM and Microsoft began to explore ways of breaking through the fundamental limitations in DOS. Of the many goals outlined for the project, the four most important were breaking the DOS 640KB memory barrier, allowing true multitasking, providing a consistent application program interface, and adding a graphic user interface. Although first conceived as a product for all Intel microprocessors all the way back to the 8088, difficulties in implementing compatible memory-handling with older chips forced the developers to draw the starting line at the 286. Intel had already announced—but not delivered—the 386 microprocessor but had promised it would have full backward compatibility with the 286, so the new operating system would work with both.

During its development, what became OS/2 wore a number of names including Big DOS, CP DOS, DOS 286, and DOS 5 (although it had no relation to the commercial product later released with that designation). In addition, the product was conceived as twofold, a basic package called Standard Edition and an enhanced version with built-in database functionality called Extended Edition.

The commercial announcement of OS/2 came in April, 1987, coinciding with IBM's release of its redefined hardware standard, the Personal Systems/2. Only in December of that year did the product actually become available as Version 1.0 Standard Edition. Although this first release did incorporate three of the promised operating system innovations—memory handling extended to 16MB, standard API, and true multitasking—it lacked the promised graphic interface.

Presentation Manager, as the interface was called, did not arrive until nearly a year later, November, 1988, with the introduction of OS/2 Version 1.1. On the screen, Presentation Manager offered overlapping windows and moveable icons. Behind the scenes, it gave programmers a hardware-independent graphical interface in a protected multitasking environment.

In truth, Presentation Manager in OS/2 1.1 was preliminary, and the whole of the system had not been finished in 16-bit code. With the introduction of Version 1.2 at the end of 1989, Presentation Manager was updated with a new three-dimensional look, a new integral file management application, and an entirely new file system. Called the High Performance File System or HPFS, it broke through the DOS 32MB partition addressing limit (which DOS itself broke shortly thereafter) while improving performance and allowing longer file names.

The final 16-bit release of OS/2 was Version 1.3, first marketed in October, 1990. Chief innovations in 1.3 included better support of device drivers and more modest memory requirements so that it could run on a larger share of PCs. OS/2 1.3 could run in as little as 2MB of RAM. It also incorporated Adobe Type Manager for more efficient handling and scaling of fonts. In addition, Version 1.3 was also the final version of OS/2 on which IBM and Microsoft jointly worked on all parts.

The step to OS/2 Version 2.0 pushed the operating system into 32-bit territory. IBM, now working on OS/2 essentially on its own, designed Version 2.0 specifically to match the 386 microprocessor (which, of course, also includes its offspring, the 486 and Pentium).

The most visible change in the step to Version 2.0 was a new graphic look based on an object-oriented interface that used a nested folder metaphor. Called the Workplace Shell, the new design brings Mac-like drag-and-drop control to file management, printing, and configuration processes and takes advantage of a properties menu and standardized setting notebook to bring greater consistency to setup and operation of applications.

More important was the revised internal design of the operating system. IBM rewrote the kernel in full 32-bit 386 code and took advantage of other microprocessor-specific features. OS/2 abandoned the segmented memory model required by earlier Intel processors. In addition, Version 2.0 is based on a demand-paged design that allows easier portability of program code between microprocessor families. For backward compatibility with DOS applications, Version 2.0 took advantage of the Virtual 8086 mode of the 386 microprocessor to devote a dedicated virtual machine to each program so it could multitask multiple programs. In addition, it gave similar support to Windows 3.0 applications.

The advance to OS/2 Version 2.1 removed the last chunks of 16-bit code from the system by adding full 32-bit graphics engine for handling screen input and output operations. In addition, the new OS/2 incarnation incorporated support for Windows 3.1 applications including those running in Enhanced Mode. Version 2.1 also improved the multimedia capabilities of the operating system with the addition of a number of new drivers and the bundling of Multimedia Presentation Manager/2.

In addition to the 386 microprocessor, the various OS/2 Version 2.X implementations require about 8MB of RAM to operate.

In November, 1994, IBM introduced Warp, OS/2 Version 3.0. Although the numerical increase implies an momentous update on par with transition from 16-bit Version 1.3 to 32-bit Version 2.0, Warp represents a smaller step, one perhaps better considered a refinement. Buried in the code, you'll even see self-references to itself as version 2.3.

Chief among Warp innovations is a reduction in resource demands. Warp runs in as little as 4MB of RAM, essentially the same hardware requirement as Windows 3.1. Other refinements include a more understandable installation process and a refined user interface with a new "launchpad" to speed access to frequently run applications.

Structure

OS/2 is built from three essential layers, one providing hardware support that handles most device drivers, a layer of operating system engines, and a layer that provides environments to support various applications.

The driver layer includes three components: drivers for physical devices such as the keyboard, mouse, disk drives, and SCSI peripherals; display system drivers; and printer drivers. As with all drivers, the code in this layer links the operating system to the underlying hardware of your PC and its peripherals. Each hardware device or subsystem requires one or more drivers. When you configure OS/2, you or the configuration program selects the proper drivers to match your hardware, which are loaded into memory every time you start OS/2.

The heart of OS/2 is its layer of operating system engines, and central to it is its main control program, which itself has two essential elements. The kernel comprises the main management function of the operating system that controls and coordinates the operation of programs, memory allocation, and interprocess communication. The file system side of the control program manages mass storage. In addition, the operating system layer includes two interface programs, the System Object Model (SOM) which empowers OS/2's object-oriented control system and the print subsystem which manages multiple print jobs.

The application support layer of OS/2 is unified by Presentation Manager, which handles the needs of native OS/2 applications, multimedia software, and the Workplace Shell user interface. Separate modules provide support for Windows and DOS applications.

Kernel

IBM structured the OS/2 kernel around a design created at Carnegie Mellon University called Mach 3.0. Two primary concepts underlie its basic design: machine-specific code was kept to an absolute minimum and functions common to all operating systems are kept separate from those unique to OS/2. The aim of both of these attributes is to make the operating system and the code written for it as portable as possible. Such a design is inherently modular and allows OS/2 and the programs that run under it to be readily adapted to other computer and microprocessor environments.

To achieve these goals, IBM uses what it calls a microkernel design, which modularizes the kernel itself. In this design, the primary machine-specific part of the operating system kernel is the actual microkernel. IBM assigns five functions to it. These include managing tasks and threads, managing communications between them, controlling virtual memory, interrupt and input/output processing, and system support such as microprocessor control and time and date functions. Although the microkernel itself is necessarily machine-specific, most of the code in it is not so even it can be readily rewritten for other hardware environments.

In managing the execution of programs, the OS/2 microkernel separates the streams of instructions into individual threads and assigns address space and resources to each. The various threads, even those of a single program, need not be contiguous is memory. The microkernel keeps track of them and controls their accesses to memory. Each thread gets effectively protected from the rest.

The interprogram communications (IPC) system in the microkernel allows the isolated threads to share data with one another without otherwise interacting. Ordinary communications get channeled as messages through ports; large blocks of data are exchanged by moving control of memory areas between threads. This tight control of communications isolates problems and prevents a crash in one program or thread from harming others.

OS/2 uses a flat memory model, which means that it does not work with 64KB segments as do real mode operating systems. The microkernel assigns memory to threads as it is needed in 4KB blocks called pages. When it runs out of memory to assign, becoming overcommitted in the number of memory pages it must supply to applications, it uses virtual memory. That is, the microkernel swaps inactive pages to hard disk memory, retrieving the pages as they are needed. These excess pages are stored in a swap file on your hard disk called SWAPPER.DAT. You can tell OS/2 where to put this swap file and how large it can be by adjusting settings in your CONFIG.SYS file. The process works much as it does in Windows 3.*x* running in enhanced mode.

The SWAPPATH= setting controls the swap file, the minimum disk space to keep free, and the initial size of the swap file. You indicate the location of the file by indicating the subdirectory in which OS/2 should put it immediately after the equals sign. The default location is in the C:\OS2\SYSTEM directory. After the directory name, you tell OS/2 how much disk space (in kilobytes) you want to keep free in case the swap file swells to fill the whole thing, the Minfree value. The final entry in the SWAPPATH= setting is the starting size of the swap file. OS/2 will allocate a swap file of this size, increasing it as needed to accommodate more memory pages until it reaches the Minfree value. Normal OS/2 housekeeping reduces the size of the swap file as your programs reduce their memory needs, but it will never shrink the size of the swapfile below the minimum size you specify in CONFIG.SYS.

A typical SWAPPATH= statement might look like this:

```
SWAPPATH=C:\OS2\SYSTEM 4096 2048
```

This statement forces OS/2 to put your swapfile in the C:\OS2\SYSTEM directory with a minimum size of 2MB. It will allow OS2 to enlarge the file until only 4MB remain available on your hard disk.

File System

To give it the greatest flexibility, OS/2 is not tied to any specific file system. Instead, it supports installable file systems in which the structure of the disk and operation of the file system are controlled by drivers. Through this mechanism OS/2 can run multiple file systems are once (on different drives or partitions). Two file systems are supplied with OS/2 Warp—a FAT system compatible with that of DOS (called *Super-FAT*) and the OS/2 High Performance File System (OS/2 HPFS). Although HPFS has advantages, its irrelevant to multimedia because most software comes on FAT-compatible discs.

As with DOS, OS/2 imposes a logical structure on disks called the partition, which is simply a convenient unit for the operating system to manage. When you work with a drive, each partition roughly corresponds to a separate drive letter, although some partitions may be invisible to you and others may be subdivided into more than one logical drive. As with DOS (and for backward compatibility with DOS), OS/2 is allowed up to four partitions by the design of the PC BIOS.

OS/2 recognizes three individual types of partitions: a special boot manager partition, which must be within the first gigabyte on the drive; primary partitions; and an extended partition. Each drive may have only one boot manager and one extended partition but may have more than one primary partition. However, only one primary partition can be accessed without rebooting your PC. This primary partition is called the *active partition* and is by default assigned the drive letter C: The extended partition may be subdivided into multiple virtual drives, each of which gets assigned its own drive letter. The boot manager partition has no drive letter. It is dedicated to a specific purpose, loading code that lets you choose among different operating systems on your disk. It is dedicated to storing special program code for the boot process and cannot be used for ordinary storage. It becomes the active partition on your drive when it is used.

OS/2 and DOS can readily share a single partition. For convenience, however, you can make a primary partition for each operating system that you want to use on your hard disk. For example, you might want one for DOS and one for OS/2. Your operating system boots from its primary partition. The extended partition is shared by all operating systems that use your PC. Some logical drives in the extended partition may not be recognized by some operating systems, however. Because DOS does not understand the OS/2's High Performance File System, logical drives that use the HPFS will be invisible to DOS and not assigned drive letters when your PC runs under DOS (although HPFS drives are accessible to DOS sessions that run under OS/2).

With current versions of DOS, you can freely mix FAT and HPFS logical drives in an extended partition. (DOS 5.0 and earlier requires the HPFS drives to come after the FAT drives.)

Getting the OS/2 file system started can be a problem, particularly with the High Performance File System, in that an installable file system has to be installed before it can be used—and it has to be installed from somewhere. Normally OS/2 loads whatever file system it has been installed under in the boot partition of your drive. It checks the master boot record—the first physical sector on the drive—to find which partition is marked for booting. It then starts reading the first sector of that partition, which is called the *partition boot record*, which stores the program code necessary for loading the balance of the operating system. Under OS/2's FAT-based file system, the partition boot record loads and executes OS2BOOT, which copies the OS/2 kernel loader (OS2LDR) from disk into memory. OS2LDR, which has built in FAT support, then loads and initializes OS/2 and shifts the system into protected mode.

When loading the High Performance File System, the partition boot block is extended by an extra 16 sectors called a *Super Boot Block*. Extra code stored there loads a basic protected mode file system called mini-FSD, which then transfers control to OS2BOOT. The mini-FSD handles the disk operations during the loading of basic kernel files until the drivers in CONFIG.SYS are running.

OS/2 also offers the ability to interactively select boot partitions at start-up time using a feature called *Boot Manager*. Installing Boot Manager causes OS/2 to set aside a dedicated 1MB disk partition called the Multi-Boot Block that stores the code needed to control the selection process. The Boot Manager installation process makes the Boot Partition active, writing a pointer to the Multi-Boot Block in the disk's master boot record at the first physical sector on the disk. When you start your PC, the Multi-Boot Block loads and gets enough of OS/2 running to enable you to select the partition from which you want to boot.

Super-FAT

To achieve backward compatibility with DOS and DOS applications, OS/2 needs to simulate the DOS disk environment. The mechanism is simple: OS/2 uses the same disk structure as does DOS, assigning disk space through the use of a file allocation table. OS/2 divides the storage space on a disk into consecutively numbered clusters. The directory entry of a file points to the first cluster, and the entries of each cluster in the FAT point to the next cluster used by the file. When using a FAT-based file system, OS/2 uses a FAT with 16-bit entries as has been standard since the introduction of DOS 4.0 but remains backwardly compatible with older 12-bit entry FATs as well.

Directory entries for FAT-based OS/2 files are the same as those for DOS with one important exception. OS/2 adds extended attributes to directory entries by commandeering 10 bytes of reserved storage in the directory entry. These 10 bytes do not hold the extended attributes themselves—10 bytes is far too little room for that—but instead store a pointer that indicates where the extended attributes are found.

The extended attributes get stored in a special file called EA_DATA._SF. One cluster (2,048 bytes) of this file is allocated to each file that has extended attributes even if the attributes require only a few dozen bytes. The pointer in a file's directory entry simply enumerates which cluster in EA_DATA._SF holds the file's extended attributes.

DOS does not understand this extended attribute system, so it does not preserve the values stored in the ten bytes of the directory entry used for the extended attribute pointer. When DOS creates, copies, or moves a file, it automatically makes these 10 special bytes all zero and breaks the association of a file with its extended attributes. You'll consequently want to avoid using DOS on files that have extended attributes under OS/2, although you can usually restore the association between a file and its extended attributes using OS/2's CHKDSK and EAUTIL utilities. Making a backup after you've booted from DOS may wipe out the extended attributes of every file backed up because DOS will reset each file's attributes to reflect that it has been backed up. This problem happens only when you boot directly into DOS, for example using OS/2's dual boot option or a floppy disk. You will not encounter this problem when running DOS functions under OS/2.

High Performance File System

The High Performance File System used by OS/2 uses an entirely different storage scheme from DOS. The basic unit of storage used by the HPFS scheme is the sector. Sectors are identified by Relative Sector Numbers, each of which is 32-bits long—sufficient to encode 4,294,967,296 sectors or a total disk space of 2,048GB. Sectors are numbered sequentially, starting with the first one in the HPFS partition. Files are allocated in multiples of single sectors; directories, however, are made from one or more blocks of four sectors. OS/2 doesn't have to limit itself to the 504MB volume size enforced by the system BIOS code because it loads its own disk routines that replace those of the BIOS.

Each file or directory on the disk is identified by its *File NODE*, which stores descriptive data about the file or directory. This information includes file attributes, creation date, modification dates, access dates, sizes, and a pointer that indicates in which sector the data in the file begins. Each File NODE is one sector (512 bytes) long. Up to 254 bytes of the File NODE of a disk file store an extended filename, which can include upper- and lowercase characters, some punctuation (for example, periods), and spaces. Although OS/2 allows normal DOS programs to read and write HPFS files, these programs cannot usually accommodate extended file names. In general, such programs truncate extended file names after the normal DOS 8 + 3 characters. Extended file names that begin with the same characters will be ambiguous to these programs and can cause errors.

As with a DOS file system, an HPFS disk organizes its storage from a root directory. In an HPFS system, however, the root directory does not have a fixed location on the disk. Instead, the root directory is identified by reference to the disk Super Block, which is a special sector that is always kept as the sixteenth sector from the beginning of the HPFS partition. The twelfth and thirteenth bytes—that is, at an offset of 0C(Hex) from the start of the block—of the Super Block points to the location of the root directory File NODE. Free space on the disk is identified by a bitmapped table.

As with other FNODEs, a pointer in the root directory FNODE stores the location of the first block of four sectors assigned to the root directory. The root directory is identical to the other directories in the HPFS hierarchy, and like them it can expand or shrink as the number of files it contains changes. If the root directory needs to expand beyond its initial four sectors, it splits into a tree-like structure. The File Node of the root directory then points to the base File Noted of the tree, and each in the tree points to one directory entry and possibly a pointer to another directory node that may in turn point to entries whose names are sorted before the pointer entry. This structure provides a quick path for finding a particular entry, along with a simple method of scanning all entries.

The HPFS shares with DOS the ability to accommodate any length file (that will fit in the partition, of course) by assigning multiple allocation units (sectors in the case of the HPFS) which need not be contiguous. However, the HPFS pre-allocates sectors to a file at the time it is opened, so a file may be assigned sectors that do not contain active data. The File NODE of the file maintains an accurate total of the sectors that are actually used for storing information. This pre-allocation scheme helps prevent files from becoming fragmented. Normally, the block of sectors assigned to a file will be contiguous, and the file will not become fragmented until all the contiguous sectors have been used up.

Two types of sector are used to track the sectors assigned a given file. For files that have few fragments, the File NODE maintains a list of all the Relative Sector Numbers of the first sector in a block of sectors used by the file as well as the total number of sectors in the file before those of each block. To capture all the data in a file, OS/2 find the Relative Sector Number of the first block of sectors used by the file and the total number of sectors in the block. It then checks the next Relative Sector Number and keeps counting with a running total of sectors in the file.

If a file has many fragments, it uses a tree-style table of pointers to indicate the location of each block of sectors. The entry in the file's File NODE table then stores pointers to the sectors that themselves store pointer to the data. Each of these sectors identifies itself as to whether it points to data or more pointers with a special flag.

Besides its huge capacity, the HPFS has significant advantages when dealing with large hierarchies of directories, directories containing a large number of files, and large files. Although both the HPFS and DOS use tree-structured directory systems, the directories in the HPFS are not arranged like a tree but each directory is stored in a tree-like structure that, coupled with the presorting of entries automatically performed by the HPFS, allows faster searches of large directories. The HPFS also arranges directories on the disk to reduce the time required to access them—instead of starting at the edge of the disk, they fan out from the center.

Device Drivers

Although IBM wrote OS/2 to be as independent as possible from specific hardware, software must somehow interact with your hardware if it is to be at all useful. After all, without a hardware connection, OS/2 couldn't read your keystrokes or paint an image across your monitor screen. OS/2 uses software drivers to make these links.

In most cases, OS/2 routes the commands your applications issue to hardware devices through several layers of drivers. For example, one driver might handle the signals at your PC's serial port and pass the data along to a mouse driver that converts the raw data from the mouse into data in a common OS/2 format. Another driver might be used to translate that data into the form needed by your Windows applications.

OS/2 uses several types of drivers. Physical device drivers handle the essential hardware in your PC. These include the basic device drivers that link your keyboard and mouse to OS/2, disk device drivers to connect your mass storage devices, and SCSI device drivers for your CD-ROM drive. Display drivers tie in your PC's video system and include base video handlers for text-oriented routine functions, Presentation Manager display drivers for graphics in OS/2 sessions, and WIN-OS/2 display drivers to match the needs of Windows applications to the OS/2 system. Printer drivers include those that actually link OS/2 Presentation Manager to your printer and those that link the Windows subsystem to the OS/2 printer system. In addition, your Windows applications use their own virtual device drivers that then link to OS/2's driver system before tying in to your hardware.

As with Windows, OS/2 has its own control system for device drivers. Its function and operation are described in Chapter 8.

Plug-and-Play

OS/2 Warp includes limited Plug-and-Play abilities. The current version of the operating system does *not* take control of Plug-and-Play expansion boards, so it cannot be considered a true Plug-and-Play operating system. However, OS/2 Warp can automatically configure PCMCIA accessories. IBM calls this feature "Plug-and-Play for PCMCIA." Although primarily of interest to the owners of notebooks computers with built-in PCMCIA slots, the feature also works with desktop systems in which you've installed PCMCIA card readers.

When Plug-and-Play for PCMCIA works best, it is invisible. You slide a card into your PCMCIA slot, Warp reads identification data stored on the card, then the operating system automatically recognizes the card and configures itself to accept it. You don't have to run any additional software.

You can check the operation by running the Plug-and-Play PCMCIA program that installs by default inside your OS/2 System folder. When the program initially loads, it lists what PCMCIA cards you've slid into your PC and their status, as shown in Figure 7.8.

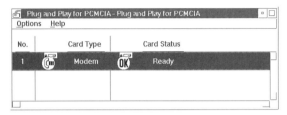

FIGURE 7.8. OS/2 Plug and Play for PCMCIA program listing.

You can configure the Plug-and-Play for PCMCIA program to automatically show card status when you change cards and to beep a warning upon the occurrence of pre-defined conditions such as inserting or removing a card. You adjust these actions using the program's Customize option, as shown in Figure 7.9.

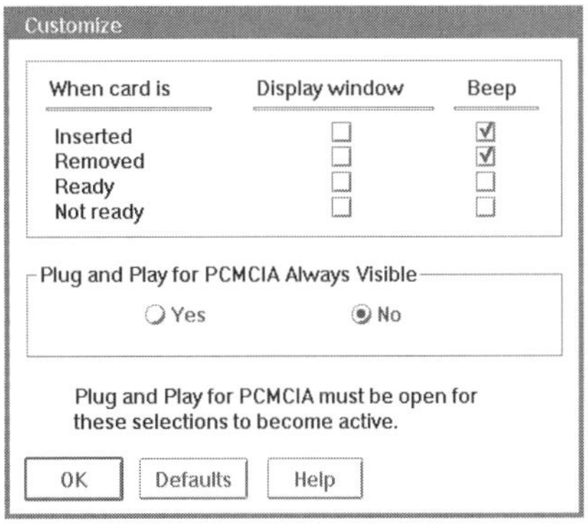

FIGURE 7.9. Customize option of OS/2 Plug and Play for PCMCIA program.

OS/2 Warp can automatically carry out specific functions when you insert a specific PCMCIA card. For example, you can key Warp to load your communications program when you slide in your modem.

In order for Warp to know what to do with what card, you must *register* each card type and the action to carry out. To register a card, open the Options menu to the Plug-and-Play for PCMCIA program and choose Register. You'll see a screen like the one shown in Figure 7.10.

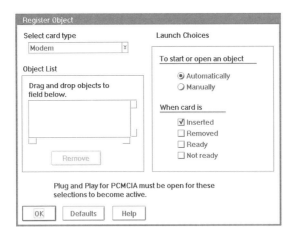

FIGURE 7.10. Register option of OS/2 Plug and Play for PCMCIA program.

To key a program to an action, simply drag the program's icon into the displayed Object List area when you've set the appropriate card type and launch choices.

Although OS/2 Warp will recognize most PCMCIA cards without your loading the Plug-and-Play for PCMCIA program, the program must be running (in the foreground or minimized in the background) to carry out its warning and automatic operations. If you use PCMCIA accessories, you'll want to put Plug-and-Play PCMCIA in your Startup folder.

Chapter 8
Device Drivers

What do a tee at the country club, the asphalt oval of the Brickyard in Indianapolis, and your multimedia PC have in common? They are all infested with drivers of one sort or another, and as different as their drivers are, they all share a few characteristics. Drivers are troublesome. Golf would be easier if balls would fly straight down the fairway without them. The Indianapolis 500 would be safer without drivers piloting their cars around its corners. And getting multimedia to work on your PC would be far easier if your every peripheral and program would spring to life without the need for yet another driver program.

Although you'd like to live without them, you can't. You can't putt off a tee (unless the golf course is decorated with fiberglass dinosaurs and miniature windmills). You can't expect a championship race car to spin around the track without someone at its helm. And you can't expect your scanner to scan, your printer to print, or your mouse to do whatever mice do without loading the right device drivers. Under Windows your PC won't talk, won't show anything, and may not do anything at all without the right drivers.

PC device drivers are different from the golf clubs and race car jockeys because they aren't anything tangible you can hold in your hand or talk to, except in the most extreme frustration. They are no more than program instructions that tell the microprocessor in your PC what to do. But what they tell your PC is mighty important. They act as a guide book or set of instructions that tell your system how to control a given piece of hardware or software.

Device drivers also provide some of the biggest headaches involved in making multimedia work. Without the right drivers, your multimedia will be no medium.

Background

Device drivers have exactly the same purpose as the interface side of BIOS code. They link your system to another device by giving your PC a handy set of control functions. In fact, the BIOS code of every PC includes several built-in drivers to handle floppy disk drives, the keyboard, printers, video, parallel and serial port operation. But BIOS code does not hold all the drivers that your system, its software, and hardware need. When you have to go beyond the reach of the BIOS, you need to add external device drivers. These add-on drivers tell your PC how to run some device or use another piece of software about which the BIOS or operating system writer has no knowledge. Although strictly speaking, the major portion of the BIOS is devoted to device drivers, when most people speak of drivers, they mean these external, add-on links. Driver code can be software or firmware—code contained in the ROM chips on expansion boards. In the latter form, however, the driver code is usually termed a *BIOS extension*.

As with the BIOS links, the external device driver provides a library of programs you can easily call to carry out a complex function of the target hardware or software device.

All device drivers have to link with your existing software somehow. The means of making that link varies with your operating system. As you should expect, the fundamental device driver architecture is that used by DOS. Drivers that work with DOS are straightforward, single-minded, and sometimes dangerous. Advanced operating systems like Windows and OS/2 have built-in hooks for device drivers that make them more cooperative and easier to manage.

You need to tangle with device drivers because no programmer has an unlimited imagination. No programmer can possibly conceive of every device that you'd want to link to your PC. In fact, programmers are hard pressed to figure out everything you'd want to do with your PC—otherwise they'd write perfect programs that would do exactly everything that you want.

With their limited imaginations, programmers cannot conceive that you'd ever want to connect an Inksmear Model 500 Sputterprinter to your PC. Worse, they might not even guess the 24-digit code that Inksmear thought was perfect for eliciting puce-colored ink from the special sputter-print head. And, of course, that's exactly what you want to do—print a poison-pen letter to Bill Gates in puce ink to complain that Windows can't control your Sputterprinter.

Just about every class of peripheral has some special function shared with no other device. Printers need to switch ribbon colors; graphics boards need to put dots on-screen at high resolution; sound boards need to blast fortissimo arpeggios; video capture boards must grab frames; and mice have to do whatever mice do. Different manufacturers often have widely different ideas about the best way to handle even the most fundamental functions. No programmer or even collaborative program can ever hope to know all the possibilities. It's even unlikely that you could fit all the possibilities into a BIOS with fewer chips than a Las Vegas casino or operating system with code that would fit onto a stack of disks you could carry. There are just too many possibilities.

Drivers let you customize. Instead of packing every control or command you might potentially need, the driver packages only those that are appropriate for a particular product. If all you want is to install a sound board, your operating system doesn't need to know how to capture a video frame. The driver contains only the command specific to the type, brand, and model of a product that you actually connect to your PC.

Device drivers offer another advantage. You can change them almost as you change your mind. If you discover a bug in one driver—say sending an upper case F to your printer causes it to form feed through a full ream of paper before coming to a panting stop—you can slide in an updated driver that fixes the problem. In some cases, new drivers extend the features of your existing peripherals because the programmer didn't have enough time or inspiration to add everything to the initial release.

The way you and your system handle drivers depends on your operating system. DOS, 16-bit versions of Windows, Windows 95, and OS/2 each treat drivers somewhat differently. All start with the model set by DOS, then add their own innovations. All 16-bit versions of Windows run under DOS, and so require that you understand (and use) some DOS drivers. In addition, these versions of Windows add their own methods of installing drivers as well as several new types of drivers. Windows 95 accommodates both DOS and 16-bit Windows drivers to assure you of compatibility with your old hardware and software. In addition, Windows 95 brings its own 32-bit protected-mode drivers and a dynamic installation scheme. OS/2 also follows the pattern set by DOS but also adds its own variations.

DOS

When the PC was created, it included several drivers for basic hardware such as the video display, keyboard, and input/output ports in its BIOS code. When DOS was created, device drivers were unnecessary. After all, when DOS was created the only available peripherals were those offered by IBM, and the BIOS of the PC took care of the necessary functions. In a few short months after the PC's introduction, however, device drivers popped up like mushrooms after a rainstorm. A lot of what we take for granted today was missing from the device driver repertory of the original PC—fanciful things like hard disk drives. Over the years, IBM and Microsoft added direct support for device drivers to DOS. Even so, for DOS device drivers are essentially Band-Aids, quick-fix add-ons.

DOS drivers load into memory much like terminate-and-stay resident programs, software you load once and may access later by pressing a "hot key." Originally, in fact, the only device drivers *were* TSR programs. Like TSRs, all DOS device drivers sequester themselves in memory. Unlike true TSRs, however, today's DOS device drivers are not complete programs in themselves but small sections of program code that can be called by applications to carry out a specific small task.

In normal programs, execution gets to sections of code by jumping, changing an address in the register of the microprocessor. Because drivers must load into any computer in any order, neither the program nor the driver has any way of knowing the address it will occupy in memory until it actually loads in the system in which it is to be used. Consequently, normal jump instructions don't work. Instead, drivers must rely on different strategies. For example, the mouse drivers commonly use the interrupt vector system. Functions that call the driver know to look at a specific location in memory to find a vector, which acts as a map to show the location to the code added in by the driver.

When the driver loads into memory, it checks its own address, and loads that address into a specific address reserved in the lower part of the PC's memory. Programs needing to access the driver can thus find its location by checking the right place in memory. Several programs may link their code through the same vector, a process called "hooking an interrupt."

Loading

DOS drivers get loaded into memory in two ways. Modern versions of DOS supply a dedicated means of installing drivers through the CONFIG.SYS file. When DOS initially loads itself, it first reads the CONFIG.SYS file to see what it needs to do to set up your system for normal operation. A `DEVICE=` or `DEVICEHIGH=` line in CONFIG.SYS instructs DOS to load a file into memory as a driver.

The difference between the two commands, `DEVICE` and `DEVICEHIGH`, is that the latter will load drivers into high DOS memory if you've loaded a memory manager and a large enough contiguous memory range is available for holding your driver. If both conditions have not been satisfied, DOS loads the driver into the normal DOS program range. When successfully loaded with `DEVICEHIGH`, drivers take up no memory that could be used by your DOS programs. Otherwise, drivers steal memory from your programs.

Drivers can also load themselves like TSR programs from the command line. They can also be loaded through batch files. In fact, they are most often loaded through the special batch file, AUTOEXEC.BAT, which your system executes immediately after it starts up CONFIG.SYS. Many mouse drivers load in this way. You can use the `LOADHIGH` command to tell DOS to load these drivers so that they do not steal away program memory if your system has sufficient space in the High DOS memory area to accommodate them. Some drivers have been designed to automatically load high and do a better job than using the `LOADHIGH` command. Their instructions should warn you when `LOADHIGH` is superfluous.

When programmers create external DOS device drivers, they write them as if they are ordinary programs. In fact, some device drivers load and run like ordinary programs. Most of these take advantage of DOS's device architecture. Although they have different filename extensions—.SYS and .BIN being the most common—they get written as ordinary executable .COM or .EXE files. Even when they have the .COM extension, however, they will not run properly at the command line like other programs because they are designed to take advantage of special installation hooks DOS uses for drivers it finds in CONFIG.SYS.

All recent versions of DOS have built-in abilities to install, manage, and use device drivers, and give programs a standard means of accessing drivers. The drivers themselves work like software interrupts or function calls. DOS provides a special function call, 044(Hex), for servicing drivers. When DOS loads the driver into memory and initializes it, DOS reads the name of the driver from its code and thereafter uses that name to identify the driver. When a program needs a driver to access another program or piece of hardware, it calls function 044(Hex), specifying the driver name and operation it needs to carry out.

Load order. DOS chains all of the drivers together and treats them essentially equally. But order is important. If two device drivers of the kind used for multimedia peripherals (technically speaking, "block devices") use the same name to define a device, the first one loaded by DOS is recognized. DOS ignores the second and later attempts to use a name by device drivers. This strategy helps the writers of device drivers substitute new functions and hardware for features otherwise built into the operating system. DOS defines several devices on its own—for example, the console device through which it receives character codes from the keyboard. Before it sets up these default devices, however, DOS sets up those specified in CONFIG.SYS. A new keyboard driver, for example, would thus get its name recorded first and prevent the default DOS keyboard driver from getting used. This polite arrangement that allows the visitor to go first also assures that you can redefine DOS devices to be anything that you want (with the right driver, of course).

The order in which DOS device drivers load is also important when one driver depends on another driver. The independent driver must be loaded first. For example, if you have a driver that uses high memory, you must load your memory manager device driver first. After all, without loading the memory manager, your system would not be able to access the high memory to let your second driver use it.

Interactions between DOS drivers can be subtle. Two drivers may vie for the same resources, and you may not recognize the conflict although the trouble will be obvious: your system may crash or even fail to boot up. Such problems are likely to develop when you use an older device driver that may not follow the current DOS design recommendations. In many cases, you can resolve such conflicts by changing the order in which you specify the loading of the external device drivers in CONFIG.SYS.

When setting up your system, the best arrangement for device drivers is to put those handling memory first, those working with disk drives next, and those dealing with other devices last. With current versions of DOS, you'll want to load your extended memory manager (HIMEM.SYS) first, followed by the expanded memory manager (EMM386.EXE) should you decide to use it. A few device drivers require loading before memory management software, which should be explained in the instructions that accompany them.

Although you don't have to load your disk drivers next, it's a good idea. One reason is that it enables you to store subsequent drivers on the disk or disks that are brought to life by the driver. This arrangement is sometimes necessary with some SCSI host adapters. Old disk compression software (that predating DOS 6.0) should also be loaded early so you can take advantage of the compressed disk volume to store your subsequent drivers and TSR programs. With current disk compression programs like DOS's DRIVESPACE, your don't have such concerns. DOS now loads these compression utilities even before it starts reading the CONFIG.SYS file.

Automatic driver installation. At one time, you were responsible for adding the device driver entries to your CONFIG.SYS file manually. That is, you had to pull out a text editor, open your CONFIG.SYS file, and type in the proper entries. Today most hardware and software devices that require drivers include automatic installation programs that modify CONFIG.SYS for you. Unfortunately these installation programs vary in quality. The best do a better job than you can by eliminating even the possibility of typographical errors. The worst may bring you new nightmares. They may not remove conflicting drivers (for example, when upgrading disk caching programs) so you get two drivers in your system bent on doing the same thing, overloading your PC with overhead until it comes crashing down—or worse, corrupting your system. Some particularly noxious installation programs don't even remember that you've already used them once and may try to install the same driver over and over again until you have five or six extra entries in CONFIG.SYS. Although duplicate entries shouldn't cause any damage (enlightened driver designs prevent total chaos), it will definitely keep your CONFIG.SYS file from winning any good housekeeping award.

Command-line drivers. Some drivers are meant to load as TSR programs from the command line as ordinary programs, most typically through batch files including your PC's AUTOEXEC.BAT file. Among these are mouse drivers and Microsoft's CD-ROM drive extensions for DOS, MSCDEX.EXE. Loading through AUTOEXEC.BAT provides additional load-order flexibility, which you'll sometimes need. For example, MSCDEX.EXE must be loaded after some network drivers, which also load through AUTOEXEC.BAT, so this configuration enables you to put it after the network drivers. Then again, if your disk cache can handle CD-ROM drives, you'll need to load the cache *after* you load MSCDEX.

Drivers that you install through AUTOEXEC.BAT or through the command line have loader code built into them. They set themselves up, so they don't require or get any extra help from DOS. They run like any other program and install part of their code as TSR routines in memory.

Mandatory Drivers

Any multimedia PC that uses a 16-bit version of Windows (including Windows 3.1 and Windows for Workgroups 3.11) needs to have at least three device drivers installed in CONFIG.SYS. These include two memory managers and a CD-ROM driver.

HIMEM.SYS. As noted previously, the first entry in your CONFIG.SYS file should be the extended memory driver HIMEM.SYS. Because your PC's memory cannot be managed without this driver and you need managed memory to load drivers high, you cannot load HIMEM.SYS high. Windows assures that this driver is present during its installation process, and most DOS installation programs automatically add the entry to your CONFIG.SYS file. If you manually modify CONFIG.SYS file, however, you should insure that this driver gets loaded properly. You normally need no options or switches, so the proper CONFIG.SYS entry is simply as follows:

```
DEVICE=HIMEM.SYS
```

EMM386.EXE. Although not necessary to bring multimedia to life, you'll usually want to install DOS's expanded memory manager EMM386.EXE, too. This driver lets you use some of the extended memory in your PC as expanded memory for the programs that need it. It also enables you to relocate the code and data of other device drivers and TSR programs to high DOS memory, giving you space to run larger programs directly under DOS and when running DOS inside Windows. It does not interfere with the operation of Windows. In fact, recent Windows versions switch the EMM386.EXE off when they load and reclaim the memory it uses. If the DOS programs you run under Windows need expanded memory, Windows synthesizes it for them. Neither Windows nor Windows applications need expanded memory.

The settings you chose for EMM386.EXE will determine how much high DOS memory you can use to relocate drivers. MS DOS's MEMMAKER and PC DOS's RAMBOOST both attempt to create as much space as possible in high DOS. You can also take manual control to resolve conflicts or squeeze out more space.

You can specify to EMM386.EXE which memory ranges to make available for relocating programs and which to avoid. EMM386.EXE uses two options for these indications: I= specifies the "include" option, memory ranges that can be used for relocating other drivers and TSRs; X= specifies an "exclude" range that tells EMM386.EXE to keep its hands off a given range because that range is used for another purpose. For example, the entry

```
DEVICE=EMM386.EXE X=A000-BFFF I=C800-DFFF
```

tells EMM386.EXE to specifically avoid the memory range used by display adapters (A000-BFFF) but to take advantage of the option code range often used by hard disks and other devices (C800-DFFF).

These memory range assignments are typically the most sensitive part of the setup of modern PCs. Specifying the wrong ranges can cause your system not to run at all, dying during the boot process. The most common problem is to include for remapping purposes a memory range used by a peripheral such as an expansion board. To troubleshoot such problems, start by excluding the entire high DOS memory area, then whittle down the exclude range one segment (this is, a 64KB memory range) at a time.

CD-ROM drivers. You'll also want to load the drivers associated with your CD-ROM drive. In most systems running 16-bit Windows, you'll need two or more drivers: those for your SCSI interface (or other interface used by your CD drive) and MSCDEX.EXE, the Microsoft CD-ROM Extensions. (MSCDEX.EXE is discussed fully in Chapter 12, "The Compact Disc.") The SCSI drivers almost always install through CONFIG.SYS while you can install MSCDEX.EXE through either it or your AUTOEXEC.BAT file. This program is a device driver that provides additional routines for using CD-ROM drives.

The SCSI driver you use will depend on the SCSI host adapter you install. For example, Adaptec host adapters use the driver ASPI4DOS.SYS. If you have a SCSI hard disk, you'll also need the hard disk driver (Adaptec's is ASPIDISK.SYS). CD drives using IDE or proprietary interfaces may also use special drivers. For example, the Sound Blaster Pro requires you to load the driver SBPCD.SYS in your CONFIG.SYS file for DOS to properly recognize the CD drive. Although most better SCSI adapters have a built-in BIOS and will run your hard disk without drivers, you should still use the disk drivers. They may have more recent code and more complete functions.

Windows 3.1 Family

If the half-dozen or so drivers you use with DOS seem like about six too many, you need to drastically revise your thinking for Windows. Straight from the box, Windows 3.1 uses dozens of drivers besides those you load through DOS. Windows 95 and OS/2 Warp use even more, layering them on top of one another. The good news is that you almost never need to tangle with the drivers used by advanced operating systems. They get added in automatically during the installation process of the driver or application that requires them. The bad news is that when you have to tangle with them, it's inevitably bad news.

Drivers connect Windows to everything, software and hardware. They link applications, help them share code, and enable them to link to hardware devices.

Background

Depending on how you look at or define things, Windows uses four kinds of drivers. At the most primitive level, it uses standard DOS drivers just like other software. Beyond those, it uses standard mode drivers to link to ports and hardware. Virtual device drivers take advantage of 386 and better microprocessors and exploit 32-bit instructions and extended memory.

DOS Drivers

Even when running Windows, DOS drivers are the same old, familiar programs loaded through CONFIG.SYS as you use with ordinary DOS applications. But DOS device drivers can be a real challenge for Windows because they can run and access data only in real mode memory; that is, the first megabyte of memory in your PC. Windows applications, on the other hand, use protected mode (extended or XMS) memory—all the rest of the stuff in your PC. While that sounds wonderful in that the device drivers and Windows applications won't have any conflicting memory needs, it presents a big problem for Windows. A microprocessor can only run in real mode or protected mode, not both simultaneously. The microprocessor must be in real mode to run the driver and in protected mode to run your Windows applications. (Real and protected mode are covered in Chapter 10, "The Basic PC—Hardware Essentials.")

To work around this memory mismatch, Windows uses a translation buffer located in real mode memory, controlled by the Windows application DOSMGR. To move data between real and protected mode memory, DOSMGR breaks memory requests into 8KB blocks and copies the data from one range to the other. Along the way, it must convert the linear addressing used in protected mode into the segmented memory used in real mode as well as switch back and forth between extended and real modes. Each step of this operation—copying data, translating addresses, and shifting modes—steals microprocessor time and slows down the execution of your applications. In other words, DOS drivers are hardly the ideal performance solution for Windows.

Using DOS drivers with Windows has another disadvantage—it wastes memory. Windows does its multitasking of DOS applications by dividing up the resources of your PC into a number of virtual machines—essentially a simulated computer that has its own address space, I/O ports, interrupt vector table, and device drivers independent all the other virtual machines that may be running. The first virtual machine created by Windows runs all of your Windows applications in protected mode. Any DOS device drivers (or terminate-and-stay resident programs) that are loaded before Windows boots also run in this virtual machine. When Windows creates another virtual machine, for example to run a DOS application, it maps the drivers to that virtual machine as well, subtracting from the resources available. Consequently, every byte you devote to DOS device drivers or TSRs eats away at the address space available to Windows applications (no big deal because they can use nearly all of your expanded memory) but also from every DOS application you run under Windows (a big deal because you have only the real mode memory range and could lose much of it to drivers and other code).

Dynamic Link Libraries

Drivers for Windows are a special case of *Dynamic Link Libraries*, program code made to be shared among Windows applications. A DLL is essentially an extension to Windows code, adding new functions that can be called by individual applications or by several applications in turn. For example, the library COMMDLG.DLL holds program code for the routines used by the Windows interface to build dialog boxes on your screen. All (or nearly so) programs that use dialog boxes call the same routines from COMMDLG.DLL. As a result, all dialog boxes in different programs have the same look and operation. Programmers benefit because they can use the same calls for all applications. They don't have to write (and rewrite) the routines themselves. Moreover, the use of DLLs makes Windows more flexible and easier to update. For example, should Microsoft want to alter the look of all your Windows applications, it only needs to change the code associated with the dialog box functions in COMMDLG.DLL. Substitute a new COMMDLG.DLL for the one accompanying Windows, and the changes would take effect identically for all Windows applications.

As you may have noted, most DLLs can be identified by their filename extension, .DLL. But DLLs may wear other extensions as well. Some that are used as drivers use .DRV. Some core Windows 3.1 libraries are written as .EXE files, including GDI.EXE, KRNL286.EXE, KRNL386.EXE, and USER.EXE.

DLLs promote economy and flexibility. Windows itself doesn't have to be built to cover all situations. Whenever it needs to be extended to a particular situation, a DLL can fill in the gaps. As the needs of hardware or software change, only the DLLs need to be altered. The core of Windows stays the same. Both debugging and upgrading become modular and are thus easy to manage. Several of the common drivers used by Windows 3.1 are written as DLLs. Some of these include MOUSE.DRV, KEYBOARD.DRV, COMM.DRV, and TIMER.DRV.

Although a blessing for you and programmers, DLLs can be problematic. DLLs are like coat hangers in a forgotten closet, mysteriously multiplying when you're not looking. DLLs are not a problem for memory management under Windows because Windows knows enough to load a DLL only once no matter how many applications need to use it (that's one of the advantages of using DLLs). Unfortunately, neither Windows nor its applications are as smart when it comes to managing DLLs on disk. While just about every Windows program you install adds one or more DLLs to your system, few programs actively delete unnecessary DLLs. Updates also bring the potential for many different versions of a DLL sitting in your directories. Ill-conceived installation programs may salt your PC's entire directory structure with obscure .DLL files that you erase only at your peril. Zap the wrong file, and your Windows applications may never again run. (At least until you resurrect the vital link.) Even worse, you could install a new program and it could overwrite a DLL with a new version. Programs that depend on the old version of the DLL could stop running.

You can check the DLLs that are present in your system and those that are active in memory using the *System Information* program that Windows 95 installs by default in the \WINDOWS\MSAPPS\MSINFO directory as the program MSINFO.EXE. Once you've loaded the program, select the option System DLL's from the Choose a Category box, and after searching through memory and your hard disk, Windows 95 will list *all* the DLLs it finds, the version number, date, size, and whether the DLL is active, as shown in Figure 8.1.

Even in simple installations the list is long, so you'll probably want to print it out rather than page through it on the screen.

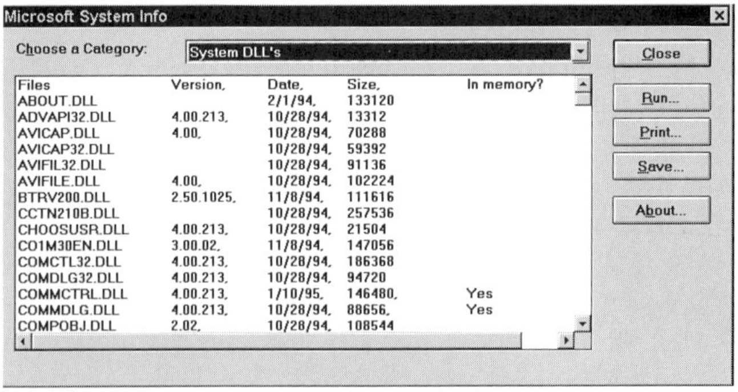

FIGURE 8.1. MSINFO.EXE showing DLLs available on disk.

Standard Drivers

Just as you'll find a wealth of drivers built into your PC's BIOS, you'll find many built into the core of Windows. These drivers are essentially invisible, loaded as part of Windows itself and residing inside basic Windows program modules. These integral drivers are essential to Windows' operation and never changed. As with the BIOS-based drivers, they are usually not considered in general discussions of Windows drivers.

The external Windows drivers share the strengths and weaknesses of DLL technology because they are a particular implementation of it. They build upon the core of Windows to extend its reach and abilities, both into hardware and software. And, although Windows offers some help, they can be a headache to manage.

Standard and virtual device drivers load when you start Windows or an affiliated application. You instruct Windows which drivers to load by listing their names in one of the various .INI files.

Standard mode drivers are peppered throughout your SYSTEM.INI file under Windows 3.1. They are generally distinguished by their filename extension, .DRV, although you'll find exceptions. Drivers with names with an asterisk (*) are built into Windows and don't need a separate file at all.

Virtual Device Drivers

Windows 3.0 added a new kind of driver to its repertory, the virtual device driver. They are often called *VxD drivers*. In fact, when discussing virtual device drivers, VxD is the general term, and more specific acronyms refer to individual driver types.

For example, a virtual device driver that interfaces with a display device is termed a VDD for *Virtual Display Driver*; one for a printer is a VPD for *Virtual Printer Driver*; one for a timer is a VTD for *Virtual Timer Driver*. The names of actual drivers take the form VxD where up to six alphanumeric characters replace the "x" to give the driver a unique identity, and the filename extension .386. Note, however, that this VxD naming convention applies only to virtual device drivers that Microsoft ships with the Windows package, however. Microsoft recommends aftermarket suppliers use some other form for their virtual device driver names, however. Typically these drivers will combine characters from the manufacturer or product name, followed by the extension .386.

As with other drivers, VxDs can link hardware and software to the Windows system. VxDs differ in being written for 32-bit, protected-mode operation and are designed so that multiple applications can use a given resource at the same time. A VxD is charged with complete resource management responsibilities. The VxD must track the operation of the device it controls as different tasks take control to prevent interactions from disrupting the operation of the device and your system. Consequently, any hardware device that can be shared between tasks requires a

VxD. VxDs can also manage software and, used judiciously, can improve the performance, particularly of shared applications.

Although virtual device drivers are 32-bit, flat-model DLLs (that is, they don't use memory segments as do old DOS programs), they are formatted differently from ordinary Windows DLLs. They cannot be loaded by applications but run as overall Windows system resources, managed by Windows itself. One virtual device driver serves all applications running under Windows and gives each the illusion it's the only application using the device controlled by the driver.

When Windows loads a virtual device driver for a function handled by a DOS or BIOS device driver, the virtual device driver takes command, substituting its 32-bit instructions for the 8- or 16-bit instructions of the older code. As a result, virtual device drivers can dramatically improve the performance of the tasks they handle, an enhancement particularly welcome for everyday functions such as hard disk access (for example, Windows for Workgroups' VFAT.386, which empowers 32-bit file access) and serial communications.

Virtual device drivers are listed primarily in the [386Enh] section of your PC's SYSTEM.INI in the \WINDOWS directory.

Under Windows 3.1, virtual device drivers are loaded statically. That is, they get loaded once and stay in memory whether they are used or not. This simple approach is exactly the same as with DOS and suffers the same disadvantages. A profusion of drivers can cause conflicts if you become careless. Worse, each driver steals the memory that it needs and doesn't release it until you exit Windows. Although device driver memory demands are not ordinarily onerous, you may notice the effects should you try to squeak by with your PC equipped with as little RAM as possible (or affordable) and you have a long list of drivers to handle the needs of a multimedia authoring system.

Media Control Interface

In multimedia PCs, the drivers used by the *Media Control Interface* are particularly important. The Media Control Interface is a software standard developed by Microsoft as its preferred method of linking applications to multimedia hardware. It's used not only by Windows 3.1 but also by many DOS-based multimedia systems and Windows 95 as well.

The MCI is designed to manage the recording and playback of multimedia files through hardware peripherals such as audio boards, CD-ROM drives, audio CD players, MIDI sequencers, video disc players, and videotape recorders and players. It is implemented as a meta-driver that translates a common set of program commands (for example, to start playback from the CD player) into more specific instructions for the device driver associated with particular hardware. Not all Windows multimedia functions and applications use the MCI. For example, the *Sound Recorder* relies on lower-level commands to do its work. Because Microsoft has standardized the MCI and built it into its latest products, however, using it assures current and future compatibility between applications and hardware.

MCI drivers interpret and direct the MCI commands. Although your operating system software may take care of some of the basic data-management tasks involved in multimedia, all the multimedia playback, presentation, and recording get routed through the various individual MCI drivers.

The MCI mechanism requires several steps to command a given multimedia device. First you must "open" the device to get its attention. Next you send the commands to the device to tell it what to do. Finally, you close the device. MCI commands are the language you use for telling the devices what to do.

A single set of core commands is shared by all MCI devices for the most common functions, for example, play and stop. Devices are also grouped as to MCI *device type,* which share a common command set for features shared by that class of devices. However, the MCI architecture enables manufacturers to customize the command range of the drivers they write. For example, while the record command is normally available to MIDI sequencers, the Microsoft MCISEQ.DRV driver does not understand this command. Currently Microsoft has defined 11 (including a catchall "undefined" classification) of these MCI device types. These types are listed in Table 8.1.

TABLE 8.1. MCI device types.

Device type	*Description*	*Constant*
Animation	Animation device	`MCI_DEVTYPE_ANIMATION`
CD audio	Audio CD player	`MCI_DEVTYPE_CD_AUDIO`
DAT	Digital audio tape player	`MCI_DEVTYPE_DAT`
Digital video	Digital video in a window	`MCI_DEVTYPE_DIGITAL_VIDEO`
Other	Undefined device	`MCI_DEVTYPE_OTHER`
Overlay	Video overlay device	`MCI_DEVTYPE_OVERLAY`
Scanner	Image scanner	`MCI_DEVTYPE_SCANNER`
Sequencer	MIDI sequencer	`MCI_DEVTYPE_SEQUENCER`
VCR	Videocassette recorder	`MCI_DEVTYPE_VCR`
Video disc	Video disc player	`MCI_DEVTYPE_VIDEODISC`
Wave audio	Audio waveform player	`MCI_DEVTYPE_WAVEFORM_AUDIO`

Although all device types understand the same commands, they may carry them out differently. For example, any digital video device understands commands to stop, start, and rewind movies. However, one digital video device may play Video for Windows .AVI files while another plays QuickTime for Windows .MOV files. To distinguish between different devices of a given type, the Media Control Interface uses *device names.* Standard Windows device names appear in Table 8.1 in the Constant column as the characters following the `MCI_DEVTYPE_` characters. (The full Constant entry is used in MCI programming.)

More complex systems may have more than one driver that needs to use a given device name. When an MCI driver needs to be installed using a device name that already exists in SYSTEM.INI or the Registry, during the installation process the operating system adds an integer to the device name that is assigned to each driver of that name that is subsequently added. For example, in a system that already has a `digital_video` driver installed for .AVI files, the second driver for .MOV files would get named `digital_video1`.

The various MCI devices are assigned their names in different ways depending upon the operating system. Within the Windows 3.1 family, the names are given in the `[mci]` section of the SYSTEM.INI file. The Registry stores the names used under Windows 95.

The Windows 3.1 family uses the information in SYSTEM.INI to identify all MCI drivers that are available to it. It makes its identity assignment by assigning a device name to each driver that it uses. The entries in the `[mci]` section that make this assignment take the following form:

```
device_name = driver_filename.extension
```

For example, the following listing shows a typical `[mci]` section from SYSTEM.INI in a basic multimedia system:

```
[mci]
CDAudio=mcicda.drv
Sequencer=mciseq.drv
WaveAudio=mciwave.drv
AVIVideo=mciavi.drv
```

Three MCI drivers accompany Windows 3.1 and, when installed, are listed in the `[mci]` section of your SYSTEM.INI file. These enable your PC to play back CD audio, .WAV files, and run your sequencer. In addition, you'll likely install other MCI drivers for video playback under Video for Windows or QuickTime for Windows. Table 8.2 lists these common MCI functions and their associated drivers.

TABLE 8.2. Common MCI drivers.

Function	Name	Driver
Compact Disc audio playback	CDAudio	MCICDA.DRV
MIDI sequencer control	Sequencer	MCISEQ.DRV
Wave file playback	WaveAudio	MCIWAVE.DRV
Video for Windows playback	AVIVideo	MCIAVI.DRV
QuickTime for Windows playback	QTWVideo	MCIQTW.DRV

Windows 95 also installs a videodisc driver (MCIPIONR.DRV) and a videocassette recorder driver (MCIVISCA.DRV) as its defaults.

Installation

As with DOS driver software, merely copying a Windows driver to your hard disk is not sufficient to do anything other than take up disk space. You have to specifically empower your Windows drivers by instructing Windows to load them.

Because drivers are an essential extension to the core of Windows' code, they must be integrated with Windows as the operating system loads itself. Consequently, any additions or alterations you make to your Windows drivers only take effect the next time you start Windows after making the change, even though you make the change from inside Windows.

You have your choice of three methods of changing your Windows 3.1 drivers, two of which must be internal to Windows, one of which can be. Programs may automatically add drivers to your SYSTEM.INI file when you install them. You can specifically add or remove drivers using the Windows Control Panel. Or you can manually edit your SYSTEM.INI file using an ASCII editor, either from within Windows or from DOS.

Automatic installation. Autopilot is always the easiest way of getting there, at least if you don't mind flying into a hillside now and then. Most Windows applications and Windows-oriented peripherals now include their own installation disks. Start the installation program and you can be mesmerized by the whirring of your floppy or CD-ROM drive as files are copied and software written by some unknown hacker who tinkers away at the most vital and vulnerable of your Windows files. While actual malevolent intent is rare in commercial software, even the best intentions oft go awry.

Installation programs carry out several functions. They copy an array of files from the distribution disks to your PC's hard disk, often decompressing and renaming them along the way. To help you maintain order in the ever-increasing chaos of your hard disk directory tree, they may create their own tree branches. They check (you hope) your various .INI files and entries as necessary, one part of which is the adding of the names of required drivers and other DLLs. The installation program may probe even deeper and explore your PC's CONFIG.SYS and AUTOEXEC.BAT files to assure they are compatible with whatever is getting installed. Some installation routines may even add drivers at the DOS level. Many installation programs carefully intertwine your name and that of your company with program code as kind of a treasure map that leads to software pirates. Some installation programs routinely paste a huge new program group across the desktop that took you months to pare down to its essence. And an increasing number of installation programs automatically call in to their maker to register themselves, sometimes sending home a profile of your PC just in case Big Brother is interested.

In this blizzard of activity, it's easy for something to get lost. On rare occasions, an installation program may miss its marks and botch planting the name of a driver where it belongs. More likely, the poorly thought-out installation routines may not adequately survey the lay of the land. It might not ferret out old drivers that need to be replaced or even duplicate listings of the drivers it wants to install. At best, such programs may leave clutter in your .INI files. At worst, your prized new peripheral or program won't work as advertised and you'll broaden your list of friends and acquaintances to include the harried technician at the end of the support line.

There. Now with all the paranoia out of the way, you can appreciate the state of Windows installation software. In the vast majority of cases, the installation software will take care of all the details of drivers and leave you with the choices that only you can make: the aesthetics of arranging your Windows and icons.

The mechanics of automated installation are simple because that's what they were designed to be:

1. Slide the distribution disk into your floppy drive or your CD-ROM player.

2. Pull down the File menu and select Run (or type Alt+F, R). Your specific product may tell you exactly what file name to type in on the command line or your can select Browse from the menu (press Tab three times if you prefer to keep your hands on the keys) and then look for the installation program—it will typically be named SETUP or INSTALL—on the distribution disk. Usually (but hardly always), SETUP is for Windows installations and INSTALL is for setting up under DOS.

3. Click to add it to the command line, run it, and sit back for the least exciting entertainment this side of the CBS fall schedule.

The only difficulty you're likely to encounter with automated installation is that it doesn't go far enough. The software will assume that you've already gotten your system set up exactly as you want it. It won't push limits. Although a product may be able to take advantage of voice synthesis with the sound board that you have, its installation program won't enable your sound board's speech driver. It will leave that opportunity to your sound board's installation, and you may not think of reinstalling a sound board simply because you've changed spreadsheets.

Automatic installation certainly is the easiest way to get things running. But it's not without its worries, and it has its limitations. That's where the other two installation processes come in.

Control Panel. One of the functions of Windows' Control Panel is to give you an easy way to edit your PC's SYSTEM.INI file. You choose what you want from menus, then Control Panel handles the actual editing of the file.

The menu selection process does more than simplify matters, however. It also guards against stupid typing mistakes. It gets the file names right the first time. It also adds a bit more sense to what you're doing. Instead of staring at an opaque name like VGBRSHD.386, you can choose from a list of descriptive names.

Adding or altering drivers through Control Panel conforms to the standard Windows procedure:

1. Select Control Panel, then Drivers. You'll see a display like the one shown in Figure 8.2 that lists available drivers to choose from.

2. If the driver you want to install is one of those that comes with Windows or has been copied to your hard disk by an automatic installation program (or even you in a moment of mastery), select with the highlight bar and then click Add, as shown in Figure 8.2.

FIGURE 8.2. Choosing a listed driver.

3. If the driver you want to add hasn't yet been copied to your disk, the Control Panel will take care of that for you.

4. Select the option for Unlisted or Updated Drivers at the top of the list, then click Add. (See Figure 8.3.)

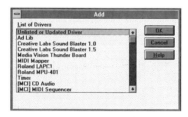

FIGURE 8.3. Adding an unlisted driver.

5. Windows will then prompt you to put a disk holding the driver in drive A: if you're not in an argumentive mood, slide the driver floppy that came with the product that you want to install into your A: drive. You can also tell Windows to look elsewhere for drivers by replacing the A:\ in the prompt with another drive letter or directory.

6. When you're satisfied that you've entered the proper place for Windows to look, click OK. (See Figure 8.4.)

FIGURE 8.4. Specifying the location of an unlisted driver.

Windows will then scan the appointed disk or directory for drivers. Specifically, it looks for a file called OEMSETUP.INF, which supplies it with setup information about the drivers on the disk. If it finds all the files associated with a Windows driver, the screen will change to one resembling the initial driver selection screen but with only the drivers in the new location listed. Select the driver you want, click Add, and Control Panel will do the rest.

But Control Panel isn't as smart as it seems. It will happily install multiple copies of the same driver. And if you don't have an OEMSETUP.INF file or all the rest of the files associated with a driver, it won't even recognize that you have a driver to install even if the driver is alive and well and waiting to be copied. In other words, when all goes well Control Panel keeps things flowing. When you have a knotty situation, however, you can count on Control Panel getting twisted up.

Manual file editing. If you do things yourself, you have complete command. You can do what you like. And you have no one to blame when something goes wrong. So it is when adding drivers manually. You trade complete control for zero tolerance of errors. A single typing mistake can mean your driver won't load when it's called for; it may even mean that Windows won't load. On the other hand, if you take precautions, none of the errors that you can make are fatal. You can try again and again. And again.

The other problem with manual file editing is that you have to know *where* to put the entry associated with loading a driver and the proper syntax for its entry. Most drivers are installed through Windows' SYSTEM.INI file. Although SYSTEM.INI has a special [drivers] section, driver entries are actually spread throughout the file. If you want to replace an existing driver with a new one, you can just find the old driver name and put the new driver name in its place. Otherwise you'll need to check the documentation accompanying the driver to determine how to enter it into the appropriate file.

Manual editing works for the same reason it works for DOS. Windows' configuration files are nothing more than formatted ASCII text. Any ASCII editor—any program or text editor that avoids adding odd control codes to what you type—can modify Windows' files. Manual editing enables you to get a device working as long as you have the driver even if you've lost the original disk and its OEMSETUP.INF file.

Windows 95

In developing Windows 95, Microsoft's engineers rethought the role of drivers. One change that brings improved support of hardware devices was the adoption of a universal driver/mini-driver architecture. Under Windows 3.1, the manufacturers of all but a few devices were required to develop their own drivers to match the operating system. Each driver was an entity to itself incorporating all the functions needed for a particular device. As a result, developing drivers was akin to blending your own paint when you wanted to redecorate a room—a lot of time wasted on preparatory efforts that could be better handled by something ready-made.

The Windows 95 approach builds on a set of universal drivers that handle an entire family of devices, for example all modems that use standard AT commands. The universal driver links the hardware to the appropriate parts of Windows 95 and in most cases is the only driver you need to take care of your PC's hardware. As part of the Windows 95 package, Microsoft provides universal drivers for most types of hardware, including display adapters, modems, and printers. Hardware vendors can write specific mini-drivers for their devices which do not run with Microsoft's universal drivers.

Windows 95 uses virtual device drivers much as did previous Windows versions. Unlike previous versions, however, Windows 95 loads virtual device drivers dynamically. Only those that are actually needed take up RAM.

You can identify many of the Windows 95 virtual device drivers by their filename extension, .VXD. Some third-party protected-mode drivers for Windows 95 retain the extension .386. A few special extensions are reserved for specific Windows 95 driver types. The extension .PDR indicates a port driver such as those used by some SCSI and ESDI hard disk systems. *Miniport drivers* use the extension .MPD.

Windows 95 accommodates all the various sorts of drivers used by DOS and earlier Windows versions. Because its 32-bit protected mode drivers offer a distinct performance advantage, however, you should prefer them over the holdovers from the past. In most cases, Windows 95 will attempt to use 32-bit protected mode drivers instead of 16-bit real mode drivers. If a protected mode driver is available, Windows will unload the corresponding real mode driver and replace it.

Not all real mode drivers are replaceable. Windows 95 doesn't guess which ones it can safely replace. Rather, it depends on outside instruction in the form of a safe driver list. A file called IOS.INI in your Windows directory lists all the drivers that can be safely replaced by Windows 95 protected mode drivers as well as those explicitly declared to be unsafe to replace.

For a driver to be safely replaced, the corresponding Windows 95 protected mode driver must supply exactly the same functions. Because several advanced disk functions are not built into Windows 95, drivers that use such functions cannot be safely replaced. These functions include data compression except for that provided by DOS, disk mirroring, and data encryption.

Windows 95 only looks at the file name in the safe driver list to determine whether a driver can be safely replaced. If you add a new real-mode driver to your system with the same name as one on the list, Windows 95 will assume it is safe even if it is not—and may unload it with disastrous results. You can alter the safe driver list by editing the IOS.INI file with a text editor.

When Windows 95 starts, it diligently checks your CONFIG.SYS file and loads the drivers it finds there exactly as DOS does. When you start a 16-bit Windows application, Windows 95 also loads the drivers and libraries associated with that application listed in your SYSTEM.INI file, as well as whatever may be specified in the .INI file dedicated to that application. But Windows 95 relies on its own Registry for overall system drivers, and Windows 95 applications do likewise.

Windows 95 has the least control over the drivers you load in CONFIG.SYS. In effect, these are force-fed to Windows 95, which must accept them and load them in real mode memory. As with any version of DOS, the memory given over to these drivers steals from that available for your DOS applications. Pile too many drivers in CONFIG.SYS and you may have too little memory left to run DOS programs, even under Windows 95. In addition, there's a second penalty for loading drivers from CONFIG.SYS under Windows 95. Ordinary DOS remains a 16-bit operating system running in real mode, and its drivers match. Not only does their 16-bit nature slow them down compared to Windows 95's 32-bit drivers, but because they run in real mode, Windows must switch back and forth between real mode (to run the drivers) and protected mode (to runs its own code and application). The overhead involved in the switchover also steals time from your microprocessor and slows down your system. That's why Windows 95 loads its protected-mode drivers whenever it can.

Operation. Microsoft calls its approach to handling input and output devices such as removable and nonremovable hard disks, floppy and floptical disk drives under Windows 95 *layered block device drivers.* The name reflects the design. The device drivers move information as *blocks* instead of individual characters; they are layered under the universal/mini-driver architecture. Under Windows 95, these layered block device drivers use 32-bit code and run under protected mode. Windows 95 loads each of these device drivers individually and dynamically. Only those drivers actually needed are put into memory.

In the Windows 95 scheme, a single virtual device driver called the *I/O Supervisor* manages all of the operating system's layered block device drivers and the protected-mode file system. The I/O Supervisor loads the drivers into memory as they are needed, initializes them to operate properly, and takes care of all of their input and output needs. It registers drivers, manages input and output requests, routing them to the proper destinations and scheduling their execution, and notifies drivers when the system needs their attention. It also doles out whatever memory the drivers need to operate.

The I/O Supervisor lodges itself between the file system and the type-specific device driver that handles the block-accessed hardware. The I/O Supervisor also links to real-mode drivers when a device requires them, for example, when no protected mode driver is available for a specific product. The file system—either the VFAT or CDFS—sends drive access requests to the I/O Supervisor. If the driver needed to access a given device has not been loaded, the I/O Supervisor loads the appropriate driver. In loading layered block device drivers, it works through the layers from the operating system to the hardware, loading the hardware-specific driver (or *type-specific driver,* in Microsoft jargon) last. Once the I/O Supervisor has loaded the drivers it needs, it then passes the request through the layers down to the type-specific driver. The type-specific driver then checks the request to be sure that it is valid for the specific device, converts the block addresses used by Windows to the physical addresses used by the device, sends the request to the device, and signals the I/O Supervisor when it completes the action. The type-specific drive can also take care of simple errors (such as a single disk read error) when they occur.

The I/O Supervisor itself gets loaded by Windows 95 through a `device=` entry in the SYSTEM.INI file. Because it must register devices and carry out their requests, it is one of the first drivers that Windows 95 initializes in its boot-up process.

The Windows 95 I/O Supervisor requires that the drivers its uses be located solely in one place, the subdirectory \WINDOWS\SYSTEM\IOSUBSYS.

Installation

Windows 95 makes no provision for separately installing drivers and making the appropriate entries into CONFIG.SYS, SYSTEM.INI or the Registry. Instead, driver installation is an integrated part of Window's hardware installation and configuration system. As Windows 95 runs through its automatic Plug-and-Play setup, it matches the drivers it has on file with those required by the hardware. Hardware vendors can take advantage of the automated Windows 95 driver installation system or devise their own installation programs.

When you install new hardware, Windows 95 gives you the opportunity to choose from its integral drivers or those accompanying the hardware. The process is part of the hardware installation wizard you'll find in the Control Panel as the icon labeled "Add New Hardware."

Once you've double-clicked the icon to start the hardware wizard, you'll see an initial screen, as shown in Figure 8.5.

FIGURE 8.5. The initial screen of the Windows 95 hardware wizard.

Although the default choice, automatically detecting installed hardware, looks easiest, it's also time-consuming and unnecessary. Most of the time you should select Install Specific Hardware, then click next. Windows will then list for you all of the hardware it knows about of the type you've chosen. It has either a built-in driver or a previously installed driver for everything it lists. If you want to install a new driver from disk, click the Have Disk button, as shown in Figure 8.6.

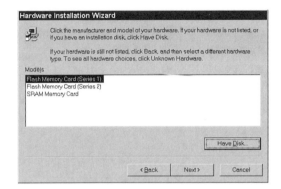

FIGURE 8.6. Installing a disk-based driver using the Windows 95 hardware wizard.

Another window will pop on the screen and ask for the location of the installation disk with the driver on it, just as it always has, as shown in Figure 8.7. You only need to indicate where to find the files, either by directly typing in the disk and directory or browsing through your system for it.

Windows takes it from there, diligently copying the files that it needs and making the appropriate entries where they are needed.

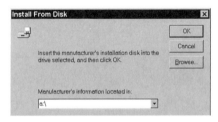

FIGURE 8.7. Specifying the location of disk-based driver files.

OS/2

Exactly as you'd expect from an operating system that combines the features of DOS and Windows with its own magic, OS/2 uses device drivers like DOS and Windows combined—with a few twists of its own. In fact, at times OS/2 seems little more than glue that holds an incomprehensible set of drivers together. OS/2 uses both its own drivers and those from DOS, the latter only when running DOS applications. As with DOS, OS/2 has its own version of a CONFIG.SYS, down to the very same moniker. It also uses .INI files much like those of Windows. But where Windows enables you to use protected mode driver software, everything (except the old DOS drivers) in OS/2 runs in protected mode with 32-bit code. There's no confusion of driver types, no 16-bit slowdown, no multiple modes to deal with—until you run a Windows application.

Memory Use

The big advance you make when moving from DOS to Warp is freedom from worries about the memory your drivers require. Because OS/2 has the full memory of your PC as well as virtual memory on disk for your OS/2 applications to work with, adding OS/2 drivers usually has a negligible effect on the amount of memory available for them. DOS applications are another matter. Because OS/2 must simulate a real-mode PC to run your DOS programs, it has to bring all the limitations of DOS along, too, including the old 640KB addressing constraint. All the DOS drivers that you load steal memory from the 640KB available to your DOS programs, resulting in exactly the same RAM-cram you faced with irritable old DOS. Even though OS/2 creates a separate virtual machine for each individual DOS application you run, it still loads all the DOS device drivers that you specify in CONFIG.SYS into each of these virtual machines.

To avoid these problems, OS/2 gives you two options for loading DOS device drivers. Those drivers specified in CONFIG.SYS get automatically loaded into each and every DOS virtual machine. In addition, you can specify DOS drivers that will be loaded only into the one virtual machine associated with a specific application. These individualized drivers have no effect on other DOS sessions. You assign DOS device drivers to specific applications by adjusting the `DOS_DEVICE` setting under DOS Settings.

To get the most from your OS/2 system and its applications, you'll want to be judicious about the DOS device drivers you load through CONFIG.SYS. Automatic installation programs for DOS applications will confound your management efforts, however. Most of these won't know or expect that you're using OS/2 and will gleefully stuff your OS/2 CONFIG.SYS file with all their drivers. You'll want to clean up after these installation programs perform their magic and put the calls to specific drivers where you really want them.

Installation

In the quest to make OS/2 easier to handle, IBM automated most of the driver installation process. If the features of your system are drawn from the lengthy list of those that OS/2 supports, you might not ever need to know that layer upon layer of driver is passing code around. For example, your mouse may need up to five separate drivers to bring it to life. During installation, OS/2 hunts through your system to determine the equipment and applications that you have, matches the appropriate drivers, and installs only what you need, quietly, invisibly, inevitably.

This automatic process does you no good when you make a change to your system. But OS/2 Warp takes care of you there, too. It supplies you with menu-controlled means of installing and changing drivers in your system. Unfortunately, instead of a single, integrated system of driver control, it has several, including separate utilities for installing drivers, maintaining normal system drivers, and handling multimedia drivers.

The device driver installation utility, which you'll find inside your OS/2 System folder, is essentially aimed at hiding the command prompt and COPY command from people with an innate fear of computers. Run the utility, and it searches out drivers on the disk or directory you specify and installs them on your PC. The interface is obvious, as shown in Figure 8.8, and most of the time requires only that you slide the driver disk that accompanies your hardware in drive A: and click the Install button.

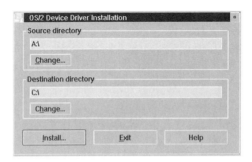

FIGURE 8.8. The OS/2 Warp installation utility.

To configure the drivers after they have been installed, including those supplied as standard equipment with OS/2 Warp, choose System Setup from your OS/2 System folder. The installation software accompanying some vendor-supplied hardware may automatically launch this utility and drop you into the middle of it. After the utility loads, you'll see a display listing the essential hardware in your PC, as shown in Figure 8.9.

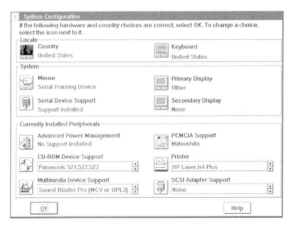

FIGURE 8.9. OS/2 Warp hardware, which lists selecting device driver installation.

Clicking the icon representing the hardware and device driver you want to configure will show you the available options, if any, and let you choose between them. For example, you may select the interrupt and memory addresses that you've configured with jumpers on your sound board. Once you've selected the appropriate values, click OK, and Warp will automatically make the necessary entries in CONFIG.SYS.

Unlike Windows 95, OS/2 Warp does *not* automatically check for and resolve conflicts between devices and device driver options. It will happily set half a dozen hunks of hardware to fight over the same interrupt. It will sometimes also add illegal switches and options to some device drivers. Most of the time Warp or the device driver will complain about conflicts or improper settings. Sometimes, however, your system will crash on take-off, and you'll have to boot from a clean floppy to do your troubleshooting.

The only way to resolve these problems is manually. You may need to adjust hardware settings, reconfigure the driver entries using the System Configuration utility, or manually change CONFIG.SYS entries using an ASCII editor.

Chapter 9

Data Storage

Storage always seems to get the short shrift. Marco Polo gained renown as a traveler and merchant, transporting goods from Occident to Orient, but never mentioned are the staunch warehousemen from whose larders came the goods that made his fortune. Generals get medals but the Supply Corps only gets fat and forgotten. Application software brings the excitement to your multimedia PC but digital storage makes it all possible. Where would your programs be if they had nowhere to put their bytes of data and code? Without a storage system, you'd be stuck keying in every program anew every time you wanted to run it—not a trivial task in these days of programs with encyclopedia-size source code.

The modern PC gives you a number of places to store information: hard and floppy disks, tapes in various guises, and memory cards. More important than the location of the information is its format. Remember, all bits are the same. Their meaning comes from the patterns in which they are arranged. The structure of data files provides the pattern that makes the bits they contain meaningful.

Text

The easiest form of data storage to get a handle on is that for text. Text comes closest to what we humans are used to seeing—the letters and words that represent our languages. Moreover, text and thus text files have a simple linear structure. Just as one letter simply follows another in a word and one word follows another in a sentence, one byte comes after another in the text file. The resemblance goes deeper. Each byte stores a single character, typically a letter or number although a few special characters format the text following simple grammatical rules. To mark sentences, text files follow the human convention using periods and initial capital letters. Indentations or extra lines mark paragraphs, represented electronically, of course. Grammar supplies a well-defined set of rules that governs the overall structure of the textual data.

Missing, however, is the code key. Over thousands of years, humankind developed a system of symbolic representation for spoken sounds, which eventually became the letters of the alphabets. Through convenience and necessity, the alphabet became standardized, in Western culture dominated by the variations, Cyrillic and Roman.

While these alphabets work well for physical representations of letters and words, they fail in the realm of electronics. Oddly, ancient scribes never thought of applying digital techniques to their fledgling alphabets. Only in modern times have people sought to standardize a correspondence between digital bit patterns and alphabetic characters. When electronic calculators first appeared, the code was obvious: simply to use the binary value to indicate the corresponding numeral. In that there are 10 numerals, a 4-bit code with 16 possibilities suffices. The resultant code was called *Binary Coded Decimal* or BCD and is still used in some data systems. Table 9.1 lists the simple BCD code.

TABLE 9.1. Binary Coded Decimal.

Binary code	Numeral
0000	0
0001	1
0010	2
0011	3
0100	4
0101	5
0110	6
0111	7
1000	8
1001	9

Useful as it is, BCD doesn't go far enough. It encodes only numbers. Adding letters and control information requires something more.

EBCDIC

When IBM developed its 360-series of mainframe computers, it developed its own 8-bit data code to encompass the alphabet. Building on the BCD, IBM extended the code by adding four more bits and created what it called the *Extended Binary Coded Decimal Interchange Code* or EBCDIC. Characters were not assigned to all of the potential code values, leaving many of them undefined. Although this code is still used by many larger computer systems, few PC applications understand it. With any luck, you should never encounter EBCDIC files when working with multimedia. For the sake of completeness, however, Table 9.2 lists EBCDIC codes.

TABLE 9.2. The Extended Binary Coded Decimal Interchange Code.

Decimal	Hex	Mnemonic	Function
0	0	NUL	Null
1	1	SOH	Start of heading (indicator)
2	2	STX	Start of text (indicator)
3	3	ETX	End of text (indicator)
4	4	PF	Punch off
5	5	HT	Horizontal tab
6	6	LC	Lower case
7	7	DEL	Delete
8	8		
9	9		
10	A	SMM	Start of Manual Message
11	B	VT	Vertical tab
12	C	FF	Form feed
13	D	CR	Carriage return
14	E	SO	Shift out
15	F	SI	Shift in
16	10	DLE	Data link escape
17	11	DC1	Device control 1
18	12	DC2	Device control 2
19	13	TM	Tape mark
20	14	RES	Restore
21	15	NL	New line
22	16	BS	Backspace
23	17	IL	Idle
24	18	CAN	Cancel
25	19	EM	End of medium
26	1A	CC	Cursor control
27	1B	CU1	Customer use 1
28	1C	IFS	Interchange file separator
29	1D	IGS	Interchange group separator

continues

TABLE 9.2. continued

Decimal	Hex	Mnemonic	Function
30	1E	IRS	Interchange record separator
31	1F	IUS	Interchange unit separator
32	20	DS	Digit select
33	21	SOS	Start of significance
34	22	FS	Field separator
35	23		
36	24	BYP	Bypass
37	25	LF	Line feed
38	26	ETB	End of transmission block
39	27	ESC	Escape
40	28		
41	29		
42	2A	SM	Set mode
43	2B	CU2	Customer use 2
44	2C		
45	2D	ENQ	Enquiry
46	2E	ACK	Acknowledge
47	2F	BEL	Bell
48	30		
49	31		
50	32	SYN	Synchronous idle
51	33		
52	34	PN	Punch on
53	35	RS	Reader stop
54	36	UC	Upper case
55	37	EOT	End of transmission
56	38		
57	39		
58	3A		
59	3B	CU3	Customer use 3
60	3C	DC4	Device control 4

Decimal	Hex	Mnemonic	Function
61	3D	NAK	Negative acknowledge
62	3E		
63	3F	SUB	Substitute
64	40	SP	Space
65	41		
66	42		
67	43		
68	44		
69	45		
70	46		
71	47		
72	48		
73	49		
74	4A		Cent sign
75	4B		
76	4C	<	Less than sign
77	4D	(	Open parenthesis
78	4E	+	Plus sign
79	4F			Logical OR
80	50	&	Ampersand
81	51		
82	52		
83	53		
84	54		
85	55		
86	56		
87	57		
88	58		
89	59		
90	5A	!	Exclamation mark
91	5B	$	Dollar sign
92	5C	.	Period

continues

TABLE 9.2. continued

Decimal	Hex	Mnemonic	Function
93	5D	)	Close parenthesis
94	5E	;	Semi-colon
95	5F		
96	60	-	Minus sign, hyphen
97	61	/	Slash
98	62		
99	63		
100	64		
101	65		
102	66		
103	67		
104	68		
105	69		
106	6A		
107	6B	,	Comma
108	6C	%	Percent sign
109	6D	_	Underscore
110	6E	>	Greater than sign
111	6F	?	Question mark
112	70		
113	71		
114	72		
115	73		
116	74		
117	75		
118	76		
119	77		
120	78		
121	79		
122	7A	:	Colon
123	7B	#	Number sign
124	7C	@	At sign

Decimal	Hex	Mnemonic	Function
125	7D	'	Single quote
126	7E	=	Equal sign
127	7F	"	Double quote
128	80		
129	81	a	
130	82	b	
131	83	c	
132	84	d	
133	85	e	
134	86	f	
135	87	g	
136	88	h	
137	89	i	
138	8A		
139	8B		Open curly bracket
140	8C		Bar
141	8D		Close curly bracket
142	8E		Tilde
143	8F		
144	90		
145	91	j	
146	92	k	
147	93	l	
148	94	m	
149	95	n	
150	96	o	
151	97	p	
152	98	q	
153	99	r	
154	9A		
155	9B		
156	9C		

continues

TABLE 9.2. continued

Decimal	Hex	Mnemonic	Function
157	9D		
158	9E		
159	9F		
160	A0		
161	A1		
162	A2	s	
163	A3	t	
164	A4	u	
165	A5	v	
166	A6	w	
167	A7	x	
168	A8	y	
169	A9	z	
170	AA		
171	AB		
172	AC		
173	AD		
174	AE		
175	AF		
176	B0		
177	B1		
178	B2		
179	B3		
180	B4		
181	B5		
182	B6		
183	B7		
184	B8		
185	B9		
186	BA		
187	BB		
188	BC		

Decimal	Hex	Mnemonic	Function
189	BD		
190	BE		
191	BF		
192	C0		
193	C1	A	
194	C2	B	
195	C3	C	
196	C4	D	
197	C5	E	
198	C6	F	
199	C7	G	
200	C8	H	
201	C9	I	
202	CA		
203	CB		
204	CC		
205	CD		
206	CE		
207	CF		
208	D0		
209	D1	J	
210	D2	K	
211	D3	L	
212	D4	M	
213	D5	N	
214	D6	O	
215	D7	P	
216	D8	Q	
217	D9	R	
218	DA		
219	DB		
220	DC		

continues

TABLE 9.2. continued

Decimal	Hex	Mnemonic	Function
221	DD		
222	DE		
223	DF		
224	E0		
225	E1		
226	E2	S	
227	E3	T	
228	E4	U	
229	E5	V	
230	E6	W	
231	E7	X	
232	E8	Y	
233	E9	Z	
234	EA		
235	EB		
236	EC		
237	ED		
238	EE		
239	EF		
240	F0	0	Zero
241	F1	1	One
242	F2	2	Two
243	F3	3	Three
244	F4	4	Four
245	F5	5	Five
246	F6	6	Six
247	F7	7	Seven
248	F8	8	Eight
249	F9	9	Nine
250	FA		
251	FB		

Decimal	Hex	Mnemonic	Function
252	FC		
253	FD		
254	FE		
255	FF		

ASCII

In small computer systems, the most popular system for coding alphabetic characters is the *American Standard Code for Information Interchange* or ASCII. Originally the developers of ASCII code used seven bits to encode all the letters of the alphabet, numerals, punctuation marks, and a range of message formatting codes.

The first 32 characters are reserved as control codes, instructions that tell data processing equipment how to handle the data. Alphabetic characters are stored in two ranges, from 65 through 90, for the capital letters "A" through "Z" and from 97 to 122 for lower case "a" through "z." The two ranges work neatly together because the codes for a specific capital and lowercase letter will always differ by only one bit. Adding 20(Hex) to the code of a capital letter results in the code for its lowercase equivalent. The numerals run from 48 (representing zero) to 57 (representing nine). Table 9.3 lists the basic 7-bit ASCII code.

TABLE 9.3. The American Standard Code for Information Interchange.

Decimal	Hex	Symbol	Mnemonic	Function
0	0	^@	NUL	Used as a fill character
1	1	^A	SOH	Start of heading (indicator)
2	2	^B	STX	Start of text (indicator)
3	3	^C	ETX	End of text (indicator)
4	4	^D	EOT	End of transmission; disconnect character
5	5	^E	ENQ	Enquiry; request answer back message
6	6	^F	ACK	Acknowledge
7	7	^G	BEL	Bell; sounds audible bell tone
8	8	^H	BS	Backspace
9	9	^I	HT	Horizontal tab
10	A	^J	LF	Line feed
11	B	^K	VT	Vertical tab

continues

TABLE 9.3. continued

Decimal	Hex	Symbol	Mnemonic	Function
12	C	^L	FF	Form feed
13	D	^M	CR	Carriage return
14	E	^N	SO	Shift out; changes character set
15	F	^O	SI	Shift in; changes character set
16	10	^P	DLE	Data link escape
17	11	^Q	DC1	Data control 1, also known as XON
18	12	^R	DC2	Data control 2
19	13	^S	DC3	Data control 3, also known as XOFF
20	14	^T	DC4	Data control 4
21	15	^U	NAK	Negative acknowledge
22	16	^V	SYN	Synchronous idle
23	17	^W	ETB	End of transmission block
24	18	^X	CAN	Cancel; immediately ends any command
25	19	^Y	EM	End of medium (indicator)
26	1A	^Z	SUB	Substitute (also, end-of-file character)
27	1B	^[	ESC	Escape; introduces escape sequence
28	1C	^\	FS	File separator (indicator)
29	1D	^]	GS	Group separator (indicator)
30	1E	^^	RS	Record separator (indicator)
31	1F	^_	US	Unit separator (indicator)
32	20		SP	Space character
33	21	!		Exclamation mark
34	22	"		Double quotes
35	23	#		Pound sign
36	24	$		Dollar sign
37	25	%		Percent sign
38	26	&		Ampersand
39	27	'		Single quote
40	28	(		Open parenthesis
41	29	)		Close parenthesis
42	2A	*		Asterisk
43	2B	+		Plus sign

Decimal	Hex	Symbol	Mnemonic	Function
44	2C	,		Comma
45	2D	-		Minus sign (hyphen)
46	2E	.		Period
47	2F	/		Slash
48	30	0		Zero
49	31	1		One
50	32	2		Two
51	33	3		Three
52	34	4		Four
53	35	5		Five
54	36	6		Six
55	37	7		Seven
56	38	8		Eight
57	39	9		Nine
58	3A	:		Colon
59	3B	;		Semi-colon
60	3C	<		Less than sign
61	3D	=		Equals sign
62	3E	>		Greater than sign
63	3F	?		Question mark
64	40	@		At sign
65	41	A		
66	42	B		
67	43	C		
68	44	D		
69	45	E		
70	46	F		
71	47	G		
72	48	H		
73	49	I		
74	4A	J		
75	4B	K		

continues

TABLE 9.3. continued

Decimal	Hex	Symbol	Mnemonic	Function
76	4C	L		
77	4D	M		
78	4E	N		
79	4F	O		
80	50	P		
81	51	Q		
82	52	R		
83	53	S		
84	54	T		
85	55	U		
86	56	V		
87	57	W		
88	58	X		
89	59	Y		
90	5A	Z		
91	5B	[		Open bracket
92	5C	\		Backslash
93	5D	]		Close bracket
94	5E	^		Caret
95	5F	_		Underscore
96	60	`		
97	61	a		
98	62	b		
99	63	c		
100	64	d		
101	65	e		
102	66	f		
103	67	g		
104	68	h		
105	69	i		
106	6A	j		
107	6B	k		

Decimal	Hex	Symbol	Mnemonic	Function
108	6C	l		
109	6D	m		
110	6E	n		
111	6F	o		
112	70	p		
113	71	q		
114	72	r		
115	73	s		
116	74	t		
117	75	u		
118	76	v		
119	77	w		
120	78	x		
121	79	y		
122	7A	z		
123	7B	{		Open curly bracket
124	7C				Bar
125	7D	}		Close curly bracket
126	7E	~		Tilde
127	7F			

The 128 possible symbols of the 7-bit ASCII code have been augmented to 256 by extending the code by an extra bit (to a full 8-bit byte), allowing the set to include foreign language characters and other odd symbols. You're likely to run into two different sets of extensions. When working with DOS, you're most likely to use the *IBM extended character set* that puts many of the extra codes to work specifying additional symbols that are often used for drawing block graphics on monitors and printed output. Windows has its own *Windows extended character set* that omits the block graphics (after all, they are hardly necessary for an interface built around bitmapped graphics) and instead includes more foreign language characters and symbols.

Word Processor Formats

ASCII and other codes work at the character level. People, however, work with documents. Where the simple ASCII code is sufficient for simply putting words into electronic form, it makes only rudimentary provisions for the details of a document—indentations, pagination, fonts, and all the other typographic conventions that make text more readable.

One of the early attempts at adding formatting codes was used by the word processor *WordStar*, first created for the CP/M operating system by Micropro (which eventually changed its name to WordStar International). To preserve the formatting of a document, WordStar embedded simple printer control codes in it. For example, one code instructed the printer to start underlining, another to stop. The relatively few available control codes limited the fonts and other printer features that could be controlled by the characters embedded in a file. Moreover, to store document formats, WordStar, like most primitive word processors, simply used spaces, tabs, and line feed. While this works acceptably when you use nothing more than monospaced printing (in which every character has the same width like the Courier characters produced by old-fashioned typewriters) it falters with modern proportionally spaced fonts and fails when confronted with today's need to include multiple fonts, graphics, and other objects inside documents.

Modern word processors don't embed actual printer codes in documents. Instead, they use their own proprietary systems for indicating a standard repertory of printer functions. When making a printout, the stored codes get translated into actual instructions for the printer by the printer driver used by the word processor (under DOS) or operating system.

Rich Text Format

The Rich Text Format (RTF) gives text files a standard means of coding text, page formatting, and graphics using nothing more than universally compatible 7-bit ASCII characters. The format provides for all normal page layout options such as typefaces and font sizes, line justification, paragraph alignment, tab control, and embedded objects. It gives formatted files an interchange format that can be used not only between applications but also platforms. The same characters and controls are easily transferred between DOS, Windows, and OS/2 applications and even with Apple Macintosh programs. Many Microsoft hypertext-based multimedia authoring systems are designed to work with .RTF files. E-mail systems like Lotus Notes use .RTF files to exchange fully formatted text.

The RTF world has its own language. A program that converts a formatted text file into an .RTF file is called a *writer*. A program that transforms an .RTF file into a file compatible with a word processor, desktop publishing system, or multimedia authoring system is called a *reader*. Writers and readers are often embedded in other applications as file export and import features. A *control word* is an RTF command that marks printer control codes and formatting instructions. Control words do not print.

Every control word follows a strict format. Each is introduced by a backslash, identified by a letter sequence, and described by a delimiter. It takes the following form:

`\ LetterSequence<Delimiter>`

Similarly, a *control symbol* takes the form of a backslash followed by a single, non-alphabetic character but no delimiter. Each control symbol has its own special meaning under RTF. For example, `\[td]` is the code for a non-breaking space.

The characters in the letter sequence of a control word are drawn from the lowercase alphabet, "a" and "z" inclusive. Control words are generally mnemonic and have an English-like look to them, for example `colortbl` and `stylesheet`, but can be any character combination. Because RTF is case sensitive, all characters in the control word must be lowercase to be properly interpreted.

The delimiter marking the end of an RTF control word can take one of three forms, a space, a numeric value, or any character other than a letter or digit.

When a space ends the control word, any text following the space before the beginning of the next control word will be printed. The space itself does not print.

Numerical values used as delimiters generally pass their values to the application reading the .RTF file. For example, in the hypothetical command `PointSize18`, the `18` delimits (and ends) the command as well as specifying to use 18-point type. The numerical digit directly follows the character sequence or it may be preceded by a hyphen (–), indicating a negative value. Numerical delimiters in general can take any integral value from –32767 to 32767, although Microsoft Word (regardless of platform) restricts the range to –31680 to 31680. The numeric delimiter is considered part of the control word and does not print. It must be followed by a space or a non-numeric, non-alphabetic character to mark the end of the control word.

A control word can also be delimited by any character other than a letter or a numeral.

Many control words act as toggles, turning a feature such as underlining or italics on and off. In RTF, the appearance of the control word with a space delimiter is assumed to turn the feature or property on. A delimiter of zero turns the feature off. For example, a `\b` would turn on boldface printing and `\b0` would turn boldface off.

Text, control words, and control symbols can be tied together as an RTF *group* by enclosing them in braces or curly brackets. An opening brace signals the start of the group, and a closing brace ends it. The control words in the group specify the attributes of the text in the group. Special groups also serve as a file header, preceding the text with descriptive details of the document such as the color, font, style, and summary information. Other groups may be used to specify annotations, fonts, footers, footnotes, headers, images, page-formatting, and other style features.

When a format is specified for text within a group, that formatting applies only to the group. However, when no formatting is specified, the second group will inherit the formatting of the first. In Microsoft's implementation of RTF, however, certain groups do not automatically assume the formatting of a previous group. In particular, annotations, footnotes, headers, and footers maintain their own formatting.

All characters that are not part of a control word or control symbol are considered *plain text* and print as the text of the document using the formatting specified by the RTF control features. The backslash and brace characters serve as signals within the RTF format and do not ordinarily print. To include them in plain text, each must be preceded by a backslash.

The control words and sequences of the complete RTF language take dozens of pages to document. Microsoft offers a full listing as well as source code for an RTF reader in the form of the file GC0165.EXE, which is distributed free through the Microsoft Software Library on CompuServe (type GO:MSL), the Microsoft Download Service (MSDL) at (206) 936-6735.

Numerical Storage

Storing numerical values might seem more straightforward than text. After all, binary data is simply numbers, so where's the problem? BCD works well, so the whole world should be happy with that.

Unfortunately, BCD is an inefficient means of packing numerical data into bytes, particularly with multiple digit numbers. Worse, calculating BCD values requires your PC to translate the coded numbers into different binary form, perform the calculations, and translate the results back into BCD. Most of the time programmers find storing numbers as simple binary values to be more convenient. For example, the 256 different byte patterns can store values from 0 to 255.

Unlike with BCD, where you simply add another digit to increase the maximum number you can represent, the range of values in this binary form is constrained by the number of bits in the storage unit. The more bits, the wider the range. PCs generally use Intel nomenclature for these storage units, as listed in Table 9.4.

TABLE 9.4. Names of storage units (Intel).

Bits	Bytes	Name
4	0.5	Nibble
8	1	Byte
16	2	Word
32	4	Double-word
64	8	Quad-word
96	16	Line

Integers

The actual code used for the bit patterns of these units can be anything a programmer wants. The basic numerical storage method is *unsigned integers.* That is, the binary value of the storage unit represents a positive integer, a whole number, that starts counting with zero and increases by one unit up to the maximum value that can be coded by the number of bytes in the data unit. For example, a 16-bit word can code unsigned values from 0 to 65,535 using the full range of hexadecimal values from 0000 to FFFF.

Signed integers span a negative to positive range centered on zero. As with unsigned values, the binary value of the storage starts at zero and increases uniformly by one unit, but the increase only goes up half the maximum value that can be coded by the number of bytes in the data unit. Negative values also start at zero and decrease uniformly subtracting a binary one from the previous value to represent the next lower integer. For example, to store a byte value of –1, you subtract a binary one from 00 to get FF. These values decrease down uniformly until they butt into the positive values at one-half the maximum coding value of the storage unit. A 16-bit digital word, for example, can code integers from –32768 to 0 to +32767 using the range of hexadecimal word values from 8000 (representing the lowest negative value) climbing upward as numbers become less negative to 0000 (zero is zero) then climbing upward again to 7FFF (representing the highest positive value).

In the Intel scheme of things, integer values are most often stored in three formats. A *word integer* uses 16 bits of storage (an Intel word) to represent values from –32,768 to 32,767. A *short integer* takes 32 bits of storage (in Intel double-word and can represent values from –2,147,483,648 to 2,147,483,647. A *long integer* uses 64 bits of storage (an Intel quad-word) to store values from –9,223,382,027,854,875,808 to 9,223,382,027,854,875,807.

Floating-Point Numbers

Numerical values used in calculations can take other forms. The most common are *floating-point numbers*. The essence of a floating-point number is that its decimal point "floats" between a pre-defined number of significant digits rather than being fixed in place the way dollar values always have two decimal places.

Mathematically speaking, a floating-point number has three parts: a *sign*, which indicates whether the number is greater or less than zero; a *significant*—sometimes called a mantissa—which comprises all the digits that are mathematically meaningful; and an *exponent*, which determines the order of magnitude of the significant, essentially the location to which the decimal point floats. Think of a floating-point number as being like those represented by scientific notation. But where scientists are apt to deal in base 10—the exponents in scientific notation are powers of 10—math coprocessors think of floating-point numbers digitally in base two, all ones and zeros in powers of two.

Intel microprocessors recognize three kinds of floating-point numbers. *Single-precision* floating-point numbers use a 32-bit double-word of storage; *double-precision* floating-point numbers use a 64-bit quad-word; and *extended floating-point* numbers use a block of 10 bytes. In all three cases, the first bit of the format stores the sign of the floating-point number. In single-precision, the next eight bits store the exponent; in double-precision, the next 11 bits; in extended precision, 15 bits. The balance of each serves as the significant. Table 9.5 lists the range of values these number types can represent.

TABLE 9.5. Floating-point number ranges.

Type	Width	Range of values
Single-precision	32-bits	5.8775×10^{-39} to 3.4028×10^{38}
Double-precision	64-bits	1.1125×10^{-308} to 1.7977×10^{308}
Extended	80-bits	$1.68105 \times 10^{-4932}$ to 1.1897×10^{4932}

Byte Order

Once the different data types make sense to you, it's time to add a further complication, byte order. When digital values span more than one byte, the order in which you examine and evaluate the bytes becomes important. Just as some human writing systems consider word order from left to right and others thing right to left (or top to bottom), you can evaluate the bytes of digital values from left to right or right to left. Either order works perfectly well, and as long as the computer industry standardizes on one, then you should face no problems.

You should know better than that. Someone always has a better idea, and it usually involves confusing the alternatives. In fact, the major microprocessor manufacturers have chosen exactly the opposite means of evaluating bytes. Motorola chose the equivalent of Western left-to-right ordering of bytes. The first byte in a sequence is the most significant. Intel, on the other hand, went the opposite direction. The first byte in a sequence is the least important.

Engineers have given these two alternatives quaint names. The Motorola scheme is termed *big-endian* because the byte with the biggest value is at the front end. The Intel scheme is called *little-endian.* (A movement by some hard-of-hearing New Age engineers to replace those names with "big Native American" and "little Native American" has reportedly not been well received.)

The difference is important. To an Intel-based little-endian computer, the word value of the byte sequence E8 02 would be 02E8, a decimal value of 744. To a Motorola machine, E8 02 would have the value E802, in decimal 59,394.

The chasm between the 2-byte ordering scheme looms large, particularly when you consider that the two most important multimedia platforms use different byte ordering schemes. Intel-based PCs use little-endian byte order. Motorola-based Apple Macintosh and PowerMac machines use big-endian byte order. Although some modern processors can work with either format, you still need to know which one you're giving them.

Images

Images are what make multimedia worth a second look. Although an image may seem a simple thing, something you can take in with a mere glance, from the computer's perspective an image presents a complex challenge. The machine sees not only a single picture (as a block of data) but also looks at its deconstruction as if it were some kind of modern art critic. Sometimes it dissects the complete image into its individual pixels and assigns one or more values to each pixel—brightness, color, transparency, or whatever. Or it may look at how the image was drawn and compile a list of every stroke that went into sketching it. In either case, it must somehow organize the resulting data and find a means of storing and transmitting it that preserves every detail.

The art of working with images is a matter of finding the best method of image construction and deconstruction. The issues are many, and all affect how you can store and use the image data.

Vectors Versus Bit Images

PCs use either of two ways of storing an image, as drawings or vectors and as bitmaps. The two schemes represent entirely different philosophies. The former is the realm of the *drawing* program; the latter, the *painting* program.

A drawing or vector file doesn't store an image at all. It comprises a set of instructions used to create an image. Every time the image is used, it gets created anew, reconstructed from the instructions in the vector file.

A bitmapped file stores an image as pixel information, usually arranged as a raster like the pixels on a television or monitor screen. Information for every pixel of the image gets locked into the file.

Vector Images

Vector images have three chief advantages. They are independent of the resolution of the system that creates them. They can be more compact. And they can encapsulate multiple views of three-dimensional objects.

Because a vector image gets drawn anew every time it is used, the on-screen image gets created with whatever resolution level is prevailing in the system drawing it. The image gets scaled to the prevailing resolution, revealing more detail with every increase in resolution. Vector files can be platform independent, enabling you to create a drawing on a low resolution system and later transfer it to one with higher resolution while taking advantage of the full capabilities of each. Vector images may not be application independent, however, and may need access to their original program under which they were created to get reconstructed.

Vector image files are compact because a large image can be coded as a few brief instructions. For example, drawing a black box on half a screen may take a couple dozen bytes of instructions that actually control hundreds of thousands of pixels. But this size advantage applies only to simple images. When a vector drawing gets complex, the number of instructions, each of which may be several or several dozen bytes long, can approach the number of pixels in the image.

Some vector files encode image data in three dimensions. With the appropriate software, you can construct a view of the image from any direction, even cross sections.

On the downside, reconstructing a vector image can be time-consuming. A complex image may take hours to generate because every pixel on every line needs to be calculated separately, and each pixel may suffer several drawing strokes. Consequently, vector images are not suited to real time display.

Moreover, vector files aren't suited to recording photorealistic images. Even the complex set of drawings can only approximate a natural object. Certainly you can capture a life-size image, but you lose the scalability that gives vector files their strength.

Bitmapped Images

Bitmapped images reproduce the original exactly (or as exactly as possible within the constraints of the storage format). Each bit gets captured in its full glory. The bits of the image constrain the resolution at which it may be displayed, however. All the image information is in its pixels. There's nothing available for constructing an image with higher resolutions than the original. Pixel interpolation may make an image fit a higher resolution screen, but interpolation adds nothing—in particular, no increase in sharpness—to the image. Bitmapped images are consequently resolution-dependent.

Because your PC can transfer a bitmapped image directly from a file to your monitor screen, they are relatively fast to display. Actual processing is minimal. The limit on display speed becomes the size of the image and the speed of the channel through which it gets transferred.

Compressed bit images fall in between vector and raster images. The compression system breaks the exact one-to-one correspondence between bits and pixels. Expanding the compressed image data is essentially a drawing system that uses commands to change formatted data into a bit image.

Resolution

Resolution is one of those wonderful terms in computing that means what it means except when it doesn't. Once upon a time, resolution meant much the same thing as sharpness. It indicated the most detailed image that could be displayed on a monitor. Over time, however, resolution has also come to mean the *logical size* of a bitmapped image.

This last meaning of resolution is most common in image storage. A bitmapped image described as having 640×480 pixel resolution would comprise a total of 307,200 pixels that need to be stored. This kind of resolution helps define the format of a stored image by presenting the number of pixels in one line and the total number of lines in an image.

In monitors (more fully discussed in Chapter 14, "Cameras and Monitors"), resolution often means the addressability of the screen. A monitor with 1024×768 resolution would be capable of displaying 1024 individual pixels horizontally and 768 pixels vertically across the face of its screen, no matter the size of the screen. At a given monitor resolution level, a smaller screen would appear sharper (or need to be sharper) because its pixels would be packed closer together.

Absolute resolution or physical resolution is measured in dots or pixels per unit of measure such as inches or millimeters. It is invariant (hence the "absolute"), producing the same size and sharpness of image regardless of the display system.

Color Depth

In any image storage system, some amount of memory must be allocated to each pixel in a bitmap. The amount of storage required depends on the number of colors in the image—or, alternately, the number of colors in an image determines the amount of memory required to store each pixel. Typically the memory assigned each pixel is quantified in bits and is called the *bit-depth* or color-depth of the image.

Monochrome images have a bit-depth of one or more. A single bit can encode whether a given pixel is black or white, so images with a bit-depth of one have the same absolute black-or-white look of line drawings. These images are sometimes called black-and-white. With more than one bit per pixels, monochrome images become *grayscale images.* That is, they can have shades of gray in addition to absolute black or white. The more bits, the more shades of gray. Two bits per pixel allows four grayscale levels: black, two shades of gray, and white. Four bits per pixel allows for 16 grayscale levels. Eight bits per pixel allows for 256 grayscale levels. Grayscale images with more than eight bits per pixel are uncommon.

Most color display systems allocate the same number of bits for each primary color, but this relationship does not hold in all bit-image storage systems. To conserve memory, lower-quality images often use color-mapping to reduce memory requirements. Nevertheless, the number of bits allocated to each pixel determines the maximum number of colors that the stored image can contain. For example, an 8-bit-per-pixel image can store a range of 256 colors. Other common formats include 16-bit images and 24-bit images, which are sometimes called True Color images because their range of 16.7 million hues can truly mimic the full range of colors, representing more hue than most people can distinguish.

2-D Versus 3-D

The current trend among graphics applications is a shift from two-dimensional drawing to three dimensions. The result is more realistic renderings that can be rotated convincingly as if they were true physical objects. The difference between 2-D and 3-D is one dimension, depth. In simplest form, depth indicates when one part of a drawing is in front of another, hiding it. In most complete form, depth adds a third coordinate to the image, making a bitmap of space.

Still Image Compression

Images require immense storage, on the order of hundreds of thousands of bytes for a single screen. With still images, keeping a library is onerous. With moving images, storing raw data is ridiculous. A few seconds of full-screen, real time video will fill a hard disk. Little wonder engineers have worked hard to reduce the data needs for both still and moving images. The key technology they have called upon is *data compression.*

Normal data compression systems like file archive programs work in one dimension. That is, they work on sequences of bytes. One of the most common algorithms is Lempel-Ziv compression, which works by encoding repeated strings of data as short tokens. The mapping between token and data string is kept in a dictionary, which is continually refreshed so that the most common byte patterns get the shortest tokens.

Normal still-image compression programs work two-dimensionally. They analyze areas. For example, JPEG compression (the initials stand for the Joint Photographic Experts Group, which developed the standard) evaluates an eight-pixel square area, eliminating frequencies too high to observe, and encoding it as a pattern of bytes. It also reduces color according to a sliding scale keyed to the compression ratio. The resulting data stream gets standard Lempel-Ziv data compression again.

Color Mapping

One straightforward way of reducing the data needs of image storage is to simply trim the amount of data that is stored or transmitted. The most commonplace way to pare away data is with color. By constraining the number of colors in an image, its data needs can be dramatically reduced. Black-and-white images require fewer bytes than color. The fewer bits per pixel, the less storage that's required for a given image.

Unfortunately, reducing the number of colors in an image often leads to comical effects—that is, images begin to look like the Sunday comics with broad patches of color and little detail, laughable rather than realistic. The problem is that the human eye can perceive a wide range of colors, millions of them. Restricting an image to a few hues strips it of its reality.

Long ago, however, engineers discovered that few scenes include all the millions of visible colors. After all, the number of different colors in a scene can never exceed the number of pixels making up the image, typically a few hundred thousand. Moreover, scenes tend to be dominated by a few hues. For instance, an image of a forest would be predominately green; a seascape, mostly blue; pornography, mostly fleshtones. By ignoring unused colors and adroitly choosing a few key tones, image engineers discovered they could produce nearly realistic images with as few as 256 distinct hues.

Unfortunately not just any 256 colors works. The best 256 hues to make the most realistic image depend on the color content of the image itself.

Moreover, eliminating colors alone doesn't save storage. To make the best blends and more realistic colors still requires the flexibility of having a wide range of hues to choose from. That is, although you might restrict the number of discrete colors in an image to 256, those colors must still be drawn from a range of millions. To specify any color from the million range still requires using the same storage-wasting scheme as using the full multi-million range.

But by using a code, the storage requirements for an image with a limited range of colors can be dramatically trimmed. For example, if you only need 256 hues you can use an 8-bit code to specify each different color in the image. Each pattern in the code points to a color drawn from a range of millions. The 256 codes serve as a map to locate the actual colors that are used to build the image. Consequently this technique is called *color mapping.*

The range of color that can be produced by a display system, the range from which the map is drawn, is called its *color palette,* exactly as the colors used by an artist are his palette. As with the work of an artist, the palette of an image determines its overall ranges of color and tones. The color map determines the actual colors that are used in the image.

In this example, the amount of data required to store an image is reduced by nearly two-thirds. Instead of each pixel needing three bytes per pixel to store individual color values, a 1-byte pointer serves to store the color map information for each pixel. The only overhead is the storage needed by the color map itself. In this example, the color map would be an array of 256 3-byte color values.

Video hardware uses a similar technique to conserve memory used by display adapters. In the hardware application, the color map is usually called a Color Look-Up Table (CLUT).

Image formats that do not use color mapping are sometimes called *direct-mapped images.*

Run Length Encoding

Bitmapped images often consist of long strings of repeated codes because most images have areas of uniform color. For example, the sky in a landscape or the background of a word-slide are uniform (or nearly so) areas of color that often dominate an image. Storing a long string of identical pixel values is inefficient. A better way is to indicate the repeated pixel value and a multiplier that tells how many times the pixel should be repeated. Using this technique, a string of 100 pixels could be stored as two characters, compressing the data by a factor of 50. This technique is called *Run-Length Encoding,* or RLE, because it encodes the length of the running string of repeated pixel values.

In practical application, the pure form of RLE is modified somewhat to minimize its one inherent handicap: pure RLE becomes terribly inefficient with non-repeating data. When every pixel is different, each one requires two characters of storage—one for the pixel value and one for a meaningless multiplier.

One way to limit the damage RLE inflicts on non-repeating data is to add sophistication to the code. In the PC Paintbrush system, for example, half of the potential values of a byte are reserved to serve as multipliers. The other half store non-repeating data. In the Targa RLE scheme, half the codes of the multiplier byte indicate the number of repeats of the following byte; the other half indicate the number of non-repeating bytes that follow. In any case, RLE is most efficient at compressing images (or other data) with lengthy repeats of individual bytes. It is least efficient at compressing non-repeating data.

Dictionary-Based Compression

Another way to compress strings of data is to use a dictionary-based code system. Sometimes called *Lempel-Ziv compression* after the investigators who first published the algorithm, dictionary-based compression works by finding patterns that occur multiple times in a data stream. The compression system stores a copy of each repeated pattern in a dictionary and assigns a short *token* (a digital code) to represent the pattern. The compression system then substitutes the short token for the longer repeated pattern wherever the pattern occurs in the data stream. When the data is reconstructed, the decompression software uses the tokens to look up the appropriate patterns in the dictionary to restore the original data stream.

Basic dictionary-based compression allows for many options such as the maximum number of tokens and dictionary entries that are permitted, how often the dictionary is updated (so that entries are not wasted if a given pattern disappears from the data stream), and how the tokens are distinguished from ordinary data. In general, however, dictionary-based compression systems are able to reduce the amount of storage required by a typical text file by about half. Images can often be reduced to about one-fifth their original size.

JPEG

Standards

In order to provide a universal standard for lossy compression (a way of reducing data storage requirements by sacrificing information that is not significant), an industry committee called the Joint Photographic Experts Group (JPEG) developed an image storage format based on studies of human sight perception. The group designed the standard to start with a 24-bit image at virtually any resolution level and reproduce it in the same form as closely as possible, trading off the separation of individual colors and fineness of spatial resolution with the demands of reducing transmission bandwidth and storage requirements. The resulting standard has many variations to serve a variety of purposes and is now sanctioned by the International Standards Organization as ISO 10918.

At heart, the JPEG compression system works within a luminance/chrominance signal framework. To reduce the data content of an image with the least apparent loss in quality, the JPEG system first manipulates the spatial resolution by evaluating the luminance of an image area measuring 8×8 pixels. Within this area, the compression algorithm eliminates spatial signals at frequencies that would be too high to perceive, essentially setting an upper limit to signal resolution based on the visibility of details.

Next the JPEG system works on the chrominance. It adjusts the separation between hues by varying the quantization of color gradations, limiting the color information that needs to be stored. Rather than fixing a predetermined bit-depth, the JPEG system is based on a sliding scale that trades off the ability to resolve fine differences in hue against the amount of compression. By sacrificing smooth transitions, you can raise the compression ratio dramatically.

The resulting stream of spatially and color compressed data is next linearly compressed using an algorithm derived from the familiar dictionary-based Lempel-Ziv compression system. Frequently occurring data sequences are stored in a dictionary and assigned a token. Every time the compression system finds the key sequence in the data stream, it replaces it with the corresponding token. When the data stream gets reconstructed, the decompression system uses the token to find the original sequence in the dictionary, which is then put into the data stream.

Because of the elimination of high frequencies and adjustment of hue scale, the JPEG process loses some data during the compression process that cannot be recovered by decompressing the image data. However, the JPEG standard discards only details that are invisible, at least at low compression ratios. As you increase the degree of compression, the loss of image detail becomes increasingly apparent. At moderate compression ratios, in the range of 10:1 to 20:1, no loss will likely be visible on PC monitors. The system can be used for ratios of 200:1, but at such high ratios, image degradation is readily apparent. JPEG also includes a lossless mode used in some technical applications but rarely in multimedia.

Video Compression

Video signals have an added dimension so they can be compressed three dimensionally. In addition to compressing an image spatially, a video compressor can also work across time. The compressor can take advantage of how little the average image actually changes from frame to frame in a video image. Instead of storing every frame in complete detail, the video compressor needs to worry about only what changes from one frame to the next. The static parts of the image can be ignored because they add no new information to the video. For example, when someone moves against a backdrop, only the pixels in the moving character need to be relayed to the data stream. The background stays the same so there's no reason to duplicate it time and again.

As with any compression technology, this store-only-what-moves approach has an inherent drawback. Any noise, distortion, or other error in one stored frame ripples through all that follow. Mistransmission in one frame gets multiplied through all those that come after. To minimize such effects, most video compression systems periodically update the entire image.

Another way to trim the storage needed for video data is akin to cutting the number of colors in a still image file, reducing the frame rate. To maintain the illusion of smooth motion, most video systems update the images on the screen between 25 and 30 times per second. PC-based video systems can hack their video storage requirements in half by slowing the frame rate by the same factor. Some video compression systems simply drop frames. More sophisticated systems adjust the period at which frames or parts of frames are upgraded in accord with movement in the image so as to minimize the visible jerkiness of the on-screen picture. It's not unusual for PC-based video systems to operate with frame updates from five to 15 per second.

Video compression is sometimes classed as symmetrical or asymmetrical. *Symmetrical video compression* means that the coding and decoding processes require the same processor power and take the same amount of time. In other words, the data stream can be compressed in real time. *Asymmetrical video compression* requires more power to compress than decompress. Compression does not take place in real time but may require hours for a few minutes of playback time. The benefit of asymmetrical video compression is that it allows for more sophisticated processing, which means higher compression ratios and more compact files.

Video compression remains on the leading edge of PC and communications technology, and many companies have invested heavily in developing the most efficient systems. In the American way, they believe that they should profit from their investment, so they keep their techniques secret, and the various video compression systems remain staunchly proprietary. Among the more popular of these video compression systems are the following, all of which come as standard equipment with Windows 95.

Cinepak

Developed by Supermac, a manufacturer of peripherals principally for Apple Macintosh computers, Cinepak provides a strong combination of good-looking video quality with good playback performance. The typical Cinepak system produces images with quarter-screen (compared to VGA) resolution of 320×240 pixel images at the relatively high rate of 15 frames per second, and even better on faster PCs. Cinepak is highly asymmetrical—decompression takes place in real time, compression does not. In fact, compressing 10 minutes of video can take as long as 12 to 16 hours. Although for that reason alone you're unlikely to compress your own videos with Cinepak, the system is often used for adding video to both Widows and Macintosh CD-ROM software. Microsoft's Cinemania uses Cinepak video compression. Apple also added a Cinepak decompressor to Video for Windows with version 1.1.

Indeo

Intel's entry into the video compression marketplace is Indeo, which delivers video quality and playback performance on par with Cinepak with the added advantage of much faster compression. In fact, you can capture video images and compress them in real time using Indeo and special capture hardware developed by Intel. Versions of QuickTime for Windows after 1.1 include Indeo decompression.

Microsoft Run-Length Encoding (RLE)

For simple compression chores, Microsoft developed this simple algorithm that is based on Run-Length Encoding. The goal was to minimize microprocessor overhead on uncomplicated images such a bar charts with limited animation. It is not intended for more complex images or those that rapidly change, on which both performance and quality will suffer.

Microsoft Video 1

Sacrificing ultimate video quality, Microsoft developed this compression algorithm to give you a means to quickly compress video images without requiring a lot of processor power. Video 1 handles full motion well but it may make fast-changing images obviously blocky.

Performance Issue

Two other video compression algorithms—Motion JPEG and MPEG—have been sanctioned by industry organizations and serve as standards, particularly in the television and video industries. They are sometimes used for PC images (particularly with add-on hardware to service their heavy processing needs). Windows 95 enables you to optionally install these compression/decompression systems.

Motion JPEG

The still-image JPEG compression standard (discussed previously) includes provisions for using the same compression algorithms with additional enhancements for compressing moving images. The Motion JPEG system compresses spatially as with the still image algorithm and also compresses temporally by setting key frames and encoding subsequent frames with the same data tables. Microsoft has endorsed a subset of the ISO definition as an interchange standard that makes all frames in a Motion JPEG sequence key frames using predefined tables so that each one will be directly and independently addressable.

Motion JPEG capture and playback are demanding. In a typical application, the compressed code for a VGA- or video-quality full-motion (30 frames per second) movie requires a hard disk to stream data at about 3MB/second, a rate sustainable only by high-performance drives—most of which are classed as "AV hard disks" by their manufacturers. Compressing and decompressing such images, which in raw form involve video data transfers at about 27MB/second, is beyond the capabilities of even today's fastest PC microprocessors and requires specialized hardware for real time operation.

Performance Issue

MPEG

Developed by an industry group called the *Motion Picture Experts Group* from which the system takes its name, MPEG is probably the most popular standard for video compression at the professional level. By combining both spatial and temporal compression, MPEG achieves very high compression ratios that allow full-screen, full-motion video at reasonable data rates that are

Performance Issue

within the capabilities of today's hard disk drives and CD-ROM players. The double-speed CD-ROM drives with a 300KB/second transfer rate that are required by the MPC-2 standard have sufficient performance for playing back MPEG-compressed movies. Even single-speed drives work for MPEG-1 playback, but you'll not otherwise be satisfied with their performance.

Performance Issue

As with Motion JPEG, however, achieving that low data rate requires intense image processing. MPEG demands performance that is beyond the capabilities of the general purpose processors in today's PCs including the fastest Pentium chips. In other words, you need special hardware for MPEG capture and playback.

Audio

Sound also presents a challenge to computers. Sound is a physical phenomenon caused by variations in air pressure that are most commonly converted into analog electrical signals (see Chapter 15, "Sound," for a discussion of the nature of sound and its electrical representation). Computers, of course, want to deal with sound information as a digital code, which we call digital audio.

Digitization

As with any coding system, digital audio can use any of a variety of codes to store sound information. The most common digital audio code is *pulse code modulation* or PCM, which turns sounds into numbers—digital bits are represented as pulses that code the numbers. The value of the number corresponds to the strength of the sound at a given moment.

To record sounds using PCM, a digital recording device measures the sound source (typically an analog audio signal) thousands of times each second and assigns a numerical value to the strength of the sound every time it looks. The resulting series of signal-strength numbers can then be stored, recorded, or transmitted.

Reproducing the music or noise only requires working backward. The digital audio device takes the recorded numbers and regenerates the corresponding signal strength—again, typically as an analog audio signal—at intervals exactly corresponding to those at which it examined the original signal. The result is a near-exact duplication of the original audio.

The process of digitally coding sound involves several arbitrary variables. The two most important are the rate at which the original audio signal is examined—called the *sampling rate*—and the numeric code assigned to each value sampled. The code is digital and is defined as a given number of bits, the *resolution* of the system. The quality of sound reproduction is determined primarily by the values chosen for these variables. In practical digital audio systems, the actual code is more complex than a simple correspondence of binary value to signal strength. Scientists have developed more exotic coding systems that minimize the effects of bit-errors on the resulting signal.

Sampling Rate

The sampling rate limits the frequency response of a digital recording system. The highest frequency that can be recorded and reproduced digitally is half the sampling frequency. This top frequency is often called the *Nyquist frequency*. Higher frequencies become ambiguous and can be confused with lower frequency values producing distortion. To prevent problems, frequencies higher than half the sampling frequency must be eliminated, typically removed using a low-pass filter, before they are digitally sampled. Because no audio filter is perfect, most digital audio systems have cut-off frequencies somewhat lower than the Nyquist frequency. The Compact Disc digital audio system was designed to record sounds with frequencies up to about 15 KHz, and it uses a sampling rate of 44.1 KHz.

Resolution

The number of bits in a digital code determines the number of discrete values that it can record. For example, an 8-bit digital code can represent 256 distinct objects, be they numbers or sound levels. A recording system that uses an 8-bit code can thus record 256 distinct values or steps in sound levels. Unfortunately, music and sounds vary smoothly rather than in discrete steps. The difference between the digital steps and the smooth audio value is distortion. This distortion also adds to the noise in the sound recording system. Minimizing distortion and noise means using more steps. High-quality sound systems—that is, CD-quality sound—require a minimum of a 16-bit code.

Sampling rate and resolution determine the amount of data produced during the digitization process, which in turn determines the amount that must be stored or transmitted. In addition, full stereo recording doubles the data needed because two separate information channels are required. The 44.1 KHz sampling frequency and 16-bit digital code of stereo CD audio result in the need to process and record about 150,000 bits of data every second, about 10.5MB per minute. As with other digital data, digital audio signals are often compressed to reduce the amount of data that you need to store.

Audio Compression

Sound data is notoriously difficult to compress—but that doesn't stop engineers from trying. The long list of compression schemes detailed in the following paragraphs attest to their imagination. Nearly all are aimed at telephone-quality audio, and that's readily understandable. Telephone companies strive to fit as many conversations as possible in a given bandwidth, and compression helps to squeeze more in. With this strong profit motive, telecommunications companies have invested heavily in finding the most efficient compression algorithms. The various schemes involve not only purely mathematical data reduction but also sophisticated modeling of the human vocal apparatus to mimic speech production.

Many of these compression systems have been adapted to multimedia use because they give a compact means of storing voice annotation to documents and packing speed on CD-ROM for distribution. Some operating systems, such as Windows 95, have one or more of these compression systems built-in and permit you to install codecs (coder/decoders) to support others. Here's a quick look at some of the more popular audio compression systems:

CCIT G.711 A-Law and u-Law (although written as a lowercase *u*, the correct name is µ-law, µ being a character of the Greek alphabet) are compression standards aimed primarily at telephone communications. The A-law system is used primarily in Europe; u-law is used in the United States and Japan. Either algorithm allows for a 2:1 compression ratio by making the correspondence between analog level and the steps of the digital code nonlinear. In effect, these coding systems enable you to get the equivalent of 16-bits of apparent quality from an 8-bit audio sample.

Code Excited Linear Predictor speech compression works like the linear predictive code model (below) but takes an additional step, computing the errors in the reconstructed speech by comparing the input to the synthesized output. It stores or transmits both the speech model instructions as well as the error information. The result is better quality than the linear predictive model at the expense of heavier processing needs.

GSM 6.10 Audio was developed by the Groupe Special Mobile (its recommendation 6.10) of the European Telecommunications Standards Institute. With fast hardware, this audio compression system can deliver real time compression at high compression rates with voice quality. The standard supports a number of sampling rates.

IMA ADPCM takes its name from the Interactive Multimedia Association, which created this compression standard to work on a variety of computer platforms. It uses a form of Adaptive Delta Pulse Code Modulation similar to Microsoft ADPCM and works in real time.

Linear Predictive Coding transforms speech into an analytic model of the human vocal tract that would utter the sounds. The system reduces the speech to a description of the changes in the vocal tract, and records the description as a kind of program. The description can then be used to generate synthetic speech. The result does not retain the exact tone qualities of the original speech (it sounds like a machine talking) but is intelligible.

Microsoft ADPCM is a versatile compression system based on *Adaptive Delta Pulse Code Modulation* (instead of recording actual signal levels, it records only the difference or *delta* between successive samples) with options that operate both in real time and non-real time. This is the compression system used by the Encarta multimedia encyclopedia.

Truespeech is a proprietary product of DSP Inc. that delivers high compression ratios for voice-quality sound. Its quality does not extend to the satisfactory compression of music or other high quality audio. Compared to GSM, Truespeech decompresses faster but does not compress in real time.

File Formats

Image and audio sizes, shapes, resolutions, bit-depths, and compression mean nothing if you can't store and transfer the data. You might as well try to grab the electrical signals that outrace your reach with the speed of light. To make digital images and sounds useful, they must be storable and exchangable. They must somehow fit into files that your programs can read and deal with.

Various application developers have devised their own formats for storing images and sounds. At one time, nearly every computer platform and program had its own image file format, and as sound came into the computer realm its formats similarly proliferated. While this freedom-of-format did a lot for preserving data and keeping audio and graphics technologies proprietary, it did little to foster communications.

Over the years, developers have gradually focused on a handful of formats, which have become as close to universal standards as any get in today's fast-changing PC industry. As the potential for multimedia technology became obvious, IBM and Microsoft got together and created a single overall standard that they hoped would unify multimedia storage. They called the standard the *Resource Interchange File Format* or RIFF.

Standards

To make the RIFF system as flexible as possible, the resulting files are structured to be self-describing. Code words in the file itself tell you want kind of data it contains (for example, still image, video, or audio) as well as the organization of that data. One file can store multiple data types as separate structures. Each structure is called a *chunk*. Each chunk is entirely self-contained and self-descriptive.

Several file formats are patterned on the RIFF framework. These include PAL (palette format), RDIB (device independent bitmap format), RMID (a MIDI format), RMMP (multimedia movie format), and WAVE (waveform audio).

A number of other file formats pop up in multimedia. Some are drawn from other computer systems, others linger around from the olden days of PCs. Herewith are the most popular of the formats used in still image, video, and audio storage—the ones you're most likely to see when putting together your multimedia magnum opus.

Still Image Formats

Over the years, images have been packed into dozens of different file formats. Only a few of these now survive into the age of multimedia. The principal formats are those native to Microsoft Windows, BMP, and WMF, attesting to the dominance of the operating system in PC multimedia. A few older formats hang on chiefly because they have long been used as exchange standards. For example .GIF and .PCX files are widely used to exchange graphic images on-line and for print publishing.

BMP

The native format for Windows bitmapped images is the .BMP file, and consequently this format has become an important image exchange standard. As multimedia shifts its primary base to Windows platforms, this format will undoubtedly become ever more popular.

There's little magical about the BMP format. It simply offers a straightforward means of packing bits into a file that follows Microsoft's device-independent bitmap standard. The file tells your programs all they need to know to decode the size and shape of the image pixels. No aspect of a BMP image is absolute—that's why it's device-independent.

The first structure in a .BMP file is the *Bitmap File Header,* which is 14 bytes long. The first two define the file as a bitmap and must be the ASCII text characters "BM." The next four bytes indicate the size of the file in bytes, allowing a maximum length of 4GB. The next four bytes are reserved and must be set to zero. The final four bytes express an offset, the distance between the bitmap file header and the start of the actual bitmap in the file. Table 9.6 lists the contents of the Bitmap File Header.

TABLE 9.6. .BMP file Bitmap File Header.

Offset (bytes)	Length (bytes)	Description	Function
0	2	bfType	Identifying characters, BM in ASCII
2	4	bfSize	Length of file in bytes
6	2	bfReserved1	Reserved, must be 0
8	2	btReserved2	Reserved, must be 0
10	4	bfOffBits	Offset after header to image start

One of two data structures must immediately follow the bitmap file header, a bitmap info block or a bitmap core info block. The former defines the dimensions and colors for a Windows 3.0 (or later) device-independent bitmap; the latter applies to OS/2 versions through 1.3 Presentation Manager bitmaps.

The Bitmap Info block itself has two parts, a header and a color table. The header is 40 bytes long. The first four bytes specify the length in bytes of the header itself, which should be 028(Hex) for 40 bytes.

Four bytes indicate the absolute horizontal resolution of the image in pixels per meter. The next four indicate the absolute vertical resolution of the image in pixels per meter. These values are typically disregarded in reconstructing the image, and are typically set to zero.

Four more bytes specify the number of color indexes in the color table actually used by the bitmap. Zero indicates that the image uses the maximum number of colors allowed by the number of bits assigned to each pixel. When these bytes are not zero, they give the actual count of the number of colors in the image—except for 24-bit color images, in which case these bytes indicate the size of the reference color table used to optimize performance of Windows color palettes.

The final four bytes indicate the number of color indices deemed important in reconstructing the image. When these bytes are set to zero, all colors in the file are deemed important. Table 9.7 summarize the Bitmap Info Header structure.

TABLE 9.7. Bitmap Info Header structure.

Offset (bytes)	Length (bytes)	Description	Function
0	4	biSize	Length of header in bytes
4	4	biWidth	Image width (pixels)
8	4	biHeight	Image height (pixels)
12	2	biPlanes	Image planes (must be 1)
14	2	biBitCount	Bits per pixel
16	4	biCompression	Compression type
20	4	biSizeImage	Image size in bytes
24	4	biXPelsPerMeter	Horizontal resoluton (pixels)
28	4	biYPelsPerMeter	Vertical resolution (pixels)
32	4	biClrUsed	Number of colors in image
36	4	biClrImportant	Number of important colors

The color table takes on one of four structures depending on the bit-depth of the image. When the bit-depth is one, the image is monochrome and the color table must contain two entries for the two available colors, foreground and background. With a bit-depth of four, the color table stores up to 16 entries. Each image pixel in the file is encoded as a 4-bit index to this color table. With an bit-depth of eight, the color table holds up to 256 entries, and one byte is assigned to each pixel. When the bit-depth is 24, the color table is not used, and each pixel is stored as a 3-byte value, one byte for each of the primary colors.

Each color table entry is four bytes long. The first indicates green intensity; the second, blue; the third, red. The fourth byte is reserved.

The core header structure used by OS/2 versions through 1.3 differs in that it uses only two bytes for some values where Windows uses four. In addition, it omits absolute resolution descriptions and does not support color tables or data compression.

The first four bytes of the core header specify the length of the header itself. This value is fixed at 12 bytes or 0C(Hex). You can distinguish an old OS/2 bitmap from a Windows bitmap by examining this value—028(Hex) indicates Windows and recent OS/2 versions; 0C(Hex) indicates old OS/2 bitmaps.

As with the Windows header, that for early OS/2 versions begins by defining the size of the image, with two bytes devoted to describing the width of the image in pixels followed by two more bytes specifying the height of the image in pixels.

The next four bytes define the number of colors in the image. The first two of these indicate the number of planes for the target device, but is always set to one. The next two indicate the number of bits of storage that are devoted to each pixels. The four values currently supported are 1, 4, 8, and 24.

All pixel data gets encoded as 3-byte triplets. The first byte stores blue intensity; the second, green; the third, red.

EPS

Encapsulated PostScript files contain the a list of commands written in the PostScript page description language. .EPS files do not contain bit images but rather text-based commands in pure ASCII. A printer or other device (which can include a file input filter to a graphics program) interprets the PostScript commands to render the image of a page.

The PostScript language includes a wide array of commands to make images. Among the commands are those to select fonts and use them to print strings of text, simple drawing commands, and paint bit images. Although PostScript is meant primarily as a device independent printer language that allows the same set of commands to generate pages at any resolution level, it is sometimes used for graphic images.

Standards

Ordinary PostScript files usually have the filename extension .PS and are typically multi-page documents that are mostly text meant for a publishing system. In contrast, Encapsulated PostScript images consist of a single page and are often used for exchanging graphics. Some painting programs are able to import Encapsulated PostScript images. As a practical matter, this approach is useful because PostScript is a fully documented standard that offers a convenient means of storing a simple image.

An Encapsulated PostScript file is essentially an ordinary PostScript file that contains one extra line that describes a bounding box giving the limits of the image on the page. This bounding box allows applications to determine how to import the image, position it on the page, and resize it when necessary.

The bounding box is described by the command `%%BoundingBox:` followed by four numbers giving the coordinates of the upper-left and lower-right corners of the image in measuring units of 1/72 inch. For example, the first two lines of an Encapsulated PostScript file that contains a full page image in portrait format would read as follows:

```
%!PS-Adobe-1.0 EPSF-2.0
%%BoundingBox: 0 0 612 792
```

GIF

CompuServe developed the Graphics Interchange Format as a means of economically exchanging large files of graphic information through dial-up connections. Rather than a file format, the GIF format defines a stream of information that can be transcribed into a disk-based file. GIF works above the image level and envisions several related images grouped together to make transmission and reconstruction more efficient. To minimize connection time (and incidentally reduce storage requirements) GIF incorporates data compression. It does not include internal error detection or correction codes.

In early 1995, the future of the GIF standard became clouded when Unisys announced it had patent rights to the compression algorithm used by the files and was intent on charging royalties. Although individual users would not have to pay such royalties, program developers using the algorithm would—which may make developers leery of incorporating GIFs into their products. (Most large companies have cross-licensing agreements with Unisys allowing them to use the technology freely.)

The GIF standard builds its data stream from a series of blocks classed as three groups, control, graphic-rendering, and special purpose. Each of these classes is subdivided. Control blocks regulate the transmission of the overall data stream or setup hardware parameters when the file is used. Graphic-rendering blocks contain the actual image data (image descriptor). Special purpose blocks handle everything else including comments and controlling the processing of the data stream.

GIF specifically defines five major control blocks: the header, the logical screen descriptor, local or global color table blocks, image descriptor blocks, and the trailer. GIF also defines three extension blocks.

Every GIF data stream and file begins with a header block, which denotes the file type and version. Only one header block is allowed in each data stream. The header block is six bytes long. The first three bytes are the ASCII characters "GIF," which are followed by three more characters describing the version. In general, the version is the last two digits of the year of the release of the version and a lowercase letter to allow multiple revisions within a single calendar year. You likely find one of two version numbers in extent .GIF files, "87a" and "89a."

A logical screen descriptor block defines the layout of the image data. In most applications, it describes the size of the image as it will appear on your monitor screen in pixels. Every GIF data stream must incorporate one and only one logical screen descriptor block.

The first two bytes of the logical screen descriptor describe the width of the image in pixels in the range 0 to 65,535. The next two bytes indicate the image height in pixels. A bitmapped flag byte follows to describe whether a global color table is present (one bit), the size of the global color table (three bits), a "sort" flag (one bit) that indicates whether the global color table is sorted, and the bit-depth of each color in the image (three bits). GIF codes the color depth as the actual value minus one, so a value of seven (all three bits high) would indicate eight bits per primary color or a 24-bit True Color image.

The sixth byte in the logical screen descriptor block indicates the background color index. The value is a pointer that indicates a position in the global color table for the hue used for those pixels on the screen that are not covered by the image. The seventh and final byte in the block describes the pixel aspect ratio. This coded value indicates the approximate aspect ratio of the image encoded to allow a 4:1 range. The value in this byte position is added to 15 and the sum divided by 64 to determine the actual aspect ratio. In other words, the formula to compute the aspect ratio from this byte value is as follows:

```
Actual Aspect Ratio = (Byte Value + 15) / 64
```

A GIF data stream optionally includes global or local color table blocks. A global color table applies to all image data in a stream except if overridden by a local color table. A local color table applies only to a single image.

A global color table block is a series of triplets of bytes, each triplet comprising a 1-byte value encoding red intensity, green intensity, and blue intensity (in that order). The logical screen descriptor block defines the number of triplets in the global color table—you calculate the number of triplets by raising two to the power of one plus the 3-bit value encoded in the logical screen descriptor block. The most common global color table size is 768, that is 256 color triplets, the value of which would be coded in the logical screen descriptor as two. If the global color table flag in the logical screen descriptor block is high, then the global color table immediately follows the logical screen descriptor block.

The local color table block takes exactly the same form as the global color table block. The only difference is that its presence and length are described in an image descriptor block, which immediately precedes the local color table, and that its values only pertain to the image data that immediately follow the table.

An image descriptor block defines each image in a GIF data stream. The image descriptor sets the image size, defines the size and presence of a local color table, and introduces a series of data sub-blocks containing the actual image information. The image data either follows immediately after the image descriptor when no local color table is present, or follows the local color table.

The first byte of the image descriptor is a fixed-value separator, 02C(Hex). Four 2-byte values follow to describe the position and size of the image. First listed is the pixel column number of the left edge of the image with respect to the logical screen defined by the logical screen descriptor block. When the image starts at the left edge of the screen, this value is zero. The next two bytes indicate the top of the image as the pixel row number referenced to the logical screen. A zero indicates that image begins at the top of the screen. The next two bytes describe the width of the image in pixels, and two more bytes indicate the height of the image in pixels.

The final byte in the image descriptor block is bitmapped and encodes whether a local color table is present, the size of the table, whether the table is sorted, and whether the image is interleaved. Two bits of this byte are reserved. Note that interlacing does not refer to monitor flicker but rather a four-way interleave of the lines of image data that gradually builds the image.

The image data is packed into one or more data sub-blocks that store from 1 to 255 bytes of data. The first byte in a data sub-block is a single size indicator byte, which stores the number of data bytes in the sub-block. The indicated number of data bytes follow. The byte after the last data byte is the size indicator byte of the next data sub-block.

When a GIF data stream uses a color table, the image data comprises a list of pointers that index triplets in a global or local color table. The pointer values follow in sequence from left to right and top to bottom across the image and are encoded using Lempel-Ziv compression. When an image uses a color table, the series of data sub-blocks must be preceded by a 1-byte value indicating the minimum code size or initial number of bits used by the Lempel-Ziv compression system.

A data sub-block with zero data bytes—that is, a size indicator byte of zero—is a special case, the block terminator. It indicates the end of the series of data sub-blocks and thus the end of the image.

The trailer block indicates the end of a GIF data stream or file. It comprises one byte of the fixed value 03B(Hex).

A GIF data stream may also incorporate several types of extension blocks, which do not contain image data and may be deleted from the data stream to minimize transmission time or file size. All extension blocks begin with an extension introducer or signature byte of the value 021(Hex).

The graphic control extension block encodes instructions on how to display and dispose of an image. It begins with an extension introducer byte of 021(Hex) and its own graphic control label of 0F9(Hex) and a length-indicator byte that has a value fixed at 04(Hex).

Four data bytes follow. The first is bitmapped and includes codes indicating the disposal method, that is the treatment of the screen after the image is erased (four possibilities are defined: 0 for no action; 1 for leaving the image in place; 2 for replacing the image with the background color; and 3 for restoring the original content of the image area), a 1-bit flag that signals that the display of the image should await user input, and a 1-bit transparent color flag.

The next two bytes indicate the number of hundredths of a second the display program should wait before processing the data stream. The next byte codes the transparency index, a pointer to the color table value. When the display program encounters this value in the data stream, it skips the corresponding pixel position, in effect letting the old image data shine through. A null byte 00(Hex) ends the graphic control extension.

The comment extension block stores text that does not get displayed as part of the image, for example a verbal description of the image or a photo credit. A comment extension block begins with an extension introducer byte of 021(Hex) followed by a comment label byte with the value 0FE(Hex). One or more data sub-blocks containing textual information follow. A null byte block terminator 00(Hex) ends the comment extension block.

A plain text extension block also stores text, but in addition, contains control information to display the text as in graphic mode as mono-spaced characters in a matrix defined by the block. The colors of the text are based on a global color table, which must be present.

The plain text extension block begins with an extension introducer byte of 021(Hex) followed by a plain text label of 01(Hex) and a length indicator byte fixed at the value 0C(Hex). The next eight bytes indicate the position and size of the character matrix. The first two bytes indicate the starting pixel column of the text area described as an offset from the edge of the logical screen. The next two bytes specify the position of the top edge of the text area as an offset from the top of the logical screen. The next two bytes indicate the width of the text area in pixels; two more bytes describe the height of the text area in pixels.

Two more bytes describe the size of each character; first the width of the character cell in pixels, then the height in pixels. The next byte indicates the foreground color for the text in the form of a pointer to a triplet in the global color table. One more byte indicates the background color as a table pointer.

One or more data sub-blocks containing the actual text in ASCII format follow. The plain text extension block ends with a null byte of 00(Hex).

The application extension block provides control information for specific applications. Although the GIF specification defines the form of the block, its contents and their meaning are specific to third-party applications.

The block begins with an extension introducer byte of 021(Hex) followed by an extension label bytes of 0FF(Hex) and a length indicator byte with a fixed value of 0B(Hex). The application extension format then allows eight bytes of ASCII text to identify the application and three bytes for an application authentication code. One or more data sub-blocks follow, and the application extension block ends with a null byte of 00(Hex).

JPEG

As Windows and multimedia applications move to 16- and 24-bit color, the JPEG compression system is gaining momentum. Using JPEG, you can pack 24-bit color images in a file the same size and often smaller than those required by color-mapped 8-bit images, such as those using the .BMP or .GIF file formats. Necessity being the mother of imposition, Microsoft has published a standard for JPEG files that fits within the RIFF framework.

The JPEG compression scheme was used long before Microsoft published its standard. Files storing images using the Joint Photographic Experts Group compression scheme use the .JPG filename extension. Sometimes files of the same format use the extension .JIF, which stands JPEG Image File (Format). Most are readily identified by the signature JFIF (for JPEG File Interchange Format) that appears at the eighth through twelfth bytes in a file.

Under Microsoft's recommendations, a JPEG file contains essentially the same data and has the following three or four structures in its format to conform with Microsoft's bitmap file format:

➤ Device-independent bitmap file header

➤ Bitmap information header

➤ Color table (optional)

➤ Image data

The device-independent bitmap file header is exactly the same as that described under the .BMP file specification. Microsoft considers the JPEG file simply to be a variation of its device-independent bitmap scheme.

The JPEG bitmap information header is a simple structure that describes the essential qualities of the image and the form of JPEG compression used to package it. This header is also much like that of .BMP file except that it is extended by additions that help describe the JPEG image. Table 9.8 lists the structure of this header.

TABLE 9.8. JPEG bitmap info header structure.

Offset (bytes)	Length (bytes)	Description	Function
0	4	biSize	Length of header in bytes
4	4	biWidth	Image width (pixels)
8	4	biHeight	Image height (pixels)
12	2	biPlanes	Image planes (must be 1)
14	2	biBitCount	Bits per pixel
16	4	biCompression	Compression type
20	4	biSizeImage	Image size in bytes
24	4	biXPelsPerMeter	Horizontal resolution (pixels)
28	4	biYPelsPerMeter	Vertical resolution (pixels)
32	4	biClrUsed	Number of colors in image
36	4	biClrImportant	Number of important colors
40	4	biExtDataOffset	Points to JPEG data
44	4	JPEGsize	Size of JPEG fields
48	4	JPEGprocess	Format type (must be 0)
52	4	JPEGColorSpaceID	Color space used by images
56	4	JPEGBitsPerSample	Bits per pixel (must be 8)
60	4	JPEGHSubSampling	Horizontal sampling factor
64	4	JPEGVSubSampling	Vertical sampling factor

The image data in the file follows the ISO standard (10918, paragraph 3.9.1, "Interchange Format." Microsoft has published its description of the JPEG device-independent bitmap format as a Technical Note, "JPEG DIB Format."

PCD

Files with the extension .PCD store images based on the PhotoCD system developed by Kodak. These files have a peculiar format based on the needs of both photographics and video display systems, and are particularly designed to facilitate fast retrieval of images at several resolution levels. To conserve storage, the system stores a reference image at base resolution (essentially that of a normal video image, 768×512 pixels) together with compressed difference information that enables the reconstruction of several successively larger and smaller images from 3072×2048 pixels down to 192×128 pixels. Colors are stored in a video-like luminance/chrominance format that translates to 12 bits per color. Chapter 12, "The Compact Disc," discusses the details of this format.

PCX

One of the most common formats for storing still images was developed by ZSoft in conjunction with its program PC Paintbrush. This system stores files with the extension .PCX.

All PCX files have a 68-byte header that's padded out to 128 bytes with 60 null characters, that is 00(Hex). The format supplies sufficient flexibility to accommodate virtually any image size and number of colors. Image compression is integral to the format.

The first byte of the PCX header is used to identify the manufacturer. ZSoft uses the value 0A(Hex) as its own signature. This value can vary without affecting the image content.

The next byte indicates the PCX version of the standard under which the file was written. Four version numbers commonly appear: 0 for version 2.5; 2 for version 2.8 files that include palette information; 3 for version 2.8 files lacking palette information (direct color); and 5 for version 3.0.

This last version (3.0) indicates the file has a more elaborate structure that may contain a color palette table at its end. A byte outside the header indicates the presence of palette data. The actual flag is stored 769 bytes from the end of the file. If this flag byte has a value of 0C(Hex), the next 768 bytes store the VGA color palette used by the image.

The third byte in the header indicates the compression method used in encoding the image. Uncompressed files have a value of zero at this location. A 1 here indicates PCX run-length encoding (RLE).

In its 8-bit mode, the PCX RLE system uses the two most significant bits of data bytes in its code. When the first byte of pixel data has zeros as its two most significant bits, the remaining six bits get directly interpreted as pixel value. If the two most significant bits are high (ones), the byte is a multiplier. The decoded data stream comprises a series of bytes of the value of the byte following the multiplier. The multiplier indicates the number of repetitions of this byte value, so up to 63 bytes can be coded by two. Note, however, this system cannot code a single byte value greater than 63. Instead, higher individual pixels require two bytes—a multiplier of one—actual value, C1(Hex)—followed by the actual pixel value as a second data byte.

The next nine bytes encode the depth and dimensions of the image window, independent of screen size or resolution. The first of these bytes describes the color depth in bits per pixel per image plane. The next two bytes store the x-coordinate of the first pixel and are followed by the y-coordinate of this initial image position. Similarly, the next two bytes encode the x-coordinate of the last pixel in the image, followed by the y-coordinate of that pixel.

The dimensions of the screen itself are stored in the next four bytes. The first two indicate the horizontal size of the screen in lines, and the last two indicate the vertical size in pixels per line.

A block of 48 bytes follows. This block encodes the color palette setting of some of the image formats stored in .PCX files.

The following byte (the 64th) was originally designed to specify the video mode used by the display system. For practical purposes, however, this byte is ignored by current systems.

The next byte indicates the number of color planes in the image. This value, multiplied by the number of bits per pixel per plane (the fourth byte of the header) yield the total number of colors available in the image.

Two more bytes indicate the number of bytes used to store the data of each scan line. This number will always be an even integer.

The last significant header byte is a flag that indicates how the palette is to be interpreted. A value of one indicates the palette information should be rendered in color; a value of two means that it is grayscale data. The last 58 bytes simply pad out the header to a length of 128 bytes.

The actual image data gets stored as a line-by-line sequence of pixels in serial order.

TGA

Files following the standard used by the TrueVision Targa video board (and related products) are identified by their .TGA filename extension. The Targa system first gave PCs the ability to directly manipulate standard video images (though mostly still rather than moving images), and the formats used by Targa files have lingered as standards for video-quality images exchange.

Standards

In fact, Targa is not one but more than half a dozen different image formats, several of which are popular image formats. All of the popular Targa formats have the same basic file structure, however. The first 18 or so bytes in each file identify the image type, size, and storage format. Table 9.9 lists this generalized format.

TABLE 9.9. Generalized Targa file format.

Start byte	Length in bytes	Function
0	1	Length of identification field
1	1	Data type field
2	1	Image type code
3	2	Color map origin
5	2	Color map length
7	1	Color map entry size
8	2	X-coordinate of image
10	2	Y-coordinate of image
12	2	Width of image
14	2	Height of image
16	1	Image pixel size
17	1	Image descriptor (bitmapped)
18	Varies	Image descriptor field
Varies	Varies	Color map data
Varies	Varies	Image data field

The different types of Targa files are identified by a byte called the *Data Type Field*, which is always the third byte in the file. Nine values are defined for the Data Type Field, listed in Table 9.10. Of these, types 1, 2, 9, and 10 are most commonly used.

TABLE 9.10. Targa data type field descriptors.

Data field	Image type	Compression type
0	None	None
1	Color-mapped	None
2	RGB	None
3	Black-and-white	None
9	Color-mapped	Run-length encoded (RLE)
10	RGB	Run-length encoded (RLE)
11	Black-and-white	Run-length encoded (RLE)
32	Color-mapped	Huffman, delta, and RLE
33	Color-mapped	Huffman, delta, and RLE, 4-pass

Uncompressed Color-Mapped Image

Uncompressed color-mapped image files start with a 1-byte value describing the size of the file's Identification Field. This one byte allows the Identification Field (which starts at byte 18) to be from 0 to 255 bytes long.

The next two bytes are always a binary one for uncompressed color-mapped images; the second byte in the file indicates color map type 1; the third byte is the Data Field byte, which defines the file type as 1.

The next five bytes provide a color map specification. The first two bytes of this field (the fourth and fifth in the file) indicate the origin of the color map as an integral value in Intel format (least significant byte first). The next two bytes indicate the color map length as an integral number of color map entries. The next byte (the seventh in the file) specifies the number of bits in each color map entry, which can be either 16, 24, or 32.

Ten bytes follow to describe the size and location of the image. First comes the x-coordinate of the lower left corner of the image as a 2-byte integer value. Following that is the y-coordinate of the lower left corner of the image as a 2-byte integer value. The next two bytes list the width of the image as an integral number of pixels, followed by the height of the image as an integral number of pixels. The next byte describes the number of bits in each pixel. It is followed by an image descriptor byte which uses a bitmapped code as shown in Table 9.11. For all practical uncompressed color-mapped Targa files, this byte is always zero.

TABLE 9.11. Targa image descriptor bytes.

Bit	Function	Code
0-3	Number of bits per attribute (in binary)	
		0000=0
		0001=1
		1000=8
4	Reserved	
		Always 0
5	Screen origin bit	
		0-lower left
		1=upper left

continues

TABLE 9.11. continued

Bit	Function	Code
6-7	Interleave flag	
		00=no interleave
		01=two-way interleave
		10=four-way interleave
		11=reserved

Next comes the Image Identification Field, which stretches from the eighteenth byte for the length specified by the first byte in the file. In most Targa files, the first byte is zero, and this field has zero length.

The actual image data follows. The Color Map Specification indicates the number of entries and the size of each. The three color formats—16, 24, and 32 bits—make for entries of two, three, or four bytes. Two-byte entries encode the color of each pixel with a 5-bit value. The leftover bit stores attribute information. The 3-byte entry stores one byte for each primary color. Four-byte entries include an extra byte of attribute data following the color data. Color values are always listed blue-green-red in 3- and 4-byte per entry files. In 2-byte files, the order is attribute-red-green-blue, but with the least significant byte first.

Uncompressed RGB Image

Uncompressed RGB image files start with a 1-byte value describing the size of the file's Identification Field. This one byte allows the Identification Field to be from 0 to 255 bytes long.

The next byte indicates whether a color map is included with the file and must be zero (indicating the absence of a color map) or one (indicating the presence of a color map). This byte is usually ignored by programs because this form of image does not use a color map, although Targa paint software sets the image border color to the first value indicated in the color map. The next byte, the third in the file, is the Data Field byte and must be set to 2 to indicate an uncompressed RGB image file.

The next five bytes provide a color map specification. If the second byte in the file is zero (indicating no color map), these bytes are ignored. Otherwise, the first two bytes of this field (the fourth and fifth in the file) indicate the origin of the color map as an integral value in Intel format (least significant byte first). The next two bytes indicate the color map length as an integral number of color map entries. The next byte (the seventh in the file) specifies the number of bits in each color map entry, which can be either 16, 24, or 32.

Another byte, number 17, serves as the Image Descriptor Byte, and it is bitmapped. Bits 0 through 2 indicate the number of attribute bits associated with each pixel. Bit 4 is reserved and is always set to zero. Bit 5 indicates the location of the origin of the image, zero indicating the lower left corner, one indicating the upper left corner. All TrueVision images have an origin in the lower left. The remaining two bits indicate the interleaving of the image: 00 for no interleaving; 01 for two-way interleaving; 10 for four-way interleaving; with a value of 11 reserved.

Following the Descriptor Byte comes the Image Identification Field, which stretches from the eighteenth byte for the length specified by the first byte in the file. In most Targa files, the first byte is zero, and this field has zero length.

The actual color map comes next, if one is present in the file. It is followed by the image data. The Color Map Specification indicates the number of entries and the size of each. The three color formats—16, 24, and 32 bits—make for entries of two, three, or four bytes. Two-byte entries encode the color of each pixel with a 5-bit value. The leftover bit stores attribute information. The 3-byte entrée stores one byte for each primary color. Four-byte entries include an extra byte of attribute data following the color data. Color values are always listed blue-green-red in 3- and 4-byte-per entry files. In 2-byte files, the order is attribute-red-green-blue but with the least significant byte first.

Run-Length Encoded, Color-Mapped Image

Run-Length Encoded, color-mapped image files start with a 1-byte value describing the size of the file's Identification Field. This one byte allows the Identification Field to be from 0 to 255 bytes long.

The next byte is always a binary one to indicate that the image is color-mapped. It is followed by the Data Field byte, which must be 9 to define the file as an RLE color-mapped image.

As in the generalized Targa format, the next five bytes provide a color map specification. If the second byte in the file is zero (indicating no color map), these bytes are ignored. Otherwise, the first two bytes of this field (the fourth and fifth in the file) indicate the origin of the color map as an integral value in Intel format (least significant byte first). The next two bytes indicate the color map length as an integral number of color map entries. The next byte (the seventh in the file) specifies the number of bits in each color map entry, which can be either 16, 24, or 32.

The next byte, number 17, is the Image Descriptor Byte, and it is bitmapped per Table 9.11. Bits 0 through 2 indicate the number of attribute bits associated with each pixel. Bit 4 is reserved and is always set to zero. Bit 5 indicates the location of the origin of the image, zero indicating the lower left corner, one indicating the upper left corner. All TrueVision images have an origin in the lower left. The remaining two bits indicate the interleaving of the image: 00 for no interleaving; 01 for two-way interleaving; 10 for four-way interleaving; with a value of 11 reserved.

Next comes the Image Identification Field, which stretches from the eighteenth byte for the length specified by the first byte in the file. In most Targa files, the first byte is zero, and this field has zero length.

The actual color map comes next, if one is present in the file. It is followed by the image data. The Color Map Specification indicates the number of entries and the size of each. The three color formats—16, 24, and 32 bits—make for entries of two, three, or four bytes. Two-byte entries encode the color of each pixel with a 5-bit value. The leftover bit stores attribute information. The 3-byte entrée stores one byte for each primary color. Four-byte entries include an extra byte of attribute data following the color data. Color values are always listed blue-green-red in 3- and 4-byte per entry files. In 2-byte files, the order is attribute-red-green-blue but with the least significant byte first.

The run-length encoding scheme puts image data into two types of packets: those that actually use run-length encoding and raw packets that do not. Both types of packets have a 1-byte header followed by one or more color entry. Each color entry comprises two, three, or four bytes depending on the bit-depth of the pixel it encodes. The header byte identifies the packet type and gives the count for the number of repeats for encoded color entries or the number of unrepeated color entries that follow. The most significant bit of the header is always a digital one for a run-length encoded packet and always zero for a raw packet. The header of a run-length encoded packet indicates one less than the number of repetitions of the color entry that follows. The 7-bit code allows specifying a repeated string of up to 128 color entries. This string may cross the border between scan lines, so one packet can specify the ending pixels on one scan line and the beginning pixels on the next. The header for a raw packet is constructed similarly and specifies one less than number of non-repeating color entries that follow, up to 128 repeated color entries.

Run-Length Encoded RGB Image

Run-length encoded RGB image files start with a 1-byte value describing the size of the file's Identification Field. This one byte allows the Identification Field to be from 0 to 255 bytes long.

The next byte indicates whether a color map is included with the file and must be zero (indicating the absence of a color map) or one (indicating the presence of a color map). This byte is usually ignored by programs because this form of image does not use a color map, although Targa paint software sets the image border color to the first value indicated in the color map. The next byte, the third in the file, is the Data Field byte and must be set to 10 to indicate a run-length encoded compressed RGB image file.

Conforming with the generalized Targa format, the next five bytes provide a color map specification. If the second byte in the file is zero (indicating no color map), these bytes are ignored. Otherwise, the first two bytes of this field (the fourth and fifth in the file) indicate the origin of the color map as an integral value in Intel format (least significant byte first). The next two bytes indicate the color map length as an integral number of color map entries. The next byte (the seventh in the file) specifies the number of bits in each color map entry, which can be either 16, 24, or 32.

The next byte, number 17, is the Image Descriptor Byte, and it is bitmapped per Table 9.11 (shown previously). Bits 0 through 2 indicate the number of attribute bits associated with each pixel. Bit 4 is reserved and is always set to zero. Bit 5 indicates the location of the origin of the image, zero indicating the lower left corner, one indicating the upper left corner. All TrueVision images have an origin in the lower left. The remaining two bits indicate the interleaving of the image: 00 for no interleaving; 01 for two-way interleaving; 10 for four-way interleaving; with a value of 11 reserved.

Next comes the Image Identification Field, which stretches from the eighteenth byte for the length specified by the first byte in the file. In most Targa files, the first byte is zero, and this field has zero length.

The actual color map comes next, if one is present in the file. It is followed by the image data. The Color Map Specification indicates the number of entries and the size of each. The three color formats—16, 24, and 32 bits—make for entries of two, three, or four bytes. Two-byte entries encode the color of each pixel with a 5-bit value. The leftover bit stores attribute information. The 3-byte entrée stores one byte for each primary color. Four-byte entries include an extra byte of attribute data following the color data. Color values are always listed blue-green-red in 3- and 4-byte per entry files. In 2-byte files, the order is attribute-red-green-blue but with the least significant byte first.

As with plain color-mapped Targa files, image data in run-length encoded RGB files is stored in two types of packets: those that use run-length encoding and raw packets that do not. Both types of packets have a 1-byte header followed by one or more color entry. Again, each color entry comprises two, three, or four bytes depending on the bit-depth of the pixel it encodes. The header byte identifies the packet type and gives the count for the number of repeats for encoded color entries or the number of unrepeated color entries that follow. The most significant bit of the header is always a digital one for a run-length encoded packet and always zero for a raw packet. The header of a run-length encoded packet indicates one less than the number of repetitions of the color entry that follows. The 7-bit code allows specifying a repeated string of up to 128 color entries. This string may cross the border between scan lines, so one packet can specify the ending pixels on one scan line and the beginning pixels on the next. The header for a raw packet is constructed similarly and specifies one less than number of non-repeating color entries that follow, up to 128 repeated color entries.

WMF

Files that bear the .WMF extension are usually Windows Metafiles and contain graphics information. A metafile stores an image as a drawing in the form of a series of Windows Graphic Device Interface functions. The file itself is a sequence of records, each of which stores a GDI function. Every time the image is viewed or imported into an application, the GDI functions get executed to recreate the drawing. Because Windows uses GDI functions to draw its screens and printer output, and because a metafile can store any GDI operation, a metafile can record

Standards

anything you can see in Windows. Because Microsoft has defined a standard format for metafiles, they serve as a ready exchange medium.

Because metafiles are essentially drawings rather than bit-images (although they can contain bit-images), they have a singular advantage over ordinary bitmapped images. The drawing commands lend themselves to scaling. Each function in a metafile can be individually scaled, so the images are essentially independent of the resolution of the display system or application using them.

Metafiles images have other advantages. Because their commands can be directly interpreted by the Windows GDI, individual applications need not deal with the data in the file to display it. Moreover, as with any drawing format, metafiles use less storage than bitmapped images for simple pictures.

Windows version 3.0 and earlier impose severe limits on metafiles. The maximum size of each record was limited to 64KB, and the number of objects in the file was limited by the size of the memory heap in the GDI. With the Windows 3.1 family, these restrictions were removed so that the maximum size of a metafile is 4GB, which means essentially unlimited.

Bitmapped images can be included as part of the metafile content as device-independent bitmaps—after all, bitmaps are an essential part of Windows screen displays generated by the GDI—but packaging a bitmap in metafile format can be counterproductive. You can even embed metafiles within metafiles.

Metafiles take their internal structure from the GDI instructions that they contain, using several layers of header to identify themselves and their internal components. The file itself and each record is individually identified by its own header. Table 9.12 lists the metafile record format.

TABLE 9.12. Metafile record format.

Offset (bytes)	Length (bytes)	Description	Function
0	2	mtType	Type descriptor (always 1)
2	2	mtHeaderSize	Length of header
4	2	mtVersion	Windows (GDI) version
6	4	mtSize	Size of metafile in words
10	2	mtNoObjects	Number of objects
12	4	mtMaxRecord	Size of largest record in words
16	2	mtNoParameters	Unused

Windows understands several commands for creating, copying, and using metafiles. The complete format, structure, and commands are documented in the Windows Software Development Kit.

Video Formats

AVI

The movies that you play with Video for Windows use the *Audio/Video Interleaved* or .AVI file format devised by Microsoft expressly for that purpose. The name describes the overall file structure: audio and video are typically interleaved throughout the file as multiple streams. Sometimes an index is added to allow quick random access of individual parts of the file. You can identify an .AVI file by its first four bytes, which identify it as an RIFF file (with the characters RIFF, of course). The eighth through twelfth characters in the file identify it as an .AVI file. These are always the capital letters "AVI" followed by a space.

.AVI files follow the general RIFF specification and are made from nested data chunks. The file itself comprises three main chunks into which other chunks are nested. The first chunk must be a LIST chunk called `hrdl`, which defines that format of the data in the file. The second chunk, also a LIST chunk, is called `movi` and stores the audio and video data as chunks nested inside it. The third main chunk is an optional index chunk called `idx1`.

Because the RIFF specification rigidly defines file structure and the AVI specification requires the particular ordering and nesting of chunks in a file, several elements of the first bytes of an .AVI file are consistent no matter its content or size. Table 9.13 lists these invariant values.

TABLE 9.13. Starting bytes of .AVI file structure.

Offset (bytes)	Length (bytes)	Data	Function
0	4	RIFF	Identifies RIFF file
4	4	[data]	Size of file
8	4	AVI	Identifies .AVI file
12	4	LIST	Marks first LIST chunk
16	4	[data]	Size of LIST chunk
20	4	hrdl	Identifies hrdl chunk
24	4	avih	Identifies AVI stream

The `hrdl` chunk begins with a header that identifies the contents of the .AVI file. This header is 60 bytes long and describes video image parameters such as size and display rate as well as the number of streams in the file. The bytes in the header are defined as listed in Table 9.14.

TABLE 9.14. AVI chunk header.

Offset (bytes)	Length (bytes)	Description	Function
0	4	`"avih"`	Identifies header
4	4	`dwMicroSecPerFrame`	Video frame length
8	4	`dwMaxBytesPerPixel`	Approximate top data rate
12	4	`dwReserved1`	Reserved
16	4	`dwFlags`	Flag bits
20	4	`dwTotalFrames`	Length of Sequence (frames)
24	4	`dwInitialFrames`	Frames before start if interleaved
28	4	`dwStreams`	Number of data streams
32	4	`dwSuggestedBufferSize`	Playback buffer
36	4	`dwWidth`	Image width (pixels)
40	4	`dwHeight`	Image height (pixels)
44	4	`dwScale`	General time scale
48	4	`dwRate`	General time scale
52	4	`dwStart`	Start of file
56	4	`dwLength`	File length

After the header come one or more `strl` chunks, one for each data stream. Each of these chunks must contain one stream header chunk, identified by the four-character code `strh` at its start, and a stream format chunk, identified as `strf`. The `strl` chunk may also contain a stream data chunk, prefaced by the characters `strd`.

The stream header describes the contents of the chunk. The first four characters in the header identify the contents of the chunk as video or audio information. Video chunks are identified by the characters `vids`; audio chunks by `auds`. The format of the stream header is given in Table 9.15.

TABLE 9.15. .AVI file stream header.

Offset (bytes)	Length (bytes)	Description	Function
0	4	`fccType`	Stream type
4	4	`fccHandler`	Compression type
8	4	`dwFlags`	Data stream flags
12	4	`dwReserved1`	Reserved

Offset (bytes)	Length (bytes)	Description	Function
16	4	dwInitialFrames	Frames before start when interleaved
20	4	dwScale	Playback rate
24	4	dwRate	Playback rate
28	4	dwStart	Starting time of stream
32	4	dwLength	Length of stream
36	4	dwSuggestedBufferSize	Playback buffer size
40	4	dwQuality	Quality of data sample
44	4	dw	Sample size

The stream format chunks that follow the header describe the format of the data in the stream. For a video stream, the structure is essentially identical to a RIFF device-independent bitmap. The audio stream format is structured as RIFF waveform format. If a stream data chunk follows the stream format chunk, the data chunk usually contains setup information for the decompression drivers.

The actual image and sound data follows the hrdl chunk in the movi chunk. The movi chunk is further subdivided into chunks, each one of which directly corresponds to a strl stream chunk in the hrdl chunk. For example, the first information in the first strl chunk describes the structure of the first chunk of data stored here.

These data chunks are identified by two digits which give the serial position of the corresponding strl chunk, starting with zero. Two characters follow to identify the type of data in the chunk. Table 9.16 lists the three codes currently defined.

TABLE 9.16. AVI data type identifying characters.

Characters	Meaning
db	Uncompressed device-independent bitmap video
dc	Compressed device-independent bitmap video
wb	Wavetable audio

All data chunks may be contained directly in the movi chunk or they may be grouped together in rec chunks within the movi chunk. The rec chunks store data chunks that are meant to be read from disk together as a group without interruption. Used for CD-ROM data, this grouping helps kept data in sync despite the low transfer rate of the storage system.

The final optional chunk in an .AVI file is the index chunk, which contains a list of all the data chunks in the file and their location. Using the data in the index chunk, playback software can find a given audio or video sequence without scanning through the entire file.

MOV

QuickTime for Windows uses files wearing the extension .MOV, short for *movie*. The structure of these files is the same whether they are meant to play on their native Macintosh computer or on PCs using QuickTime for Windows. Most QuickTime movies for PCs can be recognized by the signature *mdat* (for movie data) that occurs as the fifth through eighth bytes in the file.

A QuickTime movie is made from blocks of homogeneous data which are called *QuickTime tracks*. A simple movie might contain solely a video track or both audio and video tracks. A complex presentation might pack multiple video tracks into a single file, each of which may use a separate form of compression.

As with files that conform to the RIFF specification, in QuickTime movie files the description of the data is stored separately from the data itself. The format of the data gets described by a header structure. Video and audio tracks use distinct headers. Apple has documented the video structure as shown in Table 9.17.

TABLE 9.17. QuickTime image header structure.

Offset (bytes)	Length (bytes)	Description	Function
0	4	idSize	Structure size
4	4	CodecType	As below:
			rpza=Apple video
			jpeg=Apple JPEG
			rel=Apple animation
			raw=Apple raw
			smc =Apple graphics
			cvid=Compact video
8	4	resvd1	Reserved, always 0
12	2	resvd2	Reserved, always 0
14	2	dataRefIndex	Reserved, always 0
16	2	version	Always 0
18	2	revLevel	Revision level, always 0
20	4	vendor	Reserved, always 0
24	4	temporalQuality	Reserved, always 0

Offset (bytes)	Length (bytes)	Description	Function
28	4	spatialQuality	Reserved, always 0
32	2	width	Source image width in pixels
34	2	height	Source image height in pixels
36	4	hRes	Horizontal resolution
40	4	vRes	Vertical resolution
44	4	dataSize	Reserved, always 0
48	2	frameCount	Reserved, always 0
50	32	name	Specifies compression system
62	2	depth	Pixel depth of image
64	2	clutID	Reserved, always 0

The header structure for audio tracks is shown in Table 9.18.

TABLE 9.18. QuickTime audio header structure.

Offset (bytes)	Length (bytes)	Description	Function
0	4	descSize	Structure size
4	4	dataFormat	Data format, always "raw"
8	4	resvd1	Reserved, always 0
12	2	resvd2	Reserved, always 0
14	2	dataRefIndex	Reserved, always 1
16	2	version	Reserved, always 0
18	2	revLevel	Reserved, always 0
20	4	vendor	Reserved, always 0
24	2	numChannels	1=mono; 2=stereo
26	2	sampleSize	Bit in sample size (8 or 16)
28	2	compressionID	Reserved, always 0
30	2	packetSize	Reserved, always 0
32	4	sampleRate	Sample rate in Hertz

Apple intends that the .MOV file format will remain consistent across all platforms that use it and has published its full specifications. The complete format makes provisions for additional features such as posters and previews. *Posters* are still images that are shown on-screen as icons for the movie or used for printing out hard copy that includes a window of movie video. *Previews* are short video clips that can be used to preview the movie when scanning through a movie database or similar listing. Although the first release of the MOV format definition only included definitions of audio and video tracks, the format is designed to be extensible to include other data types.

Audio File Types

Posterity being as it is, you might be tempted to horde everything for yourself and not save anything for it. But even you alone have good reason for committing your efforts at and explorations of multimedia sound to a record more long-lasting than the vibrations of air waves. You might want to play that song one more time, tinker with an arrangement, or savor a particularly satisfying simulated explosion you've created. So your efforts are not in vain—or at least not vanishing—you need some way to preserve your work, a means of storing your sound data.

Engineers have developed three technologies for storing data for sound reproduction. Each technology uses its own type of file. These include descriptor, control, and waveform files.

Descriptor Files

Descriptor files actually hold no sound information at all. These files merely describe a means of making a sound. They define one or more synthesized instruments that can be used by sound boards to play sounds either interactively or from stored files. These files enable you or your programs to dream up a particular instrument sound and recall it for later use. Because different sound boards use a number of different synthesizer chips and means of synthesis, instrument descriptions and even the means of making the description can vary between products. Consequently sound board makers have developed their own file formats to suit their particular creations. Some have developed several formats to suit their products. For example, Creative Labs uses both .SBI and .IBX files to define instruments; the former for individual instruments, the later for mass descriptions of up to 128 instruments handled by a complete MIDI system.

Control Files

Control files store the information used for controlling an instrument or other audio device in making a sound. They are like sheet music for digital synthesizers. Rather than store sounds, they list the notes to be played—pitch, duration, rhythm, and so on. The synthesizer acts on them.

Control files are like drawing or vector graphic files. They store sound data in a compact language instead of an intimate bit description of the sound. The actual sounds that are created depend on the settings of the synthesizer. Just as Middle C played on a piano and clarinet look the same in sheet music but sound entirely different, one control file can sound wildly different when played through different synthesizers or even the same synthesizer with different instrument assignments.

Of course, to be properly understood the control language must be specific to the device that uses it. Most electronic instruments and synthesizers speak and listen to a common language, MIDI, so files of MIDI instructions make a convenient means of storing music. In fact, the MIDI specifications detail the construction of MIDI files and their contents. Most MIDI files wear the extension .MID, although a MIDI file can also be encapsulated in Microsoft's overall Resource Interchange File Format as an .RMI file.

.VOC files are another kind of control file. These store voice synthesis instructions that enable Sound Blaster boards to mimic human speech.

Waveform Files

Waveform files are bit-images of sound. They store every nuance of the sound. For example, the most common variety of waveform file stores every sample made in the progress of pulse code modulation. For CD-quality music, that would be two 16-bit samples 44,100 times per second—that's more than 10MB per minute of playing time.

Understandably, many waveform files aren't exact instant-by-instant replicas of waveforms but are instead compressed. Standard waveform file formats allow for storing both compressed and uncompressed versions of waveform data.

The most common waveform files for multimedia on PCs have the file extension .WAV. These are the files that Windows plays and most Windows-based programs generate. Other computer systems have their own file formats.

Audio File Formats

In that it is data, you handle it exactly like any other data—write it to disk. Bytes are bytes, after all, and all you need is a SAVE command and all should be well. At least until you try to make sense of what's on the disk at some later time. Bytes are bytes and 10 seconds of harp solo are to the human eye pretty much indistinguishable from a check-balancing program or even random data. Computer programs, having even less discrimination than your eye, are even more befuddled. They need some kind of hint as to what's in the file and how to decipher the data that's there. The following sections detail some standards for audio files.

AIFF Format

Both Macintosh computers and Silicon Graphics workstations store audio in Audio Interchange File Format (AIFF) developed by Apple that uses the filename extension .AIF. A variation on the theme, AIFC files compress the audio data they contain. Files that follow either of these formats are self-descriptive. That is, they begin with a header that describes the internal format of their audio data in terms of sampling rate, bit-depth, number of channels, identifying data, and so on. Formatted audio data follows the header.

Macintosh

Because most of the computers that use AIFF files are based on Motorola microprocessors, these files use big-endian byte ordering. Unlike most data formats used by Intel-based computers that put the least significant bytes and bits first, in AIFF files the most significant byte in a data word comes first, the most significant bits in a byte are first. As a consequence, AIFF files are not directly compatible with PCs but must be converted before they can be used.

IBK Format

Files with the extension .IBK are Sound Blaster Instrument Bank files, which are used to define a group of up to 128 instruments. Each .IBK file has a fixed length and format. .IBK files are 3,204 bytes long and include space to give each of 128 instruments a 9-byte name along with 16 bytes of descriptive parameters.

The first four bytes of an .IBK file identify it as such. These bytes store the characters "IBK" in standard ASCII code followed by an end-of-file character, 01A(Hex).

Next follows a sequence of 128 records, each 16 bytes long. The bytes in each of these records define an instrument with the following characteristics, as shown in Table 9.19.

TABLE 9.19. .IBK file instrument definitions.

Byte	Bits	Function
0	All	Modulator sound characteristic
1	0–3	Frequency multiplier
	4	Envelope scaling
	5	Sustaining sound
	6	Amplitude vibrato
	7	Pitch vibrato
2	All	Modulator scaling/output level
3	0–5	Output level
	6–7	Carrier level scaling
4	All	Modulator attack and decay rates
5	0–3	Carrier attack rate
	4–7	Carrier decay rate
6	All	Modulator sustain and release
7	0–3	Carrier release rate
	4–7	Carrier sustain level
8	All	Modulator wave select

Byte	Bits	Function
9	0–1	Carrier wave select
	2–7	Not used
	0	Connection
10	1–3	Modulator feedback
	4–7	Not used
11	All	Reserved
12	All	Reserved
13	All	Reserved
14	All	Reserved
15	All	Reserved

Following the instrument definitions are 128 records, each nine bytes long, storing the name of each instrument. The last (ninth) character of each name must be a null byte, 00(Hex).

MID Format

The MID format used by files following the Musical Instrument Digital Interface standard are the most widely used audio control files in multimedia. MIDI embraces a complete system that specifies not only a file format but also a signaling and hardware system. The MIDI standard is covered in depth in Chapter 16, "MIDI."

Standards

MIDI files store a stream of commands for MIDI synthesizer systems. The files themselves are built from chunks, which come in two types, header chunks and track chunks. Each MIDI file comprises one header chunk and one or more track chunks.

Each chunk devotes its first four bytes to a signature identifying its type. Header chunks begin with the characters "MThd" in ASCII code. Track chunks begin with "MTrk" in ASCII. The signature is followed by four bytes which specify the length of the data in the chunk (which does not include the eight bytes of descriptive data), permitting any chunk to be up to 4GB long. Header chunks always have a length of six bytes, encoded as 06 00 00 00 in Intel little-endian format in the MIDI file.

The first eight bytes of a header chunk are followed by a format word (two bytes) that indicates the arrangement of the data in the file. A zero (00 00 on disk) indicates that the file defines a single multichannel track. One (01 00 on disk) indicates the file holds one or more tracks of a sequence that are meant to be played simultaneously. Two (02 00 on disk) in this position indicates that the file compresses one or more single-track patterns that are independent in playing sequence.

The next word position (the eleventh and twelfth bytes) indicates the number of separate MIDI track chunks contained in the file. This format allows up to 65,535 data chunks per file. The last word (the thirteenth and fourteenth bytes) in the header chunk specifies the meaning of the delta-times in the track chunks. The data in these bytes take one of two formats. When the most significant bit of the word is zero, its lower 15 bits indicate the number of ticks per quarter note. When the most significant bit of this word is one, it indicates that timings are in a time code. The remaining seven bits of the upper byte are in negative SMPTE time-code format, and the lower byte indicates the number of ticks per SMPTE frame.

A track chunk start with the 8-byte identification preamble (four bytes as "MTrk" followed by four bytes indicating length) followed by a MIDI track event.

Each MIDI track event has two parts, a variable length (one to four byte) delta time indication, which describes the time before the event, and the event itself. The event can be one of these kinds: a MIDI event, which is simply a MIDI channel message; a system-exclusive message (also called a *sysex event*); or a Meta event, which is non-MIDI information for the sequencer.

A system-exclusive message is a data string that takes a three-part form: an identifying byte, which may be either F0(Hex) or F7(Hex), followed by one to three bytes indicating the length the data string, and the data string itself.

A meta event has a similar four-part form. Its first byte is always FF(Hex). Next comes a 1-byte type code. Next is a variable length (one to four byte) indication of the length of the data in the meta event. The final part is the meta event data itself. Table 9.20 lists the currently defined MIDI meta events.

TABLE 9.20. MIDI file meta event codes.

Byte 0	1	2	3	4	5	6	7	Definition
Meta event byte	Type	Length						
FF	00	02	#	#				Sequence number
FF	01	<length>	<text>					Text event
FF	02	<length>	<text>					Copyright notice
FF	03	<length>	<text>					Sequence or track name
FF	04	<length>	<text>					Instrument name
FF	05	<length>	<text>					Lyric
FF	06	<length>	<text>					Marker
FF	07	<length>	<text>					Cue point

Byte								
0	1	2	3	4	5	6	7	*Definition*
Meta event byte	Type	Length						
FF	20	01	#					MIDI channel prefix
FF	2F	00						End of track
FF	51	#	#	#				Set tempo
FF	54	05	Hour	Minute	Second	Frame	Fraction	SMPTE offset
FF	58	04	#	#	#	#		Time signature
FF	59	02	#	#				Key signature
FF	7F	<length>	<data>					Sequencer-specific event

*Notes: # represents a function- or action-specific byte value

*<length> is one to four bytes encoding the number of data bytes following <text> and <data> are variable length fields

In several places the MIDI file specification allows for lengths to be specified by a variable number of bytes. MIDI uses a special encoding format so that the bytes themselves indicate their number. The last byte in the variable length sequence must have its highest bit set to zero. All other bytes in the sequence have their highest bit set to one. The MIDI scheme uses only the remaining seven bits of each byte to encode numbers. In effect, this system uses 7-, 14-, 21-, or 28-bit binary values depending on whether the length value comprises one, two, three, or four bytes. This scheme allows encoding any value up to 268,435,455 (which is written to disk as FF FF FF 7F). Most practical values—those 127 and below—are written as they would normally appear using a single byte.

MOD Format

.MOD files are control files that were created for use with the sound systems of Commodore/ Amiga computers but have been adapted for PC sound systems. The format has a dedicated though modest following and is used for distributing interesting arrangements of musical combos. The MOD format is particularly suited to programming instrument combos because of its basis in the Amiga sound system, which was capable of synthesizing and playing four notes simultaneously. Rather than pre-defined instruments, the Amiga synthesizer accepted waveform samples for the notes it played, and the .MOD file system includes storage for the required waveform samples.

Waveform samples are applied to individual notes rather than channels. Consequently any channel may play any sample. Instruments may move between channels as they play notes (which makes no difference in PC sound systems that blend all four channels into one), and a single channel may play multiple instruments on sequential notes. This note-by-note versatility gives MOD the ability to simulate arrangements with more instruments than four channels might otherwise permit.

The instructions for triggering the samples are stored as patterns of notes, each pattern storing four channels, each of which is split into 64 increments called *placeholders*. Each placeholder stores four parameters for playing a note—the pitch, identity of the waveform sample associated with the note, volume, and a special effect to be applied. A pattern may correspond to a portion of a musical measure or several measures at the discretion of the programmer creating the .MOD file. The span of the pattern determines the degree of control over the timing of each note. If a pattern corresponds to a single measure, then resolution (the briefest discrete timing period) corresponds to a 64th note in 4/4 time. In the MOD scheme, a note plays until another note is triggered in the same channel (which may be silence to stop the note without playing another).

Patterns are not necessarily played in the order in which they are stored in the file. Instead, the order is determined by the order table created by the MOD programmer and stored in the file.

Waveform samples for .MOD files on Amiga computers were originally made with an 8 KHz sampling rate with an 8-bit depth stored in files with the extension .IFF. Newer adaptations have expanded the range and quality of MOD samples. In the PC environment, waveform samples usually wear the .SAM filename extension.

RMI Format

IBM and Microsoft has integrated MIDI files into the generalized RIFF format. These files often wear the filename extension .RMI (short for RMID indicating they are the RIFF version of MIDI).

.RMI files are nothing more than standard MIDI files that are enclosed in a standard RIFF chunk. This encapsulation helps the file be consistently identified by applications. The RIFF MIDI chunk is identified by the label RMID. After the label, the chunk contains data that is the equivalent of a standard MIDI file.

SBI Format

File with the extension .SBI are Sound Blaster Instrument files. Each of these short files (they're only 51 bytes long) defines a single instrument by setting program parameters for the Sound Blaster FM synthesizer.

The first four bytes of an .SBI file identify it with the characters "SBI" in ASCII code followed by an end-of-file character, 01A(Hex). The next 31 bytes store the name of the instrument as 30 ASCII text characters followed by a null character, 00(Hex).

The next 16 bytes supply the parameters necessary to program the FM synthesizer. Creative Labs defines the function of each bit as shown in Table 19.21.

TABLE 9.21. .SBI file synthesizer programming definitions.

Byte	Bits	Function
36	All	Modulator sound characteristic
37	0–3	Frequency multiplier
	4	Envelope scaling
	5	Sustaining sound
	6	Amplitude vibrato
	7	Pitch vibrato
38	All	Modulator scaling/output level
39	0–5	Output level
	6–7	Carrier level scaling
40	All	Modulator attack and decay rates
41	0–3	Carrier attack rate
	4–7	Carrier decay rate
42	All	Modulator sustain and release
43	0–3	Carrier release rate
	4–7	Carrier sustain level
44	All	Modulator wave select
45	0–1	Carrier wave select
	2–7	Not used
	0	Connection
46	1–3	Modulator feedback
	4–7	Not used
47	All	Reserved
48	All	Reserved
49	All	Reserved
50	All	Reserved
51	All	Reserved

SND Format

The extension .SND is an obvious one to use for files containing sounds, so obvious that it has been used by several manufacturers for entirely different file types. .SND files are used by Amiga computer, Apple Macintosh computers, and NeXT computers. In each case the format and audio parameters are different.

In the Apple version of .SND files, the audio format is fixed in monophonic form with eight bits of resolution. The file may use any of several sampling rates. The basic Macintosh sampling rate is 22254.545 samples per second, a frequency derived from the line rate (horizontal frequency) of the original 128KB Mac. Sometimes half this rate is used for sampling; rarely are one-third or one-quarter this basic sampling frequency used. Amiga .SND files encode a similar monophonic, 8-bit format.

The .SND files used by NeXT computers are structured to begin with a header that describes the attributes of a sound which is followed by the audio data itself. The first characters in the header and the file are ASCII for the identifying code *snd*. Table 19.22 lists the various format types used in the .SND files used by NeXT Computers.

TABLE 9.22. .SND file audio format types.

Value	Code word	Audio data format
0	SND_FORMAT_UNSPECIFIED	Format not specified
1	SND_FORMAT_MULAW_8	8-bit μ-law
2	SND_FORMAT_LINEAR_8	8-bit linear
3	SND_FORMAT_LINEAR_16	16-bit linear
4	SND_FORMAT_LINEAR_24	24-bit linear
5	SND_FORMAT_LINEAR_32	32-bit linear
6	SND_FORMAT_FLOAT	Floating-point
7	SND_FORMAT_DOUBLE	Double-precision float
8	SND_FORMAT_INDIRECT	Fragmented data
9	SND_FORMAT_NESTED	Nested audio data
10	SND_FORMAT_DSP_CORE	Program for DSP
11	SND_FORMAT_DSP_DATA_8	8-bit fixed-point
12	SND_FORMAT_DSP_DATA_16	16-bit fixed-point
13	SND_FORMAT_DSP_DATA_24	24-bit fixed-point
14	SND_FORMAT_DSP_DATA_32	32-bit fixed-point
16	SND_FORMAT_DISPLAY	Non-audio display data

Value	Code word	Audio data format
17	SND_FORMAT_MULAW_SQUELCH	Mu-law coded and gated
18	SND_FORMAT_EMPHASIZED	16-bit linear with emphasis
19	SND_FORMAT_COMPRESSED	16-bit linear with compression
20	SND_FORMAT_COMPRESSED_EMPHASIZED	A combination of the two above
21	SND_FORMAT_DSP_COMMANDS	Commands for Music Kit DSP
22	SND_FORMAT_DSP_COMMANDS_SAMPLES	Commands for other DSP

Sun computers use files with the .AU extension that have a nearly identical data structure to .SND files. Often you can simply rename an .AU file to have the .SND extension and play its sound content without a hitch.

VOC Format

The native format used by Creative Lab's Sound Blaster products is the .VOC file. These files are normally processed by Creative Labs' CT-VOICE driver. Although nominally designed for storing digitized voice data (hence the .VOC extension), this format can also handle any digitized sound in any of a variety of formats. Originally designed solely for 8-bit samples, a new data definition has extended VOC capabilities to include full 16-bit samples.

All .VOC files have a two part structure, a header block that defines the contents of the file and a data block that contains the actual audio information. The header block serves for identifying the file type. Each data block includes its own processing information such as sample size and rate. The header block starts with 20 bytes of text to identify itself—the text "Creative Voice File" followed by an end-of-file marker, 1A(Hex). If you try to use the DOS TYPE command to view a .VOC file, this end-of-file marker prevents your system from displaying anything but the three-word file description.

The next two bytes indicate the where the data block begins as an offset from the beginning of the file. In most .VOC files this offset is 32 characters, so these bytes will have the value 20 00—that is 20(Hex) in Intel little-endian notation, which puts the least significant byte first.

The next two byte identify the version of the VOC format used by the file. The sub-version precedes the version number. The most common values for these bytes are 0A 01 (version 1.10) and 14 01 (version 1.20). This value is repeated in slightly altered form in the next two bytes. They store the complement of the file format version number added to 1234(Hex). For example, the complement of 010A(Hex) is FEF5(Hex), which when added to 1234(Hex) results in 11129(Hex). The entry ignores the carried value (the most significant one), so the resulting value in the .VOC file would appear as the byte pattern 29 11.

The data block comprises one or more subblocks, each of which follows a standard format. The first byte defines one of 10 subblock types (with values 0 through 9), the next three bytes of all but subblock type 0 define the length of the data contents of the subblock, and the data follows. In processing a data subblock, your software reads the identifying byte and the length data, then reads the appropriate number of data bytes. It then expects another identifying byte marking the next subblock. An identifying byte of 00 indicates the end of the file. A given sound may extend through one or more subblocks. Special subblocks allow embedding markers and ASCII text within a .VOC file as well as repeating a given sound (which may be one or more blocks) up to 65,534 times or continuously.

Three subblock types define and encode sounds: 1, 8, and 9.

Subblock type 1 was the first format used by Creative Labs and allows monophonic digital coding with a resolution of eight bits. The first four bytes of the subblock identify it and give the length of the data that follows.

The first byte of data defines the sampling rate of the signal. Creative Labs uses a time constant to indicate the sampling rate. The time constant represents the sampling rate divided into 1 million subtracted from 256. For example, a sampling rate of 22,050 samples per second would result in a byte value of D3. (One million divided by 22,050 is approximately equal to 45, which, subtracted from 256 results in 211 or 0D3(Hex).)

The second data byte defines one of four byte-packing schemes as follows:

> 00 indicates 8-bit unpacked data
> 01 indicates 4-bit packed data
> 02 indicates 2.6-bit packed data
> 03 indicates 2-bit packed data.

The remaining bytes in the subblock encode the actual audio information.

Type 8 subblocks extend the Type 1 block to allow the handling of stereophonic (two-channel) audio data. The Type 8 subblock itself contains no actual voice data. Instead it stores a substitute definition for the data in the Type 1 subblock. If a Type 8 subblock appears in a .VOC file, it must immediately precede a Type 1 block, and the audio parameters defined by the Type 8 block replace those indicated in the Type 1 block.

Type 8 subblocks are always eight bytes long. The first byte is always 08 to define the block, and it is followed by the 3-byte length indicator 04 00 00 that specifies that the subblock contains four data bytes.

The first two of these data bytes store a time constant from which your software can derive the sampling rate of the audio data. To derive this time constant, the sampling rate is divided into 256,000,000 and the quotient is subtracted from 65,535 (the maximum value that can be represented with two bytes). For stereo signals, the sampling rate is doubled, then divided into 256,000,000, then subtracted from 65,535. A CD-quality stereo signal sampled at 44,100 samples per second would result in a byte value of A9 F4. (That is, 256,000,000 divided by 88,200 is about 2902 or 0B56(Hex). Subtract 0B56(Hex) from FFFF(Hex) and the result is F4A9(Hex).)

Subblock Type 9 replaces Types 1 and 8. All new Creative Labs drivers use Type 9 subblocks for storage. In addition to monophonic and stereo 8-bit coding, Type 9 blocks can also store 16-bit data. They can also use ADPCM and CCITT compressed audio formats.

The first four bytes of a Type 9 subblock follow the standard pattern: one identifying byte (09) followed by three bytes storing the length of the data area.

The first four bytes of the data area store the sampling rate used in the audio. Instead of a time constant, the sampling rate is stored directly as the number of samples made per channel per second. The next byte stores the number of bits in each sample, for example 08 (eight bits per sample) or 10 (16 bits per sample). The next byte codes the number of channels in the signal, 01 for monophone, 02 for stereo.

The next two bytes constitute a format tag that describes the coding of the signal. Currently Type 9 subblocks allow for eight formats as shown in Table 9.23.

TABLE 9.23. VOC type 9 subblocks.

Tag value	*Encoding*
0000	8-bit unsigned Pulse Code Modulation
0001	Creative Labs 8-bit to 4-bit ADPCM
0002	Creative Labs 8-bit to 3-bit ADPCM
0003	Creative Labs 8-bit to 2-bit ADPCM
0004	16-bit signed PCM
0006	CCITT a-Law
0007	CCITT u-law
0200	Creative Labs 16-bit to 4-bit ADPCM

The next four bytes in the Type 9 subblock data area are reserved for future use and normally are all zero. Audio data then follows to fill out the number of bytes indicated in the subblock header.

To allow sounds to span multiple subblocks and transcend the inherent 4MB subblock limit imposed by the three bytes used to encode subblock length, Creative Labs uses Type 2 subblocks. Called Voice Continuation subblocks, these subblocks contain only a 1-byte identifier (always 02), three bytes indicating data length, and additional data up to 4MB. The resolution and sampling rate remain as set in the previous Type 1, 8, or 9 subblock which the Type 2 subblock continues.

You can also prolong sounds in loops using subblock Types 6 and 7. Subblock Type 6 indicates that the subblocks following should be repeated for a designated number of repetitions or continuously. A Type 7 subblock indicates the end of a loop, so all audio subblocks between a Type 6 and Type 7 subblock will be repeated.

Type 6 subblocks are always six bytes long. The first byte identifies the subblock (06), the next three bytes encode the length of the data area (always two bytes) and the two bytes of the data area encode the number of repetitions, 1 to 65,534. A value of 65,535—that is, FF(Hex) signifies an endless loop.

Type 7 subblocks are four bytes long—one byte identifies the subblock type (07) and the three length bytes are zero because the Type 7 subblock needs no data bytes.

Type 3 subblocks insert silence. They are seven bytes long—an identifying byte (03) followed by three length bytes (indicating a fixed length of three data bytes), two bytes indicating the length of silence in units of the sampling rate, and a final byte reiterating the time constant applied in the format of a Type 1 block time constant.

Type 4 subblocks enable your software to put markers in .VOC files. Markers may be used to synchronize sounds with text or images. The marker is a 2-byte value that your program may refer to. Type 4 subblocks are always six bytes long—an identifying byte (04) followed by three length bytes (always specifying two data bytes) and two bytes storing the marker value.

Type 5 subblocks enable your software to add ASCII text to a .VOC file. The first byte identifies the subblock type (05), and the next three blocks indicate the number of characters of ASCII text (plus one for the end marker). The fifth and following bytes are standard ASCII text, terminated with a null byte (00) as an end marker.

WAV Format

The most common format for storing digitized sounds in the world of the PC is the .WAV file format, which was designed for use by multimedia applications running under Microsoft Windows. .WAV files store digitally sampled waveforms in one or more channels that use any sampling rate and bit depth within a wide range. The .WAV file itself encodes a description of its data that your software uses to reconstruct the original audio waveform. The WAV format is flexible enough to handle both compressed and uncompressed storage formats and can readily be adapted to accommodate new technology. The file format imposes no realistic limit on the length of the file or duration of sound it encodes—the standard format is capable of handling files up to 4GB long.

.WAV files follow Microsoft's Resource Interchange File Format (RIFF) structure, which uses a subdivision called the chunk. One chunk can contain one or more constituent chunks. Two types of chunks are used in .WAV files: data chunks, which each bears an identification, an indicator of its length, and data; and format chunks which add descriptive data to the length information they contain. In a .WAV file, two chunks store digital audio waveform information, a format chunk that defines the structure of the file and a data chunk that contains that actual waveform data.

As a standard RIFF file, the outer structure of a .WAV file comprises four bytes of identification—the characters "RIFF" encoded in ASCII format—followed by four bytes that indicate the length of the data chunk in the file, and the data chunk itself. The WAV format of the data chunk includes an identification (the letters "WAVE" coded in ASCII), a format chunk, and a data chunk.

The tightly defined format chunk is key to making the WAV format work. It defines encoding method, number of channels, sampling rate, and transfer rate of the audio waveform data. The first four byte of the format chunk identify it as that, a format chunk, with the letters "fmt" encoded in ASCII (the fourth character is a space, ASCII 20). The next four bytes code the length of the format chunk itself. Note that this number, as with all under the RIFF format, follow the Intel little-endian format. That is, the least significant byte comes first, so a byte sequence of 10 00 00 00 would indicate a format chunk 16 bytes long (that is, 0010 in hexadecimal notation).

The next two bytes of the format chunk define the WAV format category of the data in the file. This tag identifies the modulation or compression method used by the file. Most commonly these bytes encode the value 01, which indicates standard digital pulse code modulation (PCM).

The two next bytes encode the number of audio channels—01 indicates a single-channel monophonic sound; 02, two-channel stereo; and so on.

The next two bytes encode the sampling rate of the encoded signal in samples per second. For example, the byte pattern 22 56 encodes a value of 5622(Hex), which translates to 22,050 samples per second. Standard CD audio with a 44.1 KHz sampling rate (44,100 samples per second) would appear as the byte pattern 44 AC in a .WAV file.

The next two bytes indirectly indicate the bit depth of the signal, coded in the form of the average number of bytes per second of signal transfer. The value coded here is the number of channels times the sampling rate times the number of bytes in each sample. Dividing this value by the sampling rate, then the number of channels then multiplying by eight (the number of bits in a byte) yields the bit depth of the encoded signal.

The next two bytes encode the block alignment of the signal, another value interrelated with the above. This value indicates the number of bytes that the sound board needs to process in each sample. This value is the number of channels multiplied by the resolution bit depth (in bytes) of the audio signal.

The final two bytes of the format chunk are format specific parameters.

The data chunk of the WAV format follows the standard RIFF pattern. The first four bytes define it as a data chunk with the characters "data" encoded in ASCII. These are followed by four bytes indicating the length of the data, and finally by the data encoded in the given number of bytes.

Format Conversion

What you get isn't always what you want. A friend may send you his latest magnum opus musicum on floppy disk, but your friend is a hard core musician with a Macintosh and you're a hapless hacker with a PC. The music's on the disk, but it's in Mac format and you want to play it through Windows. What can you do? Or you might get a copy of a picture for which you have a great fondness—say a portrait of Andrew Jackson complete with several 20s decked about with seals and serial numbers—but it won't display in your multimedia presentation.

Any of a number of file conversion programs are ready to help you out, whether you need to transform text, images, sounds, or movies. They can convert files made under one standard to play under another, in some cases transforming a control file into bitmapped or wavetable files. Many are available as freeware or shareware through most bulletin board services. In addition, most graphics program import files in a variety of formats and most can save in a similar diversity of formats. Sound editing systems (such as Sound Forge, mentioned in Chapter 5, "Authoring Multimedia") typically will convert audio file formats. Most video display systems, such as those built into OS/2 Warp and Windows 95, handle standard .AVI and .MOV files indiscriminately, eliminating the need for conversion software.

All that said, OS/2 Warp includes its own file format converter aimed particularly at multimedia applications. The Multimedia Data Converter installs by default in your Multimedia folder. Open it, and you'll see a screen like the one shown (see Figure 9.1) that lets you select a file for conversion.

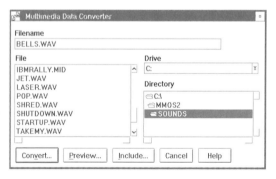

FIGURE 9.1. File listing in OS/2 Warp Multimedia Data Converter.

Once you've chosen a file, click Convert and you'll have another screen from which to choose the file format into which to transform your original, as shown in Figure 9.2. The Multimedia Data Converter comes with built-in algorithms to convert several image file types and a scanty number of audio filters. After you select the destination format of your choice, click another Convert button for the program to work its magic.

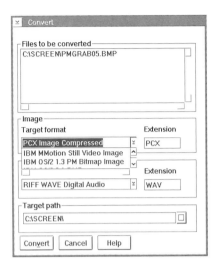

FIGURE 9.2. OS/2 Warp Multimedia Data Converter showing available file formats for conversion.

You can install additional filters to extend the breadth of the Multimedia Data Converter. However, you'll probably be able to find complete freeware format conversion programs more easily than filters for the data converter. Nevertheless, it's reassuring to know that moving from format to format takes little more than a few seconds and a free or inexpensive program.

Section III
Hardware Guide

Chapter 10 The Basic PC—Hardware Essentials 301

Chapter 11 Input and Output 353

Chapter 12 The Compact Disc 387

Chapter 13 Images 415

Chapter 14 Cameras and Monitors 477

Chapter 15 Sound 511

Chapter 16 MIDI 555

Chapter 10

The Basic PC— Hardware Essentials

The stench of hellfire and brimstone once used to mean only one thing—you've walked into the showroom and were about to face a torture worse than Old Scratch himself, the car salesman. Today, however, there's a terror most mortals face with even greater trepidation—buying a PC.

Unsuspecting, you walk into the megastore to buy a PC, and hear the buzz of the salespeople huddled in a corner hashing out their strategy against you. One approaches you with a golden gleam in his eye—the gleam of your gold, which he is intent of taking from you. He opens his mouth and words spill out. At least they sound like words, but the language is unfamiliar, alien as the array of hardware heaped in front of you. He chants the words "Mega this, turbo that, a 100 million muons per second" as he straps you over a barrel, binding your hands, and extracting the plastic cards from your wallet. The world shakes in a spasm like MTV gone awry, and you, mesmerized, sign something briefly waved past your dazed eyes. Hours later, you emerge from your trance with a tremendous headache, a DOS prompt on a screen you've never seen before on your desk, a helpful prompt asking "Press any key when ready," and an annoying, ever-louder beep each time you do.

You're up against tremendous odds, facing not just a language barrier but a culture clash. They know they have you beat as soon as you walk in the door. They spread the jargon around you like an incantation until your mind is so woozy from the onslaught of words you'll believe—and likely buy—anything they tell you to.

But you can wield a secret weapon that will leave them defenseless—knowledge. Once you understand a few basic terms and the underlying concepts, you'll be able to unjumble the jargon and cut through the cant to see the truth: Most PC salespeople don't know all that much more about computers than you do. Take a few minutes to learn the basics, and you'll be able to blow away the smokescreen and make your own judgment about what's best for you.

The most surprising thing is that all the gobbledygook makes sense once you know the fundamentals. All you need is a bit of background. And that's the purpose of this chapter. It's a jump-start on PC technology, all the essentials that will help put you above par when it comes to making a purchase decision.

This quick overview covers the general issues to consider when buying any PC, emphasizing the particular needs of multimedia. Certain peripherals that distinguish multimedia systems—sound and image hardware—are treated in chapters of their own, which follow.

The place to begin is with the circuits that define the power and abilities of any PC, the microprocessor.

Microprocessors

If there are electronic vampires, multimedia software is a likely candidate. Not only are you more likely to rev up your favorite multimedia application in the dark of the night when the rest of the world has gone to sleep, but the uninitiated will approach your PC with unholy awe. More telling still, your multimedia software will silently suck all the life out of your system. Every bit of your PC's performance will be tapped and drained in flinging around high-resolution images and ear-shattering sound. Even with the fastest PCs, you'll still suffer delays that seem interminable while you wait for your system to respond to your keystrokes, images to load, and sounds to emerge. Given a slow PC, you'll be sorely tempted to drive a stake through its heart every time that little hourglass pops on the screen.

When running multimedia, satisfaction is owning the fastest possible machine—and that means getting the fastest possible microprocessor. But searching out the quickest chip is a task more daunting than figuring out a medieval formula for ridding your residence of more earthly vampires. You have to worry about model designations and generations, bits and buses, and worse, the curse of the megahertz.

Definition

A microprocessor is a computer-on-a-chip, the chip being a flake of silicon crystal about a centimeter or two square. Everything else in a PC is meant only for serving the needs of the microprocessor. The name is a nutshell description: it's a "processor" because it processes commands to make changes in data; it's "micro" because it's smaller than a breadbox. In fact, the microprocessor is crafted from circuits that are microscopic and becoming submicroscopic.

Intel Architecture

The company name "Intel" is recurrent in any discussion of microprocessors. It has to be. Mercian "Ted" Hoff invented the microprocessor while working at Intel Corporation, and his design set the pattern for the most popular microprocessors in the world. Every computer that claims to be PC-compatible is based on a microprocessor rooted in the first Intel design.

Although other companies have developed their own microprocessors, every different chip family must have software specially written to the features of the chip design. For example, without special emulator software (that simulates the Intel design) Apple's Macintosh computers, which are based on Motorola microprocessors, cannot run software designed for PCs based on Intel chips (at least not with special hardware or software emulators which make the Mac act like a PC—a particularly slow PC). Because the Intel design is the most popular in small computers, more programs have been written for it than any other chip design. Although other microprocessor designs claim performance superiority, the Intel architecture remains the chief choice for multimedia due to its wide acceptance, huge software library, and low cost fostered by healthy competition among compatible chip (and computer) makers.

Operating Principles

Although even the simplest microprocessor ranks among the most complex electrical devices yet conceived, all chips operate on the same elementary principle: stimulus/response. Send a signal in, and another signal comes out. The relationship between those signals is the magic.

Microprocessors recognize certain patterns of electrical signals as commands or instructions. The complete group of all commands that the microprocessor understands is called the microprocessor's instruction set. Each command tells the microprocessor to carry out a specific logical or mathematical operation on bits of data temporarily stored in the chip.

A computer program is a series of microprocessors instructions that give the chip step-by-step guidance in carrying out a specific task, anything from adding two numbers to morphing the face of Lincoln into that of Lenin.

Registers

The temporary storage areas inside a microprocessor are called registers. To carry out a command, the microprocessor alters the pattern of bits stored in its registers. Commands can instruct the microprocessor to alter the bits in a pre-defined way (for example, to shift the bits one place to the right) or to let the pattern of bits in one register guide the change of bits in another. For example, an instruction might command the microprocessor to compare the bits in two registers and send a signal if they match.

The number of bits in a register is only one measure of microprocessor power. The more bits, the more work that can be done at a time. A chip with registers having twice as many bits can carry out operations twice as fast, all else being equal. The very first microprocessor had registers four bits wide. The first PCs had 16-bit registers. The chips suitable for multimedia PCs have 32-bit registers.

Bus Connections

For a microprocessor to do anything useful, you must connect it to a circuit. All commands and data are passed to the microprocessor through that connection. The greater the number of bits in the connection, the more information that can be loaded into the chip at one time. A bigger bus connection also means a wider range of possibilities of bit patterns for controlling the chip. Ideally the bus connection of a microprocessor will match or even be greater than the number of bits in each register in the chip. When the bus and register widths match, the microprocessor can load a register in a single operation. When the bus size is twice the size of a chip's registers (as with Intel's Pentium), the chip can load two registers at once. Except for the old 386SX chip, microprocessors for today's multimedia PCs have 32-bit (386DX and all 486 chips) buses or 64-bit buses (Pentium).

Clock Speeds

A computer program is series of discrete steps for carrying out a task. Disorganize the steps and there's no telling what will happen. Imagine messing up the instructions in making a cake by baking the mix before beating it. Without proper guidance, a microprocessor could confuse its instructions too and, worse than indigestible, the results might be indecipherable.

To keep programs straight, the microprocessor and computer built around it use clocked logic. The microprocessor reads off each step of its program to the beat of a metronome called the *system clock* or oscillator. The rest of the computer is synchronized to the same clock. In contemporary computers, these clock speed is measured in megahertz, millions of cycles per second. Although many modern microprocessors operate with internal speeds different from the system clock, circuitry in the chip derives its internal speed from the same system clock.

Not only does the clock organize the computer, it also sets the rate at which programs are executed. A faster clock ushers programs along quicker. Unfortunately, you can't set an arbitrarily high clock speed. Manufacturers rate all their clocked-logic circuits with a maximum operating speed. Exceed that speed and the operation of the chips can become erratic—they might make a mistake at any time. Although you can run most microprocessors at speeds below their rating without a problem, exceeding the rating of a chip is best left to the dare-devil and experimenter.

When all else is equal, the relationship between clock speed (megahertz) and PC performance is exactly linear. Double the clock speed, and performance doubles as well. But all microprocessors are not equal. Older microprocessors often required several ticks of the clock to carry out a single instruction. The latest chips carry out one or more instructions in every tick. A newer chip can consequently perform more work per tick, giving you more whiz per megahertz.

Within a microprocessor family, clock speed determines performance. A 100 MHz Pentium is 50 percent faster than a 66 MHz Pentium. Between microprocessor models and generations, however, this relationship falls apart. A 66 MHz Pentium is about 70 percent to 90 percent faster than a 66 MHz 486. Each newer generation from 386 to 486 to Pentium marks about a factor of two increase in performance per megahertz.

Complicating matters even more are those microprocessors with different internal and external speeds. Within the Intel microprocessor family used in most multimedia PCs, the listed speed for a microprocessor is its higher internal processing speed. These chips connect to external circuitry at a lower speed. DX2 chips link to external buses running at half their internal speed. DX4 chips link to buses nominally running at one-third their internal speed (although other ratios are possible). Pentium chips make their internal multiplier programmable so that system designers can adjust the ratio between internal and external speed for their own purposes. Designers can choose to operate the Pentium at an internal speed that is the same, 1.5 times faster, or twice as fast as the external clock. Although PCs achieve best performance when the internal and external clock speeds of their microprocessors match (when that is possible), by keeping external speed lower they can hold down the price of the overall system (if just to make it buildable at all). Early Pentium systems (those with 60 and 66 MHz internal speeds) often operated at the same speed internally and externally. Higher-speed Pentiums (90 MHz and 100 MHz) typically operate 50 percent faster inside as do most 75 MHz Pentiums.

Modern system designs make internal speed the most important factor in overall PC performance. Rather than judging a system simply by its microprocessor speed—almost universally quoted as the higher internal clock—you should also consider the clock speed used by the system board. When a PC spends most of its time on input and output operations, as is typical of most multimedia *playback* systems, a higher external speed is often preferable. When the principal task for your PC's microprocessor is internal calculating, as is typically the case of multimedia *authoring* systems, a high internal speed is your first concern.

Caching

Helping even out the differences between internal and external clock speeds as well as smoothing over the inadequacies of slow memory chips, is *memory caching*. The cache is a block of memory that operates at high speed and duplicates part of the contents of a larger block of lower speed memory. A circuit called the cache controller attempts to ensure that the cache holds the data required for the next operation of the microprocessor. When the right data is in the cache, the microprocessor gets a cache "hit" which allows it to read from the fast cache memory. When the right data is not in the cache, the microprocessor suffers a cache "miss" which causes the chip and the system to wait while the data gets fetched from slower memory.

Caches are classed as *primary caches* (or level one caches) and *secondary caches* (or level two caches). The former are built into microprocessors; the latter are external. All 486 and Pentium microprocessors include primary caches. PCs built from these chips may or may not include secondary caches at the discretion of the system manufacturer.

Primary caches are superior to secondary because of the way the modern microprocessor addresses memory—the smallest block that Pentiums and 486s use is called a line (of memory), four 32-bit double words. Because the 486 has only 32 data lines, reading a line takes at least five clock cycles from best caches—a burst mode in which one cycle is needed to send out the address and four to read the data. The Pentium does better because it has 64 data lines, but still requires three cycles to read a line. The internal connections between the primary cache and the rest of these chip is 128-bits wide, allowing the primary cache to be read in two cycles—one address, one data.

External caches are useful because they can be larger. Standard Intel 486SX, DX, SX2, and DX2 chips have 8KB of primary cache; DX4 chips and Pentiums have twice that. External caches can be as large as you can afford memory for.

An internal or external cache can be *direct-mapped* or *associative*. A direct-mapped cache looks at memory in blocks, and assigns one line of cache memory to each block. Only one line from each block can be held in the cache.

The advantage of the direct-mapped cache design is ease in design and implementation. Its simplicity brings quick operation. All the cache control circuitry must do is check the block address in the cache to see if the data that's needed is stored there.

Performance Issue

The disadvantage of the direct-mapped cache is that repeated requests for different lines in the same block result in cache misses. Although this is not a large problem for DOS, which only steps through one program at a time, it handicaps most multimedia software that runs under Windows or OS/2. Multimedia applications alternate between many threads, and each thread may call a different line in the same block. The cache repeatedly loads and unloads between tasks, slowing down rather than speeding up performance, a problem which is called thrashing.

A set-associative cache assigns multiple lines to each main memory block. A two-way set-associative cache gives two caching locations to each block; a four-way set-associative cache, four; and so on. The ability to keep multiple lines in the cache substantially reduces thrashing.

This advantage comes at the penalty of complexity and speed. The cache controller must track two or more lines from each block, checking two or more places to determine whether needed data is in the cache. With every additional "way," the cache becomes more complex and this complexity can impose its own speed limits. Most designers believe a four-way associative cache to be the best trade-off between complexity and performance.

Caches may operate on all memory operations or be restricted to memory reading. The latter kind of memory cache, called a *write-through cache*, ignores data to be written to memory, passing writing instructions directly through to system memory without trying to cache it. If the microprocessor writes to a line that's already stored in the cache, that line will be updated in the cache and main memory simultaneously.

A *write-back cache* intercepts both read and write operations. Although the write-back cache improves performance substantially (some sources believe 30 percent of all memory operations are writes), it also increases complexity and adds its own problems. The cache controller must constantly assure that cache memory and main memory contain the same information so that other devices in the system do not try to read data from main memory before it's updated from the cache. Ensuring reliability makes write-back caches more complex to design than write-through.

EDO Memory

Many new multimedia PCs forego secondary caches entirely and rely on the primary cache and a new kind of memory called *Extended Data Out* (EDO) memory. Rather than a radical new development, EDO is a variation on fast page mode memory (which allows waitless repeated access to bits within a single page of memory). In effect, EDO removes the remaining wait states, thereby boosting memory performance. In the latest PCs, the best EDO implementations boost performance by 10 percent to 20 percent compared to older systems that use memory caches. Some system designers believe you'll get even better performance combining EDO and a cache.

In multimedia applications, the difference between a large cache and EDO memory probably won't be noticeable. In other words, you'll want to consider EDO to be an alternative to a secondary cache—at least for the time being.

Coprocessor

When Intel Corporation first designed its microprocessors, it elected to limit the mathematical ability of its chips to simple integer math to keep the chip design simple, affordable, and on-time. Complex math functions, such trigonometric and transcendental calculations, could be approximated by repeated integer math. For heavy-duty math applications, Intel designed a separate chip called the floating-point unit or math coprocessor to take care of these advanced functions. This design allowed Intel to get its microprocessors to the market faster and cheaper, free from the development time and expense required for the floating-point circuitry. Most applications do not require hardware floating-point work, so the math coprocessor could safely be left as an option.

Starting with its 486 series, however, Intel built floating-point circuitry into its microprocessors. Intel and other manufacturers generally use the suffix letter D to indicate a 486-level chip that has an internal cache and the letter S to indicate one lacking a coprocessor. The 486DX and 486DX2 series of chips have integral math coprocessors. The 486SX and 486SX2 chips lack them (as do all earlier Intel chips). All current versions of the Pentium include floating-point circuitry as do nearly all RISC microprocessors (including the PowerPC series).

For people who change their minds after buying a PC with a chip lacking a coprocessor, Intel offers two choices of upgrades, a straight coprocessor and the OverDrive upgrade. These easy-to-plug-in chips endow a PC with the same math abilities as in one having a microprocessor with an internal math coprocessor. A coprocessor, designated the 487, only improves the floating-point performance of a PC. OverDrive chips also add an internal clock-speed boost, which may be by a factor of two or three. (A DX2 OverDrive upgrade doubles the internal processing speed of your existing chip; a DX4 upgrade runs three times faster internally than externally.) Most of the time, the OverDrive makes more sense for an upgrade in a multimedia system than does a plain coprocessor.

Multimedia applications in general do not make heavy use of floating-point math, although some programs that may be used in authoring multimedia software may. Drawing and statistic programs are the most math-intensive applications usually run on PCs. Adding a math coprocessor consequently offers only a modest performance increase to most multimedia systems. The exceptions to this rule are multimedia applications that do 3-D rendering, which can make heavy math demands.

Operating Voltages

From the first days of the PC, computer logic circuits have operated at one standard voltage, 5 VDC (volts of direct current), the standard operating potential for the Transistor-Transistor Logic (TTL) family of electronic components used in computers. Microprocessors, memory chips, and support circuits designed to run at 5 volts were cheap and readily available. The 5-volt level worked—and worked well—so even though the level was arbitrary, no one doubted its usefulness.

The rise of notebook PCs bred a new race of iconoclasts who cast aside the standard. They had good reason. The amount of power used by an electrical circuit rises by the square of the voltage in the circuit. Double the voltage, and you need four times the power. To increase battery life, engineers wanted to reduce the power consumption of notebook PCs. With the advent of the Pentium, the power used by microprocessors in desktop systems approached (and sometimes exceeded) the limits of passive convective cooling—that is, the chip couldn't keep its cool without the help of a fan. Engineers needed to reduce the power needs of these chips as well.

By reducing the operating voltage of microprocessors by more than 70 percent, engineers reduced the power used by electrical circuits by half. The first circuits to adopt the new 3.3 volt operating potential were specialized microprocessors for notebook systems. However, the power savings of the low-voltage design have spread into a variety of computer circuits. The Intel 486DX4 and Pentium series of microprocessors all run at 3.3 volts. All future Intel chips are likely to run at the new potential.

Logic circuits designed for 5 VDC and 3.3 VDC operation don't readily combine together. Consequently you cannot directly replace your old 5-volt microprocessor with a new 3.3-volt chip. Early systems that use 3.3-volt microprocessors must use special buffering circuits to match the chip with the conventional 5-volt circuits used in the rest of the system. Intel's DX4 OverDrive series incorporates its own voltage-changing circuits grafted onto the chips, readily visible through the heatsinks. The makers of support circuits and other electrical components are developing new 3.3-volt designs so that eventually an entire PC can run at the new voltage level. All of the latest Pentium processors (those rated at 75, 90, 100, and 120 MHz) operate at 3.3 volts.

Power Management

Another way to cut down the power needs of a PC is to turn off or slow down the circuits that you're not using. The latest microprocessors incorporate power-saving circuits that do exactly that. Using a facility called system management mode, they can selectively switch off portions of their own circuitry not actively in use, even signaling to other PC components to similarly shut down. Although these microprocessors were first crafted as special-purpose designs for notebook machines, the technology has now spread throughout the Intel line. Other manufacturers now also work to insure that their products minimize power consumption. Compared to the last generation of chips, today's microprocessors squeeze out substantially more processing power for every microwatt they consume.

Commercial Chips

The history of the microprocessor begins more than a generation ago when in 1969, Intel Corporation conceived the first truly programmable chip, the 4004. (The chip went into production in 1971.) Through the years, Intel added power by increasing the size of the chip's registers from four bits (in the 4004) to eight, 16, and finally, 32 bits. Recent efforts have shifted to superscalar designs that have more than one microprocessor core inside a single chip. Table 10.1 lists some of the characteristics of the Intel and compatible microprocessors up to the Pentium. At the Pentium level, manufacturers have veered from strict Intel compatibility, as noted. Pentium-level chips are listed in Table 10.3.

TABLE 10.1. Multimedia-level Intel-compatible microprocessors.

Chip	Manufacturer	Data bus width	Address bus width	Internal clock	Integral cache	Integral FPU
386SX	Intel	16	24	1x	No	No
	AMD	16	24	1x	No	No
38600SX	C&T	16	24	1x	No	No
386SLC	IBM	16	24	1x	8KB	No

continues

TABLE 10.1. continued

Chip	Manufacturer	Data bus width	Address bus width	Internal clock	Integral cache	Integral FPU
38605SX	C&T	16	24	1x	0.5KB	No
386DX	Intel	32	32	1x	No	No
	AMD	32	32	1x	No	No
38600DX	C&T	32	32	1x	No	No
38605DX	C&T	32	32	1x	0.5KB	No
486SL	Intel	32	32	1x	8KB	Yes
486SLC	Cyrix	16	24	1x	1KB	No
486SLC/E	TI	16	24	1x	1KB	No
486SLC2	IBM	32	32	2x	16KB	No
486SX	Intel	32	32	1x	8KB	No
	AMD	32	32	1x	8KB	No
486SXLV	AMD	32	32	1x	8KB	No
486SX2	Intel	32	32	2x	8KB	No
486DLC	Cyrix	32	32	1x	1KB	No
486DLC/E	TI	32	32	1x	1KB	No
486DX	Intel	32	32	1x	8KB	Yes
	AMD	32	32	1x	8KB	Yes
486DXLV	AMD	32	32	1x	8KB	Yes
486DX2	Intel	32	32	2x	8KB	Yes
486DX4	Intel	32	32	3x	16KB	Yes
486BL	IBM	32	32	3x	16KB	No
Pentium	Intel	64	32	1x, 1.5x, 2x	16KB	Yes

Multimedia requires so much processing power that early chips—those before the 386—are unable to deliver sufficient performance to keep you awake at your keyboard. (They also lack several features used by modern multimedia applications, such as the ability to remap memory and run multiple DOS applications simultaneously in separate virtual machines.) Consequently all the early generation of microprocessors can safely be left behind like baby shoes—you might even consider having your first microprocessor bronzed. Consigned to the Hall of Fame and fading memories are the 8088, the chip that powered the first IBM PC and started the personal computer revolution; the 8086, the forerunner of the 8088; and the 286 that powered the IBM AT and its clones.

The oldest Intel microprocessors now considered adequate for multimedia was the 80386, usually abbreviated as simply 386. Intel's first true 32-bit microprocessor, the 386 ushered in a new generation of PCs, different and more powerful than their predecessors. Initially, its chief claim to fame was not its 32-bit power, which was not fully tapped by operating systems until the introduction of OS/2 version 2.0, Windows NT, and Windows 95.

The real difference in the 386 was its virtual 8086 mode that allows the chip to divide itself into several virtual machines, which can each run a DOS application or session, simultaneously but in isolation from the other sessions. This feature enabled true multitasking that extended to existing applications, which gave the second generation of operating systems—Windows and OS/2—a foothold.

In addition, the 386 incorporated a novel memory management scheme that allows it (and succeeding Intel chips) to remap physical memory to different logical locations. This ability allows the chip to sidestep some of the limitation of DOS and squeeze more useful memory out of the 1MB constraint built into all standard versions of DOS. OS/2 and Windows 95 make these features nearly irrelevant because new operating systems have been designed without the memory limitations of DOS.

386 Family

First introduced in 1985, the 386 family was the first Intel chip to be built around a 32-bit core. Created in full awareness of the personal computer and microprocessor marketplace, one of its primary design goals was compatibility with DOS software. The 386 was designed to understand all of the instructions used by earlier Intel microprocessors so even the most ancient PC software could run without a hitch. The 386 was also the first Intel microprocessor to incorporate 16 bytes of pre-fetch cache memory, allowing the chip to store the next few instructions of the program being executed.

The first 386 chips were manufactured by Intel. Later, Advanced Micro Devices introduced its own version based on the Intel design to which AMD claimed rights under a technology sharing agreement with Intel (a right not acknowledged by Intel). Intel did license IBM to manufacture its own 386 chips, and IBM later extrapolated on the Intel design to create its own version of the architecture. A fourth company, Chips and Technologies, developed its own version of the 386 not in association with Intel.

The needs of multimedia have left the entire 386 family in the dust. Even the quickest of 386 chips are not fast enough to deliver adequate multimedia performance. However all chips in the 386 family are capable of running all multimedia PC-based applications, albeit slowly.

Performance Issue

Intel 386DX. The first member of the 386 family was introduced simply as the 80386 (later redesignated the 386DX) and operated at the fast-for-then but modest-for-now speeds of 12.5 MHz and 16 MHz. With further refinement of the 386 design, Intel gradually increased its top speed to 33 MHz. AMD, manufacturing nearly identical 386 chips under a putative license, extended the top speed of the 386DX to 40 MHz.

One distinguishing characteristic of the 386DX is its set of external connections, providing 32 data lines (to match its 32-bit registers) and 32 address lines, which allow the chip to directly address up to 4GB of physical memory. The chip can actually track even larger memory addresses up to 64 terabytes (that's a trillion bytes) of virtual memory.

Intel 386SX. The 386DX became the flagship of the Intel line. To allow software written for the new features of the 386 at a lower cost, Intel introduced a less powerful alternative, the 386SX. Internally, the 386SX is nearly identical to the 386 the same full set of 32-bit registers and all the same operating modes. Instead of interfacing to a 32-bit memory bus, however, the 386SX is designed for a 16-bit data and 24-bit address buses. The 16-bit external data interface allowed PC makers to build systems using time-proved (and cost-effective) AT-based designs much like the 286-based PCs they had been building for years.

Intel 386SL. The 386SL was Intel's first 386-level chip designed specifically for low-power portable computers. The chip combines reduced power consumption with a high degree of integration to allow the construction of small, lightweight computers. The 386SL introduced System Management Mode for power saving in battery-based PCs. Although considered by some as simply a low-power version of the 386SX microprocessor, the 386SL is both more and less than a 386SX. On the short side, it requires an external support chip (the 82360SL) to operate. Together, however, the two-chip 386SL implementation also incorporates an AT-bus interface and the ability to address 32MB of memory (instead of the 16MB limit of the 386SX). Otherwise the 386SL can run all 386-specific programs because it has the same internal 32-bit register structure as all 386 chips.

AMD 386 chips. The line-up of 386 microprocessors manufactured by AMD follow Intel's design exactly. The only important difference is that AMD extended the top speed of its chips to 40 MHz, giving its flagship products about a 20 percent performance edge over Intel's own line. AMD has added its own refinements to the 386 architecture, however. Most notable is its Am386DXLV chip, the final two letters standing for low-voltage. This chip was the first Intel-compatible microprocessor designed to operate at supply voltages from 3.3 volts to 5 volts.

Chips and Technologies 386s. Just like AMD and IBM, which had access to Intel's own designs, Chips and Technologies designed their version of the 386 from scratch using reverse engineering. The resulting products are electrically and functionally identical to Intel's chips to the extent that they will plug into the same sockets. Chips and Technology developed a 386SX clone as the 38600SX and a 386DX clone called the 38600DX.

Chips and Technology also extrapolated on the 386 design with its "super" chips, the SX-like 38605SX and DX-like 38605DX. While making these microprocessors code-compatible but not socket-compatible with Intel chips, C&T enhanced them with a 512-byte instruction cache, pipelining, and the company's own SuperState V management system for greater control over this chip's operations. Software must be specially written to take advantage of the SuperState management system, which never found wide market acceptance.

IBM 386SLC. IBM negotiated a license from Intel to manufacture its own 386 chips to assure a ready supply. (At the time, IBM was the largest personal computer maker in the world.) The licensing terms allowed IBM to use the Intel designs and microcode to develop improved products. In return, Intel gets rights to whatever new creations flow from the minds of IBM's engineers.

The first product of this agreement was IBM's 386SLC, basically a 16-bit 386SX microprocessor with an infusion of later technology. Although electrically compatible with the 385SX, the 386SLC also understands commands used for the next-generation 486 chip (which had been introduced before the 386SLC was released in 1991). IBM also made several performance improvements to the 386SLC. For example, it can execute most of its instructions in far fewer clock cycles than does the Intel 386 design. It also incorporates an 8KB two-way, set-associative internal cache.

486 Family

Introduced in 1989, the 486 microprocessor was Intel's better 386. The new chip ran all 386 software, differing only in some details inconsequential to nearly all software (specifically one flag, one exception, two page-table entry bits, six instructions, and nine control-register bits). In fact, to smooth over the transition between 386 and 486 technologies, Intel at first called the 486 a member of the 386 family.

Today, however, Intel has essentially disowned the 386 and considers that its best 486 chip rates only as a low-cost, entry-level microprocessor. From the multimedia perspective, this is a valid approach. Only the fastest chips in the 486 family deliver adequate multimedia performance. Despite its software compatibility with the 386, the 486 incorporates several hardware innovations to improve performance. In fact, a 486 can accomplish about twice as much work as a 386 chip running at the same clock speed, even though both are full 32-bit chips.

Performance Issue

Intel 486DX

The matriarch of the 486 family is the 486DX. The 486DX has the same number of 32-bit registers as the 386 family and incorporates full 32-bit address and data buses. Its improved internal design adds an 8KB internal cache and floating-point coprocessor. Although software-compatible with the 386DX, the 486DX is not a direct replacement. It is not socket-compatible. Moreover, its cache must be specifically activated by software (usually by code in the system BIOS).

Intel 486SX

Intel's low cost version of the 486DX is designated the 486SX. The two chips are identical except for a minor packaging difference (one pin) and the lack of a math coprocessor in the budget model.

Intel Clock-Doubled Models

The Intel 486DX2 has the same features as the basic 486DX but runs its internal logic at twice its external clock speed. Hence a 66 MHz 486DX2 plugs into a 33 MHz motherboard. This design enables you to use lower cost motherboards—or to upgrade an existing PC to nearly double-speed by simply replacing the microprocessor. The 486SX2 follows the same pattern. As with the DX2, its internal clock runs at double the external rate. The SX2 differs only in its lack of an integral math coprocessor.

Intel 486DX2

Intel's DX2 OverDrive chips have the same internal designs as the DX2 chips. The OverDrives differ in two ways, however. Intel puts the OverDrives in a variety of packages to fit different sockets—those specifically designed for upgrades and the sockets of other 486-level microprocessors. In addition, the OverDrive series is a consumer product, designed to be sold to you as an end user. Intel's other microprocessors are aimed at manufacturers rather than the retail channel.

Intel Clock-Tripled Models

The latest (and final) addition to the 486 family was DX4, which runs internally at three times its external clock rate. Otherwise the 486DX4 is functionally identical to the rest of the 486DX series. It runs the same applications only faster. Electrically, however, the DX4 boasts two significant differences over its forebears. Its integral cache measures 16KB bytes, double the rest of the 486 family, to help smooth over the huge speed difference between the internal and external speeds of the chip. In addition, Intel builds the DX4 using 3.3-volt logic. This saves enough power so that the DX4 actually generates less heat than a slower DX2 chip. The DX4 OverDrive is the same chip with voltage regulators added so that it plugs directly into 5-volt sockets.

Intel 486SL

In 1992 Intel introduced its portable 486 alternative. Although similar in concept with the 386SL, the 486SL proved a more formidable design. Unlike the 386SL—essentially a 386SX engineered for power savings—the 486SL doesn't sacrifice performance for portability. Instead it incorporates power-saving features into a full 486DX design. In other words, the 486SL is a true

32-bit chip with internal 32-bit registers, external 32-bit address and data buses with a built-in floating-point unit, and an 8KB four-way, set-associative combined instruction and data cache of the 486DX.

To conserve power in portable applications, the semiconductor design of the 486SL was altered to make it fully static—it can hold its memory even if the clock stops. The silicon circuitry of the 486SL is also designed to operate in mixed-voltage environments. The microprocessor part of the chip itself operates from a 3.3 volt supply, but the bus control and memory interfaces can work at 5 volts or 3.3 volts.

Intel discontinued development of the 486SL series in favor of transferring the power saving technology to the rest of the 486 (and Pentium) family. Current 486 chips are all SL-enhanced, meaning they have the same frugal internal design as the 486SL.

Cyrix 486SLC and DLC

Cyrix Corporation started in the microprocessor business with the 486DLC and 486SLC, a pair of products reverse-engineered to be compatible with Intel's 486. These products earn their name through their recognition of the same instructions as the Intel 486-series of microprocessors, but they are not identical to Intel's products. The Cyrix chips resemble the Intel 386 design in that they require a clock that runs at double the speed of the microprocessor, while Intel 486 chips operate at the clock speed supplied to them. Neither Cyrix chip includes floating-point circuitry but instead has a hardware multiplier that carries out integer operations more quickly than the original Intel 486 design. (Intel has since enhanced its own products similarly.) The 486DLC uses a 32-bit external data bus and 32 address lines, so it has the same data-handling and addressing abilities as the 386DX and 486-series of Intel microprocessors. The 486SLC is patterned after the 386SX, with a 16-bit data bus and 24-bit address bus. Both chips have 1KB internal caches.

IBM 486SLC2

IBM's 486SLC2 reworks the 386SLC design to recognize the complete 486 command set and deliver improved performance, although the chip still retains the 16-bit data bus and 16MB addressing limit of the 386SX. The 486SLC2 does not incorporate an integral floating-point unit.

To accelerate the performance of the chip to the low-end of the 486 range, IBM grafted on a full 16KB of integral four-way set-associative write-through cache. In addition, the chip can optionally internally double the clock speed supplied to it while maintaining its external connections at the slower original speed. As with all IBM microprocessors using technology licensed from Intel, the 486SLC2 is available only already installed in motherboards by IBM.

IBM Blue Lightning

IBM's take at clock-tripling first took the form of its enhanced 486 chip called Blue Lightning. Built from essentially the same processor core and 16KB cache as the earlier 486SLC2, the newer chip puts a true 32-bit processor in a package that fits a 386DX socket—that means 32-bit registers, 32-bit data bus, and 32-bit address bus. Because it uses 3.3-volt logic, however, the Blue Lightning is not a direct replacement for the 386DX (nor is it available individually from IBM; it can only be sold pre-installed in motherboards). The Blue Lightning does not include an internal floating-point unit.

Intel Pentium

Today Intel's top-performing microprocessor is the Pentium, first introduced in 1993. Pentium chips break with the 386/486 family by sporting a 64-bit interface rather than the 32-bit connections of the older microprocessors. Inside, however, the Pentium is a radical departure from previous Intel designs. Intel likes to say that it combines two central processing units in one chip. Strictly speaking, however, the Pentium is still a 32-bit microprocessor with a single set of 32-bit registers that lead to a split pipeline and the equivalent of two arithmetic/logic units similar to those of the 486 microprocessor. Although this design and sequential nature of programs doesn't allow the chip to split most programs neatly between the two pipelines (in fact, it cannot because the two pipelines are not truly identical), the logic of the Pentium can divvy up data and instructions well enough that a Pentium works about 70 percent faster than a 486 running at the same clock speed. Despite its revolutionary design, the Pentium will still run all the same programs that execute on the 386 and 486, including all multimedia applications.

This superscalar engineering was a necessary step because Intel had seemingly wrung all the speed it could from their basic architecture. With the 486, the company got their core logic down to needing just one clock cycle to execute most instructions—earlier chips needed five to eight clock cycles for a typical instruction. The 486 uses a processing pipeline that's divided into discrete steps that each handles part of the execution of an instruction. Each step operates in parallel, each on a different instruction.

At the 486 one-instruction-per-clock efficiency, the only way of increasing performance of a single Intel architecture pipeline was to kick up the clock. As microprocessor speed has climbed into the frequency range of television stations, system design has become more expensive, almost the equivalent of building microwave transmitters.

Two processing cores means that the Pentium can move more than one instruction per clock tick, accomplishing more at lower speeds (and lower cost). The Pentium breakthrough was to add logic that could split a single instruction stream of today's software (which was written for single pipeline processors) so the work got divided between cores. The division of labor isn't always neat so the gain isn't exactly a factor of two, but with most software the Pentium can dash through 70 percent more instructions than a 486 running at the same speed.

Strictly speaking, the Pentium is a 32-bit chip—its principal registers are 32 bits wide, and it understands the same 32-bit instructions as its 386 and 486 predecessors. It also has a 32-bit address bus to directly access 4GB of physical RAM.

To help fill both processor pipelines at the same time, Intel doubled the width of the Pentium data bus to 64 bits. And to further speed the loading and unloading of bytes, current Pentiums include a 16KB cache that is divided into equal-size, four-way set-associative data and instruction caches. The relationship between the internal and external speed of the Pentium is programmable using special pins on the chip. Which multiple a given PC uses (1x, 1.5x, or 2x) is the choice of the PC manufacturer. To help match the Pentium to the slower memory chips found in most PCs, Intel built in a 16KB internal cache, functionally split into two sections—8KB used for managing program instructions and 8KB for buffering data. The bifurcated design is not a result of having two processing units—the cache comes before the program-splitting circuitry of the Pentium—but is a more efficient way of dividing data for processing by any microprocessor.

The most powerful enhancement to the Pentium is not in its regular microprocessor circuitry but its internal coprocessor section. According to Intel, the Pentium coprocessor is three to five times faster than the floating-point unit in a 486 running at the same clock speed (megahertz).

The Pentium is, in fact, better at handling modern multimedia software and multitasking operating systems than it is at running ordinary DOS applications. Its dual nature requires programs to be optimized to be split among its nearly twin processing sections for best performance, which means applications with multiple threads naturally run better because they are more easily split. DOS is a one-thing-at-a-time operating system.

Performance Issue

While today's Windows and OS/2 versions have more power to exploit the potential of the Pentium, the double-cored chip works best with operating systems and applications specially written for it. In other words, to get the most out of the Pentium, programs will have to be recompiled by their publishers. Unfortunately the result may be that programs optimized for the Pentium may not work on older Intel processors if they use Pentium-specific instructions.

On a few rare occasions, programs may not even work with Intel's own Pentiums. In late 1994, Intel revealed that the first Pentiums that it marketed had a design flaw in its floating-point unit that, when some specific numbers were divided, resulted in a wrong result. Although this flaw probably would not affect most applications, after substantial media pressure Intel announced a policy to replace defective chips. Only Pentiums of the B1 and B3 level—the first two implementations of the chip that operated at 60 and 66 MHz—suffer from the problem. You can identify the defective chips in several ways—by testing the chip, by examining the markings on the chip itself, or by making the calculation that results in the error.

You'll find dozens of Pentium test programs on various on-line services. Better still, you can download Intel's official test program and documentation from the Internet with the following three instructions:

```
ftp.intel.com:/pub/IAL/pentium/cpuidf.exe
ftp.intel.com:/pub/IAL/pentium/cpuidf.txt
ftp.intel.com:/pub/IAL/pentium/cpusup.txt
```

The first file contains the actual chip identification program; the second, the instructions for using it; the third, how to get a replacement if you need it (in the United States and Canada, call 1-800-628-8686). The test program does not actually test the microprocessor. Rather, it checks the internal identification of the chip to see if it matches Intel's list of bad batches. It will work properly even if you run a bug-fix program that bypasses the problem (and the entire floating-point unit).

If you have access to the actual Pentium chip inside your PC, you can check the codes stenciled on it to determine whether it has the problem. Table 10.2 lists the markings on the two defective series of chips as well as those of the first bug-free version.

TABLE 10.2. Identifying Pentium processors with FPU bug.

Process Step	Initial ship date	Marking	Feature
B1	April, 1994	SX879, SX909, SX885	First commercial versions of P54C chip; sometimes produce floating-point errors
B3	June, 1994	SX923, SX922, SX921	Green PC capabilities added; sometimes produce floating-point errors
B5	December, 1994	SX957, SX958, SX959	Mask revised; no floating-point errors

Experimenters have found more than 200 combinations of floating-point numbers in division operations that demonstrate the Pentium bug. One such calculation (which, of course, requires that you use a language that exercises the floating-point unit) is the following:

```
4195835 - (4195835/3145727)*3145727
```

The correct answer is zero. A Pentium with a floating-point problem gives 256 as the result.

Odds are you will never run into this problem with multimedia—and if you do, it won't hurt anything. But you might still want a new chip for your peace of mind.

Pentium OverDrives

Pentium OverDrives, the upgrades that can be installed in special sockets in most 486 machines, break with Intel tradition by substantially altering the base microprocessor. The first Pentium OverDrive, best known by its development name of P24T, only starts with the Pentium core logic: twin 486-like 32-bit central processing units and enhanced floating-point unit. The bus interface and cache were substantially revised and the packaging was augmented to reflect system needs. Instead of the 64-bit external interface of the real Pentium, the OverDrive chips sport a 32-bit design meant to match the sockets of the 486-based machines into which they plug. To compensate for the narrower bus, the OverDrives double the integral level one cache to 32KB. Because of these changes, the Pentium OverDrive approximates but does not match the performance of standard Pentium chips. To keep heat under control (although the OverDrives use 3.3 volt logic internally, they need heat-generating built-in voltage regulation to match the 5 volt supply used by the 486 chips they augment), the Pentium OverDrives incorporate special heatsinks with built-in fans.

TABLE 10.3. The Pentium and its competitors.

Manufacturer	AMD	Cyrix	Intel	NexGen
Product	K5	M1	Pentium	586
Release date	Q3, 95	Q2, 95	March, 93	Sept, 94
DOS/Windows Compatible?	Yes	Yes	Yes	Yes
Socket-compatible with P54C?	Yes	Yes	Yes	No
Register width	32 bits	32 bits	32 bits	32 bits
Data bus width	64 bits	64 bits	64 bits	64 bits
Address bus width	32 bits	32 bits	32 bits	32 bits
Maximum addressable memory	4GB	4GB	4GB	4GB
Internal cache	16KB instruction, 8KB data	256-byte instruction, 16KB combined	8KB data, 8KB instruction	16KB data, 16KB instruction
Internal cache architecture	4-way set-associative; write through or write back	4-way set-associative; write through or write back	4-way set-assoiative; write through or write back	4-way set-associative; write through or write back

continues

TABLE 10.3. continued

Manufacturer	AMD	Cyrix	Intel	NexGen
Secondary cache controller	External	External	External	Internal
Floating-point unit	Internal	Internal	Internal	External
Pipeline stages	6	7	4	6
Core architecture	RISC	CISC	CISC	RISC
Performance edge over Pentium	30%	30%–50%	0%	0%

AMD K5

The last Pentium clone to be announced comes from the leading supplier of 486 compatibles, Advanced Micro Devices. Best known as a second source to Intel, a licensed manufacturer of 286 and disputed licensee of 386 designs (recent court decisions bolster AMD's contention of a valid license), AMD has taken a new direction with its Pentium-level product, the K5 family. Instead of building on its Intel-derived logic, AMD has instead taken the same tack as NexGen, using a RISC core with translation logic.

AMD is, in fact, well prepared in the RISC field, having developed its own RISC microprocessor family, the AMD 29000-series. AMD's director of advanced microprocessor design, engineered both the AMD 29000 and K5—and wrote the book on superscalar RISC (literally—his is a standard text).

Although the idea behind the AMD effort resembles that of NexGen, the implementation is very much different. Unlike the NexGen 586, AMD's K5 will be socket-compatible with today's Pentium. Consequently control for the secondary cache is left to external circuitry while a floating-point unit is integrated into the K5 silicon. The core logic of the K5 FPU is the same as was developed for the AMD 29000.

Like the NexGen 586, the K5 relies on a translator to convert Intel instructions into fixed-length RISC commands that can be processed more efficiently, each one in a single cycle. The uniformity of instructions helps the K5 architecture chip process four instructions simultaneously; the variable length of the execution time of Intel instructions makes running more than two simultaneously difficult. (Intel's P6, however, will have four parallel integer units.)

AMD gets this high throughput by routing the K5's instructions through six independent functional units—two integer processors, the floating-point processor, two load/store units, and a branch unit. According to AMD, their design will allow the K5 to run through programs about 30 percent faster than a Pentium operating at the same clock speed.

As with the Pentium, the external bus speed of the K5 is programmable to run at a fraction (one-half, two-thirds, or unity) of the internal clock. To match with slower external memory, the K5 uses a four-way set-associative cache split like that of the Pentium between separate instruction and data cache. The instruction cache, however, is double the size of the Pentium's—16KB versus 8KB. The data cache is 8KB.

Cyrix M1

Having proven its ability to duplicate the function of Intel's older microprocessors with its line of 386 upgrades and 486 clones, Cyrix elaborated on its theme by combining its classical designs with new technologies to produce its M1 architecture. The company hopes to usher a Pentium level—and socket-compatible—chip to market by the end of June this year. Several companies have already committed to using the chip in future systems.

The Cyrix approach is to build on its core of strength, the core logic of its 486-compatible microprocessors. The company took two processors derived from the CISC-based logic of its 486 chips and combined them in one superscalar package. As with the Pentium, the two pipelines are somewhat asymmetrical, but where the Pentium is pipelined with four stages, Cyrix uses seven in a design the company calls "superpipelined."

To eliminate problems that might arise in parallel execution, Cyrix takes advantage of several techniques popular in RISC designs.

Branch prediction and speculative execution help keep the pipelines full without stalling—they don't clog waiting for the microprocessor to get ready. (According to Cyrix, its four-state branch prediction algorithm achieves 90 percent accuracy.)

Register renaming allows each pipeline to simultaneously execute instructions in registers that appear to have the same name, so two instructions that try to access the same register can run in parallel.

Data forwarding allows the M1 chip to route the results of execution in one pipeline to the other when the operation of one instruction is dependent on the other.

Out-of-order execution lets the M1 complete the execution of a simple instruction in one pipeline before the other finishes a more complex instruction that appears earlier in the program.

The 64-bit data bus of the M1 operates at half the internal processing speed of the chip, 50 MHz for a 100 MHz part. Cyrix uses a cache unlike that of any other current microprocessor to make up the difference. The M1 internal cache has a two layered structure. To speed up loading instructions, the M1 design used a special 256-byte primary instruction cache, which Cyrix calls the "microcache." Another cache, much larger, combines the functions of primary data cache and secondary instruction cache. Although the size of this large unified cache is not set by the architecture's specifications, in initial implementations it will be the same 16KB size as the Pentium. The unified cache uses a four-way set-associative design.

Other elements of the hardware design of the M1 are much like the Pentium. The M1 is built around 32-bit registers but uses a 64-bit data path to more quickly fill its parallel pipelines. A

32-bit address bus allows direct access to up to 4GB of physical RAM. The internal hardware design is optimized for high-speed operation at 100 MHz or higher.

As does the Pentium, the M1 design incorporates an integral floating-point unit in addition to its two integer units. The Cyrix floating-point unit operates fully in parallel with the integer units when the instruction stream permits. Floating-point instructions can be executed out-of-order with related integer instructions, and a set of four write buffers permit speculative execution of floating-point instructions. The floating-point unit itself links to the rest of the M1 processor through a 64-bit internal bus and follows the IEEE 754 standard. It recognizes and executes all standard Intel coprocessor instructions.

Unlike the RISC-based competitors, the Cyrix M1 requires more silicon than the Pentium, making it more expensive to manufacture. Competition will keep its price down, but M1 gains its primary advantage in performance.

NexGen 586

The first chip to deliver Pentium-class performance came from NexGen, a Milpitas, California company that has been working on the design of its 586 microprocessor since 1988, before Intel introduced even the 486. The company announced its chip in March, 1994 and began shipping in September of that year. By the end of the March, 1995, it moved to the second generation of its 586, one that uses about 30 percent less silicon for comparable cost savings. At that time 71 companies were shipping PCs based on the chip.

The NexGen built its 586 around a RISC core (calling its architecture RISC-86), and uses a hardware preprocessor called a Decoder/Scheduler that converts Intel instructions into RISC code. The resulting instructions are all the same length (32 bits), which permits more efficient operation of the chip's pipeline.

Besides performance, this design offers other benefits. The Decoder/Scheduler determines compatibility, so designers can tinker with the integer units without worrying about causing problems when running software. Because the integer units use the latest RISC designs, as RISC core logic improves, so will the potential of the 586.

As with the Pentium, the NexGen 586 is a superscalar design with twin 32-bit integer units, each capable of processing separately and simultaneously. The dual pipelines in the 586 use branch prediction logic. The NexGen chips, however, uses a branch prediction algorithm that attempts speculative execution. (Other chip cloners also use branch prediction.) The on-chip logic not only guesses at which branch a program will take, but also it follows that branch's stream of instructions. If it encounters a second branch, it attempts to predict the course the program will take at that juncture and continues to go forward until it encounters a third branch (before resolving the actual path taken on the first branch). When the predictions are successful, the NexGen 586 can race through a many-branched program without the need to flush its cache

Where in the USA is Carmen Sandiego? The best way to scare kids away from something is to let them know that the something is good for them or—worse—educational. Several developers have chosen to make their kid's software look like games that belie their underlying educational content. The "Where in the....is Carmen Sandiego?" series from Brøderbund Software is a classic in this regard, a game that teaches geography. The screens on this page are from the "Where in the USA..." title. The latest incarnation, "Where in the World is Carmen Sandiego?" lets your kids stalk arch-criminal Carmen across the territory of CD-ROM. The object is to chase Carmen's gang around the world, gathering clues to solve a crime before the clock runs out. Of course, no one can travel dozens of times around the world without learning landmarks and locations, particularly considering that making progress requires answering geographic questions. Unlike early floppy-disk versions, this CD-based version is a true multimedia experience complete with enough exquisite photographs, foreign languages, and folk music to make education almost inadvertent.

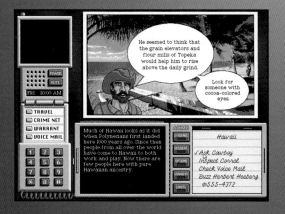

Wild Blue Yonder from Spectrum Holobyte is brought to you by the Emmy award-winning producers of the A&E Network TV show "Brute Force: The History of Weapons at War." You discover the most celebrated aircraft of the past 50 years and meet the aces and designers who propelled them into history. This combination of state-of-the-art multimedia interviews, videos, official reports, combat photos, personal mementos and more, covers the four most exciting eras in modern aviation: the Jet Age, Vietnam, Desert Storm and Tomorrow. Wild Blue Yonder brings all the sights, sounds and feel of the world's hottest jets to life!

SimCity The classic edutainment simulation is SimCity, by Maxis. The player assumes the role of mayor of the simulated city. As such, the player must allocate resources to create and maintain the city. He is faced with difficult choices: build more police stations to fight crime or invest in land development schemes? Renovate the subway system or build an airport? Urban planning becomes fun when it is done on-screen instead of in real life. Whatever the player builds actually appears on the screen, and the city actually bustles with life and activity. Natural disasters strike and the player has to cope with them. The program lures us into its depths of realistic detail, to the point that we may find it difficult to remember that this only a complex simulation.

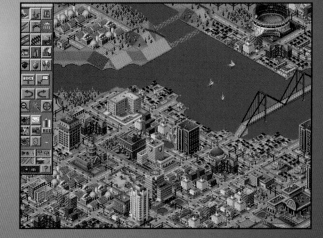

Microsoft Encarta, issued annually as part of the Microsoft Home series of multimedia products, is Microsoft's demonstration of what a multimedia reference should be—lots of flash and excitement and even some reference material. If you're looking for information, you might find it obscured rather than enhanced by 100 videos, 83 animations, and 6,500 photographs. Consider it an exploration tool rather than a reference work.

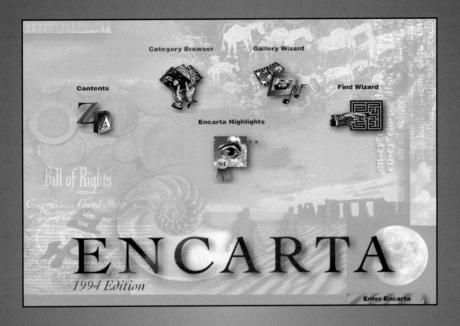

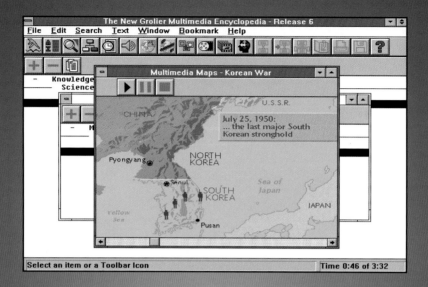

The New Grolier Multimedia Encyclopedia from Grolier Electronic Publishing attempts to be an in-depth research aid with multimedia capabilities. In fact, it is essentially a from-paper translation enhanced with some video (such as interviews with contemporary figures like Buzz Aldrin and Kurt Vonnegut) and multimedia overviews of broad topics such as architecture, the human body, and world history. Although it uses many of the usual search methods, it's sometimes quirky.

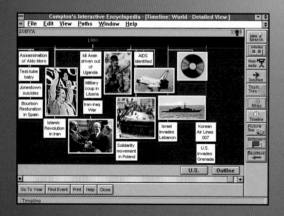

Compton's Interactive Encyclopedia from Compton's NewMedia emphasizes depth more than flashiness, making it a better choice for serious research (though not in the same league as Brittanica). Offering true multimedia, it includes video and a few animations in addition to its generous hyperlinked text base that allows you to instantly seek out individual topics. In addition, its "idea search" feature will let you find related topics in which the item of your interest plays a secondary role. It's at its best helping your kids prepare single-page homework assignments.

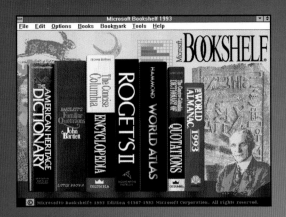

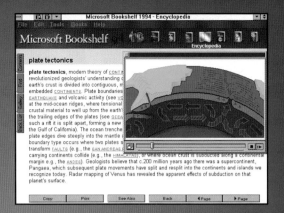

Microsoft Bookshelf, issued annually by Microsoft, sounds promising from what it includes—seven major reference works: *The Columbia Dictionary of Quotations, The American Heritage Dictionary of the English Language, The People's Chronology, The Concise Columbia Encyclopedia, The Hammond World Atlas, The Original Roget's Thesaurus,* and *The World Almanac Book of Facts.* The work as a whole has been augmented with video animation and sound clips. Unfortunately, although the breadth is wide, none of the references delve very deeply. The encyclopedia introduces new topics, the almanac adds a bit of perspective to recent events, the dictionary gives quick definitions, the atlas includes rough maps that will help locate major cities and nations but little more. It holds the promise of being exactly what you need when you are immersed in research and something unfamiliar appears that you're assumed to know. A new program called QuickShelf drops a Windows toolbar on top of your other Windows applications so you can visit this reference with a single click.

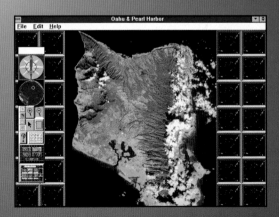

PharmAssist   Beyond general references, publishers have attempted to find topics that interest you as multimedia titles. One of the leading choices is health care. PharmAssist from SoftKey International is like having your local druggist on call. Start with the brand or generic name of a drug, and you can discover significant (and potentially dangerous) interactions and side effects.

Small Blue Planet: The Real Picture Atlas from Cambrix Publishing is a photographic atlas of the world that doesn't so much show you where things are as how they look when viewed from on high. Visual only, Small Blue Planet gives you a spy satellite view that lets you zoom in on a city, geographic feature, or meteorlogical event. This is a collection for gawkers rather than researchers, however, because the images stand on their own.

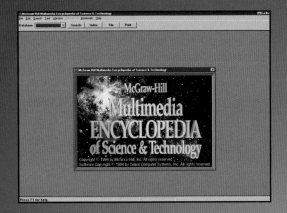
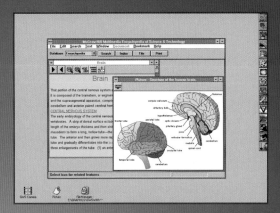
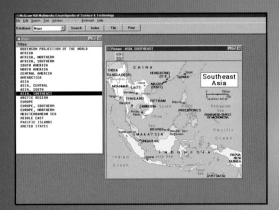
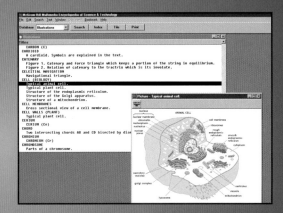

McGraw Hill Multimedia Encyclopedia of Science and Technology from McGraw-Hill Inc., shows the other extreme from Microsoft Bookshelf. It's an expensive collection of in-depth information that delves into more than 100,000 entries, 7,300 of them full-length articles on hard-core scientific topics suitable for pending college-level papers or helping shore up professional research. Although generalist in coverage, articles zero in on specifics such as individual chemical compounds. Emphasis is on depth and ease of access using searching and hypertext links. But what you gain in depth you lose in flash. Multimedia power is minimal, limited to coarse full-screen bitmapped illustrations, tiny, short animation, and low-quality sound.

"The full-color, photo-realistic world and the seamless CD technology provide top-notch suspension of disbelief and an intensely satisfying experience."

Computer Gaming World

Multimedia means interaction, and to many, interactive entertainment means games. Don't look down your nose at the computer game. The best games show new computer technologies at their finest. In fact, computer games were a multimedia experience even before multimedia was hatched. Game designers didn't just embrace multimedia early, they have continually pushed the limits of every technology they've bumped into.

If you just want to play action games, the dedicated video game systems are superior. Thanks to things like 64-bit technology, they present superior—that is, more realistic and faster moving—graphic images. Of course, the graphics used in video games get their edge from slighting somewhere else. They only need to generate resolution at the lowest end of the PC range. The multimedia games on your PC have to deal with the overhead of an operating system, several times more pixels, and probably a lot more creativity on the part of the programmers. On the other hand, a video game is solely an investment in neuro-anesthesia. A multimedia PC is a full-power system that can also play games when the left side of your brain needs to recharge.

For example, **Iron Helix** from Spectrum Holobyte, Inc. gives you the chance to save a planet from a doomsday weapon streaking toward it out of control. You can't shoot it down, but you can outsmart it—if it doesn't get you first. This multimedia tour-de-force includes top-quality video and music that will challenge all but the most powerful PCs.

The Journeyman Project, a multimedia 3-D adventure game from Quadra Interactive, takes you into a 21st century that's happy in having finally found world peace, and unsettled because the creation of a time machine could potentially rewrite history and end the new Nirvana. Your role in the game is as a member of the Temporal Protectorate, going back in time to undo the dastardly deeds that may unravel time's fabric. There are multiple solutions to the problems and puzzles. The game itself mixes adventure with arcade-style action (slow and sometimes jerky because it runs directly from CD), with enough sardonic humor to keep your soul alive.

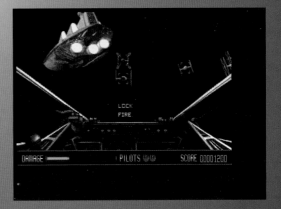

Rebel Assault from LucasArts Entertainment takes action gaming into outerspace and into a galaxy far beyond our own. You sit in the hot seat—the cockpit of a Star Wars X-wing fighter. You start as a neophyte and earn your wings on training flights. Eventually you work your way up through several levels of difficulty in half a dozen scenarios until the final challenge, an attack on the Death Star that by rights (and script) only Luke Skywalker should succeed at. The simulations are as good as the Star Wars special effects, with three-dimensional graphics combined with video images that will make you believe that you're actually there, wherever there might be.

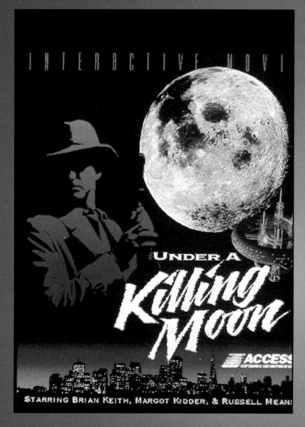

Under a Killing Moon from Access Software is a good example of how professional Hollywood actors have been lured into the world of interactive video games. Brian Keith, Margot Kidder, and Russell Means star in this mystery movie that occupies two entire CD-ROMs and includes more than two hours of digital video. You enter into this world and have to interact with the various characters in order to solve the case.

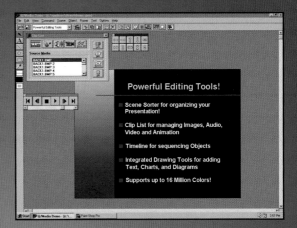

Where hypertext deals primarily with words, presentation products are chiefly visual. You need a completely different array of tools for writing presentation-style multimedia, authoring programs that are image oriented (see Chapter 5, "Authoring Multimedia"). In building a presentation, commercial authoring tools most commonly use a slide show metaphor for their primary interfaces. A slide show is simply a presentation of images arranged in a predetermined sequence, the end of one slide triggering the start of the next.

Presentation packages offer a variety of transitions between slides, from the basics through dissolves, wipes, and so on, to exotic effects like tile transition that replaces an old image with a new one as a sequence of individual blocks and a louver transition updates the image in a series of synchronized broadening bands. Modern packages enable you to fill your screen with multiple images and change each one independently. You can even superimpose a small image over a larger one. Most packages enable you to incorporate video images along with graphic stills. Sprite animation allows you to move a small bitmapped image called a Sprite across the screen to draw attention to an image or issue.

Commercial presentation authoring software tends to fall into one of three classes based on power and price. The least expensive programs offer first-time authors easy entry into multimedia programming.

Most are based on a slide-show metaphor but can incorporate any standard multimedia object. Moderately priced packages may give you a choice of control systems and often give you a programming language that you can use for greater flexibility and control. Most of these packages will gather the files you need for your presentation to help you package and master a CD-ROM and to enable you to compile a distributable program. The high end authoring packages give the serious multimedia professional a complete array of tools, a programming language, and extensive links to all sorts of multimedia devices. Most of these packages are designed to help develop training systems. Nearly all provide run-time versions that you distribute with your compiled presentation.

Q/Media from Q/Media Software Corp. extends the slide show abilities of ordinary presentation products into the realm of multimedia by allowing you to add animated objects and sound. You start by building a presentation from scratch or importing one from another presentation program. You can then drag in objects from a dialog box or any application that supports OLE 2.0 and precisely set the instant the object appears in a scene. Q/Media slows interactive branching so you can let your audience jump from scene to scene, run programs or play video clips. Basically a beginner's program, Q/Media is easy to use but lacks many of the fine control mechanisms of more expensive presentation packages.

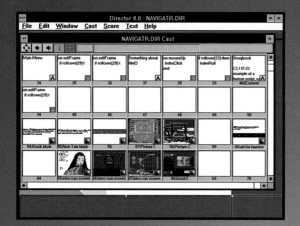

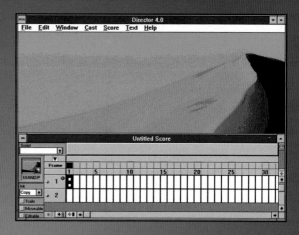

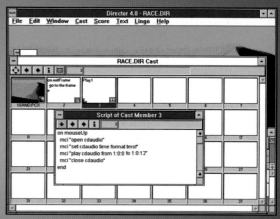

Macromedia Director from Macromedia, Inc. uses a movie metaphor instead of the slide show as its basis for building multimedia presentations. The Hollywood side of the program runs deep,

infecting the product with a language of its own that will become familiar as you build your multimedia projects. In fact, the presentations you shoot with Director are called movies, and the multimedia objects and starring roles, such as Sprites, scripts, sounds, and palettes are called the cast. You write a script by placing these objects on a stage and setting the timing of their movements and transitions.

You can take intimate control using the Director's own object-oriented language, called Lingo, that includes its own debugger and enables you to control not only devices in your PC but external hardware such as VCRs and video disc players. Many people regard Director (or its Mac-based sibling version) as the best program for developing presentation-style multimedia applications.

Page 15: Multimedia Toolbook (3 screens)

A morph is a transformation, a change in form, short for *metamorphosis* : any image can become another. Making a compelling morph in practice is a challenge. The trick is to lock certain key points in place and let all the shapes around them change. When faces morph, for instance, the eyes are likely to be locked in place and the rest of the face distorts from the old shape into the new. Morphing software lets you pick the key points or makes its own guess at what's best. It then generates the steps in between the starting and ending images, tweening the intermediate frames. Morphing programs differ in the flexibility and control they offer, both in selecting key points and in the formats they handle (see Chapter 5).

PhotoMorph from North Coast Software only starts with morphing. The package includes animated transitions, distortion effects, screen capture, and titling. It is powerful enough to transform images of different formats, bit depths, or even sizes. Control is easy: point and shoot with your mouse to set key points, choose a transition effect, and start the morph. PhotoMorph displays starting and ending images side-by-side so you can easily find the optimal key points. Link morphs into mini-movies or save single frames. Best of all, it's one of the fastest morphing programs.

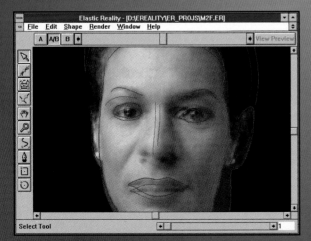

Elastic Reality from Elastic Reality Inc. Makes you into a morphing magician. You can transform anything into anything else in a few short steps. You use conventional drawing tools to select an image area to morph, putting barriers around what you want to keep from changing. Elastic Reality then tweens the intermediate frames to make the transformation. You can make multiple simultaneous transformations, and even run each at a different speed for truly complex changes. Included are 32-bit extensions to bring Windows 3.1*x* up to full speed and a package of 60 editable transitions called Transjammer. This is probably the most powerful morphing program currently available for the Windows platform.

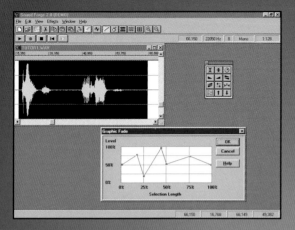

Professional recording engineers refine and doctor raw sounds with a variety of tools. They use equalizers to balance the bass and treble, add reverb to give life to flat sounds, shift pitches for dramatic effect, flange sounds for alien effects, add in choruses and echoes, maybe even stretch sounds to perfectly match a visual effect. With the right software, you can do the audio preparatory work yourself on your PC. **Sound Forge** from Sonic Foundry (see Chapter 5) gives you full command of any sound you can get onto your PC. Multimedia producers will find the equivalent of a rack of digital audio processing gear at their fingertips while musicians can sample, sync, and synthesize. It reads and writes nearly any audio file format, converts one to another, changes sampling rates and bit depths, and even synthesizes MIDI files into Windows waveform (.WAV) files.

Photoshop from Adobe Systems is regarded as today's premiere photo editing program. It ranks as the most powerful, with a fast graphics engine and built-in abilities to take advantage of multi-threading (available in Windows NT and Windows 95 operating systems) and its own plug-in API that has become an industry standard for adding on utilities. It can undetectably edit reality or make truly surreal images from ordinary photos. In its latest incarnation, it has more alpha channel control than ever before and new anti-aliasing algorithms for banishing jagged edges.

Picture Publisher from Micrografx Inc. may be the most intuitive photo editor. It offers a full range of professional-level tools that are readily customized and includes some welcome touches such as the ability to paint in extra sharpness in selected details. It also includes a unique Command List that records every change you make while editing: you can replay the list to recreate the image, editing the list in the process so that you can rethink any step you make in editing an image.

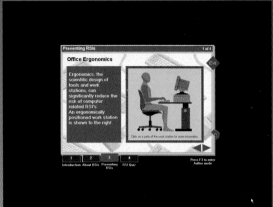

ToolBook can import text in Rich Text Format. It also understands most standard graphic formats including PhotoCD and Video for Windows, QuickTime, and motion JPEG in addition to bitmaps. The latest versions of ToolBook incorporate its own multimedia engine to handle animation and full-motion video. It includes a bitmap, icon/cursor, palette, .WAV file, and video editors. The last of these, Digital Video Producer, enables you to mix Video for Windows files, synchronize sound from .WAV files, and add titles.

You can build a book using nothing more than menus and dialog boxes. With Toolbook's programming language, OpenScript, you can build menu bars, control buttons, and hypertext links for more advanced coontrol. The package includes a library of common functions, minimizing your need for actual programming.

Multimedia ToolBook from Asymetrix Corp. is based on a book metaphor but extends far beyond hypertext with the ability to incorporate databases, financial functions, and custom interfaces. It enables you to run external applications, and can send and receive data from other applications.

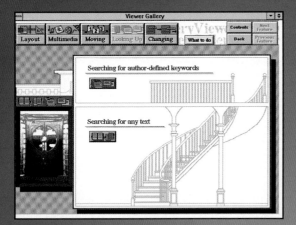

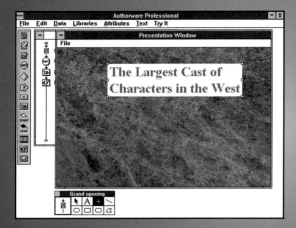

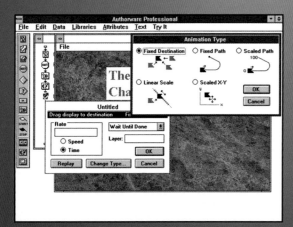

You'll find a number of commercial hypertext applications based on Microsoft's **Multimedia Viewer**. It makes a solid stand-alone package with powerful linking and search abilities as well as the ability to handle individual multimedia elements. It gives the hypertext you write an easy-to-understand user interface and features advanced text rendering and layout to let you make appealing presentations from ordinary paragraphs and graphics that automatically adapt to the display system in use. Creating applications with Multimedia Viewer requires little knowledge of programming. You only need to add special codes—lots of them—to your text. You write your text using Word for Windows formatting and embed graphics, sounds, and video in it just as you would prepare an ordinary document. When you've finished your draft, you save the result as Rich Text Format (.RTF) files which converts formatting and embedding commands into ASCII text. To produce a distribution version, you compile it using the Multimedia Viewer software.

The downside to authoring with Multimedia Viewer 2.0 is that it's the end of the line. Microsoft has announced that the package will be supported only for Windows 3.1 and some special Sony multimedia hardware. Although the application you create using it will run under Windows 95, you won't see further development of Multimedia Viewer 2.0 to enhance its operation with newer Windows incarnation.

Authorware Professional for Windows from Macromedia takes some time to learn but rewards you for your effort. It excels at handling video, both in Video for Windows format and through MCI control of external devices such as laser disc players. It lets you quickly build interactive applications complete with hyperlinks, drag-and-drop control, and integrated animation. Files made with the PC version of Authorware can be shared with those made with the Mac version, and compiled files can be distributed with a run-time module within your company without royalty. Commercial distribution requires a negotiated royalty.

at each turn. Of course, as with any branch prediction, should the prognostication be in error, all the work done in preparing for the branch not taken will be wasted.

Each NexGen integer unit can process an instruction in a single clock cycle, allowing the 586 to match the Pentium's ability to process two instructions per clock. Consequently NexGen claims performance on par with the Intel's 90 and 100 MHz Pentiums but, because the 586 is priced lower, at a price/performance advantage of about 20 percent.

Where most PCs run the external buses of their high-speed Pentiums at two-thirds the internal clock speed of the chip, NexGen runs its chips at half-speed. To make up for this difference, NexGen endowed its 586 with double the internal cache as the Pentium, devoting a full 16KB for instructions and a separate 16KB data cache. As with the Pentium, each side of the cache of the 586 is four-way set-associative with full write-back capabilities. Beyond that, NexGen 586 incorporates its own secondary cache controller on the chip itself. Not only does this integral cache controller eliminate the need for an external chip, it allows the secondary cache circuitry to be more tightly coupled with the rest of the chip. The 586 links to the secondary cache through a 64-bit interface that runs at full internal microprocessor speed. (Secondary cache memory for the Pentium runs at bus speed; Intel will use a full-speed cache bus on the Pentium's successor, now code-named P6.)

As with the Pentium, the normal data bus of the 586 is a full 64 bits wide to allow its twin 32-bit integer units to fill with external data simultaneously. The 586 has another 64-bit bus to link with its optional external floating-point unit. According to NexGen, its floating-point chip is a thoroughly modern, high-speed design on par with Intel's fourth-generation Pentium floating-point processor.

Expansion Buses

One reason that PCs have popped up in more odd applications than duct tape is their versatility. You can make a PC into just about anything you can imagine—as long as you can buy an expansion board suited to the task. Add in a pro sound board, and your PC can become a radio station editor. Plug a bank of analog-to-digital converters into your PC and you can delegate data-gathering authority to your PC for your next Ph.D. dissertation. With the right mix of expansion boards you can even make your ordinary PC into a multimedia powerhouse.

Expansion distinguishes the multimedia PC from a game machine. A game machine is a game machine is a game machine. You can slide in cartridges and switch from Sonic to Super Mario and strap on a gut-thumping vest but you still have nothing more than a game. A multimedia PC, however, can transcend modest roots thanks to expansion. You can graft on more power as it is invented or when you can afford it. You can change the entire complexion of your computer, from self-contained check balancer to international negotiator, from idle-time mind candy to capitalistic tool.

Function

Key to any PC customization project is a place to plug in your choice of enhancements, the expansion slot. The slot gives you a physical place to put circuit boards. More importantly, it provides the link you need to connect more circuitry to your PC, the expansion bus.

The expansion bus is more than a wire. It must provide enhancements with the means to share the entire resources of your PC. The various enhancements will need access to all the memory addresses and I/O ports in your PC (or at least a sufficient number to support their own functions). They need a means of synchronizing their operations with those of your PC and sharing control functions so they can take and give commands. And enhancements must have their mundane needs filled, too, needs such as a physical place to live and electricity to keep them going. The expansion slot needs to supply all these essentials.

The expansion slot is the physical place where accessories connect with your system. It must hold the hardware firmly in place and provide a place where you can plug in cables to connect external peripherals. The slot defines the physical size of the board (which limits the amount of circuitry it can hold) and how you install boards.

The expansion slot provides the electrical connections needed to link a board to your PC. In addition, it supplies the logical connection that allows a board to communicate with the rest of the circuitry in your system. The design of the bus determines whether an expansion accessory integrates as a simple extension to your system's microprocessor or as a separate entity, linked but independent. The former design—termed the *local bus*—allows for design simplicity; the latter—the *arbitrated bus*—give greater control. Given the same clock speeds, the arbitrated bus can deliver greater performance both in bus transfer speed and for host throughput (by cutting overhead). But the local bus design lends itself to quicker clocks and races ahead of conventional designs by virtue of brute horsepower. Today's so-called "local buses" actually combine features of a true local bus and an arbitrated bus.

With multimedia PCs, a single bus often isn't enough. Most of today's machines incorporate two expansion buses: one, a conventional (old-fashioned) expansion bus for backward compatibility with general-purpose accessories that need versatility and control, and a second, a "local bus" that also incorporated arbitration, for specialized high-performance expansion. Rather than mere compromise for the indecisive, this combination usually is your best choice in a new system.

History

Once upon a time, expansion bus meant one thing only. Every PC shared exactly the same design to its expansion bus, and every enhancement board plugged into every slot. At one time, Elizabeth Taylor was really the young girl she pretends to be and Apatosauri munched on fronds on the tops of tree ferns—perhaps even at the same time. But times have changed. Taylor has gone from thrill to shill, Apatosauri have gone the way of all things, and that original PC expansion bus still lingers in PCs like the scent of bad perfume. Although you might not find a slot matching the original 8-bit expansion standard of the first PCs in your next system, nearly all PCs have a slot little more than one step removed.

When the PC was first crafted, the expansion bus was an expedient. All the circuitry needed to make a working computer wouldn't fit on the PC's motherboard. Even then, however, the engineers designing the PC had the notion that you just might want to slide in boards to customize it. So they added an expansion bus. Their design was truly an expedient—they just took the signals the microprocessor in the PC needed to connect and operate with other circuits and extended them, through buffers, to a set of expansion connectors. From an electrical standpoint, sliding a board into one of these slots was no different than soldering another circuit onto the motherboard. In other words, the PC expansion bus was originally contrived as the local bus of the 8088 microprocessor inside the first PCs. The 8088 used an 8-bit connection, and so did the PC bus. The 8088 operated at 4.77 MHz and so did the PC expansion bus. The 8088 quickly became obsolete and was set aside, but the old bus clung on because everyone wanted new PCs to be able to use their old expansion boards. So we continue to live with its heritage. With the exception of IBM's aberrant Micro Channel, all PC expansion bus designs were based on the original 1981 PC bus until the 1993 advent of Intel's PCI specification.

Standards

Access is what you want from an expansion bus. Not accessibility, being able to easily slide in new enhancements, but access to the widest possible variety of products to plug in. You want wide access in this area so you'll be more likely to find the one perfect peripheral for your PC. You'll also enjoy the benefit of competition—lower prices.

Standards help assure you wide access. When a PC follows an open expansion standard, any manufacturer can build peripherals to match. Proprietary expansion standards limit access and allow peripheral makers to charge higher prices (in fact, they often have to charge higher prices because their development costs are spread over a smaller market).

In general, the longer a standard exists, the more products that follow it become available. The problem with standards is that as soon as one is set, it is obsolete. A standard that is cast in bronze can't reflect new technological developments. Picking a standard for a new PC becomes the tough choice between age and beauty. The number of PC expansion standards is a surprisingly wide half dozen: ISA, EISA, MCA, PCI, PCMCIA, and VL Bus. Unfortunately, there is no one best choice or even combination today. The marketplace is in transition from an old (the oldest) standby to the contender with the most potential, from ISA to PCI.

Standards

If you can't find what you want in PCI, the interim choice is a combination, ISA or EISA plus VL Bus. The one rule is that any multimedia PC requires one of the local buses. Base your choice of which on the availability of the expansion boards that you want.

Buying Tip

Table 10.4 lists some of the characteristics of popular PC expansion buses, including the top transfer rates claimed by its developers. All of these ratings are optimistic, based on unsustainable peak or burst rates. For example, the PC/XT bus and EISA speeds only apply to DMA transfers; the high MCA and EISA rates only apply to systems and peripherals that use advanced transfer modes, and no basic PC peripherals use these modes. The VL Bus and PCI rates are based on full 64-bit data buses, which are yet unrealized in practice. The actual transfer rate depends on so many variables that an exact number you can expect from a given system is nearly impossible to state. But the peak values are all similarly exaggerated so their relative values are an indication of how one bus would fare in comparison with another.

TABLE 10.4. Comparison of expansion buses.

Feature	Units	PC/XT	ISA	MCA	EISA	VL Bus	PCI
Introduction	Year	1981	1984	1987	1988	1992	1993
Data bus width	Bits	8	16	32	32	64	64
Addressing	Bits	20	24	32	32	32	32
Clock speed*	MHz	4.77	8	10/20	8	33	33
Transfer rate	MB/sec.	5.33	8	80	132	264	264

* Note: Clock speed at introduction. VL bus currently can go up to 50 MHz, PCI to 66 MHz.

The following sections offer closer looks at the various PC expansion standards.

ISA

The one real standard among PCs remains Industry Standard Architecture or ISA. Interestingly, the ISA standard dates from 1987 when it was officially sanctioned under the imprimatur of the Institute of Electrical and Electronic Engineers. The bus was first used, however, in 1984 as the expansion bus of the IBM AT. Consequently it is sometimes called the AT bus or, occasionally, the "classic" bus. In today's world, geriatric bus might be more appropriate.

The AT bus was designed as an extension to the old PC bus, adding new address and data lines to match the capabilities of the 286 microprocessor. Its vital statistics match those of the processor—or rather, the processor frozen in time in 1984. ISA is a 16-bit bus. It has 24 address lines, limiting its addressing abilities to 16MB of RAM. Even when installed in a Pentium PC, nothing that plugs into an ISA slot can be addressed above the bottom 16MB of addressing range. The ISA bus also provides hardware signaling for 15 interrupts and seven DMA channels. Although some systems run AT buses as fast as 16 MHz, the ISA standard sets the clock speed of the bus at or slightly above 8 MHz, usually set at a fraction of microprocessor speed. The 8 MHz corresponds, of course, to the top speed of the 286 microprocessor in late 1984.

The ISA bus requires two cycles for every transfer. The first cycle puts an address on the bus, the second cycle puts data across the bus. Every transfer, even long strings of sequential bytes, requires this two-step process. As a result, the peak rate at which ISA can move data is 8MB per second—two bytes in parallel four million times a second (half the nominal clock rate). Actual bus throughput is lower because every transfer is controlled by the microprocessor (except DMA transfers, which, because of a quirk of the AT design, are slower still), and the microprocessor is typically burdened by other work—from running programs to refreshing memory.

MCA

IBM understood the limitations of the AT bus early on, and in 1987 unleashed its version of a better bus, Micro Channel Architecture. A clever design, it failed to gain wide acceptance in the marketplace because IBM made MCA too tough and expensive for other manufacturers to use and marketed it so poorly that hardly anyone wanted to use it. Although not a multimedia contender, it laid the groundwork for buses that are contenders.

MCA was designed as a full 32-bit bus with 16-bit and 8-bit subsets. In its initial implementation, it had an address limit of 16MB, which was later pushed to the full 4GB range of 32-bit addressing. (DMA transfers were still only possible within the first 16MB, however.) MCA was designed to run synchronously with a nominal clock speed of 10 MHz, though some expansion boards could push this rate higher.

The most important innovation was that MCA allowed bus mastering, so it was not limited by the performance of its host microprocessor (nor did it load down the microprocessor with its housekeeping needs). Initially, the peak transfer rate of the bus was 20MB per second. Later refinements pushed that rate to 40MB, then to 80MB per second, although those higher rates require specialized expansion boards that never became part of the mainstream market. MCA's swan song was a clock-rate boost that pushed potential throughput to 160MB/second, but no commercial product ever demonstrated transfers near this rate.

EISA

Unhappy with the MCA effort, in 1988 a consortium of nine companies (termed by industry wags as the "Gang of Nine") made up of AST Research, Compaq Computer Corp., Epson, Hewlett-Packard Company, NEC, Olivetti, Tandy, Wyse, and Zenith Data Systems developed Extended Industry Standard Architecture, more commonly known as EISA.

As an enhancement to ISA, EISA's big claim to fame was backward compatibility with ISA. It also expanded the old bus to full 32-bit potential and added new transfer modes that, in some instances, could raise its peak transfer rate to 33MB/second. As with MCA, from which it borrowed heavily, EISA freed the bus from the direct control of the host microprocessor, so bus operations did not need to impinge on overall system performance.

Despite the best efforts of its promoters, EISA never found wide success, either, at least for its first six or seven years. It added cost and complexity to PCs but, because few devices could take advantage of its potentials, didn't deliver any great performance enhancements.

However, EISA isn't dead yet. Many PC makers are capitalizing on its bus-mastering abilities as an adjunct to newer buses with even higher potential throughputs. They gain the control that EISA offers and the speed of the new designs.

In these applications, the biggest drawback of EISA is its complexity. It adds an extra step to system setup. Every time you change an expansion board, you must reconfigure the bus to reflect your changes. New Plug-and-Play PCs promise to minimize or eliminate your involvement in setup, perhaps breathing new life into the wheezing old standard.

VL Bus

Despite the addition of EISA, in the early 1990s PC makers were feeling constrained by the bus choices. Applications like multimedia demanded the fast movement of data, and no existing bus could blast bytes fast enough. Adventurous manufacturers first tried connecting video circuits directly to the microprocessor's local bus and got a visible performance edge on other systems. But these designs suffered from the lack of standardization. Without a common standard for connecting to the microprocessor local bus, the freedom of choice and upgradability taken for granted with ordinary expansion boards would not be possible.

The first true standard for a local bus was hammered out by the Video Electronics Standards Association (VESA). Called VESA Local Bus or VL Bus, and formally announced on August 28, 1992, the design was actually a return to old times. Just as the original PC bus was a simple extension of the connections of the 8088 microprocessor, VL Bus was an extension to the microprocessor standard of the time, the 486DX. More importantly, VL Bus gave the PC industry what it wanted most: a standardized connector and protocol for a local bus expansion system for PCs.

As with the 486DX, the initial VL Bus design used a full 32-bit architecture, 32 data lines and 32 address lines so that it could address a full 4GB of memory. It was designed to operate at microprocessor speed, meaning up to 33 MHz, with the potential for higher speeds (up to 50 MHz) in some systems. It also supported a burst mode patterned after that of the 486 micropro-cessor—instead of one address cycle for every data transfer, it could transfer full 16-byte lines of data in five cycle bursts, one address cycle followed by four sequential data cycles. Although promoted as having a 132MB/second transfer rate (4 bytes 33 million times per second), in this burst mode it could peak at 105MB/second.

VL Bus is not designed to replace a more traditional expansion bus but to augment it. The design works with underlying ISA, MCA, and EISA systems, and depends on the control electronics of the other buses for support. PCs that use VL Bus will thus have another bus as well.

Reflecting the introduction of the 64-bit Pentium in 1993, VESA developed a second generation VL Bus standard (Version 2.0). This design promises to double the speed capabilities of the original design, but has been overshadowed by another new bus design, PCI, which is described later.

Perhaps the largest limitation on the VL Bus design is that its high clock frequencies limit the number of expansion slots that are possible. Typically no more than three slots can be connected in a single VL Bus system, although PCs can gain more VL Bus slots by installing addition bus controllers.

Performance Issue

PCI

In July, 1992, Intel Corporation introduced Peripheral Component Interconnect. Long awaited as a local bus specification, the initial announcement proved more and less than the industry had hoped for. The first PCI specification fully documented Intel's conception of what local bus should be—and it wasn't a local bus. Instead, Intel defined mandatory design rules and included hardware guidelines that helped assure proper circuit operation of motherboards at high speeds with a minimum of design complication. It showed how to link together PC circuits—including the expansion bus—for high-speed operation. But the initial PCI announcement didn't deliver what most people wanted, guidance as to a bus connector design.

In May, 1993, Intel answered this criticism by introducing PCI Release 2.0. The new specification extended the original document in two primary ways. It broadened the data path to 64 bits to match the new Pentium chip. And it gave a complete description of expansion connectors for both 32-bit and 64-bit implementations of a PCI expansion bus.

PCI boasts many of the same characteristics as VL Bus—full 32-bit architecture and 33 MHz speed. In addition, PCI defines its own burst mode that does not limit bursts to single-line transfers. A PCI burst can stretch for hundreds of bytes. Even so, in actual systems PCI runs a bit slower than VL Bus, but not so much as you would notice the difference.

Performance Issue

The PCI design is fundamentally unlike and incompatible with VL Bus. Foremost, PCI 2.0 was designed to be microprocessor-independent rather than limited to Intel's own chips. Instead of linking almost directly to the microprocessor, the PCI 2.0 specification provided a compatibility layer, making it what some industry insiders call a mezzanine bus. Whereas VL Bus was designed to augment more traditional expansion buses, PCI tolerates older buses but can also totally replace them. PCI also provides a standard designs for both 5- and 3.3-volt expansion board.

Standards

Many manufacturers consider PCI to be the more robust design. Even though VL Bus got off to an earlier start, most PC makers are shifting their new machines to PCI. In fact, PCI has been adopted for some computers that do not use Intel architecture microprocessors. It will probably be the most important expansion bus in multimedia systems for years to come.

Buying Tip

PCMCIA

Another up and coming expansion bus is PCMCIA, an abbreviation for *Personal Computer Memory Card International Association.* PCMCIA represents the most radical change in system expansion. Instead of conventional expansion boards, PCMCIA specifies credit-card size boards that you can slide in and out of your PC whenever you want, even while it is running. Moreover, the standard embraces not only cards for PCs but for anything electronic, from synthesizers to trash compactors, and it allows the same card to run in any device.

Originally PCMCIA was developed as a standard for portable computers, but today desktop systems are gaining slots for PCMCIA cards. Its first incarnation, PC Card, Release 1.0, was introduced in September 1990. It contemplated only the use of solid-state memory on the card as a means of data storage. But the PC Card intrigued both the makers of subnotebook computers and peripheral developers, who believed that the standard could be expanded to incorporate I/O devices as well as memory.

As a result, the PC Card standard was updated in September 1991 to comprise a more generalized interface that would accommodate both storage and input/output devices. Additionally, the new Release 2.0 standard allowed the use of thicker cards, permitting the incorporation of a wider variety of semiconductor circuits. It also allowed programs stored on PC Cards to be executed in the card memory rather than requiring the code to be downloaded into standard RAM.

Standards

In keeping with good practice, backward compatibility was maintained: Cards designed under PCMCIA Release 1.0 will plug into and work in Release 2.0 machines. Because Release 2.0 adds a wealth of features that older hardware may not understand, however, all the functions of a new card may not work in an older system. Because the thickness of both generations' cards is physically the same, new cards will fit slots in old systems. No combination of card and system will result in damage at either end of the connection. Cards come in three types. Type I are 3.3mm thick and are used mostly for memory. Type II are 5mm thick and are the most popular. They are used by modems, flash disks, and the like. Type III are nominally 10.5mm thick, although many cards are 14mm to 15mm thick. Hard disks are the chief application of the Type III form factor.

The completed PCMCIA 2.0 is much more than a simple set of physical specifications for card dimensions and a bus pin-out. The standard also describes file formats and data structures, a method through which a card can convey its configuration and capabilities to its host, a device-independent means of accessing card hardware, and software links independent of operating systems.

Performance Issue

Unfortunately this universal approach has its drawbacks. Bringing a PCMCIA expansion system to life requires nearly 100KB of device drivers in the typical PC. Nevertheless, PCMCIA remains the only standard for the expansion of notebook and smaller PCs.

The only flaw in the PCMCIA design has been its need for software drivers for support of card services and socket services. In the DOS environment, these drivers consume a total of about 100KB of real-mode memory, taken either from the High Memory Area or from your DOS programs. This large memory need severely limits the applications you can run on a DOS-based PC with an added PCMCIA slot, particularly if you also plan to run a network (most of which also have extensive memory requirements.) Advanced operating systems like OS/2 Warp and Windows 95 eliminate this burden by using drivers that run in protected mode. Moreover, both OS/2 Warp and Windows 95 add Plug-and-Play functionality to PCMCIA.

Performance Issue

At the software level, PCMCIA socket services are not all the same. Two chief types dominate the market, those patterned after Intel products and those patterned after DataBook products. The former is the more widely used. Most add-in PC Card readers include the proper software that, once installed, makes the differences between the two designs irrelevant. Windows 95 has built-in support for both. It also enables you to install other PCMCIA card services drivers, although its Plug-and-Play support may be compromised by such products. Some kinds of PCMCIA cards require manufacturer-supplied drivers to function. Such devices include network or SCSI adapters that need memory-mapped input and output functions.

Memory

Memory is mindspace for the multimedia PC. Memory holds both the raw data that needs to be processed and the instructions for the processing. Your PC's microprocessor pulls both in, and slides the results back.

Unlike other ways of holding information, the main memory of your PC allows bytes to move in and out and change in nanoseconds. Getting the best performance from your PC means having enough memory that an entire programs and its data will fit into memory at once—that way there are no delays from disk access or transfer.

Technologies

Your PC arranges its main memory as memory cells which are arranged like the pigeon holes once used for sorting mail. Your programs find each byte or character they need by peeking into the appropriate pigeon hole, called an *address*. Because the software can directly access any place in main memory at random, this kind of memory is termed *Random Access Memory* or simply *RAM*.

RAM comes in two types. *Dynamic memory*, the most common form, stores individual data bits as tiny electrical charges. *Static memory* stores bits in the form of the position of a two-way electrical switch, on or off indicating a digital one or zero. These two type of memory differ in two ways, function and cost. Dynamic memory requires periodic refreshing because the charges drain away in a few dozen microseconds. Static memory requires no refreshing. Compensating for this complication, dynamic memory is substantially less expensive to manufacture. Consequently the bulk of the memory in nearly all PCs is dynamic. Static memory, which generally operates at higher speed, is usually reserved for memory caches.

Both dynamic and static memory depend on a constant supply of electricity to maintain their integrity. Dynamic RAM would quickly lose its collection of minute charges. Without electricity, there would be no current to hold the static switches in place. In contrast, all PCs have a more permanent form of memory called *Read-Only Memory* or *ROM*—your PC can read from its storage but not write to or change its contents. Moreover, even a power failure won't erase the data stored in ROM. This primary use for ROM is based on this permanency. ROM stores the BIOS code of your PC and of its add-in peripherals.

Memory Characteristics

Memory is measured in bytes, each of which represents eight bits of storage. A bit is the smallest possible unit of information, representing one state—on or off, one or zero. One byte is sufficient to store a single character.

Modern multimedia PCs deal with so much information that memory is usually measured in bulk with larger units. One kilobyte (abbreviated KB or simply K) is 1024 bytes; that is, 2^{10} (two to the tenth power) bytes. A megabyte (abbreviated MB) is 1,048,576 bytes or 2^{20} (two to the twentieth power) bytes. A gigabyte (abbreviated GB) is 1,073,741,824 or 2^{30} (two to the thirtieth power) bytes.

Memory in PCs is divided into *memory banks*, and each bank is usually the same width as the microprocessor data bus. In modern PCs, that means that the memory will be arranged in 32-bit wide banks for 486-based machines and 64-bit wide banks for PCs based on Pentiums and their cousins.

Addressing

The basic unit of memory is the *chip*, which is a bit-oriented storage device. Chip capacities are measured in kilobits and megabits. Although early PCs often used individual chips for their main memory, most modern PCs now use *memory modules*, small circuit boards on which multiple chips are mounted. Memory modules are byte-oriented storage devices with capacities measured in kilobytes and megabytes.

The most common memory modules are called *Single In-line Memory Modules* or SIMMs because they bear an edge connector that puts all of its contacts in a straight line. Two configuration of SIMMs are generally available today, those with single-byte data paths (called 30-pin SIMMs because of the number of connections on the module) and those with 4-byte data paths (called 72-pin SIMMs). The chief difference is that you need four of the former to make a single

32-bit data bank while one SIMM with a 4-byte data path suffices for a complete 32-bit bank. Although the narrower 30-pin SIMMs were once the most popular for PCs, the wider 72-pin SIMMs have become the first choice among today's computer manufacturers. They allow you to expand the memory in your PC one SIMM at a time. With the narrower modules, the smallest increment of memory you could add was four matched SIMMs. Moreover, a Pentium PC requires eight byte-wide SIMMs to make a 64-bit banks but only two 4-byte SIMMs.

Note that 30-pins SIMMs are somewhat larger than 72-pin SIMMs. One kind of SIMM will not fit in sockets meant for the other. You must match the number of pins on your SIMMs to the requirements of your PC.

Parity-Checking

SIMM are also divided by *parity-checking*, an error-detection technique. Parity-checking allocates one extra bit for every byte of storage, and allows a PC to verify the integrity of the byte in memory. When a byte is written into memory, the value stored in the parity check bit is set either to a logical one or zero in such a way that the total of all nine bits storing the byte is always odd. Every time your PC reads its parity-checked memory, it totals up the nine bits of each byte to verify that the total has remained odd. An even total reveals a change in the stored value—a memory *parity error*—which signals most PCs to shut down rather than mislead you with erroneous data.

Parity checking can only locate an error of one bit in a byte. More elaborate error-detection schemes can detect larger errors. Better still, when properly implemented, these schemes can fix single-bit errors without crashing your system. Called Error Correction Code or ECC, this scheme in most efficient form requires three extra bits per byte of memory when errors are corrected at the byte level. (Larger blocks of bits require relatively fewer ECC bits.) Currently only a few servers use ECC memory.

SIMMs that support parity-checking have an extra bit for each byte and an extra data line for parity information. Consequently, parity-checked SIMMs are often described as 9-bit or 36-bit SIMMs. SIMMs that lack parity-checking are often termed 8-bit or 32-bit SIMMs. SIMMs are designed so that most of the time you can use one with parity-checking in a system that does not use parity-checking. If you try to use a SIMM without parity-checking in a PC that requires it (as most do), the machine probably won't boot up, because the lack of parity bits will be interpreted as a parity error.

Chip Count

Manufacturers build SIMM from discrete memory chips, soldering them to small circuit boards to make a module. The actual chips they use should not matter, but some manufacturers distinguish between 3-chip and 9-chip designs in their 9-bit SIMMs. These are both byte-wide, parity-checked SIMMs. They differ in that 3-chip SIMMs use two memory chips that have 4-bit wide data channels along with a 1-bit wide chip for parity-checking. The 9-chip variety uses nine individual chips each with a 1-bit data channel. These two types of SIMMs should be interchangeable. A few PCs with marginal memory systems may encounter errors if you mix the two types of SIMMs within a single memory bank. The best strategy is to always insure that SIMMs in any given bank are matched as the number of chips.

Sides

With 36-bit SIMMs, you may face another distinction, single- and double-sided SIMMs. The difference has nothing to do with how the chips are mounted on the SIMMs but rather with addressing. Single-sided SIMMs have two row address strobe lines; double-sided SIMMs have four. Most 1MB, 4MB, and 16MB SIMMs are single-sided; most 2MB, 8MB, and 32MB SIMMs are double-sided.

PCs differ in their reaction to the sided-ness of 36-bit SIMMs. Some 486-based computers see double-side SIMMs as two separate memory banks for purpose of tallying total system expansion capacity. Such a system with four SIMM sockets may only accept the memory on two double-sided SIMMs. Most 486 systems don't impose this artificial limit.

Double-sided SIMMs might seem perfect for Pentium PCs. If each "side" could be individually addressed, then you'd only need one SIMM for a 64-bit memory bank. Unfortunately, double-sided SIMMs have only one memory bus despite their extra endowment of row access lines, so only one side can be used at a time. A Pentium system still requires two 72-bit double-sided SIMMs to make a 64-bit bank.

Speed

SIMMs are also rated by speed. The most common measure of speed is the time required to read a word, measured from the instant that the memory accepts the address given it as valid until it sends out the requested data. This figure, called *row access time*, is measured in nanoseconds. The fewer nanoseconds required, the faster the memory. SIMMs are rated at nominal values such as 60, 70, 80, or 100 nanoseconds. You can tell the speed rating of a SIMM simply by looking at it. The individual chips on the SIMM have part numbers stenciled on. At the end of one of these numbers, you'll see a hyphen followed by a single digit, for example –7. On most chips used in PCs, the number indicates the SIMM speed in tens of nanoseconds. The –7 SIMM would be rated at 70 nanoseconds.

There is no direct correspondence between the speed at which your PC runs and the speed of memory it needs. Each system board design has its own requirements. The best way to determine what speed of SIMM to buy is by checking the owner's manual of your PC. Alternately, you can examine one of the SIMMs already installed in your system to determine its speed rating. Buy expansion memory rated at the same speed.

You can always use SIMMs rated for a higher speed than your PC requires, but this is usually wasteful because faster SIMMs inevitably cost more. In theory, you should be able to mix memory speeds within a bank as long as all of the SIMMs meet the minimum speed needs of your PC. Some PCs with marginal memory systems may encounter errors when you mix SIMM speeds within memory banks. The best strategy is to insure all SIMMs in a given bank have the same rating.

This problem does not arise with 36-bit (that is, 72-pin) SIMMs with which one SIMM equals one memory bank in a 386 or 486; half a bank in a Pentium. Better still, 36-bit SIMMs incorporate a speed sensing system by which your PC can determine the speed rating of the SIMM. This system uses three reserved pins on the SIMM to indicate its speed rating.

Logical Memory Types

For practical purposes, the common distinctions between memory logical type such as DOS memory, the High Memory Area, and extended memory are a function of your operating system and not the physical memory chips in your PC. Whereas DOS distinguishes between all of these different varieties of memory, OS/2 does not and instead sees your PC RAM as one wide range. In any case, you can pile SIMMs into your PC without worrying about these logical memory types.

The one odd memory effect you might notice is that in many PCs the total amount of RAM reported by your operating system (and even by your PC's BIOS during setup) may fall short of the amount you've actually installed. Typically the amount displayed and the amount installed differ by 256KB or 384KB. Many PCs reserve this memory to serve as ROM shadow, giving the system a dedicated block of memory into which to copy the code of your BIOS. You can sometimes recover this memory by turning ROM shadowing off using your PC's advanced setup procedure.

If you plan primarily to run OS/2 or any member of the Windows family, you'll want to recover this memory. These operating systems substitute their device drivers for your BIOS code, so they do not benefit from shadowing.

Hard Disks

An essential part of any multimedia PC is a mass-storage system. In general, mass storage means a hard disk drive. Although other technologies such as magneto-optical disks give you random access to hundreds of megabytes, only hard disks combine the speed required for multimedia production.

Speed

Speed is, in fact, the essence of modern multimedia. With hard disks, performance has two aspects: how fast you can find your data and how fast you can move it. The first is called *access time* and is the delay between when a program makes a request for data and when the disk starts to send the data back to the program, how soon after you press a key does your PC react to you. This period is usually measured in milliseconds. The second performance measure is called *transfer rate* and refers to how many bytes the disk can move to your PC in a given period. The term throughput is similar (and probably more relevant), describing how fast data makes the total trip from disk, to your PC, and finally into your application. Transfer rate and throughput are measured in kilobytes or megabytes per second. To get smooth video with high frame rates, you require a hard disk with a high transfer rate.

At one time, access time mostly depended on how quickly the heads in the drive could move from track to track. As disks become smaller, so did inertia, until today when access times are on par with a more fundamental delay called latency. Latency arises because with any rotating medium, what part you want to access is on average half a spin away. The latency period is simply the time it takes the disk to spin half way around and is inversely proportional to the rotation rate of the disk. At one time all disks spun at 3600 revolutions per minute, resulting in a latency of 8.33 milliseconds. Today disks spin at 5400 RPM and faster (the current quickest is 7200 RPM), so the typical latency is near 6 milliseconds. Average access time is only slightly higher.

Older disks have access times ranging from 9 to 100 milliseconds. All disks suitable for modern multimedia PCs, that is, those with 300MB or more capacity, have uniformly low access times, typically below 12 milliseconds. Differences between individual disks are virtually eliminated by hardware or software disk caching. Consequently access time is no longer a major concern in selecting a hard disk drive.

Performance Issue

Multimedia emphasizes transfer rate because digital movies and music take the form of long, sequential streams of data that must move from storage to display or speaker quickly. High transfer rates are required to move images from disk to your monitor screen. The best hard disk is consequently the one with the highest transfer rate.

Several factors govern transfer rate: storage density, rotation rate, and interface. Today disk manufacturers have squeezed so much speed from their products that they keep bumping into the speed limits of the interface, the electrical connection between disk and PC. As a result, today getting the highest possible transfer rate means selecting the right interface.

AV Drives

A new class of hard disks has been developed that has direct application to multimedia and in particular authoring. Called AV drives because their primary application is in the storage of audio and video data, these drives are optimized for the needs of those applications. In general they are large, starting at 1GB and climbing skyward from there so that they can store workable amounts of high-quality data.

More important than capacity is speed. Unlike normal hard disks that must provide instant access to completely random data, AV drives are designed for high-speed sequential access. Audio and video files tend to be long and linear, read sequentially for long periods. Access time is not as important for such applications as is a high sustained data transfer rate. In order to handle AV data as fast as possible, AV drives generally have very high rotational rates, some up to 7200 RPM, and newer drives will undoubtedly climb higher. In addition, most include large embedded buffers so that they can maintain high data throughputs even when incrementing between tracks and encountering errors. AV drives also attempt to maintain data contiguity, keeping sequential sectors in the data stream together so that head movement can be minimized.

Capacity

The storage capacity of a hard disk drive is probably its only characteristic that remains straightforward. A disk with a higher capacity will store more megabytes—and you need as many as you can get with multimedia files that bulge like the FBI dossiers of your less reputable neighbors. Although disk makers now resort to strategies only a bit less strange than the work of Dr. Frankenstein to make more room for megabytes, the end result is the same—hard disk storage now costs about 50 cents per megabyte and falling.

The only problem with large capacity disks is addressing everything the disk makers can give you. DOS and some interface specifications impose strict limits. New operating systems and interfaces are eliminating those limits, however.

Drive capacity isn't just a matter of hardware. Software can increase the apparent capacity of whatever hard disk you have. The secret is disk compression, the free lunch of mass storage—an elusive phenomenon with undeniable allure. Just choose to compress your disk when installing DOS 6.22 or Windows 95, and you have twice the drive at no additional cost. Microsoft's DriveSpace takes over all the work for you. Alternately you can invest in a third-party compression utility like Stacker (which is also included as standard equipment in IBM's PC DOS 7.0) for a slightly higher compression ratio.

The magic underlying data compression relies on the principle that most storage systems were designed for convenience and speed rather than maximum capacity. They store information in a form that your programs can most readily use, so your applications can read it directly without time-consuming conversions. Such primitive raw storage systems don't make sense in today's world of fast Pentium and RISC microprocessors, which can process compressed files while waiting for a program to set itself up or absorb what's been read from disk. Even with an archaic 386 microprocessor, you'll usually see no penalty for pre-processing data to maximize storage capacity. In fact, compression processing can actually speed up data transfer, cutting the amount of data your disk drive needs to deal with.

With highly compressible data, disk transfer speed can accelerate by 50 percent. There is a downside, however. Unsuccessful compression processing adds overhead to disk transfers and can substantially slow your system. In certain circumstances you should avoid disk compression, however. When you must maximize transfer rate when no other processing is involved, such as when working with raw video, compression takes a definite performance toll. For example, when editing video in digital form, it's best to use a separate, uncompressed AV drive for your image data to avoid compression overhead. (Most PC video is already compressed anyhow.) In addition, permanent swap files work best on uncompressed drives.

The secret formula used by all disk compressors is *pattern matching*. The compression program scans the data you send to disk for recurring patterns at the byte or block level, and assigns each complex pattern a simple token (or symbol). Once the token and its definition (the original pattern) is stored, further occurrences of the pattern are saved as the token alone. When decompressing the data, the program simply substitutes the original data for its token.

The effectiveness of this strategy varies with the data being compressed. The bit-image graphic files so important to multimedia systems often have large areas with little detail that compress by factors of eight or more. On the other hand, compressed graphic files (for example, the .GIF files you might download from a bulletin board) already have the fat rendered out, so they don't compress at all. On the average, you can expect to come close to the capacity-doubling increase promised by the data compression vendors.

As with every free lunch, disk compression has its price—complication and worry. Disk compression adds a layer of complication to DOS—a secret boot-up file, a renamed drive, and a mysterious disk-size file. Moreover, the added layer gives you something new to worry about. The more hands something passes through, the more likely it is to get dropped. Early versions of DOS's compression were notoriously unreliable. Compressing files also makes them more vulnerable to damage. A single error can ripple along multiplying itself. You might lose your entire disk because of an errant bit. Regular backups were never more important.

Interfaces

Your hard disk connects to the rest of your PC through an interface. Over their history, hard disks have used several interfaces. First came ST506, then ESDI (the initials stand for Enhanced Small Device Interface), essentially an updated form of ST506. Both of these are essentially obsolete in multimedia PCs. Your choices today are the AT interface—which is formally standardized as the AT Attachment but often called IDE for Integrated Drive Electronics—and SCSI, the Small Computer System Interface.

The interface takes one of several forms. Most IDE connections are simply pins on your PC's motherboard into which you plug a cable linked to your hard disk. You can add an IDE interface to PCs that lack them by adding an inexpensive expansion board that's sometimes called a *paddle board*. The expansion board that provides your PC with a SCSI connection is termed a *host adapter*, although many PCs now have SCSI circuitry built into their motherboards, too.

Once upon a time, the decision whether to get IDE or SCSI was easy, a matter of speed versus sanity. If you wanted the fastest possible disk, you chose the Small Computer System Interface (SCSI) for its high data transfer rate, even though connecting up a SCSI system is the one sure source of a migraine. In contrast, IDE drives would often simply plug in and work. The times and technologies have changed that situation. Enhancements to the IDE scheme have put its performance on par with SCSI. On the other hand, Plug-and-Play features in operating systems have made SCSI drives as easy to get going as their IDE kin.

AT Attachment

ATA (which, of course, means IDE in common parlance) drives are popular for the simplicity of the interface. It rates highly with PC manufacturers because it's usually the cheaper and easier interface to use. The motherboard circuitry needed for an ATA is trivial because the connection is little more than implementation of the AT expansion bus. On drives it's simpler, too, so much so that many drive makers charge less for ATA drives than SCSI even when the drives have the same underlying mechanism. Most PC users prefer ATA, too, because ATA drives are easier to install. SCSI requires setting of addresses, terminations, chaining cables, and running software drivers. ATA drives plug in.

The basic ATA interface allows the connection of two hard disk drives. It uses a single 40- or 44-pin cable that usually has three connectors on it. Desktop applications use 40-pin cables; notebooks use the extra pins for power and control. All connectors are wired identically. The wire simply runs straight through from one end to the other. The connector on one end of the cable usually plugs into your motherboard, and the other two connectors plug into your hard disk drives.

Each ATA hard disk can be set up either as a master or a slave. The only difference is that the Master runs its diagnostics first and normally gets assigned as Drive C: in your PC. If you have only one ATA hard disk in your PC, it *must* be configured as the master. The slave is always the second hard disk and usually appears as Drive D:

Most ATA hard disks use switches or jumpers on the drive itself to designate the drive as master or slave. Some master drives require an additional setting to indicate whether a slave drive is also present. Most of the time you must adjust the settings of both master and slave when adding a new drive to your PC. If these jumpers are improperly configured, one or both drives will fail to operate properly. Typically your PC won't even boot. The settings are usually documented in the drive's owners manual. Some new drives even include a setting chart on their labels.

Ordinary ATA drives are limited to a maximum capacity of 504MB (or 528MB, depending on what you call a MB). This limit results from an interaction of the ATA design specification and the disk parameter constraints inherent in the PC BIOS. The conventional system BIOS defines the functions of hardware interrupt 013(Hex) for controlling the hard disk drive. By itself, this BIOS limit is not much of a limit at all—it limits disks to a maximum of 63 sectors per track, 255 heads, and 1024 tracks (or cylinders). That's a potential total capacity of 8.4GB with standard 512-byte sectors. The ATA interface specification is even more generous, capping capacity at 136.9GB per disk based on an ability to address 255 sectors of 512 bytes each per track, 16 heads, and 65,536 tracks.

The ATA limit arises when these two constraints are taken together. The result is that conventional ATA disks cannot address more than 63 sectors per track (the BIOS limit), 16 heads (the ATA limit), and 1024 tracks (the BIOS limit again). With 512-byte sectors, the top capacity is 528,482,304 bytes or about the same as the 16-bit FAT limit of 512MB. Bytes beyond that simply cannot be addressed.

Because the ATA interface is simply the ISA bus in a different guise, it delivers performance essentially the same as the bus. Its maximum transfer rate is constrained by system overhead, however, and it never reaches the peak rate of 8MB/second available on the ISA bus. Typical performance is on the order of 1MB/second.

Fast ATA

Drive-maker Seagate Technology saw this low transfer rate as the fundamental handicap of the ATA interface. To push up the transfer rate, Seagate adopted a new data transfer protocol that increased peak throughput up to 13MB/second along with several intermediate transfer modes. Seagate called its system *Fast ATA.*

Enhanced IDE

At the same time Seagate was promoting Fast ATA, another drive maker, Western Digital, championed its own update to ATA. Called *Enhanced IDE,* the Western Digital scheme incorporated four features: a performance increase matching Seagate's Fast ATA; an addressing change that broke the ATA 528MB capacity barrier; a means of increasing the number of ATA drives per PC beyond its definitional limit of two; and a software interface that allows adding CD-ROM drives to a standard ATA connection. (See Table 10.5.)

TABLE 10.5. Enhanced IDE features compared to Fast ATA.

Feature	E-IDE	Fast ATA	required for implementation
11.1 MHz PIO Speed	Part of specification	Part of specification	BIOS or driver+Local bus
13.3 MHz DMA speed	Part of specification	Part of specification	BIOS or driver +Local bus
LBA addressing	Part of specification	Compatible with LBA but no specific support	BIOS
Four drives per PC	Part of specification	Not part of specification but possible with host adapters with on-board BIOS	Host adapter BIOS
Packet interface (ATAPI)	Part of specification	Compatible with ATAPI but no specific support	BIOS or driver

Speed Increase

Performance Issue

Both the Enhanced IDE and Fast ATA proposals (and products) use the same means to break through the ATA speed barrier, a new spin on programmed input/output (PIO) transfers and a revised way of dealing with Direct Memory Access (DMA).

Most PCs use programmed input/output (PIO) techniques for transferring data from disk to the host computer. The host microprocessor handles each step of the transfer of information into memory. In a system using the standard AT interface for its hard disk, the host microprocessor functions as a master controlling the drive as a slave. The master issues commands to transfer data and blindly hopes that the slave can carry them out expeditiously. The overhead involved in controlling such transfers and guaranteeing their success is what cuts the actual throughput of the ATA interface from its theoretical 8MB/second to the actual 1MB/second to 2MB/second.

Unfortunately the ATA constraints are built into the drive, so ATA products behave as if they are using an ISA expansion bus (the AT interface) even when they are connected through a higher-speed advanced bus like PCI or VL Bus. Without a huge hardware cache, you lose the advantage of an advanced expansion bus when you connect an ordinary ATA drive.

The two revised ATA designs propose a shift of control from the microprocessor to the hard disk drive. They enable a hard disk drive to take control of the expansion bus using its I/O Channel Ready signal as a semaphore. Once the drive is in control, it can regulate the flow of data itself, optimizing its transfers to the available bandwidth of the bus. At the cycle times typical of today's advanced expansion buses, about 180 nanoseconds, the two improved ATA interface proposals can boost disk transfer rates up to about 11MB/second. That beats even Fast SCSI-2, which tops out at 10MB/second.

New DMA techniques overcome the limits imposed in early PCs and allow even faster transfer rates under both the Enhanced IDE and Fast ATA proposals. DMA is a long proven technique for transferring data from drives to memory without host microprocessor intervention. The ATA improvements create a new advanced transfer DMA mode for the PCI expansion bus called Type F DMA. This mode allows peak data transfer rates of up to 8.33MB per second. By further reducing the cycle time of multi-word drive transfers to 150 nanoseconds, the new DMA mode can drive peak transfer rate up to 13MB/second. New enhancements to EIDE push the potential data rate to 20 MHz with two new modes.

The downside of this aspect of updated ATA technology is that it requires modification of the host system to enable the drive to take control of the bus. In new PCs, that's not a problem. Application-specific integrated circuits (ASICs) and chipsets that support this ability have been available to PC makers for over a year. Many new PCs already can take advantage of flow control using the I/O Channel Ready signal.

Older PCs are problematic. Enhanced IDE and Fast ATA hard disks are backwardly compatible with all ATA connections. This compatibility is assured because drives made to default to operation using the older, slower transfer method. (To enable the high-speed PIO transfer mode, the host computer must send a Set Features command to cause the drive to shift into its advanced transfer modes.) Plug an advanced technology drive into an old PC that doesn't recognize the drive's abilities, and the drive will work but only at the lower, standard ATA rate.

Fortunately the fix for this problem can be made either in your PC's BIOS or by adding a software driver. But taking full advantage of the speed potential of either Enhanced IDE or Fast ATA will require an advanced expansion bus (PCI or VL bus)—which means you'll probably need a new PC anyway.

Capacity Increases

To overcome the addressing limit of the standard ATA interface, Enhanced IDE substitutes 28-bit Logical Block Addresses (or LBA) for sector-head-track addressing. Each sector on the drive is assigned a unique logical address that would be used by the BIOS to reach its contents. The 28-bit addressing scheme allows for 268,435,456 sectors, the full ATA capacity limit of 136.9GB. The limit on maximum capacity of a drive shifts to that of the BIOS sector limit—the previously noted 63 sectors per track, 255 heads, and 1024 tracks—provides a total capacity of 8.4GB. Most new ATA drives larger than 528MB now use LBA addressing.

Bringing this change to life requires not only new hard disks that recognize the LBA access method but also BIOS code that knows how to handle LBA access. Moreover, the BIOS must be able to distinguish a drive that can use LBA access from one limited to sector-head-track addressing. Consequently the Enhanced IDE design also designates a flag bit in one of the drives registers (specifically bit 6 of the drive's SDH register) to indicate which form of addressing a drive uses.

The penalty of the Enhanced IDE system is that it requires the interrupt 013(Hex) firmware code of the host computer to be rewritten to accommodate the new addressing scheme. In other words, getting full capacity from an Enhanced IDE drive will require either a new PC with a BIOS that specifically supports Enhanced IDE (several are already available) or an add-in host adapter card that has its own compatible BIOS. Many new PC BIOSs already reflect this innovation, allowing LBA access with disks that support it. Although a device driver could substitute a new interrupt 013(Hex) service routine to add LBA addressing to older systems, booting up from an LBA drive would not be possible using such a driver.

Note that Windows 95 includes enhanced support for hard disk drives that use logical block addressing for capacities up to the 136.9GB limit. The protected-mode disk handler drivers of Windows 95 extend Interrupt 13H functions to bring LBA to life automatically. However, the Windows 95 disk handler doesn't come into play until after your PC loads the operating system using the BIOS, so you'll still need an LBA-compatible BIOS even with Windows 95.

Packet Interface

With CD-ROM drives becoming standard equipment in new PCs, manufacturers are looking for a low-cost means of connecting CD-ROM drives to replace the expensive and complex SCSI scheme. The AT Attachment interface has possibilities but one drawback, a lack of control for CD functions. Hard disks merely absorb and disgorge data. Although CD-ROMs seem simpler still—they just discharge data—they do other things, too, like usher audio around. The AT interface provides no means of linking audio to your PC, nor does it give any means of controlling the audio signals or several other aspects of normal CD-ROM operation.

Solving the audio connection problem is easy—run an extra wire. SCSI drives require that, too, because SCSI makes no provisions for audio, either. But control is another matter. SCSI offers programmers a complete command language and protocol. ATA gives them a handful of registers aimed only at hard disk operations.

To endow ATA with its own language the Small Form Factor Committee, which governs the ATA standard, developed the *ATA Packet Interface*. An enhancement to the ordinary AT interface, ATAPI gives the system a means of sending packets of commands to CD-ROM players. The ATAPI specification is designed to be completely compatible with existing ATA hardware and drivers. It changes nothing on the computer side of the AT connection and it does not affect the design or operation of ATA hard disk drives. It just gives the makers of CD-ROM players and programmers guidance as to how to link their products to PCs in a standard way. Windows 95 has built in support for ATAPI drives.

The hardware side of the ATAPI enhancement is the most straightforward. It consists of nothing more than the standard 40-pin ATA connector augmented by two jacks for audio signals (one serial digital, one two-channel analog). Under ATAPI, a CD-ROM player can replace the slave AT interface drive in your PC. But the specification requires that CD-ROM players be configurable as master or slave so that you can connect two CD-ROM drives to a single ATA cable.

ATAPI doesn't invent new commands for CD-ROM players. The commands defined by ATAPI exactly match those used by SCSI. As a result, making the translation of SCSI CD-ROM products to the new system is easier for programmers. The big innovation in ATAPI is that the specification defines a means of sending those commands to a drive through an ATA connection.

Normally, an ATA hard disk gets control information through eight registers called the Task File, which passes along all the commands and parameters needed to operate the disk. Unfortunately, these eight registers are not sufficient for the needs of CD-ROM control. ATAPI adds one new command: the Packet Command, that initiates a new mode through which multiple writes to the Task File can send packets of commands to the CD-ROM player. Most ATAPI command packets contain 12 bytes, although the standard also defines 16-byte packets for compatibility with future devices.

Technical Note

The first of the 12 bytes in the ATAPI Command Packet (byte 0) is an operation code that defines the command itself. The initial ATAPI specification defined 29 operation codes, two of which are reserved for CD-ROM XA (extended architecture) systems. The third through sixth byte (bytes 2–5) of each packet hold the logical block address of the data to be used if the command involves the use of data. The CD-ROM logical addresses start with zero as the first block and increase sequentially up to the last block. The eight and ninth bytes (bytes 7 and 8) of the packet define the length of the transfer, parameter list, or allocation involved in the command. Special extended commands add an extra byte for indicating this length. The remaining bytes in the packet are not defined by the specification but are reserved for future implementations.

Although ATAPI uses many of the same block and command definitions described by SCSI— those essential for operating CD-ROM drives—it does not use many of the other features of SCSI protocol such as messaging, bus sharing with multiple computers, disconnect/reconnect, and linking and queuing of commands. In other words, ATAPI is an extension to ATA and not an eventual overall replacement for SCSI. The SFF Committee went only as far as they had to go but no further.

More Drives

The two-drive limit of ATA becomes especially constraining when you jam a CD drive onto one of the connectors. To keep the ATA interface useful in such circumstances, Enhanced IDE boosts the number of drives permitted. The strategy it uses is the same old expedient used by ancient ST506 hard disks: primary and secondary host adapters or controllers in a PC. Enhanced IDE allows you to simply put a second AT-interface system (which inherently supports two drives) in a PC. In effect, you have two ATA interfaces—two host adapter boards or two connectors on your motherboard or special host adapters with two connectors.

The second AT-interface host adapter system will move the base address used by the ATA drives and use a different hardware interrupt (interrupt 15) from that of the primary drive system. The secondary drive system will have its own ATA cable connector and cable. On the secondary Enhanced IDE link, two drives will daisy-chain as master and slave just as they would in an ordinary two-drive ATA system.

Under Enhanced IDE, ordinary ATA drives will work with both the primary and secondary host adapters. You'll still have to set drives as master and slave on the secondary host adapter just as you do on the primary adapter.

As with the other Enhanced IDE innovations, adding a secondary host adapter requires an alteration to the host system BIOS so that all four drives can be individually identified. It also requires a second ATA connector.

On the software side, adding a second ATA subsystem to a PC requires few changes in operating systems. Versions of DOS since 3.0 was introduced way back in 1987 have allowed for seven hard disks in a single PC without special drivers. OS/2 versions since 1.31 have likewise allowed for four drives. Novell NetWare makes provisions for up to eight ATA drives. Because Windows 3.1 accesses system disk drives through the interrupt 013(Hex) function of the BIOS, the basic BIOS changes will automatically add Windows support. Windows 95 has built-in protected-mode support for a primary and a secondary AT Attachment hard disk controller, so it will recognize all four drives that you can add under the EIDE specification.

SCSI

Originally developed for minicomputer systems and adopted as an official standard by ANSI in 1986, SCSI was designed to link subsystems and intelligent peripherals. Under the SCSI scheme, all devices function independently but are commanded by the host system through the SCSI adapter. Key to the control process is the SCSI command set—essentially its own computer language. The host issues commands to the devices, then lets the devices carry them out without further intervention. The SCSI system provides a full arbitration scheme that allows the devices connected to the bus to determine which of them can send data across the bus at a given time. This arbitration is handled through hardware.

Key to the scheme is the SCSI identification number, which gives the system a unique way of identifying each device connected to the SCSI system. When any device wants to access the SCSI bus, it acts as an *Initiator*. It listens to the signals on the bus and waits until the bus is free. Then it identifies itself by sending a signal down one of the SCSI data lines. At the same time, it transmits a signal down another SCSI data line corresponding to the other SCSI device that it wants to interact with, called the *Target*. Because the SCSI bus has eight data lines, eight unique device identifications are possible. Because one SCSI ID number is assigned to the host, a SCSI system has the potential for connecting up to seven different devices.

Note that SCSI devices can initiate arbitration on their own, independent of the host. Two SCSI devices can also transfer information between one another without host intervention. For instance, a SCSI hard disk might back itself up to a SCSI tape drive without requiring the attention of (and robbing performance from) its host computer. Better than background operation, this form of backup represents true parallel processing in the computer system.

In addition, SCSI provides for *reselecting*. That is, a device that temporarily does not need bus access can release the bus, carry out another operation, then resume control. For instance, you could command a disk drive to format and it could carry out that operation without tying up the bus. The net result is, again, true parallel processing.

Because SCSI is a high-level interface, it also isolates the computer from the inner workings of the peripherals connected to it. For instance, the SCSI standard allows hard disks to monitor their own bad tracks independently from the computer host. The disk drive itself reassigns bad tracks and reports back to its computer host as if it were a perfect disk. In addition, hard disk drives could be designed to automatically detect sectors that are going bad and reassign the data they contain elsewhere, all without the host computer or the user ever being aware of any problems.

Macintosh

In fact, SCSI entirely isolates the computer from concerns about disk sector and tracks. It deals with data at a higher level, as blocks. This arrangement works well in the Macintosh environment because the Mac operating system has built-in provisions for dealing with SCSI.

Performance Issue

PC DOS and MS DOS lack such provisions, however, so SCSI host adapters for IBM-standard systems must convert sector and track requests into their SCSI equivalent. As a result, the system gets, at best, an indirect look at the disk drive. At worst, the overhead required for the address conversions can considerably slow the performance of an IBM-based SCSI system. (This is essentially the same as Logical Block Addressing used by EIDE.)

The SCSI block addressing scheme allows for multiple gigabyte drives—block addresses are 32 bits long and block length varies with the device. Under DOS, however, SCSI hard disks must obey the same addressing limits as drives with other interfaces such as 504MB per partition. Other operating systems free SCSI of these limits, although some hardware such as older host adapters may also limit drive size.

During the first few years that SCSI was being adapted to PCs, its chief allure was its speed. The SCSI system provided an eight-bit data bus operating at a clock speed of 5 MHz. The resulting potential transfer rate of 5MB/second put it well ahead of the leading PC interface of the time, ST506, which moved data at less than one-eighth that speed.

When SCSI first earned prominence as a higher performance interface for PCs, it was a muddle. The original standard was designed to allow manufacturers flexibility. The interface could be used for just about any peripheral, not just hard disks, and for a while Apple Computer relied on SCSI as its only expansion bus for early Macintosh systems. But the flexibility allowed peripheral makers to take SCSI in their own directions so that initial SCSI products suffered compatibility problems. Although they might work with one another in theory, getting a combination to work together required more than a safecracker's patience. Moreover, older PCs ran so slow they couldn't take advantage of the performance or other advanced potentials of SCSI.

Standards

The change came with the introduction of SCSI-2, which made more of the software side of the interface mandatory. In addition, SCSI-2 added performance enhancements to the initial SCSI standard. Fast SCSI-2 doubles the possible peak transfer rate of SCSI to 10MB/second. SCSI-2 also allows for a broadening of the bus used by the interface to 16 or 32 bits, each increase of which doubles the potential throughput of the interface.

Besides speed, SCSI has long held another big advantage over ATA—capacity. Ordinary ATA hard disk drives suffer an addressing limit, about 528MB. SCSI, on the other hand, handles multi-gigabyte hard disks with ease and has other allures as well. A single SCSI port that takes one expansion slot can link up to seven peripherals to your PC, including hard disks, tape drives, printers, even CD-ROM players. In exchange for this versatility, however, SCSI adds a complex wiring scheme.

Moreover, the SCSI standard doesn't describe how the interface links with your PC's software. After years of confusion, two software links have been accepted as standards, Common Access Method and the Advanced SCSI Programming Interface. The difference is in the drivers. Your SCSI drivers must be matched to the standard that your SCSI host adapter follows. This concern remains an issue only under DOS and the Windows 3.1 family, however. Both OS/2 Warp and Windows 95 understand both and automatically select the correct drivers for your SCSI hardware.

Making Connections

Because SCSI has both hardware and software aspects, it's particularly fickle. It can tease you by hiding behind hardware problems that actually originate in software. Like a pretty face on a first date, it can be very misleading. Its true nature becomes apparent only after you live with it—and fight with it—for a while.

A common mistake is to plunge head first into your relationship with SCSI by connecting together a complete SCSI system—hard disk, CD-ROM, and whatever—all at once. The cabling is seductive, plugging together as easily as video equipment. It tempts you to tie together a half dozen different SCSI devices into a single cable link before you switch on your system for the first time. Such a strategy dooms you to those evenings of diagnostics, head-scratching, and hastily scrawled suicide notes.

The secret to getting SCSI to work is to install your system one device at a time, conquering problems when they occur instead of allowing them to multiply out of control. Start small and you're certain to succeed.

Simple SCSI systems—a single hard disk connected to its own SCSI host adapter—are even easier to get going than ATA (IDE) hard disks. Most SCSI host adapters have their own BIOSes that operate independently from that in your PC. When you set up your PC for a SCSI drive, you tell the setup program you have *no* hard disks. All the other details are handled by the host adapter which reads the setup parameters from the hard disk itself every time you boot up your PC.

All SCSI hardware and wiring systems must follow several hard and fast rules laid down by the standard.

> ➤ Every SCSI device requires a unique identifying number, 0 to 6. In arbitration, the higher numbers have priority. The host adapter always uses ID number 7. Many host adapters require that your first two hard disks to be devices 0 (the boot drive) and 1, others give you more freedom.

> ➤ SCSI drives daisy-chain together. That is, you run a SCSI cable from the host adapter to one drive. Then you run a second cable from the first drive to the second, and so on. External cables must be a minimum of 12 inches (0.3 meters) long. The total SCSI chain must not be longer than about 20 feet (6 meters). SCSI cables may use any of three kinds of connectors: The old 50-pin (like a big parallel printer connector); 25-pin, as used by some serial ports; or the new, miniaturized 50-pin SCSI-2. Adapter cables are readily available.

> ➤ Every SCSI chain requires two terminations, no more nor less— one on the first device in the chain, one on the last device. In systems that use only internal devices or only external devices, the host adapter will be one end of the chain and need to be terminated. If you mix internal and external devices, the host adapter should not be terminated. Instead the internal device at one end of the chain and the external device at the other end should be terminated.

> ➤ In DOS (and Windows 3.1 family) environments, every SCSI device except the first two hard disks, will require a software driver. ASPI systems will also require an ASPI driver installed ahead of any other SCSI drivers in your CONFIG.SYS file. Although it is not necessary, you usually should install drivers for your first two disks, too, instead of relying on the BIOS. The OS/2 Warp and Windows 95 setup processes should take care of these drivers for you automatically.

When you have an external SCSI device with its own power supply, switch it on before or at the same time as your PC. Most SCSI drivers require their associated drive be running to be recognized during bootup.

Troubleshooting

Single-drive SCSI systems usually present few problems. However, each device you add to your SCSI chain multiplies the potential for problems. If you encounter difficulties, the first step in sorting out the problem is to double-check your connections, ID assignments, and terminations.

If you're sure you've done everything right and followed all the rules, then try to get things working by breaking the rules. Sometimes the cable lengths between external peripherals can be critical. Try exchanging a short cable between two devices for a longer one (or vice versa). If you have external cables of various lengths, try shifting them to different links in the system. With internal wiring, try moving reluctant devices to different connectors on the SCSI cable.

SCSI signals can be sensitive to terminations and sometimes prefer something other than the official arrangement. Shifting a termination from the last device to the second last (or somewhere else in the system) will occasionally revive a long SCSI chain. As a last resort, try adding a third termination to your SCSI chain, experimenting with various placements. Never add more than one extra termination to a single SCSI chain, however.

In some cases, the assignment of SCSI ID number can be critical. Some applications, for example, may not allow you complete freedom in selection of ID. Try adjusting the identification of any reluctant peripherals.

If all else fails, you can always install a second SCSI host adapter and divide the devices between the two. This arrangement should give you dozens of combinations to try—and something to do with your spare evenings.

A final note. When tangling with the choice of interface, you'll face further complications. Drivers can severely limit performance. While the fastest drives made may use the SCSI inter- **Performance** face, they often fall behind EIDE drives when running through the Windows 3.1 family. Few of **Issue** today's SCSI adapters have true 32-bit drivers that work with Windows, while most EIDE drives do. In mid-1995 SCSI adapter makers were just releasing their 32-bit Windows drivers (which replace the *WDCTRL driver that provides Windows default "32-bit disk access").

With OS/2 and Windows 95, driver quality is less of an issue, at least for the drivers that come with the basic operating systems. But with today's systems, software rather than disk hardware or interface often is the chief speed limit.

Floppy Disks

The floppy disk is the premiere data exchange medium for PCs and the most popular backup system. Although new developments like bootable CD-ROMs (they're coming!) may spell the death knell for the floppy, if history is any guide the little critters will be crawling in and out and around inside our PCs well into the next century. Except for a few sub-notebook computers, all PCs come with at least one floppy disk drive as standard equipment.

Although a few people still cling to their vintage 5.25-inch drives floppy disk drives like their bronzed baby shoes, the only drive you'll need in your multimedia PC is one that uses 3.5-inch high-density disks. The 3.5-inch figure describes the diameter of the thin plastic disk inside the disk that provides the recording medium. The high-density refers to the packing of sectors on each track of the disk. Two other formats, double-density and extra-high density look identical but pack fewer or more sectors per track.

The hard shell protects the fragile disk while allowing you the freedom of carrying out such crimes, forbidden with older 5.25-inch disks, of writing on an already-applied disk label with a ballpoint pen. A spring-loaded sliding metal shield or shutter protects the disk when it's not in the drive but opens to allow the read/write head to do its work.

Once you've learned how to slide a floppy disk into the drive slot (shutter first, label on top) the only other instruction you might need is about using the write-protection system. The 3.5-inch floppy disk design uses a hole in one corner of the disk equipped with a plastic slider to tell your PC whether you authorize it to write on the disk or if only reading is permitted. When the slider blocks the hole, you can read, write, and format the disk. When the slider is moved back to reveal the hole (or is entirely absent, as it is on many software distribution disks) the disk is write-protected. You can always recycle software distribution floppies by covering the hole with masking tape or part of a label.

As with hard disks, floppy disks divide their storage into tracks and sectors. The number of each determines the capacity of the floppy disk. Most often, however, floppy disks are described by their data density, which directly translates into the track and sector sound. Table 10.6 lists the popular floppy disk formats, density, track, and sector count.

TABLE 10.6. Floppy disk formats.

Diameter in (inches)	Density or format	Sectors per track	Tracks per side	Capacity in bytes	Lowest DOS versions required
5.25	Double	9	40	368640	1.1
5.25	High	15	80	1228800	2.0
3.5	Double	9	80	737280	3.2
3.5	High	18	80	1474560	3.3
3.5	Extra	18	160	2949120	5.0
3.5	DMF	21	80	1720320	3.3

Double-Density Disks

The basic 3.5-inch floppy disk stuff data into tracks that are only 0.0075 inch wide, 135 of them to the inch. Although the disk itself is a full 3.5 inches wide, data gets stored in a swath only 0.6 inch wide, covering 80 tracks. By laying nine sectors in each track, double-density floppy disks achieve their nominal capacity of 720KB.

High-Density Disks

The most popular floppy disks are those that use high-density storage. Although they still lay 80 tracks across the disk, they pack 18 sectors onto each track, doubling the nominal capacity to 1.44MB. To achieve that capacity, high-density disks require special magnetic material that react differently than those of double-density disks. Consequently, double-density media do not work well when given a high-density format and the data stored on such disk become increasingly susceptible to errors as time passes.

To prevent you from yourself and efforts to squeeze more data onto a disk than it was designed to hold, high-density disks have a coding hold directly opposite the write-protect hole. Floppy disk drives can detect this hole and recognize high density media, although not all manufacturers support this feature.

Distribution Media Format

To squeeze more storage onto each high-density floppy and cut the number of disks that they have to use to distribute applications, many software publishers have started to use *distribution media format* (DMF) on their floppy disks. This variation in the high-density design allows them to fit 1,720,320 bytes on a standard high-density 3.5 inch floppy disk in place of the more normal 1,474,560 bytes (nominal 1.44MB). The DMF format differs from the standard DOS format in that it uses 21 sectors per track instead of the normal 18. DMF squeezes more sectors on each track by reducing the inter-record gap (the space between sectors) down to nine bytes. The differences go deeper, however. Each track uses a 2:1 interleave factor so that sectors do not appear in order. This interleaving results in slower reading because the disk has to spin around twice for each track to be read. The DMF format also skews the sectors on adjacent tracks by three sectors so that sector one on track four sits next to sector one on track two.

The small inter-record gap makes DMF disk difficult to write on with normal floppy disk drives. In fact, Microsoft calls DMF a read-only format. In any case, you cannot write to DMF disks using ordinary software. However several special utilities are available for copying and even creating DMF disks. Note that Microsoft enforces a limit of 16 entries in the root directory of a DMF disk by only allocating a single cluster to service as the root, so DMF formatted disks usually use a subdirectory structure for their contents.

Extra-High Density

Currently the highest capacity floppy disks—those boasting a nominal 2.88MB per disk—are those that use extra-density recording. They are able to double the number of tracks on each disk (making each half as wide) by using an entirely different magnetic material (called barium-ferrite) that has magnetic properties substantially different from all other floppy media. In addition, the magnetic particles on the disk are aligned vertically (perpendicular to the disk surface) rather than laterally like other floppy disks. This upright alignment helps increase the storage density of the disk.

As a consequence of the requirements of the unusual magnetic media, extra-density floppy disks are so different that they require a new kind of drive mechanism and disk controller. You cannot plug an extra-high density floppy disk drive in place of other floppy drives. Moreover you cannot use double- or high-density floppy disks for extra-height density recording.

Some manufacturers have developed 100MB+ floppies (the Iomega Zip Disk, for example), which are incompatible with traditional floppies. An industry consortium is developing a 120MB floppy that uses drives capable of reading and writing old floppy formats. One of these may become a new floppy standard.

Drive Compatibility

In general higher capacity floppy disk drives are compatible with lower capacity formats, but lower capacity drives cannot handle media written with higher capacity formats. In other words, a high-density (1.44MB) floppy drive with read and write double-density disks without a problem but a double-density (720KB) drive can handle only double-density media. Extra density drives handle all 3.5 inch media.

This rule does not hold for 5.25-inch drives. High-density drives can read double-density media, but when a high-density drive writes to a double-density disk the disk may no longer be readable in double-density drives. That's just one more reason why you're better off leaving the larger floppy disks well behind you.

Chapter 11
Input and Output

Your PC needs raw material on which to work its magic. Without data, its data processing simply doesn't make sense. Moreover, like all machines, a PC lacks motivation. You have to tell your PC what to do, or it won't do anything. You need some way of supplying your system with both commands and data.

Any device that supplies a PC with input is called, with elegant logic, an *input device*. At heart a transducer, an input device converts mechanical things that you do—type or point—and converts them into electronic signals that your PC can understand. As with the rest of modern technology, the concept of an input device is simple; the devices themselves, ingenious; and the translation they perform, imperfect. No one input device suits all people or situations, and all are a pain to use—or become that way in the long run.

A Multimedia PC requires at least two input devices, a keyboard and a mouse (which can take a variety of un-mouselike forms, such as a trackball). You can optionally add a variety of other input devices to your system, including scanners, cameras (discussed in Chapter 14, "Cameras and Monitors") and sound boards (discussed in Chapter 15, "Sound").

Keyboards

The primary means of interacting with most PCs is the keyboard, the typewriter gone digital. A keyboard is nothing more than a bank of switches with one switch assigned to each number and letter of the alphabet (and enough others to make typing interesting). The keyboard lets you send data to your PC one character at a time, sensed by your pressing down on a key and closing a switch. Given a roll of tape and the inventory of an electrician's supply company, anyone could build a keyboard.

As you may have guessed, most keyboards are somewhat more refined than that. In fact, the design of the keyboard has been molded by technology and practicality through more than a century. The number of variables is astounding. Although where to put each key has been reasonably well-defined for the alphabet since Christopher Sholes was granted his patent for the first typewriter, extra keys to satisfy the needs of computers have sprouted every which where. But there are other considerations, too—how far the key and switches must move, how much effort you need to make to actuate them, how the keyboard plugs into your PC and what kind of signals it produces.

All that said, keyboards are nearly a commodity—inexpensive and interchangeable. You can get used to typing on any of them. And you usually have to because most computer makers give you no choice.

That said, all keyboards are hardly alike. You'll find differences in four major areas: layout, ergonomics, sensing, and interface. In each area, one major theme dominates. The variations help match particular situations and your personal preferences.

Layout

The layout of keyboard keys (called *stations* by those in the keyboard business) differs in two major ways: the arrangement of alphabet keys and the scattering of those outside the alphabet.

The layout of the alphabet on most keyboards follows the arrangement that Sholes developed for his typewriter, an oddly unintuitive, non-alphabetic arrangement we call QWERTY for the first six letters in the upper left. For all its flaws, QWERTY is what we have, what everyone has learned, and the probable standard for years to come.

The only alternative anyone yet considers is the Dvorak-Dealy keyboard, a more informed design that facilitates your alternating hands in typing. In the Dvorak (co-inventor Dealy is usually ignored) layout, the vowels fall under the fingers of the left hand, the most-used consonants under your right. Typists trained in using the Dvorak keyboard can often achieve 10 percent more speed over those relying on QWERTY keyboards—but achieving the necessary skill level requires years.

The electronic nature of PCs makes it easy to make Dvorak keyboards. Changing one ROM inside can convert a keyboard from one layout to another. You can even find utility software that will make your QWERTY keyboard type as a Dvorak by changing the way your PC recognizes keystrokes. A few manufacturers even offer keyboards with the key legends laid out in Dvorak fashion—a more expedient solution for experimenters than laboriously popping off and replacing each cap.

Windows 95 makes trying out the Dvorak keyboard arrangement easy. You can switch the way Windows sees your keyboard (by interpreting its scan codes) through the Language section of keyboard setup. To make this adjustment, load Control Panel and double-click the keyboard icon. Select the Language tab, then click the Properties button. Click the down-arrow on the Keyboard Layout selection, and you'll see a display of all mappings Windows 95 can make of your keyboard, among them US Dvorak, as shown in Figure 11.1.

FIGURE 11.1. Windows 95 Language Properties showing a list of available keyboard layouts.

Even this small effort at making the change probably is not worth it. Contrary to myth, the QWERTY layout was not created to slow down typists. The alleged problem—jamming keys—only occurs when you touch-type using all 10 fingers, but touch typing wasn't developed until about 20 years after Sholes "perfected" his improved layout (QWERTY).

Another equally arbitrary standard governs the placement of ancillary keys. Today's PC keyboards follow a design introduced by IBM in 1987 as its "advanced" keyboard. It arranges its 101-keys to put a set of 12 function keys above the alphanumeric keypad and puts a separate cursor control pad between the alphanumeric keys and numeric pad. The result is a keyboard only slightly smaller than a surfboard that puts your hands far left of center.

Other key arrangements are essentially obsolete. Occasionally you'll find 84-key keyboards, patterned after IBM's 1984 PC AT keyboard, that put 10 function keys to the left of the alphanumeric keypad. If you rely on function keys (and don't need the last two, F11 and F12), you may prefer this layout, but it is becoming rare.

Ergonomics

The human interface with the keyboard—its ergonomics—also has a dual nature. Of concern are the feel of each key and the way in which your hands fit the overall key layout.

The feel of the keys is called the touch of the keyboard. It involves the pressure required to actuate each key, the distance the key must travel to actuate, and the relationship between force and distance (generally described as feel).

The greater the force required to actuate a key, the less likely you are to type erroneously but the more tiring typing becomes. Most keyboards require between one and three ounces of force to actuate. Actuation distance has similar effects. Full-travel keyboards require you press down at least one-tenth. Most people find more than 0.070 inch adequate travel. Notebook computers often have less travel. Linear-travel keyboards require you to exert uniform pressure through the full travel of the key. Over-center keyboards first gradually increase the force required to press down a key then dramatically reduce it after the key actuates, providing you with tactile feedback that you've in fact actuated the key. Touch is a personal matter, and you'll want to try out different keyboards to find the kind you favor—if you have a choice.

Several vendors now offer keyboards designed to reduce repetitive stress injury (best known as carpel tunnel syndrome). Instead of a rigidly rectangular keypad, these keyboards angle the areas for your right and left hands or even enable you to pivot the keyboard in two sections to adjust it to fit your particular typing style. Any physical arrangement that keeps your wrists straight (as they would naturally hang with your arms at your sides) reduces typing stress and would be preferable for people who must type for long periods.

Technology

Somehow the keyboard must sense your efforts at typing. Over the years, manufacturers have developed elaborate strategies for detecting your finger motion, resulting in rather complex keyboard designs. In early keyboards, capacitive designs dominated. The keyboard detected your press of a key as a change in capacitance of a sensor. This design allowed for a long life (in excess of 15 million operations of each station). The sensors typically outlasted the springs and latches that made up the rest of the keyboard. As the computer market matured, keyboard makers developed ways of making a much simpler design—the mechanical switch—last adequately long. Consequently, mechanical keyboards now dominate the market.

Because the sensing element of the keyboard is essentially independent of the keyboard's touch, the technology is not a significant factor in your purchase decision. Engineers now can give any key-sensing technology any "touch" or "feel" they want. This means that any keyboard technology can deliver adequate life and acceptable touch.

Interface

The connection between the keyboard and your PC also has two factors: the physical connection and the logical interface. The physical connection determines whether you can plug in a keyboard; the logical interface determines whether it will work with your PC.

Four wires are required for a keyboard connection. One carries the actual keyboard data, sent as a serial string of bits known as scan codes. A second wire carries a synchronizing signal called the keyboard clock. Your PC provides power for the keyboard through a third wire, and a four provides a ground return for all three circuits (data, clock, and power).

Most PCs follow the keyboard wiring system IBM designed for its original series of personal computers, based on a standard five-pin DIN connector. Pin one of the connector is assigned the keyboard clock signal; two, the keyboard data signal; four, the ground; five, the 5-volt electrical supply. One of the connections provided by the keyboard plug—pin three—is assigned to carry a signal to reset the keyboard, but it is normally not used and need not be connected in normal keyboard cabling. Table 11.1 shows the pin-out of a standard PC keyboard connector.

TABLE 11.1. PC keyboard connector pin-out 5-pin DIN connector.

Pin	Description	Direction
1	+Keyboard clock	In
2	+Keyboard data	In
3	+Keyboard reset	Out
4	Ground	N/A
5	+5 V	Out

Many manufacturers have adopted an alternate connector, a six-pin miniature DIM connector, which IBM designed for its PS/2 series of computers. As with the classic keyboard connection, only four pins are significant in the miniature connector: pin one carries keyboard data; pin three, ground; pin four, 5 volts; pin five, keyboard clock. Pins two and six are reserved, and the shield is attached as a chassis ground. The pin-out of this connector is shown in Table 11.2.

TABLE 11.2. PS/2 keyboard connector pin-out (system end) 6-pin miniature DIM connector.

Pin	Description	Direction
1	Data	In
2	Reserved	N/A
3	Ground	N/A
4	+5 V	Out
5	Clock	In
6	Reserved	N/A
Shield	Ground	N/A

Some keyboards also put a connector between the keyboard and its cable, again pioneered by IBM in its PS/2 series. This keyboard-to-cable connection uses a modular (AMP) jack on the rear of the keyboard with a matching plug on the cable. The pin-out for this connector is shown in Table 11.3.

TABLE 11.3. PS/2 keyboard connector pin-out (keyboard end).

Pin	Description
A	Reserved
B	Data
C	Ground
D	Clock
E	+5 V
F	Reserved
Shield	Ground

When looking at the gold contacts of the connector, the contacts are labeled in reverse alphabetical order from left to right.

Although all keyboards send out essentially the same scan codes, some keyboards are smarter than others and recognize commands from your PC. The two intellectual levels of keyboards are distinguished as AT (smart) and XT (dumb). The distinction is becoming academic—XT keyboards are becoming ancient history. Moreover, many PCs will use either kind of keyboard interchangeably. Many replacement keyboards have switches to change modes between AT and XT keyboard emulation. Some old PCs are particular, however, and may require replacement keyboards to match the standard they follow. Modern multimedia PCs almost universally use smart AT-style keyboards.

Mice

Multimedia makes the most of graphics, and if you want to do the same you'll need a graphic input device. The chief choice is the mouse, a device small enough to fit under the palm of a hand with the button under a fingertip. With a cord connecting the device to its computer host trailing like a tail and the need to make the device scurry around the desktop to carry out its function, you can easily see how it earned its name.

As with keyboards, mice can be distinguished by four chief differences—the technology they use, the number of buttons they have, the manner in which they connect with their computer hosts, and the protocol or language they use to encode the information they send to your PC.

Technology

By far the most popular mouse technology is mechanical sensing. A mechanical mouse is based on a small ball that protrudes through its bottom and rotates as your push the mouse along. Sensors inside the mouse detect the movement and relay the direction and distance of the ball's rotation to your PC.

A few mice use optical technology. You move the mouse across a patterned pad. Optical sensors in the mouse detect the changes in the pattern as you move the mouse and translate that information into direction and distance data. Optical mice have no moving parts, making them more reliable. But they also require special pads to operate, some of which are easily damaged. With mechanical mice priced as low as $10, the cost of replacing one after a failure is not a big issue.

Buttons

You press a button on your mouse to select something you point at on your monitor screen. In purest form, you need only one button. The Apple Macintosh uses a one-button mouse.

Most PC applications are designed around two-button designs, however, and the MPC specifications require a two-button mouse. In that you can simulate a one-button mouse with a two-button mouse (just ignore one button), two button mice dominate the PC marketplace.

Some mice have three buttons. You can use them as two-button mice using the same emulation mode as you would to make a two-button mouse behave like one with one button. Few applications require a third mouse button, although some programmers like to take advantage of the additional control versatility of a third button.

The right and left mouse buttons have separate and distinct functions which vary with application and operating system. For example, Windows 95 uses the left button for its select and drag functions and the right button for popping up its context menus and special dragging. The driver software included with a given mouse often allows you to reverse the button functions using command line options.

In the Windows 3.1 family, you'll get control of Window's own mouse drivers by clicking the Mouse icon in Control Panel. Using the controls in the small window, as shown in Figure 11.2, you can swap mouse buttons, adjust the tracking and double-click speeds, and test the mouse.

FIGURE 11.2. Mouse settings screen in the Windows 3.1 control panel.

The universal mouse driver included with Windows 95 also enables you to reverse the function of the button of your mouse as well as control other functions. You can select the button assignment by clicking the mouse icon in the Windows 95 Control Panel and choosing the Buttons tab, as shown in Figure 11.3.

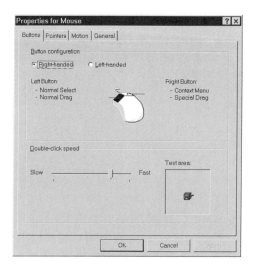

FIGURE 11.3. Mouse button settings in the Windows 95 control panel.

This same screen also gives you control of the double-click speed of the left button on your mouse. After you make a speed setting, you can test it by double-clicking with the mouse pointer in the test area.

Interfaces

Mice connect with PCs in any of three ways: through a serial port, through a built-in dedicated mouse port, and through motherboard connections. Mice that use these methods are called serial mice, bus mice, and proprietary mice, respectively.

Serial mice simply plug into any standard serial port. In general, mice make no onerous demands on the serial port in that they operate at a low communication rate, 1200 bits per second. They adapt to any available port, although you may have to specify the port (and occasionally, interrupt) you plan to use when setting up the mouse driver software. Modern drivers can locate a mouse no matter which port you plug it into.

Bus mice are handy when your PC lacks sufficient serial ports or you want to avoid interrupt conflicts. In most cases, bus mice plug into ports that conform to the RS-232 standard and act just like serial ports except that they cannot be directly accessed by DOS because the operating system doesn't know the I/O addresses to which the port is assigned. Bus mice require their own slot-stealing host adapters. When installed in 16-bit slots, however, they give you the option of using interrupts off-limits to serial mice.

If you have a spare serial port, you'll probably want a serial mouse because you pay extra for the bus mouse's adapter card. If you're short on serial ports or interrupts, however, you'll likely want a bus mouse.

Proprietary mice are matched to your PC by its manufacturer, which means one fewer thing to worry about. Some multimedia PCs come equipped with serial or bus mice, but major manufacturers typically use a special motherboard port for the mouse. These motherboard ports eliminate interrupt worries, although they substitute compatibility concerns when and if you need a replacement.

Protocols

Mice send distance and direction information to your PC in packets of three or five bytes. At one time manufacturers used one of four different languages or protocols for this control information. Each of these languages originated with a particular manufacturer—IBM, Logitech, Microsoft, and Mouse Systems—and was known by the manufacturer's name. Driver software matches your mouse to your PC, so you never have to deal with this protocol yourself.

In recent times, most manufacturers have moved to the Microsoft (3-byte) protocol. Nearly all mice you can buy emulate the Microsoft mouse. In any case, your mouse driver isolates you from the need to know the details of the protocol your mouse uses. Install the driver, and your mouse should work without a hitch.

Trackballs

Essentially a mouse turned upside down, the trackball is much like it sounds—an often big ball that, when rotated, causes the screen pointer (mouse cursor) to track its movements. The trackball spins in place and requires no more deskspace than its base, a few square inches. Portable trackballs are designed to clip onto laptop and notebook computers, extending the width of the machine by no more than a couple of inches. Most modern notebook PCs now have built-in trackballs.

Trackballs have the same button, interfacing, and control concerns as mice. In addition, the trackball adds two additional concerns: ball size and handedness.

Most freestanding trackballs have balls that match the dimensions of standard pool balls, about 2.5 inches in diameter. This situation is hardly a coincidence. It provides a ready source of supply to trackball makers. For size and weight reasons, portable computers typically use smaller balls. Some desktop trackballs also use portable-size balls. If you have a choice, which size is better is a matter of preference.

Most freestanding trackballs are symmetrical, so you can operate them equally adeptly with either hand. A few have a definite handedness and are more easily operated with either your right hand or left. Again, which is best is a matter of preference.

Lightpens

A lightpen lets you perform mouse functions by pointing at the screen. Shaped like a pen but trailing a cord, the lightpen lets your computer register positions on the screen by your pointing at them. The trick is inside the pen. At the tip are photodetectors that can detect changes in brightness. The picture tube in a computer monitor is lit by a scanning electron beam that lights tiny patches on the screen, scanning them back-and-forth and top-to-bottom. As each patch of the screen is struck by the beam, it briefly glows. The beam repeats its scan of the tube face so fast—50 to 70 times a second—that it appears continuously lit to you—but not to the sharp eye of the light pen.

The light pen registers the instant the patch on the screen lights up, then signals to your computer at that instant. Your computer can figure out exactly where the pen is because it knows where the scanning electron beam is all the time. From the light pen, then, the computer can tell where you are pointing on the screen.

The strength of the lightpen is the naturalness of the interface. You point directly at what you want instead of moving your hand at some distant location. The weakness of the lightpen is the weakness that seeps into your arm as you hold it up to the screen all day long. Extended use of lightpens is fatiguing.

Digitizing Tablets

A digitizing tablet is a mouse turned inside out. The sensing element is in the pad or tablet instead of being inside the mouse or pointer you hold in your hand. Moreover, the digitizing tablet turns the concept of the mouse on its head. The mouse senses only relative motion without regard to its previous position. The digitizing tablet can sense absolute positions (although most digitizers can emulate mice as well).

The part of a digitizing tablet system you hold in your hand takes one of two forms. One resembles the mouse and is usually called a cursor, although some manufacturers call it a puck or sometimes tracer. Another resembles a pen and is called either a pen or a stylus. Pens are best for freehand drawing; cursors work best for tracing from blueprints and other exacting applications.

As with mice, digitizing tables give you a choice as to buttons, but your choice is much wider. Cursors often offer from two to 16 buttons; pens, two or three. Two buttons give you the same point-and-click ability as a mouse. A 16-button cursor will mean that you might rarely have to go back to your keyboard to elicit functions.

Many digitizer pens have internal ink supplies so you can draw on paper as you transmit data back to your PC. Sometimes a manufacturer distinguishes its digitizer pens from a digitizer stylus in that the latter doesn't contain an ink supply. With few exceptions, pens can be equipped with dummy inkless cartridges to make them into styli. Some pens are pressure-sensitive, which enables you to press harder to indicate the width, weight, or color of a line drawn in that application, which is particularly useful in freehand sketching. Pressure pens vary in the range of forces they can detect and the number of pressure levels they can digitize, typically from 64 to 256.

Digitizing tables also differ by technology (most use a kind of electromagnetic sensing), size (both 8 1/2-by-11- and 11-by-17-inch tablets are popular), and resolution (most are accurate to one-hundredth of an inch). Nearly any will deliver adequate performance for general multimedia applications.

Scanners

When you want to assimilate an existing drawing or photograph into a multimedia presentation, a scanner is often the easiest way to capture an image. A scanner can convert anything you have on paper—or, for that matter, anything reasonably flat—into computer-compatible electronic form. Like a slow-scan television system, a scanner can reproduce photos, line drawings, even collages dot-by-dot in detail sharper than your laser printer can duplicate. Better yet, equip your PC with optical character recognition software and the images your scanner captures of typed or printed text can be converted into ASCII files for your word processor, database, or publishing system.

A scanner detects differences in the brightness of reflections off an image or object using a linear array of light sensors. Circuitry inside the scanner reads each sensing element in the line one after another and creates a string of serial data representing the brightness of each point in each individual scan line. Once the scanner has collected and arranged the data from each dot on the line, it advances the sensing element to read the next line.

Either a mechanism or your own hand moves the scanner from one line to the next. Hand scanners put you to work and are inexpensive but usually only capture a three to four inch image width. Mechanical scanners capture a sheet-size image automatically.

Mechanical scanners come in both drum and flatbed varieties. Drum scanners only work on thin images that can be wrapped around a large-diameter drum. Most inexpensive flatbed scanners can read thin sheets, books, or even three-dimensional objects.

The *hand scanner* is least expensive because it requires no precision scanning mechanism. The hand scanner also is compact and easy to carry. You could plug one into your notebook PC (with an appropriate interface adapter) and carry the complete system to the neighborhood library to scan from books in its collection. Hand scanners can also be quick because you can make quick sweeps of small images instead of waiting for the lumbering mechanism of another scanner type to cover a whole sheet. Hand scanners may also adapt to some non-flat surfaces and three-dimensional objects. For example, most will easily cope with the pages of an open atlas or gothic novel—although few can do a good job on a globe or watermelon.

Performance Issue

On the downside, the small size of the hand scanner means a single pass of the scanner will cover an image no more than about four inches wide. Although that's enough for a column of text and most scanners offer a means of pasting together parallel scans of larger drawings and photos, the narrow strips of scan make dealing with large images inconvenient. On the other hand (and in the other direction), because a hand scanner is not limited by a scanning mechanism, it can enable you to make absurdly long scans, typically limited only by the scanning software you use.

Note that hand scanning is like typing—a learned skill. To use a hand scanner effectively, you'll have to practice until you learn to move the scanner smoothly and at the proper speed, which means very slowly at high resolutions.

Drum scanners are moderate in price and compact in size because their mechanisms are relatively simple. However, that mechanism imposes a stiff penalty—only thin, flexible images can be scanned. In general, that means normal paper. Books (at least while intact) and solid objects are off-limits. Only certain sizes of paper may be accepted. While this may be no disadvantage in a character-recognition application, it may be frustrating when you want to pull an image off a large sheet without resorting to scissors or a photocopier first.

Flatbed scanners are like copying machines in that anything that you can lay flat on their glass faces can be scanned—books, magazines, sections of poster, even posteriors and other parts of your anatomy if you get imaginative, bored, or drunk. Of course, the scanned image can be no larger than the scanner bed. The big drawback of the flatbed scanner is price. Their precision mechanisms makes the technology the most expensive among popular scanners.

Scanners are also divided into color and greyscale units. Color scanners are clearly the best because they can make both color and monochrome scans. Most register from 256KB to 16.7 million different hues. Some require three passes (and nearly three minutes for a full sheet) to acquire an image. One-pass color scanners work in one-third the time.

Standards

Although at one time all scanners had proprietary software interfaces, today most scanners follow the *Twain* standard. First released in early 1992, Twain was developed by an industry consortium called the Working Group for Twain, which included Aldus Corporation, Caere Corporation, Eastman Kodak Company, Hewlett-Packard, and Logitech. (The Twain name is not an acronym but a descriptive label that expresses how the standard unites applications and input devices—making the twain meet.)

Twain links programs and scanner hardware, giving software writers a standard set of function calls by which to control the features of any scanner. One set of Twain drivers will handle any compatible scanning device. Because the Twain connection has two ends—your scanner and your software—to take advantage of it requires both be Twain-compatible. If you want to be able to use a scanner with the widest possible array of software, ensure that it supports the Twain standard.

Resolution is the most important figure of merit when selecting a scanner. A scanner with a higher resolution can image greater detail. Of course, more detail means more data—that means larger files and larger on-screen images from your scans. Scanner resolution is normally measured in dots per inch. The most common scanner resolution is 300 dpi, although newer models claim up to 1,200 dpi. In general, higher is better. You don't need to work at the highest resolution all the time, however. Most scanner software enables you to work at lower resolutions to save storage space or create smaller on-screen images.

You need to distinguish two kinds of scanner resolutions to get a fair picture of a given device. *Mechanical resolution* describes the limit of the scanner mechanism itself—essentially how closely spaced the scanner's photosensors actually are. Beyond mechanical resolution, many scanners promise significantly higher *interpolated resolutions*. To interpolate a higher resolution, the scanner calculates dots in between those mechanically scanned. Interpolation adds no new information, but it can give you a larger digital image to work with when you're scanning postage-stamp size pictures.

> Because interpolation adds no information, however, there's no point in storing an interpolated image in its raw form. You can save disk space by saving your original images at the highest mechanical resolution of your scanner and interpolating the high resolutions when you need them. Only after you've overlaid other details do you need to store an image at its interpolated resolution.

Ports

To your PC, a port is a gateway to the great unknown. It is both a passageway and control point. Through the port, your PC can link to the vast outside world and affect its surroundings, be it to print in a single sheet of paper or level a forest with its needs for foolscap. Your PC's signals can find their way in and out of your PC only through a port. Moreover, a port also serves as a sentry to prevent the unwanted from entering and the errant and addled from exiting. It controls the flow of information and prevents enthusiasm on the inside or outside from swamping the resources of the other side.

The embodiment of a port is a jack or connector on the rear panel of your PC. Contacts on the jack link with mating contacts on a plug to establish an electrical connection and let signals flow. But there's more to a port than just a few jabs of electricity; the port must arrange the signals in a standard way that can be understood by equipment connected to it. The port establishes the width of the data path and a code for its signals, usually based on time.

The port also has to link logically to your PC. That is, your PC needs a means of addressing the port, sending it data, and taking data away from it. Not being able to find your PC's ports is as good (or bad) for your programs as not having any ports at all.

Three kinds of connections are usually classed as ports in describing PCs. These are the parallel, serial, and game ports—the last sometimes called a *joystick port.* Strictly speaking, the connections for your monitor, video camera, speakers, and microphone are all ports, as is the SCSI connection that is usually reserved for mass storage devices. These are specialized ports reserved for particular applications and are called ports only by advertisers wishing to inflate the virtues of their offerings. In this book, these specialized ports will be discussed in their area of application. (For example, Chapter 10, "The Basic PC—Hardware Essentials," discusses ATA and SCSI ports in the context of mass storage.)

Windows 95

Windows 95 groups serial and parallel ports as communications ports because both serve the same purpose, communicating with external devices, and both share a common virtual device driver, VCOMM. Port drivers link to Windows 95 through VCOMM. The arrangement recognizes that new designs have extended the versatility of parallel ports to make it nearly universal in application. Already some manufacturers are designing high-speed modems to take advantage of the greater speed potential of advanced parallel ports.

The three general-purpose ports that should be part of the native endowment of any multimedia PC (one of each—serial, parallel, and game—is required by both the MPC I and MPC II specifications) are discussed in the following sections.

Serial Ports

The closest to a universal connection for PCs is the standard serial port. Its wide application is understandable because the serial connection had a headstart—it was in wide use long before PCs became popular. But PCs added momentum and applications, making the standard serial port ubiquitous.

Serial ports go by several nicknames: *RS232C* refers to the Electronic Industry Association standard which defines serial port signals. *Asynchronous port* refers to the data signal on the port's wires. The data signal is a serial stream of self-contained code that need not lock itself with an external clock. That is, equipment on two ends of a connection can distinguish the significance of the bits in each digital word and the words themselves without locking their clocks together (synchronizing their timebases), hence the ports operate asynchronously. *COM port* refers to the name DOS gives serial ports in a PC, COM1 through COM4, a contraction of communication ports because serial ports were once the primary link for communicating between PCs. Most PCs have two serial ports, but one to four are possible, designated COM1 through COM4. OS/2 added support for an additional four serial ports. Windows 95 makes provisions for up to 128 serial ports in a PC, although shortages in system resources make the practical limit substantially lower and system-dependent.

From a practical standpoint, serial ports have two big advantages: widespread use and low cost. They are everywhere, and they are cheap. These factors are probably not unrelated. On the other hand, serial ports suffer one big disadvantage—they are slow. Standard data rates for serial ports in PCs range from 50 to 115,200 bps, and even these speeds are optimistic. Overhead consumes at least two bits of every ten in a serial connection (these overhead bits define a data frame, a function required by the asynchronous nature of the signal), so the useful speed is only 80% of the nominal bit-per-second rate. At 115,200 bps, the most information you can hope to press through a serial connection is 92,160 bits per second or 11,520 bytes per second. A network or hard disk connection is about 100 times faster.

The basic serial connection involves only three wire connections, one through which the port sends out signals, one through which it receives them, and a ground common to both. Two implementations of the basic RS232C serial port assign these signals to the pins of connectors differently. The function of the two different pin assignments of serial ports belong to devices defined as Data Terminal Equipment (DTE) or Data Communications Equipment (DCE). For example, the pin one which a DTE device sends out data is used by a DCE device to receive it. This difference in pin assignment allows you to connect a DTE device to a DCE device using a straight-through cable. Connecting two DTE or two DCE devices requires a *cross-over cable* that reverses the pin assignments of the send and receive signals.

Most devices that you're likely to connect to PC serial ports are DCE and use straight-through cables. However, some peripherals—printers and plotters in particular—are classed as DTE and require cross-over cables. Table 11.4 lists common serial devices, their type of serial port, and whether they require a cross-over cable.

TABLE 11.4. Common serial device types.

Peripheral	Device type	Cable needed to connect to PC
PC	DTE	Cross-over
Modem	DCE	Straight-through
Mouse	DCE	Straight-through
Trackball	DCE	Straight-through
Digitizer	DCE	Straight-through
Scanner	DCE	Straight-through
Serial printer	DTE	Cross-over
Serial plotter	DTE	Cross-over

Serial ports use *handshaking* to control the exchange of data. When a given device cannot accept data, it sends out a signal to the device with which it is communicating. This signal could take the form of a code character sent down the data lines, in which case it is called *software hand-shaking.* The most common form of software handshaking uses the control characters XON and XOFF to indicate readiness and unreadiness to receive data and is consequently termed XON/XOFF handshaking. Alternately, serial ports use special signal wires in the serial connection for handshaking, in which case it is called *hardware handshaking.* As with the data lines, DTE and DCE devices assign different pins to the signals used by hardware handshaking.

In the PC environment, two sizes of connectors are often used for serial ports, 25-pin D-shell connectors and 9-pin D-shell connectors. The pins used by various signals are different in the two connector types. Table 11.5 lists the signals and their pin assignments for 25-pin and 9-pin connectors.

TABLE 11.5. PC serial port signals and their pin assignments.

Mnemonic	Function	Connector size	
		25-pin Pin number	9-pin Pin number
TXD	Transmit data	2	3
RXD	Receive data	3	2
RTS	Request to send	4	7
CTS	Clear to send	5	8
RTS	Data set ready	6	6
GND	Signal ground	7	5
CD	Carrier detect	8	1
DTR	Data terminal ready	20	4
RI	Ring indicator	22	9

Although the signals generated by serial ports are interchangeable, the port circuitry is not always the same. Differences abound, and the differences put further limits on serial port per-formance. If your PC uses an old, slow circuit, you won't be able to get full serial port speed from modem connections.

UARTs

The circuit at the heart of most PC serial ports is the Universal Asynchronous Receiver/Trans-mitter or UART chip that transforms the parallel data inside your PC into a series of pulses.

The oldest, cheapest, slowest, and least desirable UART is the 8250. This chip was standard equipment in IBM PCs from 1981 to 1984, at which point IBM pronounced it too slow for the needs of PCs. Many serial ports—particularly those in cheap I/O or port adapter boards that lack brand names—still use 8250 UARTs. This chip is incapable of sustaining the high communica-tions rates of today's modems, although it will suffice for low-performance applications such as the connection of serial mice and digitizing tablets.

Next in line in the UART hierarchy is the 16450. Essentially an improved 8250, the 16450 has the same hardware features and controls but greatly improved performance. It is capable of sustaining today's fastest modem communications rates in modern high-speed PCs, but suffers one handicap. In multitasking environments, it can't keep up and may lose characters. At high communications rates, the 16450 can decode characters faster than a PC can deal with them, particularly if the PC has shifted to other tasks. By the time the PC turns its attention to the UART to unload the character, the UART may have moved on to the next character in the transmission, overwriting the previous one.

The 16550 UART overcomes this problem with a small integral buffer. In this buffer the 16550 can store up to 16 bytes of data while it waits for your PC to unload them. In most PCs, this small buffer is sufficient to assure error-free communications. Because the operating systems used in multimedia all perform multi-tasking, you'll want any serial port your PC uses for communications to have a 16550 UART.

In order that the 16550 be fully compatible with its predecessors, the buffer in the 16550 is normally ignored. It operates only when specifically enabled by your communications software or your modem driver.

The buffer in the 16550 was first supported by Windows 3.1 but for Windows applications only. The Windows 3.1 family does not use the 16550 buffer for DOS applications that run within Windows. Through the COMM.DRV driver these versions of Windows take advantage of the 16550 receive buffer (actually, 14 bytes of its 16) to prevent character loss as data comes in. The transmit buffer is not enabled by Windows—it's unnecessary because there's no chance of character loss during transmission.

You can selectively enable and disable the 16550 buffer in ports that have the appropriate hardware by altering the COMxFIFO entries in the [386Enh] section of your SYSTEM.INI file when using the Window 3.1 family. Setting COMxFIFO to one enables the buffer for port x; setting it to zero disables the buffer. For example, these settings would turn on the buffer for COM3 only:

```
[386Enh]

COM1FIFO=0
COM2FIFO=0
COM3FIFO=1
COM4FIFO=0
```

The default is to turn on the buffer if Windows finds one. If you don't make COMxFIFO entries in SYSTEM.INI, the Windows 3.1 family will automatically try to enable the buffer. Under Windows 3.1, DOS applications that run under Windows cannot take advantage of the FIFO buffer. With Windows for Workgroups, however, Microsoft extended FIFO support to DOS applications. In addition, Windows for Workgroups enables you to set the trigger point for the buffer (with the default being reduced to 8 bytes from 14 bytes). The standard communications drivers for OS/2 Warp and Windows 95 automatically take advantage of the 16550 buffer.

Motherboard-based serial ports as well as some I/O boards often do not have discrete UART chips. Instead, all the required UART circuitry is built into an application-specific integrated circuit. Even so, the internal circuitry of these chips duplicates the function of one of the three UART standards. You can determine what sort of UART is in your PC or one you're investigating by running Microsoft Diagnostics (the MSD.EXE program included with Windows) or system-snooping software.

Some modem makers offer enhanced serial ports along with their high-speed modems. These usually go the 16550 UART a hundred times (or so) better by incorporating substantially larger buffers, from a few kilobytes to hundreds. In general, these look to your PC as if they were ordinary 16550 UARTs but grant you an extra measure of communications security. They are most useful in linking slower PCs to the fastest modems.

Interrupts

When a serial port receives a character from the outside world, it must discharge it to your PC. To gain the attention of your PC's microprocessor, the serial port sends out an interrupt. The procedure is simple and straightforward but suffers one inevitable complication. By rights, each serial port needs its own interrupt so that your PC knows which port requires service, but PCs are notoriously deficient in hardware interrupts. As a result, sometimes two ports use the same interrupt.

By convention, interrupt 4 is assigned your PC's first serial port and interrupt 3 is assigned the second, so no conflicts arise in two-port systems. Under DOS, the third port also uses interrupt 4 and the fourth serial port uses interrupt 3, so conflicts can and often do arise when you have more than two ports. The problem can be sneaky because internal modems have hidden serial ports (which correspond to the COM number used to reference the ports by your software).

The usual suspects in COM port interrupt conflicts are your mouse and modem. When you go on-line, particularly with background communications, you're likely to use both your modem and mouse simultaneously. Their interrupts can get confused, and your system may crash. Although Windows and OS/2 try to navigate through this morass, you should always ensure that your modem and mouse use separate interrupts.

Initializing Serial Ports

Before you use a serial port, you must program its UART to operate at a given speed and with specific communications parameters. How you initialize your serial ports depends on your operating system and what you plan to do with your ports.

If you're simply going to use commercial software, you can forget entirely about initialization. Most communications and data exchange programs that use serial ports—no matter whether they run under DOS, OS/2, or Windows—automatically handle the initialization for you. If you just use application software, you should therefore never need to worry about port initialization.

If you're going to do your own exotic things with a serial port using DOS, however, you'll probably have to do the initialization manually. DOS uses its MODE utility to initialize serial ports (and for several other purposes). To initialize a serial port under DOS, you run the MODE program and specify a complex command-line switch. You must indicate the port to initialize, the speed at which you want it to operate, whether or not to use parity checking (using the first letter to indicate None, Odd, Even, Space, or Mark), the number of data bits in a word of data you want to use through the port (usually either 7 or 8, although the command accepts other values), the number of stop bits (usually 1, 1.5, or 2), and whether to retry (using Y or P for yes, N for no). In general you must separate each option with a comma. The command

```
MODE COM1:9600,n,8,1,p
```

configures the first serial port (COM1) to operate at a speed of 9600 bps without parity using 8-bit data words, one stop bits, and enabling retries.

Using the Windows 3.1 family, you specify the initialization parameters for your serial ports in the [ports] section of your WIN.INI file. The individual entries follow the same form as the DOS MODE command. A typical listing would look like this:

```
[ports]
COM1:=9600,n,8,1
COM2:=9600,n,8,1
COM3:=9600,n,8,1,p
COM4:=9600,n,8,1
```

Under Window 95, you specify the initialization parameters for your serial ports using the Device Manager, which you access by clicking the System icon in Control Panel. Click the Ports (COM and LPT) listing to expand it, then double-click the port for which you want to set the initialization parameters. Windows 95 will give you a menu, like that shown in Figure 11.4, through which you can adjust initialization parameters at the Connections tab or the I/O port and interrupt assignments at the Resources tab.

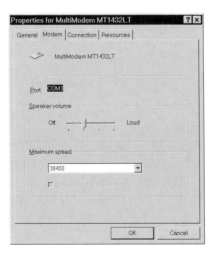

FIGURE 11.4. Adjusting port properties in the Windows 95 device manager.

Maximizing Serial Port Speed

Under DOS, serial port speed depends mostly on your software. Programs that rely on the BIOS for controlling the serial port may be limited to 9600 to 19,200 bps, while those that take direct hardware control can scream up to 115,200. Window 95, too, will operate most serial ports at full speed.

The situation with earlier Windows versions is not as promising. Although the Windows 3.1 family enables you to select communications rates up to 57,600 bps, you may be constrained to a much slower speed if your PC is not particularly fast (say a 386 machine) and you are running multiple applications. If you suspect that your serial port performance is below normal or you lose characters in serial communications, there are several tricks you can use to speed things up, according to a Microsoft technical note—about as close as you can get to the word of God about Windows.

First, minimize the amount of shifting that Windows must do between real and protected modes by minimizing the number of real-mode drivers and TSR programs that you normally run in your system. Keep the DOS kernel out of upper memory by removing the DOS=HIGH line from your CONFIG.SYS file. In the unlikely event you have a 286-based PC and run in standard mode, add this line to the [standard] section of your SYSTEM.INI file:

```
FasterModeSwitch=1
```

> **Tip**
>
> If you run a DOS-based communications program, run it full-screen when in the foreground and minimized (as an icon) when you want it to execute in the background to avoid the Windows screen-update overhead. You can also allocate more microprocessor time to your communications applications by adjusting their priority upward in the .PIF file associated with the application. If you have a permanent swap file and enable 32-bit disk access, also check the Lock Application Memory box in the .PIF file of your communications program to prevent Windows from trying to move its code into virtual memory.

Parallel Ports

Once upon a time, parallel port and printer port were synonymous, but today the parallel port has become a universal port that can connect PCs, link to networks, and even tie in modems, tape, and hard disk drives. Two reasons underlie this change. Faster PCs need the quicker communications made possible by parallel technology. And new parallel port designs have expanded the capabilities of the parallel port far beyond just sending characters to your printer.

Reflecting its printing origins, the three parallel ports that may be installed in a PC are designated LPT1 through LPT3. The LPT abbreviation stands for Line PrinTer. The limit carries through to OS/2. Windows 95, however, makes provisions for up to 128 parallel ports in a single PC, subject to system-dependent resources constraints that make the practical limit much lower.

The first parallel printer ports, today termed Standard Parallel Ports (SPP), operated at speeds high for their day but modest today—between 50KB and 150KB per second. True to their design goal, they were designed to push information in one direction only, from PC to printer. (Clever engineers have since found ways of force-feeding these ports in reverse by redefining signals.) The second generation of ports, the PS/2 Parallel Port, made parallel technology a two-way street, allowing the interface to mate a variety of devices that expect communications to be give-and-take. The next step in port design, the Enhanced Parallel Port, gave the venerable design added impetus, upping the potential parallel transfer rate to about 2,000KB/second. That puts the parallel port in league with some expansion buses—it's nearly the same as a slot in an 8-bit PC and close to the limit of ISA. Seeing the potential of the EPP design, Hewlett-Packard and Microsoft enhanced it into a complete connection system with a well-defined protocol as the Extended Capabilities Port (ECP), which is destined to become the next parallel standard.

Standard Parallel Ports

In designing the now-standard parallel port that appeared first inside its original PC, IBM elected to follow the pattern of control signals set by one once-prominent printer manufacturer, Centronics. The connection was not formalized at the time IBM borrowed the design—Centronics had just developed a set of control signals that served well the control of computer printers. Other printer companies were adopting the Centronics design when IBM appropriated it, too.

IBM, however, chose to go in its own direction for parallel port connectors. Where a true Centronics printer port uses a 36-conductor Amphenol connector, IBM selected a 25-pin D-shell connector so the connector fits in the space available. Since then, printer makers have stuck with the 36-pin design, and IBM and nearly every other computer maker has maintained the 25-pin standard. Consequently, connecting a printer to a standard parallel port inevitably requires an adapter cable. Today these are ubiquitous and inexpensive, a standard PC accessory.

The Standard Parallel Port is the basic printer port in the PC environment. It is the minimum parallel connection—and usually all you get when you buy inexpensive I/O cards.

Bi-Directional Parallel Ports

In that Standard Parallel Ports were originally conceived to serve solely as printer outputs, the flow of data was designed to be in one direction only—from PC to printer. Only a few of the parallel port control signals needed to go the other way. Consequently, all early PCs were equipped with unidirectional parallel ports. That is, they could send but not receive data.

IBM evidently rethought this design after the first PCs were produced and began to make parallel ports that were capable of bi-directional operation. The standard parallel port of the AT allows for bi-directional data flow. However, IBM did not officially support bi-directional operation until it introduced the PS/2 line.

This bi-directional support does not otherwise alter the signal definitions, connector pin assignments or other aspects of the design of standard parallel ports. PS/2 parallel ports are backward compatible with standard parallel ports.

The parallel port support built into the very early models of IBM personal computers does, in fact, permit reading of the various data lines. As long as care is taken to keep from grounding the data lines (for instance, controlling them through resistors to keep currents low), it is possible to use even the earliest PC parallel ports bi-directionally.

The whole issue of unidirectional and bi-directional ports would be academic if not for the former being easier and cheaper to build. While all reputable computer makers install bi-directional ports in their products, the makers of inexpensive parallel adapters or multifunction boards are apt to skimp on the circuitry. They may equip their parallel ports with unidirectional buffers. You can only be sure by asking. But as long as you're asking, you should ask for more—more recent technology that can give your parallel connections greater speed.

Enhanced Parallel Ports

Making parallel ports was never intended to make them into a general-purpose interface. For the most part, bi-directionality was only an expedient that IBM offered to help people switch from 5.25-inch to 3.5-inch disks. The bi-directional ports were designed to support IBM's Data Migration Facility, a combination of cable and software that anticipated your use of the connection once to copy your floppy disk data from one PC to another (and then forget all about 5.25-inch disks as you reveled in the glee of having spent too much money on your PS/2).

As with many products introduced by IBM, the idea behind the Data Migration Facility was intriguing but the implementation left a lot to be desired—little things like a comfortable interface and performance. It was enough, however, to inspire other designers to develop data transfer programs that took advantage of the speed advantage that the PS/2 parallel port held over ordinary PC serial ports.

Although standard parallel port speed was sufficient for most people (at least, at the time), some folks found it limiting. Specifically, engineers at Xircom Incorporated discovered that the low speed of the standard parallel port put the external network adapters they developed in 1989 at a severe disadvantage compared to slot-mounted host adapters. Engineers at Zenith Data Systems struggled with the parallel port speed limit in looking for a way to get information in and out of notebook computer systems without adding mass and complexity to their products. As a result, Zenith and Xircom banded together with Intel (a company that supports just about any new technology that will sell more PCs and, with them, microprocessors) to form the Enhanced Parallel Port Partnership.

Standards

On August 10, 1991, the EPP Partnership released the initial description of an Enhanced Parallel Port. After a few revisions, the standard reached its present form (Release 1.7) in March of 1992, when it was submitted to the IEEE as a prospective industry standard. The design was first implemented in Zenith's MasterPort SLE notebook computer and Intel's 386SL microprocessor chipset.

The Enhanced Parallel Port earns its speed in two ways: a streamlined logical interface and explicit definition of electrical parameters. The former lets your PC move data into the port faster. The latter assures that the data gets where it's going.

Extended Capabilities Ports

Although the Enhanced Parallel Port provides means for making high-speed data transfers to peripherals, the specifications don't tell designers exactly how each transfer should be carried out every step of the way from program to printed page.

Hewlett-Packard combined efforts with Microsoft to create the Extended Capabilities Port, an extension that takes up where the EPP left off. Version 1.0 of the ECP specification for ISA-based computers was first published in November of 1992, and numerous refinements have been made since then. ECP adds two modes to the EPP design, a fast two-way communication mode between a PC and its peripherals, and another two-way mode with performance further enhanced by simple integral data compression.

As with EPP, the ECP design is aimed at compatibility. An ECP port functions as a standard parallel port with old-fashioned devices like printers. With advanced devices, however, the ECP port can adeptly transfer data at the same high speeds as EPP but with additional versatility.

ECP includes a complete protocol for exchanging data across a parallel connection. Every ECP (as opposed to standard parallel port) transfer is negotiated. The host computer can query a given device connected to the ECP system to determine its capabilities. Peripherals that support ECP signal that they can accept high-speed transmissions and the format of the data they are capable of receiving, for example, compressed or uncompressed. The ECP system includes full handshaking and error detection so that you and your system know when transfers are unsuccessful. ECP promises to be a new connection standard that will let you add high-performance devices to your multimedia PC quickly and cheaply.

The ECP standard defines the names and functions of parallel ports somewhat differently from those used by standard parallel ports. Table 11.6 lists the pin assignments and compares the functions of the various connections under the SPP and ECP definitions.

TABLE 11.6. Parallel port connections and definitions.

Pin	SPP name	ECP name	ECP function
1	Strobe	nStrobe	Registers address or data into slave
2	Data bit 0	Data 7	Data bit
3	Data bit 1	Data 6	Data bit
4	Data bit 2	Data 5	Data bit
5	Data bit 3	Data 4	Data bit
6	Data bit 4	Data 3	Data bit
7	Data bit 5	Data 2	Data bit
8	Data bit 6	Data 1	Data bit
9	Data bit 7	Data 0	Data bit
10	Acknowledge	nAck	Indicates valid data when asserted
11	Busy	Busy	Indicates peripheral can receive data when not asserted
12	Paper end (Out of paper)	PError	Acknowledges change in direction of transfer
13	Select	Select	Indicates printer is on-line
14	Auto feed	nAutoFd	Requests byte of data when asserted
15	Error	nFault	Generates interrupt when asserted
16	Initialize printer	nInits	Sets transfer direction (asserted=reversed)
17	Select input	nSelectIn	Never asserted in ECP mode
18	Ground	Ground	Aux-Out
19	Ground	Ground	Return for strobe
20	Ground	Ground	Return for data 1
21	Ground	Ground	Return for data 3
22	Ground	Ground	Return for data 5
23	Ground	Ground	Return for data 7
24	Ground	Ground	Return for busy
25	Ground	Ground	Return logic ground

Game Ports

The Multimedia PC standard requires a game port in a system to garner the MPC trademark. In the PC scheme of things, a game port is also called a joystick port. The port provides connections for one or two joysticks using one 15-pin connector. Alternately, you can connect four paddles to one game port, two in place of each joystick.

A joystick is a two-dimensional absolute position sensor. That means it distinguishes a specific location on a plane, the position you want to point to. A mouse, on the other hand, indicates relative positions. The joystick indicates a place while the mouse indicates motion. A paddle is a one-dimensional joystick—it indicates a position on a line.

The joystick indicates locations as resistance values, one value for the x-coordinate of the location, a second value for the y-coordinate. When you move the joystick, you shift the arms of a pair of variable resistors arranged perpendicular to each other, changing the resistance value. Over its complete range, the resistance value changes from near 0 to 100,000 ohms.

Your PC senses the resistance of the joystick position as a voltage. This voltage changes linearly as you move the joystick. Consequently, game port inputs are analog signals. The game port converts each of the analog signals it senses into a single digital pulse, the duration of which is directly proportional to the resistance values in the joystick sensor. By timing the length of this pulse, your PC can determine the position of the joystick.

Each joystick or paddle also has a button. Pressing a joystick or paddle button simply closes a circuit—it acts as a switch. The game port has one input for each joystick to sense whether this switch is open or closed. Table 11.7 lists the functions of the 15 pins of the standard game port when used for joysticks or paddles.

TABLE 11.7. Game port joystick and paddle pin definitions.

Pin	Name	Joystick function	Paddle function
1	+5 VDC	Joystick A coordinate common	Paddle A coordinate high
2	Button 4	Joystick A pushbutton high	Paddle A pushbutton high
3	Position 0	Joystick A x-coordinate wiper	Paddle A coordinate wiper
4	Ground	Joystick A pushbutton return	Paddle A pushbutton return
5	Ground	Not used	Paddle B pushbutton return
6	Position 1	Joystick A y-coordinate wiper	Paddle B coordinate wiper
7	Button 5	Not used	Paddle B pushbutton high
8	+5 VDC	Not used	Paddle B coordinate high

continues

TABLE 11.7. continued

Pin	Name	Joystick function	Paddle function
9	+5 VDC	Joystick B coordinate common	Paddle C coordinate high
10	Button 6	Joystick B pushbutton high	Paddle C pushbutton high
11	Position 2	Joystick B x-coordinate wiper	Paddle C coordinate wiper
12	Ground	Joystick B pushbutton return	Paddle C/D pushbutton return
13	Position 3	Joystick B y-coordinate wiper	Paddle D coordinate wiper
14	Button 7	Not used	Paddle D pushbutton high
15	+5 VDC	Not used	Paddle D coordinate high

Technical Note

For a game port, determining what you've done with your joystick is a matter of timing. Your PC checks both the joystick position and switch condition interactively by sending an OUT instruction to the joystick port at 0201(Hex). This instruction starts the timing pulses. The first four bits of the output of the 0201(Hex) port go high at the start of the timing pulse and remain high for the period corresponding to the resistance value of the associated joystick position. The upper four bits of this port indicate the status of the associated switches.

Technical Note

The minimum length of this pulse is 24.2 microseconds. Each ohm of resistance stretches the pulse by 0.011 microsecond, so at maximum resistance the length of the pulse is 1124.2 microseconds.

Data Modems

If you want to link your multimedia system to the world beyond your office, you need a modem. Modems are key to exchanging files, snooping bulletin boards, downloading images and movies, and computing interactively with someone halfway around the world. Modems are also a vestige of the Stone Age of civilization. They are a link between the modern world and the Victorian realm of pipe-smoking armchair scientists and brave engineers taking their first few steps into the modern world of electronics. The modem connects the high-speed digital logic of your PC with the archaic analog signals developed in the middle of the nineteenth century that wend their way through the international telephone system.

This vast difference in time and technologies makes the modem a necessary evil. The worldwide telephone system was designed only to handle analog signals because that's all that speaking into a microphone creates. Over the years, telephone companies have pushed technology ahead and developed elaborate digital multiplex and switching systems. But the first and final link to this network remains the same old wire-and-analog-signal system that Alexander Graham Bell would recognize as his own, at least if he were alive.

Background

The word "modem" is a contraction of *mo*dulator/*dem*odulator, which describes its function. The modem produces one or more constant (or nearly so) tones called *carrier waves* that are altered or modulated by digital data. The simplest form of modulation shifts the frequency of the carrier wave so that one frequency represents a digital one and another a digital zero. This technique is called *frequency shift keying* and is used by only the slowest modems that follow the Bell 103 standard.

The speed of a modem, its transfer rate, is measured in bits per second, representing the number of digital code bits that, when one modem is connected to another through a telephone line, actually emerge from the output of the distant modem. The speed of data across the telephone line does not necessarily correspond to the actual throughput because most modems add an extra layer of code to their signals. Instead of simply passing data along as individual bits, the modem looks at digital data in groups of bits, then assigns a code to the group. The higher speed the modem, the bigger the group and the more different codes are required to send them. Each group is represented by a modulation state on the telephone line, and advanced modems define as many discrete states as possible by altering not only the frequency but also the phase of the carrier wave.

The rate at which the modem changes the state of the telephone line is measured using a unit called the *baud,* named after J. M. E. Baudot who invented the first widely used telegraph code. Although, strictly speaking, the baud rate and modem throughput in bits per second are the same only for modems operating at 300 bps because of the complex modulation systems used by higher speed modems, the term baud is often used to mean modem throughput in bits per second.

Modems operate at a number of different speeds, and each speed is governed by one or more communications standards that assure that two modems can talk to one another no matter their origins. The standards define not only the kind of modulation used by a modem but also its *handshaking*, the signals that two modems exchange to establish a connection. Through handshaking, modern modems negotiate the highest common speed at which they can operate (and a given telephone connection can support) as well as the error correction and compression protocols that may be used. The various tones and noise burst you hear when a modem answers the telephone line are the signals used in handshaking.

Standards

The specifications for any modem look like an alphabet soup of names of the various standards it follows. These include the Bell standards, set years ago by AT&T before its divestiture of the regional operating companies; Microcom standards developed by a modem maker; and ITU standards, promulgated by the International Telecommunications Union, part of the United Nations that was once known as Comité Consultatif Internationale Télégraphique et

Standards

Téléphonique or CCITT (in English, that's International Telegraph and Telephone Consultative Committee). In addition, other standards cover error detection and correction and data compression.

From a practical standpoint, the most important of these standards are those that govern the operating speed of a given modem. The principal modem standards in use today are listed in Table 11.8.

TABLE 11.8. Summary of modem standards.

Standard	Speed (maximum) in bps	Comments
Bell 103	300	US standard only
Bell 212A	1200	US standard only
V.22	1200	Like Bell 212A but different handshaking
V.22bis	2400	First widely used ITU standard in US
V.32	9600	Also falls back to 4800
V.32bis	14,400	ITU standard
V.32FC	28,800	Rockwell proprietary protocol
V.32terbo	19,200	AT&T proprietary protocol
V.34	28,800	ITU standard
V.42	DNA	Error correction
V.42bis	DNA	Data compression (up to 4X)

Note that two standards operate at today's top modem speed, 28,800 bits per second. Of the two, V32.FC (or *Fast Class*) never was accepted as a true standard, but was offered by modem chipmaker Rockwell International as a means for impatient people to get V.34 speed without waiting for the ITU to officially ratify the V.34 standard. In fact, V.32FC and V.34 use the same technology for communications; they differ principally by the handshaking that establishes the connection. Nevertheless, a V.32FC modem will *not* communicate with a V.34 modem. Today, V.34 is the accepted standard, and the only reason to consider a slower modem is cost. Even so, V.34 modems are inexpensive enough that only the penurious should bother with anything less.

None of these standards are mutually exclusive in a given modem. Most modems understand several of the standards, shifting between them as you adjust the speed of the modem (or as the modem adjusts itself). Most of today's modems use *digital signal processors* (DSPs) to synthesize their signals, and adding a new standard requires nothing more than changing the programming of the DSP. Consequently, most newer modems include nearly all standards in their repertories, and they can accommodate new standards by simply downloading software. Some modern modems have separate programmable support circuitry that further adds to their versatility.

In general, the more complex the modulation used by a modem, the smaller the changes between states that the modem must distinguish and the greater the likelihood of error. At today's high communications speeds, error detection and correction is mandatory. The V.42 standard provides a means by which you can assure the integrity of your modem communications. Modems negotiate the use of error correction, so you should always enable error-correction so that your modem will try to negotiate an error-free connection.

Data compression can further increase the speed of your modem communications. Some compression systems are more effective than others. The V.42bis system, which is now the preferred international standard, yields about a 4:1 compression ration on typical data. In general, it is most effective during the exchange of uncompressed text and graphics files. It doesn't speed up the transfer of previously compressed files (such as files processed with PKZip software with the ZIP filename extension or graphics files that use internal compression like run-length encoding). Again, you should always enable V.42bis in the hope that the modems you connect to also use it and will negotiate the highest speed connection.

Performance Issue

Sometimes you may encounter a modem that follows a Microcom Networking Protocol standard for compression or error control. For example, MNP5 compression was popular before the V.42bis standard was ratified and is still sometimes a feature included in new modems. The various MNP standards are defined in the following list:

MNP Class 1—A protocol to eliminate transmission errors that sacrifices modem speed.

MNP Class 2—A similar error-correction protocol that takes a smaller toll on performance (about a 16 percent hit).

MNP Class 3—A synchronous protocol that removes start and stop bits from the data stream and improves data throughput by 25 percent or more.

MNP Class 4—An error-correcting protocol that also yields modest data compression through Adaptive Packet Assembly and Data Phase Optimization.

MNP Class 5—A data compression protocol that squeezes some kinds of data up to a factor of two, effectively doubling the speed of data transmissions.

MNP Class 6—A protocol that helps modems negotiate the highest possible transmission speed (with or without compression).

MNP Class 7—A more efficient data compression algorithm (Huffman encoding) than MNP5.

MNP Class 9—A streamlined communication protocol that reduces packet overhead.

MNP Class 10—A set of enhancements that help modems work better through poor telephone connections.

Configuration

Modem speed applies only to the link established between two modems. When a modem uses data compression, the speed at which you supply data to it and the speed at which it communicates with another modem will often be different because the modem packs your PC's data more efficiently for transmission. Consequently, the speed you set for the serial port connected to your modem should be as high as possible. Your modem will use handshaking to make your PC pace the rate at which it sends data to the modem.

Trouble-
shooting

Note that some modem speeds are not the same as the speeds used by UARTs. In particular, the 14,400 bps speed of the V.32bis standard and the 28,800 bps of V.34 are not standard UART speeds. Some communication programs enable you to set their data rates to one of these speeds, ostensibly matching your modem's speed. Often these settings will not work because the UART in your PC or in the modem will not accept them. To avoid problems, always set your communications parameters at a standard UART speed such as 9600, 19,200, 38,400, 57,600, or 115,200 bps. Again, the highest speed at which your PC and modem will reliably communicate is the top choice. Setting a speed lower than your modem's highest speed will usually force your modem to use a slower standard.

While at one time you had to worry about the particular commands that your modem used so that you could match it with your software, times have changed. Not only do nearly all modems use the same basic repertory of commands (the Hayes or AT command set), nearly every modem comes with its own communications software, often in both DOS and Windows versions (either of which, of course, you can run under OS/2 or Windows 95). The software takes care of sending all the commands, so you never have to deal with the minutiae of modem instructions.

The one tricky issue that you may encounter when you want to use particular communications software with your modem is the *setup string* of your modem. The setup string is a list of modem commands that tell the modem how to configure itself to match your software and carry out communications. The software that comes with your modem should default to the setup string used by the modem it accompanies. Most communications programs that you actually go out and buy let you match your modem from a list when you install the program, eliminating your concern with setup strings. All that said, sometimes you need to get a reluctant modem working with an obscure program that doesn't recognize the model, brand, or national origin of your modem. The closest to a general-purpose setup string with a modern modem (V.32 or V.34) is the following:

`AT&F0S0=0`

This simple command tells the modem to reset itself to its factory defaults (`&F0`) and originate rather than wait for calls (that is, do not enter Answer mode) by setting `S`-register 0 to a value of zero. Some modems may require the command `AT&F1` to restore their factory defaults.

Both OS/2 and Windows 95 come complete with communications programs that require use of a modem. In OS/2 Warp, you configure the particular application (such as those in the Bonus

Pack) to match your modem. With Windows, one overall setup configures all of Windows 95's communications powers.

You access the Windows 95 modem setup procedure through Control Panel. You must first install your modem using the Hardware Installation Wizard. Click Add New Hardware, and the Wizard will let you select the hardware, including modems, by model and manufacturer. If Windows 95 does not recognize your particular modem, choose one that follows the same standards (say a generic 28,800 bps modem). You can also install a new modem by clicking the Modem icon from Control Panel.

In general, installing your modem this way is all the setup that's necessary. If you need to alter specific modem parameters, the same folder that you access through the Modem icon in Control Panel will give you several setup tabs to let you alter any important modem setting. Selecting Properties at the initial screen will give you access to the General tab for choosing the modem's COM port and speed. The controls are simple and self-explanatory, as you'll see from Figure 11.5.

FIGURE 11.5. Choosing COM port and speed on the General tab of the Windows 95 modem properties screen.

The Connection tab lets you select communications parameters. Its Advanced button controls error detection and correction, handshaking, and selects American or European standards for low-speed operation.

PCMCIA modems can sometimes be confusing. Normally, your PCMCIA driver will assign a communications port to your modem from the standard COM repertory, and you use this port value in your communications software. The Plug-and-Play PCMCIA drivers that come with OS/2 Warp allow the mapping of the same serial port to different programs, so your modem may appear as COM1 even though you have some other device attached to that port. Both will work fine, even if the other device is a mouse (a modem and mouse sharing even an interrupt is an anathema for most operating systems).

Advanced Technologies

Multimedia, and particularly videoconferencing, presents modems with a particular challenge: combining voice, data, and images in a single connection, one with bandwidth hardly adequate for carrying the full range of the human voice, let alone television. Fortunately, two companies, Radish Communications Systems and AT&T, have devised methods of shoehorning voice and data together on a single phone line, a technology called *Simultaneous Voice and Data*, or SVD. An industry consortium is further developing these ideas to make a universal voice and data standard. The data in SVD can be anything, for example ASCII text, software commands, a graphic image, an executable program file, or compressed video data.

VoiceView, developed by Radish in 1992 as a proprietary product, was released as an open SVD protocol a year later. It has quickly gained support of major modem makers such as AT&T, Hayes, Rockwell, and U.S. Robotics, as well as Intel and Microsoft because it could be grafted into standard communications chipsets while adding relatively little cost—probably under $50—to the cost of a conventional modem.

In truth, VoiceView is a mode-switching system that only simulates true SVD. As you switch from describing to doing, it quickly and inaudibly toggles between sending voice and data without altering the actual signals. When you talk, VoiceView simply steals the line from your data. Voice takes priority because computers have better handshaking signals than people. Your voice stays analog, your data digital.

On the other hand, the *VoiceSpan* system developed by AT&T works as a packet-based multiplex system. VoiceSpan converts your voice into digital form, and organizes the bytes of your voice and data into individual fixed-length packets. The mix of packets depends on what you do and say during a call. When you don't speak, VoiceSpan fills the line with data packets. Speak up, and it mixes in voice packets. The result is that data transmission slows as the stream of data packets get diluted. Even when you talk, however, some data always gets through.

DSVD is the latest development in combining voice and data on a single telephone line. Backed by an industry consortium led by Intel, DSVD works like AT&T's VoiceSpan by digitizing voice information into packets that can be handled like ordinary digital data. It uses the same sampling rate and bit-depth as long-distance telephone systems (8 KHz sampling with a sampling depth of eight bits) so it does not affect voice quality. Although the digitization process adds a slight delay (on the order of two to three milliseconds) to voice transmissions, the lag is generally not perceptible.

Neither VoiceView, VoiceSpan, nor DSVD increases the data capacity of a telephone line. Because of the severe bandwidth restraints of a dial-up connection, telephone-connected multimedia applications like videoconferencing and whiteboarding deliver adequate performance only by minimizing the data that it must move. For example, when it needs to update a screen, it sends out commands instead of hauling full-screen images through the narrow telephone channel. Because the same application software runs at each end of the multimedia modem connection, each responds identically to the shared commands. All the screens in the connection always look the same no matter who draws on them.

Fax Modems

Nearly all modems today include fax abilities; some people even consider the graphic aspect of fax to be part of the requirements of a multimedia system. As far as technology is concerned, fax is mostly a matter of software. Modern fax is just digital data that gets transmitted the same way as bytes of ASCII characters do. The difference is that fax software converts bit-image data into a compressed digital form before handing it off to modem circuitry.

Fax and data modems grew up independently, however. Fax started as an analog photomechanical technology with its roots in the wire photos used by newspapers to relay pictures across the continent. Only after two generations of development did fax go digital. This change led to its wide acceptance and integration into the PC fold. The various generations of fax technology are classified as *fax groups,* of which four have been defined:

Group 1—An analog modem standard equivalent to a Bell 103 data modem that can transmit a page of information in six minutes.

Group 2—An improved analog technology that doubles the speed of transmission to three minutes per page.

Group 3—The world-wide digital fax standard that allows a page to be sent in 20 to 60 seconds.

Group 4—A 1984 super-performance fax standard, that allows resolutions of up to 400×400 dpi as well as higher-speed transmissions of lower resolutions (not widely used).

You don't have to worry about what group your fax modem falls into. All PC-based fax modems follow the Group 3 standard.

Group 3 allows a great deal of flexibility in communications speed. Early fax modems operated solely at 9600 bps, although some inexpensive models restricted their speed to half of that. New fax modems run at the same speed as data modems, although they follow different communications standards at speeds less than 28,800 bits per second. The principal standards used in facsimile communications are:

V.17—The world-side standard for modem communications at 7200, 9600, 12,000, and 14,400 bps.

V.27ter—The world-wide fax modem standard for data rates of 2400 and 4800 bps.

V.29—An older standard for fax modems operating at 7200 and 9600 bps (these modes are now incorporated in the V.17 standard).

V.34—A world-wide standard shared with data modems for data rates up to 28,800 bps.

Standards

As with data modems, fax modems must link up with your PC and its software. Unlike data modems, which were blessed with a de facto standard since early on (the Hayes command set), fax modems lacked a single standard. In recent years, however, the Electronics Industry Association and the Telecommunications Industry Association have since created a standard of fax modem commands that is essentially an extension to the Hayes AT command set. The standard embraces two classes, 1 and 2:

Class 1 is the earlier standard. Under the Class 1 standard, most of the processing of fax documents is performed by PC software. The resulting fax data is sent to the modem for direct transmission.

Class 2 shifts the work of preparing the fax document for transmission to the fax modem itself. The modem hardware handles the data compression and error control for the transmission. The Class 2 standard also incorporates additional flow-control and station identification features.

These classes hint at the most significant difference between PC-based fax systems—software. Fax modem hardware determines the connections that can be made, but the software determines the ultimate capabilities of the system. A fax modem that adheres to various standards (classes as well as protocols) will open the widest selection of software and the widest range of features for you.

Because fax deals with images instead of ordinary text characters, its software is inherently more complex than that for data communications. Far from making things more confusing, however, fax simplifies your modem worries. Everything is handled through applications software, so you don't need to deal with the details of running a modem.

Chapter 12

The Compact Disc

Without a doubt, the Compact Disc is the enabling factor for today's multimedia systems. Without it, you might have to rent a truck to cart around your favorite applications, the heavy megabytes bursting from floppy disks and bending axles as you drag down the highway. The now-familiar CD gives you the perfect package—hundreds of megabytes on a five-inch disc that costs little to make and stores anywhere. Every kind of software is shifting from floppy to CD-ROM, everything from lowly DOS to the latest adventure games and reference libraries. CDs are convenient, too. In a few seconds you can switch your PC from being an expert sports jock to a scientific research nerd.

For the distribution of digital information—music or data—the Compact Disc is typically the most affordable alternative for moving hundreds of megabytes to thousands of locations. This low cost makes the CD-ROM the premiere digital publishing medium. Already hundreds of CD-ROM titles are available, each one holding an encyclopedia of data.

In fact, today the CD has become so common that many PC manufacturers are making them standard equipment in their PCs. Both the MPC 1.0 and 2.0 specifications require a CD drive. Some systems now come with two. And CD changers can put from 5 to 100 discs on-line.

Background

Developed by the joint efforts of Philips and Sony Corporation in the early 1980s when the digital age was taking over the stereo industry, the Compact Disc was first and foremost a high-fidelity delivery medium. Initially released in the United States in 1983, within five years it had replaced the vinyl phonograph record as the premiere stereophonic medium because of its wide dynamic range, lack of noise, invulnerability to damage, and durability.

The 70 minutes of music that was one of the core specifications in designing the Compact Disc system—enough to hold Beethoven's Ninth Symphony in D-minor—was a lot of data, more than 600MB worth. With a covetous gleam, computer engineers eyed the shiny medium and discovered that data is data (okay, data are data) and the Compact Disc could be a repository for more megabytes than anyone had reason to use. (Remember, these were the days when the pot at the end of the rainbow held a 20MB or 30MB hard disk.) When someone got the idea that a plastic puck that cost a buck to make and retailed for $16.99, could be filled with last year's statistics, and marketed for $249, the rush was on. The Compact Disc became the CD-ROM (which stands for Compact Disc, Read-Only Memory), and megabytes came to the masses—at a price.

Soon sound became only one of the applications of the Compact Disc medium. The original name had to be extended to distinguish musical CDs from all the others. To computer people, the CD of the stereo system became the CD-DA, Compact Disc, Digital Audio.

Cheap and easy duplication make CD-ROM an ideal distribution medium. Its versatility—the same basic technology stores data, sound, and video—came about because all engineers eagerly search for big, cheap storage. The Compact Disc has both of those virtues by design. Hardly coincidentally, the same stuff that the Compact Disc stores so well are the core of multimedia. Quite naturally those little silver discs are the enabling factor behind the multimedia explosion in PCs. Moreover, the Compact Disc is central to the digitalization and computerization of photography, or at least photographic storage. The PhotoCD system promises to hold your images longer and more compactly than long-familiar photographic film. The CD-ROM has become as mandatory in your next PC as the hard disk was a few years ago.

Technology

One of the great virtues of the Compact Disc is storage density—little discs mean a lot of megabytes. The enabling technology behind that high density is optics. Unlike virtually all other PC storage media, the Compact Disc and CD-ROM use light waves instead of magnetic fields to encode information.

The virtues of light for storage are numerous. Using lenses you can focus a beam of light—particularly coherent laser light—to a tiny spot smaller than the most diminutive magnetic domain writeable on a hard disk drive. (Although today's newest hard disk has passed the 10-year-old CD in storage density, new optical designs will soon push the CD ahead again.) Unlike the restricted magnetic fields of hard disks that have to be used within a range of a few millionth of an inch, light travels distance with ease. Leaping along some 5.9 trillion miles in a year, some beams have been traveling since almost the beginning of the universe 10 to 15 billion years ago. The equipment that generates the beam of light that writes or reads optical storage need not be anywhere near the medium itself, which gives equipment designers more freedom than they possibly deserve.

Optical technology underlies the CD-ROM. The basic idea is that you can encode binary data as a pattern of black and white splotches just as on and off electrical signals can. You can make your mark in a variety of ways. The old reliable method is plain, ordinary ink on paper. The bar codes found universally on supermarket products do exactly that.

Reading the patterns of light and dark takes only a photodetector, an electrical component that reacts to different brightness levels by changing its resistance. Light simply lets electricity flow through the photodetector more easily. Aim the photodetector at the bar code, and it can judge the difference between the bars and background as you move it along (or move the product along in front of it). The read lasers in the check-out aisle quicken the scan. The photodetector watches the reflections of the red laser beam and patiently waits until a recognizable pattern—the bar code as the laser scans across it—emerges from the noise.

You could store the data of a computer file in one gigantic bar code and bring back paper tape as a storage medium. Even if you were willing to risk your important data to a medium that turns yellow and flakes apart under the unblinking eye of the sun like a beach bum with a bad complexion, you'd still have all the joy of dealing with a sequential storage medium. This means you'd have a lot of waiting to do—you might want to buy a magazine to read while you're waiting. Or a book. Or the complete works of Charles Dickens.

The disk, with its random access abilities, is better suited as a storage system. That choice was obvious even to the audio-oriented engineers who put the first Compact Disc systems together. They had a successful pattern to follow: the old black vinyl phonograph record. The ability to drop a needle on any track of a record had become ingrained in the hearts and minds of music lovers for more than 100 years. Any new music storage system needed equally fast and easy access to any selection. The same fast and easy access suits computer storage equally well.

Media

The heart of the CD-ROM system is the disk itself. Once you've stepped past the obvious decision to choose the disk for its random-access abilities, you face many pragmatic decisions: What size disk? What should it be made from? How fast should it spin? What's the best way to put the optical pattern on the disk? What's the cheapest way to duplicate a million copies when the album goes platinum? Audio engineers made pragmatic choices about all of these factors long before the idea of CD-ROM had even been conceived.

Size is related to playing time. The bigger the disk, the more data it will hold, all else being equal. But a platter the size of a wading pool would win favor with no one but plastics manufacturers. Shrinking the size of every splotch of the recorded digital code increases the storage capacity of any size disk, but technology and manufacturing tolerances limit the minimum size of the storage splotch. Given the maximum storage density that a workable optical technology would allow (about 150MB per square inch), the total amount of storage dictates the size of the disk. With the "Ode to Joy" as a design goal and the optical technology of 1980 to take them there, engineers found a platter about 4.75 inches (exactly 120mm) in diameter their ideal compromise. A nice, round 100mm was just too small. The center hole in a CD is 15mm in diameter.

The form of the code was another pragmatic choice. For a successful optical music storage system, normal printing and duplication methods all had their drawbacks. Printing the disk with ink was out of the question because no printing process can reliably recreate detail as fine as was necessary. Photography could keep all the detail—an early optical storage system prototype was based on photo technology—but photographic images are not readily made in million-lot quantities.

Besides printing, the one reproduction process that was successfully used to make millions was the stamping of ordinary photograph records, essentially a precision molding process. Mechanical molding and precision optical recording don't seem a very good match. But engineers found a way. By altering the texture of a surface mechanically, they could change its reflectivity. A coarse surface doesn't reflect light as well as a smooth one; a dark pit doesn't reflect light as well as a highly polished mirror. That was the breakthrough: the optical storage disk would be a reflective mirror that would be dotted with dark pits to encode data. A laser beam could blast pits into the disk. Then the pits, a mechanical feature, could be duplicated with stamping equipment similar to that used in manufacturing ordinary phonograph records.

Those concepts underlie the process of manufacturing Compact Discs. First a disk master is recorded on a special machine with a high-powered laser that blasts the pits in a blank recording master making a mechanical recording. Then the master is made into a mold. One master can make many duplicate molds, each of which is then mounted in a stamping machine. The machine heats the mold and injects a glob of plastic into it. After giving the plastic a chance to cool, the stamping machine ejects the disk and takes another gulp of plastic.

Another machine takes the newly stamped disc and aluminizes it so that it has a shiny, mirror-like finish. To protect the shine, the disk is laminated with a clear plastic cover that guards the mechanical pattern from chemical and physical abuse (oxidation and scratches).

This process is much like the manufacture of vinyl records. The principal differences are that the CD has only one recorded side, its details are finer, and it gets an after-treatment of plating and laminating. The finishing steps add to the cost of the Compact Disc, but most of the cost in making a disc is attributed to the cost of the data it stores—either royalties to a recording act or the people who create, compile, or confuse the information that's to be distributed. That $50 disc might cost 50 cents to press—disregarding royalties, distribution costs, and (of course) profits.

CD-ROM disks themselves store information exactly the same way it's stored on the CDs in your stereo system—only instead of getting up to 75 minutes of music, a CD-ROM disk holds about 680MB of data. That data can be anything from simple text to SuperVGA images, to programs, and the full circle back to music for multimedia systems.

Compared to vinyl phonograph records or magnetic disks, Compact Discs offer a storage medium that is long-lived and immune to most abuse. The protective clear plastic layer resists physical tortures (in fact, Compact Discs are more vulnerable to scratches on their label side than the side that is scanned with the playback laser) and because the system is designed so that nothing actually touches the playback surface of the CD. The data pits are sealed within layers of the disk itself and are never touched by anything other than a light beam—they never wear out and acquire errors only when you abuse the disks themselves purposely or carelessly (for example, by scratching them against one another when not storing them in their plastic jewel boxes. Although error correction prevents errors from showing up in the data, a bad scratch can prevent a disk from being read at all. Little scratches can add up to unreadability, too.

Compact Discs show their phonograph heritage in another way. Instead of using a series of concentric tracks as with magnetic computer storage systems, the data track on the CD is one long, continuous spiral much like the single groove on a phonograph record. The CD player scans the track from near the center of the disk to the outer rim.

To maximize the storage available on a disc, the CD system uses constant linear velocity recording. The disc spins faster for its inner tracks than it does for the outer tracks so that the same length of track appears under the read/write head every second. The spin varies from about 300 RPM at the inner diameter to 100 RPM at the outside edge.

Recordable CD

CDs have a lot going for them—in particular compact high capacity and a long life without chance of losing bits. But they suffer the singular disadvantage of being a one-way medium, stamped at the factory and forever sealed with their digital contents. Without access to a mastering machine and stamping factory, CDs are off-limits to your personal data.

A new twist to the CD, the recordable system called CD-R (for Compact Disc, Recordable, of course) changes all that. With a CD-R drive, you can make your own CDs filled with hundreds of megabytes of data. You can mail them anywhere in the world, certain that they will be immune to the ravages of x-ray machines and even strong magnetic fields, knowing your data is forever safely inscribed. Better still, any ordinary CD drive can play the disks you make. Any true multimedia machine can play back a CD-R disc. If you need to send your own multimedia presentation from one place to another, CD-R is the most compact, inexpensive, and reliable means of doing it. Moreover, CD-R is the technology that enables your local photolab to make PhotoCD discs.

Besides an exchange medium, CD-R works as an archiving system. Each disc is like a stone tablet carved for the ages, unchanging and unchangeable. What you write becomes a permanent record, your mark for posterity. If you need to keep archives or make an unalterable audit trail, no medium keeps you as honest as CD-R. At that, CD-R is much like an older technology called WORM, which stands for Write-Once, Read Multiple times (or Many times). In fact, CD-R systems are refinements of the WORM concept with a different disc package (actually, the lack of the package, as WORM systems permanently encased their optical discs in plastic cartridges). The underlying technology is much the same.

That makes a CD-R disc entirely different from an ordinary CD. The CD-R disc relies on exotic compounds sealed underneath the clear acrylic outer layer of disc. A laser beam reacts with the inner media of the CD-R disc and blasts spots dark, forever changing the disk. The pattern of light and dark spots made by the laser correspond to pits of an ordinary CD and the bits of the data that's stored. Instead of digging a pit, the CD-R works by chemically darkening or evaporating the reflective medium inside their disks.

CD-R discs are not duplicated as readily as ordinary CDs. They have no stampable pattern of pits. With their optical medium safely sealed under plastic, the only way to duplicate a CD-R is by running disks through the CD-R drive one at a time. Every CD-R disk must be written individually. Each disk is either an original—or that wonderful oxymoron, an original copy. The discs themselves are no more indestructible than any computer medium you can throw in the fireplace. But the CD-R medium has a life comparable to that of mechanically stamped CDs. Although the medium is generally credited with a 10-year life span, the data you store will outlast the computer that you created it on—and maybe even you.

Price may also give you reason to think twice about using CD-R to distribute multimedia— where stamping an ordinary CD costs little more than 25 cents, a blank recordable CD costs 50 or more times more!

Physical Format

As with other disk media, the CD divides its capacity into short segments called *sectors*. In the CD-ROM realm, however, these sectors are also called *large frames* and are the basic unit of addressing. Because of the long spiral track, the number of sectors or large frames per track is meaningless—it's simply the total number of sectors on the drive. The number varies but can reach about 315,000 (for example, for 70 minutes of music).

Large frames define the physical format of a Compact Disc and are defined by the CD-ROM media standards to contain 2352 bytes. (Other configurations can put 2048, 2052, 2056, 2324, 2332, 2340, or 2352 bytes in a large frame). The CD-ROM media standards allow for several data formats within each large frame dependent on the application for which the CD-ROM is meant. In simple data storage applications, *data mode one*, 2048 bytes in a 2352-byte large frame actually store data. The remaining 304 bytes are divided among a synchronization field (12 bytes), sector address tag field (four bytes), and an auxiliary field (288 bytes). In *data mode two*, which was designed for less critical applications not requiring heavy-duty error-correction, some of the bytes in the auxiliary field may also be used for data storage, providing 2336 bytes of useful storage in each large frame. Other storage systems allocate storage bytes differently but in the same large frame structure.

The four bytes of the sector address tag field identify each large frame unambiguously. The identification method hints at the musical origins of the CD-ROM system—each large frame bears an identification by minute, second, and frame that correspond to the playing time up to that point on a musical disc. One byte each is provided for storing the minute count, second count, frame count in binary coded decimal form. BCD storage allows up to 100 values per byte, more than enough to encode 75 frames per second, 60 seconds per minute, and the 70-minute maximum playing time of a Compact Disc (as audio storage). The fourth byte is a flag that indicates the data storage mode of frame.

In data mode one, the auxiliary field is used for error detection and correction. The first four bytes of the field stores an error-detection code, and are followed by eight bytes of zeros. The last 276 hold a layered error-correction code. This layered code is sufficient for detecting and repairing multiple-bit errors in the data field.

Extended Architecture, abbreviated XA, rearranges the byte assignment of these data modes to suit multi-session applications. In XA Mode 2 Form 1, the 12 bytes of sync and four of header are followed by an 8-byte subheader that helps identify the contents of the data bytes, 2048 of which follow. The frame ends with an auxiliary field storing four bytes of error detection and 276 bytes of error correction code. In XA Mode 2 Form 2, the auxiliary field shrinks to four bytes; the leftover bytes extending the data contents to 2324 bytes.

The bytes of the large frame do not directly correspond to the bit pattern of pits that are blasted into the surface of the CD-ROM. Much as hard disks use different forms of modulation to optimize both the capacity and integrity of their storage, the Compact Disc uses a special data-to-optical translation code. Circuitry inside the Compact Disc system converts the data stream of a large frame into a bit pattern made from 98 small frames.

Each small frame stores 24 bytes of data (thus 98 of them equal a 2352-byte large frame) but consists of 588 optical bits. Besides the main data channel, each small frame includes an invisible data byte called the subchannel and its own error-correction code. Each byte of this information is translated into 14 bits of optical code. To these 14 bits, the signal processing circuitry adds three merging bits, the values of which are chosen to minimize the low frequency content of the signal and optimize the performance of the phase-lock loop circuit used in recovering data from the disk.

The optical bits of a small frame are functionally divided into four sections. The first 27 bits comprise a synchronization pattern. They are followed by the byte of subchannel data, which is translated into 17 bits (14-bit data code plus three merging bits). Next comes the 24 data bytes, (translated in 408 bits), followed by eight bytes of error correction code (translated into 136 bits).

The subchannel byte actually encodes eight separate *subchannels*, designated with letters from P through W. Each bit has its own function. For example, the P subchannel is a flag that is used in controlling audio muting. The Q subchannel is used to identify large frames in audio recording.

As with hard disk, this deep structure is hidden from your normal application software. The only concern of your applications is to determine how the 2048 (or so) bytes of active storage in each large frame are divided up and used. The CD-ROM drive translates the block requests made by the SCSI (or other interface) into the correct values in the synchronization field to find data.

The basic addressing scheme of the Compact Disc is the *track*, but CD tracks are not the same as hard disk tracks. Instead of indicating a head position or cylinder, the track on a CD is a logical structure akin to the individual tracks or cuts on a phonograph record.

A single Compact Disc is organized into from 1 to 99 tracks. Although a single CD can accommodate a mix of audio, video, and digital data, each track must be purely one of the three. Consequently a disc mixing audio, video, and data would need to have at least three tracks.

The tracks on a disc are contiguous and sequentially numbered, although the first track containing information may have a track number greater than one. Each track consists of at least 300 large frames (that's four seconds of audio playing time). Part of each track is devoted to transition areas called pre-gap areas and post-gap areas (for data discs) or pause areas (for audio disks).

Each disk has a lead-in area and a lead-out area corresponding to the lead-in and lead-out of phonograph records. The lead-in area is designated track zero, and the lead-out area is track numbered 0AA(Hex). Neither is reported as part of the capacity of the disk, although the lead-in contains specially coded subchannel data that stores the table of contents of the disc. The table of contents lists every track and its address, which is given in the standard format of minutes, seconds, and frames.

Each track can be subdivided into up to 99 *indices* by values encoded in the subchannel byte of nine out of 10 small frames. Part of the data is packed into each of a sequence of nine small frames, but other data takes its place in the tenth. An index is a point of reference that's internal to the track. The number and location of each index is not stored in the table of contents. The pre-gap area is assigned an index value of zero. An index lets you target a place in a track—the beginning of a movement on an audio CD or a specific image on a data CD.

Standards

The Compact Disc medium has proven so compelling that everyone wants to use it. Unfortunately, everyone wants to use it in his own way. And everyone want to have his own standards. Not quite everyone gets his own standards, but nearly every application does. Moreover, as with other systems of PC mass storage, the standardization of CD-ROM occurs at several levels—hardware and software.

At the hardware level Compact Disc systems are governed by several different standards that depend on what the system will be used for. The industry standards are commonly known by the color of the cover of the book that governs them. These include (in spectral order):

Red Book, which describes CD-DA, the original Compact Disc application which stores audio information in digital form. The name Red Book refers to the international standard (ISO 10149), which was published as a book with a red cover (hence the name) to specify the digitization and sampling rate details including the data-transfer rate and the exact type of pulse code modulation used. Under the Red Book standard, two disc capacities are supported: one can hold 500MB of data or 63 minutes of music, the other 680MB of data or 74 minutes of music.

Green Book, which governs CD-I, Compact Disc-Interactive, developed by Philips in 1986 as a hardware and software standard for bringing together text, sound, and video on a single disk. Under the Green Book standard, CD-I uses Adaptive Delta Pulse Code Modulation to squeeze more audio on every disk—up to two full hours of full-quality stereo or 20 hours of monaural voice-quality sound. CD-I allows the audio, video, and data tracks to be interleaved on the disc so they can be combined by your PC into an approximation of a multimedia extravaganza.

Orange Book, the official tome that describes the needs and standard for CD-R, recordable Compact Disc systems, turning the otherwise read-only medium into a write-once or read/write medium so you can make your own CDs or use CDs as general-purpose mass storage medium.

Yellow Book, which describes the data format standards for CD-ROM disks, and includes CD-XA, which adds compressed audio information to other CD-ROM data. This is the most important standard for multimedia.

In addition, several manufacturers have tried to take the Compact Disc medium their own directions and have developed what are still proprietary standards which they hope will someday sweep through the industry (along with the product). Among these are the *Video Interactive System*, developed by Microsoft and Tandy Corporation; *CD-TV*, a proprietary video storage standard developed by now-defunct Commodore International; *MMCD*, a multimedia standard for hand-held Compact Disc players developed by Sony Corporation; and *PhotoCD*, a standard for storing high-quality photographic images developed by Eastman Kodak Company.

Although these hardware standards define Compact Disc formatting and data storage methods, they do not specify how your operating systems and applications will use the disk-based storage. They are like the low-level format of a hard disk. In dedicated hardware applications—like audio Compact Disc systems—that level of standardization is sufficient. Your PC, however, needs some means of finding files equivalent to the FAT and directory structure of ordinary disk systems.

Here's a look at the more important CD standards and systems:

CD-DA

Developed jointly by Philips and Sony Corporation, the CD-Digital Audio system was first introduced in the United State in 1983. The standard CD-DA disc holds up to about 70 minutes of stereo music with a range equivalent to today's FM radio station—the high end goes just beyond 15 KHz; the low end, nearly to DC. The system stores audio data with a resolution of 16 bits, so each analog audio level is quantified as one of 65,536 levels. With linear encoding, that's sufficient for a dynamic range of 96 decibels, that is $20\log(2^{16})$. To accommodate an upper frequency limit of 15 KHz with adequate roll-off for practical anti-aliasing filters (which eliminate supersonic frequencies produced in the digital audio process), the system uses a sampling rate of 44.1 KHz.

Under the Red Book standard, this digital data is restructured into 24-byte blocks, arranged as six samples of each of a pair of stereophonic channels (each of which has a depth of 16 bits). These 24 bytes are encoded along with control and subchannel information into the 588 optical bits of a small frame, each of which stores about 136 microseconds of music. Ninety-eight of these small frames are grouped together in a large frame, and 75 large frames make one second of recorded sound.

In CD-DA systems, the large frame lacks the sync field, header, and error correction code used in CD-ROM storage. Instead, the error-correction and control information is encoded in the small frames. The necessary information to identify each large frame is spread through all 98 bits of subchannel Q in a given large frame. One bit of the subchannel Q data is drawn from each small frame.

From the subchannel Q data, a sector is identified by its ordinary playing time location (in minutes, seconds, and frame from the beginning of the disk). The 98 bits of the subchannel Q signal spread across the large frame is structured into nine separate parts: a 2-bit synchronization field; a 4-bit address field to identify the format of the subchannel Q data; a 4-bit control field with more data about the format; an 8-bit track number; an 8-bit index number; a 24-bit address counting up from the beginning of the track (counting down from the beginning of the track in the pre-gap area); eight reserved bits; a 24-bit absolute address from the start of the disk; and 16 bits of error correction code. At least 9 of 10 consecutive large frames must have their subchannel Q signals in this format.

In the remaining large sectors, two more subchannel Q formats are optional. If used, they must occur in at least 1 out of 100 consecutive large frames. One is a disc catalog number which remains unchanged for the duration of the disk; the other is a special recording code that is specific and unchanging to each track.

PhotoCD

Seeing the writing on the wall and in various books and magazines claiming that silver-based photography will disappear faster than free samples at the Federal Reserve Bank, Eastman Kodak Company developed the PhotoCD system as a way to bridge the gulf between classic cameras and modern video. Take pictures with your Nikon or Minolta, send the film to Kodak, and see the results on your television set.

Compared to lugging out the old slide projector, yanking out a reluctant screen, squaring things up, pulling the shades to make the room almost dark enough, and then having your last projector bulb flash out two seconds into the slide show, the PhotoCD sounds like a compelling idea. Video similarly simplifies soporific home-movie viewing. But you don't have to process videocassettes and you can recycle them. Moreover, PhotoCD targeted the slide-projection market—one dying its own ignoble death for other reasons. Its impact on the snapshot market proved negligible—after all, you can't put a CD or television screen in your wallet.

But PhotoCD has proven benefits. Not only is a slide-show on PhotoCD more convenient than wrestling with a Carousel projector, but the PhotoCD also gives you control and permanence. You can crop PhotoCD images electronically, and have your photofinisher print matching pictures. Better still, translating your color photographs to digital PhotoCD gives them added life. While the dyes used in most color photographic processes inevitably fade, even when the images are stored in the dark, the digital image data on the PhotoCD remains constant.

Although the PhotoCD hasn't instantly replaced the old home slide show, its success seems assured thanks to other applications to which people have put the technology. The PhotoCD serves as a catalog, exchange, and storage system for visual images. Professional photographers have embraced PhotoCD for distributing portfolios and preserving images without worries of shifting and fading colors. Graphic artists have found that the commercial PhotoCD system is a fast, inexpensive way of scanning photographs into a format compatible with their visual editing systems. Instead of tangling with a scanner and trying to maintain consistent color and quality, the PhotoCD system lets you give the difficult work to your photo finisher. Have a roll of film developed, and you can simultaneously get clear, uniform digital scans of every image, ready for incorporation in presentations, newsletters, and ransom notes.

Kodak's choice of Compact Discs for image storage was natural. They could capitalize on the familiarity, capacity, and longevity of the medium. But the PhotoCD system was not designed for mass production but for the writing of individual disks. Instead of requiring mastering at some stamping plant, Kodak envisioned ordinary photofinishers writing PhotoCD discs. Consequently, PhotoCD is based on CD-R technology. However, some PhotoCDs, such as those used to distribute stock photographs, are stamped out (but use the normal PhotoCD format).

At the hardware level, the PhotoCD system follows the Green Book standard of the Compact Disc-Interactive system. At the software level, however, it required bending the normal standards. The most important change required by the PhotoCD system is that the disc medium be capable of storing multiple sessions. That is, instead of the entirety of the disk being mastered all at once, you can add images to a partly used CD. This multi-session use frustrates the standard CD-DA system of encoding a catalog on the lead-in track because the track would have to be changed to reflect the additions to the disc—an impossibility with a write-once medium.

Color

Because Kodak envisioned standard television sets as the primary playback medium for the PhotoCD system, the company optimized the on-disc image format for television compatibility. Instead of breaking the image into red, green, and blue components, it is stored in luminance/chrominance form with one primary channel corresponding to brightness (Y) and two color signals (C1 and C2). This YCC format also makes image compression easier. Data loss in the C1 and C2 channels is much less apparent because of the human eye's low acuity in resolving colors (as opposed to brightness).

The PhotoCD process begins with the scanning of the original photographic images, positive (slides) or negative. The Kodak system uses a 36-bit scanning system that devotes a full 12 bits of resolution to each primary color. At this step, image processing standardizes basic color characteristics so that the image, no matter its origins, will reproduce properly on a standard television set (specifically, a screen that conforms to the recommendation for high-definition TV, CCIR 709). Because every film has its own spectral characteristics, the scanning system compensates using a *Scene Balancing Algorithm*—essentially a color look-up table—specific to each film type.

Instead of directly translating the brightness into digital values, the Kodak system uses a nonlinear transformation to optimize the range of brightness levels the system can accommodate. Table 12.1 shows the relationship between the reflectance of the original image (as revealed in the density of the film being scanned) to the encoded brightness level that's recorded.

TABLE 12.1. Relationship between brightness and code value in Kodak PhotoCD System.

Brightness	PhotoCD code value
1	8
2	16
5	34
10	53
15	67
20	79
30	98
40	114
50	128
60	141
70	152
80	163
90	173

Brightness	PhotoCD code value
100	182
107	188
120	199
140	215
160	229
180	243
200	255

So that specular highlights (bright reflections) and fluorescent colors in the original image will properly reproduce, the PhotoCD system encodes brightness values as high as 200 percent of white, defined by Kodak as "a perfect, non-fluorescent white-reflecting diffuser in the original scene." Photographic materials are designed to capture this brighter-than-white information, up to about 200 percent of the reference white point. In addition, this extended range also allows balance adjustments and other manipulations during the encoding process.

The math in the conversion from primary colors (red, green, and blue) signals to the luminance/chrominance format results in values that exceed the dynamic range of the brightness encoding possible within the constraints of the digital system chosen by Kodak. Consequently, the PhotoCD system uses more refined mapping, which compresses the brightness levels in excess of 100 percent. The playback system compensates for this compression of brightness values so that the levels reproduce properly.

Resolution

The PhotoCD system originally was designed to be hardware-specific. Consumers would buy a special PhotoCD player to connect to their television sets. To ease the price burden somewhat, PhotoCD players could also play back audio discs.

Compared to a modern PC, dedicated PhotoCD players are dumb. After all, were they smarter they would be computers. PhotoCD players are designed like audio machines—not to manipulate images but simply to reproduce them. Their most advanced controls allow lingering on one or another image or jogging across a disk to find a view you like. Consequently, the PhotoCD player has no complex image manipulation circuitry. However, Kodak wanted to provide the PhotoCD system with means of quickly reviewing a catalog of thumbnail images, producing TV quality images, storing high-resolution photographic quality images, and not waste time converting from one resolution to another. The logical solution was to put multiple copies of each image on a disc at different resolutions. The system need only recall the image of the required resolution without wasting time converting it or even reading through a larger data file. Compared to the needs for high-resolution images, the additional storage requirements of low-resolution pictures is minimal. The convenience gained and cost saved are large.

For consumer-quality PhotoCDs, the highest resolution of any image is 3072×2048 pixels, which translates to just under 100 lines per millimeter resolution across a 35mm slide.

Because the PhotoCD system was designed primarily for playback through television sets, the resolution for this level—768×512 pixels—is classed as its base image. Higher and lower resolution formats on the disc are classed by how much more or less information they contain. These include 4Base with resolution of 1536×1024 pixels and 16Base with photo-quality resolution of 3072×2048 pixels. 4Base images have 384×256-pixel resolution, and 16Base images have 192×128-pixel resolution. Professional PhotoCDs include one more higher resolution mode to accommodate the potentials of medium and large format film, 64Base with 6144×4096-pixel resolution. Table 12.2 summarizes the various image formats available in the PhotoCD system.

TABLE 12.2. Images resolutions under the PhotoCD system.

Format	Resolution
Base/16	192×128
Base/4	384×256
Base	768×512
4Base	1536×1024
16Base	3072×2048
64Base	6144×4096

Image Compression

The data of each of these images is grouped together into an *Image Pac*, which corresponds to a separate file on the disc. The five separate images in each consumer-level Image Pac would require 25,264,128 without compression. Kodak uses a successive-difference system to compress the image with minimal information loss. In effect, the original is first scanned at maximum resolution (16Base), then scanned at the next lower resolution (4Base). The lower resolution is extrapolated up to the higher resolution, and the differences between the extrapolated and actual images (called *residuals*) noted and recorded using a lossless Huffman code. This compression is repeated down to the Base image, which is stored uncompressed, as are the lower resolution Base/4 and Base/16 images. This compression of the high resolution images reduces the space needed for each Image Pac down to a range from 3 to 6.5MB. Foregoing compression at lower resolutions allows for faster rasterization and minimizes the need for in-drive intelligence in PhotoCD systems meant to playback through ordinary video displays which cannot handle the higher resolutions. The data for the high-resolution 64Base image for the Professional PhotoCD system is stored in the form of residuals in a separate file called the *Image Pac Extension*.

Every PhotoCD includes an on-disc image catalog, a set of thumbnail pictures, stored in a file called OVERVIEW.PCD as a collection of the Base/16 images on the disk. Each disc also includes a digital data directory in its lead-in track. When you use a disc for multiple sessions, the OVERVIEW.PCD file gets updated by building a new one on the disc. Kodak has not revealed the inner structure of the files used for the PhotoCD system.

CD-ROM

As its name implies, CD-Read Only Memory is fundamentally an adaptation of the Compact Disc to storing digital information—rock-and-roll comes to computer storage. Contrary to the implications of the name, however, you can write to CD-ROM discs with your PC, providing you buy the right (which means expensive) equipment. The discs have to be mastered somehow. For most applications, however, the CD-ROM is true to its designation—it delivers data from elsewhere into your PC. Once a CD-ROM disc is pressed, the data it holds cannot be altered. Its pits are present for eternity.

In the beginning, CD-ROM was an entity into itself, a storage medium that mimicked other mass storage devices. It used its own storage format. The kind of data that the CD-ROM lent itself to was unlike that of other storage systems, however. The CD-ROM supplied an excellent means for distributing sounds and images for multimedia systems, consequently engineers adapted its storage format to better suit a mixture of data types. The original CD-ROM format was extended to cover these additional kinds of data with its Extended Architecture. The result was the Yellow Book standard.

Format

The Yellow Book describes how to put information on a CD-ROM disc. It does not, however, define how to organize that data into files. In the DOS world, two file standards have been popular. The first was called High Sierra format, named after the hotel in which the first conference was held in hopes of hammering out the standard, the High Sierra Casino in Lake Tahoe, Nevada, in November, 1985. An even dozen companies participated in that original standard-setting conference: Apple Computer, Digital Equipment Corporation, Hitachi, LaserData, Microsoft, Philips, Reference Technology, Sony, TMS Incorporated, Videotools, Xebec, and 3M Company. They sought a common standard for digital storage on the Compact Disc medium and decided on one that combined the standard physical format used by audio disks with a file structure based on and compatible with the popular computer operating systems DOS, the Macintosh System, and UNIX. Later this format was upgraded to the current standard, the ISO 9660 specification.

Standards

The only practical difference between these two standards is that the driver software supplied with some CD-ROM players, particularly older ones, meant for use with High Sierra formatted disks may not recognize ISO 9660 discs. You're likely to get an error message that says something like `Disc not High Sierra`. The problem is that the old version of the Microsoft CD-ROM extensions—the driver that adapts your CD-ROM player to work with DOS—cannot recognize ISO 9660 discs. Of course, ISO 9660 drives can read High Sierra discs.

ISO 9660 uses a directory structure much like that of DOS, with filenames that look amazingly similar. Filenames are written with any alphabetic character A through Z, Arabic numbers from 0 to 9, and the underscore characters. ISO 9660 does not recognize lower case characters. Note that under DOS the characters @, &, and ~ can legally be used in filenames but cannot on ISO 9660 CDs.

Directory path names are specified with backslashes separating levels, just as in DOS. Under ISO 9660, paths are limited to eight levels deep, and a path name can have no more than 255 characters in it, including the backslashes. DOS has a variety of limits on the length of path names, depending on the function and version of the operating system. The most severe is a limit of 64 characters in its `Make Directory` function. These longer names are easily accommodated by the Windows 95 system, but must be truncated for handling by conventional MS (or PC) DOS.

To meld CD-ROM technology with DOS, Microsoft Corporation created a standard bit of operating code to add onto DOS to make the players work. These are called the DOS CD-ROM extensions, and several versions have been written. The CD-ROM extensions before Version 2.0 exhibit the incompatibility problem between High Sierra and ISO 9660 noted above. The solution is to buy a software upgrade to the CD-ROM extensions that came with your CD-ROM player from the vendor who sold you the equipment. A better solution is to avoid the problem and ensure any CD-ROM player you purchase comes with version 2.0 or later of the Microsoft CD-ROM extensions.

CD Drives

In that a computer CD-ROM player has the same basic job as a CD-Digital Audio machine in your home stereo, you'd expect the technology inside each to be about the same. In fact, all have similar mechanisms.

At one time, CD-ROM players were substantially more expensive than stereo models. Today, however, you can buy a CD-ROM player for little more than the stereo version. The high demand for multimedia capabilities has pushed volume so that economies of scale have really come into play. That's all the more amazing in that retrieving computer data is more demanding than playing Smashing Pumpkins or Harry Connick, Jr. A tiny musical flaw that might pass unnoticed even by trained ears could have disastrous consequences in a data stream. Misreading a decimal point as a number, even zero, can have disastrous consequences on calculations. To minimize, if not eliminate, such problems, computer CD-ROM players require different error correction circuitry than is built into stereo equipment—a system that uses much more powerful algorithms. CD-DA errors are corrected at the small frame level, 24 bytes at a time. CD-ROM data errors are corrected at the large frame level, 2048 or more bytes at a time. The CD-ROM system can thus correct for much longer errors in the data stream (which are more likely in a dense medium).

Compared to audio CD players, CD-ROM drives require more intimate control and faster access times. The toughest job a digital audio player faces is moving from track to track when you press a button. A CD-ROM player must skate between tracks as quickly as possible—in milliseconds if your human expectations are to be fulfilled.

Even the link between your PC and CD-ROM player complicates the drive and makes it more expensive. By itself a CD-ROM player does nothing but spin its disk. Your computer must tell the player what information to look for and read out. And your computer is needed to display—visually and aurally—the information the CD-ROM player finds, be it text, a graphic image, or a musical selection. Sending those commands requires an interface of some kind, in most cases either SCSI or ATAPI. Neither is needed (nor given to you) with a digital audio player.

Even though you get more with a CD-ROM drive, there's only one reason you need pay more than you would for an audio-only drive, to get higher performance. Today's best CD-ROM drives—the ones that you should really consider if you're serious about multimedia—run two, four, six or more times faster than audio CD drives.

Transfer Rate

Unlike music and video systems which require real-time playback of their data (unless you prefer to watch the recorded world race by as if overdosed on adrenaline), digital data is not ordinarily locked to a specific time frame. In fact, most people would rather have information shipped as quickly as possible from disc to memory.

For real-time playback, the original CD-Digital Audio system required a 150KB/second data transfer rate. In the data domain, however, that's almighty slow—one-quarter to one-tenth the throughput of a modern hard disk even after you account for all overhead. The transfer rate of a Compact Disc system is a direct function of the speed at which the disc itself spins. Increasing the data transfer rate requires higher rotation speeds. Consequently, most of today's CD-ROM players operate at multiples of the standard CD DA spin rate. Double-speed drives spin twice as fast to deliver 300KB/second transfer rates; triple-speed drives, 450KB/second; and quadruple-speed drives, 600KB/second In early 1995, Pioneer introduced the first drive to break the integer multiple rule, one that operates at a 4.4× rate for a raw transfer rate of 660KB/second.

Performance Issue

Raw transfer rate by itself does not guarantee optimum CD-ROM performance. The driver software, your operating system, and your applications all have to be matched to yield the best throughput. With DOS and the Windows 3.1 family, performance leveled off at about the 3× level. Even many 486-based PCs cannot handle CD-ROM data at the rate that triple-speed drives deliver it because of software overhead. With its improved driver and file system, Windows 95 can take advantage of the fastest CD drives.

Windows 95

High-speed drives can retain their compatibility with Red Book audio by buffering. They read the audio data at their higher rate and pump it into a buffer built into the drive. Then they unload the buffer at the real-time audio rate.

Access Time

Compared to magnetic hard disks, CD-ROM players are laggardly beasts. Mass is the reason. The optical head of the CD system is substantially more massive than the flyweight mechanisms of hard disks. Instead of a delicate read/write head, the CD-ROM player has a large optical assembly that typically moves on a track. The assembly has more mass to move, which translates into a longer wait for the head to settle into place.

Besides the mass of the head, the constant linear velocity recording system of CD-ROMs slows the access speed. Because the spin rate of the disk platter varies depending on how far the read/write head is located from the center of the disk, as the head moves from track to track, the spin rate of the disk changes. With music, which is normally played sequentially, that's no problem. The speed difference between tracks is tiny, and the drive can quickly adjust for it. Make the CD system into a random-access mechanism, and suddenly speed changes become a big issue. The drive might have to move its head from the innermost to outermost track, requiring a drastic speed change. The inertia of the disk spin guarantees a wait while the disk spins up or down.

Some old CD-ROM players required nearly a second to find and read a given large frame of data. Modern designs cut that time to 100 to 200 milliseconds, still about 10 times longer than the typical hard disk drive. In any case, you want the lowest possible access time for a CD drive; the fewer milliseconds the better.

Buffers

To smooth out transfers and to make audio playback possible with high-speed drives, all CD-ROM players incorporate built-in buffer memory. The buffer also helps trim your PC's overhead in running the drive. Using the buffer, the CD drive can accumulate data and send it as a quick burst instead of continuously tying up the bus.

The typical buffer on a modern CD-ROM player ranges from 64 to 256KB. The larger the buffer the better. The only penalty to increasing buffer size is cost.

Early disk-caching programs did not accommodate CD-ROM drives. Most modern caches do, including the latest incarnation of Microsoft's SMARTDRV.EXE. The Windows 95 CD File System incorporates intrinsic caching. Disk-caching software supplements rather than eliminates the need for buffering on CD-ROM drives. You need both for best performance and smooth audio and video playback.

Mechanism

Nearly all CD-ROM players fit a standard half-height 5.25-inch drive bay for one very practical reason: A 4.6-inch disc simply won't fit into a 3.5-inch drive slot. Drives can be internal or external, the latter usually including a power supply. The best choice is what works for you—internal for lower cost if you have expansion space inside your PC, external if you don't (for example, if you have a notebook computer).

Disk handling and how you get a disc into a CD-ROM player is an important aspect of drive design. Some mechanisms incorporate a sliding drawer much like that on most audio CD systems. The drawer slides out under the control of a either micromotor or spring. You simply drop the disc in and slide the drawer closed. The only important drawback to this design is that drives must be mounted horizontally lest the discs fall out.

Some CD-ROM players make the job even easier—and safer for your discs. You load your discs into a special carrier called a *caddy* which resembles the plastic jewel-box case that most commercial music CDs come in. When you want to load a disk into the CD-ROM player, you slide the whole carrier into a waiting slot. Most people buy a carrier for each CD-ROM disk they have because of this convenience and the extra protection the carrier affords the disk—no scratches and no fingerprints, guaranteed! If your CD system gets heavy use by younger folk or uncaring office personnel, use of a caddy will extend the life of your investment in CD media. Most drives that use caddies will operate either in horizontal or vertical orientation.

Buying Tip

Today three forms of caddies are used. The most common is used by Denon, Hitachi, some Matsushita, Sony, Toshiba, and newer NEC drives and most resemble a 3.5-inch floppy disk in a 5-inch clear package. Its single metal shutter slides back to let the drive optics see the disk. In general, you open the caddy by squeezing tabs at the end opposite the shutter to drop in a disc. The Philips-style caddy is clear smoked plastic. You open it by pressing two tabs and the CD slides inside between large white plastic pincers. The other style is that used by the old NEC CDR-77/88 drive, and has fallen from favor.

CD-ROM changers use multiple-disc cartridges exactly like those used by audio CD changers. The most popular size is the six-disc cartridge that was developed by Pioneer (which holds a patent on the technology). You'll find this multidisc cartridge identical to those used by six- and 18-disc audio CD changers, so you can get replacements inexpensively at the local stereo store.

Controls

The MPC specification requires a volume control on the front panel of any CD drive you have in your Multimedia PC. This control is useful if you decide to use your drive for playing back music while you work. You can plug headphones into the jack, also on the front of the drive, and use the volume control to adjust the loudness of the playback independent of the CD control software you run on your PC.

Other than the volume control, CD drives need no physical controls. All of their functions are operated by the software you run on your PC.

Interface

The connection between CD-ROM players and your PC also has been, for the most part, standardized. This connection has several aspects. In addition to the physical connection through a hardware interface, the drive also needs to link to your PC using driver software.

If you buy an already-configured Multimedia PC, you won't have to deal with the CD drive interface. Nor is it a concern from a performance standpoint. Standard equipment drives in today's PCs use either the SCSI or ATA (IDE) interface which have bandwidth more than adequate for the needs of a CD drive.

Control and Data Connections

If you're wanting to add a CD drive to your existing PC to move it into the multimedia area, you need to concern yourself with the hardware connection it makes with your PC. Most drives require three connections: one for control and data, one for audio, and one for power. For control and data movement, most CD drives use the same standard (or near-standard) system-level interfaces as hard disk drives.

SCSI

Most CD-ROM players use SCSI connections for their control and data signals. These connect exactly as SCSI hard disk drives do. Although the high performance of the SCSI interface is not necessary for handling CD-based data, it doesn't hurt. Moreover the SCSI connection gives you the option of connecting several drives to one host adapter.

Performance Issue

Many sound boards provide a suitable interface to match these SCSI CD-ROM players. The SCSI connection on sound boards is best avoided if you want to attach more than one SCSI device to your PC, however. Most sound board SCSI connections lack the high performance attributes of dedicated SCSI host adapters. If you try to plug in a hard disk or other peripheral to your sound board in addition to your CD-ROM player, you'll be disappointed. You'll probably have difficulty getting it to work. And if you do, the performance you'll get from a sound board SCSI port will be on the shy side of satisfactory, shortchanging the high-speed potentials of today's hard disks. Nor will you be able to boot from a hard disk connected to a sound card because such SCSI systems lack the ROM needed to add boot code to your PC.

You can install two SCSI host adapters in one PC by configuring them so that their resource needs do not conflict. Thus you can use the SCSI port on your sound board for a CD-ROM player and a separate, high-performance host adapter for your hard disk. Alternately, with the correct driver software, you can connect your CD-ROM player to the high performance host adapter used by your hard disk. The drive will allow program commands to get to the CD-ROM player without needing to go through the sound board.

The details of wiring a SCSI CD-ROM drive are the same as for a SCSI hard disk as discussed in Chapter 10, "The Basic PC—Hardware Essentials." You have to assign a SCSI ID to the drive, daisy-chain the cables between drives and host adapter, and properly terminate the SCSI chain. Then you get to worry about the drivers that you need—fortunately there's hope, see the following section.

Often you can use a SCSI-interface CD drive with notebook PCs by adding a PCMCIA-to-SCSI card. Slide the PC Card into a slot in your notebook PC, then plug the CD drive into the card's adapter cable.

IDE

The CD interface of choice is quickly becoming the AT Attachment (or IDE) connection long popular among hard disks. It combines more than adequate performance (CDs hardly strain even the slowest of IDE connections) with low cost and easy wiring. Using the AT Attachment Packet Interface, your system gets exactly the same degree of control over your CDs as with the more complex SCSI link.

Connecting a CD drive using the ATA/IDE system is a breeze. All you need is a few connectors on your IDE cable. If you already have two IDE hard disks in your PC, a secondary host adapter will give you the connection you need. Several manufacturers offer low-cost ($10 to $20) secondary adapters designed specifically for CD drives. The only rule you need follow is to be sure of the proper orientation of the IDE cable. Most cables and connectors are keyed to prevent inadvertent mis-insertion. In any case, the red or blue stripe on the edge of the ribbon cable indicates the side of the connector holding the lower numbered pins.

Parallel

You have exactly one reason to use a parallel connection for your CD drive—you have no other choice. The most common situation is with a notebook PC that makes no provision for an external IDE or SCSI connection and has no expansion slots into which you can install an adapter.

You might also use a parallel-interfaced CD drive if you have to share a single drive with multiple PCs. For example, you could use one parallel-interfaced drive to load software onto individual PCs. With the price of the basic CD drive falling to the $100 level, however, this strategy doesn't make sense in the long run. Some people might find parallel installation easier, but it doesn't cut the confusion of drivers, and the performance penalty can be large.

Performance Issue

Outside of these particular circumstances, you have two excellent reasons for avoiding CD drives with a parallel interface: they are expensive and they are slow. Parallel-interfaced CD drives are naturally external units. After all, that's where the parallel port is, on the back of your PC. You have to pay for a case and sometimes a power supply in addition to the basic drive to get the parallel interface. In addition, the garden variety parallel port is slow, unable to keep up even with the data rates of single-speed CD drives.

The performance of parallel-interfaced CD drives depends on both the speed of the drive and the type of parallel port you use. Linked to an ordinary (that is, PC-style unidirectional) parallel port, you can expect to get no more than a 75KB/second data transfer rate from *any* CD drive, no matter how fast it spins. A CD drive connected through a PS/2-style bidirectional parallel port should be able to push out data at about 250KB/second, not quite up to the speed of a normal 2X drive. With an Enhanced Parallel Port (or an Extended Capabilities Port) the primary speed limit shifts back to the drive.

Proprietary

At one time several manufacturers offered CD drives with their own host adapters which linked together using proprietary interfaces. These have fallen from favor, replaced by the ATAPI connection scheme. The only significant proprietary interface on the market is that used by Creative Labs to link its drive (usually made by Matsushita/Panasonic) to its sound boards. Although the Creative Labs interface is similar to the AT Attachment design, Creative Labs will not guarantee that other ATA devices will work with the connection or that the Panasonic drives designed for it will work with other ATA boards.

Buying Tip

Although this proprietary connection is effective, it forecloses on you from plugging in a better CD-ROM player—one with faster access or a higher transfer rate. Bottom line, the reason to avoid the proprietary connection is because it's proprietary.

Audio Connections

When you play CD audio through your sound board, the signal is analog not digital audio. The digital PCM data on the disk get transformed by digital-to-analog conversion circuitry that's built into the drive itself. This analog signal must somehow get transported to the sound board. The ribbon cable used by the control interface is a poor choice. The unshielded wire in close proximity to raucous digital signals would be particularly prone to picking up noise. Besides, none of the standard interfaces make provisions for analog audio signals.

Consequently, nearly all CD drives use a separate shielded cable for the stereo audio signals from the drive. Most drives have miniature white nylon three-pin connectors at the rear of their circuit boards for these signals. Your sound board has a matching connector. You only need run a short audio cable, usually supplied with the CD drive, between board and drive.

Power Connections

As with all disk drives, a CD-ROM player requires an electrical connection to power its circuitry and motors. CD drives use exactly the same power and connector as other disk drives, a four-pin white nylon Molex connector. The connector is keyed so that you can plug it in only one way, the right way.

The only problems you're likely to encounter with a power connector when plugging in a CD drive is not having a connector or forgetting to plug it in. If your Multimedia PC already has several disk drives of various types, you may run out of power connectors before you get your CD drive installed. The solution is to get a Y-cable from your dealer or favorite mail-order supplier. Forgetting to plug in the drive (which is especially easy to do when you don't have a free power connector) is certain to give you interesting error messages when you attempt to load your CD drivers. The drive light won't light. Nothing will happen. Nothing can without power to the drive. Avoid the surprise by taking an extra step and counting that you have all three necessary connections plugged into your CD drive.

Drivers

As with other peripherals, a hardware connection is not enough to bring a CD-ROM drive to life. It must be recognized by your software. While some operating systems naturally know how to work with SCSI ports and CD-ROM drives, others may require special driver software. As noted in Chapter 8, "Device Drivers," all operating systems require drivers of some kind. OS/2 Warp and Window 95 minimize your involvement with the driver software and do a respectable job of automatically configuring your CD drives.

With DOS and the Windows 3.1 family, however, you have to specifically load two drivers: one to match the IDE or SCSI port to your PC and a separate driver to match the drive to your operating system. For DOS and the Windows 3.1 family the latter driver takes the form of the Microsoft CD-ROM extensions, MSCDEX.EXE.

Windows 3.1x

MSCDEX.EXE is one of the most necessary and worst documented pieces of operating system software you normally have to deal with. You won't get help either with the DOS Help command or with the normal command-line help options /? or /H. Worse, half a dozen different versions are floating around in the marketplace, not all of which are compatible with all operating systems.

As noted in Chapter 8, most CDs require one or more drivers in CONFIG.SYS. A SCSI CD-ROM typically requires two, one general SCSI driver and a second driver for the CD-ROM. In addition to these drivers, you need to install MSCDEX.EXE in your AUTOEXEC.BAT file or whatever file you use to enable your CD-ROM drive.

A typical entry for MSCDEX.EXE might look like this:

```
LOADHIGH C:\DOS\MSCDEX.EXE /D:MSC_001 /M:4 /L:D
```

This command specifies loading the MSCDEX.EXE driver, assigns the name `MSC_001` to the CD drive, assigns the CD the drive letter D:, and uses about 8KB of RAM to buffer CD read operations. By loading this driver high, its impact on DOS memory is cut from about 36KB to 5KB. Table 12.3 summarizes the command line options available with most versions of MSCDEX.EXE:

TABLE 12.3. MSCDEX.EXE command line switches.

Switch	Requirement	Function
/D:[*name*]	Mandatory	Name of drive; must match that in CD-ROM device driver.
/L:[*drive letter*]	Mandatory	Assigns drive letter to CD-ROM drive
/M:[*number*]	Optional	Buffer size for caching CD data, in 2KB sectors
/E	Optional	Uses EMS memory
/K	Optional	Enables Kanji (Japanese) file structure
/S	Optional	Server switch, makes CD appear as local instead of network drive
/V	Optional	Verbose switch, adds diagnostic information display when loading

You can add multiple drive names to a single MSCDEX command by piling on multiple /D: switches followed by names matching those of the CD-ROM given in drivers in your CONFIG.SYS file. MSCDEX.EXE loads code for each driver, so the more names you pile on, the more memory it uses. Each name adds about 8KB to the memory used by MSCDEX.EXE.

The latest version of MSCDEX.EXE is 2.25, and it comes as standard equipment with PC DOS 7.0. The latest versions of MS DOS include 2.23. Version 2.22 is widely available from CD drive manufacturers (it came standard with MS DOS 6.0 and early releases of 6.20) and provides essentially the same functionality. Earlier versions do not and should be updated if possible.

In general, you should not need to worry about MSCDEX.EXE if you run Windows 95. Its CD File System serves in place of the CD-ROM extensions. CDFS has several advantages over MSCDEX.EXE: it uses 32-bit code, runs in protected mode, and takes advantage of Windows 95 disk caching. However, if your drive is not recognized (or if you need to make your CD-ROM work in order to *install* Windows 95, you may still need to load MSCDEX.EXE. Windows 95 should automatically eliminate it from your startup files for you after it installs its own drivers.

When running under Windows 95, you can check the driver that your CD system uses through Control Panel. Double-click the System icon and choose device manager. Among the devices listed on the screen should be your CD-ROM drive and CD-ROM controller (if you're using a dedicated controller). If you're using another interface, you should check under its host adapter.

When you double-click the CD-ROM Controller line, the first page you see will simply identify what kind of drive Windows thinks you have. Click the Driver tab, and you'll see the driver currently in use, as shown in Figure 12.1. Clicking the Resources tab to reveal the ports and other system resources used by the controller.

FIGURE 12.1. Windows 95 Device Manager showing the driver currently assigned to the CD-ROM Controller.

Windows 95 makes its best guess at the driver it should use for your particular controller and CD-ROM drive. Sometimes, however, several driver choices may be available for a particular hardware combination. If you click the Change Driver button, you'll see a window like that shown in Figure 12.2 through which Control Panel will let you see the driver choices for your hardware. When you click the name of the manufacturer of your hardware, Control Panel will list the compatible drivers that are available to the system. Simply choose the one you want. Alternately you can install a new driver from a floppy disk or CD-ROM (providing your CD-ROM works without the new driver!)

The CD-ROM drive listing in Device Manager takes you to a setup screen through which you can change the details of the operation of your drive. The first screen identifies what drive Windows 95 thinks you have installed. Clicking the Setting tab will flip to a page like that shown in Figure 12.3. In general, you'll want to leave the details of the Options selections alone unless you have a particular purpose in mind or think you know more than Windows does about the best way to run your drive.

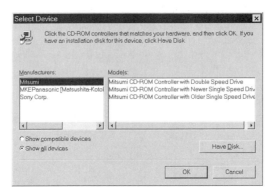

FIGURE 12.2. Windows 95 Device Manager's Change Drive window showing the available drivers compatible with the installed CD-ROM Controller.

The one setting with which you may want to tinker is the assignment and reservation of drive letters for your CD. Normally Windows 95 will assign the first available drive letter after your hard disks to your CD-ROM. You can alter its selection or assign multiple drive letters to CD-ROM use by altering the entries for Start and End drive letter.

FIGURE 12.3. Settings for the installed CD-ROM Drive as shown in Windows 95 Device Manager.

Loading the proper drivers should be sufficient to make your CD drive work, but it may not be enough to use a specific CD-ROM disc. Many CD-ROMs contain their own searching or operating software that you must run to read the data stored on them. This software may run from the DOS prompt, or (as is more likely with modern multimedia software) from within Windows or OS/2. You can usually setup CD software by selecting Run from the file menu or start bar, then browsing your CD-ROM drive for a file called SETUP or INSTALL.

If you have a profusion of CDs, you will likely discover that each publisher (and sometimes each product) will likely require its own control or data access software. If you acquire a lot of CD-ROM discs, you may overpopulate your system with a multitude of odd little icons, most of which won't work because you'll have the wrong disc in your drive. The moral to this story is not to try running a program unless you're sure you have the right disc in your drive—or you don't mind reading error messages.

Troubleshooting

Installing a new CD drive and getting it to work is usually a quick and easy process. You should be up and running within an hour. Sometimes, however, your new CD drive will prove recalcitrant. The causes of such problems are as varied as PCs, but several installation problems are common.

Trouble-shooting

Startup Problems

Some of most common problems when attempting to get a new CD-ROM installation to work are hardware-related, most often usually cabling problems. With IDE/ATA drives, connectors sometimes are not keyed, so you can plug in the cables improperly. Many motherboard IDE connectors lack a shell, enabling you to miss a full column or row of pins. Or you may plug in the cable backwards, with Pin 1 appearing where Pin 44 should be. The first step in troubleshooting is to double-check the wiring. SCSI has its own peculiarities, which are discussed in Chapter 10 under Hard Disk Drives. Improper termination sometimes results in obscure error messages, such as `CDR-103`.

Other strange error messages arise from dirty lenses on CD drives or dirty or scratched CD discs. Commercial lens cleaning kits for audio CD players will do the trick for CD-ROM drives. You can also clean CDs. Regular window cleaner works well. Lightly spray the disc, then wipe it clean with a soft, lint-free cloth (cotton is a good choice), stroking the disk radially from the center outward.

When you first install a CD-ROM drive in a PC, the message you're most likely to encounter is `Incorrect DOS Version`. This error arises from using an older version of the MSCDEX.EXE driver with a newer version of DOS. The usual culprit is that you've got more than one version of the driver on your hard disk—one that got installed with the CD software and one that came with DOS. The best one to use is the most recent version, of DOS or Windows, which should be installed in your DOS directory by default. Check your AUTOEXEC.BAT file, and ensure that it loads from the DOS directory. Even if you have an older DOS version, using the MSCDEX.EXE file in your DOS directory should assure you of the proper version number match.

When you get the error message `Disk Not High Sierra` or `CD is not High Sierra format or is not ISO-9660 format` on every disc you try, it's likely you're using too old a version of MSCDEX.EXE or have a physical problem with your drive—such as a bad termination or dirty lens. When you get this message only with a specific disc, the disc may need to be cleaned.

Audio Problems

Trouble-shooting

Problems playing back audio from CDs usually result from a loose or disconnected audio cable on your CD-ROM drive. If you've never heard audio from the drive, check to be sure both ends of the cable have been properly plugged in (and not inadvertently reversed). In most installations, the CD drive uses a separate audio cable that resembles nothing more than a thick, gray length of spaghetti. Insure that one end of the audio cable is plugged into your CD drive and the other end into your sound board. Sometimes, however, the failure to play back audio results from a lack of the proper driver or the driver improperly installed.

Windows 3.1x

This is particularly true when using the Windows 3.1 family. (OS/2 Warp and Windows 95 should automatically find and properly load the drivers you need.) Audio playback requires the Media Control Interface CD Audio driver, MCICDA.DRV. To ensure that you have the driver installed, open Control Panel and click Drivers. If you don't see the driver listed as installed, click Add and the MCI CD Audio driver. The driver is part of Windows standard equipment, so you should be prompted to insert the appropriate Windows distribution disk into your PC. If the driver is already installed, sometimes uninstalling then reinstalling it will cure playback problems.

Video Problems

Windows 3.1x

When running under the Windows 3.1 family, you'll sometimes encounter an error message that claims, `This AVI too large to be played in selected video mode`. This is often Windows' way of complaining that it cannot translate the image properly to cover the full screen. You can usually get the video to play by running Control Panel and clicking the icon for Video for Windows. In the driver configuration screen, change the selection from Full Page to Window, and you should be able to play the offending video.

Chapter 13

Images

Multimedia's greatest strength (indeed, its definition) is the bringing together of images and sound. That combination hides a number of other convergences that are implicit in multimedia technology. Nowhere are the challenges of combining seemingly similar technologies, which are faced by developers, designers, and users, more visible than in multimedia images. Certainly you can see all the problems—images that take on the wrong color or shape or become a confusing crazy-quilt of patterns unlike anything you've ever seen (or want to). But the trouble is more than skin-deep or just on your screen. Multimedia means the bringing together myriad imaging technologies that seem to be separated only by subtle distinctions but are actually worlds apart—still and moving images, drawings and bitmaps, text and pictures, and video and computer graphics.

Multimedia brings the convergence of two technologies that have coyly courted each other for more than decade—computer graphics and video.

Video deals with moving images, images that, until recently, almost always originated in reality, captured by the video camera. The only time motion stopped was when you hit the pause button or a television network decided to drive down its rating a half a dozen points. After all, television itself was the offspring of the movie industry, which descended from the theater—all of which involve motion. And all of which have conditioned us to expect action—with the result our rising expectations have granted us the action movie in which if something doesn't move you expect it to be part of the theater architecture.

Computer graphics have long been a technology of still images. Part of it is heritage. Computers are the offspring of office equipment. And the fodder of office equipment is paper. Nothing on paper moves, and in many offices the paper itself doesn't move for weeks at a time, at least when you're trying to get government approval or make an insurance claim. Computer graphics took on the primary characteristic of the charts and graphs that inspired, then generated, them—the chilling stare of stability. Of course, the ascent of multimedia has shown us the other reason computer graphics has dealt primarily with still images: making things move was just too much work—too much brainwork for programmers struggling just to make unmoving images, too much work for hardware that took seconds to paint a single screen.

Multimedia brings together computer graphics and video, still images and moving. Along the way, however, the multimedia systems crashes into nearly impassable frontiers, the land separating the standards used by the two technologies. Although both computers and video systems put images on monitor screens, they play their games by different rules so that a monitor made for one rarely works with the other and images made by one are ordinarily off-limits to the other.

Where's there's trouble, there's usually new products brewing, and multimedia images have inspired a wave of hardware and software tools that help build bridges between video and computer graphics. Today you can readily exchange images between the two technological worlds. Unfortunately crossing the board often requires a Visa—or MasterCard—and a credit limit high enough to inspire the awe of your neighbors.

Background

Seeing may be believing, but what you see isn't the whole story. Just as you can only see the surface of things and miss what's going on underneath, looking at an image on a monitor screen hides a wealth of technologies and concepts.

Human Vision

The best place to begin any discussion of images is where you and they meet, your eye. The ability and deficiencies of the human eye make computer graphics possible and movies acceptable.

Optically, the eye is a simple device. It uses a lens to focus light on an organ called the retina, which is comprised of nerve cells specially endowed with light sensitivity thanks to a protein called phototopin. When light reaches one of the retina's cells, it sends out a tiny voltage, a nerve impulse, that travels to the brain. On its way, the nerve impulse is compared and contrasted with the impulses from other retinal cells, and the optic system of your brain organizes the pulses to make sense from them so that you can see and recognize patterns and motion. Somewhere along the line your image of reality is created—a vast visual world that encircles you, filled with the tiniest details. Strangely enough, it's all an illusion.

At any given moment, your eye registers only a tiny part of that visual world. The eye actually perceives in detail only a tiny circle of the real world—that's all you see at any given moment. When you shift your attention to another part of your visual world, your eyes move to put it within its field of sharp vision. Because sharp vision occurs wherever your attention wanders, you get the illusion that you see the entire visual world sharply.

Moreover, that world looks like a continuous image without gaps or grain, even though only separate spots are registered on your retina by its cells. Your mind fills in the spaces between the dots. Scientists and philosophers can argue over the details of viewing the world as discrete nerve impulses. For you, however, the result of this process is more important because it lays a limit on the sharpness of human vision. At some point details blur together because when they are focused in your eye, they are smaller than the individual cells. In reality, other aspects of the eye further limit the sharpness of human vision, but one rule nevertheless holds: On-screen images that are sharper than you can see are just not necessary.

Your ability to see detail varies with the contrast and illumination. You see better in brighter light and you can better distinguish detail when it's in sharp contrast. Under the best conditions and looking at an image 10 inches from your eye under normal room illumination (about 10 foot-lamberts) you can expect to distinguish detail no finer than 1/20th millimeter (about 2/1000th inch). At normal viewing distances under typical viewing conditions, you'd be hard-pressed to distinguish two dots a 0.25 of a millimeter apart. This limitation is inherent to your eyes and, though it limits the detail you can see, it is a godsend to computer engineers. It makes the amount of visual information that must be managed by a PC within the range of possibility.

Moving Images

Even before Thomas Edison invented the motion picture in 1873, experimenters were exploiting one novel aspect of the persistence of vision to create the illusion of motion in images. Because people simply cannot see visual changes that occur faster than their visual systems bridge over, if you change an image quickly enough they won't see the individual changes. Instead, their eyes will average out the images over a period (about 1/15th second). Show a proper set of images, such a sequence of photographs of a changing scene, at that rate or faster, and people will see smooth continuous motion.

Movies work by putting a new image in front of your eyes every 1/24th second. (A shutter in the camera flashes each movie frame twice in that period, so most movies flicker at a rate of 48 Hz.) American television and video change frames 30 times per second, doubled through a technique called interlacing (discussed below) to 60 Hz.

This flashing is not apparent because of the inability of the human eye to resolve closely spaced individual flashes of light. This effect, termed the persistence of vision, allows a flashing light to appear constantly glowing if it flashes fast enough. Although some sources indicate a flash rate of 15 per second is sufficient to make most people see a continuous glow, some people see instability in images flashing at twice that rate. By the time the flash rate reaches about 50 times per second (50 Hz), however, nearly everyone sees a continuous glow.

Again, this facet of vision that might be classed as a defect is a blessing for the engineer. It not only makes motion pictures possible, but it enables you to live happily with fluorescent lights, televisions, and computer monitors all flashing and flickering away at a level below your threshold of perception.

Image Geometry

All computer and video imaging systems work by the same process, one analogous to the human eye. Every image is broken down into discrete parts called picture elements or pixels. A single pixel, sometimes called a dot, is the finest detail that the system is able to produce or reproduce. All images are made from patterns of pixels. The number of pixels in an image determines how much information it can convey, the total of all details that it can hold.

In general, display systems arrange pixels in rectangles. The resolution of the image describes the size of the display rectangle, usually expressed as the number of horizontal pixels by the number of vertical pixels. For example, a graphics image in the PC's basic VGA display system has a resolution of 640×480 pixels. Because a higher resolution image contains more information, it requires more memory to store and more bandwidth to transmit (in a given period).

The sharpness of the display image describes how tightly together pixels are packed and thus how sharply defined image details appear. Sharpness is expressed as the number of pixels that extend across a given distance, typically inches or millimeters. For example, a monitor image can be describe with a sharpness of 72 dots (or pixels) per inch. Sharpness is related to but not the same as resolution. Given two images of the same size, the one with the higher resolution will have higher sharpness because it will pack more dots per inch. Given two images of the same resolution, the smaller will appear the sharper.

Because your PC generates the image as an electrical signal completely independent from your computer monitor—it would make the same image no matter whether your monitor is connected to the computer at all—physical properties of the monitor (such as its physical dimensions) play no part in resolution measurements. In other words, the number of pixels in an image does not vary with the size of the screen that it is displayed upon.

Video

Images that you see differ from the input to your other sense organs in that they have two dimensions. The retina in your eye covers an area, while your ears (for example) receive a one-dimensional stream of information. The added dimension of images makes life interesting for those who would like to encode them electrically, store, and send them. If images were stored the same way as sounds, a television set could only make its screen brighter and darker. The problem is encoding. Recording and transmitting images requires more variables in the signal.

Televisions and computer systems use entirely different encoding methods. In television and conventional analog video signals, coding image information is a matter of timing. The position given to the information pertaining to a particular pixel of a picture depends on when that pixel's information occurs in the signal. Located at one instant in the signal, and a pulse might make a white spot in the upper left of the image. Delay the signal, and the image may shift right across the screen.

The principle is well-known to comedians—successful television is a matter of timing. All of the concerns of analog video are essentially matters of timing: special effects, the position of the picture on a monitor screen, even whether a monitor syncs up with the output of a video board. Timing is so important that, in critical applications, analog video cables must be cut precisely to length. Even though the electrical signals in cables travel at nearly the speed of light (186,000 miles or 300,000,000 meters per second), a one-foot difference in a video cable can make a discernible difference in an image. (At one time television stations matched the lengths of cables from cameras so that image color would not shift when switching between them.)

With computers, everything is a matter of math. Putting a pixel in a given place in an image requires only the right address. The only time timing becomes critical is when the computer system must match with conventional analog video technology.

Scanned Video Systems

When television was first created, engineers faced a big problem. A typical image comprises hundreds of thousands of pixels—a total of 307,200 pixels in a standard computer (VGA) graphic image, about the same in a television or video image. Because moving all the pixel data in an image at once would give electrical engineers a pain that all the milk of magnesia in the world would not make bearable, most transmission systems move pixels serially, one at a time. Images don't fit into disk files easily, either, because files are one-dimensional strings of bytes while images are two-dimensional. Moreover, you can't just send or store those pixels in any order. To properly reconstruct an image, whoever or whatever receives it must know how to arrange the pixels it receives. Sending and receiving, storing and retrieving systems need a common standard for serializing and deserializing pixels. We call those systems graphic (or video) standards.

For no other good reason than that we grew up reading left to right, top to bottom, the pixels in rectangular images are read in that order under most display standards. As a result the image is divided into horizontal lines of pixels, all of which are read sequentially. All of the lines in a image are sent one after the other to make the entire image or frame. This method of scanning an image is sometimes termed linear scanning because the scan sweeps linearly down the screen. It's also called progressive scanning.

The only aberration in the left-to-right, top-to-bottom scanning convention is the system used by conventional television sets and monitors. Because of the relatively primitive state of electronics when engineers developed the first commercial television standard in the United States, the lines of video and television images use interlaced scanning. Under the interlaced rubric, an image is scanned down from the top, but only every other line is skipped. That is, the system first scans line one, then line three, then line five, all the way to the bottom of the image. The process starts over again to complete the image by scanning the lines passed over the first time. A complete frame thus comprises two fields, one made from the odd-numbered lines, a second made from the even-numbered lines. In reconstructing the image, the two fields are woven together (interlaced) to make one frame.

From the standpoint of image geometry and resolution, interlacing makes no difference in what you see. Its advantages and disadvantages accrue only when the frequencies used in transporting and updating images come into play.

Refresh Rate

A single scan is sufficient to create an image: At least all the dots are there. Unfortunately, with most display technologies the dots don't stay there long. For example, on a conventional television picture tube (called a cathode ray tube or CRT by engineers and most computer folk) a single scan is nothing but a bright flash. Picture tubes are based on the exotic characteristics of a particular range of chemical compounds called phosphors that glow when struck by a high voltage beam of electrons. Physicists explain that phosphors glow because they absorb the energy from the electron and enter an excited or unstable high-energy state. To return to their stable rest state, they emit photons of light, usually within a fraction of a second of being excited. Touch the phosphor once with an electron beam, and it will flicker briefly. In order to continuously emit light, the phosphors must be continuously excited.

This complex process puts the engineer in a poor predicament. To produce a viewable image, the phosphors must glow continually. But to draw the image, it must be scanned with a narrow beam that touches each pixel individually. The beam must move. Physics comes to the rescue— all the phosphors don't immediately emit light photons; some delay a bit so that the collective glow of a pixel lasts a fraction of a second. This extended glow is called the persistence of the phosphor, and it can be tailored by adjusting the chemical composition of the phosphor. Short persistence phosphors glow for a few milliseconds; long persistence phosphors may glow for more than half a second. By assuring the electron beam strikes each pixel during the period that persistence makes the pixel glow, the moving electron beam can cause a continuous glow of the phosphor. After first painting an image across the frame, the electron beam repeats the chore for as long as you want to view the image, refreshing the image within the persistence period to keep the image constantly glowing. The period between two sweeps of the electron beam is termed the refresh rate of the image.

If all images were constant and unchanging, this system would work flawlessly. But if all you wanted were constant and unchanging images, you could paste a photograph on your monitor screen and forget all the complication of electron beams, phosphors, and energy states. Television images move; even supposedly "still" computer images change—for example when you scroll a screen full of text.

Lingering persistence is exactly contrary to the concept of motion. When part of an image moves, a long persistence will keep the glow going in the place from which the image moved long after it has gone. The result is a blurry ghost that trails behind every moving part of the on-screen image. This afterglow is particularly bothersome in images that seem as if they should still be like that old scrolling text.

Eliminating this afterglow requires tailoring the persistence of the phosphor to the rate at which the electron beam scans the screen. With a good match, the phosphors glow only long enough to bridge between scans, and you see little or no ghosting lingering behind moving images.

In reality, the story of the stable screen image isn't quite so simple. Phosphors don't glow constantly for the length of their persistence. They start bright and slowly fade.

Scanning Signals

When television was invented, the only suitable display system was the cathode ray tube. The signals used for scanning images had to be adjusted to compensate for some of the practical necessities of using CRTs and of the electronic circuits needed to control the CRT. The result was the system currently used for television sets and monitors for both computers and video systems today.

Retrace

CRT-based systems have particular signal requirements. To make the image you see, the electron beam in the CRT traces a nearly horizontal line across the face of the screen then, in an instant, flies back to the side of the screen from which it started but lower by the width of the line it already traced out. This quick zipping back is termed horizontal retrace and, although quick, it cannot take place instantly due to the inherent inertia in electrical circuits. Consequently, the smooth flow of bytes must be interrupted briefly at the end of each displayed line (or else the video information would vanish in the retrace). The video controller must take each retrace into account as it serializes the image.

In addition, another variety of retrace must occur when the electron beam reaches the bottom of the screen when it's finished painting a screen-filling image: vertical retrace. The beam must travel as quickly as possible back up to its starting place, and the video controller must halt the flow of data while it does so.

Blanking

During retrace, should the electron beam from the gun in the tube be on, it would paint a bright line diagonally across the screen as the beam returns to its proper position. To prevent the appearance of this distracting line, the beam is forcibly switched off, not only during retrace but also during a short interval on either side to give the beam time to stabilize. The interval in which the beam is forced off and cannot be turned on by any degree of programming is called blanking because the electron beam can draw nothing but a blank on the screen.

Most computer monitors don't fill their entire screens with data. They center (or try to) the image within darkened borders to minimize the image distortions that sneak in near the edges of the screen. To produce these darkened, protected areas, the electron beam is held at the level that produces a black image for a short while before and after the data of each image line is displayed. These short intervals are termed the front porch and back porch of the signal. If you examined the signal, you'd see that it dips down for blanking, pops up to an intermediate height (called black level to create the porches between blanking and data. Use your imagination and the black-level signals look like shelves—or porches.

Television and video signals also feature front and back porches. You don't see the effects as a black border around the screen because consumer television set and video monitors display overscanned images. The electron beam inside the CRT is deflected so that it starts its image trace well beyond the screen edge. The signal for the black border from the front porch and even the first few pixels of the image are blasted off to the left of the edge of the screen, so when the electron beam reaches the edge, it's already sending out images. The black border is suppressed. Similarly, the trace extends beyond the right, top, and bottom edges of the screen.

Professional television and video monitors often have a switch to permit them to view underscanned images so they can judge the quality of every pixel. Pressing the "underscan" button puts a big black border around the screen which shows the entire active image area (and then some). Both the cause and effect are the same as with computer monitors.

Vertical Interval

The period while the screen is blanked during the vertical retrace is called, appropriately, the vertical interval. Its physical manifestation is the wide black horizontal bar that's visible between image frames when your television screen or computer monitor picture rolls and requires adjustment of the vertical hold control.

The vertical interval causes an effect similar to the underscanning of the image. Because the electron beam is kept in constant synchrony, it must continue to scan even when the monitor screen is blanked. As a result, a number of scan lines are rendered invisible during the vertical interval. In standard NTSC video, about 45 lines are blanked. The result is that although the NTSC standard allows for 525 lines, only about 512 contain picture information and about 480 are actually visible in an on-screen image.

Synchronizing Signals

The electron beam in the monitor is swept across the screen by a combination of magnetic fields. One field moves the beam horizontally, and another vertically. Circuitry in the monitor supplies a steadily increasing voltage to two sets of deflection coils to control the sweep of the beam.

These coils are electromagnets, and the increasing voltage causes the field strength of the coils to increase and deflect the beam farther. At the end of the sweep of a line, the field that controls the horizontal sweep of the electron beam is abruptly switched off, returning the beam to the starting side of the screen. Likewise when the beam reaches the bottom of the screen, the field in control of the vertical sweep switches off. The result is that the electron beam follows a tightly packed zigzag path from the top of the screen to the bottom.

The primary difference between the two sweeps is that several hundred horizontal sweeps take place for each vertical one. The rate at which the horizontal sweeps take place is called the horizontal frequency or the line rate of the display system. The rate at which the vertical sweeps take place is called the vertical frequency or frame rate of the system because one complete image frame in created every time the beam sweeps fully down the screen.

The electronics that generate the sweep frequencies used by a monitor are inside the monitor itself. However, the signals themselves must be synchronized with the data stream coming from the computer so that characters appear at their proper positions on the screen. Lose sync, and the ordinarily orderly screen display takes on the countenance of the Tower of Pisa—or the present day appearance of the Colossus at Rhodes.

To keep things organized, the video controller sends out special synchronizing signals, one kind—horizontal sync—before each line is sent to the display, and another—vertical sync—before each frame. The monitor detects these synchronizing signals and knows to reset its sweep to the beginning of a line or frame.

Color

A color video image has the same underlying construction as monochrome. Images are built from stacked lines of pixels. They are scanned and the information is moved serially.

The difference between color and monochrome in video starts when the image is made. Whatever the camera sees is optically separated into three signals representing the primary colors of light, usually described as red, green, and blue. The three signals are synchronized with one another, and the synchronization carefully maintained throughout professional video systems.

To television signals, color is an interloper, someone who jumped on the bandwagon well after it started on its journey. Television started out without color. After all, getting any image at all was enough of an accomplishment when television was being developed in the 1920s. When television broadcasting was authorized, no signal space was left for color. After all, even without color a single television station stole six times as much spectrum space as did the entire Standard Broadcast band—all the AM radio stations in the country.

Color finally came to television in 1953, but it was added almost as an afterthought. The overriding concern at the time was compatibility with monochrome television sets. After all, somewhere around 100,000 monochrome television sets had been sold before the color standard was made official. To assure backward compatibility with existing television sets, color was relegated to the role of a *subcarrier*, a signal that monochrome sets could safely ignore and that color televisions could, with some difficulty, recover.

Although using a subcarrier for color need not be bad in itself, another requirement of backward compatibility was: the color television signal was allowed no more bandwidth, no more space on the radio spectrum, than the original monochrome signals. Something had to go, and it did. Resolution in conventional color video signals fall apart in color, particularly in the red region. Considering the technology of 1953, however, color television was a miracle.

RGB

In television or video, color signals start by separating an image into three primary colors, generally considered to be red, green, and blue. A video camera makes this separation optically (as described in the next chapter), and develops three separate signals. One corresponds to the red image; one green; one blue. These three signals, together with one or two synchronizing signals, make up the RGB video used in professional applications.

The synchronizing signals usually are arrayed one of three ways. A composite sync system combines the horizontal and vertical synchronizing signals into one that can be carried across a single wire. A complete composite sync system requires four cables: one for each color, and one for sync. Separate sync leaves the two sync signals independent and sends them down separate wires, so a complete hook-up requires five cables. Sync-on-green combines the composite sync signal with the green color signal so that you need only three connections for a complete color system. This combination works because the sync signals and image information occur at different times (or positions in the waveform) so they never become confused. (Remember, television is mostly a matter of timing!)

Composite Video

Television posed the problem that these three, four, or five signals must be squeezed into only one that would fit in the place of an ordinary monochrome signal. To find a answer to this challenge, a new organization called the National Television Standards Committee, or NTSC, sought out the best means of fitting color into television signals.

Engineers found a way by combining and manipulating the signals. For three independent variables—three colors—they needed three signals, but these signals could be mathematical combinations from which individual color signals could be derived.

For compatibility with monochrome, they combined all three signals together. This produced a signal they called *luminance*, which encoded all the brightness information in the television image. The luminance signal was essentially a monochrome signal and produced an entirely compatible image on black-and-white television sets. The name of the luminance signal is often abbreviated as Y.

The other two signals represented difference information—the difference between luminance and the red signal and the difference between luminance and the blue signal—which allowed the reconstruction of the original red and blue signals. Subtract red and blue from the luminance signal, and the remainder was green. This method of encoding colors assured monochrome compatibility. In the NTSC system the difference signals are called I and Q. They sometimes wear other names; in computer graphics they are more often familiar as U and V. The signals together create the *YUV color system.*

Unfortunately, making this combination of signals does nothing to reduce the needed bandwidth. After all, the manipulation still leaves three full-bandwidth signals. The next step that the NTSC used was to combine the two difference signals into a single signal that can carry all the color information, one called *chrominance* (abbreviated as *C*). Engineers developed a process called quadrature modulation to combine the two signals into one. The result is that colors are encoded into the chrominance signal as a phase angle.

Together the luminance and chrominance signals provide a guide to a map of colors, a polar chart. The chrominance encodes the angle between the color and the X-axis of the chart, and the luminance indicates the distance from the origin to the color.

To fit the chrominance signal in where only luminance should fit, engineers resorted to putting chrominance on a subcarrier. That is, they modulated a carrier wave with the chrominance signal, then added it to the luminance signal. The result is called the NTSC composite video signal or NTSC video for short.

The NTSC chose a frequency of 3.58 MHz as the color subcarrier frequency. The result is an amplitude modulated signal centered on 3.58 MHz. To avoid interference with the luminance signal, the NTSC process eliminates the carrier and lower sideband of the chrominance signal after the modulation process.

The NTSC process has two drawbacks. The luminance signal must be cut off before it reaches 3.58 KHz to avoid it interfering with the subcarrier. This frequency cap limits the highest possible frequencies in the luminance signal, which means that the sharpness of the image is reduced from what it would be using the full bandwidth (4.5 MHz for the video signal) of the channel. Worse, there's even less room for the chrominance signal, putting an even harsher limit on image detail. Fortunately, the detail in the luminance (black-and-white) image masks much of the lack of detail in the chrominance, so the shortcomings are not objectionable to the human eye.

S-Video

Because television signals are broadcast over the airwaves, governments have begun stepping in to regulate them to prevent chaos. Before the United States began to regulate broadcasters, even the few radio stations that were on the air showed what would happen if the broadcast marketplace were left to itself. Every broadcaster chose his own frequency, power for transmission, even level of modulation with little concern for other broadcasters. No one cared about interference, except the people trying to listen in who heard audio goulash. The first concern in regulating broadcasters has always been the minimization of interference. But soon the goal became more far-reaching—assuring that you could receive the widest possible range of signals (expanded in more modern times with the emphasis on minority ownership of many broadcasting stations to ensure that you receive the widest possible range of viewpoints). Promulgating (and enforcing) technical standards has been one result of that policy.

By their nature, these standards are conservative. The audience using current technology will always be larger than the audience for future technologies—until the future technologies become current. This approach led to the adoption of the NTSC broadcasting standard. It also keeps television locked to that standard.

Video signals that never make it to the airwaves need not suffer the indignities of broadcast standards. They also leave experimenters free to tinker with the signals for whatever end they hope to reach. As a result, advanced technologies now flourish everywhere except in broadcasts. Signals traveling in wires no longer conform with broadcast standards. Professional videotape has moved to digital technology. Recorded images have broken free from synchronous operation.

Although some studio signals have always transcended broadcast standards (RGB signals have been common since the development of color television), only with the VCR revolution has a new consumer video wiring standard developed. Called S-Video for "separate video," this standard breaks through the biggest shortcoming of the NTSC composite video signal with minimal changes in existing equipment.

The part of the NTSC process that most limits visual quality is the squeezing of the color signal onto its subcarrier. One place the PAL system gets superior color is by upping the subcarrier frequency, allowing for greater bandwidth in both the luminance and chrominance signals.

S-Video eliminates the subcarrier entirely by providing two separate channels for the two video signals, luminance (or Y) and chrominance (C), consequently the system or its signals are often termed Y/C. Both luminance and chrominance are unlimited in their upper frequency and thus resolution (at least by the cable) by keeping the two separate. The difference is dramatically apparent on quality equipment.

Otherwise the color encoding method used by S-Video is identical to that of NTSC. The three RGB color signals are combined into luminance and chrominance using exactly the same formulae. Although you cannot substitute one signal for the other (if just because you can't cram two S-Video connections in the place of one NTSC), the innards of S-Video monitors need not be radically different from those of NTSC displays.

Performance Issue

Note that once a signal is encoded as NTSC, information is irretrievably lost. There's no point to decoding an off-the-air television signal to S-Video. The only time S-Video helps is when you have a source of the signals that has never been NTSC encoded. Some videocassette recorders and LaserDisc players provide such signals. Better quality video monitors have S-Video inputs to take advantage of these higher-quality outputs.

International Standards

NTSC composite video modulates the carriers of all television broadcasters in North America, Japan, and several other nations. But it is far from an ideal solution.

PAL: European nations got into color television in the late 1950s—long after the United States—so they had the benefit of hindsight. They added a twist to the signals they used for color television. By reversing the phase of one of the chrominance signals (R-Y) after every scan line, they were able to make the color in image more stable. Any phase distortion that arises during the broadcast of such a signal can be reduced by the use of a simple delay line in a television receiver. Signals that use this method of color modulation are termed PAL for *Phase Alternating Line*. Instead of a 3.58 MHz subcarrier, most PAL systems use a subcarrier frequency of 4.43 MHz. This also improves image quality because it allows the chrominance signal a wider bandwidth.

SECAM: In 1959 France developed its own system, called *Sequence Couleur à Memoire* (in English, sequential color with memory) but more commonly known by its abbreviation, SECAM. Instead of one quadrature modulated color subcarrier, SECAM uses two FM subcarriers. The luminance portion of its signal is the same as PAL.

Most PAL and SECAM systems also differ geometrically from the NTSC standard. When television was developed in the United States, it was based on a 30 Hz frame rate or 60 Hz field rate, which could easily be derived from the 60 Hz power line frequency. By the time NTSC was working, the desirability of synchronizing televisions to the power line frequency was doubtful, so the NTSC adopted a slight variation, using a field rate of 59.94 Hz.

European nations use a power frequency of 50 Hz, so it was natural for them to develop their own television standards based on a 50 Hz field rate. The slower field rate allows more lines in the same bandwidth of signal, so both PAL and SECAM chose to use 625 lines per frame as opposed to the 525 specified by NTSC. Consequently, the number of pixels on a PAL or SECAM screen is almost 40 percent higher (about 20 percent greater horizontally and vertically) and images look sharper. Moreover, because the PAL and SECAM standards were developed with color in mind, they allow a greater bandwidth for their color signals, making them even sharper. In South America, two hybrid formats, PAL-M and PAL-N, combine PAL technology with NTSC timings. Table 13.1 summarizes the characteristics of the major television standards used in the world today.

TABLE 13.1. International television standards.

Standard	Name	Field rate	Frame rate	Lines per frame	Subcarrier modulation	Subcarrier frequency	Audio carrier offset	Channel bandwidth
NTSC	National Television Standards Committee	59.94	29.97	525	AM	3.58 MHz	4.5 MHz	6 Mhz
PAL	Phase Alternating Line	50	25	625	AM	4.43 MHz	6 MHz	8 MHz
PAL-M	Phase Alternating Line	59.94	29.97	525	AM	4.43 MHz	6 MHz	8 MHz
PAL-N	Phase Alternating Line	50	25	625	AM	3.58 MHz	4.5 MHz	6 MHz
SECAM	Sequence Couleur a Memoire	50	25	625	FM	4.43 MHz	6 MHz	8 MHz

Unfortunately, the different number of pixels alone is sufficient to guarantee incompatibility with NTSC television and video, and the different frame rates clinches it. Videotapes must be translated to move them between the two standards using a device appropriately called a standards converter. The equipment to make the conversion is expensive—professional quality gear can cost tens of thousands of dollars. A television, video monitor, camera, or videocassette recorder designed for NTSC won't work with PAL or SECAM broadcasts of video tapes. The opposite also applies. If you travel or plan to ship videotapes abroad, you'll have to be careful about the standard you and your recipient use. Table 13.2 lists the standards followed by most of the nations of the world.

TABLE 13.2. Television standards used in various nations.

Nation	Standard	Nation	Standard
Afghanistan	SECAM	Lebanon	SECAM
Albania	PAL	Lesotho	PAL
Algeria	PAL	Liberia	PAL
Angola	PAL	Libya	SECAM
Argentina	PAL-N	Lithuania	SECAM
Australia	PAL	Luxembourg	PAL

Nation	Standard	Nation	Standard
Bahrain	PAL	Madagascar	SECAM
Bangladesh	PAL	Malawi	PAL
Belarus	SECAM	Malaysia	PAL
Belgium	PAL	Maldives	PAL
Benin	SECAM	Mali	SECAM
Bermudas	NTSC	Malta	PAL
Bolivia	NTSC	Mauritania	SECAM
Botswana	PAL	Mexico	NTSC
Brazil	PAL-M	Monaco	PAL
British Virgin Islands	NTSC	Mongolia	SECAM
Brunei	PAL	Montserrat	NTSC
Bulgaria	SECAM	Morocco	SECAM
Burkina Faso	SECAM	Mozambique	PAL
Burma	NTSC	Netherland Antilles	NTSC
Burundi	SECAM	Netherlands	PAL
Cameroon	PAL	Nevis	NTSC
Canada	NTSC	New Guinea	PAL
Central African Republic	SECAM	New Zealand	PAL
Chad	SECAM	Nicaragua	NTSC
Chile	NTSC	Niger	SECAM
China (People's Republic)	PAL	Nigeria	PAL
Colombia	NTSC	North Korea	PAL
Congo	SECAM	Norway	PAL
Costa Rica	NTSC	Oman	PAL
Cuba	NTSC	Pakistan	PAL
Cyprus	SECAM	Panama	NTSC
Czech Republic	SECAM	Paraguay	PAL-N
Denmark	PAL	Peru	NTSC
Djibouti	SECAM	Philippines	NTSC
Dominican Republic	NTSC	Poland	SECAM
Ecuador	NTSC	Portugal	PAL
Egypt	SECAM	Qatar	PAL

continues

TABLE 13.2. continued

Nation	Standard	Nation	Standard
Equatorial Guinea	PAL	Romania	PAL
Estonia	SECAM	Russia	SECAM
Ethiopia	PAL	Rwanda	SECAM
Faroe Islands	PAL	Saudi Arabia	SECAM
Finland	PAL	Senegal	SECAM
France	SECAM	Sierra Leone	PAL
Gabon	SECAM	Singapore	PAL
Germany	PAL	Slovakia	SECAM
Ghana	PAL	South Africa	PAL
Gibraltar	PAL	South Korea	NTSC
Great Britain	PAL	Spain	PAL
Greece	SECAM	Sri Lanka	PAL
Greenland	PAL	Sudan	PAL
Guatemala	NTSC	Surinam	NTSC
Guinea	SECAM	Sweden	PAL
Haiti	NTSC	Switzerland	PAL
Honduras	NTSC	Syria	PAL
Hong Kong	PAL	Tanzania	PAL
Hungary	SECAM	Thailand	PAL
Iceland	PAL	Togo	SECAM
India	PAL	Tunisia	PAL
Indonesia	PAL	Turkey	PAL
Iran	SECAM	Uganda	PAL
Iraq	SECAM	Ukraine	SECAM
Ireland	PAL	United Arab Emirates	NTSC
Israel	PAL	United States	NTSC
Italy	PAL	Uruguay	PAL-N
Ivory Coast	SECAM	Venezuela	NTSC
Jamaica	NTSC	Vietnam	SECAM
Japan	NTSC	Yemen (No. & So.)	PAL
Jordan	PAL	Yugoslavia	PAL

Nation	Standard	Nation	Standard
Kazakhstan	SECAM	Zaire	SECAM
Kenya	PAL	Zambia	PAL
Kuwait	PAL	Zimbabwe	PAL
Latvia	SECAM		

Recording

By the time television had become commonplace, sound recording was a proven and alluring art. Engineers wanted to capture television images the same way that they could sound and music. The tape recorder was the target technology because tape was inexpensive, reusable, easily edited, and instantly reviewable. Because both recorded sound and television were basically the same stuff—analog electrical signals—capturing pictures to tape was assumed to be possible.

Practicality was the problem. The highest frequency that can be recorded in a tape systems depends on the tape speed—the faster the tape, the higher the frequencies that can be recorded (because the faster tape stretches out the waveforms). The problem is that the technology at the time recorded about 1,000 bits per inch. Sound, with a top frequency of 15,000 Hz, was recorded with tape traveling at 15 inches per second. All else being equal, video, with a top frequency around 4,500,000 Hz, would need a tape speed of 4,500 inches per second (that's more than the length of a football field). A standard reel of tape would last about five seconds.

An inspired idea led to the first practical video tape recorder: the absolute tape speed is not important. Rather, the relative speed between the head and tape limited the upper frequency. Moving the head in relation to the tape would be equivalent to speeding up the tape. Move the head fast enough, and video could be recorded at a reasonable tape speed.

The first videotape machines made the head move nearly perpendicular to the tape movement. Machines that used this technology were the mainstay of professional video recording for more than 20 years. Called by video professionals *quad tape* (for quaduplex recording because the signal was divided into four parts, and each part was assigned to a separate head), these machines used two-inch tape wrapped around about a quarter of the way around a set of four fast spinning heads so that one head was constantly in contact with the tape. The machine switched to the video signal from the head in contact with the tape. Each pass of a head recorded only a small part of a frame, so the signals from the four heads had to be carefully balanced.

The four-head problem was eliminated by extending the head path across the tape to the length of an image field. To do so, the tape machine wound the tape at a slight angle around a large drum in which two heads spun. In these machines, the head traces out a section of a helix against the tape, so the resulting process is called *helical scan recording*. Different companies have developed many helical-scan formats. Several have been used by video professionals who are now switching to digital formats. Two helical formats are popular in commercial and home video,

VHS (for Video Home System, developed by Japan Victor Corporation, JVC) and *8-millimeter tape* (developed by Sony Corporation). Although the older Sony Beta tape system is still used, consumers have relegated it to the same esteemed position given 8-track car stereos.

In a helical scan recording system, the rotating heads are mounted on a drum. The tape wraps around the drum outside its protective cartridge. Two arms pulls the tape out of the cartridge and wraps it about halfway around the drum. So that the heads travel at an angle across the tape, the drum in canted at a slight angle, about 5° for 8mm systems.

An 8mm video cassette resembles an audio cassette in that it has two hubs within its plastic shell, but the tape is much wider (8mm, of course, that's 0.315 inch compared to 0.150 inch for cassette tape) and a hinged door on the cassette protects the tape from physical damage. The cassette itself measures 3.75-inch by 2.5-inch and about half an inch thick.

In the 8mm system, the head drum rotates at 1,800 revolution per minute while the tape travels past it at 10.89mm/second to achieve a track density of 819 per inch and a flux density of 54 kilobits per inch.

Only a few professional videotape recorders achieve speed high and stable enough to permit direct recording of NTSC composite video in its pure encoded form. Consumer video recorders don't have sufficient bandwidth to record the highest frequencies of video information. With unadulterated composite video, this shortcoming would translate to a total lack of color.

Engineers solved this problem by separating the luminance and chrominance subcarrier signals in composite video before recording them. They then down-converted the chrominance subcarrier (without decoding it) to reduce the frequency of the 3.58 MHz subcarrier so that it was lower than the frequencies used by the luminance signal. Then they combined the down-converted chrominance back in with the luminance to create a color-under-video signal less sensitive to color degradation.

VHS videocassette recorders take one more step to accommodate the video signal. They convert it to a frequency-modulated (FM) signal and record the FM signal on tape. Specifically, a VHS recorder turns the color-under-video signal into an FM signal ranging in frequency from 3.4 MHz to 4.4 MHz. Super VHS machines achieve their higher quality by broadening the bandwidth from 1.0 MHz to 1.6 MHz, putting the FM signal in the range 5.4 MHz to 7.0 MHz.

All of these tricks are sufficient to produce a watchable video picture but one far short of the quality of broadcast television. Most VCRs are able to produce horizontal resolution ranging from 200 to 240 pixels.

Cabling

Video signals are more particular about wiring than are electric lights or stereo systems because they involve higher frequencies. All AC (alternating current) electrical signals—which includes house current, audio, and video—travel down wires like puffs of air flow down a pipe. In a perfect connection, the puff flows completely out of the pipe and disperses. But if you partly block the end of the pipe, part of the puff bounces back, and if the connection at the other end of the pipe is imperfect, part of the puff will bounce back and forth, wasting its energy. If you extend the puff into a long breath, however, your breath continually forces the air out of the pipe. The imperfect connection makes you blow harder, but you don't have to worry about puffs bouncing back and forth. Imperfect connections thus waste some of the energy in the puff. The shorter the puff, the greater the potential for problems.

Electrical signals are analogous. The shorter the wavelength or the higher the frequency, the greater the chance of problems. In electrical circuits, the connections are inevitably imperfect, and they lead to losses. At the frequencies used by lights and sound, the only significant problem is a loss of power. These wavelengths stretch out for miles. At video frequencies, however, wavelengths approach practical cable lengths (about 250 feet) and interference problems become legion.

The ideal channel for a video signal is one of constant impedance. Impedance (the resistance to the flow of AC current) changes with the inductance and capacitance of the cable, and is influenced by such diverse elements as the construction of the cable, material, and spacing of the conductors. These variables can change dramatically at connectors, resulting in an imperfect connection.

All cables and connectors have characteristic impedances. The accepted standard impedance for video circuits is 75 ohms. Every part of a video wiring circuit should demonstrate a 75-ohm impedance to prevent signal reflections and a corresponding loss of signal strength and quality.

Standards

The source impedance of most video equipment (that is the impedance of video outputs) is set at 75 ohms. Video inputs can be one of two types, terminating or bridging. A terminating input has a load impedance of 75 ohms and is meant to be the end of the line for a video signal. A bridging input has a high impedance (several thousand or more ohms). Bridging inputs are meant to latch onto a video signal in the middle of its travel, listening in without changing the signal. Most equipment with bridging inputs has a loop-through connection, two jacks connected together, one for an incoming signal and one for an outgoing signal. To maintain the proper impedance in a video circuit when a bridging input device is connected at the end of a video cable, you should plug a terminating resistor into the second jack of the loop-through connection. The terminating resistor typically takes the form of a dummy connector.

Some equipment, notably monitors, have switchable internal terminating resistors so they can act as terminating or bridging inputs. When such equipment is located at the end of the line, move its switch to the 75-ohm position.

Most video circuits use one of three kinds of connectors which differ in quality and price. The most expensive and most precise are *BNC connectors*, which are universally used in professional video circuits. One step down is the low-cost coaxial connector often used in cable television circuits. At the bottom end is the *pin plug* (also known as the RCA plug or phono plug), which is not truly a constant impedance connector. With consumer video circuits involving cable lengths of but a few feet, these connectors work fine. However, when cable length approaches signal wave length you should use constant impedance connectors. Television signals, such as those from your antenna to VCR or from the modulator of your VCR to your television set use broadcast instead of video frequencies, a dozen to a hundred times higher.

A video signal is not directly connected to a picture tube or CRT but is amplified (and often conditioned) first. The voltage of the video signal control the brightness of the image. The normal signal level in video circuits is an arbitrary one volt peak-to-peak. In general, the voltage of all video signals should match providing they are correctly terminated.

This one volt measurement extends from the brightest white the signal is meant to carry to the blackest black, which is the bottom of a horizontal or vertical synchronizing pulse. Some computer circuits and RGB systems use signals similar to composite video but that lack sync pulses. The lack of sync means that the peak-to-peak voltage of the signal will be somewhat lower for the same on-screen brightness. The nominal 0.7 volts of these sans-sync signals represents the same on-screen brightness as a one volt composite video signal.

Memory-Mapped Systems

If this discussion of signals, optical effects, and electron beams seems overly complex to you, you're on the right track. It's wasteful as well. There's no need for all the complication, at least in light of current technologies. Persistence, blanking, retrace, overscan and underscan are all remnants of old technology, practical needs required by the cathode ray tube and analog electronics. In the digital domain with flat-panel displays, such concerns remain only as artifacts of technologies gone by—like television.

For example, most flat-panel systems don't flicker at all. Each pixel can be kept constantly aglow and never needs to be refreshed. There's no need for retrace or blanking signals because each pixel can be directly addressed digitally at any time. Even synchronizing signals are superfluous except in the most general sense (moving images should move at the rate they are supposed to).

Monitors with flat panel displays operate more like ordinary computer memory than CRTs. The screen isn't scanned. Instead each pixel has its own address, and software can move image data to pixels exactly the same way it moves bytes between memory addresses. Instead of blasting frame after frame of the same old data to the screen, the image can be held intact, screen updates altering only the pixels that change. The changes need not occur at evenly spaced frame rates but whenever the data changes. In fact, a flat panel display has no need for synchronized picture signals. It can build an image from commands and data bytes, perhaps reconstituting a picture from highly compressed data.

The flat-panel display is a visible embodiment of a memory-mapped display system. Using this technology, each position in the display has an address, and software can route a given pixel to any position by using the right address. You can alter individual pixels whenever you want, without special regard to tides or timing. Although a flat-panel display may be scanned, the motivation in making the scan is to conserve interconnection wiring, not something required by the display technology.

The computer's representation of an image is a *memory map* of the image, with an address corresponding to each pixel position. Because this map is a block of memory that stores an entire image frame, it is often termed a frame buffer. While most people find it convenient to think of the frame buffer as a two-dimensional array that is a memory analog of the image, there's no reason it has to be. In fact, most images are stored with data for individual pixels split between several arrays.

The signals used by television and video systems are shifting from synchronized analog voltages to streams of digital data, but their input and output connections retain the same old analog signals. Even in the most optimistic projections, those old analog signals will be around for a long while. Even the most aggressive proposals for a new digital broadcast standard all allow for an extended, decade-long transition period in which broadcasters will transmit both digital and conventional analog signals to accommodate the tens of millions of old-fashioned television sets out there. Even new, all-digital, distribution systems like cable and satellite convert their digital signals to analog on your set-top for backward compatibility with old sets.

Color

Computer and video systems view color differently. In television and video, color is the stepchild of monochrome. Even the brightest, most colorful signals are basically monochrome with a dab of color piggybacked on top. PCs, however, put color in a leading role. Color is integral to display standards.

In computers, however, color is treated in accordance with its fundamental nature. All hues are effectively subdivided into the *primary colors* that make them up, and the primary color data stored and transmitted. In all but critical and application-specific systems, monochrome compatibility is good but not perfect—but that's okay because no one expects monochrome to be perfect.

To a computer system, a single pixel is nothing more than a position in an image with a corresponding position in memory. The memory associated with a pixel stores information needed to describe the essential qualities of the image at the point of the pixel. In our visual world, every place we look has its own quality that excites our retina. During the day, the predominant quality is color. At night, it is brightness. In the language of computer display systems, these pixel qualities are called *attributes*.

Every pixel holds the potential to have any of an infinity of attributes—it could be bright, black, green, orange, or something in-between. Although analog recording and transmission systems have, in theory, the ability to assign any of an infinity of attributes to a pixel, digital systems don't fare so well. All digital systems are restricted by the code chosen for storing the pixel data.

More importantly, the number of bits in the digital storage code constrains the number of available attributes per pixel. The more bits devoted to the code by a digital system, the more storage available for the attribute of each pixel. In theory, you'd want to devote as many bits as possible to each pixel so you'd have the same infinity of choices as with an analog system. Unfortunately, infinity has its drawbacks. The more bits the system uses, the more memory or bandwidth it requires. A single pixel with infinite attribute storage would require an infinity of memory itself, an expensive proposition even at $25 per megabyte.

The question for the system designer becomes how few bits can he get away with and still store a respectable image. The answer depends on what the engineer wants to do, which depends on what you expect—or at least will tolerate. The minimum the engineer can assign is one bit of storage per pixel. He can use that bit to code either of two attributes or conditions—whether the pixel is bright or dark, illuminated on the screen or invisibly black.

This minimum condition, one bit per pixel, makes no provision for color or contrast. Images look as drab as newspapers before *USA Today* brought color to the daily world. Every image is a single-hued picture with no variation or shading, essentially the same sort of an image as a line drawing. While this minimalist approach to display imaging can be sufficient for some purposes—for instance, the display of a chart or graph that mimics the monochrome look of ink-on-paper—many applications (multimedia included) demand color.

Adding color means assigning more bits to store the attribute information, and that means more memory and bandwidth. For example, instead of assigning each pixel a single bit, an extended attribute system could assign each a number, with the number corresponding to a particular color. The result is an electronic paint-by-numbers system that can specify as many hues as you have colored pencils—and numbers available for indicating them.

Standards   The one remaining problem is to come up with standards so that a color image made in one application comes up the with same hues in another. After all, without a key of which color corresponds to each number, your paint-by-numbers artwork may take on a unique look— orange sky, purple grass, and mauve seas—that might win awards at art shows but would reveal little about the real look of the scene (or the original artists intentions).

The color-to-number correspondence can be completely arbitrary, just as it is in the color-by-number sets. But because of the way computers generate images and colors, certain ways of encoding hues work better (meaning, generally, easier for programmers) than others.

Color Planes

In conventional color printing, pictures are separated into several images, each corresponding to a color of ink. These are called color separations. The separate color images are printed one over the other, and their inks combine to make a full-color images. Four colors (cyan, magenta, yellow, and black) suffice to make any color of the rainbow.

Some computer systems use a color coding method analogous to color separations. This method overlays images of different colors, termed color planes, much as four colors of ink are printed on top of one another. In each color plane the data for each pixel is represented by a single bit of memory, so the color of the corresponding plane can only be on or off. By stacking several color planes, a display system can make large number of different hues, essentially two raised by the number of color planes (this is, 2^n where n is the number of color planes). The number of color planes corresponds to the number of bits of storage for every pixel in the image. In fact, most of the time you'll find the color depth of a image described as a given number of bits—typically 4, 8, 16, or 24. The color bit-depth is the same as the number of color planes.

Unlike in the print industry, four planes do not suffice to make any color on a computer screen. Color separations are continuous-tone (or nearly so); they allow for different shades of the color they represent typically by using different sizes of dots. Color planes, on the other hand, are not continuous tone; they have no provision for encoding shades. As a result, making realistic on-screen storage requires more than four color planes. True color systems, those that can encode and reproduce more colors than most people can distinguish, have 24 color planes, enough to encode 16,777,216 different hues and shades.

True color systems are popular not because you need that many hues on-screen—after all, most monitors top out at about 262,144 colors—but because they offer an easy-to-work with system that eliminates color ambiguity even in critical applications. True color encoding is easy to work with because it assigns eight bits of storage, an even byte, to each primary color. Its superabundance of colors helps computers store images for other display systems that may be able to display a wider range of shades (like movie film).

To conserve on memory, other graphic systems use a lesser number of color planes. The VGA system used by most PCs produces colors with a bit-depth of 18 bits, six for each primary color, although the VGA system normally operates in modes with lower bit depths (four or eight bits) to conserve frame buffer memory.

The math for finding the amount of memory required to display a color graphics screen at a given bit-depth is straightforward. Simply multiply the number of pixels on the screen—that is, the resolution—by the bit-depth of each pixel, then divide by eight to translate bits into bytes. For example, a VGA graphics screen comprises 307,200 pixels (that's simply 640 pixels times 480 pixels). With a bit depth of four (which allows for 16 different colors on the screen at the same time), the minimum memory required is 1,228,800 bits. Divided by 8 bits per byte, that equates 153,600 bytes of storage. The next-highest standard increment of memory is 256KB, so you'd need at least 256KB of RAM to store a 16-color VGA image. You need to know the amount of memory required when buying a display adapter for your PC. Buy one with too little memory, and you'll shortchange yourself on the number of colors that your PC can display.

Color planes are related to memory banks but are not exactly the same thing. For instance, to map more memory into the limited address space reserved for video in PCs, VGA and SuperVGA video adapters used bank-switching techniques to move video memory bytes in and out of a limited address range in the High DOS memory area. In some video modes, these banks correspond exactly to the color planes used by the video adapter. In other modes, several planes of video information may be stored in each bank by using bits in each byte of screen memory to indicate individual colors.

Color Coding

The best and the worst display systems assign the same number of bits to each of the three primary colors—a bit or an entire byte. For intermediary color depths, however, the binary digital nature of the PC which makes numbers that are power of two easier to work with and the three-fold nature of color vision come into direct collision. For example, if you want to assign a single byte to store the colors of each pixel, how can you evenly allocate eight bits among three colors? With two bytes per pixel, how do you divide 16 colors into three primaries evenly?

You don't, but there's no need to. You don't even have to code colors as a mix of red, green, and blue. As long as the encoding process can be reversed, any storage format works.

Because the human eye is most sensitive to green and its shadings (probably something to do with primitive humans living in a nature lush with chlorophyll-green plants), some color coding systems split their bit assignments evenly and assign the odd bit to green. For example, when IBM's engineers designed a 16-bit color system, they assigned five bits to red and blue and gave six to green.

There's nothing magical about storing images as red, green, and blue values. Print-oriented workers prefer to think and store colors in correspondence with the ink colors used in printing, cyan, magenta, and yellow, which are often abbreviated CMY (or sometimes, CMYK—the K stands for black, which is used in four-color process printing to add "depth" to the colors). Some memory-mapped image storage systems encode colors to reduce the number of variables per pixel that must be stored in the same manner that the NTSC reduces three RGB signals to two. For example, the Kodak PhotoCD system encodes colors by brightness or luminance (which Kodak abbreviates as Y) and two color or chromaticity values (which Kodak abbreviates as C1 and C2) that essentially correspond to an NTSC co-ordinate map of colors. Although the same color would be stored as entirely different values under these other systems, any of these systems allow the encoded color to be reconstituted to its proper value.

These coding methods are useful to particular output devices—CMYK colors for storing images that eventually with be printed and published; luminance and chrominance coding for images that will eventually be used in broadcast-style video systems. (The Kodak PhotoCD system was originally intended for playback on ordinary television sets.) To be displayed by normal computer monitors, they must be translated by hardware or software from their native format to the RBG signals used by PC monitors. The different ways of expressing colors are called the *color space* used by the signal, and translating from one system to another is called *color space conversion.*

Color Mapping

Another method of encoding colors in memory that requires translation has found greater use in PCs. A technique called color mapping stores only code numbers, each of which could refer to almost any color. Each pixel is assigned a place to hold one code number in display memory. The display system matches the stored numeric values to a *Color Look-Up Table* or *CLUT* that tells which color corresponds to each number, then that color is sent along to the monitor. Because of the nature of colors in the real world, color mapping can lead to substantial economies in display memory.

When the values stored in screen memory directly indicate what color will appear on the screen, as it does in the above example, the colors are said to be direct mapped.

Direct mapping allows any pixel to be any color, but most images are made from far fewer colors. After all, there are only 307,200 pixels on the VGA screen so you can't possibly display them all at once. If you're judicious about your color pruning and the colors you display, you can make amazingly realistic images using a few bytes of storage by limiting the number of colors you put on the screen (which limits the storage you need). The problem is, of course, the optimum color selection for one image isn't the same as another. A polar bear in a snowstorm is predominantly white; a black bear in a cave on a starless night would be predominantly black; and a still frame from a blockbuster movie would likely be mostly red.

The colors assigned to storage can be made to adapt to the image using the Color Look-Up Table. In effect, the CLUT serves as a spectral map. A limited amount of storage makes up the guideposts or pointers which indicate which particular color in an wide overall selection called a palette belongs to a particular pixel. The number of guideposts determines how many different colors can be on the screen at the same time. The number of colors in the palette is constrained by the size of the pointer. Each pixel on the screen needs only enough storage to indicate which pointer to use. For example, a VGA system using a single byte of storage for each pixel could access a color lookup table with 256 pointers—allowing 256 different colors on the screen at a time. Each pointer has 18 bits of storage, allowing access to a palette of 262,144 different hues.

The Color Look-Up Table conserves both memory and speed. The march of technology makes these issues increasingly irrelevant, however. As memory and microprocessor power becomes cheaper, CLUTs will become rarer, at least in new display standards. With progress currently stuck on VGA, however, CLUTs will be around for a long while.

Windows and Color

The number of colors that you can actually use sometimes differs from the number that your video system can display depending on the software that you run. One important consideration is Microsoft Windows. Windows reserves a group of colors it calls the *system colors* for use in displaying elements of the graphical user interface such as the scroll bars and menu structure.

Your application software may also reserve colors. As a result, the actual number of colors that a foreground window can display is equal to the total number of colors that can be simultaneously produced by your video hardware, minus the number of colors reserved for Windows' system colors, minus those reserved by the application running in the window. In a 256-color system, Windows reserves 20 colors.

In palette-based display systems like VGA, these 20 reserved colors are located as the top and bottom entries in the color look-up table, ten on top, ten on the bottom. Software can force Windows to give up its reserved colors but doing so reduces the Windows screen elements to black and white. To give you the best on-screen color quality, some multimedia software takes over the system colors, and you'll see this effect, briefly, as the program takes over and switches the screen to its own display.

Compression and Codecs

Full-color video, which requires three bytes per pixel, at 640×480 resolution equals nearly 1MB of digital data per frame. This means that a developer could easily use up 1GB of hard disk space by storing less than one minute of uncompressed digital video information. The problem is severe when packaging video clips on CD and is even worse when you try to make a multimedia link through a modem.

Fitting megabytes of video onto a CD or where only a voice should go is today's top challenge for image-processing engineers. The problem is that huge compression ratios are required to gain adequate play time with digital media or when fitting a video signal down the limited bandwidth of a telephone connection—for example, where conventional video images were designed around a communication channel 6 MHz wide, telephones are constrained to a bandwidth of about 3,000 Hz, one two-thousandth that given to television.

The big breakthrough in image processing was the introduction of digital technology to both telephones and television. Today's most advanced communications techniques can push data at 28,800 bits per second through a telephone line. Digitizing video images makes them amenable to video compression, reducing the data required in every picture near the level that fits through the phone line. All dial-up video systems make heavy use of digital image compression.

Unlike normal data compression used in file archiving and data transfer across modems, most video compression systems are lossy. That is, part of the image information is discarded to reduce the data it contains. The trick to throw away only things that you can't see or don't notice. The more you throw away, the less data you need but the more obvious the omissions become, typically as fuzziness, blockiness or streaky ghosts in the display. How successful it is depends on the loss of quality you'll tolerate.

Modern video compression mixes together several technologies to achieve compression ratios of hundreds to one (compared to the nominal 2:1 average compression ratio of non-lossy systems).

Before compression begins, however, video phone systems give their engineers a headstart by keeping image resolution low. Most video phone systems display images that measure only 160×120 pixels, which trims image data to one-sixteenth that required by a 640×480-pixel VGA image. Similarly, video phone systems keep the number of colors available well under the 16.7 million for true photorealistic reproduction. The actual number of colors available varies with the image and compression scheme, but it is typically around 256, a factor of three savings.

Normal data compression systems like file archive programs work in one dimension. Still-image compression programs work two-dimensionally. Video compression works in three dimensions —in addition to working over areas, it works in time. It takes advantage of how little actually changes from frame to frame in a video image. Only the changes get stored or transmitted; the static parts of the image can be ignored. For example, when someone moves against a backdrop, only the pixels in the moving character need to be relayed to the data stream.

This system has one inherent problem. Any noise, distortion, or mistransmission in one frame is multiplied through all those that come after. To minimize such effects, most video compression systems periodically update the entire image.

One further way to reduce video data is simply to cut the frame rate, and most video phone system avail themselves this technique. To maintain the illusion of smooth motion, they don't simply drop frames but tie the frame rate to image movement so as to minimize the visible jerkiness of the image. Most videophone systems achieve frame rates from five to 15 frames per second.

The software or hardware that actually performs the compression operation is called a *codec*, short for *compressor/decompressor*. The most efficient codecs are proprietary designs that rely on patented technology. Each has its advantages that make it best for a given type of application. Consequently, many codecs remain in common use. Most multimedia applications include the appropriate codec in their playback software or work with those assumed to be installed in your operating system.

Windows 95 includes support for the Cinepak, Intel Indeo, Microsoft Run-length encoding, and Microsoft Video 1 codecs as standard equipment. You can view the video codecs installed in your Windows 95 system by opening the Multimedia icon in Control Panel, choosing the Advanced tab, and double-clicking Video Compression Codecs. You'll see a display like that shown in Figure 13.1.

Windows 95

Windows 95 handles codec installation as part of its *hardware* installation wizard. Codecs install as drivers. As you step through the wizard's menus, simply specify that you want to install specific hardware, then choose Sound, Video, and Game controllers from the list on the first screen. The wizard will give you the installation menu, as shown in Figure 13.2.

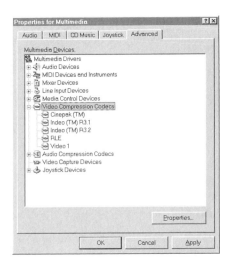

FIGURE 13.1. Listing of available Video Compression Codecs in the Windows 95 Multimedia Advanced Properties screen.

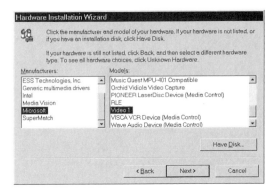

FIGURE 13.2. Windows 95 Add New Hardware Wizard showing installation menu for various sound, video, and game controllers.

Select the hardware that will use the codec. Slide the disk containing the codec in a drive, click Have Disk, and Windows 95 should find the codec and install it in your system.

Standards

The pixels in a memory-mapped display can be arranged any way you want—circles, star, squares, dodecahedrons—but usually they are arrayed as simple rectangles, probably because the most common images we see (paintings, photographs) are rectangular. The number of pixels varies, however, with the application, ambition of the engineers promoting it, and the amount people are willing to spend to get it.

Vector Graphics Systems

Some imaging systems are not based on image rasters or even individual pixels. Instead of tracing scan lines, they draw figures the same way you would as a series of strokes of a paintbrush. To keep the phosphors on the screen lit, these systems constantly retrace the figures.

Because the signals controlling the monitor drive the electron beam in the CRT as a series of vectors, this image-making technique is termed vector graphics. Alternatively, this kind of display system is sometimes called a *stroker* because of the kinship to drawing brushstrokes. Although not used in video system or PCs, the term pops up occasionally in the descriptions of expensive computerized workstations. It is also the basis of some specialized display systems such as radar and oscilloscope.

Linking Scanned and Memory-Mapped Systems

PCs in general and multimedia in particular bring together the worlds of scanned and memory-mapped display systems. Nearly all modern professional video systems do the same, and new consumer television systems likely will also. Memory-mapped digital systems combine the noise immunity of digital systems with computer power. Image manipulations are easier in the digital mode, particularly when they are controlled by a personal computer. But scanned systems linger as the exchange standard for signals, and they are still the fodder for monitors.

Rasterization

Converting from a memory-mapped system to a scanned system is easy. Every PC has done it since the PC was invented. A video system reads pixel data as bits and bytes from memory, scanning addresses as needed to construct a perfectly timed video waveform. Special hardware like the 6845 video controller of the first PCs and successor chips like graphic accelerators make the process easy.

Going the other way is more complex. The technology is called video capture and uses special hardware called the analog-to-digital converter. Video capture works by sampling the voltage level of the video at each pixel position and assigning a digital value to it. In most systems, the signal is first decoded to determine the strengths of individual colors before sampling.

The most difficult process is combining video with memory-mapped data from a PC on one monitor screen. Most video signals follow the NTSC standard while computer signals abide by the very different VGA (or VESA) standards. These systems use wildly different frequencies, making them impossible to place on one monitor at the same time. Moreover, VGA signals cannot be combined with other video signals to make composite images. Nor can they be recorded or transmitted as ordinary NTSC video.

One way to sidestep the incompatibility of VGA with ordinary video is to install a video board that generates NTSC instead of VGA. Many ancient CGA boards including the prototype IBM Color Display Adapter generated NTSC composite video signals. However the limited resolution (320×200 pixels with a maximum of 16 colors) of this product makes it a poor choice for modern multimedia. Specialized products, such as those from TruVision, generate professional-quality NTSC video that can be gen-locked and mixed with other video signals. Several companies also offer external VGA-to-composite video adapters that produce compatible signals.

Overlay Boards

You can mix video signals with your computer's output with video capture products, but displaying captured video in real time requires too much processing power for today's PCs. *Overlay boards* solve this problem by using dedicated processors for converting the video data into VGA or SuperVGA compatible signals. To minimize the load on your system, the overlay board combines the video and VGA without the intercession of your PC's microprocessor. This arrangement permits you to add a hardware codec to your display system that is not constrained by the overhead involved in shifting signals through your PC's expansion bus. It also makes video performance within the overlay independent of that of your PC's microprocessor. Overlay boards permit your PC to display full-frame video in real-time at frame rates near or including the 30 frames per second of standard NTSC video.

In general, an overlay board latches onto your PC's VESA Feature Connector and plugs directly into your monitor. The video signal plugs into the overlay board and never gets sent further into your system. Instead, the overlay board digitizes the video and keys it into the VGA output of your PC. In other words, the software for the overlay board instructs Windows to send a special signal (typically a unique color) to the area in which the video image should appear. The hardware on the overlay board keys to that color, suppressing it and substituting the video image wherever the color appears. Your PC must manage only a block of fixed color—not a great chore—while the overlay board handles the video image.

Because the video image gets combined after the VGA circuitry inside your PC, it cannot be captured by ordinary screen capture software such as the print screen feature of Windows. If you attempt to use a screen capture program to latch onto the overlay, all you'll be able to grab is the block of solid color used for the overlay's key. To make up for this shortcoming, most overlay boards include their own capture facilities for grabbing video frames.

Step Capture

Most PCs, in fact, most computers are not fast enough to produce a series of video frames in real-time. That's why frames get dropped and PC-based video appears jerky. But PCs can still create smoothly moving video images using a process called *step capture*. Instead of moving a complete multiframe image, a step capture system sends out a single frame at a time that is captured to a special video device, one that is able to address individual frames. The frames are strung together across a disk or tape. Later they can be played back in real time to make smoothly flowing video or animation. The process works in both directions. You can move a video sequence one frame at a time to your PC, then compress the sequence into a form that your PC can play back at a reasonable frame rate. Although step capture is a slow process, it is the best way to achieve the highest possible video quality from a PC.

The key to making step capture work is a video device that can record with single frame accuracy and a means to control that device. Such control is afforded through the Media Control Interface. The VISCA device driver for MCI operates with Sony Corporation's VISCA interface to control the tape transport, input and output channels, and even the tuner in the VCR.

Performance Issue

Time Code

In digital production and editing, you need to be able to individually address each frame of the image. For example, when you edit, you must indicate the starting and ending frames of each segment. You also need to indicate individual frames when you synchronize multiple sources, either when running several simultaneous related video clips or when linking a soundtrack to a video image.

This need for addressing individual frames has long been a problem with motion picture and video production. In movies, it was easy to physically mark the film—both the mark and each individual frame were easily visible. With video tape, however, individual frames are much more elusive and take final form only on the screen. The *Society of Motion Picture and Television Engineers* or SMPTE developed a system of identifying each frame by its time of display. This SMPTE *time code* is the basis of the synchronizing systems used in modern video.

SMPTE time code is a simple concept. Each frame gets identified by the hour, minute, and second in which it occurs, and the multiple frames occurring within a single second get consecutively numbers. In other words, a frame is identified in the format HH:MM:SS:FF, where HH is the hour, MM the minute, SS the second, and FF the frame number.

Unfortunately SMPTE time code is not a single thing because no single video standard exists. The NTSC video standard displays at about 30 frames per second: PAL and SECAM use 25 frames per second; motion pictures display 24 frames per second. Although the same time format could be used for each, the three would not be compatible because the frame counts would be

Standards

different in any given second. Consequently, each of these system has its own variation or variations of SMPTE time code. The system used by PAL and SECAM is called SMPTE 25 EBU (for European Broadcast Union), and that for movies is SMPTE 24 Film Sync.

Another problem arises with NTSC video. Under NTSC, the frame rate is not exactly 30 per second but rather 29.97 frames per second. Time code cannot accommodate fractional frames. Instead, the seconds in the code for NTSC color don't exactly follow seconds in reality. Each second is kept 30 frames long. Without some way of compensating, the time code clock would soon veer wildly away from real time. The SMPTE solved this problem by developing *Drop-frame time-coding*. As necessary—about once every minute—this time code system skips two frame addresses, simply dropping its number from the count. Only the frame number is dropped, not the actual frame. The code jumps ahead two frame numbers.

Dropping two frames every minute doesn't quite achieve the right multiple, so drop-frame systems do *not* drop frames at any minute that is divisible by ten. Consequently at minutes numbered 00, 10, 20, 30, 40, and 50 no frames are dropped.

Note that drop-frame time-coding is never needed with PAL, SECAM, or motion picture signals because those standards specify integer frame rates. There are no fractional parts to muck things up.

There's one further complication to SMPTE time code; in two circumstances drop-frame coding is not used.

Some NTSC television signals are coded with *non-drop time code.* Under the non-drop code, every frame is counted and the system assumes 30 frames make a second. As a result, the time code clock runs 1 percent faster than real time. Time according to the code and time according to a stop watch will gradually veer apart. For video engineers, this is usually no problem when they are editing images together because they use the code only to identify frames, not to precisely time a sequence.

When SMPTE time code is used with audio signals without video, as it is in many MIDI systems, the frame rate is held at exactly 30 per second. Unburdened by the fractional frame rate, non-drop coding works perfectly. Every second gets 30 frames and the time code and real-time stay in sync. At least until you try to synchronize the MIDI playback with a video. The two non-drop systems are usually called by the same name, SMPTE 30 non-drop even though they are quite different. You have to know what you are dealing with—the real frame rate—to be sure your time code will sync with your clocks. Table 13.3 summarizes the variations in the SMPTE time codes.

TABLE 13.3. SMPTE time codes.

Standard	Use	Frames per second	Sync with real-time
SMPTE 24 Film Sync	Motion pictures	24	Yes
SMPTE 25 EBU	European-style video	25	Yes
SMPTE 30 Non-drop	Audio/MIDI	30	Yes
SMPTE 30 Non-drop	Video production	29.97	No
SMPTE 30 Drop-frame	USA-standard Video	29.97	Yes

To avoid ambiguity, sometimes people dealing with audio and MIDI reserve the name SMPTE 30 Non-drop for audio coding that actually puts 30 frames in every second. They distinguish the video form by calling it SMPTE 29.97 Non-drop, although that term likely won't be recognized by people working in the video industry.

Image Hardware

Although the PC is perhaps the premiere memory-mapped device, most of the time it must make its images on a scanned device, the computer monitor. Getting from memory-mapped form into a scanned format is a straightforward process, but doing it well requires an array of sophisticated hardware most often combined into a single circuit card called a graphics adapter or video board.

The graphics adapter handles all aspects of image making, from accepting and storing bytes in memory to generating the waveforms that constitute a standard video signal. The image-making process begins, however, with your multimedia (or other computer) software. Under the direction of the software, your system's microprocessor loads bytes into the frame buffer or, more commonly these days, sends instructions to the graphics adapter on how the adapter should arrange the bytes in video memory.

In simple display systems, your PC's microprocessor does all the work with either direct commands from your software to move bytes to specific memory locations or through program calls to your PC's BIOS, which then handles the detailed work (and commands the microprocessor to load values into particular screen memory locations). In more complex display systems, the microprocessor sends codes to the video processor which either directly moves the data into screen memory or generates the image, then moves it into memory. In any case, the final destination for screen-bound data is your PC's frame buffer.

Getting those bytes from buffer to monitor is a much more complex matter. The graphics adapter must scan the frame buffer in synchrony with the scan of the electron beam in your monitor. The conversion from buffer to scan is not as direct as you might think. The resemblance between the memory map and the on-screen image is only metaphoric. The bytes of video information are often scattered between eight or more memory chips and several color planes. Somehow all the bits, bytes, and pixels must get organized and sent on their way. Along with ordering the pixel data, the graphics adapter must also generate the synchronizing signals the monitor uses to lay out the video information in two logical dimensions—horizontal and vertical.

Video Controllers

The process of changing memory maps into scans is called rasterization and is the job of a special circuit called the video controller. In most PCs, the video controller is a special VLSI chip designed specifically for the task of turning memory bytes into video. The first PC color and monochrome adapters relied on an off-the-shelf chip, the 6845, to handle its displays. Today, however, most manufacturers have switched to custom-designed and manufactured chips with the power of microprocessors.

The principle underlying the memory map-to-scan conversion is elegant in its simplicity. The video controller just reads addresses in the memory map in sequential order as they would appear on the screen, one row at a time. However to make sure the one-dimensional video information is not misinterpreted by your monitor, the timing and arrangement of the data must be precisely controlled.

Your PC commands the video controller through a number of registers. By writing appropriate bit values, your PC can change nearly every aspect of the video signals created by the controller chip, from the number of pixels in each line to the refresh rate. Table 13.4 lists the registers and functions of the VGA controller that serves as the basis of most PC video systems.

TABLE 13.4. VGA registers.

Register name	Class	Read or write	Mono mode address	Color mode address	Index
Miscellaneous output	General	Write	03C2	03C2	N/A
Miscellaneous output	General	Read	03CC	03CC	N/A
Input status 0	General	Read only	03C2	03C2	N/A
Input status 1	General	Read only	03BA	03DA	N/A
Feature control	General	Write	03BA	03DA	N/A
Feature control	General	Read	03CA	03CA	N/A
Video subsystem enable	General	Read/write	03C3	03C3	N/A

Register name	Class	Read or write	Mono mode address	Color mode address	Index
Address	Attribute	Read/write	03C0	03C0	N/A
Palette (x16)	Attribute	Write	03C0	03C0	00-0F
Palette (x16)	Attribute	Read	03C1	03C1	00-0F
Attribute mode control	Attribute	Write	03C0	03C0	10
Attribute mode control	Attribute	Read	03C1	03C1	10
Overscan color	Attribute	Write	03C0	03C0	11
Overscan color	Attribute	Read	03C1	03C1	11
Color plane enable	Attribute	Write	03C0	03C0	12
Color plane enable	Attribute	Read	03C1	03C1	12
Horizontal PEL panning	Attribute	Write	03C0	03C0	13
Horizontal PEL panning	Attribute	Read	03C1	03C1	13
Color select	Attribute	Write	03C0	03C0	14
Color select	Attribute	Read	03C1	03C1	14
Index register	CRT controller	Read/write	03B4	03D4	N/A
Horizontal total	CRT controller	Read/write	03B5	03D5	00
Horizontal display enable end	CRT controller	Read/write	03B5	03D5	01
Start horizontal blanking	CRT controller	Read/write	03B5	03D5	02
End horizontal blanking	CRT controller	Read/write	03B5	03D5	03
Start horizontal retrace	CRT controller	Read/write	03B5	03D5	04
End horizontal retrace	CRT controller	Read/write	03B5	03D5	05
Vertical total	CRT controller	Read/write	03B5	03D5	06

continues

TABLE 13.4. continued

Register name	Class	Read or write	Mono mode address	Color mode address	Index
Overflow	CRT controller	Read/write	03B5	03D5	07
Present row scan	CRT controller	Read/write	03B5	03D5	08
Maximum scan line	CRT controller	Read/write	03B5	03D5	09
Cursor start	CRT controller	Read/write	03B5	03D5	0A
Cursor end	CRT controller	Read/write	03B5	03D5	0B
Start address high	CRT controller	Read/write	03B5	03D5	0C
Start address low	CRT controller	Read/write	03B5	03D5	0D
Cursor location high	CRT controller	Read/write	03B5	03D5	0E
Cursor location low	CRT controller	Read/write	03B5	03D5	0F
Vertical retrace start	CRT controller	Read/write	03B5	03D5	10
Vertical retrace end	CRT controller	Read/write	03B5	03D5	11
Vertical display enable end	CRT controller	Read/write	03B5	03D5	12
Offset	CRT controller	Read/write	03B5	03D5	13
Underline location	CRT controller	Read/write	03B5	03D5	14
Start vertical blanking	CRT controller	Read/write	03B5	03D5	15
End vertical blanking	CRT controller	Read/write	03B5	03D5	16
CRTC mode control	CRT controller	Read/write	03B5	03D5	17

Register name	Class	Read or write	Mono mode address	Color mode address	Index
Line compare	CRT controller	Read/write	03B5	03D5	18
Address	Sequencer	Read/write	03C4	03C4	N/A
Reset	Sequencer	Read/write	03C5	03C5	00
Clocking mode	Sequencer	Read/write	03C5	03C5	01
Map mask	Sequencer	Read/write	03C5	03C5	02
Character map select	Sequencer	Read/write	03C5	03C5	03
Memory mode	Sequencer	Read/write	03C5	03C5	04
Address	Graphic	Read/write	03CE	03CE	N/A
Set/reset	Graphic	Read/write	03CF	03CF	00
Enable set/reset	Graphic	Read/write	03CF	03CF	01
Color compare	Graphic	Read/write	03CF	03CF	02
Data rotate	Graphic	Read/write	03CF	03CF	03
Read map select	Graphic	Read/write	03CF	03CF	04
Graphics mode	Graphic	Read/write	03CF	03CF	05
Miscellaneous	Graphic	Read/write	03CF	03CF	06
Color don't care	Graphic	Read/write	03CF	03CF	07
Bit mask	Graphic	Read/write	03CF	03CF	08
PEL address	DAC	Read/write	03C8	03C8	N/A
PEL address	DAC	Write only	03C7	03C7	N/A
DAC state	DAC	Read only	03C7	03C7	N/A
PEL data	DAC	Read/write	03C9	03C9	N/A
PEL mask	DAC	Read/write	03C6	03C6	N/A

Graphics Accelerators

Originally PCs used a technology for managing video memory called the dumb frame buffer. This design puts your PC's microprocessor in command. The software that draws an image tells the microprocessor where to move every byte in memory to light each individual pixel. Although this is the simplest possible design from a software standpoint, it is hardly the most efficient. The microprocessor must spend a large fraction of its time managing the frame buffer for relatively trivial operations. For example, scrolling one line up the screen means the microprocessor has to move every byte one position on the screen, throw away one line, and generate a new one. Given a big screen and a slow processor and you can wait seconds for a simple scroll, seconds in which your PC can do little else.

One way to minimize this slow down is to give the mundane work of managing the frame buffer to another chip. Instead of drawing an image itself or scrolling the screen, the microprocessor can send commands to the other chip. The microprocessor then can go on to other chores while the screen is independently updated.

Two technologies are built around this concept. The graphic accelerator is a VLSI chips that's specially designed for carrying out important commonly used graphic operations such as drawing lines, filling areas, or creating Windows dialog boxes. A graphic coprocessor is a full-fledged microprocessor that has been designed especially for carrying out such graphic operations. The difference between a graphic accelerator and a graphic coprocessor is that the functions and commands handled by the accelerator are fixed by its silicon circuitry. Consequently the accelerator is often called a fixed-function chip. As with a true microprocessor, a graphic coprocessor can be fully programmed—for example to carry out the operations of a graphic accelerator. Because of its programmability, a graphic coprocessor can do more than an accelerator, almost anything within the imagination of its programmer. The functions normally required by computer graphics are well-defined, however, and the less versatile accelerator has proven adept enough to almost totally replace graphic coprocessors in PC video systems.

Performance Issue

Both graphic accelerators and graphic coprocessors add intelligence to your PC's display system. Instead of the microprocessor needing to execute the instructions to create on-screen images, the graphics chips take over the chore. More importantly, these chips take a big load off the bus connection between your PC's microprocessor and the frame buffer. In a conventional dumb frame buffer video system the microprocessor must move all screen-bound data into display memory through either the I/O bus or local bus. With a graphics accelerator, both the microprocessor and the graphic accelerator are linked to the frame buffer, but the accelerator is linked directly instead of through a bus. On most operations, the graphics accelerator moves bytes without bothering to push data across a bus. Your PC's microprocessor sends only the software drawing commands to the graphics chips, pushing a few bytes instead of thousands of them across the bus. This lowers the load on the bus and prevents bus speed from limiting video performance.

The graphics chips bring another performance advantage. Just as numeric coprocessors can help your PC crunch through transcendental functions faster, these special purpose graphics chips can accelerate the performance of your system in drawing images on your monitor. The instruction set of a general purpose microprocessor is designed for versatility. The creators of the chip have no idea what some designer will do with their product so they add in the ability to do nearly anything, sacrificing overall efficiency at any particular task. The makers of the graphic processor know exactly what their creation will be used for—graphics—so they can optimize the chip's command set for graphics functions.

As with the microprocessors, graphic accelerators come in wide variety with different levels of performance and features. In fact, the number of different graphic accelerators available to display board builders appears limited only by the number of different chip makers. After just a few years of development, the chips have jumped into their second generation with overall performance several times improved over their forebears.

The first significant fixed-function graphic accelerators were made by S3 Corporation (the company prefers to think of its name as "S-cubed" but it is generally pronounced "S-three"—the name is derived from Solid State Systems). The company's 86C911 chip set the pace for the first generation of accelerators. Stripped to its essentials, the chip was a hardware implementation of the features most relevant to Windows applications drawn from the instruction set of the IBM Extended Graphics Array (XGA) coprocessor. Designed to match the ISA bus, the S3 86C911 used 16-bit architecture all around—internally and linking it to its 1MB maximum of VRAM. Although it could handle resolutions up to 1280 to 1024, its color abilities were limited by its circuitry that converts digital-to-analog signals.

Other manufacturers followed with their own 16-bit chips; most jumped directly into the second generation with 32-bit chips. Now video chipmakers are using 64-bit and wider technology, both for internal processing and for accessing the frame buffer. More than a dozen companies now offer graphic accelerator chips.

The performance and output quality of a graphic accelerator depends on a number of design variables. The following are among the most important variables.

Register Width

Graphic accelerators work like microprocessors dedicated to their singular purpose, and internally they are built much the same. The same design choice that determines microprocessor power also affects the performance of graphic accelerator chips. The internal register width of a graphic accelerator determines how many bits the chip works with at a time. As with microprocessors, the wider the registers, the more data that can be manipulated in a single operation.

The first generation of graphic accelerators were 16-bit chips. Second generation chips moved to 32-bit architecture, while a few jumped all the way to 64-bit designs.

Because each graphic accelerator has its own language or command set, you should have no concern about wasted width as with 16-bit DOS running on 32-bit microprocessors. Each chip runs at its full potential.

Bus Type and Width

Bus bandwidth is extremely important to graphic accelerators because they are the element inside your PC with the most voracious appetite for information.

The first generation of graphic accelerators had 16-bit interfaces because they were designed before local bus technology appeared on the scene. They only needed to match to ISA, and 16-bits sufficed. The advent of local buses forced the new generation of chips onto the scene to take advantage of the higher possible bus throughput. Most current-generation graphic accelerators have full 32-bit interfaces to match with the leading local buses.

Besides needing a link to the system bus, graphic accelerators also couple with their own frame buffers. The width of this connection need not match that of the bus interface. For better performance, many graphic accelerators use wider connections to their video memory. Some chips have a 64-bit memory connection. Chips with 128-bit memory buses are in development.

Memory Handling

The maximum amount of memory in the frame buffer sets upper limits on the color and resolution support of a graphic accelerator, although other design choices may further constrain these capabilities. The more memory, the higher the resolution and the greater the depth of color the accelerator can manage.

You can easily compute the frame buffer memory required by any graphic accelerator for a given resolution level and color depth. The minimum memory is the product of the horizontal resolution, vertical resolution, and color depth in bytes. For example, at the 1280×1024 resolution level with True Color capabilities (24-bit color—3-byte color depth), the required memory for the frame buffer is 1280×1024×3 or 3,932,160 bytes.

Memory Type

Graphics accelerators can be designed to use standard dynamic memory (DRAM), dual-ported video memory (VRAM), or either type. VRAM memory delivers better performance because it can handle its two basic operations (writing and reading, corresponding to image updates and writing to the screen) simultaneously. VRAM is, however, substantially more expensive than DRAM and, in the quantities used with modern display adapters, the cost difference can be substantial. Only boards aimed at squeezing out the last bit of video performance are likely to use VRAM.

Resolution Support

Every graphic accelerator supports three basic resolutions: standard VGA 640×480 pixel graphics, SuperVGA 800×600 pixels, and 1024×768 pixels. Beyond the basic trio, designers often push higher, depending on other constraints. Besides the standard increments upward—1280×1024 and 1600×1200 pixels—some makers throw in intermediate values so that you can coax monitors to their maximum sharpness.

Color Depth Support

Many of today's graphics accelerators are all-in-one video solutions so they contain DACs as well as control circuitry. These built-in DACs obey the same rules as stand-alone chips. Foremost in importance is the color-depth the chips can produce. Some graphic accelerators rely on standard VGA-style DAC and are limited to 18-bit VGA-style color—six bits of each primary color—and can put only discriminate between 262,144 colors. Most newer graphic accelerators with built-in DACs have full 24-bit (or 32-bit) color support, enabling them to display the 16.7 million hues of True Color.

Speed Rating

The higher the resolution a graphic accelerator produces, the more pixels it must put on the screen. At a given frame rate, more pixels means each one must be produced faster—it gets a smaller share of each frame. Consequently higher resolution accelerator chips must be able to operate at higher speeds. For 1024×768 resolution with a 75 Hz frame rate, 80 MHz is sufficient; for 1280×1024, 100 MHz is sufficient (110 MHz is better); for 1600×1200 resolution, 150 MHz is needed, although 135 MHz is sufficient for lower frame rates.

VGA Support

Every video board boots up in an IBM-compatible mode. In modern PCs, that means VGA. So every video board must have VGA support of some kind. Many graphic accelerator makers have integrated all the needed VGA functions into their chips. Others rely on external chips for VGA text and images. Functionally your software won't notice a difference between the location of the VGA support circuitry. You may, however. Because the design of VGA circuits vary with different chipsets, their performance varies, too. Some graphic accelerators have indifferent VGA performance. As a result, DOS screens and low resolution graphics may be slow while high resolution graphics perform superbly. Of course, accelerators with external VGA support can suffer the same indignity if their designers don't choose top VGA chips.

From a practical standpoint, VGA support may be irrelevant to you if you jump immediately from the DOS prompt to Windows or run OS/2. If, however, you often work in text mode or rely on standard VGA graphics, you should concern yourself with the performance of a given graphic accelerator both in its native high-resolution modes and in VGA.

Performance Issue

A graphic accelerator does not automatically guarantee a performance improvement on all graphic applications. Software not designed to link with the application interface of the graphic accelerator won't gain any of the benefits of the acceleration. Often, the opposite is the case; a standard DOS program may operate more slowly through a graphic system designed to accelerate Windows performance. As with other PC hardware, your choice of a graphic accelerator depends on the applications that you want to run.

One kind of image data never benefits from the speed-up brought by the graphic accelerator—bit-images. Unfortunately, bit-images are the most common form of data in many multimedia systems. For example, if you have a bit-image saved on hard disk that you want to put on the screen—for example, a photograph that you scanned in—the disk-based data must be transferred without modification directly to display memory.

Bus Connections

Fortunately the speed limits of the bus connection to the frame buffer have been raised by another technology, the local bus. Most frame buffers connect through the I/O bus, of which your PC's expansion bus is part. The I/O bus is driven through special bus-control logic that, among other things, controls the width and speed of data transfers. Most I/O buses are designed to match the one principal expansion standard used by PCs for the last decade, the ISA bus.

ISA severely constrains the speed of data. It operates at a fraction of microprocessor speed (typically whatever fraction comes closest to 8 MHz) with a fraction of the microprocessor's bus width—half that of a 32-bit 486, a quarter that of the 64-bit Pentium. A local bus is a more direct connection with your PC's microprocessor that operates closer the microprocessor's speed and bus width.

Performance Issue

Local bus is a technology not a single design. A local bus can be integrated into your PC's motherboard and often was. Today, however, local bus generally refers to a fast expansion bus that supports an array of third-party expansion boards. Two separate and incompatible designs are popular in multimedia PCs today, VL Bus and PCI, described in Chapter 11, "Input and Output." Either of these local bus designs will allow transfers between your system and the frame buffer at substantially faster rates than through the traditional I/O bus. They are particularly efficient at moving full-screen bit-images, the greatest throughput challenge faced by any display system and the most frequent fodder of multimedia images. Neither local bus will speed up other video operations or lighten the load on your PC's microprocessor. Consequently, local bus technology benefits your system most when added in conjunction with a high-speed graphic accelerator.

RAMDACs

The data inside your PC and its memory is held in digital form but today's computer and video monitors all use analog signals. Consequently, every graphics adapter must somehow convert information from one form to the other. Display adapters use special integrated circuits called Digital-to-Analog Converters for this translation. Often abbreviated as DAC, the same chips also masquerade under the name RAMDAC, which is short for Random Access Memory Digital-to-Analog Converter.

DACs are classified by the number of digital bits in the digital code they translate. For example, an 8-bit DAC converts the levels encoded in 8-bit digital patterns (eight color planes) into 256 analog levels. In color display systems, each primary color or channel requires a separate DAC, a total of three. Total up the number of bits of each DAC, and you'll get the number of bit-planes of color which a system can display. This color range directly corresponds to the palette of the display system. As noted above, the amount of display memory constrains the number of colors that can be displayed on-screen simultaneously. Backed by adequate storage, three 8-bit DACs yield a 24-bit True Color system. The number of bits describing a RAMDAC represents the maximum it can use. Nearly all RAMDACs can also translate less complex codes than their maxima. For example, 24-bit RAMDACs typically handle 18-bit, 16-bit, 8-bit, and 4-bit color as well.

In most display systems, all DAC channels have the same bit-depth. Most modern RAMDACs integrate all three color channels into a single chip which may in turn be integrated with the video controller. Some older graphics adapters, however, use separate DACs for each color channel.

One other figure of merit describes a RAMDAC speed. A RAMDAC must be fast enough to make one conversion for each pixel that gets displayed on the monitor. The speed rating of a RAMDAC must exceed the dot-clock of the graphic standard it is operating under. Today medium performance RAMDACs are rated at about 80 to 90 MHz; high performance RAMDACs run at 135 to 150 MHz.

Display Control Interface

To give hardware developers and software writers a common means by which they can quickly write to the video frame buffer in Windows, Microsoft and Intel developed the *Display Control Interface* or DCI standard. The standard defines a repertory of commands for video device drivers that handle moving data to the frame buffer as well as enabling special features of today's advanced video hardware. The common interface allows programmers to create software without worrying about the exact hardware that will run it while still taking advantage of advanced features such as overlaying, chroma keying, double-buffering, hardware scaling, and color-space conversion.

The details of DCI and help in creating DCI drivers are available in the form of the *DCI Level 2 Specification,* which you can get through the Microsoft Developer Network by calling (800) 759-5474; or (402) 691-0173).

Video Boards

Among PCs today one standard ranks as truly universal. Called VGA, it's the least common denominator among peripherals, programs, and possibilities. It's the minimum built into nearly every PC, and the one that nearly every program supports. The name comes from the IBM circuit used in the first systems to follow the standard, the Video Graphics Array.

VGA was designed to yield a television-quality image. Its resolution matches what you'd get from a top-quality TV—640 pixels horizontally by 480 pixels vertically. (Although the NTSC standard specifies 525 lines, only about 480 are active; the other 45 are given over to the miracle of blanking.) The design is a blessing for multimedia systems because the images made by a VGA system are compatible with video images. The signals used by video and VGA are not compatible, however. Video systems use a frame rate of about 30 Hz and rely on interlacing to hide flicker. VGA images use a field rate of 60 Hz (in most graphics modes) to minimize flicker. Consequently computer VGA signals are not directly compatible with video systems.

With today's multimedia PCs, VGA is only a point of departure—your PC boots up in VGA mode but heads for higher resolution as soon as you load Windows or OS/2. Beyond VGA, you'll find images of a number of different sizes and an even greater variety of signals all under a single guiding light called SuperVGA. By itself, SuperVGA simply means anything with more pixels than VGA, but SuperVGA works for the majority of multimedia systems because it is united not by an image standard but by a control standard called VESA.

Standards
The initials stand for the Video Electronics Standards Association, a group of equipment makers who joined together in 1987 to insure that their products would work together. To bring unity to the universe of images, VESA developed a common means of accessing video boards called the VESA BIOS extensions. To insure that monitors will match with video board signals, VESA developed a set of monitor timing specifications. The organization has also developed other standards relating to power saving, bus access, and data transfer.

Before VGA was introduced, three standards were used in PCs. All were developed by IBM for its PC products. MDA, which stands for the Monochrome Display Adapter, the first product to embody the standard, was designed solely for text modes. CGA (for Color Graphics Adapter) was a low-resolution graphic display system with limited color capabilities (16 possible colors). EGA (for Enhanced Graphics Adapter) increase the resolution of CGA and quadrupled the color count. None of these systems is suitable for a multimedia PC, however.

After VGA, IBM developed two more display systems, 8514/A and XGA. Both found limited initial success, but both have been adopted by VESA and merged into its standards. In other words, VGA and SuperVGA are all that count in memory-mapped multimedia today.

VGA

The native graphics modes of the VGA system operates with a resolution of 640 pixels horizontally and 480 pixels vertically. This resolution is the highest supported by standard VGA systems. Because most monitor screens have an aspect-ratio of 4:3, each pixel occupies a perfectly square area on the screen. Other display standards (indeed, other VGA display modes) produce elongated pixels that complicate the math needed to draw shapes on the screen.

At its highest resolution, the most basic VGA systems operate with either of two color-depths, one or four bits, allowing for either two or 16 simultaneous on-screen colors. These color depths are constrained by the 256KB of memory used by bottom-line VGA boards. The 307,200 pixels require at least 153,600 bytes of frame buffer for 16-color operation.

To accommodate older software, the VGA system has compatibility modes that are addressed as 320×200 pixels, 640×200 pixels, and 640×350 pixels. The first of these allows for up to 256 simultaneous on-screen colors; the others, 16 colors. The latter limit results not from inherent constraints of the VGA system but rather carry through the capabilities of earlier display systems. Most modern video boards with VGA abilities have more than 256KB of memory, but this excess memory is not supported under the VGA standard.

To broaden its apparent range of colors and generate more life-like images, the VGA standard takes advantage of a color look-up table to maps hues. Each of the 256 entries in the color look-up table encodes one of 262,144 hues.

The hue limit results from the color generation system of the VGA electronics. The VGA system produces analog signals to drive its monitors, and these analog signals are derived from three 6-bit digital-to-analog converters. In the prototype IBM VGA circuitry, all three DAC channels were integrated into a single chip, an Inmos 6171S. Each 6-bit DAC channel encodes 64 levels of intensity of a primary color (red, blue, or green). Combined together, 64×64×64 (that is 64^3 or 2^{18}) distinct combinations of color levels are possible, the 262,144 hue potential.

The actual color look-up table in the original VGA circuitry was part of the Inmos DAC chip, which provided 256 registers each capable of storing the necessary 18-bit color code.

The VGA system faces a small problem in addressing its full 256KB memory capacity: not enough address space was reserved for such a large frame buffer in the original PC specification. The available address ranges are simply too small. To fit the frame buffer within the confines of the available addresses, the VGA uses the time-honored trick of bank-switching. The full expanse of the system's display memory is usually split four ways into 64KB banks, although a two-way 128KB-bank split is also possible. A register called the Map Mask Register, which is part of the VGA chip, controls which banks the system microprocessor addresses through a 64KB range of high memory addresses. The VGA specification puts the Map Mask Register at I/O port 03C5(Hex). Several registers actually share this port address to economize on port usage. The VGA Sequencer Register at port address 03C4(Hex) controls the function of the port used by the Map Mask Register. When the Sequencer Register is set to the value 02(Hex), port 03C5(Hex) gives access to the Map Mask Register.

The Map Mask Register has four control bits. In the VGA's native 16-color mode, each bit nominally controls a bit plane and switches on or off the intensity, red, green, and blue signals (listed from most significant bit to least). Unlike most bank switching systems, the VGA system allows multiple banks to be switched on simultaneously. This scheme allows an on-screen hue that's mixed from more than one color to be loaded in a single cycle. For example, if your system could only activate the VGA banks individually, writing a bright white dot would take four separate operations—writing a bit of one color, switching banks, then writing another color, and so on. By activating all four banks simultaneously, writing the white bit takes only one switch and write operation.

Addressing within each bank is linear in the native 16-color VGA graphic mode. That is, the memory arrangement puts on-screen pixels and lines into memory in the same order that they appear on the screen. The bit data in a byte from most significant to least significant bit corresponds to an on-screen sequence of eight pixels in a line from left to right.

In 256-color mode, each byte of memory defines the color of a single pixel. The bank-control logic of the VGA system divides the 256KB of memory for on-screen pixels into four 64KB blocks. These banks essentially duplicate one another but provide a convenient way of scanning color plane data into the DAC. Because there are eight color signals per pixels and the VGA system is designed to scan four color planes at a time, the 256-color pages are scanned twice to make the transfer.

The VGA system normally locates its frame buffer in the 64KB memory segment beginning at absolute address 0A0000(Hex). To maintain compatibility with older video standards, however, the VGA system can relocate the base address of its video memory. A VGA board uses the same physical memory no matter the base address at which it is used.

The mechanics of this relocation are relatively straightforward. A register in the VGA control circuitry acts as the switch. The Memory Map Register controls the base address of the VGA's video memory and the page size of each bank. Accessing the Memory Map Register is a two-step process. First the Graphic Address Register at microprocessor I/O port must be set with a value of 06(Hex) to enable writing to the Memory Map Register through the VGA's Miscellaneous Register at microprocessor port address 03C2(Hex), an address shared with a number of other functions. Bits 2 and 3 in the Memory Map Register control bank address and size.

Setting Bit 3 of the Memory Map Register to zero locates the base address of the frame buffer at 0A0000(Hex). Bit 2 then controls bank size. Set to zero it specifies two 128KB banks; set to one it indicates four 64KB banks.

When Bit 3 of the Memory Map Register is set to one, bank size is set at 32KB and Bit 2 controls the base address used by the two permitted banks. With Bit 2 set to zero, the buffer base address is 0B0000(Hex); when set to one, the buffer base address is 0B8000(Hex).

The default operating mode of the VGA system is a character-mapped carry-over from the very first PC display system. This enables your PC to boot up with text messages on your screen so you can read diagnostic messages and enjoy the copyright messages of the various BIOS add-ins you've installed. This text is arrayed in 80 columns across your screen, 25 rows high. Each character is formed in a 9×16 dot box, so the screen displays a total of 720 pixels horizontally and 400 vertically.

Depending on your PC and monitor, the VGA system will default to either color or monochrome operation. In color mode, the VGA system locates its character buffer at base address

0B8000(Hex) and enables you or your software to choose any of 16 foreground colors and eight background colors for each text character. You can also make individual characters blink. (Some software exchanges the ability to make individual characters blink with an extra eight background colors.) In monochrome mode, the character buffer is located at base address 0B0000(Hex). In monochrome text mode, you can select character attributes instead of colors. The available attributes include character intensity (bright or dim), underlining, reverse video, and blinking.

The VGA system provides an automatic means to detect whether you have a monochrome or color monitor attached to your PC using a special signal in the monitor cable, discussed below. Not all PC and monitor makers choose to implement this feature. You can, however, switch between monochrome and color operation using the DOS MODE command.

The distinction between color and monochrome text modes is important because software that writes directly to video memory may not be able to find the screen if your system is in the wrong mode. For example, if you've installed a program to operate in monochrome mode and your VGA system is operating in color mode, the program will write to the wrong address range. The characters will miss the character buffer and disappear—and you'll be stuck staring at a screen that's nearly completely blank; all you're likely to see is a lonely cursor. Running the mode command to switch to the proper mode (color or monochrome) before starting the offending program will solve the problem. Better still, reinstall the program so that it operates in the mode that properly matches the one your VGA system normally uses.

Trouble-shooting

In color modes, monochrome monitors won't produce colors on the screen. They will, however, translate colors into shades of gray. To approximate the way that the colors would appear to your eye in monochrome, the VGA system interprets them into 16 levels of gray with eight matching background gray levels (or 16, depending on whether the individual character blinking feature is enabled).

For compatibility with older software, the VGA system can also operate in a 40-column text mode. In this mode, characters are still formed in a 9×16 dot box but the screen is traced with 360×400 pixel resolution to produce double-width characters. The memory used for this mode always starts at base address 0B8000(Hex).

The basic VGA system includes three fonts, its native 9×16 characters and two for backward compatibility with lower resolution standards, an 8×8 font and a 9×14 font. In addition, it allows the downloading of up to eight more fonts, each with 256 characters. By sacrificing eight of the possible character foreground colors, the VGA system allows the use up to 512 different characters on the screen at a time. The necessary 512-character font (up to four may be used) are simply downloaded in the positions used by two of the smaller fonts.

A familiar part of every text mode screen is the flashing cursor that identifies the position that the next character to be typed will appear on your monitor screen. The VGA chip in your PC generates the cursor. Although you can change the on-screen size of the cursor by sending commands to registers on the VGA chip, you cannot alter the rate at which the cursor flashes.

The blink rate is forever fixed by the VGA chip. The size of the cursor is varied by altering two registers. You load the cursor start register (bits 0 to 4) with binary value of the row in the character matrix that you want to be the top line of the cursor, and you load the cursor end register (bits 0 to 4) with the last line of the cursor. By altering these values, you can make the cursor a block that fills an entire character position, a single scan line, or anything in between. Normally, the cursor is a two-scan line underline. You can turn the cursor completely off by altering bit 5 of the cursor start register.

To send values to the cursor start register, you must load the CRT Controller Address register (which is part of the VGA chip)—which is located at 03B5(Hex) during monochrome operation, 03D5(Hex) during color—to a value of 0A(Hex). You reach the cursor end register by setting the CRT Controller Address register to 0B(Hex).

In text modes, the memory banks are similarly interleaved: odd bytes of display memory in the first bank; even bytes in the second bank. In normal text mode operation, this corresponds to putting the character values in the first bank and attribute data in the second bank. The various pages of character memory start at each 2KB paragraph address boundary. For example, the first page will be based at 0B8000(Hex), the second page at 0B8800(Hex) and so on.

The VGA system is designed to enable you to interchangeably plug a color or monochrome monitor into any VGA video system. Although that seems like no great feat—you'd expect to pull your car into the garage no matter what color it's painted—this compatibility has not always been the case. Early PC video standards drew a hard line between monochrome and color. Plug one in where the other is expected, and you would get a image resembling a sleet storm splashed onto the screen by a two-year-old. Worse, the mismatch connection could lead to monitor melt-down. The VGA system eliminated all such hardware incompatibilities.

Software is another matter. Translating Technicolor into gray flannel can be tricky business. Although translating the relative brightness of colors into shades of gray seems straightforward, the aesthetics can be daunting. The human eye is color-fickle: it prefers some colors to others, being most sensitive to green, least to blue. Direct translations of brightness don't take such human prejudices into account. Moreover, color and monochrome imagery differ in how they affect your human sensitivities and make impact. A monitor screen that's striking in color may become a yawn in monochrome. In fact, the image could completely disappear in the translation.

Most of these matters are beyond the concern of hardware designers, but they still have to make a system that works well for everyone. To help software writers compensate for the individual needs of color and monochrome display systems, the hardware engineers provide a means by which your PC and its software can determine whether you've plugged a monochrome or color monitor into your VGA system. The secret is a special extra signal added to the VGA interface. This extra signal is simply feedback from the display that tells the VGA circuitry what kind of monitor you've plugged in. VGA monitors are designed to send out the proper signal—at least they are supposed to be.

Two pins in the VGA connector allow the detection of display type. Monochrome monitors assign Pin 12 the function of video ground and provide no pin or connection on Pin 11. Color displays are wired in the opposite manner: the connector from the monitor has no Pin 12 and uses Pin 11 as a video ground. This digital ground function is also duplicated on Pin 10 so monitors lacking either sensing pin will still properly receive all image signals.

As a default, the VGA circuitry sends out only the signal assigned to the color green when it detects a monochrome monitor. Of course, the color repertory of the VGA system is compromised by this operation, but the VGA compensates by translating the colors into up to 64 shades of gray, a result of the green signal being capable of handling 26 discrete intensities, limited by the 6-bit green channel of the DAC. Proper monochrome monitors don't have connections for the red or blue signals, so they naturally only get the green signal. Many PCs simply operate as if they would for color monitors even when a monochrome display is attached and let the hardware take care of the differences. Critical software can, however, detect the presence of a monochrome monitor and adjust its display palette (or even image making) to optimize the contrast that appears on the screen.

VESA

The Super VGA modes and resolutions beyond the basic 640×480 graphics mode of VGA include VESA standards at resolution levels of 800×600, 1024×768, 1280×1024, and 1600×1200 pixels.

Standards

By using software drivers, even the most esoteric display hardware can link to your applications, but driver poses a major problem. Designing display drivers for all major applications and operating environments was a big challenge to programmers—and a costly demand for display adapter makers. In fact, only the largest manufacturers could afford the development costs for a full array of application drivers for their products.

The VESA solution to this problem was to develop the VESA BIOS Extension, an add-on BIOS extension for PCs that encapsulated vital data about Super VGA display systems. The VESA BIOS Extension gave programs (in particular, software drivers) vital information about the display system. As with any BIOS code, the VESA BIOS Extension provides a intermediary link between software and hardware. By keeping the BIOS interface the same, the underlying hardware can be changed without affecting the connection with programs.

The basic VESA BIOS interface takes advantage of the standard IBM video function calls that are activated with software interrupt 010(Hex). The VESA BIOS Extension adds one additional function call, 04F(Hex), which is otherwise unused. By loading different parameters when making this function call, software can elicit a number of functions from the VESA BIOS Extension.

Compared to the standard video support built into the basic PC BIOS, that provided by the VESA extension is modest. The additional code holds no new text or individual bit-handling routines. Instead the extension simply provides information that your video drivers and applications need to be able to use the higher resolutions of a Super VGA display adapter. Rather than a secret recipe, the VESA BIOS Extension is the key that unlocks the secret. The video driver software uses the key to put display bits into the proper pixel positions.

One of the most important functions of the VESA BIOS Extension is to report which modes a particular display adapter understands and displays from among the ranges supported by the VESA standard. These cover all the major resolution levels and color depths currently used by display adapters.

VESA developed its very first mode to extend ordinary VGA systems to 800×600 pixel resolution. By the time the association had begun its work, individual manufacturers had already developed their own modes. VESA chose to number its own mode 06A(Hex) and used it as a phantom mode—when this VESA mode was elicited, the display adapter actually switched to one of its own, native modes that supported the 800×600 pixel resolution level.

Standards

Originally, IBM provided eight bits for tracking video modes. To prevent confusion between proprietary video modes and VESA standards, VESA extended the range to 15 bit values. All modes agreed upon after the original 800×600 pixel standard were given 15-bit mode numbers, and the original 06A(Hex) mode was given an alternate number, 101(Hex). Table 13.5 lists the VESA video modes.

TABLE 13.5. Commonly used video mode numbers.

Mode number	Text or Graphic	Originator	Graphic Resolution Horizontal	Vertical	Colors	Text Resolution Columns	Rows
0	Text	IBM				40	25
1	Text	IBM				40	25
2	Text	IBM				80	25
3	Text	IBM				80	25
4	Graphic	IBM	320	200	4		
5	Graphic	IBM	320	200	4		
6	Graphic	IBM	640	200	2		
7	Text	IBM				80	25
8	Graphic	IBM	160	200	16		
9	Graphic	IBM	320	200	16		
A	Graphic	IBM	640	200	4		
B	Graphic	Proprietary	704	519	16		
D	Graphic	IBM	320	200	16		

Mode number	Text or Graphic	Originator	Graphic Resolution		Colors	Text Resolution	
			Horizontal	Vertical		Columns	Rows
E	Graphic	IBM	640	200	16		
F	Graphic	IBM	640	350	2		
10	Graphic	IBM	640	350	16		
11	Graphic	IBM	640	480	2		
12	Graphic	IBM	640	480	16		
13	Graphic	IBM	320	200	256		
22	Text	Ahead			16	132	44
23	Text	Ahead			16	132	25
24	Text	Ahead			16	132	28
25	Graphic	Ahead	640	480	16		
26	Graphic	Ahead	640	480	16		
2F	Text	Ahead			16	160	50
32	Text	Ahead			16	80	34
33	Text	Ahead			16	80	34
34	Text	Ahead			16	80	66
42	Text	Ahead			4	80	34
43	Text	Ahead			4	80	45
50	Graphic	Proprietary	640	480	16		
50	Text	Ahead			2	132	25
50	Text	MXIC			16	132	25
50	Text	MXIC			16	132	30
51	Text	Ahead			4	132	28
52	Text	Ahead			2	132	44
53	Graphic	Proprietary	800	560	16		
55	Graphic	MXIC	800	600	16		
56	Graphic	MXIC	1024	768	16		
57	Graphic	MXIC	640	350	256		
58	Graphic	Proprietary	800	600	16		
58	Graphic	MXIC	640	400	256		
59	Graphic	Proprietary	720	512	16		

continues

TABLE 13.5. continued

Mode number	Text or Graphic	Originator	Graphic Resolution Horizontal	Vertical	Colors	Text Resolution Columns	Rows
59	Graphic	MXIC	640	480	256		
5A	Graphic	MXIC	800	600	256		
5B	Graphic	MXIC	1024	768	256		
60	Graphic	Ahead	640	400	256		
61	Graphic	Ahead	640	480	256		
62	Graphic	Ahead	800	600	256		
63	Graphic	Ahead	1024	768	256		
6A	Graphic	VESA	800	600	16		
70	Graphic	Proprietary	800	600	16		
70	Graphic	Ahead	720	396	16		
71	Graphic	Proprietary	800	600	16		
71	Graphic	Ahead	800	600	16		
73	Graphic	Proprietary	640	480	16		
74	Graphic	Ahead	1024	768	16		
75	Graphic	Ahead	1024	768	4		
76	Graphic	Ahead	1024	768	2		
77	Graphic	Proprietary	752	410	16		
79	Graphic	Proprietary	800	600	16		
100	Graphic	VESA	640	400	256		
101	Graphic	VESA	640	480	256		
102	Graphic	VESA	800	600	16		
103	Graphic	VESA	800	600	256		
104	Graphic	VESA	1024	768	16		
105	Graphic	VESA	1024	768	256		
106	Graphic	VESA	1280	1024	16		
107	Graphic	VESA	1280	1024	256		
108	Text	VESA				80	60
109	Text	VESA				132	25
10A	Text	VESA				132	43
10B	Text	VESA				132	50

Mode number	Text or Graphic	Originator	Graphic Resolution		Colors	Text Resolution	
			Horizontal	Vertical		Columns	Rows
10C	Text	VESA				132	60
10D	Graphic	VESA	320	200	32KB		
10E	Graphic	VESA	320	200	64KB		
10F	Graphic	VESA	320	200	16MB		
110	Graphic	VESA	640	480	32KB		
111	Graphic	VESA	640	480	64KB		
112	Graphic	VESA	640	480	16MB		
113	Graphic	VESA	800	600	32KB		
114	Graphic	VESA	800	600	64KB		
115	Graphic	VESA	800	600	16MB		
116	Graphic	VESA	1024	768	32KB		
117	Graphic	VESA	1024	768	64KB		
118	Graphic	VESA	1024	768	16MB		
119	Graphic	VESA	1280	1024	32KB		
11A	Graphic	VESA	1280	1024	64KB		
11B	Graphic	VESA	1280	1024	16MB		
11C	Graphic	VESA	1600	1200	32KB		
11D	Graphic	VESA	1600	1200	64KB		
11E	Graphic	VESA	1600	1200	16MB		

For software using the VESA BIOS Extensions, finding the available modes is only a start. Your software uses the information reported back by the VESA BIOS extension to determine whether it can operate at the resolution and color level you want. Once the software is certain it can operate in the proper mode, it must then find out how. By sending another function code to the VESA BIOS Extension, your software can determine the location and control system for the memory banks used by the frame buffer for a given video mode.

Under the current VESA specification, a SuperVGA board can provide for one or two apertures into display memory, which the spec calls (without much originality) windows. The size and number of windows is left to the designer of the display system. The VESA BIOS Extension merely reports to inquiring software where they are, how large, and how to control shifting them. It also indicates the memory map, that is, the correspondence of pixel information to display memory. A software driver can then take advantage of this information and write directly to the memory on the VESA-compatible display adapter.

Standards

Under version 2.0 of the VESA BIOS Extension (which, at the time of this writing, remains a proposal rather than a completed specification), the standard itself is extended to include multimedia facilities including control of audio and MIDI control systems. Each of these uses its own function call to send the appropriate information to inquiring software.

Signals

Standards

Both the VGA and VESA SuperVGA systems use separate-sync RGB signals. VGA requires monitors capable of synchronizing at a fixed horizontal sweep frequency of 31.5 KHz and accommodate two frame rates, 60 Hz and 70 Hz. SuperVGA systems operate at higher horizontal frequencies, up to 80 KHz, and require special multiscanning monitors.

The VGA system shifts between these frame rates depending on the mode in which it operates. Text and graphics modes designed for backward compatibility with older graphics standards (which means all those except 640×480 pixels) use the frame 70 Hz rate. High resolution VGA graphics used by multimedia programs under Windows and OS/2 slip back to the 60 Hz rate to maintain operating frequencies within acceptable limits—the slower frame rate allows squeezing more lines on the screen without significantly altering system timing.

To accommodate its text mode, native graphics mode, and two backwardly compatible graphics modes, the VGA system creates displays that may be built from one of three possible numbers of horizontal display lines—either 350, 400, or 480 lines. (To work with old graphic software that builds images 200 lines high, the VGA system uses double-scanning. This is, each pixel in the image is sent to the monitor twice, once in each of two sequential scan lines. This technique does not increase the resolution of the image; it only trims the number of different image sizes used by the system.)

The tripart VGA line count creates a tough enough problem. All else being equal, a display made out of fewer lines will fill less of the monitor screen. The image will be shorter because the width of monitor display lines is reasonably constant; the height of the image depends only on the number of lines piled up. Practically speaking, a 350-line display would be less than three-quarter the height of a 480-line image. The VGA system compensates for this height difference by requiring the monitor to alter its vertical gain in accordance with the number of lines it is displaying. Raising the vertical gain effectively makes each line wider, which can compensate for a lower line count. On many monitors you can make this adjustment yourself by twisting the control labeled vertical gain or height.

The VGA designers developed a system to tell the monitor how many lines are in an image without counting them (which would challenge the thinking abilities of most monitors that usually have the intelligence of a flatworm). The VGA circuitry simply sends a code to the monitor to indicate how many vertical lines it is sending in each frame. Instead of adding a new signal to the array of those the VGA system sends out, the engineers took advantage of two signals that were already available. By altering the polarities of the vertical and horizontal synchronizing signals, the engineers were able to send the monitor an indication of each of four distinct VGA modes.

Only three of the possible codes are used by the VGA system. The code specifies 480 line operation when both sync signals are negative-going. For 400-line mode, vertical sync is negative-going and horizontal is positive-going. For 350-line mode, the code is vertical sync positive-going and horizontal sync negative-going. The remaining combination was reserved for indicating interlaced 1024-line displays but has been subsumed by VESA to indicate any of its SuperVGA operating modes.

To standard monitor operating parameters at higher resolutions, VESA has developed a full list of *monitor timing specifications.* Although these are commonly represented (as here) as a table of horizontal and vertical synchronizing frequencies used at various resolution levels, the VESA standards go deeper. They also indicate the exact relationship between the synchronizing signals and the on-screen display, specifying the delay between blanking and on-screen information. The net result is that the specifications completely describe the shape of the display waveform at each resolution level. The wave shape directly translates to the on-screen position of the active image. In other words, if a display adapter follows the VESA specification, it will put its image at the same place exactly as every other display adapter that follows the VESA spec—no more images jumping around the screen.

Standards

The initial increment up from VGA was 800×600 pixel resolution. True to its committee origins, VESA endowed this resolution with several options. Initially the specifications describe two guidelines and a single standard. These guidelines allowed for SuperVGA systems operating at 56 and 60 Hz to earn the VESA imprimatur—and let manufacturers with monitor designs pre-dating the original standard to sell their products as VESA compliant. The 56 Hz guideline accommodated older monitors designed with a bandwidth aimed only as high as handling the 35.5 KHz horizontal frequency IBM set for its 8514/A system. The 60 Hz guideline compromised between electronics cost and refresh rate. The official VESA standard at the 800×600 pixel resolution level requires an eye-pleasing 72 Hz refresh rate.

At higher resolutions, VESA allows for several refresh rates. All standard monitor frequencies are given in Table 13.6.

TABLE 13.6. Scanning frequencies and refresh rates specified by monitor standards.

Standard	Resolution	Vert. Sync (Frame rate)	Horz. Sync (Line rate)	Sync Polarity Vert.	Horz.	Signal type (TTL or analog)
MDA	720×50	50 Hz.	18.3 KHz.	Pos.	Pos.	TTL (1 color)
CGA	640×200	60 Hz.	15.75 KHz.	Pos.	Pos.	TTL (16 colors)
EGA	640×350	60 Hz.	21.5 KHz.	Pos.	Pos.	TTL (64 colors)
MCGA (Graphics)	640×480	60 Hz.	31.5 KHz.	Neg.	Neg.	Analog

continues

TABLE 13.6. continued

Standard	Resolution	Vert. Sync (Frame rate)	Horz. Sync (Line rate)	Sync Polarity Vert.	Horz.	Signal type (TTL or analog)
MCGA (Text)	720×400	70 Hz.	31.5 KHz.	Neg.	Neg.	Analog
VGA (Graphics)	640×480	60 Hz.	31.5 KHz.	Neg.	Neg.	Analog
VGA (Text)	720×400	70 Hz.	31.5 KHz.	Neg.	Neg.	Analog
Macintosh	640×480	67 Hz.	35.0 KHz.	N/A	N/A	Analog
XGA-2	640×480	75.0 Hz.	39.38 KHz.	Neg.	Neg.	Analog
VESA	640×480	75	37.5 KHz.	Neg.	Neg.	Analog
Apple Portrait	640×870	76.5 Hz.	70.19 KHz.	N/A	N/A	Analog
VESA guideline	800×600	56 Hz.	35.5 KHz.	Either	Either	Analog
VESA guideline	800×600	60 Hz.	37.9 KHz.	Pos.	Pos.	Analog
VESA standard	800×600	72 Hz.	48.1 KHz.	Pos.	Pos.	Analog
VESA standard	800×600	75 Hz.	46.875 KHz.	Pos.	Pos.	Analog
RasterOps &	1024×768	75.1 Hz.	60.24 KHz.	N/A	N/A	Analog
Supermac	1024×768	75.1 Hz.	60.24 KHz.	N/A	N/A	Analog
VESA guideline	1024×768	60 Hz.	48.3 KHz.	Neg.	Neg.	Analog
VESA standard	1024×768	70.1 Hz.	56.5 KHz.	Neg.	Neg.	Analog
VESA standard	1024×768	75 Hz.	60 KHz.	Pos.	Pos.	Analog
8514/A	1024×768	44 Hz.*	35.5 KHz.	Pos.	Pos.	Analog
XGA	1024×768	44 Hz.*	35.5 KHz.	Pos.	Pos.	Analog
XGA-2	1024×768	75.8 Hz.	61.1 KHz.	Pos.	Pos.	Analog
Apple 2-page	1152×870	75 Hz.	68.68 KHz.	N/A	N/A	Analog

Standard	Resolution	Vert. Sync (Frame rate)	Horz. Sync (Line rate)	Sync Polarity Vert.	Horz.	Signal type (TTL or analog)
VESA standard	1280×1024	75 Hz.	80 KHz.	Pos.	Pos.	Analog

* Because 8514/A and XGA the current XGA standards operate in interlaced mode, they require monitors that are capable of synchronizing to their field rate, which is twice the frame rate, that is 88 Hz.

Connectors

As a separate sync video system, VGA should by rights require five separate connections. At the time IBM developed VGA, the company regarded such a tangle of cables as particularly unfriendly to the consumer. As a result, IBM developed a new connector that accommodated all of the required signals in a single cable. Called a high-density 15-pin connector, signals on the VGA connector as assigned as shown in Table 13.7.

TABLE 13.7. Video Graphics Array Pin-Out.

15-Pin High-Density D-Shell Connector	
Pin	Function
1	Red video
2	Green video
3	Blue video
4	Reserved
5	Digital Ground
6	Red Return
7	Green Return
8	Blue Return
9	Key (plugged hole)
10	Digital Ground
11	Reserved (monitor type indicator)
12	Reserved (monitor type indicator)
13	Horizontal Sync
14	Vertical Sync
15	Reserved

Most computer monitors now use this connector. However because this connector does not present a constant impedance and is somewhat subject to crosstalk, many monitor makers have elected to use separate video cables for each signal channel. Invariably, these high-quality monitors use BNC connectors: three for sync on green (typically labeled R, G, and B); four for composite sync (typically labeled R, G, B, and Sync); five for separate sync (typically labeled R, G, B, H, and V).

Many multimedia video products link up with VGA circuits internally to combine signals. These rely on a special connector on your PC's motherboard or display adapter called the *VESA Feature Connector.* This special connection permits add-on accessories to share signals and control with VGA circuitry. Add-ons can even overpower the VGA and switch it off, claiming the video output as their own.

VESA derived its feature connector from the VGA Feature Connector that IBM added to its VGA systems. The VESA connector includes the same signals as the VGA Feature Connector but uses a pin connector instead of the VGA's edge connector. Note that older products that expect to use a VGA Feature Connector cannot plug into a VESA Feature Connector (and vice versa). Each of the two standards requires its own particular connecting cable.

Both the VGA and VESA feature connectors are limited to the signals used by the VGA system itself. They are not useful beyond 640×480-pixel resolution in 256 colors, but higher resolution systems sometimes require interconnections, too. To satisfy the need for a high-performance channel for linking graphics and video systems, VESA designed a new, high performance connection called the VESA Advanced Feature Connector. Although it has limited backward compatibility with the standard VESA Feature Connector, the new VAFC transcends the limitations of VGA. It passes video data at a rate up to 150MB/second. The connector provides a 16-bit or 32-bit data channel that operates at a maximum clock speed of 37.5 MHz and supports resolutions up to 1024 by 768. In its fullest 32-bit implementation, the VAFC uses an 80-pin high-density connector with 0.1 by 0.05-inch pin spacing. Its pinout is shown in Table 13.8.

TABLE 13.8. VESA Advanced Feature Connector.

Pin	Name	Direction	Function
1	RSRV0	Undefined	Reserved for future use
2	RSRV1	Undefined	Reserved for future use
3	GENCLK	In/out	Genlock input
4	OFFSET0	In	Pixel offset 2
5	OFFSET1	In	Pixel offset 1
6	FSTAT	In	FIFO buffer status
7	VRDY	In	Video ready

Pin	Name	Direction	Function
8	GRDY	In	Graphics ready
9	BLANK	In/out	Blanking
10	VSYNC	In/out	Vertical sync
11	HSYNC	In/out	Horizontal sync
12	EGEN	In/out	Enable genlock
13	VCLK	In/out	Graphics data clock
14	RSV2	Undefined	Reserved for future definition
15	DCLK	In/out	Video data clock
16	EVIDEO	In/out	Video data direction control
17	P0	In/out	Video data 0
18	GND	Undefined	Ground
19	P3	In/out	Video data 3
20	P4	In/out	Video data 4
21	GND	Undefined	Ground
22	P7	In/out	Video data 7
23	P8	In/out	Video data 8
24	GND	Undefined	Ground
25	P11	In/out	Video data 11
26	P12	In/out	Video data 12
27	GND	Undefined	Ground
28	P15	In/out	Video data 15
29	P16	In/out	Video data 16
30	GND	Undefined	Ground
31	P19	In/out	Video data 19
32	P20	In/out	Video data 20
33	GND	Undefined	Ground
34	P23	In/out	Video data 23
35	P24	In/out	Video data 24
36	GND	Undefined	Ground
37	P27	In/out	Video data 27
38	P28	In/out	Video data 28
39	GND	Undefined	Ground

continues

TABLE 13.8. continued

Pin	Name	Direction	Function
40	P31	In/out	Video data 31
41	GND	Undefined	Ground
42	GND	Undefined	Ground
43	GND	Undefined	Ground
44	GND	Undefined	Ground
45	GND	Undefined	Ground
46	GND	Undefined	Ground
47	GND	Undefined	Ground
48	GND	Undefined	Ground
49	GND	Undefined	Ground
50	GND	Undefined	Ground
51	GND	Undefined	Ground
52	GND	Undefined	Ground
53	GND	Undefined	Ground
54	GND	Undefined	Ground
55	GND	Undefined	Ground
56	GND	Undefined	Ground
57	P1	In/out	Video data 1
58	P2	In/out	Video data 2
59	GND	Undefined	Ground
60	P5	In/out	Video data 5
61	P6	In/out	Video data 6
62	GND	Undefined	Ground
63	P9	In/out	Video data 7
64	P10	In/out	Video data 8
65	GND	Undefined	Ground
66	P13	In/out	Video data 13
67	P14	In/out	Video data 14
68	GND	Undefined	Ground
69	P17	In/out	Video data 17
70	P18	In/out	Video data 18

Pin	Name	Direction	Function
71	GND	Undefined	Ground
72	P21	In/out	Video data 21
73	P22	In/out	Video data 22
74	GND	Undefined	Ground
75	P25	In/out	Video data 25
76	P26	In/out	Video data 26
77	GND	Undefined	Ground
78	P29	In/out	Video data 29
79	P30	In/out	Video data 30
80	GND	Undefined	Ground

A typical application uses the VAFC to link a video system that captures images with a television camera with a computer graphic system for special effects. Equipment on either side of the connector can use signals from either side of it to create composite images.

When you want the highest quality video on a PC screen, running through a standard display system like VGA or SuperVGA won't cut it. Even the highest speed systems are pressed to make images larger than 160×120 with a 15 per second frame rate. For full-screen, real-time video you need an external video source that can be combined with the PC-generated video (both images and text) and still take advantage of the PC as a control system. Today's multimedia technology allows you to combine external video from cameras, VCRs, and laser disc players with the rest of your PC's resources.

Chapter 14

Cameras and Monitors

In a multimedia system, the PC operates as the command center, control point, and editor for video images. Although it can create some images on its own, most multimedia presentations involve video captured from the real world. You also need a means to monitor the production of your multimedia extravaganza and to view the results.

These two functions, video input and output, are served by devices running refugee from the classic world of video production. At the input end is the video camera, today a sophisticated electronic device more complex than an ordinary PC that combines a multitude of functions. At the output end comes the monitor, a stripped-down television set that's often beefed up for the needs of your PC.

Video Cameras

A true video camera has three essential parts. A lens focuses an external image on an optical transducer where the image gets converted to electrical signals. Control electronics transform the signals from the transducer into one compatible with external video systems. A viewfinder lets you see and monitor the image so you can tell what you've pointed the camera at. Today, most consumer video cameras take the form of *camcorders*, which mean that a videocassette recorder of some kind is grafted to a video camera along with a microphone. We'll discuss the individual parts of video cameras and camcorders separately as their optical, electronic, recording, and monitoring sections.

Optics

By their nature, all cameras—still, motion picture, and video—work with light. The images a video camera sees are made from photons, which are captured and focused by a lens and translated into electrical signals by a sensor or optical transducer. The video camera then organizes the video signals and prepares them for storage or transmission.

The first part of this process involves the field of optics, the manipulation of light. The output of the camera depends almost entirely on the quality of the optical components of the camera. To understand how a video camera works and what you can do with it, you need a basic understanding of its optical components.

Sensors

The primary job of any camera is to convert light into a more workable form. After all, light itself is pretty difficult to deal with. You can't hold on to it, you can't even stop it. It just keeps going off in its own direction, spreading out and mixing up with the rest of the stuff of the universe, mingling and making entropy. The camera captures a pattern of light and renders it into either a chemical or electronic image.

Conventional still cameras work by capturing the energy from photons of light and using it to disrupt silver-based molecules. Video cameras let the energy in photons cause or change the flow of an electrical current. In the camera, this current gets amplified and organized, eventually becoming a video signal.

The initial interface between light and electricity is the optical sensor, the device that actually registers the reception of photons. The first video cameras—actually television cameras—used special vacuum tubes to detect light. These had interesting names, kind of a pantheon of fire gods: for example, image orthicon, vidicon, Saticon, and Plumbicon. In the late 1970s, however, solid-state technology finally overtook image-making. Today the standard optical sensor is the *Charge-Coupled Device* or *CCD*, a special flat silicon chip that produces a small current proportional to the number of photons striking it.

The mere presence of light is not as important as its pattern, which makes up the actual image. A single CCD registers only a single point. Consequently, what's normally called a CCD is actually an array of individual CCD elements. In video cameras, the CCD elements get arranged as a matrix. (The CCDs used in scanners typically are arranged as a thin straight line.) Camera circuitry samples each element in turn to scan an image frame.

CCDs come in various sizes. Typical CCDs in video cameras measure one-quarter, one-third, or one-half inch (diagonally). All else equal, the larger the CCD, the greater the number of elements that can be packed into the array. The number of elements determines the resolution of the image signal produced by the CCD. This number is related to, but is not the same as, the number of pixels in an image.

Color

The difference between CCD elements and pixels results from the need to register color. To record a full color spectrum, each pixel normally requires three CCD elements, one each for the three primary colors (red, green, and blue). The number of pixels is consequently one-third the total number of CCD elements.

CCDs by themselves are essentially color blind. To separate colors, video cameras put *color filters* that transmit only one color (actually a well-defined range of colors) between the CCDs and light source. Professional video cameras and the best consumer models use three separate CCD arrays, each dedicated to one color. In these three-chip cameras, a beam-splitter divides the incoming light into three beams, one for each sensor. One-chip sensors put a single filter with a three-color pattern (for example, interleaved stripes) in front of a single CCD. Two-chip cameras use one sensor for luminance (green) and a single chip with a two-color filter to produce two chrominance signals, corresponding to the needs of composite video encoding. Three-chip cameras are inherently sharper because each color is measured at exactly the same point. One-chip cameras must physically offset the sensing elements of the different colors of a pixel.

Resolution

A number of factors limit the resolution of camcorder images, and the quality of both the lens and the CCD enter into consideration.

The maximum possible resolution is set by the number of pixels that the CCD can sense. If you know the number of CCD elements in a sensor (video cameras are sometimes described by this figure) you can determine its highest possible resolution using these formulae:

```
Horizontal resolution = 4 * sqr(number of pixels/12)
Vertical resolution = 3 * sqr(number of pixels/12)
```

To determine the number of pixels in the image, divide the number of CCD elements by three. Divide this figure by 12, then determine the square root of the result. Horizontal resolution is four times this figure; vertical resolution three times the figure.

A high-quality camcorder with a CCD sensor with 300,000 elements can achieve a resolution of 365×273 pixels, which is actually somewhat better than most consumer videotape formats can handle. With a one-quarter-inch CCD, the entire imaging area measures a bit more than 4×3mm, which would require a lens to be able to resolve nearly 100 lines per millimeter, quite a challenge for the lens designer. The lens would likely limit resolution to a lower level than the CCD sensor can detect. With a larger CCD, however, the larger imaging area moves the resolution limitation from lens quality to the sensor itself.

Of course, no matter what limits its resolution, a 365×273 image has pretty poor resolution, at least in comparison with computer displays that reach beyond 1024×768 pixels. In video images, however, such a low resolution often is not objectionable. You probably watch without grumbling lower quality displays every time you press the play button on your VCR. Moving images and the large, smooth color range in video signals help mask lens defects and CCD resolution limitations. Moreover, video image processing can increase apparent sharpness by accentuating edge contrast.

Lenses

As the preceding resolution calculations show, getting the best possible quality from a video camera or camcorder requires a high-quality lens. Oddly, this most important part of a video camera (or any camera, for that matter) is not electronic and, in purest form, doesn't even have any moving parts. It generates no signals but determines what's in them all.

A camera lens is actually a composite of many individual lenses, called simple lenses or elements. By properly designing and grouping the simple lens elements together, optical designers can minimize (but never entirely eliminate) the distortion and defects caused by the individual simple lenses. The trade-offs they make in selecting the simple lenses and arranging them as well as the quality of the lenses themselves determines the focal length, sharpness, brightness, and contrast of the image formed by the overall lens. By making the arrangement between the lens elements variable in the proper manner, the designers can make the lens zoom, which means change its magnification (actually, zooming in a lens changes its focal length without altering its focus, but the optical effect is the same).

The lenses in modern video cameras and camcorders are amazing optics. Ten-to-one zoom ratios are near the norm in camcorder. That is, the camera can brings things ten times closer visually than its widest setting. Even the best still camera lenses struggle with 7:1 zoom ratios. The best professional video zoom lenses triple that. You can get even more range by adding supplementary lenses to your camcorder, which typically double the telephoto reach and wide-angle breadth of the image.

Video lenses have wide zoom ranges because they otherwise don't have to be very good. Their images need only cover a small area, an image sensor a fraction of an inch across. They don't have to be very sharp because the resolution of a video system is less than one-quarter that of 35mm film.

Focal Length

Zoom ratios tell you a range but don't reveal absolute values, how wide an area you can picture or how close you can get. Buried in the specifications of most camcorders you'll find the focal length of the lens, expressed as a range matching the zoom ratio. Strictly speaking, the focal length of a lens is the distance from the center of the lens to a sharply focused image of an object an infinite distance away (from the other side of the lens). In other words, a lens with a focal length of two inches (about 50mm) would focus a distant view two inches from the lens.

The size of the image relative to the original object varies with the focal length of the lens. The shorter the focal length, the smaller replica of the original object the image will be. When the area over which the image gets projected is held constant, the focal length of the lens relates to its field of view—how much of the original object fits into the image area. By making the image replica smaller, a short focal length lens fits more of the image in a given area. Short focal length lenses fit a wider viewing angle into a given area and are hence often called wide-angle lenses. Longer focal lengths make the image appear larger.

Old-fashioned cameras—those made of wood with long black bellows and a photographer behind holding up a birdie—accommodated various lens focal lengths by lengthening and shortening their bellows. Making such changes is impractical with camcorder lenses, particularly when it must handle a 10:1 zoom range.

Optical designers solved this problem by adding extra lens elements that alter the path of light. With a proper design, they can adjust the distance from the back of the lens to the image to nearly any value they like. To make lenses interchangeable, this back focus is controlled so that the distance from the lens mounting flange to the image is constant for a given lens system.

Adding more lens elements enables optical designers to create complex lenses that change their apparent focal length—zoom—without altering the back focus of the lens. A zoom lens comprises several lens elements that act together so that they look to the outside world as a single lens. A modern camcorder zoom lens works by moving the optical center of the lens around without appreciably changing the rest of the lens assembly. (Modern optical designers can actually move the optical center of the lens so that it behaves as if it were in front or behind the entire lens assembly.) The result is that zoom lenses alter the size of the image of a given object without getting appreciably longer or shorter. This corresponds to changing the angle of view of the resulting image, letting you pull back for a wide-angle shot of a barroom brouhaha or zoom in for a telephoto view of your star's nose pores just before the impact of a punch.

Field of View

The most prominent description of any camcorder lens—its zoom ratio—tells you nothing about what you'll actually see, how wide an area the lens can spread across your monitor screen or how big it can make a distant object. Even when the manufacturer lists the focal length range of the lens, you still won't know. Although the field of view of a lens depends on the focal length, it also varies with the size of the area you devote to the image—the film size or the size of the camcorder image sensor. The larger the image area, the wider the view from a given focal length lens. For example, while a 50mm lens gives a "normal" field of view on a 35mm camera, for a camcorder a 50mm lens would be a telephoto.

Unlike 35mm cameras, which all use the same size film and have about the same size image area, camcorders use different sizes of image sensors. Most camcorders describe this as CCD size, and three sizes are common in consumer models: quarter-inch, third-inch, and half-inch. All of these values represent the length of a diagonal drawn across the rectangular sensor and are nominal rather than exact values.

Most experts believe that the "normal" field of view for a still camera lens results when the focal length of the lens equals the diagonal of the image area. This relationship results in a field of view of about 46°. (A 35mm camera has an image diagonal of about 43mm, and the nearest round value is 50mm.) The focal length required for this normal field of view for a quarter-inch CCD is about 7mm; for a third-inch CCD, 6.9mm; and for a half-inch CCD, 9.3mm. Table 14.1 compares the field of view for lens focal lengths in various imaging formats.

TABLE 14.1. Focal length for given field of view for various imaging formats.

Format	6×4.5	35mm	1-in CCD
Units	Centimeters	Millimeters	Millimeters
Diagonal	7.50	43.27	25.40
Field of view		Focal length:	
115.00	2.39	13.78	8.09
110.00	2.63	15.15	8.89
105.00	2.88	16.60	9.75
100.00	3.15	18.15	10.66
95.00	3.44	19.82	11.64
90.00	3.75	21.63	12.70
85.00	4.09	23.61	13.86
80.00	4.47	25.78	15.14
75.00	4.89	28.19	16.55
70.00	5.36	30.90	18.14
65.00	5.89	33.96	19.93
60.00	6.50	37.47	22.00
55.00	7.20	41.56	24.40
50.00	8.04	46.39	27.24
45.00	9.05	52.23	30.66
40.00	10.30	59.44	34.89

Iris

Lenses differ in their ability to collect light. Given the same scene, one lens may make an image sixteen or more times brighter than another. In still photography, the light gathering ability of a lens is called its aperture and is familiar as the *f-stop*. In movie-making and video, the same concept is sometimes called an *iris*, corresponding to your eye's light regulator, the iris.

The lens aperture or iris is usually measured by its f-stop, a measure of the relationship between the focal length of the lens and the diameter of its clear aperture. The f-stop number indicates the focal length divided by the diameter of the apparent aperture (not the physical diameter of the iris hole but the apparent size of the hole when you look through the lens). For example, a lens with a 25mm focal length with an aperture of about 9mm would be set to an f-stop of 2.8 (that's roughly 25/9).

3/4-in CCD	*1/2-in CCD*	*1/3-in CCD*	*1/4-in CCD*
Millimeters	Millimeters	Millimeters	Millimeters
19.05	12.70	8.47	6.35
6.07	4.05	2.70	2.02
6.67	4.45	2.96	2.22
7.31	4.87	3.25	2.44
7.99	5.33	3.55	2.66
8.73	5.82	3.88	2.91
9.52	6.35	4.23	3.17
10.39	6.93	4.62	3.46
11.35	7.57	5.05	3.78
12.41	8.28	5.52	4.14
13.60	9.07	6.05	4.53
14.95	9.97	6.64	4.98
16.50	11.00	7.33	5.50
18.30	12.20	8.13	6.10
20.43	13.62	9.08	6.81
23.00	15.33	10.22	7.67
26.17	17.45	11.63	8.72

continues

TABLE 14.1. continued

Format	6×4.5	35mm	1-in CCD
Units	Centimeters	Millimeters	Millimeters
Diagonal	7.50	43.27	25.40
Field of view		Focal length:	
35.00	11.89	68.61	40.28
30.00	14.00	80.74	47.40
25.00	16.92	97.58	57.29
20.00	21.27	122.69	72.03
15.00	28.48	164.32	96.47
10.00	42.86	247.27	145.16
8.00	53.63	309.37	181.62
6.00	71.55	412.79	242.33
5.00	85.89	495.48	290.88
4.00	107.39	619.50	363.68
3.00	143.21	826.14	484.99
2.00	214.84	1239.37	727.58
1.00	429.71	2478.93	1455.27

This simple math makes for complications. It results in an inversely logarithmic scale. (The focal length is a linear measurement, the aperture an area.) Doubling the f-stop lowers the amount of light that can pass by a factor of four. To make mental calculations and comparisons easier, the world has standardized a series of f-stop numbers, each of which differs from the next by a factor of two. The series runs 1.0, 1.4, 2, 2.8, 4, 5.6, 8, 11, 16, 22, 32, 45, 64, 90, 128. (The sequence is simpler than it looks. Each f-stop differs from its predecessor by the square root of two, the results rounded.) Table 14.2 lists the ISO standard (nominal) f-stops, the actual (computed) f-stop, and relative light values.

TABLE 14.2. Standard f-stops and light values.

Nominal stop (ISO)	Actual stop and half-stop	Light value (relative f/1.0)
1	1.00	1.00
	1.19	1.41
1.4	1.41	2.00
	1.68	2.83

3/4-in CCD	1/2-in CCD	1/3-in CCD	1/4-in CCD
Millimeters	Millimeters	Millimeters	Millimeters
19.05	12.70	8.47	6.35
30.21	20.14	13.43	10.07
35.55	23.70	15.80	11.85
42.96	28.64	19.10	14.32
54.02	36.01	24.01	18.01
72.35	48.23	32.16	24.12
108.87	72.58	48.39	36.29
136.21	90.81	60.54	45.40
181.75	121.16	80.78	60.58
218.16	145.44	96.96	72.72
272.76	181.84	121.23	90.92
363.74	242.50	161.66	121.25
545.69	363.79	242.53	181.90
1091.45	727.64	485.09	363.82

Nominal stop (ISO)	Actual stop and half-stop	Light value (relative f/1.0)
2	2.00	4.00
	2.38	5.66
2.8	2.83	8.00
	3.36	11.31
4	4.00	16.00
	4.76	22.63
5.6	5.66	32.00
	6.73	45.25
8	8.00	64.00
	9.51	90.51
11	11.31	128.00
	13.45	181.02

continues

TABLE 14.2. continued

Nominal stop (ISO)	Actual stop and half-stop	Light value (relative f/1.0)
16	16.00	256.00
	19.03	362.04
22	22.63	512.00
	26.91	724.08
32	32.00	1024.00
	38.05	1448.15
45	45.25	2048.00
	53.82	2896.31
64	64.00	4096.00

Lenses are usually described by the f-stop corresponding to their maximum aperture. The iris stops usually down to a much lower value, typically with a range of six to nine f-stops (a brightness range of 64 to 512). By itself this degree of control is inadequate to even out the levels of illumination of all scenes, which may differ by factors greater than 10,000, but it can aid the automatic gain control circuitry in a video camera to maintain the correct output level.

The maximum f-stop of a lens is one factor that determines how much light you need in a scene to make a usable image, measured in lux. The sensitivity of the image sensor is a more important factor.

Lens aperture also controls the depth of field of a recorded image, the distance range in which objects appear to be in focus. Wider apertures result in less depth of field; opening the iris of a lens makes the depth of field shallower and puts greater emphasis on the parts of the image that are in sharpest focus.

Depth of field depends only on absolute aperture (not f-stop). The same diameter aperture will yield the same depth of field no matter the focal length of the lens. Note, though, that as you increase the focal length of a lens while holding the aperture constant, the f-number increases. Consequently, the longer the lens, the higher the f-stop required for a given depth of field.

Shutters

Video cameras do not need shutters in the same way movie cameras do. A shutter protects motion picture film from getting exposed by light passing through the camera lens when the film moves from one frame to the next. Shutters in video cameras are used instead to freeze action. Ordinary video cameras integrate the light of an image throughout the entire period of a single frame. If the object that's being recorded moves in that period, its image will smear out into a motion blur within the frame. When watching a normal speed video, you don't notice the blur because your eye cannot follow the action. But if you run the video in slow or stop motion, the blur becomes readily apparent.

By limiting the exposure of an image to a tiny fraction of the normal frame rate, a video camera shutter freezes action. Not only will still frames appear sharper but even moving images develop a sharper presence.

Zooming

Modern video cameras enable you to zoom in on images in two ways, optically and electronically. Optical zooming takes place inside the zoom lens. The focal length of the lens changes, enlarging the image on the camera sensor. Electronic zooming requires sampling a small section of the entire image sensor and resizing the data from the sample to fill your entire screen. An optical zoom increases the visual information falling on the sensor; electronic zooming does not. Optical zooming does not affect image resolution; electronic zooming lowers resolution an amount equivalent to the zoom factor.

Note that electronic zoom need not take place in the camera. Most image editing programs let you electronically zoom in on any image you can capture into your PC. Some programs give you a choice of resizing or resampling the image. Resizing generally just duplicates pixels, making the image increasingly jagged as you raise the zoom factor. Resampling interpolates pixels to minimize the jagged effect.

Zoom range is usually expressed as a zoom "power" or zoom "factor," and it quantifies how many times greater the longest focal length of the lens is compared to the shortest. A zoom lens with a range from 5 to 50mm would be classed as a 10× or 10-power zoom. A wide optical zoom range gives you more control but makes for a more complex and expensive lens.

The optical zooming of a zoom lens is continuous. You can choose whatever intermediate value of zoom you want just by releasing the pushbutton on the zoom control. Electronic zooming usually is available only in discrete increments, factors from two to 20. In that way, electronic zooming is like adding a supplementary telephoto lens. The supplementary lens generally has less of an effect on resolution. Although the supplementary lens lowers the sharpness of the image, it does so smoothly. Electronic zooming can add objectionable blockiness to the image because it adds no additional detail or information to the image.

There is no electronic equivalent of the wide-angle supplementary lens. Modern electronics cannot synthesize the outer edges of an image that do not reach the CCD sensor.

Focusing

Zoom lenses maintain their focus throughout their zoom range (at least they should), although modern autofocus cameras make this need less important.

Focus is most critical at the longest focal lengths, when you zoom in to make your subject as large as possible in the viewfinder. (Technically speaking, focusing errors are more obvious because the depth of field for a given aperture decreases as focal length increases.) When you manually focus a zoom lens, the best practice is to zoom all the way in, focus, then pull back to frame your subject properly without further adjustment to the focus—unless your subject moves.

Stability

Cinema verité once meant prying the old Mitchell movie camera from its tripod and carrying it around like an overweight baby. Scenes sloshed around like a small yacht bound for terminal seasickness. It gave you a sense of being there—and looking for the nearest exit. Today popping the video camera off the tripod is the standard way of rebelling against the authority of the establishment image, the means of bringing the immediacy of video journalism to mundane matters, the way of making even the most polished and rehearsed efforts look like home movies.

The unstable, swimming image of a handheld video camera still has its place. But a stable image that frees the audience of suspicions that the theater is sitting atop San Andreas on an off day has a role, too. Getting the rock solid look takes a lot of attention.

The classic means of keeping images stable is locking down the camera to a tripod. The bigger, the better. The more unwieldy it is to make pictures, the better they will look. As soon as the script calls for a pan, however, the image can break free from its moorings. The secret to keeping things sane is to do them smoothly. Smooth pans require a special tripod, one with a fluid head. The fluid is a viscous oil in the bearing about which the head and camera rotates. The fluid damps the movements to prevent sudden jerks or too quick acceleration or deceleration.

If you set up a tripod for every shot, every magic moment would likely be lost for all time. Things happen quick, and absent a script or a goodly dose of precognition you'll never catch them. That's why the handheld camera works so well for memory-making home movies.

If you want the spontaneity of freedom movement but don't want your images to look like you've got terminal delirium tremens, you have your choice of two stable solutions. Portable camera steadying platforms, the most familiar being SteadiCam (or its low-cost home video offspring, SteadiCam Jr.). These platforms combine a more stable, multi-point base of support (they don't just wear down your shoulder, they poke and prod at your whole body) along with a damping mechanism to smooth out the earthquakes.

Although with a stabilizing platform the operator doesn't quite suffer as if he were bound and chained, the effect on spontaneity can be almost as stiffling. To give you both freedom and stability, several camcorder makers have put digital technology to work. Some camcorders have built-in image stablization, usually a mechanical system that uses an optical element to move the lens image when the camcorder moves.

Expensive imaging systems sometimes use electronic image stabilization, which requires no mechanical add-ons. Instead, the system exploits an extra area on a camera's CCD sensor, making the on-screen image a window that shows only the central part of the image. When a particularly inept or abrupt camera motion makes the image bounce, the camcorder compensates by moving the image window to match, then more slowly and smoothly moves the window back to its normal, central position. The jitters go away but your aspirations remain unchained. The only shortcoming is that the range of such systems is limited by the size of the CCD sensor. Again, the camera can't synthesize what it cannot see. Optical image stabilization systems, used on some better camcorders, use a variable optical element (a wedge or prism) that is varied to compensate for camera movement. Because it is optical, the stabilization system does not require overscanning and does not decrease the detail in the image.

Electronics

After an image falls on a CCD sensor, a video camera's electronics get the chore of making sense of it. The camera must arrange a scan of the image, putting each pixel in its proper place in the serial data stream; it must compensate for the non-linearities of the sensor and perform other manipulations; it must encode the colors into a format compatible with whatever destination the signal is headed; it must add synchronizing signals, and finally it must adjust the level of the signals to suit whatever standard the system follows.

Scanning

Turning the flat, two-dimensional image on the sensor into a serial data stream requires only sampling the individual elements of the CCD in the proper order at the proper times. The sampling order is easy; a few lines of BASIC code would be enough to generate the needed addresses. Timing, too, is no hardship—just supply the system with the proper clock for carrying out its sampling.

The video standard determines the clock frequency, and crystal oscillators are accurate enough that a camera can generate the signal it needs internally. Sometimes, however, even crystal precision is not enough. When there's even a slight timing difference between video signals, they won't mix smoothly together when you want to fade or wipe between them. To get smooth effects, the frequencies used by multiple video sources must be precisely locked. One way of providing the necessary synchrony between signals is to supply a single common timebase for all video sources. This technique is called gen-locking because the timebase generators of all video sources get locked together. In a gen-locked system, each camera or other video source receives a timing signal from which it derives its synchronizing frequencies.

Digital still cameras are essentially single-shot video cameras. They use the same imaging technology, but they are freed from the need of synchrony. Because they don't have to track sequences of images, they can scan at their leisure. Their job is simply to transfer pixel data from CCD sensor to a file that can be stored or transmitted to your PC. Sync signals are irrelevant to this transfer process. The camera only needs to hold the image in solid-state memory until it can be written to more lasting storage (such as disk).

Encoding

A video camera derives three raw signals from its CCD sensors, one corresponding to each primary color. Although a few professional video systems use these signals in their individual states, as a matter of connection convenience, most systems combine these signals together under one or another video standard. The most common (in the United States) is NTSC, which severely constrains signal quality. S-Video or YC coding does not suffer the limitations of subcarrier coding and allows for greater resolution. (See Chapter 13, "Images.")

Every time a signal goes through the encoding or decoding process, it suffers some degradation. More importantly, once a signal gets coded as NTSC composite, it loses quality you can never get back even if subsequently it gets changed back into S-Video. Consequently it makes sense to generate a video signal in the form that it will ultimately be used. If your multimedia system needs composite video signals, you should start with them. If your multimedia system can capture S-Video, use S-Video to get its higher quality, providing you don't have to detour to composite and back along the way.

White Balance

Light is the raw material for any camera. Just as you need light to see, the camera needs light to make an image. The image is, after all, nothing but a collection of light rays.

Light comes in surprising variety, and not only in intensity. The quality or color of light varies with every scene and situation. You may think of overall outdoor or indoor illumination as bland white light, but white light is hardly bland and rarely a real white. Strictly speaking, of course, real white is a mixture of all colors. The white of any lighting, artificial or natural, is not a pure and equal mixture, however. Some white lights are richer in blue, some in yellow.

Scientifically this shading of the different colors of white is described as *color temperature* and expressed as the number of Kelvins (degrees Celsius above absolute zero) that a perfectly luminescent body would need to be to emit that color. Why should you care? After all, multimedia images are made by artists, not rocket scientists.

The problem is uniformity. If your presentation switches from one image or scene to another and the color temperature changes, you lose unity. Instead of a flowing narration, you get an abrupt change of view and focus. Moreover, one or the other of the two scenes will be seen as wrong, off-color, distracting your audience with minutia when they should be looking for meaning. You need to eliminate the shadings of white light as a variable, to keep color temperature standardized to eliminate the distraction.

Color temperature earns its name from the glow of a perfect "blackbody" radiator, a scientist's term for a theoretic something that has a perfectly continuous spectrum. As the temperature of this blackbody gets higher, its hue shifts like the color incandescence of a hot iron horseshoe in the blacksmith's forge, first from dim red to brighter orange, then yellow and on to blue-white. Color temperature simply assigns an absolute temperature rating to these colors.

Although your eye quickly adjusts to whatever color temperature lights a scene, most people still see some of the differences. For example, ordinary lightbulbs look quite yellow when compared to noontime sunlight. Those ordinary lightbulbs range from 2,700 to 3,400 Kelvins while direct midday sun falls in the range 5,000 to 6,000 Kelvins. Most fluorescent lights have non-continuous color spectra rich in certain hues (notably green) while lacking others that makes assigning a true color temperature impossible. Other fluorescent lamps are designed to approximate daylight (with color temperatures of about 5,000 Kelvins).

Still photographers deal with these color temperature differences with special films and filters. Videographers have it much easier. They can adjust the mixture of signals coming from the three-color camera sensors to compensate, adding more red when color temperature is high, pushing up the blue when temperatures are low. They only need a reference to make the adjustment. The choice is obvious, a sample of white using which they can balance equally the three primary colors. This process is called *white balancing*, and must (or should) be done before using any color video from a camera or camcorder.

The likelihood that anyone is going to set up a standard whitecard in front of his camcorder before catching the shot of Grampa falling from the apple tree is somewhat less than negligible. Consequently most video cameras and camcorders now feature automatic white balancing. Every time the camera is turned on, periodically, or continuously the camera checks the video stream and adjusts the strengths of the red, green, and blue signals deriving its own reference from what it thinks is white.

No circuit is infallible, and off-color images remain possible, though less likely. Try to make cyberpunk images that look akin to an explosion in a ketchup factory, and the camera might deduce the prevailing redness is actually white. You'll lose the impact of your images as the camera adjusts to give everything the pale cast of pastel gore.

Effects

Were it not for special effects, Hollywood would have gone the way of the great auk. Better camcorders try to win you over the same way, with a range of video effects wide enough to occupy the most wayward mind. You have your choices of fades, wipes, and enhancements. You can edit together home movies with studio panache right in your camcorder. Some systems even include their own character generators so you can overlay titles and credits so you get your due.

For multimedia, however, camera effects are small advantage. You can do better with greater control in your PC. Instead of dissolves, you can morph. Instead of simple titles you have your choice of half a zillion fonts that you can bend and shape and crawl into anything. When you can alter speeds, drop frames, and key in backgrounds at the press of a key and try, try again with digital forgivability, you won't want to bother with in-camera features. Moreover, you're better off adding effects later from pure video. You get those valuable second, third, and three-thousandth chances when your timing just misses. You'll also get better quality.

Viewfinders

The viewfinder is named after its function: it helps you find the view that you want to photograph. On still cameras, a viewfinder can be as simple as a frame that works like a gunsight or a precision optical system. Modern *reflex cameras* use the camera lens as part of the viewfinder so you see the image seen by the lens. A mirror reflects the lens image up into the viewfinder, the reflection being the camera's reflex. Sometimes a camera incorporates a *rangefinder* in its viewfinder to help you determine the distance to the subject you want to photograph so you can focus the camera.

Low-cost video cameras often have no viewfinders. You're suppose to plug the camera into a monitor and watch the monitor to focus and compose your images. Three types of viewfinders are popular in better video cameras.

Optical reflex viewfinders do not depend on the camera's electronics. Instead, the viewfinder splits the lens image between the camera sensor and the viewfinder. You see the image produced by the lens as it is going into the camera. A reflex viewfinder enables you to see the effects of zooms. Moreover, the reflex viewfinder gives you a detailed color image without the need for expensive color LCD displays or their associated circuitry. But because you don't see how the camera's electronics are affecting the image, you can only guess at effects like fade-outs.

Conventional *video viewfinders* give you a small monitor to watch that's built into an ocular like a traditional movie camera viewfinder. The tiny screen—a small picture tube on older video cameras but usually an LCD panel in modern units—shows the image in stark monochrome along with warning lights and indicators. The miniature monitor lets you view all the effects the camera generates, even monitor tapes you've made.

Big-screen or *view-screen viewfinders* give you a larger LCD display meant to be watched like a television set instead of a pirate's telescope. It gives the best possible view of the image before and after recording. Using big-screen viewfinders can seem unnatural to anyone used to the peep-show method of previewing images in other camera formats.

Recording

Performance Issue

By their very definition, camcorders include a videocassette recorder along with a video camera. You can choose to tape images and later transfer them to your PC for inclusion in multimedia presentations, or you can ignore the recording section of the camcorder and capture live images. While the former strategy is more flexible and convenient, the latter yields higher quality. All consumer videotape systems use analog technology which inevitably degrades signals; the constraints of standard video recording formats put an even lower lid on quality. If you choose to tape before you capture, select the highest quality recording system, S-VHS or Hi-8.

Microphones

Most camcorders have built-in microphones as a convenience feature, allowing them to record sound as well as images without further ado. Camcorder microphones are capable of high quality—most use electret capsules, which have outstanding frequency response. But camcorder audio inevitably suffers because of proximity—or the lack of it. The camcorder microphone gets no closer to a sound source than the rest of the camera, which means it can be pretty distant. All the other sounds that are nearby are equally likely to be sensed and recorded—background noise, room echoes, the snide comments of the camera operator. Chapter 15, "Sound," includes a full discussion of microphone technology.

To help minimize these distractions, most camcorder microphones are highly directional. They are most sensitive to sounds directly ahead of them and least sensitive to those behind. But they still lack the proximity needed to give a real presence to human voices.

Professional movie-makers and videographers almost universally use auxiliary microphones close to the subject they are taping—boom mikes just above the top of the image frame, desktop microphones in front of talk-show hosts, handheld microphones waved beneath the faces of foreign correspondents, or tiny microphones clipped to neckties and lapels of interviewers. To get the best audio quality in your multimedia presentations, you'll want to do the same. Microphones are fully discussed in the next chapter.

Monitors

Multimedia systems often involve two kinds of monitors, one for the PC and one for video. Although the two work the same way, they work with different kinds of signals.

Although the terms are often used interchangeably, a display and a monitor are distinctly different. A display is the image-producing device itself, the screen that you see. The monitor is a complete box that adds support circuitry to the display, This circuitry converts the signals sent by the computer (or some other device, such as a videocassette recorder) into the proper form for the display to use. Although most monitors operate under principles like those of the television set, displays can be made from a variety of technology including liquid crystals and the photon glow of some noble gases.

Because of their similar technological foundations, monitors to a great extent resemble the humble old television sets. Just as a monitor is a display enhanced with extra circuitry, the television is a monitor with even more signal conversion electronics. The television has incorporated into its design a tuner or demodulator which converts signals broadcast by television stations or a cable television company into about the same form as those signals used by monitors. Beyond the tuner, the television and monitor work in much the same way. Indeed, some old-fashioned computer monitors will work as television as long as they are supplied the proper signals.

New monitors have developed far beyond their television roots, however. They have greater sharpness and purity of color. They accept signals that could never be broadcast, using higher frequencies and different standards.

The PC revolution parallels a different kind of revolution in monitor technology. Ever since the beginning of television in the 1920s, monitors have been based on vacuum tube technology, far out-living the application of tubes in any mainstream consumer application. Vacuum tubes survive only in X-ray machines, some high power/high frequency equipment, and technically less-sophisticated nations—and high-end audio equipment! The move to portable computing has energized the flat-screen monitor revolution, putting new technologies behind the images you see. Although the flat-panel television has a long history of unfulfilled prediction (at least as far back as the 1950s they were thought but a few years away), notebook PCs gave financial incentive to move the technology into the mass market. Although most people would balk at spending $2,000 for a 10-inch television set, they readily pay as much for an active-matrix color display for their notebook computers. Currently old-technology monitors survive in general-purpose applications (home television, video, desktop computers), and the newer flatscreens remain the realm of the niche (notebook PCs, handheld televisions, projection systems, and viewfinders).

Cathode Ray Tubes

The needs of old technology shaped our existing video and television standards, and video signals remain subservient to these requirements. When you think of television, it's still that old blue eye glowing in the living room. That glow comes from a special kind a vacuum tube called a cathode ray tube or CRT.

The name is purely descriptive. The tube of a CRT is a glass bottle that's been partially evacuated and filled with an inert gas at very low pressure. The cathode—another name for a negatively charged electrode—of the CRT shoots a beam or ray of electrons toward a positively charged electrode, the anode. It's not so much target practice as a certainty—electrons, having a negative charge, are naturally attracted to positive potentials. Because it works like a howitzer for electrons, the cathode of a CRT is often called an electron gun.

Phosphors

The first trick of the CRT is controlling those projectile electrons. Get them going fast enough and you can make X-rays as they plunge to a stop. That's not exactly a desirable consequence in that, outside of Superman, most people can't see X-rays or even the original beam of electrons. The CRT relies on special compounds called phosphors (because they are based on phosphorus) that have the wonderful property of glowing when excited by or struck by sufficiently (but not too) energetic electrons.

At the end of the short flight of the electrons, from the gun in the neck of the tube to the inside of its wide, flat face there lies a layer of these phosphors. That gives light, but absent some other force all you would see is a tiny, bright spot glowing its life away. To form an image, the electron beam must trace across the screen.

To move the beam across the breadth of the tube face (so that the beam doesn't light just a tiny dot in the center of the screen), a group of powerful electromagnets arranged around the tube called the yoke bend the electron beam in the course of its flight. The magnetic field set up by the yoke is carefully controlled and causes the beam to sweep each individual display line down the face of the tube.

Monochrome monitors have their CRTs evenly coated with a single, homogenous phosphor so that wherever the electron beam strikes, the tube glows in the same color. The color of the phosphors determine the overall color that the screen glows.

Different compounds and mixtures glow various colors and for various lengths of time after being struck by the electron beam. Color CRT displays use special brews of three different phosphors painted in fine patterns across the inner surface of the CRT. The patterns are made from dots or stripes of the three additive primary colors—red, green, and blue—arrayed next to one another. A group of three dots is called a color triad or color triplet. One triad of dots makes up a called a picture element, the familiar pixel. The makers of color monitors can individually choose each of the three colors used in forming the color triads on the screen. Most monitor makers have adopted the same phosphor family (P22), so the basic color capabilities of most multi-hued monitors are the same.

The color monitor screen can be illuminated in any of its three primary colors by individually hitting the phosphor dots associated with that color with the electron beam. Other colors can be made by illuminating combinations of the primary colors. By varying the intensity of each primary color, a CRT can generate a nearly infinite spectrum. (According to one monitor maker, the color range actually embraces about 300,000 different hues.)

Color Temperature

As with video cameras, color temperature (white balance) concerns arise with monitors. Although you set may your video camera to perfect white balance so that it matches all the other cameras in the world, your CRT-based monitor may give everything its own interpretation. CRT displays have a color temperature, too, like lightbulbs and other light generators. Unlike ordinary lightbulbs, you can adjust the color temperature of a CRT by changing its mix of primary colors. Tweak up the red and the color temperature of your monitor slips down.

Most monitors makers design their products to glow with the approximate color temperature of daylight, the one true unchanging standard. Unfortunately, they fall into two schools of thought regarding the color temperature of the day. When color television first came on the scene, engineers agreed that the best color temperature was about 6,000 Kelvins, and this temperature became an international standard. At least until the Japanese television industry decided that a higher temperature gave screens a whiter look. They developed an alternate standard of 9,500 Kelvins.

If you sit in the dark and watch your video or computer monitor, you need worry about color temperature about as much as you worry about the temperature of your reading light. As long as it's the only light source in the room or you make no comparisons, you eyes adjust to it and everything looks natural.

When you have other sources of light—particularly incandescent bulbs—most monitors look decidedly blue. Although only overly critical interior designers might notice, the hot glow of the monitor can become a concern when you want to make critical matches of color. For example, your client demands the red of his soup in the presentation you're preparing for him exactly match the real can sitting next to the monitor. Now you have a big problem. The pigments and paper on the can only reflect light, so their actual color depends on the temperature of the light illuminating them. Your monitor screen emits light, so its color is independent of illumination— it has its own color temperature that may be (and is likely) different from that lighting the rest of your work. You must either match the room light to the monitor or match the monitor to the room light. The latter is easier, and several companies now offer software products that will help you get an exact match. Moreover, you might find that you prefer a cooler screen that's rich in warmer colors.

Persistence

Besides color, CRT phosphors also differ in persistence—how long they glow after the electron beam strikes them. Persistence is not an issue with video monitors because they all follow the same frequency standards and muck up the image with interlacing. Computer monitors, on the other hand, can make persistence an issue.

You'll notice persistence in a computer monitor only when it is too long. Images take on a ghostly appearance, lingering for a few seconds before slowly fading away. Although the effect may be bothersome, particularly in a darkened room, it's meant to offset the effect of another headache-producer, the flicker that results when the refresh frequency is too low. Some manufacturers depend on long persistence phosphors to reduce the flicker in interlaced display systems. Fortunately, interlaced standards and the need for them are disappearing almost as fast as the ghosts on the screen. The only time you'll even want to consider a CRT monitor with long persistence phosphors is when you have an old IBM 8514/A or XGA display adapter.

Electron Guns

The brief flight of an electron in a CRT begins with getting shot from a gun—the cathode. The electron gun, oddly enough, looks like a gun with a long metal tube that points down the neck of the CRT bottle toward the screen. Ordinary monochrome CRTs have a single electron gun that continuously sweeps across the screen. Most color tubes have three guns, although some color televisions and monitors boast "one-gun" tubes that put three guns into a single assembly that has three distinct electron-emitting cathodes that can be individually controlled.

In a three-gun color CRT, the trio of guns are usually arranged to form a triangle. One-gun color CRTs arrange their cathodes in a straight line, often earning the epithet in-line guns. In theory in-line guns should be easier to setup, but as a practical matter excellent performance can be derived from either arrangement.

The three guns in a color CRT emit their electrons simultaneously, and the three resulting beams are steered together by the yoke. Most monitors provide individual adjustments for each of its three beams to assure that it can point all three to fall on the same on-screen triplet of color dots. In that these controls help the three beams converge on the same triad, they are called convergence controls. The process of adjusting them is usually termed alignment.

Convergence

If a monitor is not adjusted properly—or if it is not designed or made properly—the three beams will not converge properly on their appointed triad. The result of this poor convergence can be images with rainbow-like shadows and a loss of sharpness and detail. Individual text characters no longer appear sharply defined but become two- or three-color blurs. Video displays don't reach their resolution potential. Monochrome monitors are inherently free from such convergence problems because they have but one electron beam (as are those that don't use CRT technology, which have no beams).

Convergence problems are a symptom rather than a cause of monitor deficiencies. Convergence problems arise not only from the design of the display but also from the construction and setup of each individual monitor. It can vary widely from one display to the next and may be aggravated by damage during shipping.

The result of convergence problems is most noticeable at the screen periphery because that's where the electron beams are the most difficult to control. When bad, convergence problems can be the primary limit on the sharpness of a given display, having a greater negative effect than wide dot-pitch or low bandwidth (discussed later in this chapter).

Many monitor makers will claim that their convergence is a given fraction of a millimeter at a particular place on the screen. If a figure is given for more than one screen location, the center of the screen will invariably have a lower figure—tighter, better convergence—than a corner of the screen.

The number given is how far one color may spread from another at that location. Lower numbers are better. A typical monitors may claim convergence of about 0.5mm (one-half millimeter) at one of the corners of the screen. That figure often rises 50 percent higher than the dot-pitch of the tube, making the convergence the limit on sharpness for that particular monitor.

External magnetic fields from transformers and other devices can cause misconvergence. Note, however, that misconvergence that is externally caused can be minimized or eliminated by moving the monitor or interference source. Internal misconvergence isn't cured so easily.

Trouble-shooting

Misconvergence problems often can be corrected by adjustment of the monitor. Many monitors have internal convergence controls. A few, high-resolution (and high-cost) monitors even have external convergence adjustments. But adjusting monitor convergence is a job for the specialist —and that means getting a monitor converged can be expensive, as is any computer service call.

Many monitor makers now claim that their products are converged for life. While this strategy should eliminate the need to adjust them (which should only be done by a skilled technician with the correct test equipment), it also makes it mandatory to test your display before you buy it. You don't want a display that's been badly converged for life.

Shadow Masks

Just pointing the electron beams at the right dots is not enough because part of the beam can spill over and hit the other dots in the triplet. The result of this spillover is a loss of color purity—bright hues become muddied. To prevent this effect and make images as sharp and colorful as possible, all color CRTs used in computer and video monitors (as well as ordinary television sets) use *shadow masks*. A metal sheet with fine perforations in it, the shadow mask fits inside the CRT bottle a small distance behind the phosphor coating of the screen.

The shadow mask and the phosphor dot coating on the CRT screen are critically arranged so that the electron beam can only hit phosphor dots of one color. The other two colors of dots are in the "shadow" of the mask and cannot be seen by the electron beam.

The spacing of the holes in the shadow mask to a great degree determines the sharpness of a monitor's on-screen image. For the geometry of the system to work out, the phosphor dots on the CRT screen must be spaced at the same distance as the holes in the mask. Because the hole spacing determines the dot spacing, it is often termed the dot-pitch of the CRT.

The dot-pitch of a CRT is simply a measurement of the distance between dots of the same color. It is an absolute measurement, independent of the size of the tube or the size of the displayed image.

The shadow mask affects the brightness of a monitors image in two ways. The size of the holes in the mask limits the size of the electron beam getting through to the phosphors. Off-axis from the guns—that is, toward the corners of the screen—the round holes appear oval to the gun and less of the beam can get through. When all else is equal, the corners of a shadow mask screen are often dimmer than the center, although the brightness difference may not be distinguishable. Monitors can compensate for this difference by making their beams a bit brighter in the corners.

The mask also limits how high the electron beam intensity can be in a given CRT. A stronger beam—which makes a brighter image—holds more energy. When the beam strikes the mask, part of that energy is absorbed by the mask and becomes heat which raises the temperature of the mask. In turn, this temperature rise makes the mask expand unpredictably, distorting it minutely and blurring the image. To minimize this heat-induced blur, monitor makers use materials that have a low coefficient of thermal expansion for their shadow masks. The alloy Invar is favored for shadow masks because of its ability to maintain a nearly constant size as it warms.

Aperture Grilles

With all the problems associated with shadow masks, you'd expect someone to come up with a better idea. Sony Corporation did exactly that, inventing the *Trinitron* picture tube which uses an *aperture grille*—slots between a vertical array of wires—instead of a mask. The phosphors are painted on the inner face of the tube as interleaved stripes of red, green, and blue. The grille blocks the electron beam from the wrong stripes just as a shadow-mask blocks it from the wrong dots. Just as shadow-mask CRTs have a dot-pitch, Trinitrons have a slot-pitch which describes the center-to-center distance between two grille slots. Because the electron beam fans out as it travels away from the electron gun and phosphor stripes are farther from the gun than is the mask, the distance between two sequential stripes of the same color is somewhat longer than the slot-pitch. This stripe spacing is termed screen-pitch. For example, a 0.25mm slot-pitch Trinitron might have a screen-pitch of 0.26mm.

The aperture grille wires are held taut but they can vibrate. Consequently Trinitron monitors have one or two thin tensioning wires running horizontally across the screen. Although quite fine, these wires cast a shadow on the screen that's most apparent on computer monitors that use light-colored screen backgrounds. They are invisible to most people on video images, masked by the motion and many colors on the screen.

Trinitrons hold a theoretical brightness advantage over shadow-mask tubes. Because the slots allow more electrons to pass through to the screen than do the tiny holes of a shadow mask, a Trinitron can (in theory) create a brighter image. This added brightness is not borne out in practice.

Matrix Color

The background area on a color screen—that is, the space between the phosphor dots or stripes—is called the matrix, and it is shaded from the electron beam so it does not glow. The color of the matrix determines what the screen looks like when the power is off—pale gray, dark green-gray, or nearly black. Darker and black matrices give an impression of higher contrast to the displayed images. Lighter gray matrices make for purer white. The distinctions are subtle, however, and unless you put two tubes side-by-side, you're unlikely to be able to judge the difference. Most of the difference vanishes as soon as the screen lights up.

Projection Systems

Putting a big screen on a PC extends its multimedia reach to an audience instead of a mere individual. But with the big screen comes a big loss—the multimedium no longer works interactively with every participant. While a big screen presentation is as much multimedia as a multi-projector slide show of decades past, it loses in the translation. The power of self-pacing evaporates as your entire audience must await the progress of its slowest participant. Moreover, hypertext references are lost or confounded by the demand of the least common denominator.

Projection televisions (and monitors) take a slightly different tack to produce their big-screen colored light shows. Each of the three tubes in the projection television are actually combinations of cathode ray tubes and a reflector telescope. Each tube has a single electron gun and special bright phosphors that produce an intense white image that's shot backward through the telescope and a color filter through the air to an external screen. There's no mask or color triads involved—the three colors get superimposed—so there's nothing to interfere with the sharpness of the image except the focus of the system and the grain of the screen. Projection televisions can be sharp enough to make individual scan lines readily apparent (when line width is not properly adjusted) and vividly reveal the limited resolution of conventional video signals.

Flat-Panel Displays

CRTs are impractical for portable applications, whether as televisions or computers. The glass in a small CRT weighs more than a notebook PC and draws so much power that an equally heavy battery would be drained in a few minutes. CRTs are big, too. Even a two-inch screen suitable for a handheld TV or camcorder viewfinder needs several inches of neck and several thousands of volts to run.

Flat-panel systems are a bulk and power breakthrough. The flatpanel is little bigger than the screen itself, and the latest technologies are frugal with electricity. Although they still suffer substantial handicaps to replace CRTs in mass-market video applications—prices that are too high and screens that are too small—no one doubts that someday they will dominate the viewing world.

In lieu of the tube, computer and video designers have tried just about every available alternate display technology. These include the panels packed with light-emitting diodes (LEDs), gas-plasma systems, and today's favorite, liquid crystal display panels (LCDs). LEDs are familiar as the red devil's eyes that glow as the power-on indicators of the Eighties, but they are power hungry and inherently monochromatic. Gas-plasma displays suffer the same shortcomings with the added disadvantage that they run at higher voltages not directly obtainable from conventional batteries.

LCDs differ from both LEDs and gas-plasma displays in that they don't emit light on their own. Rather, LCDs block light. They only change their light transmission abilities and instead rely on external light sources for legibility. To make patterns visible, they either selectively block reflected light (*reflective LCDs*) or the light generated by a secondary source either behind the LCD panel (*backlit LCDs*) or adjacent to it (*edgelit LCDs*). The backlight source is typically an electroluminescent (EL) panel, although some LCD systems use Cold-Cathode Fluorescent (CCF) for brighter, whiter displays with the penalty of higher cost, greater thickness, and increased complexity. LCD projector panels use transmission LCDs that, instead of having an integral light source, rely on external illumination.

Reflective LCDs are most frugal with power because they need not bother with the inefficient process of creating light. But even backlit and edgelit LCDs are more electrically economical than other flat-panel technologies because they can use the most efficient light sources.

Nematic Twists

In the few years that LCDs have been used for computer monitors and televisions, the technology has been dramatically improved. Every few years a manufacturer typically adds a new "twist" to its products. In fact, LCD panels are often described by their twists—for example, "supertwist," "double supertwist," and "triple supertwist." In effect, the twist of the crystals controls the contrast of the screen. The more twist, the more contrast; so a triple-supertwist screen has more contrast than ordinary supertwist.

An LCD display is actually a sandwich made from two plastic sheets with a very special liquid made from rod-shaped or *nematic molecules.* One important property of the nematic molecules of liquid crystals is that they can be aligned by grooves in the plastic covering sheets to bend the polarity of light that passes through them. More importantly, the amount of bend the molecules of the liquid crystal gives to the light can be altered by applying an electrical current through them.

Ordinary light has no particular orientation, so liquid crystals don't visibly alter it. But polarized light aligns all the oscillations of its photons in a single direction. A polarizing filter creates polarized light by allowing light of a particular polarity (or axis of oscillation) to pass through. Polarization is key to the function of LCDs.

LCD panels use two polarizing filters. A first filter converts light incident on the panel into polarized light. The light then passes through the panel and through a second polarizing filter. The second filter is set to pass light at right angles to the polarity of the first. This cross-polarizer design would normally stop all light from getting through, but the liquid crystal panel bends the polarity of light emerging from the first polarizing filter by about 90° so that it lines up with the second filter. Consequently, in its passive state, light normally slips through the polarizer/LCD/polarizer sandwich. Pass a current through the liquid crystal, however, and the nematic bending in the LCD changes, altering the twist of the light so that it can no longer slip through the second polarizer.

To make an LCD display, you only need to be able to selectively apply current to small areas of the liquid crystal. The areas to which you apply current will be dark; those that you don't will be light. A light behind the LCD will make the changes more visible.

Over the past few years, engineers have made several improvements to this basic LCD design to improve its contrast and color. The basic LCD design outlined above is technically termed *twisted nematic* technology or TN. The liquid molecules of the TN display in their resting state always bend light by 90°, exactly counteracting the relationship between the two polarizing panels that make up the display.

By increasing the bending of light by the nematic molecules, the contrast between light and dark can be increased. An LCD design that bends light by 180° to 270° is termed a "supertwist nematic" or simply *supertwist display.* One side effect of the added twist is the appearance of color artifacts, resulting in the yellowish green and bright blue hues of many familiar LCD displays.

This tinge of color can be canceled simply by mounting two supertwist liquid crystals back to back so that one bends the light the opposite direction of the other. This design is logically termed a "double-supertwist nematic" or simply double supertwist) display. This LCD design is currently popular among notebook PCs with monochrome displays. It does have its own drawback, however. Because there are two layers of LCD between you and the light source, double-supertwist panels appear darker or require brighter backlights for adequate visibility.

Triple-supertwist nematic displays instead compensate for colorshifts in the supertwist design by layering both sides of the liquid crystal with thin polymer films. Because the films absorb less light than the twin panels of double-supertwist screens, less backlight—and less backlight power—is required for the same screen brightness.

Active Versus Passive

LCDs also come in two styles based on how the current that aligns their nematic molecules is applied. Most LCD panels have a grid of horizontal and vertical conductors, and each pixel is located at the intersection of these conductors. The pixel is darkened simply by sending current through the conductors to the liquid crystal. This kind of display is called a passive matrix.

The alternate design, the active matrix, is more commonly referred to as *Thin Film Transistor* (or TFT) technology. This style of LCD puts a transistor at every pixel. The transistor acts as a relay. A small current gets sent to the transistor through the horizontal and vertical grid, and the transistor responds by switching a much higher current to activate the LCD pixel.

The advantage of the active matrix design is that a smaller current needs to traverse the grid so the pixel can be switched on and off faster. While passive LCD screens may update only about half a dozen times per second, TFT designs can operate at ordinary monitor speeds, ten times faster. That increased speed equates to faster response—for example, your mouse won't disappear as you move it across the screen.

The disadvantage of the TFT design is that it requires the fabrication of one transistor for each screen pixel. Putting those transistors there requires combining the LCD and semiconductor manufacturing processes. That's sort of like getting bricklayers and carpenters to work together.

To try to achieve the quality of active matrix displays without paying the price, engineers have upped the scan on passive panels. Double-scanned passive panels work exactly like the name says: they scan their screens twice in the period that a normal screen would be scanned only once. As a result, they eke out extra brightness, contrast, and speed. They do not, however, reach the quality level set by active matrix screens.

Color

Adding color complicates LCD design and manufacture because of the inherently monochrome nature of the LCD panel. Manufacturers have tried a number of technologies to give color to LCD screens, both additive (which put red, green, and blue-colored pixels side-by-side so their output can visually combine) and subtractive (which layer cyan, yellow, and magenta-absorbing screens to produce colors). The most striking results have been achieved by coupling TFT technology with color to achieve bright, fast, and expensive displays. Although the best units look wonderful—often better than color CRTs—TFT screens demand a price premium (once hefty but finally coming down) over double-scanned color panels.

Resolution

The resolution of an LCD panel is set during its manufacture by the number of discrete cells wired into the panel. Manufacturers choose a resolution suitable to the application of the display. For example, a small pocket television may display only 70,000 pixels while a computer-quality panel will have more than about five times as many. The LCD screens used in most notebook computers usually achieve VGA-level resolution, 640×480 pixels, although in early 1995 the first 800×600-pixel screens were introduced.

Electronics

To make a viewable image, every monitor requires an elaborate set of control electronics. For example, to make a CRT image, video or computer signals must be amplified to make them strong enough to light the screen. The monitor must generate sweep signals that control the position of the electronic beam. And, in video systems, the monitor has to sort out the colors coded into the signal. Although flat-panel displays don't need the high voltages or sweep signals of CRTs, their electronics still need to translate video signals into scan addresses to light the proper pixels.

The basic electronic components inside a monitor are its video amplifiers. As the name implies, these circuits simply increase the strength (amplify) the approximately one volt signals they receive from your video system or PC to the somewhat higher voltage used by LCD panels or the thousands of volts needed to drive the electron beam from cathode to phosphor. Monochrome monitors have a single video amplifier; color monitors, three (one for each primary color). These three amplifiers must be exactly matched and absolutely linear. That is, the input and output of each amplifier must be precisely proportional and it must be the same as the other two amplifiers. The relationship between these amplifiers is called color tracking. If it varies, your images will look oddly off-color.

The relationship between the input and output signals of video amplifiers is usually not linear. That is, a small change in the input signal may make a greater than corresponding change in the output. In other words, the monitor may exaggerate the color or gray scale range of the input signal—contrast increases. The relationship between input and output is referred to as the gamma of the amplifier. A gamma of one would result in an exact correspondence of the input and output signals. However, monitors with unity gammas tend to have washed out, pastel images. Most people prefer higher gammas, in the range 1.5 to 1.8, because of their more contrasted images.

Synchronizing Frequencies

If all you need is a video monitor, you can buy one without worry about things like frequency range. All video signals in the United States follow the same video standard. With computer monitors, however, the profusion of standards makes matching frequencies a major concern. You have two frequencies to worry about—vertical frequency (the refresh rate or frame rate) and horizontal synchronizing frequency (horizontal scan rate). Each PC video standard makes its own demands, as summarized in Chapter 13, Table 13.6.

Most CRT-based computer monitors are multiscanning and accept any horizontal and vertical frequency within a wide range to match whatever standard you choose to use, but all monitors do not cover all frequencies or standards. Note that very few computer monitors include video scanning frequencies in their ranges, so they cannot be used as video monitors with your VCR or camcorder.

The integral LCD panels in notebook computers usually operate at a single standard resolution (ordinary VGA), but they do not need ordinary synchronized scanning. They can be directly connected to the frame buffer and can hold their image indefinitely (as long as power is on) and address individual pixels instead of retracing an entire screen. They don't need to be periodically refreshed.

The exceptions are the LCD panel with electronics added so that it can substitute for a standard VGA monitor and LCD projector panels. These systems require circuitry to convert VGA or video signals into the memory addresses used by the LCD panel. In effect, the synchronizing signals scan through addresses instead of pulling an electron beam across a screen. These systems are usually limited to one signal standard at a resolution level corresponding to the screen pixel layout, most often VGA.

Bandwidth

Perhaps the most common specification that is usually listed for any sort of monitor is bandwidth, which is usually rated in megahertz. Common monitor bandwidths stretch across a wide range—figures from 12 to 100 MHz are sometimes encountered.

In theory, the higher the bandwidth, the higher the resolution and sharper the image that can be displayed. In the case of color displays, the dot-pitch of the display tube is the biggest limit on performance. In monochrome system, however, bandwidth is a determinant of overall sharpness.

The bandwidth necessary in a video monitor is relatively modest. A television channel is, after all, 6 MHz wide and it must accommodate both video and television audio signals. High-resolution PC displays are demanding. An ordinary VGA system needs almost 25 MHz of bandwidth. SuperVGA monitors can demand four times more. (See Table 13.6 in the previous chapter.)

Overscan and Underscan

When CRT technology was born, the face of the CRT screen was inevitably round. Today's rectangular screens were beyond the reach of the technology of the 1950s. The images they were meant to display, however, were rectangular—exactly the same shape as they are today. Manufacturers of the first televisions had two choices: putting the full image on the CRT by shrinking it down to fit, or make the picture as big as possible by letting the limits of the screen cut off the corners of the image. In that the first CRTs were also tiny and manufacturers wanted to show as much image as possible, they compromised. Part of the screen got masked off to make it look rectangular, but part of the image got lopped off to make it big. A CRT image that gets cut off by the edge of the screen is called *overscanned*.

At the television studio, engineers wanted to view the entire image all the way to the edges. They relied on the opposite strategy, shrinking the image so that all four corners fit on the face of the CRT. These undersized images are termed *underscanned*.

Most makers of computer monitors set up their products to underscan the image so that you can see everything. After all, you wouldn't want your typing to disappear and fall off the edge of the screen. Television and video remain as they were 40 years ago, overscanned in the living room, underscanned in the studio. Most video and many computer monitors have controls that enable you to switch between over- and underscanned images.

Overscanning and underscanning don't apply to LCD panels used in computer systems. Most LCDs are directly connected to the frame buffer of their host PCs. Their pixel positions are forever fixed when they are fabricated and are matched to addresses in the frame buffer. The display area exactly matches the frame buffer and pixels always appear in the right place.

Aspect Ratio

The relationship between the width and height of a monitor screen is termed its aspect ratio. Computer monitors, video monitors, and at one time even Hollywood movies all shared the same aspect ratio. They were designed for images 1.33 times wider than they are high. Expressed as a ratio of integers, this is an aspect ratio of 4:3.

In a CRT system, the aspect ratio is not set by the tube. The electronics of monitors separate the circuitry that generates the horizontal and vertical scanning signals and results in their independent control. As a result, they can adjust the relationship between horizontal and vertical to change the aspect radio of the image. For example, by increasing the amplification of the horizontal signal, the width of the image will be stretched, raising the aspect ratio.

LCDs used in computer systems have fixed aspect ratios. In better systems, the aspect ratio is fixed at the correct value (1.33) by the design of the screen. Some ultra-compact PCs use smaller LCD displays that give them permanent, overly long (squashed) aspect ratios.

With CRT-based video monitors, you can generally adjust the aspect ratio once and forget it. Normal signal anomalies don't affect it. With computer monitors, however, you may find yourself tweaking controls to adjust the aspect ratio several times a day. The variety of signals and standards used by computer monitors force you to deal with it. For example, the VGA standard allows images made with three distinct line counts—350, 400, and 480. All else being equal, an image made from 350 lines will be less than three-quarters the height of a 480-line image.

Image Sizing

Computer monitors often have to deal with another odd problem—the VGA standard is actually three standards in one. The different VGA image standards vary in the number of lines per frame but all use the same synchronizing frequencies. Ordinarily the images with more lines would appear taller on the screen, but the VGA system sends code signals to the monitor that instruct the monitor to set the proper picture height. The relative polarities of the horizontal and vertical sync signals tell the monitor the line count in the image it is sent. The monitor then compensates by adjusting its vertical gain to obtain the correct aspect ratio no matter the number of lines in the image.

Not all monitors take advantage of this sync signaling system. LCD panels typically display squashed images when a VGA signal shifts to a lower line count. Fortunately the VGA system uses these lower line-count signals only for backward compatibility with old PC display standards that are rapidly falling into disuse.

When shifting to resolutions other than standard VGA, CRT-based monitors often need to be adjusted to give the proper size and aspect ratio to the resulting image. Many CRT-based monitors use a technique called autosizing that to maintain a consistent image size no matter what video signal a display adapter sends out. (Autosizing is irrelevant to LCD systems, which usually follow only one display standard.)

Monitor makers can achieve autosizing in several ways. True autosizing works regardless of the signal going to the monitor and scales the image to match the number of display lines. Mode-sensitive autosizing works by determining the display mode used for an image from the frequency of the signal. It then switches the size to a preset standard to match the number of lines in the signal. Monitors often combine VGA sync-sensing with mode-sensitive autosizing.

Image Controls

Monitors have controls that help you deal with aspect ratio and image size. Horizontal and vertical size (or gain) controls let you to adjust the size and shape of the on-screen image to suit your own tastes. With these controls—providing they have adequate range—you can stretch a too-small PC image to touch the top, bottom, and sides of the screen bezel or you can shrink the bright area of your display to a tiny (but geometrically perfect) patch in the center of your screen.

Size and position controls give you command of how much screen the image on your monitor fills. With full-range controls, you can expand the image to fill the screen from corner to corner or reduce it to a smaller size that minimizes the inevitable geometric distortion that occurs near the edges of the tube. A full complement of controls includes one each of the following: horizontal position (sometimes termed phase), vertical position, horizontal size (sometimes called width), and vertical size (or height).

Size and position controls are irrelevant to LCD and similar alternate display technologies. LCD panels are connected more directly to display memory so that memory locations correspond nearly exactly to every screen position. There's no need to move the image around or change its shape because it's forever fixed where it belongs.

Most CRT-based displays also carry over several controls from their television progenitors. Nearly every computer monitor has a brightness control, which adjusts the level of the scanning electron beam, which in turn makes the on-screen image glow brighter or dimmer. The contrast control adjusts the linearity of the relationship between the incoming signal and the on-screen image brightness. In other words, it controls the brightness relationship that results from different signal levels—how much brighter high-intensity is. In a few CRT-based displays, both the brightness and contrast function are combined into a single "picture" control. Although a godsend to those who might get confused by having to twiddle two knobs, the combined control also limits your flexibility in adjusting the image to best suit your liking.

LCD screens usually have two controls as well. A brightness control adjust the level of back- or edge-lighting. The LCD contrast control adjusts the twist applied by the panel to light passing through it.

Other controls ubiquitous to televisions are usually absent from better computer monitors because they are irrelevant. Vertical hold, color (saturation), and hue controls only have relevance to composite video signals, so they are likely only to be found on composite-interfaced video monitors. The vertical hold control tunes the monitor to best decipher the vertical synchronizing signal from the ambiguities of the composite video signal. The separate sync signals used by computer display standards remove any ambiguity and eliminate the need for this control on computer monitors. Color and hue only adjust the relationship of the color subcarrier to the rest of the composite video signal and have no relevance at all to computer monitor systems.

Image controls come in two types, analog and digital. Analog controls are the familiar old knobs like you find on vintage television sets. They remain prevalent on video monitors. Analog controls have one virtue—simplicity. Twist one way and the image gets bigger; twist the other and it shrinks. You know the setting just by looking at the knob. The control itself is a simple memory system. It stays put until you move it again. But analog controls also become dirty and wear out with age. And they usually enable you to set but one value per knob, one value that must cover all of the monitor's operating modes.

Digital controls give you pushbutton control over image parameters. Press one button, and the image gets larger or moves to the left. Another compensates in the opposite direction. Usually digital controls are linked with a microprocessor, memory, and mode-sensing circuitry so that you can preset different image heights and widths for every video standard your monitor can display.

Digital controls don't get noisy with age and are more reliable and repeatable. But you never know when you're approaching the limit of their travel. Most have two-speed operation—hold them in momentarily and they make minute changes; keep holding the button and they shift gears to make gross changes. Of course, if you don't anticipate the shift, you'll overshoot the setting you want and you'll spend a few extra moments zeroing in on the exact setting you want.

Audio Inputs

The sound circuitry in multimedia systems is part of the PC rather than the monitor. A sound board in the PC handles all mixing, control, and amplification functions. You plug loudspeakers directly into your PC's sound board. The speakers and your computer monitor are entirely separate entities.

Video monitors (as opposed to computer displays) usually have built-in amplifiers and speakers that let you listen to the soundtracks of tapes. You may find these facilities to be helpful when you want to preview a video presentation, but they are otherwise unnecessary for a multimedia PC.

Setup

Monitors are among the most blessed of devices that you can plug into your PC. They usually require no specific setup on the part of your other hardware and software. As long as the monitor can handle the signals produced by your video adapter, you're home free. You should get a viewable image on the screen. You may have to adjust the image size and position controls on the monitor to accommodate signal timing and make the picture as large as possible and in the center of the screen. And you'll probably want to adjust the brightness and contrast to accommodate the cave or lightbulb factory in which you work.

Windows 95 gives you a monitor setup option, however, accessible through Control Panel by double-clicking the Display icon. The window that opens lets you change the look and operation of your monitor.

If you want to tell Windows 95 that you're using a specific type of display, choose the Settings tab, which will flip to the screen shown in Figure 14.1.

FIGURE 14.1. Windows 95 Display Settings screen.

From this screen, clicking the Change Display Type button will give you the option of altering the video adapter and monitor that you plan to use. The screen will look like Figure 14.2.

Selecting the right monitor at this point is not a major issue. If you tell Windows 95 the wrong kind of monitor, none of the parameters of the operating system will mysteriously change. Windows 95 uses this information only for telling your applications what kind of monitor you have, just in case they are particular. The setup program for your video adapter may access this information and use it to guide your choices of available resolutions.

You can also tell Windows 95 whether your monitor is Energy*Star compliant. This choice will affect the interaction of your monitor and screen saver. Choose the Blank Screen screen saver and Energy*Star compliance from the Screen Saver tab, and Windows 95 will signal your monitor when to shift to standby or power-down modes.

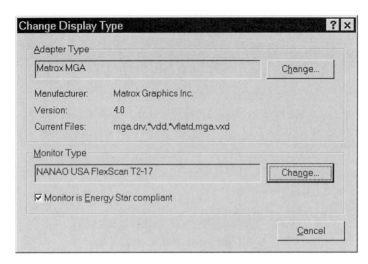

FIGURE 14.2. Windows 95 Change Display Type screen.

Chapter 15

Sound

Sound distinguishes ordinary PCs from extraordinary multimedia machines. After all, even the most rudimentary computer can change the image on a monitor screen. But at best, all an ordinary PC can manage to utter is a few beeps. The sound it creates is not so much music as alarm, annunciation rather than aural enlightenment. For all essential purposes—and that means business work in addition to games—a PC without real sound capabilities is uni-media, not multimedia.

A true multimedia machine can make a symphony of sounds ranging from realistic reproduction of acoustic instruments to synthesized ear-openers only imaginable in the nightmares of Martians. But more than that, a multimedia PC can capture just about any sound that you can hear and reduce it to a digital form that you can chop, channel, shake, and bake into music or madness. You can eke out quality on par with professional recording equipment or as appalling as a fourth-rate garage band with its feet stuck on the fuzz pedal.

The noise-making spectrum of PCs ranges from the beeps and squeaks of the tiny internal speaker to an aural rush equal in quality to today's best stereo CDs. PCs can generate, manipulate, record, and playback sounds of all sorts and even control other noise-makers such as music synthesizers. Today's high-quality sound capability distinguishes multimedia PCs from ordinary, visual-bound systems.

While most PCs are mostly limited to visual interaction, a multimedia PC extends the computer's capabilities of interacting with the world to include sound. It can generate sounds on its own, acting like a music synthesizer or noise generator. And it can control external devices that do the same thing through a MIDI interface. It can record or sample sounds on any standard computer medium (the hard disk being today's preferred choice) with sonic accuracy every bit as good (or even better) than commercial stereo CDs. All the sounds it makes and stores can be edited and manipulated: tones can be stretched, voices shifted, noises combined, music mixed. It can play back all the sounds it makes and records with the same fidelity, pushing the limits of even the best stereo systems.

The sound abilities of the multimedia PC go even further. The MPC specification requires that your PC be able to push all the right buttons—that is, link up with any of today's electronic instruments and play the keys as if you were fingering them yourself. Through a Musical Instrument Digital Interface (MIDI) connection, your multimedia PC links to the outside world and takes control of the other electronic music-makers that you might have.

The basic sound abilities of a multimedia PC are five-fold:

- ➤ Make or synthesize sounds
- ➤ Capture sounds from the outside world, be they what you hear or digital bits of a compact disc
- ➤ Mix and edit the sounds it makes or hears
- ➤ Control the sounds made by other electronic instruments through its MIDI connection
- ➤ Play back the whole cacophony through a speaker system of some kind

Each of these abilities requires its own set of technologies, hardware, and software to carry out.

Unfortunately, the native endowment of most PCs is naught but a squeaker of a loudspeaker that makes soprano Mickey Mouse sound like the Mormon Tabernacle Choir in comparison. The designers of the first PCs simply thought sound unnecessary. After all, the noise that calculating machines made was to be avoided. All they thought important were warning signals, so that's all the PC got. Images fared little better: text screen hinted little at today's graphic potential of the PC.

The audible omission of the PC's designers can be corrected by adding a soundboard. One of the basic requirements of a Multimedia PC, a soundboard, endows your PC with a range of aural capabilities beyond the chirps of its squeaker. But a soundboard alone is not enough to fully appreciate the sound of multimedia. To put the signals made by a soundboard into earshot, you'll also need loudspeakers of some kind. (A multimedia PC without speakers has the sound of one hand clapping.)

Acoustics and Transducers

From the standpoint of a computer, sound is foreign stuff. Indeed, it's something that happens to stuff—air—while the computer deals with the non-stuff of logical thoughts. Video images are much more akin to computer electronics—at least the photons that you see are electromagnetic. Sound is purely mechanical, actual moving physical things.

Acoustics

Creating and controlling sound is an entirely different science—and art—from the electronic technology of the computer. At the human level, sound involves its own, dedicated sensory system and embodies its own realm of experiences from the pleasure of music to the panic roused by sirens. The science of sound is called acoustics, and it has its own laws, issues, and quirks.

The Nature of Sound

Pictures and sound are fundamentally different phenomena and present totally different engineering challenges. Your eyes see images and respond to light. Your ears hear sounds and respond to them. The very construction of your sense organs hints at the essential difference between the visual and the audible. Although your eye is a sealed entity, as protected against the entry of foreign matter as a hermetically sealed can, your ear is open to the world. Stuff simply gets into your ear. Even when we say that something gets into your eye, we mean that a hair or chunk of dust is caught between your eye and eyelid, scratching but never penetrating inside your eye.

More scientifically speaking, pictures are visual images, patterns of photons, which are sub-atomic particles that are capable of sliding through solid walls of glass or radiating through the vacuum of space. Although strictly speaking, these light photons are actual particles, they are hardly tangible in the sense that you can touch them as you would a painting, newspaper, or saxophone.

Sound, however, is something tangible. Certainly you can hear it, but given the right circumstances—or a loud enough rock band—you can feel it as well. Sound is made from actual physical stuff that needs to enter your ear to be heard. But that's not to say that sound is made from particles like light. Rather, sound or acoustic energy is a property of particles, their movement and vibration. The sounds we hear are made from the movement of air molecules, but sound can travel through liquids and solids as well. One important property of sound follows. Sound cannot exist without molecules because there's nothing to move or vibrate. That's why there's no sound in a vacuum and the surface of the moon and outer space are silent indeed, not withstanding the efforts of Hollywood special effects teams to convince you otherwise with rumbling spaceships and explosions that blast you from your seat. But sound is not the molecules themselves; the molecules are only the medium. Sound is the message.

Light is a beam of particles, and it travels as fast as the particles move—literally at the speed of light. Sound, however, moves by a different mechanism. It requires one particle transfer part of its acoustic energy to another. In other words, sound moves when one molecule knocks another around. Without sound, the net motion of molecules is zero, if simply by definition. To make sound travel, one molecule must physically move and interact with another. How fast that can happen depends on the density of molecules—how many are how close together. Where light particles just spray out and keep going, the molecules of sound have to accelerate, move, and decelerate. Sound consequently travels much slower than light—roughly one millionth the speed. Without a headstart, sound inevitably comes in second place.

Frequencies and Wavelengths

Light and sound share a single similarity—both deal in frequencies and wavelengths, but the ranges are far different. Wavelength and frequency measure the same phenomena but differ in perspective. Wavelength refers to the definite and measurable distance between peaks or crests of light or sound waves. Frequency counts the number of peaks passing a measuring point in a given period. Assuming a constant speed, wavelength and frequency are reciprocals.

The huge difference between the phenomena of light and sound becomes immediately apparent when you consider the wavelengths of each. The wavelengths of light are measured in angstroms, tens of millionths of a meter, while the wavelengths of sound can stretch from less than a centimeter to several meters. The difference in frequency is even more dramatic. The highest sound frequencies are a couple tens of thousands of kilohertz (about 20,000 Hz) while the lowest frequencies of visible light are measured in quintahertz. (The wider difference results from the slower speed of sound, as you'll see in the following sections.)

From a sensory standpoint, the range of auditory experience is also broader than the visual. While the entire band of visible light occupies about half an octave, the human ear (in good condition, at least) covers about 10 octaves. That is, the highest perceptible frequencies are about one thousand times higher than the lowest.

All of these differences are a result of the nature of the two phenomena. Light is essentially electromagnetic while sound is mechanical. At heart, sound is a physical phenomenon, produced by physical processes—clanging hammer to anvil, blowing through the tube of a trumpet.

Air Pressure

Although as acoustic energy sound can take a variety of forms, the most familiar is a rapid change in air pressure. When a physical object moves, it forces air to move also. After all, air and the object cannot take up the same place at the same time, at least in this plane of reality. As the object moves, it pushes the air away; on the other side, air rushes into the empty place where the object was. Of course, all of this moving air has to come from and go to somewhere. Ideally, the air pushed out of the way would retreat to the vacuum left behind when the object moved. Unfortunately the air, much like any physical entity, cannot instantly transport itself from one place to another.

The speed at which the air moves depends on its density; the higher the pressure, the greater the force pushing the air around. Indeed, moving the object creates an area of high pressure in front of it—where the air wants to get out of the way—and low pressure behind. Air is dumb—or in today's politically correct language, intellectually challenged. The high pressure doesn't know there's an exactly matching area of low pressure behind the object. So the high pressure pushes out in all directions. As it does, it spreads out and the pressure decreases.

Simply moving an object creates a puff of air. Sound arises when the object moves rapidly, vibrating. As it moves one way, it creates the high pressure puff that travels off. It moves back, and a corresponding low pressure pulse pops up and follows the high pressure. As the object vibrates, a steady stream of these high-and-low pressure fronts moves steadily away from it.

The basic principles of sound should be obvious from this rudimentary picture. Sound requires a medium for transmission. The speed of sound depends not on the moving object but on the density of the air (or other medium). The higher the density, the faster the sound will move. The intensity of the sound pressure declines with distance as more and more air interacts with the compression-decompression cycles. Unconstrained, this decline would follow the infamous inverse-square law because as the sound travels in one direction, it must spread over two. By confining or directing the air channel, however, you can alter the rate of this decay.

Hearing

Human beings have a mechanism called the ear that detects pressure changes or sound waves. The ear is essentially a mechanical device that's tuned to react to pressure changes that occur over a range that's commonly listed as between 20 and 20,000 times per second. (Everyone's hearing is different, and the upper limit that an individual can perceive declines with age. Women tend to have wider hearing ranges than men.)

The job of the sound side of your multimedia PC is to set the air in motion, making noises that you can hear to alert you, to entertain you, and to amaze you. The end product of this job is to move air, make it vibrate, and to send sound waves buffeting across the room and into your ears.

Loudspeakers

From the standpoint of a PC, moving air is a challenge as great as bringing together distant worlds, the electronic and the mechanical. To make sounds audible, the PC must somehow do mechanical work. It needs a transducer, a device that transmits energy from one system to another—from the electrical PC to the kinetic world of sound.

Computers are not alone in their need to convert electrical signals into mechanical sound. Nearly every sound producing home entertainment device (with the exception of ancient hand-cranked phonographs) has the same need, as do telephones, voice pagers, even amplified bullhorns. The technology has been around since Alexander Graham Bell first sent sound through wires in 1876.

The most common audio transducer today, called the *dynamic loudspeaker*, was invented in 1921 by Kellogg Rice. In the classic dynamic loudspeaker design, an electrical current activates a *voice-coil* (a solenoid or coil of wire that gives the speaker its voice). The voice coil acts as an electromagnet. Dynamic loudspeakers wrap the voice coil around a magnet so that the coils changing magnetic field reacts with the permanent magnetic field of the magnet. The cycling audio signal causes the voice coil to move back-and-forth across the magnet.

The voice coil doesn't make much noise by itself because it is not coupled to the transmission medium, the air. To enable the voice coil to move air, it is attached to a diaphragm or *speaker cone.* As the voice coil vibrates, the cone moves like a piston—pushing out, then back in repeatedly—to moving air in response to the electrical signal fed to the voice coil.

Every PC has a speaker of some kind in it. The most common kind in the IBM world is minimal with a cone that measures a minuscule 2-1/2 inches in diameter. Although that size is sufficient to make noise, it falls short on quality, range, and loudness. The reason that a small speaker fails in these vital areas is mostly a matter of physics.

The louder a sound, the more air moves. You can make a speaker move more air by increasing its excursion (how far the cone moves in and out) or by increasing the diameter of the cone. Turning up the volume on a stereo system increases the volts of the audio signal, which increases the magnetic field of the voice coil, which forces the cone to travel further. This excursion is not unlimited, however, and it can come to an abrupt end if the voice coil pops off the magnet it encircles or, more likely, is constrained by the material holding the cone in place. Practical considerations like holding the loudspeaker together limit excursion length, so larger speakers are normally louder. The diameter of the speaker cone is, of course, fixed when the speaker is manufactured.

Sound quality is another issue entirely. Although it is partly influenced by the size of the speaker cone, other parameters also influence the quality of sound reproduced by a speaker. Two of the most important are how you package the speaker and the native free-air resonance of the voice coil/cone physical system.

Baffles

Physics also requires that more air move at lower frequencies to achieve the same pressure changes or loudness, so larger speakers do a better job generating low frequency sounds. But the packaging of the speaker also influences its low frequency reproduction. At low frequencies, the pressure waves created by a loudspeaker can travel a substantial distance in the time it takes the speaker cone to move in and out. In fact, when frequencies are low enough the air has time to travel from the high pressure area in front of the speaker to the low pressure area behind an outward-moving speaker cone. The moving air cancels out the air pressure changes and the sound. At low frequencies—typically those below about 150 Hz—a loudspeaker in free air has little sound output.

This low-frequency cancellation can be reduced or eliminated by blocking the air flow from the front to the back of the speaker. Putting the loudspeaker in an enclosure or speaker baffle accomplishes exactly that. (Strictly speaking, an enclosure and baffle are not the same: a *baffle* controls flow of sound while an *enclosure* is a cabinet that encircles the rear of the speaker. Most people use the terms interchangeably.) Although speaker baffles have their own problems—they absorb sound energy and they have resonances that alter the quality of the loudspeaker's sound—in general they improve sound quality.

The internal loudspeakers in PCs are not baffled, so they have two strikes against them when it comes to accurate sound generation at low frequencies. (Although the speaker in a PC is enclosed in the case of the PC, the speaker is actually suspended in free air inside the case.) To get realistic sound reproduction, a PC consequently requires an external baffled loudspeaker—preferably two for modern stereophonic sound.

To reproduce low frequencies well, a baffle is insufficient. In the preceding discussion, the idealized baffle simply prevents air on one side of the speaker cone from getting to the other side and canceling out the low frequency sound waves. Cutting a hole in a wall and mounting the speaker in the hole would accomplish exactly that. This kind of installation is called an infinite baffle.

Cutting holes in walls and installing speakers doesn't lend itself to casual interior decorating, and in apartments can definitely lead the landlord to raise the roof as well as the rent. Consequently, most loudspeaker baffles are designed to be more portable with sizes somewhat smaller than infinity. Instead of an open wall, these smaller baffles are made as boxes or speaker enclosures—and they bring their own concerns. Primary among these is resonance. Any closed volume will resonate at a particular frequency determined by its size and shape. Blow across a soda bottle, and it whistles at a resonant frequency. A speaker enclosure will resonate similarly, and the result is an emphasis of the resonant frequency—some sounds, and particularly some musical notes, will sound louder than others at the same signal input level. Practical loudspeaker enclosures put this resonance in the bass part of the audio spectrum (low frequencies).

The loudspeaker itself also has its own *resonance.* Typically the speaker will be most efficient at its resonant frequency, and its output (for a given level of signal input) will fall precipitously below resonance. Loudspeaker manufacturers take advantage of these resonances to optimize the sound of their products. For example, making the enclosure resonate at a frequency lower than that of the loudspeaker can extend the range of frequencies that the speaker will usefully generate at the low end of its range. In effect, the air in the enclosure acts as a spring; as the speaker cone moves inward, the internal air compresses, and it helps push the cone back out.

Because this air spring helps hold the speaker cone in place, this sealed enclosure is termed an *acoustic suspension loudspeaker.* In the early days of high fidelity sound reproduction, acoustic suspensions proved a revolution, extending speaker range to new lows and musical accuracy.

Acoustic suspension speakers have one drawback. Much of the electrical energy that goes into the speaker system as an audio signal gets used up compressing the air in the enclosure instead of becoming sound. Consequently acoustic suspension speakers are notoriously inefficient and require relatively large input powers to achieve a given sound level.

Another way to prevent the sound waves from the rear of a speaker driver from interfering with those from the front is to delay their mixing so that the two acoustic waves are no longer out of phase. Instead of getting sealed inside the enclosure, the sound waves from the rear of the driver can be routed through a long escape path before exiting the enclosure. This escape path can be a twisted and folded channel like a maze inside the cabinet, resulting in a design called the *acoustical labyrinth.* Because the escape path prevents pressure build-up inside the enclosure and its energy waste, acoustical labyrinth speakers are more efficient than acoustic suspension systems. But the labyrinth likely will not significantly extend the low frequency response of the speaker system as an acoustic suspension system would.

The tuned-port or *bass reflex* enclosure design combines the strengths of both the acoustic suspension and acoustic labyrinth designs. The bass reflex enclosure is tuned to compliment the response and resonance of the speaker driver, but it uses a port to prevent the inefficiency of sealed designs. The result is a high-efficiency system with extended bass response in a compact cabinet. Most modern high-quality stereo speakers use a bass reflex design.

Most multimedia speaker systems get designed for compactness rather than extended low frequency response. They use small drivers incapable of generating much acoustic energy at low frequencies. Typically they are small, acoustic suspension or bass-reflex systems.

Multi-Speaker Systems

In the kingdom of stereo equipment, one or more loudspeakers mounted inside a baffle is often called a speaker system. To distinguish the combination from its primary constituents, the loudspeakers inside a baffle are often termed drivers, a usage unrelated to the software drivers used by programmers, the clubs used by golfers, and the pilots of automobiles.

Most low-cost multimedia speakers designed for PCs have a single or full-range driver. Some, however, have multiple drivers to cover the extensive human hearing range more smoothly. Speakers with two drivers are called two-way systems; those with three, three-way systems; and so on.

Speaker drivers are often subdivided by the frequency range they cover using colorful terms from the early days of hi-fi aficionados. A driver meant to handle low or bass frequencies, covering a range from 20 to 50 Hz up to 150 to 500 Hz (depending on the engineer giving the designation), is termed a *woofer*. A driver meant to handle high or treble frequencies, covering a range from 15,000 to 20,000 Hz at the top down to 500 to 3,000 Hz, is termed a *tweeter*. A third driver that covers the range between woofer and tweeter (when the two do not meet) is called a *midrange driver*. Drivers specially design to extend the lower range of woofers are called *subwoofers*, and drivers that extend the upper range of tweeters are termed *supertweeters*. Two-way speaker systems comprise a woofer and a tweeter; three way systems add a midrange driver.

The term "subwoofer" is also used to describe a special, auxiliary baffled speaker system meant to enhance the sound of ordinary speakers by extending their low frequency range. Because the human ear cannot localize low-frequency sounds, you can place this subwoofer anywhere in a listening room without much effect on stereophonic imaging. The other, smaller speakers are often termed satellite speakers.

Because most multimedia speaker systems are small and lack the ability to produce strong low-frequency bass sounds, this sort of subwoofer helps make your PC sound more realistic.

Location and Coupling

In addition to the drivers and enclosure, a third physical factor influences the sound of speaker systems: where you put them. Move a speaker system from the corner of a room to the center, and its sound quality will change dramatically. This difference is particularly noticeable at low frequencies.

This difference is a result of the acoustic coupling between the speaker and the room. A speaker driver acts as a piston pushing air forward. The air in front of an ordinary cone loudspeaker, sometimes termed a direct radiator, compresses and pushes against the air in front of it, which tends to resist compression and pushes back. So part of the acoustic energy pushed out from the speaker gets pushed back, and some of the pressure wave gets squeezed and squashes out between the driver and air in front. Energy ends up wasted all over the place, and the driver does a lot of work to produce a little sound. In the lingo of physicists, the impedance of the speaker and room are mismatched so the speaker couples poorly with the room.

This coupling is improved by smoothing the transition from the small piston motion to the huge mass of air in front of the speaker. To do this, the wave front excited by the speaker driver is initially confined and gradually allowed to increase—the driver pushes air into a tube that flares outward. This flaring tube resembling the bell of a trumpet is called a *horn*.

Speaker drivers coupled with horns are substantially more efficient than direct radiators, so they need less power to produce a given sound level. Unfortunately, the size of a horn required to efficiently couple a driver depends on the wavelength of sound to be reproduced; and at bass frequencies horns have to be prodigious. A special enclosure design called the *folded horn* approximates the coupling of a true horn for lower frequencies. Typically folded horn speakers are placed in the corners of a room, and the speakers beam backward. The sound reflects from the corner walls, which act as an extension of the horn.

Locating an ordinary speaker system in a corner approximates this horn effect and results in greater efficiency in the reproduction of low frequency sounds. In other words, shoving your woofer in a corner gives you better bass. Even putting a speaker against a wall improves its low frequency coupling. With some speakers, however, corner placement exaggerates the bass and makes the overall sound unnatural.

Performance
Issue

In any case, you can control the low frequency sound of your stereo or multimedia system by the placement of your speakers. (In the case of subwoofer-and-satellite speakers, the location of the subwoofer alone controls bass response.) For the most bass, locate your speakers in corners. Against a wall gives the next most bass. Moving a speaker a few inches out from a wall oftentimes dramatically decreases its bass response. Finally, raising a speaker off the floor on a speaker stand reduces bass response to its lowest level.

Another concern in speaker placement is *stereophonic imaging,* which means how well the stereophonic illusion succeeds. With good imaging, an orchestra seems to spread out between your two stereo speakers; you can pick out the exact location of every instrument in a rock band; singers often seem to be standing directly between the two stereo speakers. With poor stereo imaging, you hear sounds coming from one or the other speaker but rarely in between.

Performance Issue

In multimedia applications, most people find that putting speakers on either side of their monitor is the most satisfactory. The symmetrical location gives good imaging (with most of the sound seemingly located inside the monitor!). Because the speakers are near your ears you hear less room noise and can operate them at a lower sound level—which usually pleases the people with whom you share your home or office.

Note that some speakers are specifically designed for corner placement (notably folded horns) while others are designed for speaker stands. The overall guiding rule is, however, that you should put your speakers where they sound best to you.

Passive and Active Systems

Multimedia speakers typically come in one of two types, active or passive. The difference is that *active speakers* have built-in amplifiers while *passive speakers* do not.

Speaker systems designed for stereo systems are almost universally passive. They rely on your receiver or amplifier to provide them with the power they need to make sound.

Active speakers are typically designed for personal stereo systems—the little radios and cassette players you clip to your belt to fend away boredom while you jog. The small stereos are typically designed for use with headphones, and consequently produce only enough power to operate headphones. Active speakers have integral amplifiers that boost this headphone-level signal to the strength needed to power normal speakers. In effect, active speakers move the amplifier from the stereo system into the speaker cabinet.

Most multimedia sound boards produce sufficient power to operate small, passive speaker systems. Their outputs are almost uniformly about four watts because all use similar circuitry to generate the power. This level is enough even for many large stereo-style passive speaker systems. Active speakers still work with these higher-powered sound boards and in many cases deliver better (if just louder!) sound through their own amplifiers.

The amplifiers in active speakers are like any other audio amplifiers with output power measured in watts (and in theory matched to the speakers) and quality measured in terms of frequency response and distortion. The big difference is that most active speakers, originally designed for portable stereos, operate from battery power. If you plan to plug active speakers into your desktop PC, ensure that you get a battery eliminator power supply so you can plug them into a wall outlet. Otherwise, if you're serious about multimedia, you'll be single-handedly supporting the entire battery industry.

Microphones

Capturing sound—turning pressure waves into electricity—requires a special transducer that's familiar in the form of the microphone. The job of the microphone is simple: to translate changes in air pressure into voltage changes. The accuracy of the microphone's translation determines the quality of the sound that can be recorded. No microphone is perfect. Each subtly distorts the translation, not making the results unidentifiable but minutely *coloring* the captured sound. One side of the microphone designer's art is to make these colorations as pleasing as possible. Another side of the art is to attempt to make the microphone work more like the human ear and tuning in only to what you want to hear, rejecting unwanted sounds.

Technology

Engineers have developed several technologies for converting mechanical sound waves into electrical signals. Each of these technologies has spawned a distinct type of microphone. The most important of these are dynamic, condensor, and piezoelectric.

Dynamic

The microphones you're most apt to plug into your multimedia PC use the same technology as electrical generators, in part because that's exactly what they do—generate small voltages. An electrical generator or dynamo uses a moving magnetic field to induce a current in a coil of wire. Microphones that use this technology are called *dynamic*.

The basic dynamic microphone starts with a diaphragm that's typically made from lightweight plastic and formed into a domed shape or something even more elaborate to stiffen it. The diaphragm is connected to a lightweight coil of wire that's wrapped around a small, usually cylindrical, permanent magnet. This voice coil is firmly connected to the diaphragm but otherwise loosely suspended to that it can move longitudinally in relation to the magnet. Sound waves press against the diaphragm and push down. The moving coil in the permanent magnetic field generates a small voltage. When the pressure drops, the suspension of the diaphragm pushes it and the voice coil back, generating a voltage of the opposite polarity.

One of the chief limits on the performance of a dynamic microphone is mass. Compared to the tenuous nature of sound waves, the voice coil and diaphragm of a dynamic microphone have a relatively large mass, requiring a relatively large force to move it. A larger diaphragm can capture more force, though making it too large both increases its mass and lowers sensitivity to the short waves of high frequencies.

One way to limit the moving mass of a dynamic microphone is to eliminate the voice coil. Ribbon microphones use a thin metallic ribbon suspended between poles of a magnet to act both as voice coil and diaphragm. The disadvantage of this design is that the ribbon and its suspension are so light in weight that they are prone to be easily damaged. Highly regarded microphones from the golden age of radio use the ribbon design. Ribbon microphones are held in esteem by many people—particularly announcers and narrators—for their "warm" sound that adds a fullness to the deeper registers of the voice.

Condenser

Today's most highly regarded professional microphones also eliminate the voice coils but they use an entirely different operating principle. Instead of generating electricity, they start with a voltage and modify that voltage in correspondence to the sound pressure. The microphone can then eliminate or cancel out the initial *bias* voltage to leave nothing but a voltage representation of the sound pressure.

The prototype design of this technology makes the microphone diaphragm one plate of an electrical capacitor, and as the diaphragm vibrates, the capacitance of the sensing element of the microphone changes, which can in turn modify the bias voltage. Such microphones are called capacitor or, more commonly from the old-fashioned word for capacitor, *condensor microphones*. These microphones are noted for their ability to produce crisp renderings of high frequencies, a characteristic "bright" sound compared to dynamic microphones.

To function properly, the capacitor of the classic condensor microphone must be polarized by a relatively high voltage. Modern microphones of this design instead use a special, permanently charged capacitor called an *electret*. In any case, the electronics of the condensor or electret microphone require a supply of electricity to operate. Most modern designs, such as the small professional lavaliere microphones used in television interviews, use small batteries. The audio signal wires can also send the necessary DC voltage to the microphone from a special power supply. This scheme is often called a phantom power system because the power sneaks through the signal wires without additional connections (the electrical circuitry easily separates the DC power from the AC audio signal and prevents them from interfering). The nominal voltage of these phantom power systems is 48 volts, a carryover from the needs of the classic condensor microphone.

Piezoelectric

The low-cost, low-quality microphones of days gone by used the piezoelectric principle. That is, some materials (notably ceramics and crystals) generate small voltages when they are stressed. Engineers took advantage of this principle by attaching a diaphragm to a thin crystal or ceramic element in such a way that sound on the diaphragm flexed the piezoelectric element and generated a voltage proportional to the intensity of the sound.

These microphones were almost elegant in their simplicity—no coils of wires, no transformers, no electronics whatsoever. Better still, back in the days when electronic circuits were built from tubes and things you're more likely to find in a plumber's kit these days, piezoelectric microphones better matched the circuitry. Tube inputs had a high impedance. They required high voltages but small currents to operate, and the piezoelectric elements delivered exactly that.

On the downside, however, the sound quality of piezoelectric transducers is subject to the resonances and mechanical limitations of the crystal element they use. Their frequency response is consequently limited and uneven.

Modern transistor circuits happily accommodate low impedance devices, including dynamic and condenser microphones. Piezoelectric microphones often require a transformer to match to transistor circuits, adding expense to their use. That disadvantage, coupled with the inevitable low quality of piezoelectric elements, has led to the virtual demise of the technology.

Directionality

Sometimes you want to hear everything, say when you've leveled your ear to a keyhole and there's some delicious sound effects on the other side of the door. Other times you want to block out everything—the screaming spouse, the moaning children, the sirens of the emergency squad—so you can concentrate on something really important, like the playoffs on television. Similarly, at times you want a microphone that hears everything and other times you want to focus on a particular sound. Engineers have obliged by producing microphones that differ in their directionality.

An *omnidirectional microphone* does not discriminate between sounds no matter what direction they come from. It hears everything the same in a full circle around the microphone.

A *unidirectional microphone* has a preferred direction in which it hears best, and it tends to subdue the sounds coming from other directions. Most unidirectional microphones are most sensitive to sounds directly in front of them. Sounds in the preferred direction are called *on-axis sounds*. Those that are not favored are called *off-axis sounds*.

Because sound occurs in waves, the most efficient way of making a microphone directional is not to absorb unwanted sounds but to make sound waves from the less desired directions cancel themselves out. The most efficient cancellation results in a pick-up pattern that has a shape vaguely resembling a heart. Consequently, most unidirectional microphones are called *cardioid microphones* from the shape of the pattern, *kardia* being Greek for heart. Hypercardioid microphones focus their coverage more narrowly while maintaining the basic cardioid shape.

Most cardioid microphones suffer a *proximity effect*. When you push a cardioid microphone close to a sound source, the acoustical design that cancels out sound from behind the microphone tends to accentuate low frequencies striking the microphone. The resulting sound is boomy (if you don't like it) or warm and full (if you do).

Bi-directional microphones are, as the name implies, sensitive to sounds coming from two directions, generally the front and rear of the microphone that resembles the numeral "8." Consequently, bi-directional microphones are sometimes called figure-eight microphones. Although the odd pattern was originally a remnant of early microphone designs, modern engineers find it useful in some stereophonic miking techniques.

Physical Characteristics

Microphones come in a variety of sizes and shapes, most of which are dictated by function. In making a video, you'll probably use *tie-tack microphones*, tiny microphones hardly an inch long (although each one may have a large lump of electronics at the end of its cord). These are favored by videographers because they can easily be hidden or placed unobtrusively on the video subject. Typically, one might be clipped onto a necktie, like a tie tack (and hence the name).

Lavaliere microphones were the tie-tack microphones of the black-and-white television age. About the size of a carrot, they hung around a subjects neck like a two pound necklace—cumbersome but better than spending your video life in front of a microphone stand.

Shotgun microphones use a ribbed tube that's so long people see a resemblance of a gun barrel in it. The design helps create a hypercardioid pattern that gives the microphone a long reach and excellent directionality. Shotgun microphones are often used in motion pictures, held just above camera range, where they are invisible in the shot but close enough to produce good sound quality. Shotgun microphones are also used much in the same way by some electronic journalists.

Parabolic microphones are the ultimate in directionality. They use a reflecting disk like a satellite television antenna to focus distant sound on a microphone element. The focusing effect increases directionality and increases the apparent level of the sound (like having a diaphragm two feet in diameter). What inevitably suffers is sound quality. Parabolic reflectors work best when the waves they reflect are substantially smaller than the diameter of the dish. The typical microphone reflector is tiny compared to low frequency sound waves, so the microphone tends to emphasize high frequencies. This works well for surveillance because high frequencies are key to intelligibility but poor for video because low frequencies contain presence and warmth.

Electrical Characteristics

The signals produced by microphones are measured in several ways. The two most important characteristics are impedance and signal level.

Impedance describes the resistance to the flow of alternating current signals of a circuit and is measured in ohms. Impedance defines the relationship between voltage and current in an AC circuit. Every AC device has a characteristic impedance, and when two are connected together the optimum transfer of power between them occurs when their impedances are matched. Microphones are known as low impedance (from 50 to 600 ohms) and high impedance (50,000 and more ohms). Some microphones have switches that enable you to change their impedance.

Plugging a microphone of one impedance into a circuit meant for another results in low power transfer—faint signals. Nearly all professional microphones and most other microphones now operate at low impedance as do most microphone inputs. If your microphone has an impedance switch, you'll usually want it set to the low (150 ohm) position.

The signal levels produced by microphones are measured in millivolts or dB (decibels) at a given sound pressure level. This value is nominal. Loud sounds produce higher voltages. Most microphones produce signals described as –60 to –40 dB, and will work with most microphone inputs. If you shout into any microphone, particularly one with a higher output (closer to –40 dB), its output level may be too high for some circuits to process properly, particularly those in consumer equipment—say your PC's soundboard. The high level may cause distortion. Adding an attenuator (or switching the microphone with output level switches to a lower level) will eliminate the distortion.

Microphone signals can be balanced or unbalanced. Balanced signals require two wires and a ground; unbalanced, one wire and a ground. Balanced signals are more immune to noise. Unbalanced signals require less sophisticated electronic input circuitry. Most sound boards use unbalanced signals. Most professional microphones produce balanced signals.

You can often convert a balanced signal into an unbalanced one (so you can connect a professional microphone to your soundboard) by tying together one of the two signal wires of the balanced circuit with the ground. The ground and the other signal wire then act as an unbalanced circuit.

Sound Quality

The figure most often given as representing quality is *frequency response*, the range of frequencies that the microphone can pick up and translate from mechanical to electrical energy. With modern microphones, the figure is almost meaningless, as all microphones claim to cover at least the 50 Hz to 15,000 Hz range, which is close to the limits of human hearing (and actually exceeds that of middle-aged men and younger folk who favor rock concerts). Microphones priced from $10 to $2,500 claim essentially the same frequency response.

The difference between microphones is *sound color*. Every facet of microphone design—the shape of the microphone, the size and construction of its capsule (the combination of voice coil and diaphragm), the technology, and other aspects all affect the translation of sound into electrical signals and change how different frequencies are emphasized or attenuated. The expensive microphones preferred by professionals simply sound better to them. And that should be enough.

Connectors

Professional microphones with balanced signals typically use XLR connectors (named after the model designation of one of the original designs) with three pins for their two signals and ground. Pin one is always the ground pin. In balanced circuits, pin two carries the positive signal; pin three, the negative. When used in unbalanced circuits, pins one and three are usually connected together.

Consumer quality unbalanced signal microphones usually use phone plugs of various sizes. The plug size refers to the diameter of the shaft of the connector. An old-style quarter-inch phone plug has a connector shaft one-quarter inch in diameter. Modern microphones use miniature (one-eighth-inch) plugs.

Phone plugs have two or three connections. The end of the plug is called the *tip*, and is always connected to the unbalanced signal. The shaft of the connector is called the *shield*, and it connects to the ground. Stereo and balanced signals use three connector plugs. The end is still called the tip, and it connects to the positive signal or the left channel of a stereo pair of balanced signals. A thin ring between the tip and the shield is called, logically, the *ring* and acts as the link for the negative side of the balanced line or for the right channel in unbalanced stereo systems.

Audio

As transducers, microphones and loudspeakers only transduce. That is, they only transform one kind of energy into another. That energy—and more importantly, its information content—needs to come from somewhere. Multimedia makes your PC the originator of both. Your multimedia software generates the information content, and the audio circuitry of your PC gives it power.

Audio is a term that refers to the electrical equivalent of sound. Any signal conveying information that represents sound qualifies, no matter how that signal is coded.

In fact, audio signals use one of two primary coding systems. Classic audio signals are *analog audio*, their electrical signal strength (usually voltage) directly corresponds to the loudness of the sound. The audio signal is an electrical analog of the mechanical sound. Audio signals are a form of alternating current that fall within the frequency range of idealized human hearing, that is about 20 to 20,000 Hz.

As with everything else, PCs prefer to deal with sound encoded in digital form, that is, as *digital audio*. Sounds are encoded in the form of digital pulses.

As with any coding system, digital audio can use any of a variety of codes to store sound information. The most common digital audio code is *pulse code modulation* or PCM, which turns sounds into numbers. The value of the number corresponds to the strength of the sound at a given moment.

Making a PCM signal requires an *analog-to-digital conversion* process. A device, usually called a PCM encoder, measures the analog sound source thousands of times each second and records each measurement. The reverse of the process, *digital-to-analog conversion*, takes the measurements and creates an analog voltage at the level each one represents. In reconstructing the original signal, the digital-to-analog converter must know two vital parameters of the digital PCM code, the sampling rate and the resolution. The sampling rate indicates how often the measurements were made, and the resolution indicates the number of bits in the digital code the system uses.

Today, most stereo systems have at least one component that uses digital signals—a compact disc player. High-tech stereo gear may use digital signals throughout. But two elements in most modern-day sound systems remain resolutely analog: microphones and loudspeakers. Both are transducers that must link to the physical world where—at least from the human (macroscopic) perspective—sounds vary smoothly and continuously in loudness and frequency, not in distinct digital jumps.

As with stereo systems, PCs similarly have both analog and digital audio aspects. Internally, all signals need to be digital because of the PC's underlying digital nature. But speaker outputs and microphone inputs remain steadfastly analog.

Although the native audio endowment of every PC is modest, it is at heart a digital audio system. Its biggest shortcoming arises at the analog end. Its tiny loudspeaker lacks even pretensions of any fidelity. Although at one time it might have been considered an adequate sound system, by today's multimedia standards the basic PC sound system is anemic indeed. But it is the least common denominator among PC sound systems.

Basic PC Sound

The quality of the standard PC sound system is marginal at best if just because of its tiny, unbaffled loudspeaker. But the abysmal loudspeaker resident in most PCs isn't the only problem. In fact, the little earsore is well-matched to the rudimentary sound-generation abilities designed into the basic circuitry of the PC.

In fact, the ancient design of the original IBM PC made no attempt to generate appealing sounds. And that disdain for aural pleasures has carried through to the machines of today— except for the select few with inherent multimedia capabilities.

When IBM's engineers designed the original PC, they realized that they needed some sort of sound-generating capacity but they didn't set their goals very high. Sound was not a high priority. After all, the world's entire experience with computers was in business, and most managers didn't exactly expect symphonies to pour out of typewriters and other office equipment. Certainly computerized games were available, but game-playing computers were cheaply made using crude technology. The best they did was beep. So the PC didn't have to do much more to match the market, and more was hardly expected.

The IBM engineers endowed the PC with a simple programmable oscillator, a device for generating tones. The little speaker they stuffed into the PC's case could beep warnings or diagnostic codes (useful if your monitor doesn't work). It could even play simple songs—softly, crudely. But the system has one shortcoming: no one thought to give it any sort of volume control!

Instead, the engineers gave a second, more direct means of controlling the speaker, essentially a direct on/off switch. One digital code sends full voltage to the speaker; a second signal shuts it off. Although this at first seems even more primitive than using an oscillator, clever programmers have exploited it to coax a form of speech from the PC's speaker and generate enough noises to make games playable. The secret is to switch the speaker signal fast enough to yield a form of pulse code modulation. The right program can vary the volume and extend the audio range of the PC far beyond the limits imposed by its loudspeaker.

All of the sounds in the PC's tone-based sound system begin in one of the channels of the PC's 8253 or 8254-2 timer/counter integrated circuit chip (or its equivalent integrated into the system's chipset). By changing the time base set for this oscillator, you or your software can alter the frequency of the audio signal bound for the system's internal speaker.

This oscillator starts with a crystal-controlled fixed frequency of 1.19 MHz. A register in the timer chip stores a 16-bit divisor by which value the timer reduces the oscillator. Loading the highest possible value into the divisor register (65,535) generates the lowest possible tone, about 18 Hz, low enough to strain the limits of normal hearing if the PC's speaker was able to reproduce it.

Because of the circuit design of the PC, these tones are produced as square waves, which means they are not pure tones but are rich in overtones or harmonics. Musically they sound harsh— exactly what the doctor (or engineer) ordered for warning tones.

To use the timer to generate tones in a PC, you must first set up the timer/oscillator chip by writing the value 0B6(Hex) to the timer's control port at I/O port address 043(Hex). The frequency divisor for the PC tone generator then gets loaded into the I/O port at 042(Hex). This 8-bit port expects to receive two data bytes in sequence, with the least significant byte first. Finally you must turn the speaker on by activating bit 0 of the register at I/O port 061(Hex). Resetting this bit to zero switches the speaker off. (You must exercise care when tinkering with these bits; other bits in this register control the keyboard.)

This design limits the dynamics of the signal. The output of the timer/oscillator chip is set at a constant level—the standard digital signal level—so the sound level produced by the speaker does not vary. All the sounds produced by the PC's motherboard have the same level. Some tones generated by the PC timer sound louder than others primarily because they are more obnoxious. They are made from the exact right combination of frequencies to nag at the aesthetic parts of your brain. That's about all they were designed to do. Listen long enough and you'll agree that the PC's designers succeeded beyond their wildest dreams at creating obnoxious sound.

Taking direct control of the speaker sidesteps these limitations. Bit 1 of I/O port 061(Hex) gives you this control. Setting this bit high sends voltage to the speaker; setting it to zero switches off the voltage. The sound generated by the speaker depends only on when you do the switching.

Using a technique called pulse-width modulation, you can use this primitive control system to add dynamics to the audio you generate. Pulse-width modulation uses the duty cycle of a high-frequency signal coupled with a low-pass filter to encode the loudness of an analog signal equivalent. The loudness of a sound corresponds to the length of a signal pulse of a high-frequency carrier wave. A soft sound gets a brief pulse while loud sounds are full-strength square waves. The low-pass filter eliminates the high carrier frequency from the signal and leaves a variable strength audio signal (the modulation).

The only shortcoming to using this system with PCs is that you are left to control the timing of the signal. If, for example, you use program loops to switch the speaker on and off, the frequency of the tone produced will vary with the processing speed of the PC. What sounds great on an old 386 machine may be supersonic on a Pentium.

Because the timer-based sound system and the direct-control system are independently controlled, you can use both techniques at once to generate more complex sounds.

The output of the chip that controls the PC's speaker (specifically, an 8255 Programmable Peripheral Interface chip) cannot supply enough current to power a loudspeaker at a listenable level. Consequently, every PC adds an amplifier to boost this signal up to speaker level. While many early PCs use a special line-driver integrated circuit to provide enough power to run the internal loudspeaker, modern systems incorporate this circuitry into the basic motherboard chipset.

The standard PC design also adds an integral low-pass filter and a current limiting resistor between the speaker driver chip and the loudspeaker itself. The low-pass filter eliminates frequencies higher than normal hearing range (and some in the upper ranges that you probably can readily hear). This filtering prevents digital artifacts (such as those from pulse-width modulation) from leaking into the speaker.

The current-limiting resistor (typically about 33 ohms) in series with the loudspeaker prevents the internal loudspeaker of a PC from drawing too much current and overloading the driver circuit. It also lowers the loudness of the speaker (because it absorbs some power as part of the current-limiting process). Although some circuit tinkerers bypass this resistor to make their PCs louder, doing so risks damage to the driver circuit.

The Windows 3.1 family normally uses only the tone-generating abilities of your PC to beep warnings. However, Microsoft developed a special driver that takes direct control of the speaker to generate complex sounds. This driver was included with the beta test versions of Windows 3.1 but not the release version. During the development of Windows 3.1, Microsoft found that this driver sometimes misbehaved with some programs. To avoid support headaches, Microsoft elected not to include the driver in the basic Windows 3.1 package. The driver is included in the Microsoft Driver Library and Microsoft does license it to developers to include with their products. It is available from a number of sources.

Windows 3.1x

A similar shareware driver written by John Ridges is available through the CompuServe Microsoft Windows Multimedia forum, where you'll find it as the compressed file SPEAKR.ZIP, which is an archive containing four files: SPEAKR.DRV, VADLIBWD.386, OEMSETUP.INF and SPEAKR.TXT. Although this internal speaker driver acts much like Microsoft's own version, it does not disable interrupts (for example, Windows is totally occupied with the speaker when sounds are playing so it cannot run other programs or respond to your typing). As a result, sound quality may suffer when an application issues a lot of interrupts while sounds are playing, but this design prevents your losing data at communications ports or from your network while you enjoy the noise it makes.

Sound Boards

The loudspeaker only reacts to the signals sent to it. They can be from a radio, television, stereo receiver, or public address system. Or from a multimedia PC. Just as all those other audio sources need some source of sound—be it a broadcast signal, a compact disc, or a microphone—so does your PC. As with everything else in your PC, the original fodder of multimedia sound is data, byte after byte of it. Bytes, unfortunately, don't translate easily into audio. Plug a loud-speaker into a digital output from your PC, say a serial or parallel port, and you'll soon appreciate the problem. To your ear, raw data bytes are as raucous as heavy metal music strained through broken glass.

The part of a multimedia PC charged with translating data to audio is the soundboard. Although some multimedia PCs may have sound circuitry built into their motherboards, in most PCs the soundboard is simply one more expansion board that plugs into a vacant slot.

To cope with the needs of multimedia software and the demands of human hearing and expectation, the soundboard needs to carry out several audio-related functions. Foremost is the conversion of digital sound data into the analog form that speakers can shake into something that you can hear. In addition, most sound boards can sample or record sounds for later play-back, a process technically called analog-to-digital conversion. They also create sounds of their own with built-in synthesizers, mix together the results of sampling, synthesis, and storage, and amplify the aural goulash to an ear-pleasing volume.

Sound boards can be distinguished in several ways. The most important of these divisions are compatibility and quality. Compatibility determines the software with which a given soundboard will work. Quality influences how satisfied you will be with the results—essentially whether you will be delighted or dismayed by your foray into multimedia.

Of the two, compatibility is often most important because if your software can't coax a whimper from your soundboard, you won't hear anything no matter how well the circuitry on the board might be able to do its job. Once you have the basic compatibility that your software wants, however, your ears will prefer the board with the better quality. A bad soundboard shrieks and crackles worse than a radio in a thunderstorm; a good one can rival the best audiophile's stereo system.

Before you consider compatibility, you need to know how a soundboard carries out its various functions. All of the work done by a given soundboard can be classified as one of three primary chores: creating sounds from instructions sent to them by your programs, playing back sounds created by some other source, and controlling these and other sounds.

Creating sounds is called synthesis, and when it's done well, it's as far from the simple oscillator of a PC as a metal toy drum is from a symphony orchestra. The sounds range from the contents of ordinary audio CDs to reproducing those that you've captured onto your hard disk, perhaps sampled by the soundboard itself. Control of other sound-making devices requires a special electrical connection.

The Multimedia PC specification also charges sound boards with two other chores. In addition to its synthesis and sampling functions, an MPC soundboard must also be able to control a CD-ROM drive (and incidentally use digital information encoded on a CD-ROM as a sound source). Often, however, the CD-ROM interface on a soundboard is better ignored and another interface used in its stead. Standalone SCSI host adapters, for example, often deliver better performance than the SCSI circuitry built into sound boards. Consequently, the CD-ROM interface aspect of MPC sound boards is separately discussed in the CD-ROM chapter.

Performance Issue

The MPC specification also requires that a compliant soundboard include a Musical Instrument Device Interface or MIDI port. Because MIDI connections are verging out of the multimedia mainstream and because MIDI is a detailed and intense topic in itself, it will be discussed in a separate chapter as well.

Audio Quality

You don't have to use CD-quality sampling rates and resolution when you capture sounds with your PC, and you have good reason not to. CD-quality sound involves a lot of data, 150KB/second. Consequently, you are well advised to use lower sampling rates when you need to conserve space and don't need the utmost in quality.

Most sound boards support 22 KHz and 11 KHz sampling; some offer a full range of other intermediate values such as 8 KHz, 16 KHz, or 32 KHz. If you want to play back the sound you sample on the widest variety of systems, you'll want to choose one of the more ubiquitous sampling rates (11 KHz, 22 KHz, or 44.1 KHz). To minimize the disk space you need for storage, select the lowest sampling rate consistent with the application (and sound quality) you want.

The basic rule is that the highest frequency that can be sampled and stored is about slightly less than one-half the sampling rate. An 8 KHz sampling rate is about equal to telephone quality (and is used by the telephone company); 22 KHz takes you halfway between AM and FM radio quality; and 44.1 KHz sampling pushes all the way up to CD sound quality.

Performance Issue

The resolution (or sample size) affects the noise level and distortion in the sampled sound. Most sound boards give you a choice of either 8-bit or 16-bit sampling. Although samples could in theory be any size, these values offer the most convenient package for storage and manipulation. As you would expect, the larger sample size yields better quality but sacrifices storage. With 16-bit sampling, you get full CD-quality with a signal-to-noise ratio of about 96 dB (not counting defects that might sneak into the output of the soundboard after it converts the digital signal to analog). Eight-bit sampling yields a signal-to-noise ratio of about 48 dB, which is nearly a thousand times worse (the dB scale is logarithmic), below the standard set for AM radio. That said, you won't notice much difference when you listen through the internal speaker in your PC or inexpensive satellite speakers. Sixteen-bit quality is only apparent in headphones and component-quality speakers. For music, you'll want to use 16-bit samples. For frugality, use eight bits.

If you're making original recordings of sounds and music, you'll want to use as high a rate as is consistent with your PC's resources. Notwithstanding the full 44.1 KHz sampling rate, don't expect to get the quality of a recording studio from an inexpensive soundboard even though it may boast full CD-level digitization. In operation, the electronic noise rattling around inside your PC will leak into the soundboard and its signals, degrading your recordings with an electronic background cacophony.

The digital signal processing circuitry inside most CD players is typically more sophisticated than that on sound boards. You'll get better sound quality from your stereo system than from a soundboard. In fact, most sound boards have analog inputs that enable you to send the audio output of a CD-ROM player that's already been converted from digital to analog form through your PC sound system. Most sound boards enable you to digitize or sample this signal, record it in digital form, or mix it with other sounds, and reproduce it through the speakers connected to your PC. Because the signals sent along to your soundboard in analog form require no further digital processing, playing them puts no load on your PC.

Synthesis

Making a sound electronically is easy. After all, any AC signal with a frequency in the range of human hearing makes a noise when connected to a loudspeaker. Even before the age of electronics, Hermann Helmholtz discovered that any musical tone was made from vibrations in the air that corresponded to a periodic (but complex) waveform. Making an electronic signal sound like something recognizable is not so simple, however. You need exactly the right waveform.

The basic frequency-generating circuit, the oscillator, produces a very pure tone, so pure it sounds completely unrealistic—electronic. Natural sounds are not single frequencies but collections of many frequencies, related and unrelated, at different strengths.

A tone from a musical instrument, for example, comprises a single characteristic frequency (corresponding to the note played) called the fundamental and a collection of other frequencies, each a multiple of the *fundamental*, called overtones by scientists or *partials* by musicians. The relationship of the loudnesses of the overtones to one another gives the sound of the instrument its distinctive identity, its *timbre*, and makes a note played on a violin sound different from the same note played on a flute. Timbre is a product of the many resonances of the musical instrument which tend to reinforce some overtones and diminish others.

Noises differ from musical tones in that they comprise many, unrelated frequencies. *White noise*, for example, is a random collection of all frequencies.

The one happy result of all sounds being combinations of frequencies (a principle discovered in relation to periodic waves by Jean Baptiste Joseph Fourier in the late Eighteenth Century) is that creating any sound requires only putting together frequencies in the right combination. So synthesizing sounds should be easy—all you need to know is the right combination. At that, synthesis becomes a little daunting. Trial-and-error experimentation at finding the right combinations is daunting at best because the number of frequencies and the possible strengths of each frequency are both infinite, so you end up dealing with numbers that strain most pocket calculators—like infinity times infinity. Add in one more variable—that natural sounds vary from one instant to the next, meaning each instant represents a different frequency combination, giving you yet another infinity to deal with—and sound synthesis suddenly seems to slip to the far side of impossible.

In truth, the numbers are much more manageable than the dire situation outlined above. For example, musical sounds involve only a few frequencies—the fundamental and overtones that are within the range of human hearing (both in frequency range and strength). But synthesizing sounds from scratch remains a challenge.

Electronic designers have come up with several strategies that synthesize sound with varying degrees of success. Two techniques are popular in today's synthesizers: Frequency Modulation and Wave Table Synthesis.

Compatibility is most important when you call upon a soundboard to create sounds from program instructions. If a given soundboard is not completely compatible with your software, it cannot produce the sounds that the programmer originally intended.

Subtractive Synthesis

The first true music synthesizers (as opposed to electronic instruments, which seek to replicate rather than synthesize sounds) used analog technology. The first of these machines were created in the late 1950s and were based on the principle of subtractive synthesis. These early synthesizers generated tones with special oscillators called *waveform generators* that made tones already rich in harmonics. Instead of pure tones of sine waves, they generated square waves, sawtooth waves, and odd intermediary shapes. In itself, the harmonic-rich complex wave each of these oscillators generated had its own distinctive sound.

These initial waveforms were then mixed together and shaped using *filters* that emphasized some ranges of frequencies and attenuated others. The filters removed or subtracted some of the harmonics, hence the name of the technology. Sometimes one tone was used to modulate another to create waveforms so strange they sounded like they originated in foreign universes.

Analog synthesis was born in an age of experimentation when creative artists explored the furthest reaches of new music. They made no attempt to mimic conventional instruments—after all, conventional instruments could already do that and the outposts of the avant-garde have traipsed far beyond the fringes of conventional music. The goal of analog synthesis was to create new sounds, sounds not found in nature, sounds never before heard, sounds like the digestive system of some giant dyspeptic dinosaur. Analog synthesizers sounded unmistakably electronic, even alien. Compared to the tones of conventional acoustic instruments, the synthesizer could be jarring—exactly the effect desired by both serious music composers and rock musicians to make their work stand out.

As the depths of new music were being plumbed, digital technology appeared as an alternative to analog designs. The first digital synthesizers sought merely to duplicate the function of the analog units using an alternate technology, transistors substituted for tubes. Suddenly room-size wiring nightmares could be compressed into human-size machines, and engineers could pile in even more circuitry for more control over the sounds. Computers added their influence, and engineers shifted from analog to digital technology. Along the way, they discovered that digital synthesis gave so much control over sounds that they could not only create new sounds but also create (or at least approximate) any sound. The goal of synthesis shifted to mimicking conventional instruments—that is, expensive, hand-crafted instruments—with cheap, sound-nearly-alike digital substitutes. With one mass-produced electronic box—the *digital synthesizer*—a musician could put an entire orchestra at his fingertips.

Additive Synthesis

When attempting to recreate the sounds of actual instruments, engineers discovered that they got better results when combining the sounds of waveform generators instead of filtering them. In effect, they turned subtractive synthesis on its head and developed the additive synthesizer.

Instead of starting with complex waves and filtering away the unwanted parts, the additive synthesizer builds sounds in the most logical way—by adding together all the frequencies that make up a musical sound. While this chore was difficult if not impossible with analog circuitry, the precision of digital electronics made true additive synthesis a reality. The digital additive synthesizer mathematically created the pattern that mixing tones would create. The resulting digital signal would then be converted into an analog signal (using a digital-to-analog converter) that would drive a loudspeaker or recording system.

The additive synthesizer faced one large problem in trying to create life-like sounds: the mix of frequencies for each note of an instrument is different. In fact, the mix of frequencies changes from the initial attack when a note begins (for instance, when a string is struck by a piano hammer) to its final decay. To produce sounds approaching reality, the synthesizer required a complete description of every note it would create at various times in its generation. As a result a true additive-type digital synthesizer is a complex—and expensive—device.

Practical sound synthesis for PC peripherals is based on much more modest technologies than purely additive synthesis. Two primary alternatives have become commercially popular in the synthesizers incorporated into PC sound boards. These are FM synthesis and wave table synthesis.

FM Synthesis

While working at Stanford Artificial Intelligence Laboratories in 1973, John M. Chowning discovered that two pure sine wave tones, when properly combined together, made interesting sounds. To make his combinations, he borrowed a radio broadcasting technique called frequency modulation and applied it to audio frequencies. Although the FM principle is completely unlike any natural phenomenon, Chowning found he created sounds that had attacks and decays that sounded quite natural.

The resulting FM synthesis works by starting with one frequency or tone called a *carrier* and altering it with a second frequency called a *modulator*. When the modulator is a low frequency of a few Hertz, the carrier frequency rises and falls much like a siren. When the carrier and modulator are close in frequency, however, the result is a complex wave. Varying the strength of the modulator changes the mix of frequencies in the resulting waveform, altering its timbre. (Changing the strength of the carrier merely makes the sound louder or softer.) By changing the relationship between the carrier and modulator, the timbre changes in a natural-sounding way.

A basic FM synthesis system needs only two oscillators producing sine waves to work. However, a synthesizer with a wider combination of carriers and modulators, can create an even more complex variety of waveforms and sounds. Each of the sine waves produced by an FM synthesizer is called an operator. Popular synthesizers have four to six operators.

The greatest strength of FM synthesis is that it is inexpensive to implement. All it takes is a chip. On the other hand, FM synthesis cannot quite duplicate real world sounds. The sounds created through FM synthesis are recognizable—both as what they are supposed to represent and as synthesized sounds.

Wave Table Synthesis

An alternate technique used for creating sounds is *wave table synthesis*. Also known as *sampling*, wave table synthesis starts not with pure tones but with representative waveforms for particular sounds. The representations are in the form of the sound's exact waveform, and all the waveforms that a product can produce are stored in an electronic table, hence the name of the technology. The waveforms for a given instrument or sound are only templates that the synthesizer manipulates to produce music or what is supposed to pass as music. For example, the wave table may include a brief burst of the tone of a flute playing one particular note. The synthesizer can then alter the frequency of that note to play an entire scale and alter its duration to generate the proper rhythm.

While wave table synthesis produces sounds that are more life-like than FM synthesis, they are not entirely realistic because the process does not replicate the complete transformation of musical sounds from attack to decay nor the subtle variation of timbre with the pitch produced by a synthesized instrument. Some wave table synthesizers have specific patterns for the attack, sustain, and decay of notes but mathematically derive the transitions between them. These come closer to reality but still fall short of perfection. In general, wave table synthesized notes all have the same frequency mix and consequently have a subtle but unreal sameness to them.

On the other hand, wavetable synthesis is the PC hardware-maker's delight. Because all the waveforms are stored digitally just like all other sounds, they can be reconstituted without any special hardware like synthesizer chips. All that's needed is an audio digital-to-analog converter, which has to be incorporated in any multimedia PC anyway. A programmer can create the necessary waveforms for any sound he can imagine using software alone. The only trouble is that putting together the necessary waveforms digitally takes a lot of processor power, so much that older, slower PCs can't handle the chore in real time. When the process need not be done in real time, however, your PC can transform synthesizer instructions (typically in the form of a MIDI file) into synthesized music without additional expensive synthesis hardware. MIDI Renderer uses this technique to endow MIDI files with top-quality synthesized sound.

Wavetable synthesizer boards sidestep the demand for processor power by incorporating their own processing abilities. To keep their performance as high as possible, many of these products put the reference waveforms they need into ROM memory, saving any delays that might be needed for disk access. The downside of this fast storage is that the waveform reference hogs storage space. Many hardware-based waveform synthesizers have hundreds of thousands of bytes of wavetable ROM; some have multiple megabytes of reference waveforms.

Advanced Techniques

Scientifically inclined musicians and musically inclined scientists are never satisfied with the sound of synthesized instruments—and never will be until they can make an all-electronic violin sound better than a Strativarius in good hands. As modern electronics puts more and more processing power in their hands, they are developing ever more elaborate techniques to generate the most realistic sounds possible.

The latest trend is modeling of actual instruments. They make mathematical models of musical instruments that reflect how the physical attributes of the instrument affect the sounds it makes. Instead of deconstructing the waveform the instrument makes, they seek to construct the waveform in the same manner as the instrument itself. For example, they might start with a basic tone generated by scraping a string with a bow (an elaborate model in itself), then temper it with the resonances of the instrument's body.

Another aspect of advanced synthesis designs is increased control. Current synthesizers distill a musician's (or program's) control of an instrument to a few parameters: the press and release of a key and "touch," the speed at which the key is struck. While this description is reasonably complete for a keyboard instrument, it ignores the modulations possible with bowed instruments or those through which the musician blows. The newest synthesizers often include a more elaborate control system focused on an additional sensor such as a instrument-like tube the musician blows through. The musician can then use his breath pressure to continuously signal the synthesizer how to modulate the music.

Although these experimental synthesizers are currently aimed at live performance, nothing prevents the acquisition of their control information for automated playback or editing. MIDI does not currently accommodate the increased data needs of such synthesizers, but new standards will undoubtedly accompany any new technology synthesizers into the market mainstream.

Compatibility and Standards

Technologies like FM and wave table synthesis don't do anything until they are put to work in an implementation. They require an architecture and method of control to be made to work. In other words, you have to build a synthesizer around the technology.

If you want to put the synthesizer under the control of your PC, it needs to link to your hardware and software. How you make this link depends on the applications you want to run. Today's multimedia software runs mostly under an all-encompassing graphic environment like OS/2 or Windows. The programs link with the environment and depend on it to control both the image and sound. The environment, in turn, links to the synthesizer circuitry through a software driver. This connection scheme gives both you and the board maker versatility. The manufacturer can develop its own version of the one true synthesizer and take advantage of the most obscure and esoteric designs. The driver clues in the operating system on how to reach the features it needs. Your only concern is getting a driver to match your operating system.

This in itself can be a challenge as the world steps from one operating system version to another, as with the move from Windows 3.1 to Windows 95. You can keep your old synthesizer circuitry working if you get a new driver, which means contacting the manufacturer or searching through bulletin board services. It also means you should look closely at the long-term prospects of the maker of any synthesizer board you consider. If the manufacturer should disappear, a victim of vicious competition, you may never be able to get new drivers to move to the next operating system version.

Upgrading Advice

When you're more concerned with fun and games instead of true multimedia, standardization becomes a bigger issue. Without the extra compatibility layer afforded by an advanced operating system, your synthesizer will depend on your DOS software to take direct control. That means your games must either have explicit support for the synthesizer board you plan to use or that the board follows one of the recognized industry standards that virtually all games will work with. For DOS-based software, two standards are widely popular for soundboard synthesizers: Ad Lib and Sound Blaster.

Ad Lib

One of the first sound boards to gain popularity was made by a company, no longer in the sound-board business, called Ad Lib. Because it had the widest user base early when noisy games were becoming popular, many game programmers wrote their products to take advantage of the specific hardware features of the Ad Lib board. The ability to mimic the Ad Lib hardware became the minimal standard for sound creation compatibility.

Standards

Sound Blaster

Standards

Another company, Creative Labs, entered the soundboard business and built upon the Ad Lib base. Its Sound Blaster product quickly gained industry acceptance as a superset of the Ad Lib standard—it did everything the Ad Lib board did and more. The Sound Blaster found a huge market and raised the standard for sound synthesis among game products. Because programmers directly manipulated the hardware registers of the Sound Blaster to make the sounds they wanted, to run most games and produce the proper sounds you need a soundboard that is hardware compatible with the Sound Blaster. Several iterations of Sound Blaster hardware were produced; the minimal level of compatibility to expect today is with version Sound Blaster 1.5.

The Sound Blaster relies on a particular integrated circuit to produce its array of synthesized sounds, the Yamaha YM3812. This chip has a single output channel, so it can produce only monophonic sound even when it is installed on a soundboard that's otherwise called stereo. Some sound boards use two of these chips to produce stereo. The YM3812 has a fixed repertory of 11 voices, six of which are instrumental and five for rhythm.

A newer FM synthesis chip has become popular on better sound boards, the Yamaha YMF262 or OPL3. Not only does the OPL3 have more voices—20—but it also uses more sophisticated synthesis algorithms for synthesis. It can also produce a full stereo output. In that it can do anything the earlier chip can do—and much more—consider it the minimum to look for in a soundboard.

Program writers can couple up with the Sound Blaster synthesizer circuitry in two ways, through function calls to the Sound Blaster driver software or through direct hardware access to the input/output ports on the board. The former technique is easier for programmers and isolates the software from changes made in the hardware, but direct hardware control can be more responsive (which is what most game programmers want).

Standards

Because the Sound Blaster has become the *de facto* industry standard, compatibility with its design is required for software that uses synthesis to generate music and sound effects. The game DOOM takes full advantage of the Sound Blaster synthesizer and is consequently used by many reviewers to judge the compatibility of particular sound boards. Note that such compatibility is a measure of the synthesizer and not other soundboard functions. Absolute Sound Blaster compatibility is unnecessary for business software and games that play WAV files for higher quality or use MIDI to synthesize music.

The degree of Sound Blaster compatibility is critical when you're investigating portable PCs because the hardware needs of the Sound Blaster are incompatible with the PCMCIA standard. The PCMCIA bus in current form (version 2.1) does not include all of the signals needed by the Sound Blaster interface: although PCMCIA-based sound boards can approximate true Sound Blaster compatibility, they cannot play DOOM. That's not to say Sound Blaster compatibility is impossible in notebook PCs. Many computer manufacturers are incorporating Sound Blaster circuitry on the motherboards of their notebook machines. (Intel, in fact, believes that sound is a necessary part of *every* motherboard.)

The Sound Blaster is controlled by sending data to its two control ports, an address/status port located at 0388(Hex) and a write only data port at 0389(Hex). These ports serve to access the Sound Blaster's 244 internal registers. The board also has four ports assigned to speakers. The addresses of these vary with the base address you assign the board. By default, the data ports for the left speaker are at 0220(Hex) and 0221(Hex); for the right speaker, 0222(Hex) and 0223(Hex). You can make music by sending data directly to these ports. Most programming, however, takes the form of sending function calls through the Sound Blaster's driver software.

Creative Labs uses a layered approach to software drivers to match with programs. One TSR program, the Sound Blaster Standard Interface Module or SBSIM, serves as the master to all other drivers and provides the entry point for function calls. SBSIM handles more than just synthesizer functions. It also links MIDI commands, synthesized voice from disk files or memory, and control over playback volume. Although SBSIM loads some drivers, it also requires others—in particular the FM synthesis and MIDI drivers—to be resident before you run it. SBSIM then loads or initializes the drivers it needs and allocates memory to them.

A single, pre-fabricated SBSIM program cannot possibly anticipate all the installation options you'll need—what drivers to use, how much memory, and how to configure the memory. Consequently, the program is designed to read a special configuration program called SBSIM.CFG that lists the drivers to use and setup parameters. In a standard installation, both SBSIM.EXE and SBSIM.CFG reside in a subdirectory SBSIM that's stored in the main directory used for Sound Blaster files (such as SBPRO, for the Sound Blaster Pro).

SBSIM uses a software interrupt for access to its functions. Programmers use it by loading the appropriate values required by each function call into specific registers of the host microprocessor, then issuing the designated software interrupt. The function to be called is designated in the BX register of the microprocessor; the BH half of the register indicates one of five major functions handled by an individual driver (control, FM synthesis, Voice from disk, Voice from memory, or MIDI), and the BL register indicates exactly what to do. Table 15.1 summarizes these functions.

TABLE 15.1. Sound Blaster function calls.

Function name	Register settings			Additional comments
	BH	BL	CX	
Get SBSIM version number	0	0	Not used	On exit, AH=major version number; AL=minor version number

continues

TABLE 15.1. continued

Function name	BH	BL	CX	Additional comments
	Register settings			
	BH	BL	CX	
Query drivers	0	1	Not used	On exit, AX bit values show drivers in use; bit 0=FM; bit 1=voice from disk; bit 2=voice from memory; bit 3=control; bit 4=MIDI
Load file into extended memory	0	16	Not used	AX indicates file type (0=VOC file); CX, SBSIM handle to use; DS:DX points to file name
Free extended memory	0	19	Not used	AX indicates SBSIM handle of file to be cleared
Start FM sound source	1	0	0	SBSIM file handle in AX
Play FM sound	1	1	0	
Stop FM sound	1	2	0	
Pause FM sound	1	3	0	
Resume FM sound	1	4	0	
Read FM sound source	1	5	0	On exit, AX=0 indicates sound is stopped; AX=FFFF indicates sound playing
Start voice from disk	2	0	0	SBSIM file handle in AX
Play voice from disk	2	1	0	
Stop voice from disk	2	2	0	
Pause voice from disk	2	3	0	
Resume voice from disk	2	4	0	
Read voice from disk	2	5	0	On exit, AX=0 indicates sound is stopped; AX=FFFF indicates sound playing

Function name	Register settings			Additional comments
Start voice from memory	3	0	0	AX point to file in conventional memory; DX:AX points to file in extended memory
Play voice from memory	3	1	0	
Stop voice from memory	3	2	0	
Pause voice from memory	3	3	0	
Resume voice from memory	3	4	0	
Read voice from memory status	3	5	0	On exit, AX=0 indicates sound is stopped; AX=FFFF indicates sound playing
Show volume level	4	0	Not used	On entry, AX shows source; on exit AH=left channel volume, AL=right channel volume
Set volume level	4	1	Not used	On entry, AX indicates source to change; DH=left volume, DL=right volume
Get gain setting	4	2	Not used	On entry, AX=1; on exit, AH=left channel gain, AL=right channel gain
Set gain	4	3	Not used	On entry, AX=1; DH=left channel gain, DL=right channel gain
Show tone settings	4	4	Not used	On entry, AX=0 for treble, AX=1 for bass; on exit, AH=left channel setting, AL=right channel
Set tone	4	5	Not used	On entry, AX=0 for treble, AX=1 for bass; DH=left channel setting, DL=right channel
Start MIDI source	5	0	0	SBSIM file handle in AX

continues

TABLE 15.1. continued

Function name	Register settings			Additional comments
	BH	BL	CX	
Play MIDI source	5	1	0	
Stop MIDI source	5	2	0	
Pause MIDI source	5	3	0	
Resume MIDI source	5	4	0	
Read MIDI status	5	5	0	On exit, AX=0 indicates sound is stopped; AX=FFFF indicates sound playing

When SBSIM loads, it chooses the first available interrupt within the range 080(Hex) to 0BF(Hex) inclusive. Programs needing to use its function calls can find the interrupt by looking for the signature "SBSIM" offset 103(Hex) bytes from the start of the interrupt vector segment address.

SBSIM loads the drivers that are specified in the SBSIM.CFG file. However, using FM synthesis requires that you load the separate driver SBFMDRV.COM before you run SBSIM.EXE. Using MIDI functions requires that you load another separate driver, SBMIDI.EXE, before starting SBSIM. If you want to take advantage of the ability to store and load .VOC files from extended memory, you'll also need to load the DOS/Windows extended memory driver HIMEM.SYS before starting SBSIM.

The [FM] entry in SBSIM.CFG indicates to load the SBFMDRV.COM driver used for controlling the FM synthesizer using .CMF files. Its BufferSize: parameter indicates the size of buffer to use in kilobytes within the range 2KB to 32KB. The default is a 32KB buffer. A lower value will reduce memory usage but may reduce overall performance.

The [DskVoice] entry loads the CTVDSK.DRV driver that allows the system to read .VOC files from disk. It gives you control of two parameters, BufferSize:, which mirrors that of the FM entry and DMABufferSize: that enables you to specify a separate DMA buffer in kilobytes from 2KB to 32KB. The default is 8KB.

The [MemVoice] entry loads the CT-VOICE.DRV that enables the system to read .VOC files that have been stored in conventional or extended memory. Three parameters are also specified. ExtendedMemory: switches on or off support of XMS memory for storing files. XMShandles indicates the maximum number of individual voice files in extended memory that the system can address. The default is 10. DMABufferSize: mirrors that of the DskVoice entry.

The [Auxiliary] entry loads the AUXDRV.DRV driver which allows access to the volume controls of the associated soundboard that support this function (for example, the Sound Blaster Pro and Sound Blaster 16). Its solitary parameter, CDswitchSpeakers:, specifies whether CD-ROM output to the system's speakers should be swapped.

The [MIDI] entry loads the MIDI driver, SBMIDI.EXE. Its two parameters control buffer size (BufferSize:) as with other entries and the MIDI mapper format to use (MidiMap:) The latter parameter has three options: 0 for General MIDI; 1 for Windows Basic MIDI; and 2 for Windows Extended MIDI.

Compression

Even the best synthesis systems only approach the sound of real-world musical instruments and not-so-musical noises. The best—or most real—sound quality produced by a soundboard is thus not synthesized but recorded. As with Compact Discs, sound boards use the high-tech high-quality high-fidelity digital sound recording system.

For full CD compatibility, most newer sound boards have the capability to digitize at the CD level of quality. But to save disk space and processing time, most give you the option of using less resource-intensive values. Many older sound boards were not powerful enough for full CD-quality. For example, basic Sound Blaster compatibility guarantees you only voice quality sampling. Even the Sound Blaster family has gone far beyond its humble beginnings, however. But even the best boards enable you to reach back to intermediary sampling frequencies and bit densities for playing back old files or more frugal storage of new ones.

To squeeze more sound into a given amount of storage, digital audio can be compressed like any other data. The more efficient algorithms take into account the special character of digital sound. The algorithms for compressing and decompression digital audio are sometimes called *codecs*, short for compressors-decompressors.

Windows 95 includes support for the CCITT G.711 A-law and u-law, DSP Group TrueSpeech, IMA ADPCM, GSM 6.10, Microsoft ADPCM, and Microsoft PCM converter codecs as discussed in Chapter 9, "Data Storage." You can view the audio codecs installed in your Windows 95 system by opening the Multimedia icon in Control Panel, choosing the Advanced tab, and double-clicking Audio Compression Codecs. You'll see a display like Figure 15.1.

FIGURE 15.1. Audio Compression Codecs listing in the Windows 95 Advanced Multimedia Properties panel.

Digital Signal Processors

In the next few years, audio in multimedia systems will likely be transformed by an upcoming technology, the *Digital Signal Processor*. More commonly called *DSP*, this technology promises to add new versatility and power to sound systems. Just as graphics resolution and speed have jumped up from a cartoon-colored caricature of reality to Technicolor artistry thanks to high-powered video systems, the DSPs will help multimedia PCs push at the limits of human perception and flexibility unmatched in the aural world. More importantly, thanks to a new DSP interface developed by Microsoft, compatibility between sound boards and applications will be easier to achieve. In a few years, all the problems associated with setting up sound boards may disappear.

At heart the DSP is the audio equivalent of the graphic coprocessor, a microprocessor optimized for the handling of sound signals. A DSP will endow sound circuits with programmability so that traditional signal processing such as filtering (to diminish or augment certain frequencies), synthesis, or even digital-to-analog conversion will be controlled by software, changeable as easily as putting a syntax error into a BASIC program.

In function the basic DSP starts a wire that conducts audio signals without alternation, then, by software command, transforms the signals any way you want. Of course, the journey through the DSP is hardly a straight path. Incoming analog signals first get converted into digital code upon which the DSP works mathematically, making its signal transformations under the control of algorithms specified by a program. Once all the processing is done, the digital audio signals are converted back into analog form.

The challenges of working with multimedia sound are entirely different from those confronted by general purpose microprocessors. For example, the DSP need not be as powerful as the main chip in your PC because sound need not be digitized with any greater precision than 16-bits (at least under current aural standards). On the other hand, the DSP must be quick, quick enough to make all of its transformations—no matter how mathematically complex—in real time. Think of the wire that the DSP emulates—signals go in and come out without slowing down. There's no delay between input and output. If there were, the DSP would put a hole in the sound it worked on. You could hear such pauses as pops or distortion—not exactly what you'd expect or desire from adding audio processing power.

Most of the work that a DSP does is simple multiplication of 16-bit numbers representing sounds. Nearly all audio filtering and other sound manipulations require multiplying signals by trigonometric functions—sines, cosines, and tangents. In other words, a DSP has to have same powerful math abilities as a floating-point processor or quick RISC microprocessor. In fact, many DSPs are built from RISC processors, and some chips classed as general purpose RISC processors do well as DSPs. Most of the time, however, application-specific DSPs can be substantially less expensive than full-blown RISC chips.

These DSP chips can be distinguished from RISC processors by special-purpose internal circuits that facilitate their use inside PCs. For example, the most popular DSPs used in PCs, the Texas Instruments TMS320M500 and TMS320M520, incorporate interface circuits to link to the ISA bus, telephone lines, microphones, and speakers. This design lets the DSP do everything audio that your PC needs. It can be a synthesizer, modem, or heart of a speech-recognition system.

Because the programs rather than hardware define the precise function of a DSP, a DSP-based modem can switch between communications standards as easily as downloading a configuration file. A DSP synthesizer can change technologies as easily as a programmer can rewrite a few hundred thousand lines of code. (Okay, that's not easy—but it is probably easier than moving around a few million transistors to design an integrated circuit.) Using DSP technology, you will be able to upgrade a DSP-based soundboard to match any new standards without touching the hardware at all.

Why doesn't every soundboard, every modem, every PC have a DSP inside? Part of the reason is newness: DSP technology is young and many designers lack experience using them. After all, building with DSPs requires a different mindset from creating with conventional audio hardware. It's a job more for programmers than chip jockeys. Moreover, getting a single standard to control DSPs has been a long, troubling process. One reason is the diversity of DSPs. While PCs are dominated by Intel microprocessors, no single DSP owns the majority of the market—at least not yet. No single design dominates. Several chip-makers manufacture DSPs to their own specifications, each with its own internal architecture. At the chip level, there's no common language among DSPs. Each DSP maker has created its own proprietary standard, hoping its design will become accepted as the one true specification by the PC industry.

Standards

These standards take several different forms. For example, the standard may be an operating system to control DSP functions; it could be an architecture based on a layered structure of software and hardware, or it may be simply a command set. Currently, three of such standards have a major presence in the industry: MWave, CVOS, and Signal Computing Architecture. A fourth standard, Microsoft Windows DSP Architecture is essentially a meta-standard. It promises the ability to link Windows and your applications to any DSP chip. As Windows becomes the multimedia platform of choice, Windows DSP Architecture stands ready to unify the world of DSPs.

Here's a brief rundown of the major DSP standards:

MWave

Originally a joint effort between Texas Instruments and IBM, MWave linked TI's coprocessor expertise with IBM's strength in software and system architecture design. The core of the design was TI's series of 16-bit DSPs coupled with an IBM-designed software kernel. The software runs on a host PC to give it control of the DSP functions.

The original goal of the MWave effort was to make it an open standard that could win industry support. IBM went so far as to develop a board that implemented the MWave specification and could function as both soundboard and modem in a PC, giving the rest of the industry a working model to copy. Early on, MWave showed promise if just because the TI DSPs had the largest share of the overall market. In 1993, however, Texas Instruments withdrew its support from MWave, leaving IBM the solitary MWave standard bearer.

Signal Computing Architecture

Analog Devices manufactures DSPs and quite naturally designed a control system to link them to computers. Called Signal Computing Architecture, the Analog Devices design is based on a layered model that functionally divides the overall DSP system. Four of the layers involve the host computer: The top layer is the user interface, how you work with the system. One step down is the application software you run on your PC to control the DSP. Next comes the API (application program interface), the set of program hooks that translate program instructions into the language understood by the DSP. The final host layer is the operating system of the computer which provides the environment for running the software, controlling how the program interacts with your PC.

The other three layers concern the DSP and its software. The fifth layer is the algorithm layer which develops the mathematical form of the commands requested by the host. The sixth layer is the DSP's own operating system, and the seventh layer is the language layer which is the actual code that runs on the DSP.

The layered approach makes the links more important than the underlying design. A hardware designer can change the internal structure of a DSP, and as long as the chip properly links with the language layer the rest of the system won't notice the difference. Similarly, programmers need only concern themselves with the upper layers, letting the lower layers and hardware take care of itself.

VCOS

To control its own line of digital signal processors, AT&T developed its own operating system called VCOS. The operating system runs on the DSP and is controlled through function calls from the host computer's software. Developers write the proper calls into their C-language or Windows programs, and AT&T offers its own set of algorithms as a multimedia module library.

VCOS is also able to allow the DSP and its host to share memory. This sharing lets either processor take a hand in signal manipulation. In addition, sharing memory can cut the overall cost of adding a complete DSP system to a PC—memory costs can be a significant part of a DSP board. To prevent memory access problems (a DSP needs fast access to operate in real time) a DSP running VCOS internally caches blocks of memory instead of randomly accessing bytes. Unlike normal PC memory caching, however, the data in the cache is controlled by the programmer writing VCOS code, giving the application developer complete control over the speed of signal processing.

The current version of VCOS (1.1, announced in August, 1993) gives designers power far in excess of that yielded by a single DSP. The operating system can spread multimedia tasks over several DSPs to further improve performance, balancing the load between chips and applications.

Windows DSP Architecture

Microsoft entered the DSP standardization fray late in 1993 with the introduction of Windows DSP Architecture. Unlike the other DSP standards, the Microsoft incarnation was not tied to a specific chip or family. In fact, when it was released, no product actually used it. The first application of Windows DSP Architecture is Windows 95.

The new system is designed to give programmers a consistent set of links through which they can control any DSP. Rather than develop its own DSP interface, however, Microsoft joined with Spectron Microsystems to create an interface to allow Windows applications to control DSPs for any communications or multimedia application. The result of this marriage was a hybrid of PC-based software and an operating system for DSPs. In concept, Windows DSP architecture can give developers a hardware-independent application interface that can be used to operate any DSP for audio or even video processing.

The foundation for Windows DSP architecture was the SPOX DSP operating system, which Spectron had developed earlier. Originally designed as a 32-bit operating system, SPOX had been revised just before the Microsoft affiliation into a product better suited to 16-bit DSP applications.

The underlying SPOX design is a three-part entity that includes a software kernel that runs on the DSP to control hardware functions, a set of communications links between the DSP and the host computer, and a set of high-level math functions for defining the actual signal processing. Microsoft added in links to the Windows environment.

Even before joining with Microsoft, Spectron was working on SPOX development kits for Analog Devices, IBM, Motorola, and Texas Instruments DSPs, so the resulting collaborative product will give programmers access to the major DSP families.

Under the Windows DSP Architecture design, drivers and service providers link to a variety of Windows application interfaces including the Multimedia Systems API, Speech API, and Telephony API using a DSP Resource Manager. To control the DSP Resource Manager, Microsoft once provided a new DSP Resource Manager Interface (the DSP RMI). This design was supposed to minimize the work programmers would have had to do for various DSP platforms. The DSP RMI design was meant to enable programmers to write drivers to a standard interface that need not be altered to accommodate a change in the DSP, its operating system, or even the interface between DSP and host PC. However, Microsoft has withdrawn its support for RMI.

The multimedia driver supports all soundboard functions and more: a microphone, a line input, a line output, CD-ROM audio, a wave table synthesizer, a mixer, a telephone handset, and two telephone lines. The specification also includes built-in compression and decompression and the ability to change sampling rates.

The minimal Windows DSP Architecture specification closely follows the MPC standard. For example, 11 KHz and 22 KHz sampling rates of 8-bit samples is all that's required. Control functions are based on the Windows Sound System; in fact, the first nineteen of its basic mixer controls match those of the WSS, as shown in Table 15.2.

TABLE 15.2. Windows DSP Architecture mixer control functions.

Source	Destination	Type of Control
Wave-in		MUX
Voice-in		MUX
Line-in	Line-out	VOL
Wave-out	Line-out	VOL
MIDI-out	Line-out	VOL

Source	Destination	Type of Control
Master Line-out		VOL
Line-in	Wave-in	VOL
Mic-in	Wave-in	VOL
Line-in	Voice-in	VOL
Mic-in	Voice-in	VOL
Line-in	Line-out	MUTE
Wave-out	Line-out	MUTE
MIDI-out	Line-out	MUTE
Master Line-out		MUTE
Line-in	Wave-in	VU
Mic-in	Wave-in	VU
Line-in	Voice-in	VU
Mic-in	Voice-in	VU
Wave-out	Line-out	VU
Mic-in	Line-out	VOL
CD-in	Line-out	VOL
CD-in	Wave-in	VOL
CD-in	Voice-in	VOL
CD-in	Line-out	MUTE
CD-in	Wave-in	VU
CD-in	Voice-in	VU
Wave-out	Handset-out	VOL
Wave-out	Tel-out 1	VOL
Wave-out	Tel-out 2	VOL
Wave-out	Handset-out	MUTE
Master Handset-out		MUTE
Wave-out	Handset-out	MUTE
Wave-out	Tel-out 1	MUTE
Tel-out 1 Master		MUTE
Wave-out	Tel-out 2	MUTE
Tel-out 2 Master		MUTE

Standards

In fact, Windows DSP Architecture is hardware-compatible with the Windows Sound System so no emulation or extra software is needed to use games designed for the WSS with products complying with the specification. In addition, the synthesizer design is compatible with the Ad Lib standard as well as Sound Blaster. Its MIDI functions are compatible with Roland's MPU-401 standard.

Microsoft recommends that DSP products venture far beyond these minimal functions, however. Table 15.3 lists the minimum and recommended functionality demanded by Windows DSP architecture.

TABLE 15.3. Minimum and recommended functionality under Windows DSP Architecture.

Function	Minimum Requirement	Recommendation
Plug and Play	Not required	Full support
Sampling rate	11.025 KHz and 22.05 KHz	5.125 KHz—48 KHz
Sample size	8-bit	16-bit
Channels	Mono	Stereo
MIDI	MIDI play	Wavetable synthesis
CD-ROM interface	Not required	One interface, internal or external, IDE or SCSI
Games compatibility	Not required	Compatibility with Ad Lib, Sound Blaster, AD1848, and MPU-401
Multimedia devices	Telephone set (wave), telephone line (wave), audio codec (wave), line in (AUX), mixer	Telephone set (wave), telephone line (wave), audio codec (wave), synthesis DAC (MIDI play), line in (AUX), mixer
Telephone interface	One line, POTS or ISDN	Two lines, POTS or ISDN
Call types	Voice only	Voice, data, fax, VoiceView
Telephony	DTMF generation and detection, CallerID, CLASS features	DTMF generation and detection, CallerID, popular CLASS features
Data standards	Not required	V.32bis, V.32, V.22bis, V.22, Bell 212A, Bell 103J, V.42 LAPM, V.42bis, MNP 2-4, MNP 5

Function	Minimum Requirement	Recommendation
Fax standards	Not required	V.18, V.17, V.29, V.21, Channel 2, V.27 ter
VoiceView	Not required	Full support

Under Windows 95, the DSP Resource Manager comprises three elements: SPMGR.DLL, an interface for 32-bit device drivers; SPMGR16.DLL, an interface for 16-bit device drivers; and SPMGR.386, a 16-bit protected mode interface for virtual device drivers and Windows 95 I/O control interface.

Installing a Soundboard

Getting a sound system to work with your PC is mostly a matter of preparation and trouble-shooting. The actual hardware part of the installation is almost trivial—you just slide in an expansion board and connect up the wires. But getting the soundboard to work is another matter entirely. The board must be prepared to match your system. Specifically, you must set its interrupt, port, and DMA channel usage to avoid conflicts.

Soundboard Setup

Almost universally, soundboards give you some means of selecting which of these resources it uses. Typically you'll be confronted with a bank of DIP switches or a row or two of jumpers. Your owners' manual should document what each of these settings does and should list the factory defaults (always a good starting place).

DMA channel choice is the most straightforward. If you want to run DOS-based games, you must use DMA channel 1. DOS games require Sound Blaster compatibility, and the Sound Blaster's DMA usage is set to channel 1. If you don't want to play games, however, another channel choice may be more appropriate. Higher DMA channel numbers are all 16-bit transfers while lower DMA channels (1, 2, and 3) are only eight bits wide.

Similarly, achieving the highest degree of Sound Blaster compatibility dictates setting the base I/O port assignment for your soundboard to 220(Hex), the default assignment of the Sound Blaster. You have some degree of freedom with your I/O port selection, however, because the Sound Blaster allows for alternate base addresses. As long as your driver software does likewise, you can alter these settings to a value that does not conflict with other system hardware.

Should you elect to move the base address of your soundboard, write down the address you choose to use. The installation programs of many soundboards require you indicate your alternate address. If you're manually setting up your soundboard's drivers, you'll probably have to add the new port assignment as a command line option.

Most soundboards require you assign them one or more interrupt channels. Multiple interrupts are sometimes required by soundboards that integrate other functions, such as a CD-ROM interface. For the utmost in compatibility, your first best choice for the interrupt to use is the Sound Blaster default, 5. DOS normally reserves interrupt 5 for your PC's second printer port. Although most PCs don't have two printers, this interrupt is often snarfed up by other peripherals. If you've already assigned some other device to interrupt 5, you'll have to move your soundboard to an alternate interrupt. For 8-bit sound boards, the second choice is interrupt 7, which interferes with the first printer. With 16-bit sound cards, you have a wider selection of interrupts to choose from, values from 8 to 15. To help you choose a suitable, non-conflicting interrupt Table 15.4 lists the standard interrupt assignments in most PCs.

TABLE 15.4. Interrupt assignments

Interrupt Number	Function
IRQ0	Timer Output 0
IRQ1	Keyboard (Buffer Full)
IRQ2	Cascade from IRQ9
IRQ3	Serial Port 2; Serial Port 4; SDLC Communications; BSC Communications; Cluster Adapter; Network (alternate); 3278/79 (alternate)
IRQ4	Serial Port 1; Serial Port 3; SDLC Communications; BSC Communications; Voice Communications Adapter
IRQ5	Parallel Port 2, Sound Blaster default
IRQ6	Floppy Disk Controller
IRQ7	Parallel Port 1; Cluster Adapter (alternate)
IRQ8	Real-time Clock
IRQ9	Software redirected to INT 0A(Hex); Video; Network; 3278/79 Adapter
IRQ10	Reserved
IRQ11	Reserved
IRQ12	Reserved
IRQ13	Coprocessor
IRQ14	Hard Disk Controller
IRQ15	Reserved

The Windows 3.1 family and OS/2 Warp require that you go through the same hardware setup process, finding acceptable resource allocation values. With the Windows 3.1 family, you'll also have to install drivers; depending on your soundboard, OS/2 Warp may automatically install the proper drivers during its installation process or may leave you to fend for yourself with manual installation.

Windows 3.1x

OS/2 Warp

The Plug-and-Play abilities of Windows 95 simplify the soundboard setup process. Although even as late as mid-1995 few sound boards supported the Plug-and-Play specification, the Windows 95 setup database covers a wide variety of boards. In most cases, Windows 95 can identify your board and the system resources that it uses. If it conflicts with some other device, it will report the problem through Device Manager, pointing out exactly what you must change.

Windows 95

If you're still using the Windows 3.1 family, you'll have to install the appropriate drivers using the familiar Control Panel process. The procedure is standardized, so you'll follow the same steps no matter the soundboard you install. It's covered in the overview of drivers in Chapter 8, "Device Drivers."

Windows 3.1x

Sometimes you'll find that you have a confusing selection of drivers to use. For example, Windows 3.1 automatically offers you two different Sound Blaster drivers, and you may have others that came with your board. The best choice is always the most recent driver version that is designed specifically for your soundboard. Even if your board claims Sound Blaster compatibility, you'll probably want to forego the Sound Blaster drivers (if you can). Remember, Sound Blaster compatibility is the least common denominator, and it gives Windows control of the smallest subset of board features. For example, the basic Sound Blaster driver only offers control of basic MIDI features; you won't get access to extended MIDI channels when using it.

When installing a new soundboard driver, you'll also want to remove any old soundboard drivers that you've previously installed. Again, the procedure is specific to your operating system. For example, under the Windows 3.1 family, you would select REMOVE from the drivers menu, highlight the old driver name, and click OK. Some sound boards may install other drivers that your operating system may not know about, however. For example, the old Sound Blaster Pro also installed VSBPD.386 and VADLIBD.386 in the [386Enh] section of your SYSTEM.INI file in Windows 3.1 systems. Should you discontinue using your Sound Blaster Pro, you may want to eliminate these by editing them out (or, better still, commenting them out) with a text editor.

Windows 3.1x

Speaker Wiring

The other side of soundboard installation is the wiring. If you want the board to play through an external speaker, you'll have to connect the speaker wires.

Connecting speakers to a soundboard can be easy. Most multimedia speakers plug directly into the rear panel of sound boards. In most cases, you'll find only one jack for two speakers. Many multimedia speakers take care of this by daisy-chaining. Plug one speaker into your soundboard, then plug the other speaker into the jack on the back of the first speaker. Other systems use cable that splits when emerging from a single plug.

If you have two separate speakers, each with its own wire, you'll need a stereo splitter. These are available either as an odd-looking adapter—a single male plug comes out one end, and two jacks decorate the back—or a short cable.

Another consideration is matching levels and impedances. Most sound boards are rated to deliver full power into loads with a four ohm impedance. Higher impedance cause no worry because a higher impedance load typically reduces the drain on an amplifier (making it less prone to overloading and failure).

Although a lower impedance can be dangerous, nearly all speakers have a four ohm or greater impedance. The only time you may encounter a lower impedance is if you try to connect two speakers in parallel to one channel of your soundboard. Don't try it.

In general, you can plug either passive or active speakers in the speaker outputs of the typical soundboard. Although strictly speaking the input of the active speakers will be mismatched as to level and impedance to a speaker output, these two mismatches tend to cancel out. The only shortcoming of connecting active speaker to a speaker-level jack is noise. The signal must go through two levels of amplifiers, each of which adds its own noise and distortion. You will get better sound quality from active speakers if you plug them into the auxiliary output of your soundboard (if it has an auxiliary output). This bypasses the sound board's amplifiers and the degradation they add. In addition, it may improve the frequency response of the system. Some sound boards have jumpers that disable their internal amplifiers for this very reason.

If you want the best sound quality, you may be tempted to plug your soundboard into your stereo system. For such purposes, you can consider you stereo as an active speaker system. Just connect an unused input of your receiver or preamp to the output of your soundboard (the auxiliary output is best, but the speaker output will likely work, too). If your PC and stereo are not both properly grounded, however, you may inadvertently cause damage. With improper grounding, there can be odd voltage differences between the chassis of your PC and stereo system—enough of a difference that you can draw sparks when plugging in the audio cable. This can have detrimental effects on both computer and stereo circuitry. In other words, make sure that you properly ground both PC and stereo.

Chapter 16
MIDI

Besides just playing back pre-recorded sounds, another way you and your PC can make beautiful music is by controlling external electronic musical instruments. Instead of generating sounds itself, your PC becomes a sequencer, a solid-state surrogate conductor capable of leading a big band or orchestra of electronic instruments in the cacophony of your own creation. MIDI is the standard that provides you with this kind of control.

You can think of the function of MIDI to be the same as sheet music. When you want to play a song someone else has written, you look at the notes on the sheet music, written in a code designed for human eyes: notes, staves, time signatures and the like. MIDI provides the same information for electronic instruments. But MIDI is an entire orchestral score, embracing not only what your two hands can play but every voice and sound your synthesizer can make. In addition, MIDI works like sheet music when you're writing your own compositions. It records every note that plays on every instrument. More than that, it records *how* each instrument plays each note, specifying effects such as tremelo and vibrato.

Under MIDI, your sequencer is nothing more than a memory and messaging system with editing abilities. It lets you arrange notes and it translates your arrangements (or files that other people have arranged) into commands for your synthesizer or other electronic instruments. In PC-based MIDI, the memory required by the sequencer is supplied by your PC's hard disk. The editing is the software you use for your music making.

Background

MIDI, the *Musical Instrument Digital Interface*, is the principal control system used for linking together electronic instruments. It's not tied to PCs or any particular computer system. In fact, although MIDI is an intrinsic part of today's multimedia standards, MIDI predates multimedia computers. MIDI is the standard connection for plugging electronic instruments and accessories together. In essence, MIDI is both hardware (a special kind of serial port) and software (a protocol for transferring commands through the port). And, amazingly, it's one of the few sound board standards that's actually standardized enough that it works with just about everything that says MIDI without compatibility worries. MIDI enables synthesizers, sequencers, home computers, rhythm machines, and so on to be interconnected through a standard interface.

Although MIDI is used for linking electronic music-making instruments, the MIDI connection itself carries no music. The MIDI wire is only for control signals. Like a remote control for your television, it turns things on and off but doesn't carry the sound (or picture) at all.

The MIDI standard is governed by the *MIDI Manufacturers Association*, an industry consortium. You can buy the complete specification directly from the association. The telephone number to reach the association is (818) 598-0088.

Hardware

The MIDI interface hardware itself is electronically and logically simple. It's just another kind of serial port designed to provide a moderate-speed port to pass commands to musical interfaces. Each device that's connected together using MIDI has either transmitting or receiving circuits, although some may have both. A MIDI transmitter packages signals into the standard MIDI format and sends them on their way. A MIDI receiver listens for commands on the MIDI bus and executes those meant for it.

Every MIDI port has at its heart a UART chip that converts parallel computer data into serial form. MIDI transmitters link to the MIDI bus using a line driver which increases the strength of the UART signal so that it can drive a five milliamp current loop. In other words, it makes the MIDI signal powerful enough to fend for itself in the outside world. The driver also buffers the UART from problems with the connection. The transmitter signal is designed to power exactly one MIDI receiver.

Each MIDI receiver links to the bus through an optoisolator, a device that uses an incoming electrical signal to power a light-emitting diode. A photocell senses changes in brightness in the LED and creates a corresponding electrical signal. The intermediary light (optical) beam isolates the incoming electrical signal from those inside the MIDI device, preventing all sorts of nasties like electrical shocks (which can harm you) and ground loops (which can harm the integrity of the MIDI signal).

The physical embodiment of a MIDI transmitter is the Out connector on a MIDI device. The In connector links to a MIDI receiver. A Thru connector, when present, is a second MIDI transmitter. Its signal comes directly from the In connector, and it shares its signals with the receiver.

The MIDI connectors themselves are standard full-size five-pin DIN jacks (such as Switchcraft 57 GB5F). Only three connections are used: pin 2 is ground; pin 4 is the positive-going side of the differential signal; pin 5 is the negative-going side. Pins 1 and 3 are not used and are unconnected. Unlike the case with serial ports, there's no need to crossover conductors in going from one MIDI port to another; all three connections are the same at both ends of the cable.

MIDI cables have matching male 5-pin DIN plugs on either end. They use shielded twisted-pair wire and can be up to 50 feet (15 meters) long. The shield of the cable connects to pin 2 at both ends of the cable.

The UARTs in the MIDI system provide an asynchronous serial connection that operates at a fixed speed of 31,250 bits per second. Because every byte transferred is framed with a start bit and stop bit, it allows information to be exchanged at 3,125 bytes per second. Each data frame measures 320 microseconds long. The actual MIDI electrical signals are inverted; that is, a logical 0 on the MIDI bus is indicated by switching the current on. Although the data rate seems slow today, it was lickety-split when MIDI was devised. Back then, 300 baud modems were the standard for serial communication.

MIDI interfaces mate with your PC exactly as does any other port. They communicate with your system by exchanging bytes through an input/output port. Most MIDI port adapters prefer to use the input/output port address of 330(Hex), because much MIDI software expects to find MIDI there and often refuses to recognize MIDI at other locations. Alternately, many sound boards use 220(Hex). This latter value is often the better choice because many SCSI host adapters also prefer the 330(Hex) base address for communications. In any case, be sure that your MIDI software is aware of the port address you choose for your MIDI adapter.

The wiring of even the most complex MIDI system can be as easy as stringing Christmas tree lights or plugging in stereo components. All MIDI devices are daisy-chained together. That is, you connect the MIDI Out of one device to MIDI In on the next. Signals will then travel from the first transmitter through all the devices down to the last receiver. Ordinarily the first transmitter will be your keyboard or sequencer; the rest of the devices in the chain will be synthesizers or electronic instruments.

Thru connectors make your MIDI project more thought-provoking. Because the signals at the Thru connector on a device duplicate those at the In connector rather than the Out connector, the information the device sends out will not appear on the Thru connector. Ordinarily this situation presents no problems because most downstream MIDI devices will be musical instruments that act only as receivers. However, if you have a keyboard connected to a sequencer, any device plugged into the sequencer's Thru connector will listen and hear the keyboard and not the sequencer. To hear both, you'll have to use the sequencer's Out connector.

Standards

If there is any standard among MIDI interface hardware, it is Roland's MPU-401, and for the widest possible access to applications you'll want a product that mimics it as closely as possible. Most MIDI interfaces plug into your PC's slots like any other expansion board would. Sound boards, which are required to include MIDI capabilities under the MPC specifications, often make the MIDI hardware connections optional, typically as adapters that you buy to give you the right jacks for your MIDI cables.

If you have a notebook computer or have run out of slots in your desktop machine, all is not lost. Several serial-to-MIDI and parallel-to-MIDI adapters are available. Unfortunately, these generally sacrifice true MPU-401 compatibility.

Channels and Voices

If you're not a serious musician, you're likely not to need the capabilities of MIDI hardware connections. Most of what you will use MIDI for in multimedia will be a file and synthesizer control standard. You're most likely simply to play back MIDI files through the synthesizer on your sound board. Other than seeing a .MID file extension, you may not even know that you're dealing with MIDI. If you do any MIDI composing or programming, you may simply rely on your PC's synthesizer. (Of course, even then the best way to play is with an external keyboard— so you're back to worrying about MIDI hardware.)

Even if your MIDI efforts don't leave your sound board, you may face a formidable MIDI challenge. The most complex part of the MIDI system—in fact, its essence—is its communications protocol, the signals sent through the wiring. MIDI devices communicate with one another through the MIDI connection by sending *messages*, which are nothing more than sequences of bytes. These bytes encode an instruction for the MIDI system, which may involve control functions (such as synchronizing MIDI devices) or playback (such as instructing the synthesizer to play Middle C as a trumpet with vibrato).

MIDI precisely defines the format of every message. Each begins with a *Status Byte* which identifies the type of message being sent, for example, to switch on or off a musical note. The Status Byte is usually followed by *Data Bytes* in groups of one or two (depending on the command), which hold the information about what to do—for example, which note to switch on. Status bytes are unambiguously identified by always having their most significant bit set high, that is, as a logical one. Data bytes always have zero as their most significant bit.

Each MIDI system has 16 channels which can be individually addressed. The sounds generated by the synthesizers or instruments in the MIDI system are called *voices*. By playing more than one voice per channel and more than one channel at a time, MIDI allows for extensive polyphony.

What a voice sounds like depends on the synthesizer generating it. A voice controls a *program* on the synthesizer, and the program is a property of the synthesizer. The MIDI system code provides for 128 different instrument programs. Individual instrument sounds are assigned or mapped to each program in a process called patching, and the complete list of instrument assignments is called a *patch map*. You can, if you want, patch any instrument sound on your synthesizer to any program. When musicians use MIDI with sequencers to program one or more synthesizers and create their own musical works, they do exactly that.

The codes of MIDI are also used like a programming language. PCs use MIDI files as a compact way of storing music and sound effects. The PC acts as a sequencer, and uses the program to elicit instrument sounds. But there's a problem. The same MIDI messages may elicit different sounds from different synthesizers. If you can assign any instrument to any program, there's no way anyone can anticipate what sounds each of their program numbers will make. A musician may write a tune that plays on piccolos only to have it play back on your PC with tubas. The effect will likely be very different. What MIDI as a distribution medium needs is a standard map of instruments to programs that everyone agrees to and uses.

At the instigation of a MIDI music publisher (Warner New Media) the MIDI industry came up with exactly that, a generalized patch map that specifies an instrument for each of the 128 MIDI programs in 16 groups of eight instrument types each. They called the result General MIDI. Table 16.1 summarizes the assignments of the General MIDI instrument patch assignment standard.

TABLE 16.1. General MIDI instrument program map.

Program Number	Group	Instrument
1	Piano	Acoustic Grand
2	Piano	Bright Acoustic
3	Piano	Electric Grand
4	Piano	Honky-Tonk
5	Piano	Electric Piano 1
6	Piano	Electric Piano 2
7	Piano	Harpsichord
8	Piano	Clav
9	Chrom percussion	Celesta
10	Chrom percussion	Glockenspiel
11	Chrom percussion	Music Box
12	Chrom percussion	Vibraphone
13	Chrom percussion	Marimba
14	Chrom percussion	Xylophone

continues

TABLE 16.1. continued

Program Number	Group	Instrument
15	Chrom percussion	Tubular Bells
16	Chrom percussion	Dulcimer
17	Organ	Drawbar Organ
18	Organ	Percussive Organ
19	Organ	Rock Organ
20	Organ	Church Organ
21	Organ	Reed Organ
22	Organ	Accordian
23	Organ	Harmonica
24	Organ	Tango Accordian
25	Guitar	Acoustic Guitar (nylon)
26	Guitar	Acoustic Guitar (steel)
27	Guitar	Electric Guitar (jazz)
28	Guitar	Electric Guitar (clean)
29	Guitar	Electric Guitar (muted)
30	Guitar	Overdriven Guitar
31	Guitar	Distortion Guitar
32	Guitar	Guitar Harmonics
33	Bass	Acoustic Bass
34	Bass	Electric Bass (finger)
35	Bass	Electric Bass (pick)
36	Bass	Fretless Bass
37	Bass	Slap Bass 1
38	Bass	Slap Bass 2
39	Bass	Synth Bass 1
40	Bass	Synth Bass 2
41	Strings	Violin
42	Strings	Viola
43	Strings	Cello
44	Strings	Contrabass
45	Strings	Tremolo Strings

Program Number	Group	Instrument
46	Strings	Pizzicato Strings
47	Strings	Orchestral Strings
48	Strings	Timpani
49	Ensemble	String Ensemble 1
50	Ensemble	String Ensemble 2
51	Ensemble	Synth Strings 1
52	Ensemble	Synth Strings 2
53	Ensemble	Choir Aahs
54	Ensemble	Voice Oohs
55	Ensemble	Synth Voice
56	Ensemble	Orchestra Hit
57	Brass	Trumpet
58	Brass	Trombone
59	Brass	Tuba
60	Brass	Muted Trumpet
61	Brass	French Horn
62	Brass	Brass Section
63	Brass	Synth Brass 1
64	Brass	Synth Brass 2
65	Reed	Soprano Sax
66	Reed	Alto Sax
67	Reed	Tenor Sax
68	Reed	Baritone Sax
69	Reed	Oboe
70	Reed	English Horn
71	Reed	Bassoon
72	Reed	Clarinet
73	Pipe	Piccolo
74	Pipe	Flute
75	Pipe	Recorder
76	Pipe	Pan Flute

continues

TABLE 16.1. continued

Program Number	Group	Instrument
77	Pipe	Blown Bottle
78	Pipe	Skakuhachi
79	Pipe	Whistle
80	Pipe	Ocarina
81	Synth lead	Lead 1 (square)
82	Synth lead	Lead 2 (sawtooth)
83	Synth lead	Lead 3 (calliope)
84	Synth lead	Lead 4 (chiff)
85	Synth lead	Lead 5 (charang)
86	Synth lead	Lead 6 (voice)
87	Synth lead	Lead 7 (fifths)
88	Synth lead	Lead 8 (bass+lead)
89	Synth pad	Pad 1 (new age)
90	Synth pad	Pad 2 (warm)
91	Synth pad	Pad 3 (polysynth)
92	Synth pad	Pad 4 (choir)
93	Synth pad	Pad 5 (bowed)
94	Synth pad	Pad 6 (metallic)
95	Synth pad	Pad 7 (halo)
96	Synth pad	Pad 8 (sweep)
97	Synth effects	FX 1 (rain)
98	Synth effects	FX 2 (soundtrack)
99	Synth effects	FX 3 (crystal)
100	Synth effects	FX 4 (atmosphere)
101	Synth effects	FX 5 (brightness)
102	Synth effects	FX 6 (goblins)
103	Synth effects	FX 7 (echoes)
104	Synth effects	FX 8 (sci-fi)
105	Ethnic	Sitar
106	Ethnic	Banjo
107	Ethnic	Shamisen
108	Ethnic	Koto

Program Number	Group	Instrument
109	Ethnic	Kalimba
110	Ethnic	Bagpipe
111	Ethnic	Fiddle
112	Ethnic	Shanai
113	Percussive	Tinkle Bell
114	Percussive	Agogo
115	Percussive	Steel Drums
116	Percussive	Woodblock
117	Percussive	Taiko Drum
118	Percussive	Melodic Tom
119	Percussive	Synth Drum
120	Percussive	Reverse Cymbal
121	Sound effects	Guitar Fret Noise
122	Sound effects	Breathing Noise
123	Sound effects	Seashore
124	Sound effects	Bird Tweet
125	Sound effects	Telephone Ring
126	Sound effects	Helicopter
127	Sound effects	Applause
128	Sound effects	Gunshot

In addition to these 128 instruments, the General MIDI specification assigns 47 drum sounds to a percussion *key map*. These assignments are shown in Table 16.2.

TABLE 16.2. General MIDI percussion key map.

Program	Instrument
35	Acoustic Bass Drum
36	Bass Drum 1
37	Side Stick
38	Acoustic Snare
39	Hand Clap
40	Electric Snare

continues

TABLE 16.2. continued

Program	Instrument
41	Low Floor Tom
42	Closed Hi-hat
43	High Floor Tom
44	Pedal Hi-hat
45	Low Tom
46	Open Hi-hat
47	Low-mid Tom
48	High-mid Tom
49	Crash Cymbal 1
50	High Tom
51	Ride Cymbal 1
52	Chinese Cymbal
53	Ride Bell
54	Tambourine
55	Splash Cymbal
56	Cowbell
57	Crash Cymbal 2
58	Vibraslap
59	Ride Cymbal 2
60	High Bongo
61	Low Bongo
62	Mute High Conga
63	Open High Conga
64	Low Conga
65	High Timbale
66	Low Timbale
67	High Agogo
68	Low Agogo
69	Casaba
70	Maracas
71	Short Whistle

Program	Instrument
72	Long Whistle
73	Short Guiro
74	Long Guiro
75	Claves
76	High Wood Block
77	Low Wood Block
78	Mute Cuica
79	Open Cuica
80	Mute Triangle
81	Open Triangle

To be controlled, voices (and thus the assigned programs) are assigned to channels, although the correspondence need not be one-to-one. For example, all voices can share one channel or one voice can be controlled by all channels. Which voice responds to which channel is controlled by setting up each receiver by sending messages through the system.

The General MIDI specification sets the first nine channels for instruments and the tenth for percussion. The remaining channels, 11 through 16, are left for individual musicians to use as they see fit. Most of the time they are not used.

As wonderful as General MIDI is, for the first generation of PC sound boards it was a high standard, indeed. Most of them were unable to support the 10 channels of General MIDI that were generally assigned to instruments, let alone the full 16. Consequently Microsoft came up with its own definitions of MIDI devices for use with Windows.

Basic MIDI devices have only four channels, corresponding to MIDI channels 13, 14, 15, and 16.

Extended MIDI devices have 10 channels, corresponding to MIDI channels 1 through 10 and assigned according to the General MIDI specification. Table 16.3 briefly summarize the three levels of MIDI implementations.

Standards

TABLE 16.3. MIDI implementations.

Standard	Creator	Number of channels	Channel numbers
Basic	Microsoft	4	13 thru 16
Extended	Microsoft	10	1 thru 10
General	MIDI	16	1 thru 16

This arrangement is effective for Microsoft's purposes. It allows the same MIDI file to be played on both Basic and Extended devices with separate and distinct programs for each. The basic devices will ignore the voices on the channels used by the extended devices, and vice versa. Programmers creating MIDI files for playback through Windows thus make two programs, one for the limited abilities of basic MIDI and one for extended. Most General MIDI programs will play through extended MIDI devices without a problem, although any voices assigned the top six channels will be silent.

These definitions have resulted in three classes of MIDI products. The Basic MIDI standard is low enough to include virtually every sound board you can buy for your PC. Both you and software publishers can depend on Basic MIDI working with any MPC-compatible PC. Extended MIDI, supported by the latest sound boards, allows complex compositions and gives you enough versatility for you to create intricate compositions. General MIDI assures the best compatibility with most mainstream MIDI products.

As a practical matter, this scheme helps assure that you don't have to worry about the details of mapping if all you want to do is playback commercially distributed MIDI files. General MIDI and the Microsoft mapping assure software developers that they can supply files that will make the best of whatever hardware you have installed in your Multimedia PC.

Messages

A MIDI file or data stream is a sequence of bytes. MIDI gains its structure by defining channels entirely through software. This structure is not specifically declared but implicit in the codes used by MIDI messages.

The least significant nibble (that is, the last four bits) of the Status Byte of a MIDI message defines the channel to which it is addressed. The most significant nibble (the first four bits) of the Status Byte define the function controlled by the channel message. The various channel messages are listed in Table 16.4. The "x" in the Status byte column is replaced in the actual message by the nibble corresponding to the channel number.

TABLE 16.4. MIDI channel mode messages.

Status	Data 1	Data 2	Function
Bx	0	7A	Local control off
Bx	7F	7A	Local control on
Bx	0	7B	All notes off
Bx	0	7C	Omni Mode off
Bx	0	7D	Omni Mode on

Status	Data 1	Data 2	Function
Bx	0	7E	Mono Mode on; Poly Mode off (see Note)
Bx	0	7F	Poly Mode on; Mono Mode off

The Mono Mode on command requires a mandatory third Data Byte which specifies the number of channels in the range 1 to 16 in which voice messages are to be sent. The receiver assigns channels sequentially to voices starting with the Basic Channel.

A MIDI system divides its channels into two types, Voice Channels and Basic Channels. A *Voice Channel* controls an individual voice. A *Basic Channel* sets up the mode of each MIDI receiver for receiving voice and control messages. Typically a MIDI receiver will be assigned one Basic Channel as a default. Later the device could be reconfigured as something else. For example, an eight-voice synthesizer could be reconfigured to respond as two four-voice synthesizers, each with its own Basic Channel. The MIDI sequencer or keyboard could then send separate messages to each four-voice synthesizer as if it were a physically separate instrument.

Messages sent to individual channels in the MIDI system are termed *channel messages*. Messages sent through the voice channel are termed *voice messages* because they control a voice; those sent through the basic channel are *mode messages* because they control the mode of the device listening to the channel. Mode messages determine how a device will respond to voice messages. Although voice messages may also be sent through the basic channel, mode messages can use only the basic channel.

MIDI allows for four modes to govern how the receiver routes the channel messages to individual voices. These modes are distinguished by three characteristics that act as flags: Omni, Mono, and Poly.

Omni controls whether the channels are treated individually or as a single-minded group. When Omni is on, the channels are grouped together. In effect the messages come in from all directions—control is omnidirectional. The MIDI voices respond as if all the control signals were all funneled together. When Omni is off, voices listen solely to the one channel to which they are assigned. Each channel and its voice are individually linked, separate from the others.

Mono is short for monophonic. If Omni is on, Mono combines together all channel messages and sends them to a single designated voice. When Omni is off, Mono allows the assigning of channels to individual voices. That is, each voice has individual control through a separate channel.

Poly is short for polyphonic and routes the messages on one channel to all the voices in the MIDI receiver. When Omni and Poly are on, all messages combine together and go to all voices indiscriminately. When Omni is off but Poly is on, one channel controls all voices. In other words, when Poly is on, all voices play the same notes.

Note that Poly and Mono are mutually exclusive. When Poly is on, Mono must be off. When Mono is on, Poly must be off. Table 16.5 summarizes the various MIDI receiver modes.

TABLE 16.5. MIDI receiver modes.

Mode number	Omni status	Poly/Mono	Function
1	On	Poly	Voice messages received from all voice channels assigned to voices polyphonically.
2	On	Mono	Voice messages received from all voice channels control only one voice, monophonically.
3	Off	Poly	Voice messages received in voice channel N only are assigned to voices polyphonically.
4	Off	Mono	Voice messages received in voice channels N thru N+M-1 are assigned monophonically to voices 1 thru M, respectively. The number of voices M is specified by the third byte of the Mono Mode Message. N is the second byte.

With MIDI transmitters, the mode effects are similar. When Poly is on MIDI transmitters send all voices through a designated channel. When Poly is off, Omni determines whether one or multiple voices are controlled. When on, voice messages for one voice are sent through the designed channel. When Omni is off, a number of channels carry voice messages for a like number of individually controlled voices. Table 16.6 summarizes MIDI transmitter modes.

TABLE 16.6. MIDI transmitter modes.

Mode number	Omni status	Poly/Mono	Function
1	On	Poly	All voice messages transmitted in Channel N.
2	On	Mono	Voice messages for one voice sent in Channel N.
3	Off	Poly	Voice messages for all voices sent in Channel N.

Mode number	Omni status	Poly/ Mono	Function
4	Off	Mono	Voice messages for voices 1 thru M transmitted in voice channels N thru N+M-1, respectively. (Single voice per channel.)

MIDI devices, whether receivers or transmitters, can operate only under one mode at a time. In most cases both the transmitter and receiver will operate in the same mode. However, if a receiver cannot operate in a mode that a transmitter requests from it, it may switch to an alternate mode (in most cases, this will be Omni on, Poly on) or it will ignore the mode message. When powered up, all MIDI instruments default to the Omni on, Poly on mode.

Mode messages affect only voice channels and don't affect the definition of the basic channel. Consequently, a receiver will recognize only those mode messages sent over its assigned basic channel, even if that device is in a mode with Omni on. Because mode commands affect how the instruments respond to channel messages, a mode command might have weird, unanticipated, and undefined effects on notes being played when the message is received. Consequently MIDI dictates that a mode command (with the exception of those turning local control on or off) automatically turns all notes off.

Besides voice and mode messages, each receiver in the MIDI system listens to all system messages. Because these are universal messages, the Status Byte of each one does not define an individual channel. Three types of system messages are defined: *common messages* are meant to be heard by all receivers in the MIDI system; *exclusive messages* are sent to all receivers but are keyed by a manufacturer's code so that only devices keyed to that code respond; and *real-time messages* which are used to synchronize the various devices in the MIDI system.

Exclusive and real-time messages are exceptions to the rule that all messages must have a Status Byte followed by multiples of one or two Data Bytes. The Status Byte of an exclusive message may be followed by any number of Data Bytes. Its length is defined by a special End of Exclusive flag byte—that is a value of 0F8(Hex) or 11110111 (binary)—or by any other Status Byte. A real-time message consists only of a Status Byte.

Manufacturers of MIDI equipment assign an ID code through which an Exclusive message accesses the equipment. The MIDI standard requests that manufacturers publish the ID codes they use so that programmers can address and control it with Exclusive messages. The manufacturer also controls the format of the Data Bytes that follow their ID. These allow manufacturers to expland on MIDI and incorporate new features without the need to alter the MIDI control system.

Real-time messages can (and often are) sent at any time, even during other messages. The action called for by a real-time message is immediately executed, then normal function of the system continues. For example, the entire MIDI system is synchronized with the real-time clock message—0F8(Hex)—which is sent from the transmitter at a rate of 24 clocks to the quarter note (sometimes called a *crotchet*). Some MIDI transmitters periodically send out Active Sensing messages—byte value 0FE(Hex)—to indicate that the transmitter is still connected to the system and operating.

The *Song Position Pointer* tracks the number of MIDI beats that have elapsed since the beginning of a song. One MIDI *beat* equals six MIDI *clocks*, one-quarter of a quarter note—a semiquaver. To move to any position in a song (with a resolution of one beat), a Song Position Pointer Status Byte can be sent followed by two Data Bytes indicating the pointer value.

Operation

MIDI works by simply sending out strings of bytes. Each device recognizes the beginning of a command by detecting a Status Byte with its most significant bit set high. With Voice and Mode messages, the Status Byte simply alerts the MIDI receiver to the nature of the Data Bytes that follow. Each device knows how many Data Bytes are assigned to each command controlled by a Status Byte, and waits until it has received all the data in a complete command before acting on the command. If the complete command is followed by more Data Bytes, it interprets the information as the beginning of another command. It awaits the correct number of Data Bytes to complete this next command, then carries it out. This feature—one Status Byte serving as the preamble for multiple commands—is called *Running Status* in the MIDI scheme of things. Running Status ends as soon as another Status Byte is received, with one exception. If the interrupting message is a Real-time message, the Running Status will resume after the Real-time message is complete. If a subsequent Status Byte interrupts a message before it is complete (for example, between the first and second Data Bytes of a message requiring two Data Bytes), the interrupted message will be ignored. The MIDI device won't do anything until it receives a full and complete message (which may be the interrupting message).

Badly formatted or erroneous MIDI commands are generally ignored. If a given MIDI receiver does not have a feature that a command asks for, it will ignore the Status and Data Bytes of that command. If a MIDI transmitter inadvertently sends out a Status Byte that's not defined by the MIDI specification, the Status Byte and all following Data Bytes are ignored until a valid Status Byte is sent.

Because of the nature of the MIDI coding system, Data Bytes can have a value only from 0 to 127. Higher values would require the most significant bit of the Data Byte to be set high, which would cause MIDI devices to recognize it as a Status Byte. Most MIDI values consequently fall in the range of 0 to 127. For example, MIDI recognizes 128 intensities and 128 musical notes as well as 128 General MIDI programs.

MIDI encodes musical notes as discrete numeric values in steps generally corresponding to the 12-tone scale used in most Western music, but it need not. For example, electronic percussion instruments may recognize note values for different non chromatic drum sounds. In the MIDI scheme of things, middle C is assigned a value of 60. Each note or semitone lower is one number lower; each semitone higher is one number higher. The MIDI coding scheme thus covers a range 40 notes wider than the 88 keys of most pianos, 21 notes below and 19 above. This range also exceeds the bounds of the hearing of most humans. Table 16.7 lists MIDI values and the corresponding chromatic notes.

TABLE 16.7. MIDI note values.

MIDI Value	Note	Frequency (Hz)
1	C#/D-flat	17.32
2	D	18.35
3	D#/E-flat	19.45
4	E	20.60
5	F	21.83
6	F#/G-flat	23.12
7	G	24.50
8	G#/A-flat	25.96
9	A	27.50
10	A#/B-flat	29.14
11	B	30.87
12	C	32.70
13	C#/D-flat	34.65
14	D	36.71
15	D#/E-flat	38.89
16	E	41.20
17	F	43.65
18	F#/G-flat	46.25
19	G	49.00
20	G#/A-flat	51.91
21	A	55.00
22	A#/B-flat	58.27
23	B	61.74
24	C	65.41

continues

TABLE 16.7. continued

MIDI Value	Note	Frequency (Hz)
25	C#/D-flat	69.30
26	D	73.42
27	D#/E-flat	77.78
28	E	82.41
29	F	87.31
30	F#/G-flat	92.50
31	G	98.00
32	G#/A-flat	103.83
33	A	110.00
34	A#/B-flat	116.54
35	B	123.47
36	C	130.81
37	C#/D-flat	138.59
38	D	146.83
39	D#/E-flat	155.56
40	E	164.81
41	F	174.61
42	F#/G-flat	185.00
43	G	196.00
44	G#/A-flat	207.65
45	A	220.00
46	A#/B-flat	233.08
47	B	246.94
48	C	261.63
49	C#/D-flat	277.18
50	D	293.66
51	D#/E-flat	311.13
52	E	329.63
53	F	349.23
54	F#/G-flat	369.99
55	G	391.99

MIDI Value	Note	Frequency (Hz)
56	G#/A-flat	415.30
57	A	440.00
58	A#/B-flat	466.16
59	B	493.88
60	Middle C	523.25
61	C#/D-flat	554.37
62	D	587.33
63	D#/E-flat	622.25
64	E	659.25
65	F	698.46
66	F#/G-flat	739.99
67	G	783.99
68	G#/A-flat	830.61
69	A	880.00
70	A#/B-flat	932.33
71	B	987.77
72	C	1046.50
73	C#/D-flat	1108.73
74	D	1174.66
75	D#/E-flat	1244.51
76	E	1318.51
77	F	1396.91
78	F#/G-flat	1479.97
79	G	1567.98
80	G#/A-flat	1661.22
81	A	1760.00
82	A#/B-flat	1864.65
83	B	1975.53
84	C	2093.00
85	C#/D-flat	2217.46
86	D	2349.31
87	D#/E-flat	2489.01

continues

TABLE 16.7. continued

MIDI Value	Note	Frequency (Hz)
88	E	2637.01
89	F	2793.82
90	F#/G-flat	2959.95
91	G	3135.95
92	G#/A-flat	3322.43
93	A	3520.00
94	A#/B-flat	3729.31
95	B	3951.07
96	C	4186.01
97	C#/D-flat	4434.92
98	D	4698.63
99	D#/E-flat	4978.03
100	E	5274.04
101	F	5587.65
102	F#/G-flat	5919.91
103	G	6271.92
104	G#/A-flat	6644.87
105	A	7040.00
106	A#/B-flat	7458.62
107	B	7902.13
108	C	8372.02
109	C#/D-flat	8869.84
110	D	9397.27
111	D#/E-flat	9956.06
112	E	10548.08
113	F	11175.30
114	F#/G-flat	11839.81
115	G	12543.84
116	G#/A-flat	13289.74
117	A	14080.00

MIDI Value	Note	Frequency (Hz)
118	A#/B-flat	14917.24
119	B	15804.26
120	C	16744.03
121	C#/D-flat	17739.68
122	D	18794.54
123	D#/E-flat	19912.12
124	E	21096.15
125	F	22350.59
126	F#/G-flat	23679.62
127	G	25087.69

*Note: Frequency values assume standard Western tuning, that is, A=440 Hz.

After a MIDI system has been set up by assigning modes and programs, tunes can be played by sending out voice messages. A *Note On* Status Byte plays a single note of the voice on the channel indicated in the byte, the pitch of the note is defined by the first Data Byte and its velocity (which approximates sensing how hard you press a key when playing expressively—at least on velocity-sensing keyboards) by the second Data Byte. The note continues as defined by the program until a *Note Off* (either a specific Note Off or a general All Notes Off) message is sent, although in the meantime the program may cause the note to decay to inaudibility. The individual Note Off message also allows the control of a release velocity, a feature rare but available on some synthesizers.

MIDI provides for further control. Messages also govern *aftertouch*, a feature of some keyboards that enables you to change the sound of a note by pressing harder on a key after you've first depressed it to sound the note. MIDI provides for two kinds of aftertouch, *general*—using Status Byte 0D(Hex)—that applies to all notes that are currently being played in the channel; and *specific*—using Status Byte 0Ax (Hex)—that applies only to an individual key.

Another Status Byte allows MIDI to send the state of dials or switches on the keyboard called controllers. One important controller, the *shift wheel* has its own Status Byte—0Ex(Hex)—assigned to its control. Another Status Byte—0Bx(Hex)—relays data to appoximately up to 122 other controllers.

Synchronizing

Time for MIDI in the scheme described previously is a relative thing, measured in clocks and beats, independent from anything else in the world. Sometimes, however, you want to synchronize MIDI music with some other event. For example, you may have a video to which you want to add a MIDI soundtrack, and you don't want the music from the chase scene to play during a moment of intimate love-making. Then again, maybe you might. But to get the effect you want on your audience, you at least want the correspondence between music and video to be predictable.

Although the basic MIDI scheme doesn't include a means to sync external devices, the versatility of the standard allows it to be extended in that direction easily. Just as you can send a message to play a note now, you can use messages to relay a time code. Some MIDI devices can generate a signal, *MIDI time code*, to synchronize the system to real time. With suitable hardware, MIDI events can be triggered to the time code and played appropriately.

If you have a reasonably smart sequencer, only it needs to be synchronized to your external source. With suitable software, you can program your sequencer to send a message at a predetermined time to any MIDI instrument and tell the instrument to play a note immediately. The sequencer acts like an orchestra conductor who has to make the music fit; it watches the clock alone, and the band just plays along.

When you are synchronizing an external source, you need a means of recording time to which you can lock your MIDI system. Several methods are in common use.

The simplest is Frequency Shift Keyed (FSK) time code. The frequencies are tones that are within the range that can be recorded on regular audio equipment. The shifts in tones define the beats of the clock. You can record FSK on one channel of a multitrack analog tape recorder to derive a signal to lock to your synchronizer.

This basic FSK has one problem. It provides no means of determining absolute time. Fast forward on the tape, and you may lose sync with your synthesizer. *Smart FSK* adds structure to the FSK signals, code that indicates elapsed time so a compatible sequencer can tell the playback position of the tape. This enables you to *chase and lock*, to fast forward to any place on the tape and have your sequencer lock on and play the appropriate music for that moment.

Of course if you're inclined to use analog tape these days, you might as well slide a wax cylinder on the old gramophone. Today audio recording is digital, and FSK makes no sense in the digital domain. That's okay because digital technology lets you directly record SMPTE time code. (See Chapter 13, "Images," for more information.) The single-frame resolution SMPTE time code lets you lock your sequencer exactly to movies and videos.

Playback

To make music with MIDI, you need sequencer software to generate the MIDI messages to make your synthesizer play. Most sound boards come with their own sequencer programs so you have an instant means of getting started with musicmaking. If you're serious about making music, however, you'll need serious music-making software. You'll find a wealth of commercial sequencer programs for PCs (and more for Macs—most musicians favor the Mac platform).

Each has its own advocates filled with a religious fervor that falls just short of hostage-taking. After all, musicmaking is an art, and it need not be rational. As such, it is beyond the scope of any book that pretends to be rational (like this one).

When all you want to do is play back a MIDI file that someone else has prepared for you, MIDI is easy to use. You can play back a MIDI file as conveniently as waveform files, particularly under Windows 95. All you need to do is bring up the Media Player, select a MIDI file instead of a .WAV file, click, and your music will be playing. Or simply click a file with a .MID extension using My Computer or Windows Explorer, and Windows 95 will start playing through whatever sequencer you have associated with those files. By default, Windows 95 uses its own *Microsoft MCI MIDI Sequencer* to control your synthesizer.

To use the Media Player for MIDI playback, start by clicking the Media Player in your Multimedia folder. Once the Media Player pops on the screen, you have two choices for selecting the file to play.

Pull down the Device menu, click Microsoft MCI MIDI Sequencer, and the Media Player will give you a file Open menu that defaults to a search for MIDI files in your current directory. You'll see a screen like that shown in Figure 16.1.

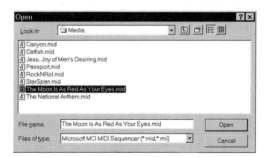

FIGURE 16.1. The MIDI Sequencer's File Open window within the Windows 95 Media Player showing available MIDI files in the current directory.

Just browse through your system to find the file you want to play. Click your choice, then the Open button and the Media Player will load and give you control.

Alternately, choose the File menu from the opening Media Player window. Again you'll have a choice of files, but as a default you'll see all the various types of files that the Media Player recognizes. You can make your selection easier by one of three ways: simply choosing a MIDI file from the display, restricting the file types displayed by choosing .MID files only, or browsing through your entire system to find the MIDI file you want.

Once you've chosen a file, your run the Media Player exactly as you would for .WAV or .AVI files. You'll have an on-screen version of a tape or disc player, like that shown in Figure 16.2. Click the play button near the lower left of the window to start playback. You can move around in the file with the fast forward button or by moving the scale to the appropriate place.

FIGURE 16.2. Windows 95 Media Player playing MIDI file.

Note the time scale for the sample file; the numbers shown represent minutes and seconds. The CANYON.MID sample file measures only 20KB but plays for over two minutes. That's the essence of MIDI, an efficient storage system for the music you make on your PC.

Section IV
Appendixes

Appendix A *Multimedia Law* *581*

Appendix B *Production Issues* *595*

Appendix C *Distribution* *599*

Appendix A
Multimedia Law

You should have known. Eventually the lawyers will get involved. After all, they have their fingers in everything. If you plan to create a multimedia extravaganza, you can bet the lawyers will be coming after you from two directions—those with microscopes, cross-references, and the conviction you've stolen every word and image in your show from their client who emerged from his drunken stupor for 15 minutes back in 1956 and wrote a paragraph from which the lawyer alleges you've lifted vital words (such as "the," "of," and of course, "and of course"); and those willing to defend your rights in your presentation until their death or until your retainer runs out, whichever comes first.

You can't avoid the law, and it's becoming increasingly difficult to avoid the lawyers, what with all their ads on TV. If you ignore them, they might just come after you. This appendix is designed to give you an appreciation for the legal issues involved in producing, consuming, and pirating multimedia. It is hardly definitive law, if there is such a thing. Although it is accurate as far as it goes, it doesn't go very far. You need a lawyer to take you the rest of the way. (Okay, now are all you lawyers happy? Let's dig in.)

The legal issues of concern when preparing a multimedia presentation for public consumption boil down to two fundamental questions: *One*, what can you borrow from other sources for your presentation without tying yourself in a legal knot from which there is no relief (such as an obligation to pay royalties)? *Two*, what kind of brick wall can you build around your work so that no one can steal the fruit of your immense labors without giving you your just due (such as paying royalties)?

Your concerns are actually two sides of a single body of law called *intellectual property*. This branch of jurisprudence concerns itself with ensuring that the work of your mind has some kind of legal protection just as the work of your hands does. After all, if you spend 15 years carving an old sassafras tree into a slide trombone and someone takes it from you, the law entitles you to its return or compensation for your loss. If you wrestle with your muse for 15 years to turn your mental ravings into a cogent novel and a publisher prints it without your permission, the law similarly entitles you to compensation. In our society stealing is stealing whether what's taken is a material thing or an artistic creation—unless of course it involves an operating system or game software.

Copyright

You can sum up all of copyright law in a single sentence. A copyright is a grant of control and ownership over what you create as an original expression of your ideas. Attorneys earn their livelihood explaining what that simple sentence means. That explanation is called copyright law.

Subject Matter

A copyright protects only the expression of your ideas, not the ideas themselves. You can't own knowledge or information, only the way in which that knowledge or information is expressed. The distinction sounds trivial at first because you cannot communicate information without expressing it somehow—without words your thoughts would be forever locked inside your head. By the act of speaking, however, you organize the knowledge that you have, you make it clear or turgid, you add your personality and style to what you say and write. The legal concept is that your knowledge is held inside your head in some abstract form and through mental effort you make it into something understandable. Take your words and distill out the meaning, the idea, that lacks your influence. Tell a story, and the words you say are an expression (and subject to copyright) but the moral behind it—good triumphs over evil—is an idea that can be freely shared.

To be able to gain a copyright, the expression of your ideas must be original. That only makes sense. The expression must be your own or else you cannot claim ownership over it. Mere slavish copying of someone else's expression is exactly what a copyright is supposed to prevent. Copying short-circuits the creative process. Instead of you applying mental effort to create an expression, adding your personality and style to it, you merely recite a tale told by someone else. You don't put any meaningful mental work into the process, so you have nothing to gain from or protect.

A big question is exactly what you must do to make an expression "original." After all, just remembering something can be work for some of us. Where do you draw the line between original and copy? How different must something be? Is sorting a list that someone else prepared sufficient effort to constitute originality? Probably not. Is editing the list? Probably. But even those distinctions are fuzzy. Organizing a list *is* editing, isn't it? Suddenly the issue becomes a judgment call. That's where the judges come in, with the lawyers arguing both sides of the issue until courts and society agree on where to draw the line. Fixing that line so that everyone knows where it is, is the essence of copyright law.

Copyrights don't apply solely to words. Well nigh anything qualifies as an expression of an idea. Although copyrights of books, magazines, and newspapers are most obvious, movies, sound recordings, and television programs can also be copyrighted. Sculpture, paintings, computer programs, images on computer screens all qualify.

The works not covered by copyright generally fall into two major classes: things that are primarily functional and things that are not original. When things are functional, they may qualify for another form of legal protection, the patent, the subject of a separate body of law.

Things that are unoriginal obviously don't qualify as original expressions, but then you're stuck with the tricky issue of drawing the line. You can create some works almost mechanically, like printing out a database. Some works are very simple, so simple that they might require little or no creative work, such as drawing boxes for a ledger sheet. Other works might expand minimally on what's come before, a new edition that corrects the punctuation errors in the original. In other words, despite your best dreams you cannot get a copyright on the alphabet and hope to roll in the royalties on anything that ever gets written.

Most people would agree that sliding the sheets of a printed play through a Xerox machine doesn't raise to the level of achievement required for originality or copyright protection. But what about someone who spends six months translating the play from English to Esperanto. Is the final Esperanto version the translator's original expression or that of the playwright? Is the movie based on the play an original expression? Is the book that's based on the movie? And what about the play based on the book that was based on the movie (stranger things have happened in Hollywood)? The Esperanto version, of course.

Other legal means of protecting intellectual property include patents, trademarks, and trade-secret laws.

Much as copyrights cover the expression of ideas, *patents* cover the applications of ideas rather than the ideas themselves. Patents only cover things that are new and useful. A patent provides more far-reaching protection than a copyright (a copyright prohibits unauthorized copying; a patent prohibits unauthorized use even if someone thinks up the same application independently) but for a shorter time. U.S. patents last only 17 years.

Trademarks give you control over an identifying name or symbol for as long as the name or symbol is used in commerce. In other words, the protection for trademarks can last forever, providing it is used as a trademark forever.

Trade secret laws prevent people with access to your secrets from selling them to others. They vary state by state. In general, they protect secrets for a reasonable period. What's reasonable? Ask a lawyer.

Each of these protections comprises an entire body of law, and each has its own application. You won't be concerned with patents in multimedia unless you develop some new means of presenting software or some truly novel approach to presentations. You need be concerned with protecting a trademark only after you establish yourself as a multimedia vendor and start selling products. Trade secrets will become a concern only when your multimedia business becomes large enough to have several employees who might share—and steal—your secrets. Copyrights, though, pertain to everything you create.

The basic concept of copyright doesn't address any of the technicalities, like how long protection should last, when does the copyright arise, what can you do with it. Lawyers and lawmakers (usually one and the same) have argued these issues for hundreds of years. The result is statutory copyright law. Alas, the lawyers and lawmakers are still arguing, so the law keeps changing. But that's good because they define answers for tricky questions—new lines that need to be drawn—as those questions arise.

The principal statute covering copyrights in the United States is the Copyright Act of 1976, which has been amended several times since (and which replaced an earlier 1909 act). It is a federal law, which means it is uniform in all states. Further, the law prohibits individual states from creating their own copyright statutes. Of course, that's not to say there are no state copyright laws. There are, but these laws are not statutory. Each state has its own *common law* copyrights, protections that arise from court decisions. These apply to subjects and circumstances that the federal law does not cover. Once your work qualifies for federal copyright law, the federal law takes over and controls.

To qualify for protection under the federal law, your work must be an *original* expression that is *fixed* in a tangible medium of expression. The requirement for "fixing" the work gives the law and lawyers something they can get their hands on. If a work were not fixed, it would change or disappear. No one could say exactly what it was. Printing, painting, sculpture, even digital codes on magnetic and optical media qualify for the fixing required by the copyright law.

Issuance

The place most people start is the end. They want a copyright they can hold in the hand as a completed thing. How can you get a copyright? Amazingly, copyrights arise by the process of spontaneous generation. They pop up without your needing to do anything at all. After that, they cling tenaciously to you, like flypaper in a slapstick routine. You can't even rely on a simple expedient like death to end them.

Wait a minute. If you've ever read a book—even this one—you've seen a copyright notice glaring on the back of the title page. That message is there for a reason, and if one's missing you'd expect there's no copyright, right? Nope. Copyrights are many splendored things, and overall copyright law embraces a number of separate laws. The copyright notice you see in books is a construction of federal copyright law and international treaty. But the state common law copyright arises without a copyright notice, and even federal law allows for works that don't have a notice (but eventually a notice must be given to qualify for federal protection).

The most familiar aspects of the federal copyright law deal with published expressions of ideas. For the most part, its protections take effect after you've made copies of something and distributed them. But as soon as you make any expression of an idea, it is protected by common law copyright. No one can steal your words—except in certain situations—without your permission. Your diary, unpublished, is still protected.

You get a federal copyright on something essentially as soon as you publish it. You don't have to send any form into the government to register your copyright to get copyright protection. Although the federal copyright law once required registration of your copyright before you could take the matter to court, this need will soon disappear as the United States moves more in conformity with international copyright treaties. (Most other nations do not require registration before the prosecution of copyright claims.)

Notice

To tell the world that you want copyright control over a published work, you must include a copyright notice on it. The lack of a copyright notice does not always indicate something is not copyrighted, however. The federal copyright law allows you a five-year grace period in which to repair your omission, so forgetting the notice is not a fatal mistake. More importantly, the lack of copyright notice on a work does not necessarily mean that the work is in the public domain, that is, available to anyone in the public to use as he sees fit.

Proper *notice* requires three parts: an indication you are claiming a copyright, who is making the claim, and when the claim was made.

You can use either of two different indications of a copyright claim. The word "Copyright" or its abbreviation "Copyr." serves the function in the United States. Worldwide, however, that language-sensitive word is not recognized. Under the Berne Convention you should use the international copyright symbol to indicate you are making a claim. The symbol is the familiar letter *C* with a circle around it (©). For good measure, many people and organizations use both forms, the word and symbol.

Often you'll see an attempt to approximate the international copyright symbol using the letter *C* enclosed within parentheses—(c). This form is not officially recognized either by the United States or the international treaty governing copyrights, the Berne Convention. Although some sources believe that it is sufficient to serve as an indication of copyright claim, its validity has not been established in court.

To show who is making a copyright claim, you only need to put in your name (or the name of your company, if you are asserting its rights to the copyrighted work). You don't have to use your full legal name, but whatever you use should be recognizable.

Finally, append the date of the first publication of the work for which you are claiming copyright. The date of publication is when you release the product to the public, not when you finish writing it, send it off to the printer (or disk duplicator), or even when you are receiving nice, new shrink-wrapped packages ready to send out. You need not be any more specific than indicating the year of publication.

Term

Unlike patents, for all intents and purposes the year in which you claim your copyright really isn't significant as to its longevity. Copyrights endure forever, at least as far as you as a normal human being are concerned. The common law copyrights on your unpublished works last your lifetime and often longer. The federal copyright law gives you a lifetime's protection on your published works, then adds 50 years for good measure. Although you might not gain any more benefit from the longer run, your starving spouse and children may.

Corporations could last forever, however. To prevent copyrights from lasting in perpetuity, federal law gives corporations a fixed term for copyrights, 75 years.

Protection

Copyright laws give you a simple protection: unauthorized copying of your work is prohibited. The law stops there. Once a copy has been made under your authority or with your permission, your power over it stops. Called the *first sale doctrine*, this policy allows someone owning an authorized copy of your work to do with it as he pleases, even selling it at a grotesque profit that makes you yearn to confine your business manager to purgatory for eternity. Although some artworks have been granted special protection beyond copyright, in general under the first sale doctrine purchasers can do what they want, including shredding copies and consigning them to the compost pile.

Infringement

When someone takes advantage of your copyrighted work without your permission, they infringe your copyright. Copyright *infringement* means simply that someone copies what you've done without your approval. That's all well and good, but you need some means of enforcing your rights. Although some forms of copying are prohibited by criminal statutes, copyrights are usually enforced by a civil lawsuit—that is, you sue infringers.

When you sue, you ask for what lawyers call *remedies*. In copyright suits you'll probably seek two kinds of relief: an *injunction* to prevent further copying and monetary *damages*. An injunction is an order from the court prohibiting someone from doing something, for example continuing to make copies of your work. If the offender doesn't obey the court order, he then becomes guilty of contempt of court, a criminal offense, for which he may be fined or jailed or whatever else the court sees fit to impose.

Monetary damages are a means of making up for the loss you suffered from the distribution of unauthorized copies. In most lawsuits you have to prove the extent of your damage to show how much compensation you deserve. In copyright cases, proving such actual damages can be difficult, so the federal copyright statute allows for *statutory damages*, an amount of damage you can claim without proving the amount of actual damage you suffered. In order to claim statutory damages under the federal law, your copyright must first be registered.

Fair Use

What the government gives, it often takes away. In the case of copyrights, the take-back is modest. The framers of the copyright law recognized that some copying must still be permitted, so a few exceptions to the complete control afforded by copyright have been recognized. These are called fair use. There are a number of different kinds of fair use. Two of the most important to you in regard to multimedia are backup copies and quotes for reviews.

Recognizing the fragility of computer storage media and the necessity of safeguarding your disk-based data, the copyright law entitles you to make a single backup copy of your copyrighted software. If the original gets destroyed, you can restore it.

Reviewers and researchers can quote excerpts to carry out their jobs, but the quotes have to be brief. Quoting a substantial amount of the work is not fair use.

Work for Hire

If someone employs you and your work involves creating things for the employer, then what you create on the employer's time becomes the property of the employer. If, however, you're hired to create a specific project, the issue becomes cloudier. In some specific circumstances, what you create becomes that of the person or organization giving you the contract. What you do is called work for hire, and you lose nearly all rights to it. (A special provision in the law enables your heirs to recapture your copyright 28 years after you've signed them away.) If certain specific requirements are not met, however, you retain the copyright to your work.

Most professional artists and writers consider work for hire nasty stuff, a way of depriving them of the fruits of their labors. The law now makes a presumption against what you do being work for hire. But any time you sign a contract to write or produce something, you should probably consult with a lawyer.

Rights

A copyright is like any other kind of property. It's yours as long as you choose to keep it. But you don't have to keep it. You can sell rights to whomever you please for however much you can negotiate. The rights you sell can be limited by time, geography, or media. For example, you can sell rights to copy your work solely in North America or worldwide. You can sell magazine rights but not book rights. You can sell exclusive rights so that only one person or organization is ever allowed to make copies, or you can sell the same rights to a number of people or organizations. Assigning rights is essentially making a contract, and the law allows you to contract for anything that is not illegal or against public policy.

Rights are limited. You can define exactly what you license to someone. The license of a work does not automatically confer any rights beyond ownership of the work. For example, simply buying the rights to a printed work does not entitle you to performance rights of that work. Even if you buy a dozen copies of a play, you cannot put on a show without a specific license to do so.

Public Domain

If you can do anything with your rights in a copyrighted work, you can clearly give them away. Some people do exactly that. For example, early computer hobbyists enjoyed working with their PCs and freely exchanged software and, not stopping there, allowed anyone to make copies. They specifically contributed their work to the public domain, the body of works that can be freely copied for whatever purpose whatsoever. Public domain works include—besides those openly contributed—works for which the copyrights have lapsed and works that have never been copyrighted. Public domain works may be freely copied by anyone for any purpose. Most public domain software is distributed either in the spirit of generosity—typically because someone solved a specific problem and doesn't want others to have to go through all that work again—or as a fishing mechanism, spreading program code around to show the author's expertise and encourage job or consulting offers.

Works that are so old that their copyrights have expired are also in the public domain. Few computer programs date back so far.

Freeware

Freeware differs from public domain works in that the author never gives away his rights to his work; he only gives away copies of the work itself. The author can later change his mind and start charging for his rights in the work and for copies of it. The copies he distributed free remain the property of those to whom they were given.

The motivation underlying freeware may be the same as public domain works—generosity, pride, status seeking—but the author wants to maintain control just in case something comes of it later on. Note that a freeware author cannot demand payment later from someone who has already legitimately gotten a copy of the program for free, although he can demand payment for copies made after he has withdrawn his free license.

Shareware

Shareware, as with freeware, differs from public domain works in that the copyright owner of a shareware work does not give up his ownership rights. Only the licensing terms change with shareware—the author of shareware delays payment for the software until after an examination or trial period. The author retains his rights. Moreover, if you do not pay for shareware, you never become a legitimate owner, so you cannot sell it. The first sale doctrine does not apply unless there's actually a sale. You can, of course, give away copies under terms of the shareware license.

Crippleware

Akin to shareware but produced by those with less faith in human nature (or suffering more from another frailty, greed) is crippleware, software distributed in crippled or not-quite-functional form. For example, a database may enable you to enter records but not generate reports. The idea is that you'll so fall in love with the data entry section of the software, you'll dutifully enter all your records then, not wanting to have wasted your time, order the fully functional version to make your report. Some shareware is less explicit and more insidious, pulling the carpet out from underneath you just when you begin to depend on a product, limiting the time you can use a program or the number of entries you can make.

These limitations, viewed by their instigators as encouragement, take on the aura of extortion to people making a commitment to a product. Legally and morally, the crippleware publishers are only exercising and protecting their own rights (after all, the only ones getting burned are people who were expecting to get something for nothing, right?). Nevertheless, according to shareware publishers, no program distributed as crippleware has ever become a commercial success.

Bannerware

Software as advertisement is the best definition for bannerware. The software is not a product but a message that promotes something else, something that may not have the least association with programs, PCs, or the least human need. A free floppy disk advertising a new automobile is the premiere example of bannerware.

Because the PC has become one of the primary communications media, getting a message across as software has become commonplace. After all, that's what multimedia is all about. Often the best way to show off a product is to give a multi-faceted, interactive view. For example, you can look under the hood of a new car, count the cylinders, look up a table of options, preview the color schemes, and get the lifestyle hard-sell all from floppy disk. The goal in promoting a product is, of course, to make as many people aware of it as possible. Giving away the demon-stration software free and allowing it to be copied freely helps guarantee it the widest popular circulation.

Although the publisher of bannerware allows its free distribution, it retains full rights to its work. The publisher may enable you to make copies but retains the right to prohibit you from copying the images or sounds for your own purposes. You can't steal pictures of cars from a bannerware demo disk for your own purposes without permission of the publisher. In other words, bannerware is not a source for multimedia.

If you're looking to build a business based on multimedia, however, bannerware can open wide opportunities to you. In effect, a multimedia bannerware disk is the modern-day sponsored film.

Licensing

Multimedia means combining materials from many sources, some of which may not be your own. For example, you may want to use a particularly striking image you've seen in a magazine or a certain rock song that you think is appropriate for the mood of your presentation. You bought the magazine and record, so you figure you can just make them part of your extravaganza. Under the first sale doctrine they are yours anyway. But you don't get performance rights with your purchase nor will you get reproduction rights—authorization to make copies. Incorporating unlicensed works in your multimedia presentation will constitute copyright infringement and may open you to all sorts of liabilities (in addition to those you incur from whatever else is in your presentation).

In order to use someone else's work in your presentation, you must obtain a license to use the work. Material prepared specifically for use in presentations may be sold with a blanket license. For example, clip art libraries include reproduction licenses (otherwise the art would be useless for its intended purpose).

Subject Matter

What must you license to use in your multimedia productions? The answer is simple, anything that you don't do yourself. If you want to include the work other people do, you'll want to protect yourself with a contract or release (which is really just a form of contract).

Photographs and videos are the most problematic. If you do the photography or videography yourself, you of course have rights to your work. Unfortunately you may not have rights to the object that makes the image. If you photograph a recognizable person, you will need a release to use that person's image if you intend to commercially distribute your final production. There are many exceptions, but the safe strategy is to obtain a release. Similarly, you'll need a release to use images of nonpublic sites.

If you don't take a photograph yourself, you'll need the photographer's permission or license to use the image. Many commercial photographers now claim copyright to their work in photographing you, so you'll need to get the photographer's permission to use your own image. Some images that you may think are in the public domain may not be. For example, the Mona Lisa, has survived long past Leonardo Da Vinci's copyright, but a photographic reproduction may be covered by the photographer's copyright.

Don't forget that you also need rights to the software you distribute as part of your multimedia program. Certainly you will have written the code yourself, but not everything in your finished production will be your own. Although in general you don't need a license for the language software you use or the compiler that generates your code, other tools that you use may require licensing. You may use routines from a software library, a code module developed by someone else, you may even need a runtime routine to make everything work. Some of these are like clip art: You get a blanket license to use the routines (even in commercial products) when you purchase the software. Others (some Microsoft runtimes, for example) can be distributed free as long as you get permission. Still others (for example, some specialized runtime libraries) require licenses and payment for each and every copy you sell. The moral is to check everything before you distribute anything.

Permissions

The mechanics of getting permission depend on what you want permission for. Most photographers get their model and site releases when and whenever they take photographs. They don't wait to see what comes out and whether it will be worthwhile because their subject may disappear and never been seen again (at least in the case of anonymous models). They keep a pad of releases handy and get one signed for every person appearing. (Some lawyers recommend giving each model a dollar upon signing a release to ensure the contract is valid in all jurisdictions, some of which still require "compensation"—money changing hands—for enforceability.) If you actually hire a model, a release should be part of your contract. You can buy standard model releases from larger photographic supply stores.

Getting permission for still photographs that others have taken requires finding the source of the image. Fortunately, most published photos are now credited, and more credits include an agency name, particularly in the case of stock photographs. If you can find the photographer or agent, a call to whoever published the photograph will usually get the information you need. Stock photo agencies earn their livelihood from licensing images, so getting permission is easy once you swallow hard and decide to pay.

Many images are in the public domain. For example, many libraries have collections of historical photographs. In general, the copyright will have expired on any image made before 1920. Before the 1976 revision to the federal copyright law, the copyright term was 28 years with one renewal of an additional 28 year period. The 1976 act extended the life of copyrights still in effect so not all copyrights after 1920 have expired.

Government-owned images are generally in the public domain (as are government-sponsored films). You can usually obtain copies of the images you want at the cost of duplication from the agency that maintains or conserves them, for example the Library of Congress.

Performance rights for music (which you'll need to distribute songs as part of your multimedia presentation) are licensed chiefly by two organizations, the American Society of Composers, Authors, and Publishers (ASCAP) and Broadcast Music, Inc., (BMI), both which are located in New York City.

Rights to other works must often be individually negotiated. You'll have to find the owner of the work and make contact. Always assume that a work has an owner, one with a vicious copyright lawyer eager to send you certified letters.

Always ensure that the permission you obtain includes what you want to use the property for—multimedia. Because rights can be sold individually, most organizations will offer the minimum they can give you for the money. If all you obtain is multimedia rights of an image, you may not be able to use that image in an advertisement for your product—or in the book or movie based on your software. You'll want to get permission for future editions so you don't have to renegotiate everything each time you revise your software. And you'll want the permission to extend over the widest possible geography so your multimedia software can accompany the astronauts on the first Mars mission.

Protecting Your Rights

If you put a lot of work into a multimedia work, you'll want to ensure that you reap all the benefits. The first step is, of course, to copyright it. You'll want to register your copyright, too, because registration costs little, takes minimal effort (send in a form), and gives you a certificate you can frame.

In the United States, the Copyright Office, part of the Library of Congress, has charge of copyrights. The Copyright Office can supply you with free and accurate information about federal copyrights. It also dispenses the forms necessary for registering copyrights and administers the registration process. For information on copyrights, you can write:

> Copyright Office
> Library of Congress
> Washington, D.C. 20559

Alternately, call (202) 707-3000 during East Coast business hours. The Copyright Office also maintains a 24-hour *Forms Hotline* at (202) 707-9100. You must know what forms you need before calling. The Copyright Office only administers copyrights. It is prohibited from giving legal advice.

Unfortunately a copyright does not automatically disable the write circuitry of disk drives. Someone somewhere (and maybe everyone everywhere) will give it a spin and end up with a few more disks holding your handiwork. What can you do to protect your rights and profits?

First, you have to identify who has infringed your copyright. You can't just have a hunch that someone is duplicating your work. You have to know who that someone is. And you'll need to be able to prove that someone did the deed—that means witnesses and evidence.

You can take a variety of approaches, from a tap on the shoulder to hanging the infringer by his thumbs. If the copying isn't egregious and you just want it to stop (or to get paid for another copy of your software), you can write a letter. Simply explain that the illegal copy is a violation of a federal criminal statute and also opens the infringer to civil liability (damages) as well. If that doesn't work, you'll want to enlist a lawyer who can first add weight to your threat (lawyer stationery helps open people's eyes, but don't fake your own as that will get you in trouble). If the letter doesn't work, your lawyer will take care of the mechanics of pressing your case. If the copying involves a substantial number of copies or is otherwise egregious, you'll want a lawyer who specializes in intellectual property.

A variety of remedies are available if you can prove infringement. These include injunctions to prevent further copying and monetary damages. If you can prove criminal wrongdoing (making and selling lots of copies), a court can impose fines and even confine the infringer to prison.

Contracts

Whatever you do in multimedia, if it involves someone else, it will likely involve a contract, too. Stripped to its essence, a contract is an agreement between two or more people that can be legally enforced. A multimedia sales agreement, a model release, and a permission letter are all likely to be contracts.

The law of contracts can be summarized in a few paragraphs, but the details take an entire course of study. Knowing the rudiments will help you negotiate the legalities involved in making multimedia.

Contracts can involve anything as long as it is not illegal or against public policy. The only requirement is that you reach an agreement and that you intend your agreement to be binding. To help people have faith in what others agree to, courts will hold you to your contractual agreement. If you don't do what you agree to, a court will try to find a way to make things right—giving the aggrieved party what lawyers call a remedy. In general, if someone breaks a contract with you, you are entitled to whatever you would have been given were the contract fulfilled. Usually the harm you suffer is measured in money, called monetary damages. Ordinarily the amount of damages is only compensatory. You are entitled to nothing more than you would have gotten under the contract had it been fulfilled. However, if the failure of the other party in a contract leads you to suffer another loss (for example, you lose a big order because your floppy disks don't come in on the agreed day) you may be entitled to consequential damages, the amount of which should be equal to your loss. You are obligated to mitigate your damages if you can, for example by running to the computer store and buying more floppies (but if they cost more, you may recover the price difference as compensatory damages). In some egregious cases, however, a court can punish someone who breaks a contract with punitive damages, which may be any amount.

A contract is only enforceable by those who agree to it. After all, a contract is binding only on those who agree to it and the rights under the contract only extend to those who agree. If you order diskettes from a computer store and they don't deliver, you can't sue the maker of the disks because your contract was with the store. You can only sue the store, although the store can sue the manufacturer.

Contracts can be verbal or written. However, the Statute of Frauds requires that contracts that involve large values (generally in excess of $1,000) or take more than a year to complete must be evidenced by writing. The writing doesn't have to be a signed agreement. Once there is a signed agreement, however, no verbal agreements can change it. In other words, get it in writing. Spelling everything out in detail is particularly important with permissions because of the range of rights involved.

If you involve anyone in creating a multimedia work, you will want a written contract that spells out exactly what rights you and your co-workers have. If you suspect (or hope) to create the first solid platinum, million-selling multimedia CD, you'd better get the advice of a lawyer in advance, lest your profits go the way of all things and lawsuits.

Appendix B
Production Issues

Multimedia is a multi-effort. Unlike producing ordinary (shall we say, old-fashioned?) software where you could simply sit behind your monitor screen amid a pile of Coke cans and Clark bar wrappers and hack out the masterpiece to make you a millionaire, multimedia needs more. You need the images (still or moving), the sounds, a story, and the software to make a full multimedia production. Getting what you need runs the gamut of possibilities.

Doing It Yourself

The easy way is to do everything yourself. Redecorate the back bedroom with background paintings and props, stick the old video camera on a tripod, hang a mirror under the lens, then stand in front and grimace until the tape runs out. Take the old point-and-shoot camera and capture the squirrels at work. Give your kids a drum set and saxophone for their birthdays, and keep the cassette recorder running. Buy yourself a one-way ticket to the rest home.

Most multimedia presentations are hardly so elaborate that they require sets, costumes, or special talent. Most will involve charts and tables you can create with a presentation package or even a decent spreadsheet, sound that is little more than narration masked by slow sampling rates, and microphone technique hardly better than Alexander Graham Bell's. Most multimedia is, in fact, dedicated to in-house presentation, and the rules are the same as for any other presentation—that is, the rules get bent because everything gets kept inside the family. You use a cartoon clipped from the newspaper to make a point even though, legally speaking, you need a license to use it.

If suddenly you discover that, "Hey, I am good. No, a genius. This little presentation I prepared about pastel egg-crates for the marketing department is a little gem. People will pay for it. Break out the CD-R machine and I'll become instantly rich!" You're likely to get a quick education in the law, licensing, and a lot of Latin words brandished on court documents that you wish you'd never seen. Untangling the mess of a jumbled-together presentation will likely be harder than starting afresh and taking care to have good rights in what you use.

Fortunately you don't have to rely on your own drawings of stick people and box houses. There are several sources of high quality drawings and images that you can use without legal hassles or royalties. Many clip-art libraries allow free use of their images. You can even find elaborate drawings and photographs available through commercial sources that allow royalty-free distribution as part of your presentation. Some are offered by commercial software vendors (Corel has several big packages). Others you'll find on on-line services. Although you might not find exactly what you want, considering the price the images will likely be close enough.

If you're looking for the perfect sound or image, however, you'll likely have to make it yourself—or find someone to do the work for you. You may need to hire a studio.

Studios

Although there is much to say for the multimedia producer as *auteur*, professional-looking presentations depend on getting professional-level work. And that means hiring a professional. Even for something seemingly as simple as a still photograph, professionalism can make a difference. The entire mood and feeling of an image depends on its lighting. The right light can make the difference between a presentation that hits the mark or misfires.

Most of the still images you need for a multimedia presentation you can get into digital form yourself or with minimal help. All it takes is a scanner or a digital camera to turn paper into a computer file. If you want top quality, the easy solution is to have your favorite photo lab transfer your film images to PhotoCD. Most multimedia software will convert PhotoCD images to whatever image format it prefers.

Video is another story entirely. You spend a week trying to get a video sequence right using a camcorder and its built-in editing. You may be able to put together simple stuff on your PC and edit it down, adding effects, and mixing in sounds. But you'll still need the original images.

If you're serious about your presentation, you'll want to hire a studio to do the work. After all, nothing says "cheap home video" like a cheap home video. The professionals working in a studio have answers for questions you didn't even know to ask.

Most larger cities have video production studios, and nearly all television studios will sell their time for production.

Renting studio time is costly because you not only have to pay for equipment but its operators as well. The cost of studio time will pay for a good camcorder in a few hours. But a few hours should be all that it takes to get the footage you need for all but the lengthiest presentations.

It's all a trade-off. In one case you get a camera that you can keep, show your friends, and lose in some foreign land. You pay for it by spending weeks to make things look like they were done professionally. With the studio-crafted tape in your hand, you have a studio-crafted tape—and several extra weeks to spend on the trickier aspects of programming your presentation.

The key to making studio time affordable is to practice. There's no bigger waste of time and your budget than sitting on a television set trying to figure out how to best open the lid of a computer case while the camera operators chat among themselves and the floor director works out the day's crossword puzzle. You can avoid a dozen takes just by rehearsing, working things out, having your talent read the lines before walking in the studio door.

Contractors

One time or another, you'll need to hire a contractor to help you out when your multimedia project suddenly gets out of hand the day before it's due. The problem with contractors is that some are very good and others simply incompetent—and you can't tell them apart by looking at a business card or resume. You have to depend on references—and a contract with the teeth of a piranha.

Avoid the pitfalls. You need to set a specific completion date and penalty for not completing on time in the contract. You need to outline exactly what will be delivered in what form. If you're not experienced with a contractor, you'll need to provide for monitoring along the way so you can catch problems before they become disasters. And you need to define exactly what you're buying, particularly if you want the rights to the final work. If you expect your assignment to be work for hire, you must explicitly state that.

If your contractor comes complete with a contract and asks only that you sign on the dotted line, you might as well kiss your first-born child good-bye. Odds are the contractor has made sure his contract is bulletproof—after all, the contractor makes his living through contracts—and all the good stuff will go to the contractor and the bad stuff to you. If you want to even things up, you'll need your own professional to look for the loopholes. Get a leather strap, bite down hard, and call a lawyer.

Appendix C
Distribution

After you craft a multimedia piece, you've got to move it out if you hope to make your fortune. Goods do you no good when they sit on the shelf.

As with other aspects of multimedia, your choice is doing it yourself or getting someone else to handle the work. Often, however, you won't have a choice. Many books are written, but few are commercially published.

But with software, at least there's hope. Although many books are self-published or printed by "vanity" presses (which charge you for printing instead of paying you for your writing), most end up on the bookshelves of friends and relatives. The rest get recycled or pulped into bedding for hamsters. Self-published software, however, supports hundreds of people and has made some authors wealthy.

Commercial Distribution

It sounds like the ideal profession. You send out some little thing that you've created, and every month thereafter you get a check in the mail. It works that way with book publishing (except, perhaps for the part about the check coming with any periodicity—and about it being a little thing. More like several years' work and thousands of gallons of ink, sweat, and tears). You need to link with a publisher who will handle the distribution and send you the check. Unfortunately, finding a publisher isn't easy. Usually publishers find you, often through an agent. Most multimedia works are commissioned.

The good part of working for a publisher is that you do the fun stuff—the creative work—and the publisher handles all the mundane details, such as manufacturing or copying, advertising, distribution, bookkeeping, and embezzlement. On the other hand, you lose control of the same factors. If the publisher screws up on publicity and advertising so that even your mother doesn't know of your grand *oeuvre*, you're out of luck and out of royalties.

The rights you give to a publisher and those that you retain are all governed by the contract between the two of you (back to Appendix A, "Multimedia Law"). As with the rest of life, everything is negotiable. If you view your creation as valuable or potentially so, you need the help of a professional in negotiating the contract. After all, the publisher is a professional or may hire a specialist to negotiate the contract. You should protect yourself with an agent or at least have an attorney read and interpret the legalese of the contract for you. It's only self-defense.

Self-Distribution

The alternative is to do the publishing yourself. If you've just inherited half the assets of General Motors, you might want to set yourself up like one of the professionals, with editors, marketers, publicists, a production department, a shipping department, and an ulcer the size of Iowa. Even if you plan to go about self-publishing in a minimal way, you still have to budget thousands and tens of thousands of dollars for duplication and packaging. Then you have to learn to love a life on the road, driving from town to town with a trunk full of packages that you have to cajole or blackmail retailers into stocking. It can be done, but it takes dedication and a certain leave of reality.

Fortunately, the computer world has developed its own, lower-cost publishing and distribution system that relies on the electronic transportability of digital code and the good nature and generosity of the common man. (Well, one out of three isn't bad.) It's called *shareware.*

Shareware has become the leading way to distribute self-published software. It is as close in concept to the vanity press as software comes, but offers greater returns at less cost for both the publisher and user.

For you as a consumer, shareware offers the benefit of relatively low prices coupled with the opportunity to try before you buy. Although you often get what you pay for (or refuse to), some shareware programs are every bit as good as higher-priced commercial alternatives. Many are even better suited to their tasks than their mass-market rivals and thus offer you an even better value.

For you operating as a multimedia developer, shareware is the most affordable way of gaining entry into the market. The shareware industry is more a meritocracy than is commercial distribution, in which sales are more dependent on publicity. Shareware succeeds on its merits. As shareware, the better product is more likely to succeed. Do a good job and you may be rewarded; do shaky work and you might as well write for yourself alone.

Getting yourself started as a commercial software vendor requires a huge investment, probably millions of dollars in today's market. If you're not independently wealthy or don't have friends who are both wealthy and speculative (often a kind way of saying foolish), you've got to depend on outside investment. That's not easy. Venture capital firms prefer a strong track record to a strong product, and usually invest only when they find both together. They want to back someone who's already proven successful because the goal is to make money, not finance your dreams. Of course you end up in the bind of not getting published the first time because you've not been published before. Philosophers have nightmares trying to sort that one out.

Shareware provides the avenue for establishing your success. If you're good, you can supplement the income from your day job. If you're great, you can live off your product. And if you're blessed, you can found a multimillion dollar business.

Now for the realism department. According to shareware experts, a really successful shareware product (one in the top 1 percent of all shareware) gets about 2,000 registrations. Most shareware offerings get far fewer than that. If you charge reasonably for your offering, you won't become a millionaire overnight. (Shareware is typically priced at about one-half the price of its commercial equivalent. Deduct your cost of registration—a disk, printed manual, and support—from the price to determine your gross margin, which may not be very gross.)

You'll find that most shareware distribution services are already stuffed full of various multimedia utilities aimed at multimedia creation and manipulation—viewers, control centers, sound systems, editors, and the like—but end-user offerings are more modest. Of course, the potential market for end-user multimedia presentations is much, much larger. Maybe you can see an opportunity.

Whatever you choose to do in shareware, you must remember to be successful you must run your business as a business. You need to plan not only your product but its marketing. One of the best guides to developing a shareware business plan is itself shareware, a book written by Bob Schenot called *The ShareBook*, which is available through many on-line services and bulletin boards. You can also order it directly from the author at PO Box 117, Portsmouth, New Hampshire 03802 by paying the $24.95 registration fee up front.

Creating a Product

If you're considering shareware, first determine whether your product lends itself to shareware distribution. Hard experience has shown that some kinds of software are better suited to commercial distribution, others to shareware. Various kinds of multimedia software fall into each realm.

Games overall have not fared well as shareware. After all, games are probably the most pirated class of commercial software. There's no reason a game copier will be more honest with shareware than commercial programs. Shareware writers are experimenting with new registration (and payment) incentives for games, but there's no wide consensus as to their success. In general, you write a game because writing it itself is a fun project. You share the game with the same pride as a mom or dad showing off pictures of the new baby. If anyone actually registers, it's a bonus. And they're likely to be a relative.

Business software, on the other hand, has been one of the great success stories in shareware. Multimillion dollar companies have emerged from shareware startups that offered business-oriented shareware. One reason for this success is that most businesses tend to pay for the

602 Section IV: Appendixes

software they use, whether commercially distributed or obtained as shareware. Efforts by the Software Publishers Association have raised awareness of the penalties for illegal copying and have encouraged companies to keep "clean." The lawsuit for illegally copying shareware is just as nasty and expensive as that for commercial software.

Next, you must be sure that your multimedia offering itself is legal. Before offering for sale any software, insure that you have rights for every screen, every sound, every story, every software routine. Then make sure that you eradicated every bug from your software. You might want to have friends or associates serves as beta testers to ensure you haven't missed anything. You have to ensure your program gets a strong positive response so that people will share their discovery with others. If they run into problems or can't get the program to work at all, your multimedia bombshell may itself bomb.

After you eliminate the bugs, eliminate the uglies and gotchas. Multimedia is about images, and not just those the user sees on the screen. The control screens, the installation process, the documentation, even the packaging (in the case of shareware, how you put modules and files together) all reflect on the quality of the product and whether people will want to use, share, and pay for it. Elegance is a big part of image. Your software should be elegant in appearance and use. The easier and more intuitive it is to use, the more people will use it.

Document it. Sure, multimedia lends itself to exploration, but what seems natural to you won't be for everyone. They won't know all the potential of your program unless you tell them—and tell them how to do it. Shareware documentation generally gets distributed as a plain ASCII file with a minimum of formatting so that it will print on the widest selection of hardware. Too much formatting and special typefaces will frustrate users who lack exactly the right equipment. Someone who has only WordPerfect doesn't look in joy at receiving a file that needs Microsoft Word. Besides, a typeset-quality manual is one of the rewards you can offer as incentive for registration.

Shareware Help

Many organizations provide more specific instructions on how to create and market shareware. There's even an industry association that promotes quality and professionalism among shareware authors named (rather appropriately) the *Association of Shareware Professionals*. The Association is an excellent source of information about shareware and can provide you with lengthy lists of support organizations that can duplicate disks, distribute your shareware, and help you gain publicity. Dues are currently $75 per year, and anyone can obtain a membership by writing, phoning, or faxing a request to the following address:

Association of Shareware Professionals
545 Grover Rd
Muskegon MI 49442

Phone: 616-788-5131
FAX: 616-788-2765
CompuServe ID: 72050,1433

Shareware is physically distributed through several different channels. The name hints at one: sharing with your friends. The entire concept underlying shareware is that you make copies of the software for people who you think might benefit from it. They pay for it if it gives them some benefit.

But shareware reaches beyond friends. It has a worldwide electronic reach. Shareware distribution is one of the most important services of the computer bulletin board service or BBS. These range from local extensions of users' groups to international commercial services like America On-Line, CompuServe, and Prodigy. The typical BBS has an extensive library of shareware programs that you can download into your PC for free. Different bulletin board services have their own rules about what software they accept for listing in their libraries. Local BBSs will often take anything that's not immoral, illegal, or too fat to fit on their file server. The commercial services exercise greater selectivity. If you don't have time to send copies of your work all over creation, you can hire a *shareware broker* who will, for a fee, distribute your program to a wide array of BBSs.

Several organizations distribute shareware on disk like commercial software. However, these distributors pay you as the program producer no royalty but neither do they charge you a commission on the registration fees you receive. They publish catalogs of the shareware they make available, and sell disks at a price that reflects their overhead (cost of producing the catalog, maintaining the library, the disk itself, and mailing) and add in their profit. Hardly parasites, they provide the shareware author an important service: they extend the reach of his product. For example, one large disk distributor, Public Brand Software, sends out over a quarter million copies of its shareware catalog. You can contact them for a catalog or to see if they will list your program at:

Public Brand Software
25 First St.
Cambridge, MA 02141
(800) 426-3475

Shareware and multimedia provide you with an opportunity. What you do with it and what you get from it depends on how much you want to do and involve yourself. With a little luck you can find a pot of gold hidden at the end of the rainbow—or you can simply sit back, look at the pretty colors, and enjoy.

Index

Numerics

16-bit processing
upgrading to 32-bit, 159-162
Windows 95 compatibility, 170
16-bit real mode drivers, 219
16450 UART chip, 368-369
16550 UART chip, 369-370
2-D images, 249
3-D images, 249
3.3-volt chips, 308-309
3.5-inch floppy disks, 350
30-pin SIMMs, 332-333
32-bit disk access, 160-161
32-bit file access, 160-162
32-bit processing
386 chips, 311-313
486 chips, 313-316
enabling, 160-161
features (Windows), 160-162
history of OS/2, 191-192
Pentium chips, 316-318
AMD K5 chips, 320-321
Cyrix M1 chips, 321-322
NexGen 586 chips, 322-323

Pentium OverDrive chips, 318-320
upgrading Windows, 159-162
Windows 95, 170
Windows 95 (history of Windows), 157-158
32-bit protected mode drivers, 219
386 chips, 311-313
386DX chips, 312
386SL chips, 312
386SPART.PAR (permanent swap files), 165
386SX chips, 312
486 chips, 313-316
math coprocessors, 307
486DX chips, 313
486DX2 chips, 314
486DX2 OverDrive chips, 314
486DX4 chips, 314
486SL chips, 314-315
486SX chips, 314
486SX2 chips, 314
5 volt chips, 308-309
5.25 inch floppy disks, 350
72-pin SIMMs, 332-333
8250 UART chip, 368
86C911 chip (graphics accelerator), 453
8mm video cassettes, 432

A

A.D.A.M. The Inside Story (educational software), 26
absolute resolution, 249
access times
CD drives, 404
hard disk speed, 336
acoustic suspension loudspeakers, 517
acoustical labyrinth speakers, 518
acoustics, 513-515
air pressure, 514-515
frequencies, 514
human hearing, 515
properties of sound, 513
wavelengths, 514
active matrix (monitors), 502-503
active partitions (OS/2), 154, 194
active speaker systems, 520
Ad Lib soundboards, 537
Adaptive Digital Pulse Code Modulation (ADPCM), 80
ADC (analog-to-digital) converters, 41, 43
additive synthesis, 534
addressability (hard drives), 48-49

addresses
device drivers, 131-133, 204
memory, 130-131
addressing
block addressing (SCSI), 346
CHS addressing, 149
LBA (Logical Block Addressing), 150
advanced synthesis, 536-537
aftertouch (MIDI), 575
AIFF (Audio Interchange File Format), 283-284
air pressure (relationship to sound), 514-515
Aldus Persuasion (graphics presentations authoring software), 96
aliases (Windows 95 filenames), 175-176
AMD (Advanced Micro Devices) 386 chips, 312
AMD (Advanced Micro Devices) K5 chips, 320-321
American Standard Code for Information Interchange (ASCII), 237-241
amplifiers (speakers), 520
amplitude modulated video signals, 425
analog audio signals, 526
analog data transmissions, compared to digital, 7-8
analog image controls (monitors), 508
analog synthesis, 533-534
analog-to-digital (ADC) converters, 41, 43

anatomy (educational software), 26
animation, 95
spline-based animation, 94
Sprite animation, 94
WinToon (authoring software), 106-107
aperture grilles (monitors), 499
apertures (video cameras), 483-486
API (Application Program Interface), 134
application-level programming, 122
applications, 135
basic multimedia applications, 61-74
CD players, 67-68
Multimedia Viewer, 64-67
system sounds, 72-74
video players, 68-72
Windows Help, 62-64
compatibility with Windows 95, 169-171
DOS support, 146
multimedia file conversions, 296
OLE (Object Linking and Embedding), 74-77
arbitrated buses, 324
ASCII (American Standard Code for Information Interchange), 237-241
aspect ratios (monitors), 506
assembly language (programming software), 120

Association of Shareware Professionals, 602-603
Astound! (graphics presentations authoring software), 96
asymmetrical video compression, 254
asynchronous ports, 366
AT Attachment (IDE) specification, 48-49
CD drives, 407
hard disks, 339-345
AT keyboards, 358
ATAPI (ATA Packet Interface), 343-344
attributes (pixels), 435-436
audio, 511-554
acoustics, 513-515
air pressure, 514-515
analog signals, 526
CDs (Compact Discs), 9-10
compression, 257-258
connections, CD-ROM drives, 408
current-limiting resistors, 529
device drivers, 553
digital music (CDs), 7
digital signals, 526-527
digitization, 256
DSPs (Digital Signal Processors), 544-551
MWave, 546
Signal Computing Architecture, 546-547
VCOS, 547
Windows DSP, 547-551
electronic integration, 33

file formats
    AIFF (Audio Inter-
        change File Format),
        283-284, 288
    converting, 296
    IBK (Instrument
        Bank), 284-285
    MIDI (Musical
        Instrument Digital
        Interface), 285-287
    MOD, 287-288
    RMI, 288
    SBI (Sound Blaster
        Instrument),
        288-289
    SND, 290-291
    VOC, 291-294
    WAV, 294-295
files
    control, 282-283
    descriptor, 282
    waveform, 283
frequencies, 257, 514
history of PC sounds,
    527-530
human hearing, 515
inputs on monitors, 508
links with video random
    access, 13
microphones, 493,
    521-526
    condenser micro-
        phones, 522
    connectors, 525-526
    directionality, 523
    dynamic micro-
        phones, 521-522
    impedance, 524-525
    physical characteris-
        tics, 524
    piezoelectric micro-
        phones, 522-523

signal level, 524-525
sound quality, 525
MIDI (Musical Instru-
    ment Digital Interface),
    555-578
    aftertouch, 575
    channels/voices,
        558-566
    connectors, 557
    encoding notes,
        570-575
    messages, 566-570
    patch maps, 559-566
    playback, 576-578
    Song Position
        Pointer, 570
    speed of processing,
        557
    Status/Data Bytes,
        570-575
    synchronizing,
        575-576
    transmitters/receivers,
        556-557
    UART chips, 556
    Windows, 565-566
MPC 1.0 performance
    standards, 41-42
multimedia
    aspects, 13
    potential, 23
oscillators, 527-528
PCM (pulse code modula-
    tion), 256
performance standards
    sound boards, 51-52
pre-production, 111-113
producing multimedia
    presentations, 37-38
properties of sound, 513
pulse-width modulation,
    528-529

recording, 256
resolution, 257
sampling rates, 257,
    531-532
sampling sounds (produc-
    ing multimedia
    presentations), 86
software, Sound Forge,
    111-113
soundboards, 512,
    530-531
    configuring, 551-553
    installing, 551-554
    wiring speakers,
        553-554
speakers, 515-520
    amplifiers, 520
    baffles, 516-518
    location/coupling,
        519-520
    multi-speaker systems,
        518-519
    resonance, 517
    stereophonic imaging,
        520
storing, 259, 282-295
synthesis, 532-551
    Ad Lib, 537
    additive synthesis, 534
    advanced synthesis,
        536-537
    compression, 543-544
    FM synthesis, 535
    Sound Blaster,
        538-543
    standards, 537-543
    subtractive synthesis,
        533-534
    wave table synthesis,
        535-536
system sounds, 72-74

timbre, 532
troubleshooting
  CD-ROM drives, 414
voice annotation
    embedding objects, 81
    recording, 78-81
wavelengths, 514
Windows 3.1 device
  drivers, 529-530
authoring software, 87-88
  computer-based training,
    88, 99-101
      TIE Authoring
        System, 100-101
      TourGuide, 100
  hypertext, 88-93
      Guide, 92-93
      MediaView
        Libraries, 91
      Multimedia
        ToolBook, 93
      Multimedia Viewer
        2.0, 90-91
      WinHelp 4.0, 91-92
  presentations (graphics),
    88, 93-99
      Aldus Persuasion, 96
      Astound!, 96
      Authorware Profes-
        sional for
        Windows, 97
      ForShow, 97
      IconAuthor, 97
      ImageQ, 97-98
      Macromedia Director,
        98-99
      Q/Media, 99
  programming languages,
    88, 101-107
      Delphi, 103
      MCI (Media Control
        Interface), 104-105

MCIWnd, 104-106
ObjectView, 103
OpenGL, 105
PowerBuilder, 103
SQLWindows, 103
Visual Basic, 104
WinG, 106
WinToon, 106-107
**Authorware Professional for
Windows (graphics
presentations authoring
software), 97**
AUTOEXEC.BAT file, 146
loading device drivers, 206
    command-line, 206
    DOS, 204
**automatic device driver
installation, 206, 215-216**
**autosizing images (moni-
tors), 506-507**
AV drives, 336-337
**AVI (Audio/Video Inter-
leaved) files, 69, 106**
  chunks
      headers, 278
      index, 277
      LIST, 277
  data type identifying
    characters, 279
  starting bytes, 277
  stream headers, 278-279
  video format, 277-280

B

**back porches (video
signals), 422**
backlit LCDs, 501
**backups, the Registry
(Windows 95), 180**
baffles, 516-518

bandwidth, 8
  color video requirements,
    435-436
  monitors, 505
**bank-switching (VGA video
adapters), 459**
**bannerware (copyright law),
589-590**
**BASIC (Beginner's All-
purpose Symbolic
Instruction Code), 120**
Basic Channels (MIDI), 567
**Basic Input/Output System
(BIOS), 48, 128-133**
  boot sequence, 128-129
  boot-strap loader, 129
  device drivers, 131-132
  hardware interface,
    130-131
  initialization code, 128
  input/output mapping, 130
  memory addresses,
    130-131
  memory mapping, 130
  Plug-and-Play, 132-133
  pointers, 128
  ports, 130-131
  POST (Power-On Self-
    Test), 129
  ROM (Read-Only
    Memory), 129
  speed, 130
**bass reflex enclosure
speakers, 518**
bauds (modem speed), 379
**BBSs (bulletin board
services) shareware
distribution, 603**
**BCD (Binary Coded
Decimal), 228**
**Beethoven's Fifth (enter-
tainment software), 33**

Beginner's All-purpose Symbolic Instruction Code (BASIC), 120
bi-directional microphones, 523
big-screen viewfinders, 492
.BIN file extension, 71
Binary Coded Decimal (BCD), 228
binary files (QuickTime movies), 71
BIOS (Basic Input/Output System), 48, 128-133
  boot sequence, 128-129
  boot-strap loader, 129
  booting up DOS (Disk Operating System), 144-146
  device drivers, 131-132
  hardware interface, 130-131
  initialization code, 128
  input/output mapping, 130
  LBA (Logical Block Addresses) access, 343
  memory addresses, 130-131
  memory mapping, 130
  operating systems, 134
  Plug-and-Play, 132-133, 181, 187-188
  pointers, 128
  ports, 130-131
  POST (Power-On Self-Test), 129
  relationship to device drivers, 202
  ROM (Read-Only Memory), 129
  storage capacity (DOS), 149-150

speed, 130
VESA BIOS Extension, 463-468
bit-images, 456
BitFAT, 150
Bitmap File Header, 260-261
bitmap info header, JPEG, 260
bitmapped images, 247
  compressed, 248
  core info block, 260
  info blocks, 260
  pixels, interpolation, 248
  resolution, 248
bits, 303-304, 332
blanking (video signals), 421-422
block addressing (SCSI), 346
blocks
  control, 263
  graphic-rendering, 263
  special purpose, 263
  memory, 152
BMP still image formats, 260-262
BNC connectors (video signals), 433-434
Boot Manager (OS/2), 195
boot manager partitions (OS/2), 194
boot sequence, 128-129
booting up
  DOS (Disk Operating System), 144-146
  Plug-and-Play expansion boards, 184-185
bootstrap loaders, 129, 145
Borland C++, 102
bounding box in .EPS files, 262

branch prediction
  Cyrix M1 chips, 321
  NexGen 586 chips, 322-323
bridging inputs (video signals), 433
brightness controls (monitors), 507
brightness levels (Kodak PhotoCD), 398-399
Britannica CD (reference software), 29
buffers
  16550 UART chips, 369-370
  CD drives, 404
  frame buffers (memory-mapped video), 435
bugs (Pentium chips), 317-318
bulletin board services (BBSs) shareware distribution, 603
bus connections (microprocessors), 304
bus mice, 360
buses, *see* expansion buses
buttons
  digitizing tablets, 362
  joysticks, 377
  mice, 359-360
byte orders (numerical values), storing, 246
bytes, 332

C

C programming language, 101-102
C++ programming language, 102

CAB32.EXE file, 171

cable connections

  SCSI devices, 348

  VESA standards, 471-475

  VGA video adapters,
    471-475

  video signals, 432-434

caching (memory), 305-307

  Cyrix M1 chips, 321

  integrated disk cache
    (Windows 95), 177

  Pentium chips, 317

  performance standards, 46

  VCache (32-bit process-
    ing), 161-162

caddies (CDs), 405

cameras (video), 477-493

  color filters, 479

  encoding images, 490

  f-stops, 483-486

  field of view, 481-482

  focal length, 480-481

  focusing, 487-488

  lenses, 477, 480-486

  microphones, 493

  optical transducers, 477

  optics, 478-489

  recording, 492-493

  resolution, 479-480

  scanning, 489

  sensors, 478

  shutters, 486-487

  special effects, 491

  stability of images,
    488-489

  tripods, 488

  viewfinders, 477, 492

  white balancing, 490-491

  zoom ratios,
    480-481, 487

capturing

  graphics, 85

  text, 84-85

  video, 443-444

    producing multimedia
      presentations, 85-86

    step capture, 445

**Card Select Number (CSN),
  185-186**

cardioid microphones, 523

cathode ray tubes, *see* **CRTs**

**CBT (Computer Based
  Training), 32**

**CCDs (Charge-Coupled
  Devices), 478-480**

**CCIT G.711 A-Law and
  u-Law audio compression,
  258**

**CD-DA (Digital Audio)
  standard, 395-396**

CD-ROM drives, 402-409

  access times, 404

  buffers, 404

  compared to audio CD
    drives, 402-403

  device drivers, 207-208,
    409-413

  interfaces, 406-409

  performance standards, 49

  physical characteristics, 405

  software applications,
    67-68

  transfer rates, 403-404

  troubleshooting, 413-414

  volume controls, 405-406

CD-ROMs, *see* **CDs**

**CDFS (Compact Disc File
  System), 169, 174**

**CDs (compact discs), 7-10,
  387-414**

  ATAPI (ATA Packet
    Interface), 343-344

CD drives, 402-409

  access times, 404

  ATA interfaces, 407

  audio connections,
    408

  buffers, 404

  compared to audio
    CD drives, 402-403

  device drivers,
    409-413

  interfaces, 406-409

  parallel interfaces,
    407-408

  physical characteris-
    tics, 405

  power connections,
    409

  proprietary interfaces,
    408

  SCSI interfaces,
    406-407

  software applications,
    67-68

  transfer rates,
    403-404

  troubleshooting,
    413-414

  volume controls,
    405-406

constant linear velocity
  recording, 391

costs, 16-17

error detection/correction,
  393

history, 387-388

large frames (sectors),
  392-393

manufacturing, 390-391

MPC 1.0 performance
  standards, 41

MPC 2.0 performance
  standards, 42-43

optical technology, 388-389
random access, 389
recordable CDs, 391-392
sector address tag field, 392-393
size, 389-390
small frames, 393
speed of data processing, 9
standards, 394-402
  CD-DA (Digital Audio), 395-396
  CD-ROMs, 401-402
  Green Book standard, 395
  High Sierra, 401-402
  ISO 9660, 401-402
  Kodak PhotoCD, 396-401
  Orange Book standard, 395
  Red Book standard, 395
  Yellow Book standard, 395
storage capacity, 16, 22, 28-29
tracks, 394
XA (Extended Architecture), 393
cells (animation), 95
channels (MIDI), 558-567
character modes (VGA video adapters), 460
Charge-Coupled Devices (CCDs), 478-480
chips (microprocessors), 302
486 chips, 307
AMD 386 chips, 312
AMD K5 chips, 320-321
bus connections, 304

Chips and Technologies 386 chips, 312-313
clock speeds, 304-305
Cyrix 486 chips, 315
Cyrix M1 chips, 321-322
direct-mapped caches, 306
DX2 chips, 305
EDO memory, 307
external clock speeds, 305
IBM 386SLC chips, 313
IBM 486SLC2 chips, 315
IBM Blue Lightning chips, 316
instruction sets, 303
Intel chips, 303
  386 chips, 311-313
  386DX, 312
  386SL, 312
  386SX, 312
  486 chips, 313-315
  486DX, 313
  486DX2 OverDrive, 314
  486DX4, 314
  486SL, 314-315
  486SX, 314
  clock-doubled 486 chips, 314
  history, 309-311
  Pentium, 305, 316-318
  Pentium OverDrives, 308, 318-320
internal clock speeds, 305
math coprocessors, 307-308
memory caching, 305-307
NexGen 586 chips, 322-323
power consumption, 309
primary caches, 305-306

registers, 303-304
secondary caches, 305-306
set-associative caches, 306
voltages, 308-309
write-back caches, 307
write-through caches, 306
Chips and Technologies 386 chips, 312-313
chrominance, 426
images, 253
video signals, 424-425, 432
CHS (Cylinder, Head, Sector) addressing, 149
chunks, 294
files, 259
headers, 278
index, 277
LIST, 277
Cinepak video compression, 254
class libraries, 122
classes (object-oriented programming), 102
clip-art libraries, 596
clipboard (Windows), 77
clock speeds
microprocessors, 304-305
NexGen 586 chips, 323
Pentium chips, 316
SCSI, 346
clock-doubled 486 chips, 314
cloning (still images), 107-108
clusters, DOS (Disk Operating System), 148-151
CLUTs (Color Look-Up Tables), 251, 439
CMYK color scheme, 438
coaxial connectors, video signals, 433-434

Code Excited Linear Predictor speech compression, 258
codecs (video compression), 441-442
color, 435-443
attributes (pixels), 435-436
CMYK color scheme, 438
codecs (video compression), 441-442
color filters (video cameras), 479
color space conversion, 438
compressing images, 266-268
direct mapping, 439
encoding, 438, 490
graphics accelerators memory requirements, 455
Kodak PhotoCD system, 398-399, 438
memory requirements, 249, 437-438
memory-mapped displays, standards, 442-443
monitors, 495, 503
color tracking, 504
convergence, 497-498
pixels, 435-436
planes, 436-438
recording video signals, 432
resolution (video), 51, 441
separations, 436-437
true color video systems, 437
VGA video adapters, 437-438, 459-463
video compression, 440-442

video signals, 423-426
Windows, 439-440
Color Look-Up Tables (CLUTs), 251, 439
color mapping, 250-251
color scanners, 364
color tables, 260-261
color temperature
monitors, 495-496
video cameras, 490-491
color-mapped image files
Run-Length Encoded, 273-274
uncompressed, 271-272
COM ports, 366
COMM.DRV, 210
command processor (DOS), 147
command sets (microprocessors), 118-119
command-line device drivers, loading, 206
command-line interfaces, 125
COMMAND.COM file, 144, 147
commands
DEVICEHIGH, 204
Edit menu, Paste Special command, 77
external commands, 147
internal commands, 147
LOADHIGH, 204
MCI (Media Control Interface), 104-105, 213
RTF (Rich Text Format) control codes, 242
Windows 95 file manipulation, 177
COMMDLG.DLL
file, 159
library, 209

commercial distribution (creating multimedia presentations), 599-600
common messages (MIDI), 569
communications methods (multimedia aspects), 12
Compact Disc File System (CDFS), 169, 174
Compact Discs, *see* **CDs**
compatibility, Windows 95, 169-171
compiled programming languages, 121
compiling
hypertext links, 89
multimedia presentations, 86-87
Complete Guide to Symptoms, Illness & Surgery (reference software), 30
complex instructions (programming software), 119
composite sync video systems, 424
compound files (OLE), 76
compressing
audio, 257-258
audio synthesizers, 543-544
bitmapped images, 248
color images, 266-268
data, 8, 252, 381
directory-based, 252
GIF (Graphic Interchange Format), 263
hard disks, 337-338
DOS file structure, 150-151
DOS files, 145

history of DOS, 142
loading device
drivers, 205
images, 250-253
JPEG (Joint Photographic
Experts Group), 252-253
Kodak PhotoCD, 400-401
Lempel-Ziv, 252
video, 253-256, 440-442
**Compton's Interactive
Encyclopedia (reference
software), 29**
**Computer Based Training
(CBT), authoring soft-
ware, 32**
producing multimedia
presentations, 88,
99-101
TIE Authoring System,
100-101
TourGuide, 100
computers, *see* **PCs**
condenser microphones, 522
CONFIG.SYS file, 145, 193
automatic device driver
installation, 206
essential DOS device
drivers, 206-208
loading device drivers
DOS (Disk Operating
System), 204
Windows 95,
219-220
configuring
DOS (Disk Operating
System), 145-146
modems, 382-383
monitors, 508-510
OS/2 device drivers,
224-225
soundboards, 551-553
Windows, 167-168

Windows 95, 178-189
accommodating old
device drivers,
182-184
hardware, 180-189
Plug-and-Play,
180-189
the Registry,
178-180
connectors, 471
microphones, 525-526
MIDI, 557
SCSI devices, 348
VESA standards, 471-475
VGA video adapters,
471-475
video signals, 432-434
**constant linear velocity
recording (CDs), 391, 404**
context switching, 123
contracts
creating multimedia
presentations, 597
licensing, 593-594
**contrast controls (moni-
tors), 507**
control audio files, 282-283
control blocks, 263
extension, 265
global color tables,
263-264
headers, 263
image descriptors,
263-264
logical screen
descriptors, 263
trailers, 263, 265
control codes (data), 237
**Control Panel (Windows),
editing SYSTEM.INI file,
216-218**

**Control Program for
Microprocessors
(CP/M), 139**
control words, 242-243
**conventional video
viewfinders, 492**
**convergence (monitors),
497-498**
converting
file formats, 296-297
formatted text files, 242
video signals between
standards, 428
**cooperative multi-tasking,
124, 159**
**coprocessors (math),
307-308**
Cyrix M1 chips, 322
Pentium chips, 317
**copying files
(Windows 95), 176**
copyright law, 582-590
bannerware, 589-590
crippleware, 589
expression of ideas,
582-584
fair use, 587
first sale doctrine, 586
freeware, 588
infringement, 586-587
issuance of copyrights,
584-585
notice of copyright,
585-586
public domain, 588-590
registering copyrights,
592-593
rights, 587-588
shareware, 589
term of copyrights, 586
work for hire, 587

Corel PhotoPaint 5 Plus (photo editing), 108
costs of multimedia, 16-17
  CDs (Compact Discs), 16-17
  online connections, 18
  presentation authoring software, 95
  upgrading PCs compared to purchasing Multimedia PCs, 55
coupling (speakers), 519-520
CP/M (Control Program for Microprocessors), 139
creating multimedia presentations, 595-597
    contractors, 597
    distribution, 599-603
    studios, 596-597
    testing, 602
crippleware (copyright law), 589
cross-platform compatiblity, QuickTime (video player), 71-72
CRTs (cathode ray tubes), 420, 494-500
  aperture grilles, 499
  color, 495
  convergence, 497-498
  dot-pitch, 498
  electron guns, 496-497
  matrix colors, 499
  persistence, 496
  phosphors, 494-495
  projection systems, 500
  shadow masks, 498-499
  white balancing, 495-496
CSN (Card Select Number), 185-186

current-limiting resistors, 529
cursors
  digitizing tablets, 362
  VGA video adapters, 461-462
Cylinder, Head, Sector (CHS) addressing, 149
Cyrix 486 chips, 315
Cyrix M1 chips, 321-322

D

DACs (Digital-to-Analog Converters), 41, 43, 456-457
data
  compression, 8, 250-253, 263, 381
  control codes, 237
  non-repeating, 251
  translation (applications), 135
  transmission, 263
  voice, storing, 291-294
Data Bytes (MIDI), 558, 570-575
Data Migration Facility, 374
Data Terminal Equipment (DTE), 367
data transfer rates (ATA hard disk interfaces), 341-342
DCE (Data Communications Equipment), 367
DCI (Display Control Interface), 457
debuggers (programming software), 122
decoding image pixels, 260

defining hot spots (producing multimedia presentations), 85
deleting images, 265
delimiters, 243
Delphi (programming authoring software), 103
descriptors
  audio files, 282
  bytes, 271-272
design of GUIs (graphical user interfaces), 127-128
desktops (interfaces), 128
Detroit (entertainment software), 33
device drivers, *see* drivers
device independent bitmap format (RDIB), 259
device names (MCI), 213-214
DEVICEHIGH command, 204
DIB (Device Independent Bitmaps) engine, 172
digital audio signals, 526-527
digital control, 6
digital image controls (monitors), 508
digital media, 6-7
digital music (CDs), 7
Digital Signal Processors (DSPs), 380, 544-551
  MWave, 546
  Signal Computing Architecture, 546-547
  VCOS, 547
  Windows DSP, 547-551
digital synthesis, 534
digital technology, 6-8
  audio software, 111-113
  bandwidth, 8

CDs (Compact Discs), 9-10
  compared to analog, 7-8
  noise (CD players), 68
  noise reduction, 7-8
  resolution, 8
  speed of data processing, 7
Digital-to-Analog Convert-ers (DACs), 41, 43, 456-457
digitial recording (voice annotation), 78-81
digitization, audio (pulse code modulation), 256
digitizing tablets, 362-363
direct color mapping, 439
Direct Memory Access (DMA), 341-342
direct-mapped caches, 306
direct-mapped images, 251
directionality of micro-phones, 523
directory-based compres-sion, 252
disk compression, 337-338
  DOS file structures, 150-151
  DOS files, 145
  history of DOS, 142
  loading device drivers, 205
disk drives, booting up, 129
Disk Operating System, *see* **DOS**
Display Control Interface (DCI), 457
displaying images, 265
dissolve (slide show transi-tion), 94
distribution (creating multimedia presentations), 599-603

DLLs (Dynamic Link Libraries), 209-210
DMA (Direct Memory Access), 341-342, 551
DMF (Distribution Media Format), 153, 351
documenting shareware, 602
DOS (Disk Operating System), 139-154
  application support, 146
  booting up, 144-146
  command processor, 147
  configuring, 145-146
  device drivers, 203-208
  disk compression, 150-151
  DOS drivers in Windows, 208-209
  essential files, 144
  file system, 148-151
  history, 139-143
  initializing serial ports, 370-371
  installing, 153-154
  loading device drivers, 204-206, 223
  memory management, 151-152
  MSCDEX.EXE (CD device driver), 409-410
  multitasking, 146-147
  OS/2 compatibility, SuperFAT, 195-196
  Windows 95 compatibility, 170-171, 174
    virtual device drivers, 173-174
  Windows memory management, 164
DOSMGR (Windows application), 209
dot-pitch (monitors), 498

double supertwist LCDs, 501-502
double-buffering (anima-tion), 94
double-density floppy disks, 351
double-precision floating-point numbers, 245
double-sided SIMMs, 334
downloading files (Pentium chip test program), 317-318
DR DOS, 139
Dr. Schueler's Home Medical Advisor Pro (reference software), 30
DRAM (dynamic memory), 454
drawing, 247
drive letters, assigning (DOS), 154
drivers, 201-225
  address conflicts, 131-133
  advantages of device drivers, 202-203
  audio device drivers, 551, 553
  BIOS relationship to device drivers, 202
  CD-ROM device drivers, 207-208, 409-413
  configuring Windows 95, 182-184
  definition of device drivers, 202-203
  device names (MCI), 213-214
  DOS device drivers, 203-208
    essential drivers, 206-208
    loading, 204-206

hard disk controllers,
32-bit processing, 160
operating systems, 134
OS/2 device drivers,
198, 222-225
Plug-and-Play, 132-133
SCSI devices, 349
Sound Blaster, 539-543
virtual device drivers, 173
Windows 3.1 device
drivers, 208-218
audio drivers,
529-530
DOS drivers (in
Windows), 208-209
Dynamic Link
Libraries (DLLs),
209-210
installing, 215-218
Media Control
Interface (MCI),
212-214
standard drivers, 211
virtual drivers,
211-212
Windows 95 device
drivers, 218-222
drivers (speakers), 518-519
drives (CD-ROM), 402-409
access times, 404
buffers, 404
compared to audio CD
drives, 402-403
device drivers, 409-413
interfaces, 406-409
physical characteristics, 405
transfer rates, 403-404
troubleshooting, 413-414
volume controls, 405-406
**drop-frame time codes,
446-447**
drum scanners, 363-364

DRVSPACE.BIN file, 145
**DSPs (Digital Signal
Processors), 380, 544-551**
MWave, 546
Signal Computing
Architecture, 546-547
VCOS, 547
Windows DSP, 547-551
DSVD (modems), 384
**DTE (Data Terminal
Equipment), 367**
**dual-ported video memory
(VRAM), 454**
Dvorak keyboards, 354-355
DX2 chips, clock speeds, 305
**Dynamic Link Libraries
(DLLs), 209-210**
**dynamic memory,
331-332, 454**
**dynamic microphones,
521-522**
**dynamic swap file (Win-
dows 95 virtual
memory), 173**

E

EA_DATA._SF file, 196
**EBCDIC (Extended Binary
Coded Decimal Inter-
change Code), 229-237**
**ECC (Error Correction
Code), 333**
**ECP (extended capabilities
ports), 375-376**
edgelit LCDs, 501
**Edit menu commands, Paste
Special, 77**
editing
embedded objects, 76
photos, 107-109

the Registry
(Windows 95), 179
SYSTEM.INI file
manually, 218
via Windows' Control
Panel, 216-218
video, 109-110
**EDO (Extended Data Out)
memory, 46, 307**
educational software, 25-28
**EISA (Enhanced Industry
Standard Architecture),
133, 327-328**
**Elastic Reality (morphing
software), 110**
**electron guns (monitors),
496-497**
**electronic image stabiliza-
tion (video cameras),
488-489**
electronic integration, 33
**electronic zooming (video
cameras), 487**
embedded data channels, 41
**embedding objects,
74-77, 81**
**EMM386.EXE file (ex-
panded memory manager),
205, 207**
**EMS (expanded
memory), 152**
**enabling 32-bit access,
160-161**
encoding
audio signals, 526-527
color, 438
musical notes (MIDI),
570-575
video, 418-419, 490
**encyclopedias
(CD versions), 29**

Enhanced IDE hard disks, 48-49, 340-341, 344-345

enhanced mode (Windows), 158, 166

enhanced parallel ports, 374-375

entertainment software, 32-34

.EPS (Encapsulated PostScript) files, 262

ergonomics, 355-356

Error Correction Code (ECC), 333

error detection/correction
CDs, 393
modems, 381

European Racers (entertainment software), 33

events, assigning system sounds, 72-74

exclusive messages (MIDI), 569

expanded memory (EMS), 152

expanded memory managers (DOS), 205, 207

expansion boards (Plug-and-Play), 184-188

expansion buses, 323-331
arbitrated buses, 324
configuring Windows 95, 182-184
definition, 324
EISA standard, 327-328
graphics accelerators, 453-454, 456
history, 324-331
ISA standard, 326-327
local buses, 324
MCA standard, 327
PCI standard, 329

PCMCIA standard, 330-332

performance standards, 50, 325-331

VL bus standard, 328-329

expansion slots, 53

Exploring Ancient Architecture (educational software), 27

exponents, floating-point numbers, 245

exporting files (Rich Text Format), 242

Extended Architecture (XA) CDs, 393

extended attributes (OS/2 file structure), 195-196

Extended Binary Coded Decimal Interchange Code (EBCDIC), 229-237

extended capabilities ports, 375-376

Extended Data Out (EDO) memory, 307

Extended Density Format (XDF), 153

extended floating-point numbers, 245

extended memory, 152

extended memory drivers (DOS), 205-207

extended partitions
DOS, 153
OS/2, 194

extension blocks, 265

external caches, 306

external clock speeds, 305

external commands, 147

external DOS device drivers, loading, 204

extra-high density floppy disks, 352

F

f-stops (video cameras), 483-486

fair use (copyright law), 587

Fast ATA interface (hard disks), 340

fast page mode memory, 307

FAT (File Allocation Table)
DOS, 148-151
Super-FAT (OS/2), 195-196

fax modems, 385-386

FDISK (installing DOS), 153

features, toggling in RTF (Rich Text Format), 243

field descriptors (TGA), 270

field of view (video cameras), 481-482

file formats
audio, 285-288
PAL (palette), 259
RDIB (device independent bitmap), 259
RMID (MIDI format), 259
RMMP (multimedia movie), 259
still images
BMP, 260-262
EPS (Encapsulated PostScript), 262
GIF (Graphics Interchange Format), 263-266
JPEG, 266-268
PCD (PhotoCD), 268
PCX, 268-269
TGA, 269-275
WMF (Windows Metafiles), 275-276
video, 277-282

File NODE (OS/2), 196
filenames
    OS/2, 196
    Windows 95, 175-178
files
    audio format
        AIFF (Audio Inter-
            change File Format),
            283-284, 288
        control, 282-283
        descriptor, 282
        .IBK (Instrument
            Bank), 284-285
        .SBI (Sound Blaster
            Instrument),
            288-289
        .SND, 290-291
        .VOC, 291-294
        .WAV, 294-295
        waveform, 283
    chunks, 259
    clusters (DOS), 148-151
    copying
        (Windows 95), 176
    DOS, 144-151
    downloading Pentium
        chip test program,
        317-318
    formats, converting,
        296-297
    import/export (Rich Text
        Format), 242
    initialization files
        (Windows), 167
    moving linked objects,
        76-77
    OS/2 file structure,
        194-198
    renaming
        (Windows 95), 177

.RTF, 242
still image (.BMP),
    263-266
text, converting, 242
upgrading
    Windows 3.1, 159
    Windows 95 file structure,
        171-172, 174-178
    Windows file
        structure, 158
    word processors, compat-
        ibility, 242
filters (photo editing), 107
first sale doctrine (copyright
    law), 586
flat memory model
    (OS/2), 193
flat-panel displays (moni-
    tors), 500-503
flat-panel video systems,
    434-435
flatbed scanners, 363-364
flattening (QuickTime
    movies), 71-72
floating-point circuitry
    (math coprocessors),
    307-308, 322
floating-point numbers, 245
floppy disk drives, perfor-
    mance standards, 47
floppy disks, 349-352
    boot sequence, 129
    history of DOS, 140-143
    storage capacity, 149, 350
flowcharts (producing
    multimedia
    presentations), 95
FM signals (VHS videocas-
    sette recorders), 432
FM synthesis, 535

focal length (video cam-
    eras), 480-481
focusing (video cameras),
    487-488
folded horn speakers, 519
fonts
    TrueType fonts (Windows
        95), 169
    VGA video adapters, 461
FORMAT.COM
    program, 154
formats
    audio files
        AIFF (Audio Inter-
            change File Format),
            283-284, 288
        .IBK (Instrument
            Bank), 284-285
        MIDI (Musical
            Instrument Digital),
            285-287
        .MOD, 287-288
        .RMI, 288
        .SBI (Sound Blaster
            Instrument),
            288-289
        .SND, 290-291
        .VOC, 291-294
        .WAV, 294-295
    files, converting, 242,
        296-297
    still image
        BMP, 260-266
        EPS (Encapsulated
            Postscript), 262
        GIF (Graphics
            Interchange
            Format), 263-266
        JPEG, 266-268
        PCD (PhotoCD), 268

PCX, 268-269
TGA, 269-275
WMF (Windows
 Metafiles), 275-276
video, 277-282
formatting
DOS hard disks, 154
low-level formatting
 (installing DOS), 153
text, 85, 242-244
word processor docu-
 ments, 242
**ForShow (graphics presen-
tations authoring
software), 97**
**frame buffers (memory-
mapped video), 435**
frame rates
video compression, 441
video signals, 423
frames (video), 445-447
**freeware (copyright
law), 588**
frequencies
audio, 257, 514
Nyquist, 257
recording video signals, 431
synchronizing monitor
 frequencies, 504
VESA standards, 468-471
VGA video adapters,
 468-471
VHS videocassette
 recorders, 432
video signals, 427
**Frequency Shift Keyed
(FSK) time code, 576**
**frequency shift keying
(modems), 379**

**front porches (video
signals), 422**
function calls
DOS (Disk Operating
 System), 146, 205
GDI (Graphics Device
 Interface), 275
Sound Blaster, 539-542
**function of operating
systems, 138-139**
**future predictions for
multimedia, 14-19**

G

game ports, 377-378
**games (software),
34-35, 601**
**gas-plasma systems (moni-
tors), 500**
**GDI (Graphics Device
Interface), 158**
functions, storing, 275
local heap (Windows
 memory
 management), 163
Windows 95 file
 structure, 172
GDI.EXE file, 159, 209
**gen-locking (video
images), 489**
**geography (educational
software), 27**
**Gettysburg Multimedia
Battle Simulation (enter-
tainment software), 33**
**GIF (Graphic Image
Format), 263-266**
global color tables, 264

**Global EMM Inport
Interface, 164**
graphic accelerators, 50
**graphic-rendering
blocks, 263**
**graphical user interface
(GUI), 125-128**
graphics
authoring software, 88,
 93-99
capturing, 85
history of Windows,
 155-158
see also images
**graphics accelerators,
451-457**
graphics adapters, 447-448
graphics coprocessors, 452
**Green Book standard
(CDs), 395**
**Grolier Multimedia Ency-
clopedia (reference
software), 29**
grouping, 243
**GSM 6.10 Audio audio
compression, 258**
**GUI (graphical user
interface), 125-128**
**Guide (hypertext authoring
software), 92-93**

H

hand scanners, 363-364
handshaking
modems, 379
serial ports, 367
**hard disk controllers,
32-bit processing, 160**

hard disks, 335-349
32-bit processing features
(Windows), 160-162
assigning drive letters
(DOS), 154
AV drives, 336-337
boot sequence, 129
disk compression, 337-338
formatting DOS hard
disks, 154
history of DOS, 140-143
HPFS (High Performance
File System), 196-198
interfaces, 338-349
ATA interface,
339-345
ATAPI (ATA Packet
Interface), 343-344
Enhanced IDE,
340-341
Fast ATA interface,
340
LBA (Logical Block
Addresses), 342-343
multiple drives,
344-345
SCSI, 345-349
SCSI-2, 347
speed of processing,
341-342
loading DOS device
drivers, 205-206
logical drives, 154
partitioning
DOS, 153-154
OS/2, 194-195
performance standards,
47-49

speed of processing, 336
storage capacity, 148-151,
337-338
Super-FAT (OS/2),
195-196
hardware
audio, 511-554
acoustics, 513-515
Ad Lib soundboard,
537
air pressure, 514-515
amplifiers, 520
analog signals, 526
baffles, 516-518
compression, 543-544
condenser micro-
phones, 522
connectors (micro-
phones), 525-526
current-limiting
resistors, 529
digital signals,
526-527
directionality of
microphones, 523
DSPs (Digital Signal
Processors), 544-551
dynamic micro-
phones, 521-522
frequencies, 257, 514
history of PC sound,
527-530
human hearing, 515
impedance of
microphones,
524-525
installing
soundboards,
551-554

location/coupling,
519-520
microphones,
521-526
multi-speaker systems,
518-519
MWave, 546
oscillators, 527-528
physical characteristics
of microphones, 524
piezoelectric micro-
phones, 522-523
pulse-width modula-
tion, 528-529
resonance, 517
sampling rates,
531-532
Signal Computing
Architecture,
546-547
signal level (micro-
phones), 524-525
Sound Blaster,
538-543
sound quality of
microphones, 525
soundboards,
512, 530-531
speakers, 515-520
standards, 537-543
stereophonic
imaging, 520
synthesis, 532-551
VCOS, 547
Windows 3.1 device
drivers, 529-530
Windows DSP,
547-551
wiring speakers,
553-554

BIOS interface, 130-131
CD-ROM drives, 402-414
CDs, 387-414
    constant linear velocity recording, 391
    error detection/ correction, 393
    history, 387-388
    Kodak PhotoCD, 396-401
    large frames (sectors), 392-393
    manufacturing, 390-391
    optical technology, 388-389
    random access, 389
    recordable CDs, 391-392
    sector address tag field, 392-393
    size, 389-390
    small frames, 393
    standards, 394-402
    tracks, 394
    XA (Extended Architecture), 393
codecs (video compression), 441-442
configuring Windows 95, 180-189
device drivers, 131-134, 203-208
digitizing tablets, 362-363
DOS interrupts (multitasking), 146-147
expansion buses, 323-331
fax modems, 385-386
floppy disks, 349-352

graphics accelerators, 451-457
    color, 455
    DCI (Display Control Interface), 457
    expansion buses, 453-456
    memory requirements, 454
    RAMDACs, 456-457
    register width, 453
    resolution, 454
    speed of processing, 455
    VGA support, 455-456
graphics adapters, 447-448
graphics coprocessors, 452
hard disks, 335-349
keyboards, 353-358
lightpens, 362
memory, 331-335
mice, 358-361
microprocessors, 302-323
    486 chips, 307
    AMD K5 chips, 320-321
    bus connections, 304
    clock speeds, 304-305
    Cyrix 486 chips, 315
    Cyrix M1 chips, 321-322
    definition, 302
    direct-mapped caches, 306
    DX2 chips, 305
    EDO memory, 307
    external clock speeds, 305
    IBM 486SLC2 chips, 315

    IBM Blue Lightning chips, 316
    instruction sets, 303
    Intel chips, 303, 309-320
    internal clock speeds, 305
    math coprocessors, 307-308
    memory caching, 305-307
    NexGen 586 chips, 322-323
    OverDrive chips, 308
    Pentium chips, 305
    power consumption, 309
    primary caches, 305-306
    registers, 303-304
    secondary caches, 305-306
    set-associative caches, 306
    video display, 447-448
    voltages, 308-309
    write-back caches, 307
    write-through caches, 306
MIDI (Musical Instrument Digital Interface), 555-578
    aftertouch, 575
    channels/voices, 558-566
    connectors, 557
    encoding notes, 570-575
    messages, 566-570

patch maps, 559-566
playback, 576-578
Song Position
  Pointer, 570
speed of processing,
  557
Status/Data Bytes,
  570-575
synchronizing,
  575-576
transmitters/receivers,
  556-557
UART chips, 556
Windows, 565-566
modems, 378-385
  configuring, 382-383
  data compression, 381
  frequency shift
    keying, 379
  speed of processing,
    379
  standards, 379-381
  SVD (Simultaneous
    Voice and Data),
    384-385
monitors, 493-510
  active matrix,
    502-503
  aperture grilles, 499
  aspect ratios, 506
  audio inputs, 508
  autosizing images,
    506-507
  bandwidth, 505
  color, 495, 503
  color tracking, 504
  compared to televi-
    sion, 493
  configuring, 508-510
  convergence, 497-498

CRTs (cathode ray
  tubes), 494-500
dot-pitch, 498
electron guns,
  496-497
flat-panel displays,
  500-503
history, 494
image controls,
  507-508
matrix colors, 499
overscanning, 505
passive matrix,
  502-503
persistence, 496
phosphors, 494-495
polarizing filters, 501
projection
  systems, 500
resolution, 503-504
shadow masks,
  498-499
synchronizing
  frequencies, 504
twisted nematic
  technology, 501-502
underscanning, 505
video amplifiers,
  503-504
white balancing,
  495-496
Multimedia PCs, physical
  requirements, 53
OS/2 device drivers,
  222-225
overlay boards (video), 444
performance standards,
  8-10, 45-53
ports, 365-378
  game ports, 377-378
  handshaking, 367

interrupts, 370
parallel ports,
  372-376
physical connec-
  tions, 365
serial ports, 366-372
speed of processing,
  366-367, 372
UART chips,
  368-370
registers (VGA video
  adapters), 448-451
scanners, 363-365
trackballs, 361
VGA video adapters,
  457-463, 468-475
video boards, 457-475
  VESA standard, 458
  VESA standards,
    463-468, 468-475
  VGA video adapters,
    457-463, 468-475
video cameras, 477-493
  color filters, 479
  encoding images, 490
  f-stops, 483-486
  field of view, 481-482
  focal length, 480-481
  focusing, 487-488
  lenses, 477, 480-486
  microphones, 493
  optical trans-
    ducers, 477
  optics, 478-489
  recording, 492-493
  resolution, 479-480
  scanning, 489
  sensors, 478
  shutters, 486-487
  special effects, 491

stability of images,
488-489
tripods, 488
viewfinders, 477, 492
white balancing,
490-491
zoom ratios,
480-481, 487
video controllers, 448-451
video image hardware,
447-457
Windows 3.1 device
drivers, 208-218
DOS drivers (in
Windows), 208-209
installing, 215-218
standard drivers, 211
virtual drivers,
211-212
Windows 95 device
drivers, 218-222
**HDTV (High Definition
Television), 7**
headers, 260, 263, 278-279
**heads (recording video
signals), 431-432**
**health care (reference
software), 30**
height of images, 263
**helical scan recording,
431-432**
**Help function (Windows),
62-64**
**high level programming
languages, 120-121**
**High Memory Area
(DOS), 152**
**High Performance File
System (HPFS), 191,
196-198**

**High Sierra standard (CDs),
401-402**
**high-density floppy
disks, 351**
**HIMEM.SYS (extended
memory driver), 152,
205-207**
**history (educational
software), 26-27**
**history (entertainment
software), 33-34**
history of
CDs, 387-388
color television, 423-424
digital technology, 6-8
DOS (Disk Operating
System), 139-143
expansion buses, 324-331
GUIs (graphical user
interfaces), 126-127
Intel chips, 309-311
monitors, 494
multimedia, 4-6
OS/2, 190-192
parallel ports, 372-373
PC sound, 527-530
Windows, 155-158
home computers, *see* **PCs**
**home movies (multimedia
potential), 37-38**
**Home Survival Toolkit
(reference software), 30**
**horizontal position controls
(monitors), 507**
**horizontal retracing (video
signals), 421**
**horizontal size controls
(monitors), 507**
**horizontal sweeps (video
signals), 422-423**

**horizontal synchronizing
frequency (monitors), 504**
host adapters, 48
hot spots, defining, 85
**HPFS (High Performance
File System), 191,
196-198**
**HSC Digital Morph
(morphing software), 110**
hue (images), 253
human hearing, 515
human vision, 416-418
hypertext
authoring software, 88-93
Multimedia Viewer, 64-66
Windows Help, 62-64

I

**I/O Supervisor (Windows
95 device drivers),
220-221**
**IBK (Instrument Bank)
audio file format, 284-285**
IBM 386SLC chips, 313
IBM 486SLC2 chips, 315
**IBM Blue Lightning
chips, 316**
**IconAuthor (graphics
presentations authoring
software), 97**
icons, 127
IDE interface, 48-49, 407
**IMA ADPCM audio
compression, 258**
image data packets, 274
image files, color, 273-275
**image resolution (scanners),
364-365**
**Image-In Professional
(photo editing), 108**

ImagePals (video editing), 109
ImageQ (graphics presentations authoring software), 97-98
images
2-D, 249
3-D, 249
bitmapped, 247-248
chrominance, 253
color depth, 249
color mapping, 250-251, 271-272
color temperature, 490-491, 495-496
compressing, 250-253, 266-268
deleting, 265
descriptors (blocks), 263-264
direct-mapped, 251
displaying, 265
height, 263
hue, 253
human vision, 416-417
layout, 263
luminance, 252
metafiles, 276
monochrome, 249
on-screen resolution, 247
pixels, 260, 418
PostScript language, 262
resolution, 248-249, 252, 418
RGB, uncompressed, 272-273
sharpness, 418
sizing, 264
storing, 247-248, 259-276

TGA, descriptor bytes, 271-272
transmitting, 263
vector, 247-248
video, 417-434
8mm video cassettes, 432
attributes (pixels), 435-436
autosizing, 506-507
bit-images, 456
BNC connectors, 433-434
bridging inputs, 433
cable connections, 432-434
coaxial connectors, 433-434
codecs, 441-442
color, 435-443
combining scanned/memory-mapped systems, 443-451
compression, 440-442
DCI (Display Control Interface), 457
direct color mapping, 439
drop-frame time codes, 446-447
encoding, 418-419, 438, 490
flat-panel video systems, 434-435
graphics accelerators, 451-457
graphics adapters, 447-448
graphics coprocessors, 452

hardware, 447-457
image controls (monitors), 507-508
impedance, 433
interlaced scanning, 419-420
linear scanning, 419
memory requirements, 437-438
memory-mapped systems, 434-435
microprocessors, 447-448
overlay boards, 444
overscanning, 505
pin plugs, 433-434
pixels, 435-436
rasterizing, 443-445
recording, 431-432
refresh rate, 420-421
resampling, 487
resizing, 487
scanning signals, 421-432
standards for memory-mapped displays, 442-443
step capture, 445
synchronizing signals, 489
terminating inputs, 433
time codes, 445-447
timing, 418-419
true color systems, 437
underscanning, 505
vector graphics, 443
VESA standards, 458, 463-475

VGA video adapters, 437-438, 457-475
video boards, 457-475
video capture, 443-444
video controllers, 448-451
voltage, 434
Windows color, 439-440
see also cameras (video)
width, 263
impedance
microphones, 524-525
video signals, 433
importing files (Rich Text Format), 242
Indeo video compression, 254
index (help functions), 63
index chunks, 277
indices (CD tracks), 394
Industry Standard Architecture (ISA), 326-327
infinite baffles, 517
info blocks, 260-261
information flow, future of multimedia, 16
infringement (copyright law), 586-587
initialization code (BIOS), 128
initialization files (Windows), 167, 179-180
initializing serial ports, 370-371
Initiation Key (Plug-and-Play), 185
injunctions (copyright law), 586

input/output (I/O) devices
digitizing tablets, 362-363
fax modems, 385-386
keyboards, 353-358
lightpens, 362
mice, 358-361
modems, 378-385
configuring, 382-383
data compression, 381
frequency shift keying, 379
speed of processing, 379
standards, 379-381
SVD (Simultaneous Voice and Data), 384-385
ports, 365-378
game ports, 377-378
handshaking, 367
interrupts, 370
parallel ports, 372-376
physical connections, 365
serial ports, 366-372
speed of processing, 366-367, 372
UART chips, 368-370
scanners, 363-365
trackballs, 361
input/output mapping (BIOS), 130
installing
DOS (Disk Operating System), 153-154
multimedia software, 60-61
Multimedia Viewer, 64

OS/2 device drivers, 223-225
QuickTime (video player), 71
SCSI devices, 347-348
soundboards, 551-554
Windows 3.1 device drivers, 215-218
Windows 95 device drivers, 221-222
see also loading
instruction sets (microprocessors), 118-119, 303
instruments (MIDI patch map), 559-563
integers, 244-245
integrated disk cache (Windows 95), 177
Intel storage units, 244
Intel microprocessor chips, 303, 311-320
interactivity of multimedia, 11-12, 23-24
interfaces
API (Application Program Interface), 134
ATA interface, 339-345
ATAPI (ATA Packet Interface), 343-344
CD-ROM drives, 406-409
CD-ROMs, 49
device drivers, 202-203
Enhanced IDE, 340-341
Fast ATA interface, 340
hard disks, 48-49, 338-349
keyboards, 356-358
LBA (Logical Block Addresses), 342-343
MCI (Media Control Interface), 212-214

mice, 360-361
MIDI (Musical Instru-
    ment Digital Interface),
    555-578
    aftertouch, 575
    channels/voices,
        558-566
    connectors, 557
    encoding notes,
        570-575
    messages, 566-570
    patch maps, 559-566
    playback, 576-578
    Song Position
        Pointer, 570
    speed of processing,
        557
    Status/Data Bytes,
        570-575
    synchronizing,
        575-576
    transmitters/receivers,
        556-557
    UART chips, 556
    Windows, 565-566
multimedia, 11
multiple drives, 344-345
operating systems,
    133, 138-139
SCSI, 345-349
SCSI-2, 347
software, 125-128
speed of processing,
    341-342
user interface
    (Windows 95 file
    structure), 171-172
visual editing interface
    (OLE), 76
Win32, 169

interference (video signals),
    425-426
interlaced scanning,
    419-420
internal clock speeds, 305
internal commands, 147
international standards
    (video signals), 427-431
Internet, 16-17, 317-318
interpolated resolution
    (scanners), 365
interpolation (pixels), 248
interpreted programming
    languages, 120-121
interrupts
    configuring
        soundboards, 552
    DOS, 146-147
    serial ports, 370
    Sound Blaster, 539-542
    standards, 552
    Windows, 160
    Windows 95 user inter-
        face, 172
IO.SYS file, 144
IOS.INI file, 219
IPC (interprogram commu-
    nications) system, 193
irises (video cameras),
    483-486
Iron Helix (games
    software), 35
ISA (Industry Standard
    Architecture), 326-327
ISO 9660 standard (CDs),
    401-402
Isolation state (Plug-and-
    Play), 186
issuance of copyrights,
    584-585

J-K

J.F.K. Assassination:
    A Visual Investigation
    (entertainment
    software), 34
The Journeyman Project
    (games software), 35
joystick ports, 377-378
JPEG (Joint Photographic
    Experts Group), 252-253,
    266-268
jumping (program execu-
    tion), 204

kernel, 158
    OS/2, 192-194
    protected-mode kernel
        (upgrading Windows
        3.1), 159
    Windows 95 file
        structure, 171
keyboard clocks, 356
KEYBOARD.DRV, 210
keyboards, 353-358
Kodak PhotoCD,
    396-401, 438
KRNL286.EXE file, 209
KRNL386.EXE file,
    159, 209

L

languages (programming
    software), 119-122
large frames (sectors),
    392-393
latency (hard disk
    speed), 336
lavaliere microphones, 524

layered block device drivers (Windows 95), 220
layered model (software), 128
LBA (Logical Block Addressing), 150, 342-343
LCDs (liquid crystal display panels), 500-504
lead-in areas (CDs), 394
lead-out areas (CDs), 394
LEDs (light-emitting diodes), 500
legal issues, 581-594
    clip-art libraries, 596
    contractors, 597
    copyright law, 582-590
        expression of ideas, 582-584
        fair use, 587
        first sale doctrine, 586
        infringement, 586-587
        issuance of copyrights, 584-585
        notice of copyright, 585-586
        public domain, 588-590
        registering copyrights, 592-593
        rights, 587-588
        term of copyrights, 586
        work for hire, 587
    licensing, 590-594
        contracts, 593-594
        permissions, 591-592
        protecting your rights, 592-593
        subject matter, 590-591

    patents, 583
    trade secret laws, 583
    trademarks, 583
Lempel-Ziv compression, 250-252
lenses (video cameras), 477, 480-486
libraries, class, 122
licensing (legal issues), 590-594
    contracts, 593-594
    permissions, 591-592
    protecting your rights, 592-593
    subject matter, 590-591
light-emitting diodes (LEDs), 500
lightpens, 362
line rates (video signals), 423
Linear Predictive Coding audio compression, 258
linear programming, 123
linear scanning, 419
lines (memory), 306
linking
    hypertext, 88-93
    multimedia compared to traditional media, 13
    objects, 75-77
    Windows Help, 63
liquid crystal display panels (LCDs), 500-504
LIST chunks, 277
load order (DOS device drivers), 205-206
loaders, memory (DOS), 152
LOADHIGH command, 204

loading
    CD-ROM drivers, 207-208
    DOS device drivers, 204-206, 223
    virtual device drivers (Windows), 212
    Windows 95 device drivers, 219-220
    see also installing
local buses, 48, 324
local color table blocks, 263
local heaps (Windows memory management), 163-164
locating QuickTime (video player), 70
Logical Block Addressing (LBA), 150, 342-343
logical drives, 154, 194
logical memory types, 335
logical screen descriptors, 263
louver transitions (slide shows), 94
low-level formatting (installing DOS), 153
lower memory (DOS), 152
luminance, 426
    of images, 252
    recording video signals, 432
    video signals, 424-425

M

machine language (programming software), 119

Macintosh
history of Windows, 155-156
QuickTime cross-platform compatiblity, 71-72

Macromedia Director (graphics presentations authoring software), 98-99

The Magic School Bus Explores the Human Body (educational software), 26

mantissas (floating-point numbers), 245

manually editing SYSTEM.INI file, 218

manufacturing CDs, 390-391

Map Mask Register (VGA video adapters), 459-460

mapping
BIOS, 130
direct color mapping, 439

master ATA drives (hard disks), 339

math coprocessors, 307-308
Cyrix M1 chips, 322
Pentium chips, 317

matrix colors (monitors), 499

MCA (Micro Channel Architecture), 327

McGraw-Hill Multimedia Encyclopedia of Science & Technology (reference software), 30

MCI (Media Control Interface), 104-105, 212-214

MCIWnd (programming authoring software), 104, 106

MDFAT (Microsoft DriveSpace FAT), 150

measurements, static compared to digital, 6-7

measuring memory, 332

mechanical mice, 358-359

mechanical resolution (scanners), 365

mechanical scanners, 363

Media Player (software application), 69, 576-578

MediaRecorder (video editing), 109-110

MediaView Libraries (hypertext authoring software), 91

megahertz (clock speed), 304-305

memory, 331-335
addresses, 130-133
buffers (CD-ROM drives), 404
caching, 305-307
Cyrix M1 chips, 321
integrated disk cache (Windows 95), 177
Pentium chips, 317
VCache (32-bit processing), 161-162
color video requirements, 435-438
dynamic memory, 331-332, 454

ECC (Error Correction Code), 333

EDO (Extended Data Out) memory, 307

expanded memory (EMS), 152, 207

extended memory, 152, 206-207

fast page mode memory, 307

graphics accelerators memory requirements, 454

High Memory Area (DOS), 152

images, color depth, 249

lines (caches), 306

loading DOS device drivers, 204-206

logical memory types, 335

lower memory (DOS), 152

managing
DLLs (Dynamic Link Libraries), 210
DOS (Disk Operating System), 151-152
flat memory model (OS/2), 193
loading DOS device drivers in OS/2, 223
Windows, 162-166
Windows 95, 172-174

mapping (BIOS), 130

measurement, 332

parity-checking, 333

pixels, 249

protected mode processing, 163, 208

RAM (Random Access
Memory), 45-47,
331-332
range assignments
(EMM386.EXE), 207
real mode memory, 151,
163, 208
remapping, 151, 311
ROM (Read-Only
Memory), 129, 332
ROM shadowing, 335
SIMMs, 332-334
static memory, 331-332
UMB (upper memory
blocks), 152
VGA video adapters
memory requirements,
459-460
video, 51, 251
virtual memory
OS/2, 193
Windows 95,
173-174
VRAM (dual-ported video
memory), 454
memory loaders (DOS), 152
**memory-mapped video
systems, 434-435**
combining with scanned
video systems, 443-451
standards, 442-443
message queues, 172
messages (MIDI), 566-570
metafiles, 276
mice, 358-361
**Micro Channel Architecture
(MCA), 132-133, 327**
**Microcom Networking
Protocols (MNP), 381**
microkernel (OS/2), 193

microphones, 493, 521-526
condenser micro-
phones, 522
connectors, 525-526
directionality, 523
dynamic microphones,
521-522
impedance, 524-525
physical characteristics, 524
piezoelectric microphones,
522-523
signal level, 524-525
sound quality, 525
microprocessors, 302-323
486 chips, 307
AMD 386 chips, 312
AMD K5 chips, 320-321
BIOS interface, 130-131
boot sequence, 128-129
bus connections, 304
Chips and Technologies
386 chips, 312-313
clock speeds, 304-305
Cyrix 486 chips, 315
Cyrix M1 chips, 321-322
definition, 302
direct-mapped caches, 306
DX2 chips, 305
EDO memory, 307
external clock speeds, 305
IBM 386SLC chips, 313
IBM 486SLC2 chips, 315
IBM Blue Lightning
chips, 316
instruction sets, 303
Intel chips, 303, 311-320
internal clock speeds, 305
math coprocessors,
307-308
memory caching, 305-307

memory modes, 208
NexGen 586 chips,
322-323
OverDrive chips, 308
Pentium chips, 305
performance standards, 45
power consumption, 309
primary caches, 305-306
programming software,
118-125
application-level
programming, 122
class libraries, 122
complex instruc-
tions, 119
context switching, 123
debuggers, 122
high-level languages,
120-121
instruction sets,
118-119
languages, 119-122
linear
programming, 123
multi-tasking,
123-124
object code, 121
run-time modules, 122
SDKs (software
development
kits), 122
source code, 121
threads, 124-125
tools, 121-122
protected mode processing
(Windows), 163
real mode processing
(Windows), 163
registers, 303-304
secondary caches, 305-306

set-associative caches, 306
video display, 447-448
voltages, 308-309
write-back caches, 307
write-through caches, 306
Microsoft ADPCM audio compression, 258
Microsoft Bookshelf (reference software), 29-30
Microsoft Cinemania (reference software), 31
Microsoft Download Service, 159
Microsoft Encarta (reference software), 29
Microsoft Run-Length Encoding (RLE) video compression, 255
Microsoft Video 1 video compression, 255
Microsoft Visual C++, 102
MIDI (Musical Instrument Digital Interface), 555-578
    aftertouch, 575
    audio file format, 285-287
    channels/voices, 558-566
    connectors, 557
    encoding notes, 570-575
    messages, 566-570
    meta event codes, 286-287
    patch maps, 559-566
    playback, 576-578
    RMID file, 259
    Song Position Pointer, 570
    speed of processing, 557
    Status/Data Bytes, 570-575
    synchronizing, 575-576
    transmitters/receivers, 556-557
    UART chips, 556
    Windows, 565-566

Midisoft Multimedia Songbook (music software), 36
Midisoft Music Mentor (music software), 36
midrange drivers (speakers), 518
mixer control functions (Windows DSP), 548-549
mixers (sound recordings), 80
MNP (Microcom Networking Protocols), 381
MOD audio file format, 287-288
mode messages (MIDI), 567-568
modems, 378-385
    configuring, 382-383
    data compression, 381
    fax modems, 385-386
    frequency shift keying, 379
    performance standards, 52-53
    speed of processing, 379
    standards, 379-381
    SVD (Simultaneous Voice and Data), 384-385
modes (Windows), 158
monitors, 248, 493-510
    active matrix, 502-503
    aperture grilles, 499
    aspect ratios, 506
    audio inputs, 508
    autosizing images, 506-507
    bandwidth, 505
    color, 495, 503-504
    compared to television, 493
    configuring, 508-510

convergence, 497-498
CRTs (cathode ray tubes), 494-500
dot-pitch, 498
electron guns, 496-497
flat-panel displays, 500-503
history, 494
image controls, 507-508
matrix colors, 499
overscanning, 505
passive matrix, 502-503
persistence, 496
phosphors, 494-495
polarizing filters, 501
projection systems, 500
resolution, 248, 503-504
selecting, 51
shadow masks, 498-499
synchronizing frequencies, 504
twisted nematic technology, 501-502
underscanning, 505
video amplifiers, 503-504
white balancing, 495-496
Mono mode (MIDI), 567
monochrome images, 249
Morgan's Trivia Machine (educational software), 27
Morph (morphing software), 111
morphing, 95, 110-111
Motion JPEG video compression, 255
MOUSE.DRV, 210
MOV (movie) video formats, 69, 280-282
movies, *see* **video**
moving linked objects (OLE), 76-77

MPC 1.0 performance standards, 40-42
MPC 2.0 performance standards, 42-44
.MPD file extension, 219
MPEG (Motion Picture Experts Group) video compression, 255-256
MS DOS, *see* **DOS**
MSCDEX.EXE (CD device driver), 207, 409-410
MSDOS.SYS file, 144
MSINFO.EXE program, 173, 210
multi-speaker systems, 518-519
multi-tasking, 123-124
multi-threading (programming software), 124-125
multimedia
   audio potential, 23
   basic software applications, 61-74
      CD players, 67-68
      file conversions, 296
      Multimedia Viewer, 64-67
      system sounds, 72-74
      video players, 68-72
      Windows Help, 62-64
   comparisions
      other communications technologies, 22
      print media, 3-4, 15
      traditional video, 12-13
      video technologies, 23
   definitions, 4
   digital technology, 6-8
   economics, 16-17
   effect on the senses, 5

electronic integration (PCs/stereos/TVs), 33
future predictions, 14-19
games (shareware potential), 601
hardware standards, 8-10
history, 4-6
installing software, 60-61
interactivity, 11-12, 23-24
interfaces, 11
legal issues, 581-594
   clip-art libraries, 596
   contractors, 597
   copyright law, 582-590
   licensing, 590-594
   patents, 583
   trade secret laws, 583
   trademarks, 583
movie format (RMMP), 259
performance standards, 40-44
personal uses, 24-25, 59-60
   educational software, 25-28
   entertainment software, 32-35
   home movies, 37-38
   music software, 36-37
   reference software, 28-31
producing multimedia presentations, 37-38, 595-597
   authoring software, 87-88
   contractors, 597
   distribution, 599-603
   overview, 84-87

pre-production, 107-113
software, 36-38
studios, 596-597
testing, 602
random access, 13
scope, 22-23
software, 117-135
   application-level programming, 122
   applications, 135
   BIOS, 128-133
   definition, 118
   layered model, 128
   operating systems, 133-135
   Plug-and-Play, 132-133
   programming, 118-125
   standards, 10-12
   user interfaces, 125-128
temporal dimension, 3-4
training uses, 31-32
video annotation, 81
voice annotation, 78-81
Multimedia Data Converter, 296
Multimedia PC Marketing Council, 40
Multimedia PCs, 8-10
   compared to upgrading PCs, 54-57
   performance standards, 40-44
      CD-ROM drives, 49
      expansion buses, 50
      hard disks, 47-49
      memory (RAM), 45-47
      microprocessors, 45

modems, 52-53
MPC 1.0, 40-42
MPC 2.0, 42-44
Plug-and-Play, 49-50
ports, 52-53
sound boards, 51-52
target requirements,
44-45
video hardware, 50-51
physical requirements, 53
speed of processing, 14
**Multimedia ToolBook
(hypertext authoring
software), 93**
**Multimedia Viewer (soft-
ware application), 64-67,
90-91**
**Multimedia Workshop
(educational software), 28**
**multiple hard disk drives,
344-345**
multiprocessors, 159-162
multitasking, 6, 311
cooperative multi-
tasking, 159
DOS (Disk Operating
System), 146-147
history of Windows,
156-158
Pentium chips, 317
pre-emptive multi-
tasking, 168
Windows, 209
**Museum Madness (educa-
tional software), 27**
**music software, 28, 33,
36-37**
**Musical Instrument Digital
Interface,** *see* **MIDI**
**musical notes, encoding
(MIDI), 570-575**

**The Musical World of
Professor Piccolo (educa-
tional software), 28**
**MusicTime (music soft-
ware), 36**
MWave (DSP standard), 546

N

**naming conventions, virtual
device drivers, 211**
negative integers, 245
NetWare file system, 177
**networks, history of
DOS, 141**
NexGen 586 chips, 322-323
noise (CD players), 68
**noise reduction, digital
technology, 7-8**
non-repeating data, 251
**notebook computers
(PC Convertible), 141**
**notice of copyright,
585-586**
Novell DOS, 139
**NTSC (National Television
Standards Committee),
424-431, 444**
numerical values
BCD (Binary Coded
Decimal), 228
delimiters (Rich Text
Format), 243
storage, 244-246
Nyquist frequency, 257

O

**object code (programming
software), 121**
**Object Packager, embed-
ding voice annotations, 81**

**Object Windows C++ Class
Library (OWL), 102**
**object-oriented program-
ming (OOP), 102, 122**
**ObjectView (programming
authoring software), 103**
OEMSETUP.INF file, 218
**OLE (Object Linking and
Embedding), 74-77**
editing embedded
objects, 76
embedding voice annota-
tions, 81
linking objects, advantages
/disadvantages, 75
moving linked objects,
76-77
versions, 76
video annotation, 81
voice annotation, 78-81
Windows clipboard, 77
Omni mode (MIDI), 567
**omnidirectional micro-
phones, 523**
**on-screen images, resolu-
tion, 247**
online connections, 17-19
**OOP (object-oriented
programming), 102**
**OpenGL (programming
authoring software), 105**
**operating systems,
133-135, 137-200**
Application Program
Interface (API), 134
BIOS, 134
device drivers, 134
DOS (Disk Operating
System), 139-154
application
support, 146
booting up, 144-146

command
  processor, 147
device drivers,
  203-208
disk compression,
  150-151
essential files, 144
file system, 148-151
history, 139-143
initializing serial
  ports, 370-371
installing, 153-154
memory management,
  151-152
MSCDEX.EXE (CD
  device driver),
  409-410
multitasking, 146-147
function, 138-139
OS/2, 189-200
  device drivers,
    198, 222-225
  file structure, 194-198
  history, 190-192
  kernel, 192-194
  Plug-and-Play,
    198-200
utility programs, 134
Windows, 155-168
  configuring, 167-168
  file structure, 158
  history, 155-158
  memory management,
    162-166
Windows 3.1
  device drivers,
    208-218
  initializing serial
    ports, 371
  upgrading, 159-162

Windows 95, 168-189
  CD device drivers,
    412-413
  compared to
    Windows NT, 169
  compatibility with
    applications,
    169-171
  configuring, 178-189
  device drivers,
    218-222
  file structure, 171-178
  initializing serial
    ports, 371
  memory management,
    172-174
OPL3 chip (audio), 538
Optical Character Recognition software, 84, 363
optical mice, 358-359
optical reflex view-
  finders, 492
optical technology (CDs),
  388-389
optical transducers, 477
optical zooming (video
  cameras), 487
optics (video cameras),
  478-489
optoisolators (MIDI), 556
Orange Book standard
  (CDs), 395
OS/2, 189-200
  device drivers, 198,
    222-225
      configuring, 224-225
      installing, 223-225
      loading DOS device
        drivers, 223
  file structure, 194-198

history, 190-192
HPFS (High Performance
  File System), 177,
  196-198
kernel, 192-194
Plug-and-Play, 198-200
OS/2 Warp, memory
  requirements, 46
oscillators, 304, 527-528
OverDrive chips (math
  coprocessors), 308, 314,
  318-320
overlay boards (video), 51,
  86, 444
overscanning
  (monitors), 505
OWL (Object Windows
  C++ Class Library), 102

P

packet-based multiplex
  systems, 384
packets, 274-275
PAL (palette format), 259
PAL (Phase Alternating
  Line) video standard,
  427-431
parabolic microphones, 524
parallel interfaces (CD-
  ROM drives), 407-408
parallel ports, 372-376
  bi-directional parallel
    ports, 373-374
  enhanced parallel ports,
    374-375
  extended capabilities ports,
    375-376
  performance standards,
    52-53
  standard parallel ports, 373

**parallel processing
(SCSI), 346**
parity-checking, 46, 333
partitioning
  DOS hard disks, 153-154
  OS/2 boot record, 195
partitions
  DOS, 149
  OS/2, 194-195
**passive matrix (monitors),
502-503**
passive speaker systems, 520
**Paste Special command
(Edit menu), 77**
pasting objects
  compared to embedding
    objects, 74-75
  OLE (Object Linking and
    Embedding), 77
**patch maps (MIDI),
559-566**
patents, 583
**pattern matching (disk
compression), 338**
pause areas (CDs), 394
PC Convertible, 141
PC DOS, 139-140
**PCD (PhotoCD) still image
formats, 268**
**PCI (Peripheral Compo-
nent Interconnect),
181, 329**
**PCI buses, compared to
VL Bus, 50**
**PCM (Pulse Code Modula-
tion) sampling, 41, 256**
**PCMCIA (Personal Com-
puter Memory Card
International Association),
330-332**
  compatibility with Sound
    Blaster, 538

configuring modems, 383
OS/2 Plug-and-Play,
  198-200
slots, 50
PCs (personal computers)
audio, 511-554
  acoustics, 513-515
  Ad Lib soundboard,
    537
  additive synthesis, 534
  advanced synthesis,
    536-537
  air pressure, 514-515
  amplifiers, 520
  analog signals, 526
  baffles, 516-518
  compression, 543-544
  condenser micro-
    phones, 522
  configuring
    soundboards,
    551-553
  connectors (micro-
    phones), 525-526
  current-limiting
    resistors, 529
  digital signals,
    526-527
  directionality of
    microphones, 523
  DSPs (Digital Signal
    Processors), 544-551
  dynamic micro-
    phones, 521-522
  FM synthesis, 535
  frequencies, 514
  history, 527-530
  human hearing, 515
  impedance of
    microphones,
    524-525

installing
  soundboards,
  551-554
location/coupling,
  519-520
microphones,
  521-526
multi-speaker systems,
  518-519
MWave, 546
oscillators, 527-528
physical characteristics
  of microphones, 524
piezoelectric micro-
  phones, 522-523
properties of
  sound, 513
pulse-width modula-
  tion, 528-529
resonance, 517
sampling rates,
  531-532
Signal Computing
  Architecture,
  546-547
signal level of
  microphones,
  524-525
Sound Blaster,
  538-543
sound quality of
  microphones, 525
soundboards,
  512, 530-531
speakers, 515-520
standards, 537-543
stereophonic
  imaging, 520
subtractive synthesis,
  533-534
synthesis, 532-551
VCOS, 547

wave table synthesis, 535-536

wavelengths, 514

Windows 3.1 device drivers, 529-530

Windows DSP, 547-551

wiring speakers, 553-554

boot sequence, 128-129

codecs (video compression), 441-442

color, 435-443

   attributes (pixels), 435-436

   CMYK color scheme, 438

   color planes, 436-438

   color separations, 436-437

   color space conversion, 438

   direct mapping, 439

   encoding, 438

   Kodak PhotoCD system, 438

   memory requirements, 437-438

   pixels, 435-436

   standards for memory-mapped displays, 442-443

   true color systems, 437

   VGA video adapters, 437-438

   Windows, 439-440

cross-platform compatiblity, QuickTime (video player), 71-72

images, storing, 247-248

initialization code (BIOS), 128

interrupts, 552

Multimedia PCs, 8-10

   compared to upgrading PCs, 54-57

   performance standards, 40-45

   physical requirements, 53

   speed of processing, 14

speed of data processing, 7

video compression, 440-442

PCX still image formats, 268-269

.PDR file extension, 219

pens (digitizing tablets), 362-363

Pentium chips, 316-318

   AMD K5 chips, 320-321

   clock speeds, 305

   Cyrix M1 chips, 321-322

   NexGen 586 chips, 322-323

   testing, 317-318

Pentium OverDrive chips, 318-320

percussion (MIDI patch map), 563-565

performance standards

   CD-ROM drives, 49

   expansion buses, 50

   hard disks, 47-49

   memory (RAM), 45-47

   microprocessors, 45

   modems, 52-53

   MPC 1.0, 40-42

   MPC 2.0, 42-44

   Multimedia PCs, 40-45

   Plug-and-Play, 49-50

   ports, 52-53

   sound boards, 51-52

   video hardware, 50-51

Peripheral Component Interconnect (PCI), 181, 329

permanent swap files (Windows memory management), 165

permissions (licensing), 591-592

persistence

   monitors, 496

   video, 420-421

Personal Computer AT, 141

Personal Computer Memory Card

   International Association (PCMCIA), 330-332

personal uses of multimedia, 24-25, 59-60

   educational software, 25-28

   entertainment software, 32-34

   games, 34-35

   home movies, 37-38

   music software, 36-37

   reference software, 28-31

PharmAssist (reference software), 30

Phase Alternating Line (PAL) video standard, 427-431

phone plugs (microphones), 526

PhoneDisc PowerFinder (reference software), 31

phosphors

   monitors, 494-495

   video, 420-421

PhotoCD, *see* Kodak PhotoCD

PhotoMorph (morphing software), 111
photos
    capturing, 85
    editing
        Corel PhotoPaint 5 Plus, 108
        Image-In Professional, 108
        Photoshop, 109
        Picture Publisher, 109
    pre-production, 107-109
Photoshop (photo editing), 109
physical requirements (Multimedia PCs), 53
physical resolution, 249
Picture Publisher (photo editing), 109
piezoelectric microphones, 522-523
pin plugs (video signals), 433-434
PIO (programmed input/ output) transfers, 341
pixels, 418
    attributes, 435-436
    color, 435-436
    flat-panel video systems, 434
    images, decoding, 260
    interpolation, 248
    memory, 249
playback (MIDI), 576-578
Plug-and-Play, 132-133
    accommodating old device drivers, 182-184
    configuring Windows 95, 180-187
        BIOS issues, 187-188
        SCSI devices, 188-189

OS/2, 198-200
    performance standards, 49-50
pointers (BIOS), 128
polarizing filters (monitors), 501
Poly mode (MIDI), 567
porches (video signals), 422
ports, 365-378
    game ports, 377-378
    input/output, 130-131
    MPC 2.0 performance standard, 43
    parallel ports, 372-376
        bi-directional parallel ports, 373-374
        enhanced parallel ports, 374-375
        extended capabilities ports, 375-376
        standard parallel ports, 373
    performance standards, 52-53
    physical connections, 365
    Plug-and-Play expansion boards, 184
    serial ports, 366-372
        device types, 367
        handshaking, 367
        initializing, 370-371
        interrupts, 370
        speed of processing, 366-367, 372
        UART chips, 368-370
    Sound Blaster, 539
positive integers, 244
POST (Power-On Self-Test), 129
post-gap areas (CDs), 394

power connections (CD-ROM drives), 409
power consumption
    microprocessors, 309
    Multimedia PCs, 53
PowerBuilder (programming authoring software), 103
pre-emptive multi-tasking, 124, 168
pre-gap areas (CDs), 394
pre-production
    producing multimedia presentations, 107-113
    still images, 107-109
Presentation Manager (OS/2), 191
presentation of multimedia, 5-6
presentations (graphics), authoring software, 88, 93-99
    Aldus Persuasion, 96
    Astound!, 96
    Authorware Professional for Windows, 97
    ForShow, 97
    IconAuthor, 97
    ImageQ, 97-98
    Macromedia Director, 98-99
    Q/Media, 99
pricing, *see* costs
primary caches, 305-306
primary partitions
    DOS, 153
    OS/2, 194
print media, compared to multimedia, 3-4, 15
printer ports, *see* parallel ports

producing multimedia presentations, 37-38
authoring software, 87-88
capturing
graphics, 85
text, 84-85
video, 85-86
compiling the finished presentation, 86-87
defining hot spots, 85
formatting text, 85
overview, 84-87
pre-production, 107-113
sampling sounds, 86
software, 36-38
Program Manager (Windows), 128
Programmable Option Select (device driver conflicts), 132
programmed input/output (PIO) transfers, 341
programming languages
authoring software (producing multimedia presentations), 88, 101-107
Delphi, 103
MCI (Media Control Interface), 104-105
MCIWnd, 104, 106
ObjectView, 103
OpenGL, 105
PowerBuilder, 103
SQLWindows, 103
Visual Basic, 104
WinG, 106
WinToon, 106-107
BASIC (Beginner's All-purpose Symbolic Instruction Code), 120

Borland C++, 102
C programming language, 101-102
C++ programming language, 102
Microsoft Visual C++, 102
RAD (rapid application development), 103-104
programming software, 118-125
application-level programming, 122
class libraries, 122
complex instructions, 119
context switching, 123
cooperative multi-tasking, 124
debuggers, 122
high-level languages, 120-121
compiled languages, 121
interpreted languages, 120-121
languages, 119-122
assembly language, 120
machine language, 119
linear programming, 123
microprocessor instruction sets, 118-119
multi-tasking, 123-124
object code, 121
pre-emptive multi-tasking, 124
programming tools, 121-122
run-time modules, 122
SDKs (software development kits), 122
source code, 121
threads, 124-125

progressive scanning, 419
projection systems (monitors), 500
properties
sound, 513
toggling in RTF (Rich Text Format), 243
proprietary interfaces (CD-ROM drives), 408
proprietary mice, 361
protected mode
32-bit processing, 160
drivers (Windows 95), 219
kernel (upgrading Windows 3.1), 159
memory, 208
processing (Windows), 163
protocols, mouse, 361
PSCRIPT.DRV file, 159
Public Brand Software (shareware distribution), 603
public domain (copyright law), 588-590
publishers (commercial distribution), 599-600
Pulse Code Modulation (PCM), 41, 80, 256
pulse-width modulation, 528-529
purchasing Multimedia PCs, compared to upgrading PCs, 54-57

Q

Q/Media (graphics presentations authoring software), 99
quad tape (recording video signals), 431

quadrature modulation (video signals), 425
quality of recording (voice annotation), 79-81
QuickTime (video player), 70-72
    compared to Video for Windows, 69
    cross-platform compatiblity, 71-72
    image header structure, 280-281
    installing, 71
    locating, 70
QWERTY keyboards, 354-355

R

RAD (rapid application development), 103-104
RAM (Random Access Memory), 331-332
    performance standards, 45-47
    virtual memory, 173-174
    Windows requirements, 166
RAMDACs (Random Access Memory Digital-to-Analog Convertors), 456-457
random access, CDs, 389
random access in multimedia, 13
rasterizing video, 443-445
raw packets, 274-275
RDIB (device independent bitmap format), 259
Read-Only Memory (ROM), 129, 332
readers, 242

real mode drivers (Windows 95), 219
real mode memory, 151, 208
real mode processing (Windows), 163
real-time messages (MIDI), 569-570
Rebel Assault (games software), 35
receivers/transmitters (MIDI), 556-557, 568
recordable CDs, 391-392
recording
    audio (pulse code modulation), 256
    video cameras, 492-493
    video signals, 431-432
    voice annotation, 78-81
Red Book standard (CDs), 395
reference software, 28-31
    Britannica CD, 29
    Complete Guide to Symptoms, Illness & Surgery, 30
    Compton's Interactive Encyclopedia, 29
    Dr. Schueler's Home Medical Advisor Pro, 30
    Grolier Multimedia Encyclopedia, 29
    Home Survival Toolkit, 30
    McGraw-Hill Multimedia Encyclopedia of Science & Technology, 30
    Microsoft Bookshelf, 29-30
    Microsoft Cinemania, 31
    Microsoft Encarta, 29
    PharmAssist, 30

    PhoneDisc PowerFinder, 31
    Select Phone, 31
    Small Blue Planet: The Real Picture Atlas, 31
    Taxi, 31
    Warplanes: Modern Fighting Aircraft, 31
    Webster's Interactive Encyclopedia, 29
reflective LCDs, 501
refresh rates
    VESA standards, 469-471
    VGA video adapters, 469-471
    video, 420-421
REG.DAT (Windows registration database), 167-168
REGEDIT.EXE file, 179
registering copyrights, 592-593
registers, 303-304
    graphics accelerators, 453
    Map Mask Register (VGA adapters), 459-460
    renaming, 321
    VGA video adapters, 448-451
Registration Database, 167-168
the Registry (Windows 95 configuration), 178-180
regulating data transmission, 263
Relative Sector Numbers (OS/2), 197
remapping memory, 151, 311
renaming
    files (Windows 95), 177
    registers, 321

resampling (video images), 487
resizing (video images), 487
resolution
  absolute, 249
  audio, 257
  digital technology, 8
  graphics accelerators
    memory requirements, 454
  images, 248-249, 252, 418
    bitmapped, 248
    on-screen, 247
  Kodak PhotoCD, 399-400
  monitors, 248, 503-504
  physical, 249
  scanners, 364-365
  VESA standards, 463
  VGA video adapters, 458-459
  video, 51
    cameras, 479-480
    phone systems, 441
resonance (sound), 517
retracing video signals, 421
RGB (Red, Green, Blue) video files, 424
  run-length encoded, 274-275
  uncompressed, 272-273
ribbon microphones, 521
RIFF (Resource Interchange File Format), 259, 288
rights (copyright law), 587-588, 592-593
RLE (Run Length Encoding), 251-252
RMID (MIDI format), 259
RMMP (multimedia movie format), 259

ROM (Read-Only Memory), 129, 332
ROM shadowing, 335
RTF (Rich Text Format), 90-91, 242-243
Run-Length Encoding (RLE), 251-252
  color-mapped image files, 273-274
  RGB image files, 274-275
run-time modules, 122

S

S-video (separate-video)
  color encoding, 490
  video signals, 425-427
S3 Corporation graphics accelerator chips, 453
sampling rates
  audio, 41, 257, 531-532
  MPC 2.0 performance standards, 43
sampling sounds (producing multimedia presentations), 86
SBI (Sound Blaster Instrument) audio file format, 288-289
SBSIM (Sound Blaster Standard Interface Module), 539-543
SCAM (SCSI Configured AutoMagically), 188-189
scan codes (keyboards), 356
scanners, 363-365
  capturing
    graphics, 85
    text, 84
  image resolution, 364-365
  Twain standard, 364

scanning
  interlaced scanning, 419-420
  linear scanning, 419
  refresh rate (video), 420-421
  video cameras, 489
  video signals, 421-432
    back porches, 422
    blanking, 421-422
    chrominance, 424-425
    color, 423-426
    combining with memory-mapped systems, 443-451
    converting between standards, 428
    front porches, 422
    interference, 425-426
    international standards, 427-431
    luminance, 424-425
    retracing, 421
    S-video, 425-427
    synchronizing, 422-423
    vertical interval, 422
scope of multimedia, 22-23
screens, *see* monitors
scripting (producing multimedia presentations), 84
SCSI (Small Computer System Interface), 345-349
  block addressing, 346
  clock speed, 346
  installing, 347-348
  interfaces
    CD-ROM drives, 406-407
    hard disks, 48

loading CD-ROM drivers,
207-208
Plug-and-Play, 188-189
troubleshooting, 349
SCSI-2 interface, 347
SDKs (software develop-
ment kits), 122
search engines, Multimedia
Viewer, 65-66
SECAM (Sequence Couleur
á Memoire), 427-431
secondary caches, 305-306
sections (initialization
files), 167
sector address tag field
(CDs), 392-393
sectors
large frames (CDs),
392-393
disk cluster size, 148
disk compression, 150-151
OS/2 file structure, 196
Select Phone (reference
software), 31
senses, effect of
multimedia, 5
sensing technology
joysticks, 377
keyboards, 356
sensors (video cameras), 478
separate sync video
systems, 424
serial mice, 360
serial ports, 366-372
device types, 367
handshaking, 367
initializing, 370-371
interrupts, 370
performance standards,
52-53

speed of processing,
366-367, 372
UART chips, 368-370
set-associative caches, 306
setup strings (modems), 382
shadow masks (monitors),
498-499
shareware
copyright law, 589
creating multimedia
presentations, 600-603
Association of Shareware
Professionals, 602-603
BBSs (bulletin board
services), 603
documenting, 602
Public Brand Software
(shareware
distribution), 603
sharpness (images), 418
SHELL.DLL file, 159
shotgun microphones, 524
shutters (video cameras),
486-487
Signal Computing Architecture (DSP standard),
546-547
signal level of microphones,
524-525
signal-to-noise ratio, 52
signals (data transmission),
noise reduction, 7-8
signed integers, 245
significants (floating-point
numbers), 245
signs (floating-point
numbers), 245
SIMMs (Single In-line
Memory Modules),
46-47, 332-333
chip count, 333-334
double-sided SIMMs, 334

parity-checking, 333
single-sided SIMMs, 334
speed ratings, 334-335
Simultaneous Voice and
Data (SVD), 384-385
Sing-Along with Elvis
(music software), 37
Single MS-DOS Application
mode (Windows 95), 174
single-precision floating-
point numbers, 245
single-sided SIMMs, 334
single-threaded operating
systems, 146
single-threading (programming software), 125
.SIT file extension, 71
size
CDs, 389-390
monitors images, 506-507
sizing images, 264
Sketchpad (history of
GUIs), 126
slave ATA drives (hard
disks), 339
Sleep state (Plug-and-Play),
186-187
slide presentations, 4-5, 94
Small Blue Planet: The Real
Picture Atlas (reference
software), 31
Small Computer System
Interface, *see* SCSI
small frames (CDs), 393
SmartDrive (caching disk
drives), 161
SMPTE (Society of Motion
Picture and Television
Engineers) time codes,
445-447
SND audio file format,
290-291

software, 24-35, 117-135
applications, 135
audio software, Sound
Forge, 111-113
authoring software
computer-based
training, 88,
99-101
hypertext, 88-93
presentations (graph-
ics), 88, 93-99
producing multimedia
presentations, 87-88
programming
languages, 88,
101-107
basic multimedia applica-
tions, 61-74
CD players, 67-68
Multimedia Viewer,
64-67
system sounds, 72-74
video players, 68-72
Windows Help,
62-64
BIOS, 128-133
boot sequence,
128-129
boot-strap loader, 129
device drivers,
131-132
hardware interface,
130-131
initialization code, 128
input/output map-
ping, 130
memory addresses,
130-131
memory mapping, 130
Plug-and-Play,
132-133
pointers, 128

ports, 130-131
POST (Power-On
Self-Test), 129
ROM (Read-Only
Memory), 129
speed, 130
codecs (video compres-
sion), 441-442
definition, 118
device drivers
SCSI devices, 349
Sound Blaster,
539-543
educational software,
25-28
A.D.A.M. The Inside
Story, 26
Exploring Ancient
Architecture, 27
The Magic School
Bus Explores the
Human Body, 26
Morgan's Trivia
Machine, 27
Multimedia Work-
shop, 28
Museum Madness, 27
The Musical World of
Professor Piccolo, 28
Where in the World
is Carmen
Sandiego?, 27
The Yukon Trail, 27
entertainment software,
32-34
Beethoven's Fifth, 33
Detroit, 33
European Racers, 33
games, 34-35
Gettysburg Multi-
media Battle
Simulation, 33

J.F.K. Assassination:
A Visual Investiga-
tion, 34
Supersonic, 34
Twain's World, 34
installing multimedia
software, 60-61
layered model, 128
MIDI (Musical Instru-
ment Digital Interface),
555-578
aftertouch, 575
channels/voices,
558-566
connectors, 557
encoding notes,
570-575
messages, 566-570
patch maps, 559-566
playback, 576-578
Song Position
Pointer, 570
speed of processing,
557
Status/Data Bytes,
570-575
synchronizing,
575-576
transmitters/receivers,
556-557
UART chips, 556
Windows, 565-566
morphing software
Elastic Reality, 110
HSC Digital Morph,
110
Morph, 111
PhotoMorph, 111
music software
Midisoft Multimedia
Songbook, 36

Midisoft Music
Mentor, 36
MusicTime, 36
Sing-Along with
Elvis, 37
Soloist, 37
operating systems,
133-135, 137-200
device drivers, 134
DOS (Disk Operating
System), 139-154
function, 138-139
OS/2, 189-200
Windows, 155-168
Windows 95,
168-189
optical character recognition software
(scanners), 363
photo editing
Corel PhotoPaint 5
Plus, 108
Image-In Professional,
108
Photoshop, 109
Picture Publisher, 109
producing multimedia
presentations, 36-38
programming, 118-125
application-level
programming, 122
class libraries, 122
complex
instructions, 119
context switching, 123
cooperative multi-
tasking, 124
debuggers, 122
high level languages,
120-121
languages, 119-122

linear
programming, 123
microprocessor
instruction sets,
118-119
multi-tasking,
123-124
object code, 121
pre-emptive multi-
tasking, 124
run-time modules, 122
SDKs (software
development
kits), 122
source code, 121
threads, 124-125
tools, 121-122
reference software, 28-31
Britannica CD, 29
Complete Guide to
Symptoms, Illness &
Surgery, 30
Compton's Interactive
Encyclopedia, 29
Dr. Schueler's Home
Medical Advisor
Pro, 30
Grolier Multimedia
Encyclopedia, 29
Home Survival
Toolkit, 30
McGraw-Hill
Multimedia
Encyclopedia of
Science & Technol-
ogy, 30
Microsoft Bookshelf,
29-30
Microsoft
Cinemania, 31
Microsoft Encarta, 29

PharmAssist, 30
PhoneDisc
PowerFinder, 31
Select Phone, 31
Small Blue Planet:
The Real Picture
Atlas, 31
Taxi, 31
Warplanes: Modern
Fighting Aircraft, 31
Webster's Interactive
Encyclopedia, 29
Sound Recorder (voice
annotation), 78-81
standards for multimedia,
10-12
Twain standard
(scanners), 364
user interfaces, 125-128
command-line
interfaces, 125
design of GUIs,
127-128
GUIs (graphical user
interfaces), 125-128
history of GUIs,
126-127
icons, 127
window interface,
127-128
VESA BIOS Extension,
463-468
video editing
ImagePals, 109
MediaRecorder,
109-110
Windows 3.1 device
drivers (MCI), 212-214
**software development kits
(SDKs), 122**
**software interrupts
(DOS), 146**

Soloist (music software), 37

Song Position Pointer (MIDI), 570

Sound Blaster, 538-543

Sound Blaster Standard Interface Module (SBSIM), 539-543

Sound Forge (audio software), 111-113

sound quality of microphones, 525

Sound Recorder (voice annotation), 78-81

soundboards, 512, 530-531
  configuring, 551-553
  installing, 551-554
  performance standards, 51-52
  wiring speakers, 553-554

sounds
  storing, 294-295
  see also audio

source code (programming software), 121

spatial video compression, 255

speakers, 515-520
  amplifiers, 520
  baffles, 516-518
  location/coupling, 519-520
  multi-speaker systems, 518-519
  performance standards, 52
  resonance, 517
  stereophonic imaging, 520

SPEAKR.ZIP file (audio device driver), 529

special effects (video cameras), 491

special purpose blocks, 263

speculative execution
  Cyrix M1 chips, 321
  NexGen 586 chips, 322-323

speed of processing, 7
  ATA hard disk interfaces, 341-342
  BIOS, 130
  business compared to home computers, 14
  CD-ROM drives, 403-404
  CDs (Compact Discs), 9
  clock speeds (microprocessors), 304-305
  fax modems, 385
  graphics accelerators memory requirements, 455
  hard disks, 336
  MIDI, 557
  modems, 52-53, 379
    configuring, 382-383
    standards, 379-381
  MPC 1.0 performance standards, 40-41
  MPC 2.0 performance standard, 42
  NexGen 586 chips, 323
  serial ports, 366, 372

speed ratings (SIMMs), 334-335

spline-based animation, 94

Sprite animation, 94

SQLWindows (programming authoring software), 103

stability of images (video cameras), 488-489

standard mode (Windows), 158, 166

standard parallel ports, 373

standard Windows device drivers, 211

standards
  audio synthesizers, 537-543
    Ad Lib, 537
    Sound Blaster, 538-543
  CD-ROMs, 394-402
    CD-DA (Digital Audio) standard, 395-396
    Green Book standard, 395
    High Sierra, 401-402
    ISO 9660, 401-402
    Kodak PhotoCD, 396-401
    Orange Book standard, 395
    Red Book standard, 395
    Yellow Book standard, 395
  DSP (Digital Signal Processors), 546-551
  expansion buses, 325-331
    EISA (Enhanced Industry Standard Architecture), 327-328
    ISA (Industry Standard Architecture), 326-327
    MCA (Micro Channel Architecture), 327
    PCI (Peripheral Component Interconnect), 329

PCMCIA (Personal Computer Memory Card International Association), 330-332
VL Bus, 328-329
fax modems, 385-386
international television standards, 427-431
memory-mapped video displays, 442-443
modems, 379-381
PCMCIA standard, 538
Sound Blaster, compatibility with PCMCIA, 538
VESA video standards, 458
standards converters (video signals), 428
startup problems, troubleshooting CD-ROM drives, 413-414
static measurements, compared to digital, 6-7
static memory, 331-332
Status Bytes (MIDI), 558, 566, 570-575
step capture (video), 445
stereophonic imaging, 520
still image compression, 250
still image formats
BMP, 260-266
EPS (Encapsulated PostScript), 262
GIF (Graphics Interchange Format), 263-266
JPEG, 266-268
PCD (PhotoCD), 268
PCX, 268-269
pre-production, 107-109

Run-Length Encoded, color-mapped files, 273-274
TGA, 269-275
run-length encoded RGB, 274-275
uncompressed color-mapped, 271-273
WMF (Windows Metafiles), 275-276
storage capacity
ATA hard drives, 340
CDs (Compact Discs), 9, 16, 22, 28-29
clusters (DOS), 148-151
DOS memory management, 151-152
floppy disks, 140-143, 149, 350
hard disks, 47-49, 140-143, 337-338, 342-343
HPFS (High Performance File System), 196-198
memory measurement, 332
MPC 1.0 performance standards, 40
MPC 2.0 performance standard, 42
RAM (Random Access Memory), 45-47, 166
registers, 303-304
SCSI interface, 347
swap files (Windows virtual memory), 165-166
storage units (Intel), 244
storing
audio, 259
audio data, 282-295
GDI functions, 275

images, 247-248, 259-276
numerical values
byte orders, 246
floating-point numbers, 245-246
integers, 244-245
sounds, 294-295
text, 227-228
video data, 277-282
voice data, 291-294
streams
headers, 278-279
video, 279
structure of DOS (Disk Operating System), 143-147
studios, creating multimedia presentations, 596-597
stylus (digitizing tablets), 362-363
subtractive synthesis, 533-534
subwoofers, 518-519
Super Block (OS/2), 197
Super Boot Block (OS/2), 195
SuperFAT (OS/2), 194-196
Supersonic (entertainment software), 34
supertweeters, 518
supertwist LCDs, 501-502
SuperVGA video adapters, 458, 463-468
SVD (Simultaneous Voice and Data), 384-385
swap files
OS/2, 193-194
Windows 95 virtual memory, 173
Windows virtual memory, 164-166
SWAPPATH= setting (OS/2), 193-194

SWAPPER.DAT file, 193
sweeps (video signals), 422-423
symmetrical video compression, 254
sync-on-green video systems, 424
synchronizing
MIDI, 575-576
monitor frequencies, 504
video signals, 422-423, 489
synthesis (audio), 532-551
Ad Lib soundboard, 537
additive synthesis, 534
advanced synthesis, 536-537
compression, 543-544
FM synthesis, 535
Sound Blaster, 538-543
standards, 537-543
subtractive synthesis, 533-534
wave table synthesis, 535-536
SYS.COM (manual DOS installation), 154
System Information program (Windows 95), 173
system messages (MIDI), 569-570
system requirements, *see* **performance standards**
system sounds, 72-74
SYSTEM.DAT file, 178
SYSTEM.INI file, 167
editing manually, 218
editing via Windows' Control Panel, 216-218

T

Targa video board, *see* **TGA**
Taxi (reference software), 31
television
compared to monitors, 493
history of color television, 423-424
interference, 425-426
international standards, 427-431
NTSC (National Television Standards Committee), 424-425
temporal dimension of multimedia, 3-4
temporal video compression, 255
temporary swap files (Windows memory management), 165
term of copyrights, 586
terminate-and-stay resident programs, 203
terminating inputs (video signals), 433
testing
multimedia presentations, 602
Pentium chips, 317-318
text
ASCII (American Standard Code for Information Interchange), 237-241
capturing text (producing multimedia presentations), 84-85
EBCDIC (Extended Binary Coded Decimal Interchange Code), 229-237

files, converting, 242
formatting codes, 242
formatting (producing multimedia presentations), 85
numerical storage, 244-246
Rich Text Format (RTF), 242-244
storing, 227-228
word processor formats, 242
text modes
interfaces, 125
VGA video adapters, 461-462
TFT (Thin Film Transistor) technology, 502-503
TGA
descriptors
field, 270
image, 271-272
still image formats, 269-275
run-length encoded, color-mapped files, 273-274
run-length encoded RGB files, 274-275
uncompressed color-mapped files, 271-273
Thin Film Transistor (TFT) technology, 502-503
thrashing, 306
threads
programming software, 124-125
single-threaded operating systems, 146

three-dimensional images, 249

throughput (hard disk speed), 336

TIE Authoring System (computer-based training authoring software), 100-101

tie-tack microphones, 524

tile transitions (slide shows), 94

timbre (audio), 532

time codes (video), 445-447

TIMER.DRV, 210

timing (video), 418-419

toggling properties in Rich Text Format, 243

TourGuide (computer-based training authoring software), 100

trackballs, 361

tracks (CDs), 394

trade secret laws, 583

trademarks, 583

trailers, 263, 265

training (computer-based), authoring software, 88, 99-101
   TIE Authoring System, 100-101
   TourGuide, 100

training uses of multimedia, 31-32

transducers, 515

transfer rates
   CD drives, 403-404
   hard disk speed, 336

transforming .RTF files, 242

transitions (slide shows), 94

translating data (applications), 135

transmission (data), regulating, 263

transmission noise reduction, 7-8

transmitters/receivers (MIDI), 556-557, 568

transmitting images, 263

Trinitrons (monitors), 499

triple supertwist LCDs, 501-502

tripods (video cameras), 488

troubleshooting
   CD device drivers, 413-414
   SCSI devices, 349

true color video systems, 437

Truespeech audio compression, 258

TrueType fonts (Windows 95), 169

tunneling (Windows 95), 176

Twain standard (scanners), 364

Twain's World (entertainment software), 34

tweeters, 518

twisted nematic technology (monitors), 501-502

two-dimensional images, 249

type-specific drivers (Windows 95), 220

U

UART chips (Universal Asynchronous Receiver/Transmitter), 368-370
   configuring modems, 382
   MIDI, 556

UMB (upper memory blocks), 152

uncompressed color-mapped images, 271-272

uncompressed RGB images, 272-273

underscanning (monitors), 505

unidirectional microphones, 523

UNIDRV.DLL file, 159

universal driver/mini-driver architecture (Windows 95), 218-219

unsigned integers, 245

updates for CDs, 28

upgrading
   PCs, compared to purchasing Multimedia PCs, 54-57
   Windows 3.1, 159-162

upper memory blocks (UMB), 152

user interfaces, 125-128
   command-line interfaces, 125
   design of GUIs, 127-128
   GUIs (graphical user interfaces), 125-128
   history of GUIs, 126-127
   icons, 127
   window interface, 127-128
   Windows 95 file structure, 171-172

User program (Windows), 158, 163

USER.DAT file, 178

USER.EXE file, 159, 209

utility programs (operating systems), 134

V

V.34 modems, 380
V32.FC modems, 380
vacuum tubes, 494
values, numerical
  integers, 244-245
  storing, 244-246
variables (configuring Windows), 167
VCache (32-bit processing), 161-162
VCOS (DSP standard), 547
vector graphics, 443
vector images, 247-248
versions of OLE, 76
vertical frequency (monitors), 504
vertical hold controls (monitors), 507-508
vertical interval (video signals), 422
vertical position controls (monitors), 507
vertical retracing (video signals), 421
vertical size controls (monitors), 507
vertical sweeps (video signals), 422-423
VESA (Video Electronics Standards Association), 458, 463-468
  Advanced Feature Connector, 472-475
  BIOS Extension, 463-468
  connectors, 471-475
  Feature Connector, 472
  frequencies, 468-471
  refresh rates, 469-471

VFAT (Virtual File Allocation Table), 161-162, 169, 174
VGA video adapters, 437-438, 457-463
  bank-switching, 459
  character modes, 460
  color, 459-463
  combining NTSC signals, 444
  connectors, 471-475
  cursors, 461-462
  frequencies, 468-471
  Map Mask Register, 459-460
  memory requirements, 459-460
  refresh rates, 469-471
  registers, 448-451
  resolution, 458-459
  support from graphics accelerators, 455-456
  text modes, 461-462
VHS videocassette recorders, 432
video, 417-434
  8mm video cassettes, 432
  bit-images, 456
  BNC connectors, 433-434
  bridging inputs, 433
  cable connections, 432-434
  cameras, 477-493
    color filters, 479
    encoding images, 490
    f-stops, 483-486
    field of view, 481-482
    focal length, 480-481
    focusing, 487-488
    lenses, 477, 480-486

    microphones, 493
    optical
      transducers, 477
    optics, 478-489
    recording, 492-493
    resolution, 479-480
    scanning, 489
    sensors, 478
    shutters, 486-487
    special effects, 491
    stability of images, 488-489
    tripods, 488
    viewfinders, 477, 492
    white balancing, 490-491
    zoom ratios, 480-481, 487
  capturing (producing multimedia presentations), 85-86
  coaxial connectors, 433-434
  codecs, 441-442
  color, 435-443
    attributes (pixels), 435-436
    CMYK color scheme, 438
    color planes, 436-438
    color separations, 436-437
    color space conversion, 438
    direct mapping, 439
    encoding, 438
    Kodak PhotoCD, 398-399, 438
    memory requirements, 437-438

pixels, 435-436
standards for
  memory-mapped
  displays, 442-443
true color systems, 437
VGA video adapters,
  437-438
Windows, 439-440
color temperature,
490-491, 495-496
combining scanned/
  memory-mapped
  systems, 443-451
compared to multimedia,
12-13, 23
compression, 253-256,
440-442
  asymmetrical, 254
  Cinepak, 254
  Indeo, 254
  Kodak PhotoCD,
    400-401
  Microsoft Run-
    Length Encoding
    (RLE), 255
  Microsoft Video 1,
    255
  Motion JPEG, 255
  MPEG, 255-256
  spatial, 255
  symmetrical, 254
  temporal, 255
drop-frame time codes,
446-447
editing
  ImagePals, 109
  MediaRecorder,
    109-110
encoding, 418-419

file formats, AVI (Audio/
  Video Interleaved),
  277-280
flat-panel video systems,
434-435
formats
  converting, 296
  MOV (movie),
    280-282
frame rates, video com-
  pression, 441
graphics accelerators,
451-457
  color, 455
  DCI (Display Control
    Interface), 457
  expansion buses,
    453-456
  memory require-
    ments, 454
  RAMDACs, 456-457
  registers, 453
  resolution, 454
  speed of processing,
    455
  VGA support,
    455-456
graphics adapters, 447-448
graphics coprocessors, 452
hardware, 447-457
  memory, 251
  performance stan-
    dards, 50-51
impedance, 433
interlaced scanning,
419-420
linear scanning, 419
links with audio, random
  access, 13

memory-mapped systems,
434-435
microprocessors, 447-448
monitors, 493-510
  active matrix,
    502-503
  aperture grilles, 499
  aspect ratios, 506
  audio inputs, 508
  autosizing images,
    506-507
  bandwidth, 505
  color, 495, 503
  color tracking, 504
  compared to televi-
    sion, 493
  configuring, 508-510
  convergence, 497-498
  CRTs (cathode ray
    tubes), 494-500
  dot-pitch, 498
  electron guns,
    496-497
  flat-panel displays,
    500-503
  history, 494
  image controls,
    507-508
  matrix colors, 499
  overscanning, 505
  passive matrix,
    502-503
  persistence, 496
  phosphors, 494-495
  polarizing filters, 501
  projection
    systems, 500
  resolution, 503-504
  shadow masks,
    498-499

synchronizing
  frequencies, 504
twisted nematic
  technology, 501-502
underscanning, 505
video amplifiers,
  503-504
white balancing,
  495-496
MPC 2.0 performance
  standard, 43
overlay boards, 444
pin plugs, 433-434
producing multimedia
  presentations, 37-38, 95
rasterizing, 443-445
recording, 431-432
refresh rate, 420-421
resampling images, 487
resizing images, 487
resolution
  Kodak PhotoCD,
    399-400
  video phone
    systems, 441
scanning signals, 421-432
  back porches, 422
  blanking, 421-422
  chrominance,
    424-425
  color, 423-426
  converting between
    standards, 428
  front porches, 422
  interference, 425-426
  international stan-
    dards, 427-431
  luminance, 424-425
  retracing, 421
  S-video, 425-427

synchronizing,
  422-423
  vertical interval, 422
step capture, 445
storing, 277-282
streams, 279
studios (creating multimedia presentations),
  596-597
synchronizing signals, 489
terminating inputs, 433
time codes, 445-447
timing, 418-419
troubleshooting
  CD-ROM drives, 414
vector graphics, 443
VESA standards, 458,
  463-468
  connectors, 471-475
  frequencies, 468-471
  refresh rates, 469-471
VGA video adapters,
  457-463
  bank-switching, 459
  character modes, 460
  color, 459-463
  connectors, 471-475
  cursors, 461-462
  frequencies, 468-471
  Map Mask Register,
    459-460
  memory require-
    ments, 459-460
  refresh rates, 469-471
  resolution, 458-459
  text modes, 461-462
video boards, 457-475
video capture, 443-444
video controllers, 448-451
voltage, 434

**video amplifiers (monitors),
  503-504**
video annotation, 81
video boards, 457-475
  VESA standards, 458,
    463-468
    connectors, 471-475
    frequencies, 468-471
    refresh rates, 469-471
    resolution, 463
  VGA video adapters,
    457-463
    connectors, 471-475
    frequencies, 468-471
    refresh rates, 469-471
video capture boards, 51
video controllers, 448-451
**Video Cube: Space (games
  software), 35**
**Video Electronics Standards
  Association (VESA),
  458, 463-468**
  connectors, 471-475
  frequencies, 468-471
  refresh rates, 469-471
**Video for Windows (video
  player), 69-70**
  compared to
    QuickTime, 69
  WinToon extensions,
    106-107
**video games (software),
  34-35**
Video Graphics Array, *see*
  VGA video adapters
**video players (software
  applications), 68-72**
  QuickTime, 70-72
    compared to Video
    for Windows, 69

cross-platform compatiblity, 71-72
installing, 71
Video for Windows, 69-70
Viewer (Multimedia Viewer), 64-67, 90-91
viewfinders (video cameras), 477, 492
virtual device drivers
Windows, 211-212
Windows 95, 219
Virtual File Allocation Table (VFAT), 161-162, 169, 174
virtual memory, 46
OS/2, 193
Windows, 164-166
Windows 95, 173-174
vision
moving images, 417-418
relationship to multimedia, 416-417
Visual Basic (programming authoring software), 104
visual editing interface (OLE), 76
VL Bus standard, 50, 328-329
VOC audio file format, 291-294
VOC type 9 subblocks, 293
voice annotation, 78-81
embedding objects, 81
recording, 78-81
Voice Channels (MIDI), 567, 569
voice data, storing, 291-294
voice messages (MIDI), 567
voices (MIDI), 558-566
VoiceSpan (modem), 384
VoiceView (modem), 384

voltages
joysticks, 377
microprocessors, 308-309
video signals, 434
volume controls (CD-ROM drives), 405-406
VRAM (dual-ported video memory), 454
.VXD file extension, 219
VxD naming convention (virtual device drivers), 211

W

Wait for Key (Plug-and-Play), 185
Wake command (Plug-and-Play), 187
Warplanes: Modern Fighting Aircraft (reference software), 31
WAV audio file format, 72, 79, 294-295
wave table synthesis, 535-536
waveform audio (WAV) files, 259, 283, 288
waveform generators, 533
wavelengths (audio), 514
Webster's Interactive Encyclopedia (reference software), 29
Where in the World is Carmen Sandiego? (educational software), 27
white balancing
monitors, 495-496
video cameras, 490-491
width of images, 263
WIN.COM file, 166
WIN.INI file, 167

Win32 interface, 169
Win32s, 159-160
WIN386.SWP (temporary swap files), 165
Windows, 155-168
assigning system sounds, 72-74
clipboard, 77
color, 439-440
configuring, 167-168
file structure, 158
history, 155-158
memory management, 162-166
DOS session memory, 164
local heaps, 163-164
RAM requirements, 166
virtual memory, 164-166
memory requirements, 46
MIDI implementations, 565-566
Program Manager, 128
relationship to multimedia, 11
serial port speed, 372
upgrading Windows 3.1, 159-162
Video for Windows, 69-70
windows (interfaces), 127-128
Windows 3.1
device drivers, 208-218
audio device drivers, 529-530, 553
DOS drivers (in Windows), 208-209
Dynamic Link Libraries (DLLs), 209-210

installing, 215-218
Media Control
    Interface (MCI),
    212-214
standard drivers, 211
virtual drivers,
    211-212
initializing serial ports, 371
MSCDEX.EXE (CD
    device driver), 409-410
Windows 95, 168-189
    audio compression, 543
    audio device drivers, 551
    CD device drivers,
        411-413
    codecs (video compres-
        sion), 441-442
    compared to
        Windows NT, 169
    compatibility with
        applications, 169-171
    configuring, 178-189
        accommodating old
            device drivers,
            182-184
        hardware, 180-189
        modems, 383
        monitors, 508-510
        Plug-and-Play,
            180-189
        the Registry,
            178-180

copying files, 176
device drivers, 218-222
    installing, 221-222
    loading, 219-220
file structure, 171-178
filenames, 175-178
history of Windows,
    157-158
initializing serial ports, 371
memory management,
    172-174
MIDI playback, 576-578
renaming files, 177
Windows DSP, 547-551
**Windows Help (software
    application), 62-64**
**Windows NT, compared to
    Windows 95, 169**
**Windows NT File System
    (NTFS), 177**
**WinG (programming
    authoring software), 106**
**WinHelp 4.0 (hypertext
    authoring software), 91-92**
**WinToon (programming
    authoring software),
    106-107**
**wipes (slide show transi-
    tion), 94**
wiring speakers, 553-554
**WMF still image formats,
    275-276**
woofers, 518

word processors, 242
**work for hire (copyright
    law), 587**
**World Wide Web
    (WWW), 16**
write-back caches, 307
**write-protection, floppy
    disks, 350**
write-through caches, 306
writers, 242
WW091.EXE file, 159

X-Y-Z

**XA (Extended Architecture)
    CDs, 393**
**XDF (Extended Density
    Format), 153**
**Xerox Corp. (history of
    GUIs), 127**
**XLR connectors (micro-
    phones), 525**
XT keyboards, 358

Y/C video system, 426
**Yellow Book standard
    (CDs), 395**
YM3812 chip (audio), 538
**The Yukon Trail (educa-
    tional software), 27**
YUV color system, 425

**zoom ratios (video cam-
    eras), 480-481, 487**

PLUG YOURSELF INTO...

THE MACMILLAN INFORMATION SUPERLIBRARY™

Free information and vast computer resources from the world's leading computer book publisher—online!

FIND THE BOOKS THAT ARE RIGHT FOR YOU!

A complete online catalog, plus sample chapters and tables of contents give you an in-depth look at *all* of our books, including hard-to-find titles. It's the best way to find the books you need!

● STAY INFORMED with the latest computer industry news through our online newsletter, press releases, and customized Information SuperLibrary Reports.

● GET FAST ANSWERS to your questions about MCP books and software.

● VISIT our online bookstore for the latest information and editions!

● COMMUNICATE with our expert authors through e-mail and conferences.

● DOWNLOAD SOFTWARE from the immense MCP library:
  - Source code and files from MCP books
  - The best shareware, freeware, and demos

● DISCOVER HOT SPOTS on other parts of the Internet.

● WIN BOOKS in ongoing contests and giveaways!

TO PLUG INTO MCP: ➤ WORLD WIDE WEB: **http://www.mcp.com**

GOPHER: gopher.mcp.com

FTP: ftp.mcp.com

CD-ROM Setup

The Multimedia Bible CD-ROM

The companion CD-ROM contains the complete text and images from the book in a multimedia hypertext application. You can find any information in the book using the word search feature or by navigating through the chapters.

In addition, you'll find working trial versions of many of the multimedia software products mentioned in the book.

Getting Started

Insert the disc into your CD-ROM drive and follow these steps to set up the software.

If you're running Windows 95, the setup program will automatically start after you insert the disc into your drive.

1. From the Windows Program Manager menu, choose **File+R**un, or choose **R**un from the Windows 95 Start menu.
2. Type D:\CDSETUP and press Enter. If your CD-ROM drive is not drive D, substitute the proper drive letter. For example, if your CD-ROM drive is F, type F:\CDSETUP.

Follow the on-screen instructions in the setup program and a group named *Multimedia Bible* will be created. When the setup is complete, the Microsoft Video for Windows installation program will automatically begin. When this installation program is complete, you need to restart Windows.

You can start the electronic book by double-clicking *The Winn L. Rosch Multimedia Bible* icon. There will also be icons for installing each of the trial software products.